The
NEW LIFE BIBLE

New Testament

Illustrated

Translated by
Gleason H. Ledyard

Illustrations by
Deborah Skufca

Christian Literature
International
P.O. BOX 777 CANBY, OREGON 97013

Twenty-fifth printing

THIS IS THE BOOK OF LIFE

From the beginning to the end of these Writings, they tell of the life of Jesus. He said, "I am the Way and the Truth and the Life. No one can go to the Father except by Me." New Life has come to many, many people who have read or heard the Word of God and have put their trust in Jesus Christ, the Son of God.

God's Written Word is as much alive today as when it was written many hundreds of years ago. Through the years, sinful men have tried to destroy It, but this living Book can never be destroyed. "Heaven and earth will pass away, but My words will not pass away."

Those early men of God wrote in a different language than we use today. When a translation is done from one language to another, it is hard to make the second language say what the first language said. Every part of the New Testament is important and should say what the Holy Spirit said to those early men of God who wrote it down. For many hundreds of years people could not have a copy for themselves because the Bible was not printed. After it was printed, only rich people could buy one. For over 350 years the King James Bible has been in print and now many people own a copy. Since about 1900 many different translations have been printed in the English language.

The New Testament has many hundreds of quotations taken from the Old Testament. Many of these references are given in this translation so they can be read and studied in the Old Testament. The New Testament is made up of 27 different Books or Writings.

The reason for this translation of the New Testament is to take difficult words that are found in most translations of the Bible and put them into words or phrases that are easy to understand. A list of some of these phrases can be found in the back of this translation. About 850 different words have been used in this translation.

The New Testament does not only tell of the life of Jesus, but it tells how to be saved from the punishment of sin. It shows the way to heaven. It tells how to live in peace and happiness. The promises God has made to all people are in it. GOD'S WRITTEN WORD IS THE GREATEST OF ALL BOOKS.

GLEASON H. LEDYARD

THE BOOKS OF THE NEW TESTAMENT

Wherever ∗ is seen, the words that follow are not in all the early writings of the New Testament. If part of a verse or more than one verse is missing in some of the early writings, it is marked (∗).

The Families Jesus Came Through [Luke 3:23-38]

1 These are the families through which Jesus Christ came. He came through David and Abraham. [2]Abraham was the father of Isaac. Isaac was the father of Jacob. Jacob was the father of Judah and his brothers. [3]Judah was the father of Perez and Zerah. Their mother was Tamar. Perez was the father of Hezron. Hezron was the father of Aram. [4]Aram was the father of Amminadab. Amminadab was the father of Nahshon. Nahshon was the father of Salmon. [5]Salmon was the father of Boaz. The mother of Boaz was Rahab. Boaz was the father of Obed. The mother of Obed was Ruth. Obed was the father of Jesse. [6]Jesse was the father of David the king.

King David was the father of Solomon. His mother had been the wife of Uriah. [7]Solomon was the father of Rehoboam. Rehoboam was the father of Abijah. Abijah was the father of Asa. [8]Asa was the father of Jehoshaphat. Jehoshaphat was the father of Joram. Joram was the father of Uzziah. [9]Uzziah was the father of Jotham. Jotham was the father of Ahaz. Ahaz was the father of Hezekiah. [10]Hezekiah was the father of Manasseh. Manasseh was the father of Amon. Amon was the father of Josiah. [11]Josiah was the father of Jeconiah and his brothers at the time the people were taken to Babylon.

[12]After they were taken to the city of Babylon, Jeconiah was the father of Shealtiel. Shealtiel was the father of Zerubbabel. [13]Zerubbabel was the father of Abiud. Abiud was the father of Eliakim. Eliakim was the father of Azor. [14]Azor was the father of Zadok. Zadok was the father of Achim. Achim was the father of Eliud. [15]Eliud was the father of Eleazar. Eleazar was the father of Matthan. Matthan was the father of Jacob. [16]Jacob was the father of Joseph. Joseph was the husband of Mary. She was the mother of Jesus Who is called the Christ. [17]So the number of families from Abraham to David was fourteen. The number of families from David to the time the people were taken to Babylon was

fourteen. The number of families after they were taken to Babylon to the birth of Jesus Christ was fourteen.

The Birth Of Jesus [*Luke 2:1-7*]

¹⁸The birth of Jesus Christ was like this: Mary, His mother, had been promised in marriage to Joseph. Before they were married, it was learned that she was to have a baby by the Holy Spirit. ¹⁹Joseph was her promised husband. He was a good man and did not want to make it hard for Mary in front of people. He thought it would be good to break the promised marriage without people knowing it. ²⁰While he was thinking about this, an angel of the Lord came to him in a dream. The angel said, "Joseph, son of David, do not be afraid to take Mary as your wife. She is to become a mother by the Holy Spirit. ²¹A Son will be born to her. You will give Him the name Jesus because He will save His people from the punishment of their sins."

> You will give Him the name Jesus because He will save His people from the punishment of their sins.

²²This happened as the Lord said it would happen through the early preacher. ²³He said, "The young woman, who has never had a man, will give birth to a Son. They will give Him the name Immanuel. This means God with us." (Isaiah 7:14)

²⁴Joseph awoke from his sleep. He did what the angel of the Lord told him to do. He took Mary as his wife. ²⁵But he did not have her, as a husband has a wife, until she gave birth to a Son. Joseph gave Him the name Jesus.

Men Who Learned From The Stars Visit The Young Child Jesus

2 Jesus was born in the town of Bethlehem in the country of Judea. It was the time when Herod was king of that part of the country. Soon after Jesus was born, some wise men who learned things from stars came to Jerusalem from the East. ²They asked, "Where is the King of the Jews Who has been born. We have seen His star in the East. We have come to worship Him.

³King Herod heard this. He and all the people of Jerusalem were worried. ⁴He called together all the religious leaders of the Jews

and the teachers of the Law. Herod asked them where Christ was to be born. [5]They said to him, "In the town of Bethlehem in the country of Judea. The early preacher wrote, [6]'You, Bethlehem, land of Judah, are not the least of the leaders of Judah. Out of you will come a King Who will lead My people, the Jews.'" (Micah 5:2)

[7]Then Herod had a secret meeting with the men who learned things from stars. He asked them about what time the star had been seen. [8]He sent them to the town of Bethlehem and said, "Go and find the young Child. When you find Him, let me know. Then I can go and worship Him also."

[9]After the king had spoken, they went on their way. The star they had seen in the East went before them. It came and stopped over the place where the young Child was. [10]When they saw the star, they were filled with much joy.

[11]They went into the house and found the young Child with Mary, His mother. Then they got down in front of Him and worshiped Him. They opened their bags of riches and gave Him gifts of gold and perfume and spices. [12]Then God spoke to them in a dream. He told them not to go back to Herod. So they went to their own country by another road.

Joseph Goes To Egypt

[13]When they had gone, an angel of the Lord came to Joseph in a dream. He said, "Get up. Take the young Child and His mother to the country of Egypt. Go as fast as you can! Stay there until you hear from Me. Herod is going to look for the young Child to kill Him." [14]During the night he got up and left with the young Child and His mother for the country of Egypt. [15]He stayed there until Herod died. This happened as the Lord had said through an early preacher, "I called My Son out of Egypt." (Hosea 11:1)

Herod Had All The Young Boys Killed

[16]Herod learned that the wise men had fooled him. He was very angry. He sent men to kill all the young boys two years old and under in the town of Bethlehem and in all the country near by. He

decided to do this from what he had heard from the wise men as to the time when the star was seen. [17]Then it happened as the early preacher Jeremiah said it would happen. [18]He said, "The sound of crying and much sorrow was heard in Ramah. Rachel was crying for her children. She would not be comforted because they were dead." (Jeremiah 31:15)

Joseph Goes From Egypt To Nazareth [*Luke 2:39-40*]

[19]After Herod died, an angel of the Lord came to Joseph in a dream while he was in the country of Egypt. [20]He said, "Get up. Take the young Child and His mother and go into the land of the Jews. Those who tried to kill the young Child are dead." [21]Joseph got up. He took the young Child and His mother and came into the land of the Jews. [22]Joseph heard that Archelaus was the king of the country of Judea. Herod, the father of Archelaus, had died. Joseph was afraid to go there. God told him in a dream to go to the country of Galilee and he went. [23]Joseph stayed in a town called Nazareth. It happened as the early preachers said it would happen. They said, "Jesus will be called a Nazarene."

John The Baptist Makes The Way Ready For Jesus [*Mark 1:1-8; Luke 3:1-18; John 1:15-28*]

3 In those days John the Baptist came preaching in the desert in the country of Judea. [2]He said, "Be sorry for your sins and turn from them! The holy nation of heaven is near." [3]The early preacher Isaiah spoke of this man. He said, "Listen! His voice calls out in the desert! 'Make the way ready for the Lord. Make the road straight for Him!' " (Isaiah 40:3)

Be sorry for your sins and turn from them!

[4]John wore clothes made of hair from camels. He had a leather belt around him. His food was locusts and wild honey.

[5]Then the people of Jerusalem and of all the country of Judea and those from near the Jordan River went to him. [6]Those who told of their sins were baptized by him in the Jordan River. [7]He saw many proud religious law-keepers and other people of the religious group who believe no one will be raised from the dead. They were coming to him to be baptized. He said to them, "You

family of snakes! Who told you how to keep from God's anger that is coming? 8Do something to show me that your hearts are changed. 9Do not think you can say to yourselves, 'We have Abraham as our father.' For I tell you, God can make children for Abraham out of these stones.

10"Even now the ax is on the root of the trees. Every tree that does not give good fruit is cut down and thrown into the fire. 11For sure, I baptize with water those who are sorry for their sins and turn from them. The One Who comes after me will baptize you with the Holy Spirit and with fire. He is greater than I. I am not good enough to take off His shoes. 12He comes ready to clean the grain. He will gather the grain in and clean it all. The clean grain He will put into a building. He will burn that which is no good with a fire that cannot be put out."

The Baptism Of Jesus [*Mark 1:9-11; Luke 3:21-22; John 1:29-34*]

13Jesus came from Galilee. He went to John at the Jordan River to be baptized by him. 14John tried to stop Him. He said, "I need to be baptized by You. Do You come to me?" 15Jesus said to him, "Let it be done now. We should do what is right." John agreed and baptized Jesus. 16When Jesus came up out of the water, the heavens opened. He saw the Spirit of God coming down and resting on Jesus like a dove. 17A voice was heard from heaven. It said, "This is My much-loved Son. I am very happy with Him."

Jesus Was Tempted [*Mark 1:12-13; Luke 4:1-13*]

4 Jesus was led by the Holy Spirit to a desert. There He was tempted by the devil. 2Jesus went without food for forty days and forty nights. After that He was hungry. 3The devil came tempting Him and said, "If You are the Son of God, tell these stones to be made into bread." 4But Jesus said, "It is written, 'Man is not to live on bread only. Man is to live by every word that God speaks.'" (Deuteronomy 8:3)

5Then the devil took Jesus up to Jerusalem, the holy city. He had Jesus stand on the highest part of the house of God. 6The devil said to Him, "If You are the Son of God, throw Yourself down. It is written, 'He has told His angels to look after You. In their hands they will hold You up. Then Your foot will not hit against a stone.' " (Psalm 91:11-12) [7]Jesus said to the devil, "It is written also, 'You must not tempt the Lord your God.' " (Deuteronomy 6:16)

[8]Again the devil took Jesus to a very high mountain. He had Jesus look at all the nations of the world to see how great they were. [9]He said to Jesus, "I will give You all these nations if You will get down at my feet and worship me." [10]Jesus said to the devil, "Get away, Satan. It is written, 'You must worship the Lord your God. You must obey Him only.' " (Deuteronomy 6:13) [11]Then the devil went away from Jesus. Angels came and cared for Him.

Jesus Preaches In Galilee [Mark 1:14-15; Luke 4:14-15]

[12]When Jesus heard that John the Baptist had been put into prison, He went to the country of Galilee. [13]He left the town of Nazareth and went to live in the city of Capernaum. It is by the lake in the land of Zebulon and Naphtali.

[14]This happened as the early preacher Isaiah said it would happen. He said, [15]"The land of Zebulon and Naphtali is along the road to the lake. It is on the other side of the Jordan River in the country of Galilee. These people are not Jews. [16]The people who sat in darkness saw a great light. Light did shine on those in the land who were near death." (Isaiah 9:1-2)

[17]From that time on, Jesus went about preaching. He said, "Be sorry for your sins and turn from them. The holy nation of heaven is near."

Jesus Calls Peter And Andrew [Mark 1:16-20; Luke 5:1-11]

[18]Jesus was walking by the Lake of Galilee. He saw two brothers. They were Simon (his other name was Peter) and Andrew, his brother. They were putting a net into the sea for they were fishermen. [19]Jesus said to them, "Follow Me. I will make you fish for men!" [20]At once they left their nets and followed Him.

Follow Me.
I will make you
fish for men!

²¹Going from there, Jesus saw two other brothers. They were James and John, the sons of Zebedee. They were sitting in a boat with their father, mending their nets. Jesus called them. ²²At once they left the boat and their father and followed Jesus.

Jesus Keeps On Preaching In Galilee [*Mark 1:35-39; Luke 4:42-44*]

²³Jesus went over all Galilee. He taught in their places of worship and preached the Good News of the holy nation. He healed all kinds of sickness and disease among the people. ²⁴The news about Him went over all the country of Syria. They brought all the sick people to Him with many kinds of disease and pains. They brought to Him those who had demons. They brought those who at times lose the use of their minds. They brought those who could not use their hands and legs. He healed them. ²⁵Many people followed Him from the countries of Galilee and Judea. They followed Him from the cities of Decapolis and Jerusalem. They followed Him from the country of Judea and from the other side of the Jordan River.

Jesus Teaches On The Mountain [*Luke 6:20-49*]

5 Jesus saw many people. He went up on the mountain and sat down. His followers came to Him. ²He began to teach them, saying, ³"Those who know there is nothing good in themselves are happy, because the holy nation of heaven is theirs. ⁴Those who have sorrow are happy, because they will be comforted. ⁵Those who have no pride in their hearts are happy, because the earth will be given to them. ⁶Those who are hungry and thirsty to be right with God are happy, because they will be filled. ⁷Those who show loving-kindness are happy, because they will have loving-kindness shown to them. ⁸Those who have a pure heart are happy, because they will see God. ⁹Those who make peace are happy, because they will be called the sons of God. ¹⁰Those who have it very hard for doing right are happy, because the holy nation of heaven is theirs. ¹¹You are happy when people act and talk in a bad way to you and make it very hard for you and tell bad things and lies about you because you trust in Me. ¹²Be glad and full of joy because your pay will be much in heaven. They made it very hard for the early preachers who lived a long time before you.

Jesus Teaches About Salt And Light

[13]"You are the salt of the earth. If salt loses its taste, how can it be made to taste like salt again? It is no good. It is thrown away and people walk on it. [14]You are the light of the world. You cannot hide a city that is on a mountain. [15]Men do not light a lamp and put it under a basket. They put it on a table so it gives light to all in the house. [16]Let your light shine in front of men. Then they will see the good things you do and will honor your Father Who is in heaven.

Jesus Teaches About The Law

[17]"Do not think that I have come to do away with the Law of Moses or the writings of the early preachers. I have not come to do away with them but to complete them. [18]I tell you, as long as heaven and earth last, not one small mark or part of a word will pass away of the Law of Moses until it has all been done. [19]Anyone who breaks even the least of the Law of Moses and teaches people not to do what it says, will be called the least in the holy nation of heaven. He who obeys and teaches others to obey what the Law of Moses says, will be called great in the holy nation of heaven. [20]I tell you, unless you are more right with God than the teachers of the Law and the proud religious law-keepers, you will never get into the holy nation of heaven.

Jesus Teaches About Anger And Killing

[21]"You have heard that men were told long ago, 'You must not kill another person. If someone does kill, he will be guilty and will be punished for his wrong-doing.' [22]But I tell you that whoever is angry with his brother will be guilty and have to suffer for his wrong-doing. Whoever says to his brother, 'You have no brains,' will have to stand in front of the court. Whoever says, 'You fool,' will be sent to the fire of hell. [23]If you take your gift to the altar and remember your brother has something against you, [24]leave your gift on the altar. Go and make right what is wrong between you and him. Then come back and give your gift. [25]Agree with the one who is against you while you are talking together, or he might take you to court. The court will hand you over to the police. You will be put into prison. [26]For sure, I tell you, you will

not be let out of prison until you have paid every piece of money of the fine.

Jesus Teaches About Husband And Wife

[27]"You have heard that it was said long ago, 'You must not do sex sins.' [28]But I tell you, anyone who even looks at a woman with a sinful desire of wanting her has already sinned in his heart. [29]If your right eye is the reason you sin, take it out and throw it away. It is better to lose one part of your body than for your whole body to be thrown into hell. [30]If your right hand is the reason you sin, cut it off and throw it away. It is better to lose one part of your body than for your whole body to go to hell.

Jesus Teaches About Marriage

[31]"It has been said, 'Whoever wants to divorce his wife should have it put in writing, telling her he is leaving her.' [32]But I tell you, whoever divorces his wife except if she has not been faithful to him, makes her guilty of a sex sin. Whoever marries a woman who has been divorced is guilty of a sex sin.

Jesus Teaches About What To Say

[33]"You have heard that it was said long ago, 'You must not make a promise you cannot keep. You must carry out your promises to the Lord.' [34]I tell you, do not use strong words when you make a promise. Do not promise by heaven. It is the place where God is. [35]Do not promise by earth. It is where He rests His feet. Do not promise by Jerusalem. It is the city of the great King. [36]Do not promise by your head. You are not able to make one hair white or black. [37]Let your yes be YES. Let your no be NO. Anything more than this comes from the devil.

Jesus Teaches About Fighting

[38]"You have heard that it has been said, 'An eye for an eye and a tooth for a tooth.' [39]But I tell you, do not fight with the man who wants to fight. Whoever hits you on the right side of the face, turn so he can hit the other also. [40]If any person takes you to court to get your shirt, give him your coat also. [41]Whoever makes you walk a short way, go with him twice as far. [42]Give to any

Whoever hits you on the right side of the face, turn so he can hit the other also.

person who asks you for something. Do not say no to the man who wants to use something of yours.

Jesus Teaches About Loving Those Who Hate You

Pray for those who do bad things to you and who make it hard for you.

43"You have heard that it has been said, 'You must love your neighbor and hate those who hate you.' 44But I tell you, love those who hate you. (*Respect and give thanks for those who say bad things to you. Do good to those who hate you.) Pray for those who do bad things to you and who make it hard for you. 45Then you may be the sons of your Father Who is in heaven. His sun shines on bad people and on good people. He sends rain on those who are right with God and on those who are not right with God. 46If you love those who love you, what pay can you expect from that? Do not even the tax gatherers do that?   47If you say hello only to the people you like, are you doing any more than others? The people who do not know God do that much. 48You must be perfect as your Father in heaven is perfect.

Jesus Teaches On The Mountain About Helping Others

6 "Be sure you do not do good things in front of others just to be seen by them. If you do, you have no pay from your Father in heaven. 2When you give to the poor, do not be as those who pretend to be someone they are not. They blow a horn in the places of worship and in the streets so people may respect them. For sure, I tell you, they have all the pay they are going to get. 3When you give, do not let your left hand know what your right hand gives. 4Your giving should be in secret. Then your Father Who sees in secret will pay you.

Jesus Teaches About Prayer

5"When you pray, do not be as those who pretend to be someone they are not. They love to stand and pray in the places of worship or in the streets so people can see them. For sure, I tell you, they have all the pay they are going to get. 6When you pray, go into a room by yourself. After you have shut the door, pray to your Father Who is in secret. Then your Father Who sees in secret will pay you. 7When you pray, do not say the same thing over and over again making long prayers like the people who do not know

God. They think they are heard because their prayers are long. ⁸Do not be like them. Your Father knows what you need before you ask Him.

⁹"Pray like this: 'Our Father in heaven, Your name is holy. ¹⁰May Your holy nation come. What You want done, may it be done on earth as it is in heaven. ¹¹Give us the bread we need today. ¹²Forgive us our sins as we forgive those who sin against us.

¹³Do not let us be tempted, but keep us from sin. *Your nation is holy. You have power and shining greatness forever. Let it be so.'

Jesus Teaches About Forgiveness

¹⁴"If you forgive people their sins, your Father in heaven will forgive your sins also. ¹⁵If you do not forgive people their sins, your Father will not forgive your sins.

Jesus Teaches About Not Eating So You Can Pray Better

¹⁶"When you go without food so you can pray better, do not be as those who pretend to be someone they are not. They make themselves look sad so people will see they are going without food. For sure, I tell you, they have all the pay they are going to get. ¹⁷When you go without food so you can pray better, put oil on your head and wash you face. ¹⁸Then nobody knows you are going without food. Then your Father Who sees in secret will pay you.

Jesus Teaches About Having Riches

¹⁹"Do not gather together for yourself riches of this earth. They will be eaten by bugs and become rusted. Men can break in and steal them. ²⁰Gather together riches in heaven where they will not be eaten by bugs or become rusted. Men cannot break in and steal them. ²¹For wherever your riches are, your heart will be there also. ²²The eye is the light of the body. If your eye is good, your whole body will be full of light. ²³If your eye is bad, your whole body will be dark. If the light in you is dark, how dark it will be! ²⁴No one can have two bosses. He will hate the one and love

the other. Or he will listen to the one and work against the other. You cannot have both God and riches as your boss at the same time.

Jesus Teaches About Cares Of Life

[25]"I tell you this: Do not worry about your life. Do not worry about what you are going to eat and drink. Do not worry about what you are going to wear. Is not life more important than food? Is not the body more important than clothes? [26]Look at the birds in the sky. They do not plant seeds. They do not gather grain. They do not put grain into a building to keep. Yet your Father in heaven feeds them! Are you not more important than the birds? [27]Which of you can make himself a little taller by worrying? [28]Why should you worry about clothes? Think how the flowers grow. They do not work or make cloth. [29]But I tell you that Solomon in all his greatness was not dressed as well as one of these flowers. [30]God clothes the grass of the field. It lives today and is burned in the stove tomorrow. How much more will He give you clothes? You have so little faith! [31]Do not worry. Do not keep saying, 'What will we eat?' or, 'What will we drink?' or, 'What will we wear?' [32]The people who do not know God are looking for all these things. Your Father in heaven knows you need all these things. [33]First of all, look for the holy nation of God. Be right with Him. All these other things will be given to you also. [34]Do not worry about tomorrow. Tomorrow will have its own worries. The troubles we have in a day are enough for one day.

Do not worry about tomorrow.

Jesus Teaches On The Mountain About Saying What Is Wrong In Others

7 "Do not say what is wrong in other people's lives. Then other people will not say what is wrong in your life. [2]You will be guilty of the same things you find in others. When you say what is wrong in others, your words will be used to say what is wrong in you. [3]Why do you look at the small piece of wood in your brother's eye, and do not see the big piece of wood in your own eye? [4]How can you say to your brother, 'Let me take that small piece of wood out of your eye,' when there is a big piece of wood in your own eye? [5]You who pretend to be someone you are not, first take the big piece of wood out of your own eye. Then you can see better to take the small piece of wood out of your brother's eye.

⁶"Do not give that which belongs to God to dogs. Do not throw your pearls in front of pigs. They will break them under their feet. Then they will turn and tear you to pieces.

Jesus Teaches About Prayer

⁷"Ask, and what you are asking for will be given to you. Look, and what you are looking for you will find. Knock, and the door you are knocking on will be opened to you. ⁸Everyone who asks receives what he asks for. Everyone who looks finds what he is looking for. Everyone who knocks has the door opened to him. ⁹What man among you would give his son a stone if he should ask for bread? ¹⁰Or if he asks for a fish, would he give him a snake? ¹¹You are bad and you know how to give good things to your children. How much more will your Father in heaven give good things to those who ask Him?

Jesus Teaches About Others

¹²"Do for other people whatever you would like to have them do for you. This is what the Jewish Law and the early preachers said.

Jesus Teaches About Two Roads

¹³"Go in through the narrow door. The door is wide and the road is easy that leads to hell. Many people are going through that door. ¹⁴But the door is narrow and the road is hard that leads to life that lasts forever. Few people are finding it.

Jesus Teaches About False Teachers

¹⁵"Watch out for false teachers. They came to you dressed as if they were sheep. On the inside they are hungry wolves. ¹⁶You will know them by their fruit. Do men pick grapes from thorns? Do men pick figs from thistles? ¹⁷It is true, every good tree has good fruit. Every bad tree has bad fruit. ¹⁸A good tree cannot have bad fruit. A bad tree cannot have good fruit. ¹⁹Every tree that does not have good fruit is cut down and thrown into the fire. ²⁰So you will know them by their fruit. ²¹Not everyone that says to me,

'Lord, Lord,' will go into the holy nation of heaven. The one who does the things My Father in heaven wants him to do will go into the holy nation of heaven. ²²Many people will say to Me on that day, 'Lord, Lord, did we not preach in Your Name? Did we not put out demons in Your Name? Did we not do many powerful works in Your Name?' ²³Then I will say to them in plain words, 'I never knew you. Go away from Me, you who do wrong!'

Jesus Teaches About Houses Built On Rock And Sand

²⁴"Whoever hears these words of Mine and does them, will be like a wise man who built his house on rock. ²⁵The rain came down. The water came up. The wind blew and hit the house. The house did not fall because it was built on rock. ²⁶Whoever hears these words of Mine and does not do them, will be like a foolish man who built his house on sand. ²⁷The rain came down. The water came up. The wind blew and hit the house. The house fell and broke apart." ²⁸Then Jesus finished talking. The people were surprised and wondered about His teaching. ²⁹He was teaching them as One Who has the right and the power to teach. He did not teach as the teachers of the Law.

The people were surprised and wondered about His teaching.

The Healing Of A Man With A Bad Skin Disease [Mark 1:40-45; Luke 5:12-16]

8 Jesus came down from the mountain. Many people followed Him. ²A man with a bad skin disease came and got down in front of Him and worshiped Him. He said, "Lord, if You will, You can heal me!" ³Then Jesus put His hand on him and said, "I will. You are healed!" At once the man was healed. ⁴Jesus said to him, "Go now, but tell no one. Let the religious leader see you. Give the gift in worship that Moses told you to give. This will show them you have been healed." (Leviticus 13:49)

Healing Of The Captain's Helper Boy [Luke 7:1-10]

⁵Jesus came to the city of Capernaum. A captain of the army came to Him. He asked for help, ⁶saying, "Lord, my helper boy is sick in bed. He is not able to move his body. He is in much pain." ⁷Jesus said to the captain, "I will come and heal him." ⁸The captain said, "Lord, I am not good enough for You to come to my

house. Only speak the word. My helper boy will be healed. ⁹I am a man who works for someone else and I have men working under me. I say to this man, 'Go!' and he goes. I say to another, 'Come!' and he comes. I say to my workman, 'Do this!' and he does it.''

¹⁰When Jesus heard this, He was surprised and wondered about it. He said to those who followed Him, ''For sure, I tell you, I have not found so much faith in the Jewish nation. ¹¹I say to you, many people will come from the east and from the west. They will sit down with Abraham and with Isaac and with Jacob in the holy nation of heaven. ¹²But those who should have belonged to the holy nation of heaven will be thrown out into outer darkness, where there will be crying and grinding of teeth.'' ¹³Jesus said to the captain, ''Go your way. It is done for you even as you had faith to believe.'' The helper boy was healed at that time.

Peter's Mother-In-Law Healed [*Mark 1:29-31; Luke 4:38-39*]

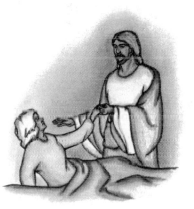

¹⁴Jesus came to Peter's house. He saw Peter's wife's mother in bed. She was very sick. ¹⁵He touched her hand and the sickness left her. She got up and cared for Jesus.

Many People Are Healed [*Mark 1:32-34; Luke 4:40-41*]

¹⁶That evening they brought to Jesus many people who had demons in them. The demons were put out when Jesus spoke to them. All the sick people were healed. ¹⁷It happened as the early preacher Isaiah said it would happen. He said, ''He took on Himself our sickness and carried away our diseases.'' (Isaiah 53:4)

Testing Some Followers [*Luke 9:57-62*]

¹⁸Jesus saw many people and told them to go to the other side of the lake. ¹⁹A teacher of the Law came to Jesus. He said, ''Lord, I will follow You wherever You go.'' ²⁰Jesus said to him, ''Foxes have holes. Birds have nests. But the Son of Man has no place to lay His head.''

²¹Another of His followers said to Him, ''Lord, let me go first and bury my father.'' ²²Jesus said to him, ''Follow Me. Let the people who are dead bury their own dead.''

The Wind And Waves Obey Jesus [Mark 4:35-41; Luke 8:22-25]

²³Jesus got into a boat. His followers followed Him. ²⁴At once a bad storm came over the lake. The waves were covering the boat. Jesus was sleeping. ²⁵His followers went to Him and called, "Help us, Lord, or we will die!" ²⁶He said to them, "Why are you afraid? You have so little faith!" Then He stood up. He spoke sharp words to the wind and the waves. Then the wind stopped blowing. ²⁷The men were surprised and wondered about it. They said, "What kind of a man is He? Even the winds and the waves obey Him."

Demons Ask Jesus To Let Them Live In Pigs [Mark 5:1-20; Luke 8:26-39]

²⁸Jesus came to the other side of the lake into the country of the Gadarenes. Two men came to Him from among the graves. They had demons in them and were very wild men. They were so bad that no one would go near them. ²⁹They called out, saying, "What do You want of us, You Son of God? Have You come here to make us suffer before it is our time to suffer?"

³⁰A long way from there many pigs were eating. ³¹The demons begged Jesus, saying, "If You put us out, send us into the pigs." ³²Jesus said to the demons, "Go!" They came out of the men and went into the pigs. At once the pigs ran down the mountain side. They fell into the water and died.

³³The men who cared for the pigs ran fast into the city and told everything. They told what happened to the men who had the demons. ³⁴Every person in the city came to meet Jesus. When they saw Jesus, they asked Him to leave their country.

The Healing Of A Man Who Could Not Move His Body [Mark 2:1-12; Luke 5:17-26]

9   Jesus got into a boat. He crossed over to the other side and came into His own city. ²They took a man to Him who was on his bed. This man was not able to move his body. Jesus saw their faith. He said, "Son, take hope. Your sins are forgiven." ³Some of the teachers of the Law said to themselves, "This man speaks as if He is God, but He is not!" ⁴Jesus knew what they were thinking. He said, "Why do you think bad thoughts in your hearts? ⁵Which is easier to say, 'Your sins are forgiven' or to say, 'Get up and walk?' ⁶But this is to show you that the Son of Man has power on earth to forgive sins." He said to the sick man, "Get up! Take your bed and go home." ⁷He got up and went to his home. ⁸All the people saw this. They were surprised and wondered about it. Then they gave thanks to God because He had given such power to men.

Jesus Calls Matthew [Mark 2:13-17; Luke 5:27-32]

⁹As Jesus went from there, He saw a man called Matthew. Matthew was sitting at his work gathering taxes. Jesus said to him, "Follow Me." Matthew got up and followed Jesus. ¹⁰Jesus ate in Matthew's house. Many men who gathered taxes and many who were sinners came to Matthew's house and sat down with Jesus and His followers. ¹¹The proud religious law-keepers saw this. They said to the followers of Jesus, "Why does your Teacher eat with men who gather taxes and with sinners?" ¹²Jesus heard them and said, "People who are well do not need a doctor. ¹³But go and understand these words, 'I want loving-kindness and not a gift to be given.' (Hosea 6:6) For I have not come to call good people. I have come to call those who are sinners."

Follow Me. Matthew got up and followed Jesus.

Jesus Teaches About Going Without Food So You Can Pray Better [Mark 2:18-22; Luke 5:33-35]

¹⁴Then the followers of John the Baptist came to Jesus. They asked, "Why do we and the proud religious law-keepers many times go without food so we can pray better? But Your followers never go without food so they can pray better." ¹⁵Jesus said, "Can the friends at a wedding be sorry when the man just married is with them? But the days will come when the man just married will be taken from them. Then they will not eat food so they can pray better.

¹⁶"No one sews a piece of new cloth on an old coat, because if the new piece pulls away, it makes the hole bigger. ¹⁷Men do not put new wine into old skin bags. If they did, the skins would break and the wine would run out. The bags would be no good. They put new wine into new skin bags and both can be used."

Two Healed Through Faith [Mark 5:21-43; Luke 8:40-56]

[18]While Jesus talked to them, a leader of the people came and got down in front of Him, and worshiped Him. He said, "My daughter has just died. But come, lay Your hand on her and she will live." [19]Jesus got up and followed him. His followers went also.

[20]Just then a woman who had been sick with a flow of blood for twelve years came from behind. She touched the bottom of His coat. [21]She said to herself, "If I only touch the bottom of His coat, I will be healed." [22]Then Jesus turned around. He saw her and said, "Daughter, take hope! Your faith has healed you." At once the woman was healed.

Daughter, take hope! Your faith has healed you.

[23]Jesus came into the leader's house. He saw the people playing music and making much noise. [24]He said to them, "Go now! For the girl is not dead, but is sleeping." But they laughed at Him. [25]He sent the people outside. Then He went in and took the girl's hand. She was raised up. [26]News of this went out into all the country.

The Healing Of Two Blind Men

[27]Jesus went on from there. Two blind men followed Him. They called out, "Take pity on us, Son of David." [28]Jesus went into the house. The blind men came to Him. Then Jesus said to them, "Do you have faith that I can do this?" They said to Him, "Yes, Sir!" [29]Then Jesus put His hands on their eyes and said, "You will have what you want because you have faith." [30]Their eyes were opened. Jesus told them to tell no one. [31]But when they had gone, they told about Him everywhere in the country.

A Demon Put Out Of A Man

[32]As they went on their way, a man who had a demon and could not talk was brought to Jesus. [33]When the demon was put out of him, the man was able to talk. Many people were surprised and wondered about it. They said, "We have never seen anything in the nation of the Jews like this." [34]But the proud religious law-keepers said, "He puts out demons by the help of the leader of the demons."

Jesus Preaches And Heals In Galilee

³⁵Jesus went on into all the towns and cities. He taught in their places of worship. He preached the Good News of the holy nation of God. He healed every sickness and disease the people had. ³⁶As He saw many people, He had loving-pity on them. They were troubled and were walking around everywhere. They were like sheep without a shepherd. ³⁷Then He said to His followers, "There is much grain ready to gather. But the workmen are few. ³⁸Pray then to the Lord Who is the Owner of the grain fields that He will send workmen to gather His grain."

Jesus Calls Twelve Followers And Sends Them Out [Mark 6:7-13; Luke 9:1-6]

10 Jesus called His twelve followers to Him. He gave them power to put out demons and to heal all kinds of sickness and disease. ²These are the names of the twelve missionaries. There were Simon who was called Peter, and Andrew his brother, and James and John who were the sons of Zebedee. ³There were Philip and Bartholomew and Thomas. There was Matthew, the man who gathered taxes. There were James the son of Alphaeus, and Thaddeaus, and ⁴Simon the Canaanite. There was Judas Iscariot who handed Jesus over to be killed.

⁵Jesus sent out these twelve missionaries. He told them to go, saying, "Stay away from people who are not Jews. And do not go to any town in the country of Samaria. ⁶But go to the Jewish people who are lost. ⁷As you go, preach. Say, 'The holy nation of heaven is near.' ⁸Heal the sick and those with bad skin diseases. Raise the dead. Put out demons. You have received much, now give much. ⁹Do not take gold or silver or brass money with you. ¹⁰Do not take a bag of things for the trip. Do not take two coats or shoes or a walking stick. A workman should receive his food and what he needs.

¹¹"When you come to a city or town, find a home that is respected and stay there until you leave. ¹²As you go into a house, tell them you hope good comes to them. ¹³And if the house is respected, give them your good wishes. If it is not respected, let

your good wishes come back to you. ¹⁴Whoever does not receive you or does not listen to what you say, as you leave that house or city, shake off the dust from your feet. ¹⁵For sure, I tell you, it will be easier for the land of Sodom and Gomorrha on the day men stand in front of God and are told they are guilty, than for that city.

¹⁶"I am sending you out like sheep with wolves all around you. Be wise like snakes and gentle like doves. ¹⁷But look out for men. They will take you up to their courts and they will hurt you in their places of worship. ¹⁸They will take you in front of the leaders of the people and of the kings because of Me. You will tell them and the people who do not know God about Me. ¹⁹When you are put into their hands, do not worry what you will say or how you will say it. The words will be given you when the time comes. ²⁰It will not be you who will speak the words. The Spirit of your Father will speak through you.

²¹"A brother will hand over a brother to be put to death. A father will hand over his child to be put to death. Children will hand over their parents to be put to death. ²²You will be hated by all people because of Me. But he who stays true to the end will be saved. ²³When they make it hard for you in one town, go to another. For sure, I tell you, before you have gone through the Jewish cities, the Son of Man will come.

²⁴"A follower is not greater than his teacher. A workman who is owned by someone is not greater than his owner. ²⁵A follower should be happy to be as his teacher, and a workman who is owned by someone should be happy to be as his owner. If they have called the head of the house Satan, how much more will they speak against those of the house. ²⁶Then do not be afraid of them. For nothing is covered up that will not be brought out into the light. There is nothing hid that will not be made known. ²⁷You tell in the light what I tell you in the dark. You must speak with a loud voice from the roofs of houses what you have heard. ²⁸Do not be afraid of them who kill the body. They are not able to kill the soul. But fear Him Who is able to destroy both soul and body in hell. ²⁹Are not two small birds sold for a very small piece of money? And yet not one of the birds falls to the earth without your Father knowing it. ³⁰God knows how many hairs you have

There is nothing hid that will not be made known.

on your head. ³¹So do not be afraid. You are more important than many small birds.

³²"Whoever makes Me known in front of men, I will make him known to My Father in heaven. ³³But whoever does not make Me known in front of men and acts as if he does not know Me, I will not make him known to My Father in heaven.

³⁴"Do not think I came to bring peace on the earth. I did not come to bring peace, but a sword. ³⁵I came to turn a man against his father. I came to turn a daughter against her mother. I came to turn a daughter-in-law against her mother-in-law. ³⁶A man will be hated by his own family.

Giving Up Things Of This Earth [Luke 14:25-35]

³⁷"He who loves his father and mother more than Me is not good enough for Me. He who loves son or daughter more than Me is not good enough for Me. ³⁸He who does not take his cross and follow Me is not good enough for Me. ³⁹He who wants to keep his life will have it taken away from him. He who loses his life because of Me will have it given back to him.

⁴⁰"Whoever receives you, receives Me. Whoever receives Me, receives Him Who sent Me. ⁴¹Whoever receives a preacher who speaks for God because he is a preacher, will get the pay of a preacher who speaks for God. Whoever receives a man right with God, because he is a man right with God, will get the pay of a man right with God. ⁴²For sure, I tell you, anyone who gives a cup of cold water to one of these little ones because he follows Me, will not lose his pay."

John The Baptist Asks About Jesus [Luke 7:18-23]

11 When Jesus finished telling His twelve followers what to do, He went away from there to teach and preach in their town.

²When John the Baptist was in prison, he heard what Jesus was doing. He sent his followers. ³They asked, "Are You the One Who was to come, or should we look for another?" ⁴Jesus said to them, "Go and tell John what you see and hear. ⁵The blind are

made to see. Those who could not walk are walking. Those who have had bad skin diseases are healed. Those who could not hear are hearing. The dead are raised up to life and the Good News is preached to poor people. 6He is happy who is not ashamed of Me and does not turn away because of Me.''

Jesus Tells About John The Baptist [Luke 7:24-35]

7As the followers of John the Baptist went away, Jesus began to tell the people about John. He said, ''What did you go out to see in the desert? A small tree shaking in the wind?   8But what did you go out to see? A man dressed in good clothes? Those who are dressed in good clothes are in the houses of kings. 9What did you go out to see? One who speaks for God? Yes, I tell you, he is more than one who speaks for God. 10This is the man the Holy Writings spoke of when they said, 'Look! I will send My helper to carry news ahead of You. He will make Your way ready for You!' (Malachi 3:1) 11For sure, I tell you, of those born of women, there is no one greater than John the Baptist. The least in the holy nation of heaven is greater than he. 12From the days of John the Baptist until now, the holy nation of heaven has suffered very much. Fighting men try to take it. 13All the early preachers and the Law told about it until the time of John. 14And if you will believe it, he is Elijah who was to come. (Malachi 4:5) 15You have ears, then listen!

Jesus Speaks Against Cities In Galilee

16''What are the people of this day like? They are like children playing in the center of town where people gather. They call to their friends. 17They say, 'We played music for you, but you did not dance. We showed sorrow in front of you, but you did not show sorrow.' 18John came and did not eat or drink. They said, 'He has a demon.'   19Then the Son of Man came and ate and drank. They said, 'Look! He eats too much and likes wine. He is a friend of men who gather taxes and of sinners!' But wisdom shows itself to be right by what it does.''

But wisdom shows itself to be right by what it does.

20Then He began to say strong words against the cities where most of His powerful works were done. He spoke to them because they were not sorry for their sins and did not turn from them. [21]"It is bad for you, city of Chorazin! It is bad for you, town of Bethsaida! For if the powerful works which were done in you had been done in the cities of Tyre and Sidon, they would have turned from their sins long ago. They would have shown their sorrow by putting on clothes made from hair and would have sat in ashes. [22]I tell you, it will be better for Tyre and Sidon on the day men stand in front of God and are told they are guilty, than for you.

[23]"And Capernaum, are you to be lifted up into heaven? You will be taken down to hell. If the powerful works which were done in you had been done in the city of Sodom, it would be here to this day. [24]But I say to you that it will be better for the land of Sodom on the day men stand in front of God and are told they are guilty, than for you."

Jesus Prays To His Father

[25]At that time Jesus said, "Thank you, Father, Lord of heaven and earth, because You hid these things from the wise and from those who have much learning. You have shown them to little children. [26]Yes, Father, it was good in Your sight.

[27]"Everything has been given to Me by My Father. No one knows the Son but the Father. No one knows the Father but the Son, and those to whom the Son wants to make the Father known.

Jesus Calls People To Follow Him

[28]"Come to Me, all of you who work and have heavy loads. I will give you rest. [29]Follow My teachings and learn from Me. I am gentle and do not have pride. You will have rest for your souls. [30]For My way of carrying a load is easy and My load is not heavy."

Jesus Teaches About The Day Of Rest [Mark 2:23-28; Luke 6:1-5]

12 At that time Jesus walked through the grain fields on the Day of Rest. His followers were hungry and began to pick off grain to eat. [2]The proud religious law-keepers saw this. They said to Jesus, "Look! Your followers do what the Law says not to do on the Day of Rest." ³He said to them, "Have you not read what David did when he and his men were hungry? ⁴He went into the house of God and ate the special bread used in worship which was against the Law for him or those with him to eat! Only the Jewish religious leaders were to eat that special bread. ⁵Have you not read in the Law how the religious leaders do that which is not right to do on the Day of Rest, and yet they are not guilty? ⁶I tell you that Someone greater than the house of God is here. ⁷If you had understood what the words mean, 'I want loving-kindness and not a gift to be given,' (Hosea 6:6) you would not say a person is guilty who has done no wrong. ⁸For the Son of Man is Lord of the Day of Rest."

Jesus Heals On The Day Of Rest [*Mark 3:1-6; Luke 6:6-11*]

⁹From there Jesus went into their place of worship. ¹⁰A man was there with a dried-up hand. The proud religious law-keepers asked Jesus, "Does the Law say it is right to heal on the Day of Rest?" They wanted something to say against Him. ¹¹He said to them, "If one of you has a sheep which falls into a hole on the Day of Rest, will you not take hold of it and pull it out? ¹²How much better is a man than a sheep! So it is right to do good on the Day of Rest." ¹³Then He said to the man, "Put out your hand." He held it out and it was made as well as the other. ¹⁴The proud religious law-keepers went out and made plans against Him. They planned how they might kill Him.

Jesus Heals Many People [*Mark 3:7-12; Luke 6:17-19*]

¹⁵Jesus knew this and went away from there. Many people followed Him and He healed all of them. ¹⁶He told them to tell no one of Him. ¹⁷It happened as the early preacher Isaiah said it would happen, saying, ¹⁸"Look! My Helper Whom I picked out! My much Loved, in Whom My soul is well pleased! I will put My Spirit in Him. He will say to the nations what is right from wrong. ¹⁹He will not fight or speak with a loud voice. No man will hear His voice in the streets. ²⁰He will not break a broken branch. He will not put out a little f   until He makes things right. ²¹In His name the nations will ha   hope." (Isaiah 42:2-4)

A Nation That Cannot Stand [Mark 3:22-30; Luke 11:14-23]

²²Then they brought to Him a man who had a demon. He was blind and could not speak. Jesus healed him and he could talk and see. ²³All the people were surprised and said, "Can this Man be the Son of David?" ²⁴But when the proud religious law-keepers heard it, they said, "This Man puts out demons only by Satan, the leader of demons."

²⁵Jesus knew their thoughts and said to them, "Every nation divided into groups that fight each other is going to be destroyed. Every city or family divided into groups that fight each other will not stand. ²⁶If the devil puts out the devil, he is divided against himself. How will his nation stand? ²⁷If I put out demons by Satan, by whom do your followers put them out? So your followers will say if you are guilty. ²⁸But if I put out demons by the Spirit of God, then the holy nation of God is come to you. ²⁹How can anyone go into a strong man's house and take away his things, unless he ties up the strong man first? Only then can he take things from his house.

The Sin That Cannot Be Forgiven

³⁰"Whoever is not with Me is against Me. Whoever is not gathering with Me is sending everywhere. ³¹I tell you, every sin and every bad word men speak against God will be forgiven, but bad words spoken against the Holy Spirit will not be forgiven. ³²Whoever speaks a word against the Son of Man will be forgiven, but whoever speaks against the Holy Spirit will not be forgiven in this life or in the life to come.

The Sin Of Saying Bad Things

³³"A good tree gives good fruit. A bad tree gives bad fruit. A tree is known by its fruit. ³⁴You family of snakes! How can you say good things when you are sinful? The mouth speaks what the heart is full of. ³⁵A good man will speak good things because of the good in him. A bad man will speak bad things because of the sin in him. ³⁶I say to you, on the day men stand in front of God, they will have to give an answer for every word they have spoken that was not important. ³⁷For it is by your words that you will not be guilty and it is by your words that you will be guilty."

A tree is known by its fruit.

Jesus Tells About Jonah [*Luke 11:29-32*]

38Then some of the teachers of the Law and the proud religious law-keepers said to Jesus, "Teacher, we would like to have you do something special for us to see." 39He said to them, "The sinful people of this day look for something special to see. There will be nothing special to see but the powerful works of the early preacher Jonah. 40Jonah was three days and three nights in the stomach of a big fish. The Son of Man will be three days and three nights in the grave also. 41The men of the city of Ninevah will stand up with the people of this day on the day men stand in front of God. Those men will say these people are guilty because the men of Ninevah were sorry for their sins and turned from them when Jonah preached. And look, Someone greater than Jonah is here!

42"The Queen of the South will stand up with the people of this day on the day men stand in front of God. She will say that these people are guilty because she came from the ends of the earth to listen to the wise sayings of Solomon. And look, Someone greater than Solomon is here!

A Person Filled With Bad Or Good [*Luke 11:24-26*]

43"When a demon is gone out of a man, it goes through dry places to find rest. It finds none. 44Then it says, 'I will go back into my house from which I came.' When it goes back, it sees that it is empty. But it sees that the house has been cleaned and looks good. 45Then it goes out and comes back bringing with it seven demons more sinful than itself. They go in and live there. In the end that man is worse than at first. It will be like this with the sinful people of this day."

The New Kind Of Family [*Mark 3:31-35; Luke 8:19-21*]

46While Jesus was still talking to the people, His mother and His brothers came and stood outside. They wanted to talk to Him. 47Someone said to Him, "Your mother and brothers are outside and want to talk to you." 48Jesus said, "Who is My mother? And who are My brothers?" 49He put out His hand to His followers and said, "Look, these are My mother and My brothers! 50Whoever does what My father in heaven wants him to do is My brother and My sister and My mother."

Jesus Teaches With Picture-Stories [Mark 4:1-34; Luke 8:4-18]

13 That same day Jesus went out of the house and sat down by the shore of the lake. ²Then He got into a boat and sat down because so many people had gathered around Him. Many people were standing on the shore.

The Picture-Story Of The Man Who Planted Seeds

³Jesus taught them many things by using picture-stories. He said, "A man went out to plant seeds. ⁴As he planted the seeds, some fell by the side of the road. The birds came and ate the seeds. ⁵Some seeds fell between rocks. The seeds came up at once because there was so little ground. ⁶When the sun was high in the sky, they dried up and died because they had no root. ⁷Some seeds fell among thorns. The thorns grew and did not give the seeds room to grow. ⁸Some seeds fell on good ground and gave much grain. Some gave one hundred times as much grain. Some gave sixty times as much grain. Some gave thirty times as much grain. ⁹You have ears, then listen."

Some seeds fell on good ground and gave much grain.

Why Jesus Used Picture-Stories

¹⁰The followers of Jesus came to Him and said, "Why do You speak to them in picture-stories?" ¹¹He said to the followers, "You were given the secrets about the holy nation of heaven. The secrets were not given to the others. ¹²He who has will have more given to him. He will have even more than enough. But he who has little will have even that taken away from him.

¹³"This is why I speak to them in picture-stories. They have eyes but they do not see. They have ears but they do not hear and they do not understand. ¹⁴It happened in their lives as Isaiah said it would happen. He said, 'You hear and hear but do not understand. You look and look but do not see. ¹⁵The hearts of these people have become fat. They hear very little with their ears. They have closed their eyes. If they did not do this, they would see with their eyes and hear with their ears and understand with their hearts. Then they would be changed in their ways, and I would heal them.' (Isaiah 6:9-10) ¹⁶But how great are your eyes

because they see. How great are your ears because they hear. [17]For sure, I tell you, that many early preachers and men right with God have wanted to see the things you see, but they did not see them. They wanted to hear the things you hear, but they did not hear them.

Jesus Tells About The Man Who Planted Seeds

[18]"Listen to the picture-story of the man who planted seeds in the ground. [19]When anyone hears the Word about the holy nation and does not understand it, the devil comes and takes away what was put in his heart. He is like the seed that fell by the side of the road. [20]The seed which fell between rocks is like the person who receives the Word with joy as soon as he hears it. [21]Its root is not deep and it does not last long. When troubles and suffering come because of the Word, he gives up and falls away. [22]The seed which fell among thorns is like the person who hears the Word but the cares of this life, and the love for money let the thorns come up and does not give the seed room to grow and give grain. [23]The seed which fell on good ground is like the one who hears the Word and understands it. He gives much grain. Some seed gives one hundred times as much grain. Some gives sixty times as much grain. Some gives thirty times as much grain."

The Picture-Story Of The Good Seed And The Weed Seed

[24]Jesus told them another picture-story. He said, "The holy nation of heaven is like a man who planted good seed in his field. [25]During the night someone who hated him came and planted weed seed with the good seed in his field and went away. [26]When the good seed started to grow and give grain, weeds came up also.

[27]"The men came who worked for the man who planted the seed. They said to him, 'Sir, did you not plant good seed in your field? Why does it have weeds also?' [28]The man who planted the seed said, 'Someone who hates me has done this.' The workmen asked him, 'Should we go and pull the weeds out from among the good grain?' [29]He said, 'No, because if you pull out the weeds, the good grain will come up also. [30]Let them grow together until the time

to gather the grain. Then I will say to the workmen, ''Gather the weeds first and put them together to be burned. Gather the good grain into my building.'' ' ''

The Picture-Story Of The Mustard Seed

³¹Jesus told them another picture-story. He said, ''The holy nation of heaven is like mustard seed which a man planted in his field. ³²It is the smallest of seeds. But when it is full-grown, it is larger than the grain of the fields and it becomes a tree. The birds of the sky come and stay in its branches.''

The Picture-Story Of The Yeast

³³Jesus gave them another picture-story. He said, ''The holy nation of heaven is like yeast that a woman put into three pails of flour until it had become much more than at first.''

³⁴Jesus told all these things using picture-stories to the many people. He did not speak to them without using picture-stories. ³⁵It happened as the early preacher said it would happen, ''I will open My mouth in picture-stories. I will tell things which have been kept secret from the beginning of the world.''(Psalm 78:2)

Jesus Tells About The Weed Seed

³⁶After Jesus sent the people away, He went into the house. His followers came to Him and said, ''Tell us what You mean by the picture-story of the weeds in the field.'' ³⁷Jesus said, ''He Who plants the good seed is the Son of Man. ³⁸The field is the world. The good seed are the children of the holy nation. The weeds are the children of the devil. ³⁹The devil is the one who got in and planted the weeds. The time to gather is the end of the world. The men who gather are the angels. ⁴⁰As the weeds are gathered together and burned in the fire, so will it be in the end of the world. ⁴¹The Son of Man will send His angels. They will gather out of His holy nation all things that cause people to sin and those who do sin. ⁴²They will put them into a stove of fire. There will be loud crying and grinding of teeth. ⁴³Then the ones right with God will shine as the sun in the holy nation of their Father. You have ears, then listen!''

The ones right with God will shine as the sun in the holy nation of their Father.

The Picture-Stories Of The Gold Buried In The Field And Of Buying A Pearl

44"The holy nation of heaven is like a box of riches buried in a field. A man found it and then hid it again. In his joy he goes and sells all that he has and buys that field.

45"Again, the holy nation of heaven is like a man who buys and sells. He is looking for good pearls. 46When he finds one good pearl worth much money, he goes and sells all that he has and buys it.

The Picture-Story Of The Fish Net

47"The holy nation of heaven is like a big net which was let down into the sea. It gathered fish of every kind. 48When it was full, they took it to the seashore. They sat down and put the good fish into pails. They threw the bad fish away. 49It will be like this in the end of the world. Angels will come and take the sinful people from among those who are right with God. 50They will put the sinful people into a stove of fire where there will be loud crying and grinding of teeth."

51Jesus asked them, "Have you understood all these picture-stories?" They said, "Yes, Lord!" 52He said to them, "Every teacher of the Law who has become a follower of the holy nation of heaven is like a man who owns his house. He takes new and old riches from his house."

They Do Not Believe In Jesus In The Town Of Nazareth [Mark 6:1-6]

53When Jesus had finished these picture-stories, He went away from there. 54He came to His own town and taught them in their places of worship. They were surprised and wondered, saying, "Where did this Man get this wisdom? How can He do these powerful works? 55Is not this the son of the man who makes things from wood? Is not Mary His mother? Are not James and Joseph and Simon and Judas His brothers? 56And are not all His sisters here? Then where did He get all these things? 57And they were ashamed of Him and turned away because of Him. Jesus said to them, "One who speaks for God is shown no respect in his own town and in his own house."

⁵⁸He did not do many powerful works there because they did not put their trust in Him.

John The Baptist Is Put Into Prison [Mark 6:14-20; Luke 3:18-20]

14 At that time King Herod heard much about Jesus. ²He said to his helpers, "This must be John the Baptist. He has risen from the dead. That is why these powerful works are done by him." ³For Herod had taken John and put him into prison. It was because of Herodias, the wife of his brother Philip. ⁴For John had said to him, "It is against the Law for you to have her." He would have killed John but he was afraid of the people. The people thought John was one who spoke for God.

John The Baptist Is Killed [Mark 6:21-29; Luke 9:7-9]

⁶On Herod's birthday the daughter of Herodias danced in front of them. Herod was made happy by her. ⁷He promised he would give her anything she asked. ⁸Because her mother told her to do it, she said, "Give me the head of John the Baptist on a plate." ⁹The king was sorry. But he told them to give it because he had promised and because of those who were eating with him. ¹⁰He sent to the prison and had John's head cut off. ¹¹It was brought in on a plate and given to the girl. She brought it to her mother. ¹²Then the followers of John came and took his body and buried it. They went and told Jesus.

The Feeding Of The Five Thousand [Mark 6:30-44; Luke 9:10-17; John 6:1-14]

¹³When Jesus heard that John had been killed, He went from there by boat to a desert. He wanted to be alone. When the people knew it, they followed after Him by land from the cities. ¹⁴When He got out of the boat, He saw many people. He had loving-pity for them and healed those who were sick.

¹⁵When it was evening, His followers came to Him. They said, "This is a desert. The day is past. Send the people away so they

may go into the towns and buy food for themselves." [16]Jesus said to them, "They do not have to go away. Give them something to eat." [17]They said to Him, "We have only five loaves of bread and two fish." [18]Jesus said, "Bring them to Me." [19]He told the people to sit down on the grass. Then He took the five loaves of bread and two fish. He looked up to heaven and gave thanks. He broke the loaves in pieces and gave them to His followers. The followers gave them to the people. [20]They all ate and were filled. They picked up twelve baskets full of pieces of bread and fish after the people were finished eating. [21]About five thousand men ate. Women and children ate also.

Jesus Walks On The Water [Mark 6:45-52; John 6:15-21]

[22]At once Jesus had His followers get into the boat. He told them to go ahead of Him to the other side while He sent the people away. [23]After He had sent them away, He went up the mountain by Himself to pray. When evening came, He was there alone. [24]By this time the boat was far from land and was being thrown around by the waves. The wind was strong against them.

[25]Just before the light of day, Jesus went to them walking on the water. [26]When the followers saw Him walking on the water, they were afraid. They said, "It is a spirit." They cried out with fear. [27]At once Jesus spoke to them and said, "Take hope. It is I. Do not be afraid!"

[28]Peter said to Jesus, "If it is You, Lord, tell me to come to You on the water." [29]Jesus said, "Come!" Peter got out of the boat and walked on the water to Jesus. [30]But when he saw the strong wind, he was afraid. He began to go down in the water. He cried out, "Lord, save me!" [31]At once Jesus put out His hand and took hold of him. Jesus said to Peter, "You have so little faith! Why did you doubt?"

[32]When Jesus and Peter got into the boat, the wind stopped blowing. [33]Those in the boat worshiped Jesus. They said, "For sure, You are the Son of God!"

People Are Healed At Gennesaret [Mark 6:53-56]

[34]When they had gone over to the other side, they came to the land of Gennesaret. [35]When the men of that land saw it was

Jesus, they sent word into all the country around. They brought all who were sick to Jesus. 36They begged Him that they might touch the bottom of His coat. As many as touched the bottom of His coat were healed.

As many as touched the bottom of His coat were healed.

Jesus Speaks Sharp Words To The Leaders [Mark 7:1-23]

15 Some of the teachers of the Law and the proud religious law-keepers from Jerusalem came to Jesus. They asked, 2"Why do Your followers not obey the teaching that was given to them by our fathers? They do not wash their hands before they eat." 3Jesus said to them, "Why do you break the Law of God by trying to keep their teaching? 4For God said, 'Show respect to your father and mother.' (Exodus 20:12) And, 'He who says bad things against his father or mother will be put to death.' (Exodus 21:17) 5But you say that if a man says to his parents that anything he has, that might have been of help to them, is already given to God, 6he does not have to show respect by helping his father and mother. You are putting aside the Word of God to keep their teaching. 7You who pretend to be someone you are not, Isaiah told about you. He said, 8'These people show respect to Me with their mouth, but their heart is far from Me. 9Their worship of Me is worth nothing. They teach what men have made up.' " (Isaiah 29:13)

Show respect to your father and mother.

10Jesus called the people to Him and said to them, "Listen and understand this! 11It is not what goes into a man's mouth that makes his mind and heart sinful. It is what comes out of a man's mouth that makes him sinful."

12His followers came to Him. They said, "Did You know the proud religious law-keepers were ashamed and turned away because of You when they heard this?" 13He said, "Every plant that My Father in heaven did not plant will be pulled up by the roots. 14Let them alone. They are blind leaders of the blind. If one blind man leads another blind man, they will both fall into a hole."

If one blind man leads another blind man, they will both fall into a hole.

15Then Peter said to Jesus, "Tell us this picture-story so we can understand it." 16Jesus said, "Do you not understand yet? 17Do you not understand that whatever goes into the mouth goes into the stomach and then out of the body? 18But whatever comes from the mouth has come out of the heart. These things make the man dirty inside. [19]For out of the heart come bad thoughts, killing other people, sex sins of a married person, sex sins of a person not married, stealing, lying, speaking against God. [20]These are the things that make the man dirty inside. It does not make a man sinful to eat with hands that have not been washed."

Jesus Puts A Demon Out Of A Girl [Mark 7:24-30]

[21]Jesus went from there to the cities of Tyre and Sidon. [22]A woman came from the land of Canaan. She cried out to Jesus and said, "Take pity on me, Lord, Son of David! My daughter has a demon and is much troubled." [23]But Jesus did not speak a word to her. His followers kept asking, saying, "Send her away for she keeps calling us." [24]He said, "I was sent only to the Jewish people who are lost." [25]Then she came and got down in front of Jesus and worshiped Him. She said, "Lord, help me!" [26]But He said, "It is not right to take children's food and throw it to the dogs." [27]She said, "Yes, Lord, but even the dogs eat the pieces that fall from the table of their owners." [28]Jesus said to her, "Woman, you have much faith. You will have what you asked for." Her daughter was healed at that very time.

Woman, you have much faith. You will have what you asked for.

Jesus Heals All Who Come To Him

[29]Jesus went from there and came to the Lake of Galilee. Then He went up the mountain and sat down. [30]Many people came to Him. They brought with them those who were not able to walk. They brought those who were not able to see. They brought those who were not able to hear or speak and many others. Then they put them at the feet of Jesus and He healed them. [31]All the people wondered. They saw how those who could not speak were now talking. They saw how those who could not walk were now walking. They saw how those who could not see were now seeing, and they gave thanks to the God of the Jews.

The Feeding Of The Four Thousand [Mark 8:1-9]

[32]Then Jesus called His followers to Him. He said, "I pity these people because they have been with Me three days and they have no food. I do not want to send them home without food. They

might get too weak as they go." [33]The followers said to Jesus, "Where can we get enough bread to feed them all in this desert?" [34]Jesus said to them, "How many loaves of bread do you have?" They said, "Seven loaves and a few small fish." [35]He told the people to sit down on the ground. [36]Then He took the seven loaves of bread and the fish and gave thanks. He broke them and gave them to His followers. The followers gave them to the people. [37]They all ate and were filled. They picked up seven baskets full of pieces of bread and fish after the people finished eating. [38]Four thousand men ate. Women and children ate also. [39]After this Jesus sent the people away. Then He got into a boat and came to a place called Magadan.

Jesus Speaks Sharp Words To The Proud Religious Law-Keepers [Mark 8:10-13]

16 The proud religious law-keepers and a religious group of people who believe no one will be raised from the dead came to Jesus. They asked Him to show something special from heaven. They wanted to trap Jesus. [2]*(He said to them, "In the evening you say, 'The weather will be good tomorrow because the sky is red.' [3]And in the morning you say, 'We will have a storm today because the sky is red and the clouds are low.' You understand the things you see in the sky, but you cannot understand the special things you see these days!) [4]The sinful people of this day go after something special to see. There will be nothing special for them to see but the early preacher Jonah." Then He went away from them.

Jesus Shows That The Teaching Of The Proud Religious Law-Keepers Is Wrong [Mark 8:14-21]

[5]The followers came to the other side of the lake. They remembered they had forgotten to bring bread. [6]Jesus said to them, "Listen! Have nothing to do with the yeast of the proud religious law-keepers and the religious group of people who believe no one will be raised from the dead." [7]They started to think about it among themselves and said, "He said this because we forgot to bring bread." [8]Jesus knew this and said, "You have very little faith! Why are you talking among yourselves about not bringing bread? [9]Do you not yet understand or remember the five loaves of

bread that fed five thousand men? And how many baskets full were gathered up? [10]Or do you not even remember the seven loaves of bread that fed the four thousand men? And how many baskets full were gathered up? [11]Why is it that you do not see that I was not talking to you about bread? I was talking to you about keeping away from the yeast of the proud religious law-keepers and the religious group of people who believe no one will be raised from the dead." [12]Then they understood that it was not the yeast of bread that He was talking about. But He was talking about the teaching of the proud religious law-keepers and of the other religious group of people.

Peter Says Jesus Is The Christ [*Mark 8:27-30; Luke 9:18-20*]

[13]Jesus came into the country of Caesarea Philippi. He asked His followers, "Who do people say that I, the Son of Man, am?" [14]They said, "Some say You are John the Baptist and some say Elijah and others say Jeremiah or one of the early preachers."

You are the Christ, the Son of the living God.

[15]He said to them, "But who do you say that I am?" [16]Simon Peter said, "You are the Christ, the Son of the living God."

[17]Jesus said to him, "Simon, son of Jonah, you are happy because you did not learn this from man. My Father in heaven has shown you this.

[18]"And I tell you that you are Peter. On this rock I will build My church. The powers of hell will not be able to have power over My church. [19]I will give you the keys of the holy nation of heaven. Whatever you do not allow on earth will not have been allowed in heaven. Whatever you allow on earth will have been allowed in heaven." [20]Then with strong words He told His followers to tell no one that He was the Christ.

Jesus Tells Of His Death For The First Time [*Mark 8:31-38; Luke 9:21-27*]

[21]From that time on Jesus began to tell His followers that He had to go to Jerusalem and suffer many things. These hard things would come from the leaders and from the head religious leaders of

the Jews and from the teachers of the Law. He told them He would be killed and three days later He would be raised from the dead. ²²Peter took Jesus away from the others and spoke sharp words to Him. He said, "Never, Lord! This must not happen to You!" ²³Then Jesus turned to Peter and said, "Get behind Me, Satan! You are standing in My way. You are not thinking how God thinks. You are thinking how man thinks."

Giving Up Riches

²⁴Jesus said to His followers, "If anyone wants to be My follower, he must forget about himself. He must take up his cross and follow Me. ²⁵If anyone wants to keep his life safe, he will lose it. If anyone gives up his life because of Me, he will save it. ²⁶For what does a man have if he gets all the world and loses his own soul? What can a man give to buy back his soul? ²⁷The Son of Man will come in the greatness of His Father with His angels. Then He will give to every man his pay as he has worked. ²⁸For sure, I tell you, there are some standing here that will not die until they see the Son of Man coming as King."

A Look At What Jesus Will Be Like [Mark 9:1-13; Luke 9:28-36]

17 Six days later Jesus took with Him Peter and James and his brother John. He led them up to a high mountain by themselves. ²He was changed in looks before them. His face was as bright as the sun. His clothes looked as white as light. ³Moses and Elijah were seen talking with Jesus. ⁴Then Peter said to Jesus, "Lord, it is good for us to be here. If You will let us, we will build three altars here. One will be for You and one for Moses and one for Elijah."

⁵While Peter was speaking, a bright cloud came over them. A voice from the cloud said, "This is My much-loved Son, I am very happy with Him. Listen to Him!" ⁶When the followers heard this, they got down on the ground on their faces and were very much afraid. ⁷Jesus came and put His hand on them. He said, "Get up! Do not be afraid." ⁸When they looked up, they saw no one there but Jesus only. ⁹As they came down from the mountain, Jesus

told them in strong words, saying, "Do not tell anyone what you have seen until the Son of Man is raised from the dead."

The Followers Ask About Elijah

¹⁰The followers asked Jesus, "Then why do the teachers of the Law say that Elijah must come first?" ¹¹He said, "For sure, Elijah will come first and get things ready. ¹²But I tell you, Elijah has already come and they did not know him. They did to him whatever they wanted to do. In the same way the Son of Man will suffer from them also." ¹³Then the followers understood He was talking about John the Baptist.

A Boy With A Demon Is Healed [Mark 9:14-29; Luke 9:37-42]

¹⁴When they came to many people, a man came up to Jesus and got on his knees. He said, ¹⁵"Lord, have pity on my son. He is very sick and at times loses the use of his mind. Many times he falls into the fire or into the water. ¹⁶I took him to Your followers but they were not able to heal him."

¹⁷Then Jesus said, "You people of this day have no faith and you are going the wrong way. How long must I be with you? How long must I put up with you? Bring him here to Me." ¹⁸Jesus spoke sharp words to the demon and the demon came out of him. At once the boy was healed.

¹⁹The followers came to Jesus when He was alone. They said, "Why were we not able to put the demon out?" ²⁰Jesus said to them, "Because you have so little faith. For sure, I tell you, if you have faith as a mustard seed, you will say to this mountain, 'Move from here to over there,' and it would move over. You will be able to do anything. ²¹*But this kind of demon does not go out but by prayer and by going without food so you can pray better."

Jesus Tells Of His Death The Second Time [Mark 9:30-32; Luke 9:43-45]

²²While they were still in Galilee, Jesus said to the followers, "The Son of Man will be handed over to men. ²³They will kill Him, but He will be raised from the dead three days later." The followers were very sad.

Tax Money For The House Of God

²⁴They came to the city of Capernaum. Those who gathered the tax for the house of God came to Peter. They said, "Does not your Teacher pay tax money for the house of God?" ²⁵Peter said, "Yes." When Peter came into the house, Jesus spoke to him first. He said, "What do you think, Simon? From whom do the kings of this earth get their money or taxes, from their own people or from those of another country?" ²⁶Peter said to Him, "From those of another country." Then Jesus said, "Then their own people do not pay taxes. ²⁷But so we will not make them to be troubled, go down to the lake and throw in a hook. Take the first fish that comes up. In its mouth you will find a piece of money. Take that and pay the tax for Me and yourself."

Jesus Teaches About The Faith Of A Child [Mark 9:33-50; Luke 9:46-50]

18 At that time the followers came to Jesus. They said, "Who is the greatest in the holy nation of heaven?" ²Jesus took a little child and put him among them. ³He said, "For sure, I tell you, unless you have a change of heart and become like a little child, you will not get into the holy nation of heaven. ⁴Whoever is without pride as this little child is the greatest in the holy nation of heaven. ⁵Whoever receives a little child because of Me receives Me. ⁶But whoever is the reason for one of these little children who believe in Me to fall into sin, it would be better for him to have a large rock put around his neck and to be thrown into the sea.

> Whoever is without pride as this little child is the greatest in the holy nation of heaven.

⁷"It is bad for the world because of that which makes people sin. Men will be tempted to sin. But it is bad for the one who is the reason for someone to sin. ⁸If your hand or your foot is the reason you sin, cut it off and throw it away. It is better for you to go into life without a hand or a foot, than to have two hands or two feet and to be thrown into the fire of hell. ⁹If your eye is the reason you sin, take it out and throw it away. It is better for you to go into life with one eye, than to have two eyes and be thrown into the fire of hell. ¹⁰Be sure you do not hate one of these little children. I tell you, they have angels who are always looking into the face of My Father in heaven.

The Lost Sheep

¹¹*"For the Son of Man has come to save that which was lost. ¹²What do you think about this? A man has one hundred sheep and one of them is lost. Will he not leave the ninety-nine and go to the mountains to look for that one lost sheep? ¹³If he finds it, for sure, I tell you, he will have more joy over that one, than over the ninety-nine that were not lost. ¹⁴I tell you, My Father in heaven does not want one of these little children to be lost.

What To Do With A Brother Who Sins Against You

¹⁵"If your brother sins against you, go and tell him what he did without other people hearing it. If he listens to you, you have won your brother back again. ¹⁶But if he will not listen to you, take one or two other people with you. Every word may be remembered by the two or three who heard. ¹⁷If he will not listen to them, tell the trouble to the church. If he does not listen to the church, think of him as a person who is as bad as one who does not know God and a person who gathers taxes.

¹⁸"For sure, I tell you, whatever you do not allow on earth will not have been allowed in heaven. Whatever you allow on earth will have been allowed in heaven. ¹⁹Again I tell you this: If two of you agree on earth about anything you pray for, it will be done for you by My Father in heaven. ²⁰For where two or three are gathered together in My name, there I am with them."

True Forgiveness

²¹Then Peter came to Jesus and said, "Lord, how many times may my brother sin against me and I forgive him, up to seven times?" ²²Jesus said to him, "I tell you, not seven times but seventy times seven!

²³"The holy nation of heaven is like a king who wanted to find out how much money his workmen owed him. ²⁴As he began, one of the workmen he owned was brought to him who owed him very much money. ²⁵He could pay nothing that he owed. So the king spoke the word that he and his wife and his children and all that he had should be sold to pay what he owed. ²⁶The workman got down

on his face in front of the king. He said, 'Give me time, and I will pay you all the money.' 27Then the king took pity on his workman and let him go. He told him he did not have to pay the money back.

28"But that workman went out and found one of the other workmen who owed him very little money. He took hold of his neck and said, 'Pay me the money you owe me!' 29The other workman got down at his feet and said, 'Give me time, and I will pay you all the money.' 30But he would not. He had him put into prison until he could pay the money.

31"When his other workmen saw what had happened, they were very sorry. They came and told the king all that was done. 32Then the king called for the first one. He said, 'You bad workman! I forgave you. I said that you would not have to pay back any of the money you owed me because you asked me. 33Should you not have had pity on the other helper, even as I had pity on you?' 34The king was very angry. He handed him over to men who would beat and hurt him until he paid all the money he owed. 35So will My Father in heaven do to you, if each one of you does not forgive his brother from his heart.''

What Jesus Taught About Marriage And Divorce [Mark 10:1-12]

19 When Jesus had finished talking, He went from the country of Galilee. He came to the part of the country of Judea which is on the other side of the Jordan River. 2Many people followed Him and He healed them there.

3The proud religious law-keepers came to Jesus. They tried to trap Him by saying, "Does the Law say a man can divorce his wife for any reason?" 4He said to them, "Have you not read that He Who made them in the first place made them man and woman? 5It says, 'For this reason a man will leave his father and his mother and will live with his wife. The two will become one.' 6So they are no longer two but one. Let no man divide what God has put together.''

7The proud religious law-keepers said to Jesus, "Then why did the Law of Moses allow a man to divorce his wife if he put it down

For this reason a man will leave his father and his mother and will live with his wife. The two will become one.

in writing and gave it to her?'' [8]Jesus said to them, ''Because of your hard hearts Moses allowed you to divorce your wives. It was not like that from the beginning. [9]And I say to you, whoever divorces his wife, except for sex sins, and marries another, is guilty of sex sins in marriage. Whoever marries her that is divorced is guilty of sex sins in marriage.''

[10]His followers said to Him, ''If that is the way of a man with his wife, it is better not to be married.'' [11]But Jesus said to them, ''Not all men are able to do this, but only those to whom it has been given. [12]For there are some men who from birth will never be able to have children. There are some men who have been made so by men. There are some men who have had themselves made that way because of the holy nation of heaven. The one who is able to do this, let him do it.''

Jesus Gives Thanks For Little Children [*Mark 10:13-16; Luke 18:15-17*]

Let the little children come to Me. Do not stop them. The holy nation of heaven is made up of ones like these.

[13]Then little children were brought to Him that He might put His hands on them and pray for them. The followers spoke sharp words to them. [14]But Jesus said, ''Let the little children come to Me. Do not stop them. The holy nation of heaven is made up of ones like these.'' [15]He put His hands on them and went away.

Jesus Teaches About Keeping The Law [*Mark 10:17-31; Luke 18:18-30*]

[16]A man came to Jesus and asked, ''Good Teacher, what good work must I do to have life that lasts forever?'' [17]Jesus said to him, ''Why are you asking Me about what is good? There is only One Who is good. If you want to have life that lasts forever, you must obey the Laws.'' [18]The man said to Him, ''What kind of laws?'' Jesus said, ''You must not kill another person. You must not be guilty of sex sins. You must not steal. You must not lie. [19]Show respect to your father and your mother. And love your neighbor as you love yourself.'' [20]The young man said to Jesus, ''I have obeyed all these Laws. What more should I do?'' [21]Jesus said to him, ''If you want to be perfect, go and sell everything you have and give the money to poor people. Then you will have riches

in heaven. Come and follow Me." ²²When the young man heard these words, he went away sad for he had many riches.

The Danger Of Riches

²³Jesus said to His followers, "For sure, I tell you, it will be hard for a rich man to get into the holy nation of heaven. ²⁴Again I tell you, it is easier for a camel to go through the eye of a needle than for a rich man to get into the holy nation of heaven." ²⁵When His followers heard this, they could not understand it. They said, "Then who can be saved from the punishment of sin?" ²⁶Jesus looked at them and said, "This cannot be done by men. But with God all things can be done."

²⁷Then Peter said to Him, "We have given up everything and have followed You. Then what will we have?" ²⁸Jesus said to them, "For sure, I tell you, when all the earth will be new and the Son of Man will sit on His place as King in His shining greatness, you who have followed Me will have twelve places to sit also. You will say who is guilty in the twelve family groups of the Jewish nation. ²⁹Everyone who has given up houses or brothers or sisters or father or mother or wife or children or lands because of Me, will get a hundred times more. And you will get life that lasts forever. ³⁰Many who are first will be last. Many who are last will be first.

The Picture-Story Of The Workmen In The Grape Field

20 "For the holy nation of heaven is like the owner of a grape field. He went out early in the morning to hire workmen to work in his grape field. ²He promised to give them a day's pay and then sent them to his grape field. ³Later in the morning he went to the center of the town where people gather. He saw men standing there doing nothing. ⁴He said to them, 'You go to my grape field and work also. Whatever is right, I will pay you.' And they went. ⁵Again he went out about noon and at three o'clock and did the same thing. ⁶About five o'clock he went out and still found others doing nothing. He asked them, 'Why do you stand here all day and do nothing?' ⁷They said to him, 'Because no one has hired us.' He said, 'Go to my grape field and work. Whatever is right, I will pay you.'

8"When evening came, the owner of the grape field said to the boss of the workmen, 'Call the workmen. Give them their pay. Start with the last ones hired and go on to the first ones hired.' 9The workmen who had been hired at five o'clock came up. Each one of them got a day's pay for his work. 10When the workmen who had been hired the first thing in the morning came, they thought they would get more. But each one got a day's pay. 11After they received it, they talked against the owner. 12They said, 'The last workmen hired have only worked one hour. You have given to them the same as to us. We have worked hard through the heat of the day.' 13But he said to one of them, 'Friend, I am doing you no wrong. Did you not agree with me when I promised to pay you a day's pay? 14Take your pay and go. I want to give the last ones hired the same as I have given you. 15Do I not have the right to do what I want to do with my own money? Does your eye make you want more because I am good?' 16So those who are last will be first and the first will be last.''

So those who are last will be first and the first will be last.

Jesus Tells Of His Death The Third Time [Mark 10:32-34; Luke 18:31-34]

17As Jesus was going up to Jerusalem, He talked also to the twelve followers by the side of the road. He said, 18"Listen! We are going up to Jerusalem. The Son of Man will be handed over to the religious leaders and to the teachers of the Law. They will say that He must be put to death. 19They will hand Him over to the people who do not know God. They will make fun of Him and will beat Him. They will nail Him to a cross. Three days later He will be raised to life."

The Mother Of James And John Asks Jesus Something Hard [Mark 10:35-45]

20The mother of Zebedee's children (James and John) came to Jesus with her sons. She got down on her knees in front of Jesus to ask something of Him. 21He said to her, "What do you want?" She said, "Say that my two sons may sit, one at Your right side and one at Your left side, when You are King." 22Jesus said to her, "You do not know what you are asking. Are you able to take the suffering that I am about to take? *(Are you able to be baptized with the baptism that I am baptized with?)" They said, "Yes, we are able.'' ²³He said to them, ''You will suffer as I will suffer. But the places at My right side and at My left side are not Mine to give. Whoever My Father says will have those places.''

²⁴The other ten followers heard this. They were angry with the two brothers. ²⁵Jesus called them to Him and said, ''You know how the kings of the nations show their power to the people. Important leaders use their power over the people. ²⁶It must not be that way with you. But whoever wants to be great among you, let him care for you. ²⁷Whoever wants to be first among you must be as one who is owned by you and cares for you. ²⁸For the Son of Man came not to be cared for. He came to care for others. He came to give His life so that many could be bought by His blood and made free from the punishment of sin.''

> He came to give His life so that many could be bought by His blood and made free from the punishment of sin.

The Healing Of The Blind Men [*Mark 10:46-52; Luke 18:35-43*]

²⁹As they went away from the city of Jericho, many people followed Him. ³⁰Two blind men were sitting by the side of the road. They called out when they heard that Jesus was going by. They said, ''Lord, take pity on us, Son of David!'' ³¹Many people spoke sharp words to them. They told the blind men not to call out. But they called all the more, ''Lord! Take pity on us, Son of David!'' ³²Jesus stopped and called them. He asked, ''What do you want Me to do for you?'' ³³The blind men said to Jesus, ''Lord, we want our eyes opened!'' ³⁴Jesus had loving-pity for them. He put His hands on their eyes. At once they could see, and they followed Jesus.

The Last Time Jesus Goes Into Jerusalem [*Mark 11:1-11; Luke 19:29-44; John 12:12-19*]

21 They were near Jerusalem and had come to the town of Bethphage at the Mountain of Olives. Jesus sent two followers on ahead. ²He said to them, ''Go to the town over there. You will find a donkey tied and her young with her. Let them loose and bring them to Me. ³If anyone says something to you, say, 'The Lord needs them.' He will send them at once.''

⁴It happened as the early preacher said it would happen, saying, ⁵''Say to the people in Jerusalem, 'Look! Your King is coming to

you. He is gentle. He is riding on a young donkey.' '' (Zechariah 9:9; Isaiah 62:11)

⁶The followers went and did as Jesus told them. ⁷They brought the donkey and her young one. They put their clothes on the donkey and Jesus sat on them. ⁸Many people put their coats down on the road. Other people cut branches from the trees and put them along the way. ⁹The people who went in front and those who followed Jesus called out, "Greatest One! The Son of David! Great and honored is He Who comes in the name of the Lord! Greatest One in the highest heaven.''

¹⁰When Jesus came into Jerusalem, all the people of the city were troubled. They said, "Who is this?'' ¹¹Many people said, "This is Jesus, the One Who speaks for God from the town of Nazareth in the country of Galilee.''

Jesus Stops The Buying And The Selling In The House Of God [Mark 11:15-19; Luke 19:45-48; John 2:13-17]

¹²Then Jesus went into the house of God and made all those leave who were buying and selling there. He turned over the tables of the men who changed money. He turned over the seats of those who sold doves. ¹³He said to them, "It is written, 'My house is to be called a house of prayer.' 'You have made it a place of robbers.' '' (Isaiah 56:7; Jeremiah 7:11)

¹⁴The blind and those who could not walk came to Jesus in the house of God and He healed them. ¹⁵The religious leaders of the Jews and the teachers of the Law saw the great things He did. They heard the children calling in the house of God and saying, "Greatest One! The Son of David!'' The leaders were very angry. ¹⁶They said to Jesus, "Do you hear what these children are saying?'' Jesus said to them, "Yes, have you not read the writings, 'Even little children and babies will honor Him'?'' ¹⁷Jesus left them and went out of the city to the town of Bethany. He stayed there that night.

The Fig Tree Dries Up [Mark 11:20-26]

¹⁸In the morning as He was coming back to the city, He was hungry. ¹⁹He saw a fig tree by the side of the road and went to it.

There was nothing on it but leaves. He said to the tree, "No fruit will ever grow on you again." At once the fig tree dried up. ²⁰The followers saw it and were surprised and wondered. They said, "How did the fig tree dry up so fast?" ²¹Jesus said to them, "For sure, I tell you this: If you have faith and do not doubt, you will not only be able to do what was done to the fig tree. You will also be able to say to this mountain, 'Move from here and be thrown into the sea,' and it will be done. ²²All things you ask for in prayer, you will receive if you have faith."

All things
you ask for
in prayer,
you will receive
if you have faith.

They Ask Jesus Who Gave Him The Power To Do These Things
[Mark 11:27-33; Luke 20:1-8]

²³Jesus came into the house of God. The religious leaders and the other leaders of the people came up to Him as He was teaching. They said, "By what right and power are You doing these things? Who gave You the right and the power to do them?" ²⁴Jesus said to them, "I will ask you one thing also. If you tell Me, then I will tell you by what right and power I do these things. ²⁵Was the baptism of John from heaven or from men?" They thought among themselves, "If we say, 'From heaven,' then He will say, 'Then why did you not believe him?' ²⁶But if we say, 'From men,' we are afraid of the people, because they all think John was one who spoke for God." ²⁷They said to Jesus, "We do not know." He said to them, "Then I will not tell you by what right and power I do these things.

The Picture-Story Of The Two Sons

²⁸"What do you think about this? There was a man who had two sons. He came to the first son and said, 'My son, go to my grape field and work today.' ²⁹He said, 'I will go.' But he did not go. ³⁰The father came to the second son and asked the same thing. The son said, 'No, I will not go.' Later he was sorry and went. ³¹Which one of the two sons did what his father wanted?" They said to Jesus, "The second son." Jesus said to them, "For sure, I tell you this: Tax gatherers and women who sell the use of their bodies will get into the holy nation of heaven before you. ³²For John came to you preaching about being right with God. You did not believe him. But tax gatherers and women who sell the use of

their bodies did believe him. When you saw this, you were not sorry for your sins and did not turn from them and believe him.

The Picture-Story Of The Grape Field [*Mark 12:1-12; Luke 20:9-18*]

33"Listen to another picture-story. A man who owned land planted grapes in a field and put a fence around it. He made a place for making wine. He built a high building to look over the grape field. He let farmers rent it and then he went into another country. 34The time came for gathering the grapes. He sent his workmen to the farmers to get the grapes. 35The farmers took his workmen and hit one. They killed another and threw stones at another. 36Again he sent other workmen. He sent more than the first time. The farmers did the same to those workmen. 37After this he sent his son to them. He said to himself, 'They will respect my son.' 38When the farmers saw the son, they said to themselves, 'This is the one who will get everything when the owner dies. Let us kill him and we will get it all.' 39They took him and threw him out of the grape field and killed him. 40When the owner of the grape field comes, what will he do to those farmers?" 41They said to Him, "He will put those bad men to death. Then he will rent the grape field to other farmers who will give him the grapes when they are ready." 42Jesus said to them, "Have you not read in the Holy Writings, 'The Stone that was put aside by the workman has become the most important Stone in the building? The Lord has done this. We think it is great!' (Psalm 118:22-23) 43I say to you, because of this, the holy nation of God will be taken from you. It will be given to a nation that will give fruit. 44Whoever falls on this Stone will be broken. And on the one it falls, it will make him like dust."

45When the religious leaders and the proud religious law-keepers heard this picture-story, they knew He spoke of them. 46When they tried to put their hands on Him, they were afraid of the many people. The people thought He was One Who spoke for God.

The Picture-Story Of The Marriage Supper

22 Again Jesus spoke to them in picture-stories. He said, 2"The holy nation of heaven is like a king who gave a wedding supper for his son. 3He sent the workmen he owned to tell the people, who had been asked, to come to the supper. But the people did not want to come.

4"He sent other workmen he owned, saying to them, 'Tell those who have been asked to come, "Look! My supper is ready. My cows and fat calves are killed. Everything is ready. Come to the wedding supper!" ' 5But they did not listen and went on working. One went to his farm. Another went to his store. 6The others took hold of the workmen he owned. They hurt them and killed them.

7"When the king heard this, he was very angry. He sent his soldiers to put those to death who had killed these workmen. He burned their city. 8Then he said to the workmen he owned, 'The wedding supper is ready. Those who were asked to come to the supper were not good enough. 9Go out into the roads and as many people as you can find, ask them to come to the wedding supper.'

10"The workmen he owned went out into the roads and brought all they could find, both bad and good. The wedding supper room was full of people. 11The king came in to see those who had come. He saw one man who did not have on wedding supper clothes. 12He said to him, 'Friend, how did you get in here without wedding supper clothes?' The man did not speak! 13Then the king said to the workmen he owned, 'Tie his hands and feet, and throw him out into the darkness. In that place there will be loud crying and grinding of teeth.' 14For many are called but few are chosen."

For many are called but few are chosen.

The Proud Religious Law-Keepers Try To Trap Jesus [Mark 12:13-17; Luke 20:19-26]

15Then the proud religious law-keepers got together to think how they could trap Jesus in His talk. 16They sent their followers to Jesus with some of King Herod's men. They asked, "Teacher, we know that You are true. We know that You are teaching the truth about God. We know You are not afraid of what men think or say about You. 17Tell us what You think of this. Is it right to pay taxes to Caesar, or not?" 18Jesus knew their sinful thoughts and said, "You pretend to be someone you are not! Why do you try to trap Me? 19Show Me a piece of money." They brought Him a piece. 20Jesus said to them, "Whose picture is this? Whose name

Pay to Caesar the things that belong to Caesar. Pay to God the things that belong to God.

is on it?" ²¹They said to Him, "Caesar's." Then He said to them, "Pay to Caesar the things that belong to Caesar. Pay to God the things that belong to God." ²²When they heard this, they were surprised and wondered about it. Then they went away from Him.

They Ask About Being Raised From The Dead [Mark 12:18-27; Luke 20:27-40]

²³The same day some people from the religious group who believe no one will be raised from the dead came to Jesus. They asked, ²⁴"Teacher, Moses said, 'If a man should die without having children, then his brother must marry his wife. He should have children for his brother.' (Deuteronomy 25:5) ²⁵There were seven brothers with us. The first was married but died before he had any children. The second brother then married the first brother's wife. ²⁶The second brother died and the same with the third and on to the seventh. ²⁷Then the woman died also. ²⁸When people are raised from the dead, whose wife will she be of the seven? They all had her for a wife."

²⁹Jesus said to them, "You are wrong because you do not know the Holy Writings or the power of God. ³⁰After people are raised from the dead, they do not marry. They are like the angels in heaven. ³¹Have you not read what God said to you about those who are raised from the dead? He said, ³²'I am the God of Abraham and the God of Isaac and the God of Jacob.' He is not the God of the dead but of the living!" (Exodus 3:6) ³³When the people heard this, they were surprised and wondered about His teaching.

The Great Law [Mark 12:28-34]

³⁴The proud religious law-keepers got together when they heard that the religious group of people who believe no one will be raised from the dead were not able to talk anymore to Jesus. ³⁵A proud religious law-keeper who knew the Law tried to trap Jesus. He said, ³⁶"Teacher, which one is the greatest of the Laws?" ³⁷Jesus said to him, " 'You must love the Lord your God with all your heart and with all your soul and with all your mind.' ³⁸This is the first and greatest of the Laws. ³⁹The second is like it, 'You must love your neighbor as you love yourself.' ⁴⁰All the Laws and the

You must love your neighbor as you love yourself.

writings of the early preachers depend on these two most important Laws.''

Jesus Asks The Proud Religious Law-Keepers About The Christ
[Mark 12:35-37; Luke 20:41-44]

⁴¹The proud religious law-keepers were gathered together. Then Jesus asked, ⁴²''What do you think about the Christ? Whose Son is He?'' They said to Him, ''The Son of David.'' ⁴³Jesus said to them, ''Then how is it that David, being led by the Holy Spirit, calls Him 'Lord?' He said, ⁴⁴''The Lord said to my Lord, ''Sit at My right side until I make those who hate you a place to rest Your feet.'' ' (Psalm 110:1) ⁴⁵If David calls Him 'Lord,' then how can He be the Son of David?'' ⁴⁶No one could answer a word, and after that day no one asked Him anything.

The Teachers Of The Law And The Proud Religious Law-Keepers
[Mark 12:38-40; Luke 20:45-47]

23 Then Jesus talked to the many people and to His followers. ²He said, ''The teachers of the Law and the proud religious law-keepers have put themselves in Moses' place as teachers. ³Do what they tell you to do and keep on doing it. But do not follow what they do. They preach but do not obey their own preaching. ⁴They make heavy loads and put them on the shoulders of men. But they will not help lift them with a finger. ⁵Everything they do, they do to be seen of men. They have words from the Holy Writings written in large letters on their left arm and forehead and they make wide trimming for their clothes. ⁶They like to have the important places at big suppers and the best seats in the Jewish places of worship. ⁷They like to have people show respect to them as they stand in the center of town where people gather. They like to be called teacher.

⁸''But you are not to be called teacher. There is only one Teacher, and all of you are brothers. ⁹Do not call any man here on earth your father. There is only one Father and He is in heaven. ¹⁰You are not to be called leader. There is only one Leader and He is Christ.

He who is greatest
among you
will be the one
to care for you.

¹¹"He who is greatest among you will be the one to care for you. ¹²The person who thinks he is important will find out how little he is worth. The person who is not trying to honor himself will be made important.

Jesus Speaks Sharp Words To The Proud Religious Law-Keepers

¹³"It is bad for you, teachers of the Law and proud religious law-keepers, you who pretend to be someone you are not! You keep men from going into the holy nation of heaven. You are not going in yourselves, and you do not allow those to go in who are about to go in. ¹⁴It is bad for you, teachers of the Law and proud religious law-keepers, you who pretend to be someone you are not! *(You take houses from poor women whose husbands have died. Then you try to cover it up by making long prayers. You will be punished all the more because of this.) ¹⁵It is bad for you, teachers of the Law and proud religious law-keepers, you who pretend to be someone you are not! You go over land and sea to win one follower. When you have him, you make him twice as much a child of hell as you are.

¹⁶"It is bad for you, blind leaders! You say, 'Whoever makes a promise by the house of God, his promise is worth nothing. But whoever makes a promise by the gold of the house of God, then his promise has to be kept.' ¹⁷You fools and blind men! Which is greater, the gold or the house of God that makes the gold holy? ¹⁸You say, 'Whoever will promise by the altar, his promise does not have to be kept. But whoever makes a promise by the gift on the altar, then his promise has to be kept.' ¹⁹You fools and blind men! Which is greater, the gift, or the altar that makes the gift holy? ²⁰Whoever makes a promise by the altar, promises by it and by everything on it. ²¹Whoever makes a promise by the house of God, promises by it and by Him Who is in it. ²²Whoever makes a promise by heaven, promises by the great place where God sits and by Him Who sits there.

²³"It is bad for you, teachers of the Law and proud religious law-keepers, you who pretend to be someone you are not! You give one-tenth part of your spices, and have not done the most important things of the Law, such as thinking what is right and wrong, and having pity and faith. These you should have done

and still have done the other things also. ²⁴You blind leaders, you take a small bug out of your cup but you swallow a camel!

²⁵"It is bad for you, teachers of the Law and proud religious law-keepers, you who pretend to be someone you are not! You clean the outside of the cup and plate, but leave the inside full of strong bad desires and are not able to keep from doing sinful things. ²⁶You blind proud religious law-keepers! Clean the inside of the cup and plate, then the outside will be clean also.

²⁷"It is bad for you, teachers of the Law and proud religious law-keepers, you who pretend to be someone you are not! You are like graves that have been made white and look beautiful on the outside. But inside you are full of the bones of dead men and of every sinful thing. ²⁸As men look at you, you seem to be good and right but inside you are full of sin. You pretend to be someone you are not.

²⁹"It is bad for you, teachers of the Law and proud religious law-keepers, you who pretend to be someone you are not! You make buildings for the graves of the early preachers, and you make the graves beautiful of those who are right with God. ³⁰You say, 'If we had lived in the days of our early fathers, we would not have helped kill the early preachers.' ³¹In this way, you are showing that you are the sons of those who killed the early preachers. ³²You might as well finish what your early fathers did. ³³You snakes! You family of snakes! How can you be kept from hell?

A Guilty People

³⁴"Because of this, I am going to keep on sending to you men who speak for God and wise men and teachers of the Law. Some of them you will kill and nail to a cross. Some of them you will beat in your places of worship. You will make it very hard for them as they go from city to city. ³⁵Because of this, you will be guilty of the blood of all those right with God on the earth. It will be from the blood of Abel who was right with God to the blood of Zachariah son of Barachias. He was the one you killed between the house of God and the altar. ³⁶For sure, I tell you, all these things will come on the people of this day.

Jesus Sorrows Over Jerusalem

³⁷"Jerusalem, Jerusalem! You kill the men who speak for God and throw stones at those who were sent to you. How many times I wanted to gather your children around Me, as a chicken gathers her young ones under her wings. But you would not let Me. ³⁸Look! Your house is empty. ³⁹I say to you, you will not see Me again until you will say, 'Great is He Who comes in the name of the Lord!' "

Jesus Tells Of The House Of God [*Mark 13:1-37; Luke 21:5-36*]

24 Jesus went out of the house of God. On the way His followers came to Him to show Him the buildings of the house of God. ²Jesus said to them, "Do you see all these things? For sure, I tell you, all these stones will be thrown down. Not one will be left standing on another."

Jesus Teaches On The Mountain Of Olives

³Jesus sat on the Mountain of Olives. The followers came to Him when He was alone and said, "Tell us, when will this happen? What can we look for to show us of Your coming and of the end of the world?"

⁴Jesus said to them, "Be careful that no one leads you the wrong way. ⁵Many people will come using My name. They will say, 'I am Christ.' They will fool many people and will turn them to the wrong way. ⁶You will hear of wars and lots of talk about wars, but do not be afraid. These things must happen, but it is not the end yet. ⁷Nations will have wars with other nations. Countries will fight against countries. There will be no food for people. The earth will shake and break apart in different places. ⁸These things are the beginning of sorrows and pains.

⁹"Then they will hand you over to be hurt. They will kill you. You will be hated by all the world because of My name. ¹⁰Many people will give up and turn away at this time. People will hand over each other. They will hate each other. ¹¹Many false religious teachers will come. They will fool many people and will turn them

to the wrong way. [12]Because of people breaking the laws and sin being everywhere, the love in the hearts of many people will become cold. [13]But the one who stays true to the end will be saved.

[14]"This Good News about the holy nation of God must be preached over all the earth. It must be told to all nations and then the end will come.

This Good News about the holy nation of God must be preached over all the earth.

Days Of Trouble And Pain And Sorrow

[15]"You will see a very sinful man-made god standing in the house of God in Jerusalem. It was spoken of by the early preacher Daniel. (Daniel 9:27;12:11) The one who reads this should understand it. [16]Then those in the country of Judea should run to the mountains. [17]The man who is on the top of his house should not come down to take anything out of his house. [18]The man who is in the field should not go back to get his coat. [19]It will be hard for a woman who will soon be a mother. It will be hard for the ones feeding babies in those days! [20]Pray that you will not have to go in the winter or on the Day of Rest. [21]In those days there will be very much trouble and pain and sorrow. It has never been this bad from the beginning of the world and never will be again. [22]If the time had not been made short, no life would have been saved. Because of God's people, the time will be made short.

The False Religious Teachers

[23]"If anyone says to you, 'Look! Here is the Christ!' or 'There He is!' do not believe it. [24]People who say they are Christ and false preachers will come. They will do special things for people to see. They will do great things, so that if it can be done, God's people will be fooled to believe something wrong. [25]Listen! I have told you before it comes. [26]If they tell you, 'Look! He is in the desert,' do not go to see. Or if they say, 'Look! He is in the inside room,' do not believe them. [27]The Son of Man will come as fast as lightning goes across the sky from east to west. [28]Birds gather wherever there is a dead body.

The Son of Man will come as fast as lightning goes across the sky from east to west.

Jesus Will Come Again In His Shining Greatness

[29]"As soon as those days of trouble and pain and sorrow are over, the sun will get dark. The moon will not give light. The stars

will fall from the sky. The powers in the heavens will be shaken. [30]Then something special will be seen in the sky telling of the Son of Man. All nations of the earth will have sorrow. They will see the Son of Man coming in the clouds of the sky with power and shining greatness. [31]He will send His angels with the loud sound of a horn. They will gather together God's people from the four winds. They will come from one end of the sky to the other.

They will see the Son of Man coming in the clouds of the sky with power and shining greatness.

The Picture-Story Of The Fig Tree

[32]"Now learn something from the fig tree. When the branch begins to grow and puts out its leaves, you know that summer is near. [33]In the same way, when you see all these things happen, you know the Son of Man is near. He is even at the door. [34]For sure, I tell you, the people of this day will not pass away before all these things have happened.

No One Knows When Jesus Will Come Again

[35]"Heaven and earth will pass away, but My words will not pass away. [36]But no one knows the day or the hour. No! Not even the angels in heaven know. The Son does not know. Only the Father knows.

[37]"When the Son of Man comes, it will be the same as when Noah lived. [38]In the days before the flood, people were eating and drinking. They were marrying and being given in marriage. This kept on until the day Noah went into the large boat. [39]They did not know what was happening until the flood came and the water carried them all away. It will be like this when the Son of Man comes.

[40]"Two men will be working in a field. One will be taken and the other will be left. [41]Two women will be grinding grain. One will be taken and the other will be left.

Watch! You do not know on what day your Lord is coming.

[42]"Because of this, watch! You do not know on what day your Lord is coming. [43]But understand this: If the owner of a house had known when the robber was coming, he would have watched. He would not have allowed his house to have been broken into. [44]You must be ready also. The Son of Man is coming at a time when you do not think He will come.

Faithful Workmen And Workmen Who Are Not Faithful

⁴⁵"Who is the faithful and wise workman whom his owner has made boss over the other workmen? He is to have food ready for them at the right time. ⁴⁶That workman is happy who is doing what his owner wants him to do when he comes back. ⁴⁷For sure, I tell you, he will make him boss over all that he has. ⁴⁸But if that workman is bad, he will think, 'The owner will not come soon.' ⁴⁹He will beat the others. He will eat and drink with those who are drunk. ⁵⁰The owner will come on a day and at an hour when the workman is not looking for him. ⁵¹The owner will punish the workman and will give him his place with those who pretend to be someone they are not. There will be loud crying and grinding of teeth.

The Picture-Story Of Ten Young Women

25 "At that time the holy nation of heaven will be like ten women who have never had men. They took their lamps and went out to meet the man soon to be married. ²Five of them were wise and five were foolish. ³The foolish women took their lamps but did not take oil with them. ⁴The wise women took oil in a jar with their lamps. ⁵They all went to sleep because the man to be married did not come for a long time.

⁶"At twelve o'clock in the night there was a loud call, 'Look! The man soon to be married is coming! Go out to meet him!' ⁷Then all the women got up and made their lamps brighter. ⁸The foolish women said to the wise women, 'Give us some of your oil because our lamps are going out.' ⁹But the wise women said, 'No! There will not be enough for us and you. Go to the store and buy oil for yourselves.' ¹⁰While they were gone to buy oil, the man soon to be married came. Those who were ready went in with him to the marriage. The door was shut.

¹¹"Later the foolish women came. They said, 'Sir, Sir, open the door for us!' ¹²But he said to them, 'For sure, I tell you, I do not know you!' ¹³So watch! You do not know what day or what hour the Son of Man is coming.

The Picture-Story Of The Ten Workmen And The Money

14"'For the holy nation of heaven is like a man who was going to a country far away. He called together the workmen he owned and gave them his money to use. 15He gave to one workman five pieces of money worth much. He gave to another workman two pieces of money worth much. He gave to another workman one piece of money worth much. He gave to each one as he was able to use it. Then he went on his trip. 16The workman who had the five pieces of money went out to the stores and traded until he made five more pieces. 17The workman who had two pieces of money did the same thing. He made two more pieces. 18The workman who had received the one piece of money went and put the money in a hole in the earth. He hid his owner's money.

19"'After a long time the owner of those workmen came back. He wanted to know what had been done with his money. 20The one who had received the five pieces of money worth much came and handed him five pieces more. He said, 'Sir, you gave me five pieces of money. Look! I used it and made five more pieces.' 21His owner said to him, 'You have done well. You are a good and faithful workman. You have been faithful over a few things. I will put many things in your care. Come and share my joy.' 22The one who received two pieces of money worth much came also. He said, 'Sir, you gave me two pieces of money. Look! I used it and made two more pieces.' 23His owner said to him, 'You have done well. You are a good and faithful workman. You have been faithful over a few things. I will put many things in your care. Come and share my joy.' 24The one who had received one piece of money worth much came. He said, 'Sir, I know that you are a hard man. You gather grain where you have not planted. You take up where you have not spread out. 25I was afraid and I hid your money in the ground. Look! Here is your money.' 26His owner said to him, 'You bad and lazy workman. You knew that I gather grain where I have not planted. You knew that I take up where I have not spread out. 27You should have taken my money to the bank. When I came back, I could have had my own money and what the bank paid for using it. 28Take the one piece of money from him. Give it to the one who has ten pieces of money.' 29For the man who has will have more given to him. He will have more than enough. The man who has nothing, even what he has will be taken away. 30Throw the

You have done well. You are a good and faithful workman. You have been faithful over a few things. I will put many things in your care.

bad workman out into the darkness. There will be loud crying and grinding of teeth.

The Sheep And The Goats

³¹"When the Son of Man comes in His shining greatness, He will sit down on His place of greatness. All the angels will be with Him. ³²All the nations of the earth will be gathered in front of Him. He will divide them from each other as a shepherd divides the sheep from the goats. ³³He will put the sheep on His right side, but the goats He will put on His left side.

³⁴"Then the King will say to those on His right side, 'Come, you who have been called by My Father. Come into the holy nation that has been made ready for you before the world was made. ³⁵For I was hungry and you gave Me food to eat. I was thirsty and you gave Me water to drink. I was a stranger and you gave Me a room. ³⁶I had no clothes and you gave Me clothes to wear. I was sick and you cared for Me. I was in prison and you came to see Me.'

³⁷"Then those that are right with God will say, 'Lord, when did we see You hungry and feed You? When did we see You thirsty and give You a drink? ³⁸When did we see You a stranger and give You a room? When did we see You had no clothes and we gave You clothes? ³⁹And when did we see You sick or in prison and we came to You?' ⁴⁰Then the King will say, 'For sure, I tell you, because you did it to one of the least of My brothers, you have done it to Me.'

⁴¹"Then the King will say to those on His left side, 'Go away from Me! You are guilty! Go into the fire that lasts forever. It has been made ready for the devil and his angels. ⁴²For I was hungry but you did not give Me food to eat. I was thirsty but you did not give Me water to drink. ⁴³I was a stranger but you did not give Me a room. I had no clothes but you did not give Me clothes. I was sick and in prison but you did not come to see Me.'

⁴⁴"Then they will ask, 'Lord, when did we see You hungry or thirsty or a stranger? When did we see You without clothes or sick or in prison and did not care for You?' ⁴⁵Then He will say to them, 'For sure, I tell you, because you did not do it to one of the least of

these, you did not do it to Me.' ⁴⁶These will go to the place where they will be punished forever. But those right with God will have life that lasts forever.''

Jesus Tells Of His Death The Fourth Time [Mark 14:1-2; Luke 22:1-6]

26 When Jesus had finished all this teaching, He said to His followers, ²''You know that the special religious supper to remember how the Jews left Egypt is in two days. The Son of Man will be handed over to be nailed to a cross.''

³The religious leaders and the leaders of the people gathered at the house of the head religious leader. His name was Caiaphas. ⁴They talked together how they might trap Jesus and kill Him. ⁵But they said, ''This must not happen on the day of the special supper. The people would be against it. They would make much trouble.''

Mary Of Bethany Puts Special Perfume On Jesus [Mark 14:3-9; John 12:1-11]

⁶Jesus was in the town of Bethany in the house of Simon. Simon had a very bad skin disease. ⁷A woman came with a jar of perfume. She had given much money for this. As Jesus ate, she poured the perfume on His head. ⁸When the followers saw it, they were angry. They said, ''Why was this wasted? ⁹This perfume could have been sold for much money and given to poor people.''

¹⁰Jesus knew what they were saying. He said to them, ''Why are you giving this woman trouble? She has done a good thing to Me. ¹¹You will have poor people with you all the time. But you will not have Me with you all the time. ¹²She put this perfume on My body to make it ready for the grave. ¹³For sure, I tell you, wherever this Good News is preached in all the world, this woman will be remembered for what she has done.''

Judas Hands Jesus Over To Be Killed [Mark 14:10-11]

¹⁴Judas Iscariot was one of the twelve followers. He went to the religious leaders of the Jews. ¹⁵He said, ''What will you pay me if

I hand Jesus over to you?'' They promised to pay him thirty pieces of silver. [16]From that time on Judas looked for a way to hand Jesus over to them.

Getting Ready For The Special Supper [*Mark 14:12-16; Luke 22:7-13*]

[17]On the first day of the supper of bread without yeast the followers came to Jesus. They said, ''What place do You want us to make ready for You to eat the supper of the special religious gathering to remember how the Jews left Egypt?'' [18]He said, ''Go into the city to a certain man and say to him, 'The Teacher says, ''My time is near. I will eat the special supper at your house with My followers.'' ' '' [19]The followers did as Jesus told them. They made things ready for this special supper.

The Last Special Supper [*Mark 14:17-21; Luke 22:14-18; John 13:21-35*]

[20]When evening came, Jesus sat with the twelve followers. [21]As they were eating, Jesus said, ''For sure, I tell you, one of you will hand Me over.'' [22]They were very sad. They said to Him one after the other, ''Lord, is it I?'' [23]He said, ''The one who will hand Me over is the one who has just put his hand with Mine into the dish. [24]The Son of Man is going away as it is written of Him. It is bad for that man who hands the Son of Man over! It would have been better if he had not been born!'' [25]Judas was the one who was handing Jesus over. He said, ''Teacher, am I the one?'' Jesus said to him, ''You have said it.''

The First Lord's Supper [*Mark 14:22-26; Luke 22:19-20*]

[26]As they were eating, Jesus took a loaf of bread. He gave thanks and broke it in pieces. He gave it to His followers and said, ''Take, eat, this is My body.'' [27]Then He took the cup and gave thanks. He gave it to them and said, ''You must all drink from it. [28]This is My blood of the New Way of Worship which is given for many. It is given so the sins of many can be forgiven. [29]I tell you that I will not drink of the fruit of the vine again until that day when I will drink it new with you in the holy nation of My

This is My blood
of the New Way
of Worship
which is given
for many.
It is given
so the sins of many
can be forgiven.

Father.'' [30]After they sang a song they went out to the Mountain of Olives.

Jesus Tells How Peter Will Lie About Him [Mark 14:27-31; Luke 22:31-34; John 13:36-38]

[31]Jesus said to them, "All of you will be ashamed of Me and leave Me tonight. For it is written, 'I will kill the shepherd and the sheep of the flock will be spread everywhere.' (Zechariah 13:7) [32]After I am raised from the dead, I will go before you into the country of Galilee."

[33]Peter said to Jesus, "Even if all men give up and turn away because of You, I will never." [34]Jesus said to him, "For sure, I tell you, before a rooster crows this night, you will say three times you do not know Me." [35]Peter said to Him, "Even if I have to die with You, I will never say I do not know You." And all the followers said the same thing.

Jesus Prays In Gethsemane [Mark 14:32-42; Luke 22:39-46]

[36]Jesus came with them to a place called Gethsemane. He said to them, "You sit here while I go over there to pray." [37]He took Peter and the two sons of Zebedee with Him. He began to have much sorrow and a heavy heart. [38]Then He said to them, "My soul is very sad. My soul is so full of sorrow I am ready to die. You stay here and watch with Me."

[39]He went on a little farther and got down with His face on the ground. He prayed, "My Father, if it can be done, take away what is before Me. Even so, not what I want but what You want."

Watch and pray so that you will not be tempted. Man's spirit is willing but the body does not have the power to do it.

[40]Then He came to the followers and found them sleeping. He said to Peter, "Were you not able to watch with Me one hour? [41]Watch and pray so that you will not be tempted. Man's spirit is willing, but the body does not have the power to do it."

[42]He went away again the second time. He prayed, saying, "My Father, if this must happen to Me, may whatever You want be done." [43]He came and found them asleep again. Their eyes were heavy. [44]He went away from them the third time and prayed the same prayer.

⁴⁵Then He came to His followers and asked them, "Are you still sleeping and getting your rest? As I speak, the time has come when the Son of Man will be handed over to sinners. ⁴⁶Get up and let us go. Look! The man who will hand Me over is near."

Jesus Handed Over To Sinners [Mark 14:43-52; Luke 22:47-51; John 18:1-11]

⁴⁷Judas, one of the twelve followers, came while Jesus was talking. He came with many others who had swords and sticks. They came from the religious leaders of the Jews and the leaders of the people. ⁴⁸The man who handed Jesus over gave the men something to look for. He said, "The One I kiss is the One you want. Take Him!" ⁴⁹At once Judas went up to Jesus and said, "Hello, Teacher," and kissed Him. ⁵⁰Jesus said to him, "Friend, do what you came to do." Then they came and put their hands on Jesus and took Him.

⁵¹One of those with Jesus took his sword. He hit the workman who was owned by the religious leader and cut off his ear. ⁵²Jesus said to him, "Put your sword back where it belongs. Everyone who uses a sword will die with a sword. ⁵³Do you not think that I can pray to My Father? At once He would send Me more than 70,000 angels. ⁵⁴If I did, how could it happen as the Holy Writings said it would happen? It must be this way."

⁵⁵Then Jesus said to the many people, "Have you come with swords and sticks to take Me as if I were a robber? I have been with you every day teaching in the house of God. You never put your hands on Me then. ⁵⁶But this has happened as the early preachers said in the Holy Writings it would happen." Then all the followers left Him and ran away.

Jesus Stands In Front Of The Religious Leaders [Mark 14:53-54; Luke 22:52-54; John 18:19-24]

⁵⁷Those who had taken Jesus led Him away to Caiaphas. He was the head religious leader. The teachers of the Law and the other leaders were gathered there. ⁵⁸But Peter followed Him a long way behind while going to the house of the head religious

leader. Then he went in and sat with the helpers to see what would happen.

Jesus Stands In Front Of The Court [Mark 14:55-65]

59The religious leaders and the other leaders and all the court were looking for false things to say against Jesus. They wanted some reason to kill Him. 60They found none, but many came and told false things about Him. At last two came to the front. 61They said, "This Man said, 'I am able to destroy the house of God and build it up again in three days.'"

62Then the head religious leader stood up. He said to Jesus, "Have You nothing to say? What about the things these men are saying against You?" 63Jesus said nothing. Then the head religious leader said to Him, "In the name of the living God, I tell You to say the truth. Tell us if You are the Christ, the Son of God." 64Jesus said to him, "What you said is true. I say to you, from now on you will see the Son of Man seated on the right hand of the All-powerful God. You will see Him coming on the clouds of the sky."

From now on you will see the Son of Man seated on the right hand of the All-powerful God.

65Then the head religious leader tore his clothes apart. He said, "He has spoken as if He were God! Do we need other people to speak against Him yet? You have heard Him speak as if He were God! 66What do you think?" They said, "He is guilty of death!"

67Then they spit on His face. They hit Him with their hands. Others beat Him. 68They said, "Tell us, Christ, You Who can tell what is going to happen, who hit You?"

Peter Said He Did Not Know Jesus [Mark 14:66-72; Luke 22:55-62; John 18:15-18; 25-27]

69Peter sat outside in the yard. A young woman who was a helper came to him. She said, "You were also with Jesus Who is from the country of Galilee!" 70But Peter lied in front of all of them, saying, "I do not know what you are talking about." 71After he had gone out, another young woman who was a helper saw him. She said to those standing around, "This man was with

Jesus of Nazareth.'' [72]Again he lied and swore, "I do not know this Man!" [73]After a little while some of the people standing around came up to Peter and said, "For sure, you are one of them. You talk like they do." [74]Then he began to say bad words and swear. He said, "I do not know the Man!" At once a rooster crowed.

[75]Peter remembered the words Jesus had said to him, "Before a rooster crows, you will say three times you do not know Me." Peter went outside and cried with loud cries.

Jesus Stands In Front Of Pilate [Mark 15:1-5; Luke 23:1-5; John 18:28-37]

27 Early in the morning all the head religious leaders of the Jews and the leaders of the people gathered together and talked about how they could put Jesus to death. [2]They tied Him and took Him away. Then they handed Him over to Pilate who was the leader of the country.

Judas Kills Himself

[3]Then Judas was sorry he had handed Jesus over when he saw that Jesus was going to be killed. He took back the thirty pieces of silver and gave it to the head religious leaders and the other leaders. [4]He said, "I have sinned because I handed over a Man Who has done no wrong." And they said, "What is that to us? That is your own doing." [5]He threw the money down in the house of God and went outside. Then he went away and killed himself by hanging from a rope.

[6]The head religious leaders took the money. They said, "It is against the Law to put this money into the house of God. This money has bought blood." [7]They talked about what to do with the money. Then they decided to buy land to bury strangers in. [8]Because of this, that land is called the Field of Blood to this day. [9]It happened as the early preacher Jeremiah said it would happen. He said, "And they took the thirty pieces of silver which was the price the Jews said they would pay for Him. [10]And they bought

land to bury strangers in, as the Lord told me." (Zechariah 11:12-13)

[11]Then Jesus stood in front of the leader of the country. The leader asked Jesus, "Are You the King of the Jews?" Jesus said to him, "What you say is true." [12]When the head religious leaders and the other leaders spoke against Him, He said nothing. [13]Then Pilate said to Him, "Do You not hear all these things they are saying against You?" [14]Jesus did not say a word. The leader was much surprised and wondered about it.

Jesus Or Barabbas Is To Go Free [*Mark 15:6-14; Luke 23:17-25; John 18:38-40*]

[15]At the special supper each year the leader of the country would always let one person who was in prison go free. It would be the one the people wanted. [16]They had a man who was known by all the people whose name was Barabbas. [17]When they were gathered together, Pilate said to them, "Whom do you want me to let go free? Should it be Barabbas or Jesus Who is called Christ?" [18]For the leader of the country knew the religious leaders had given Jesus over to him because they were jealous.

[19]Pilate was sitting in the place where he sits when he tells people if they are guilty or not. His wife sent him this word, "Have nothing to do with that good Man. I have been troubled today in a dream about Him."

[20]The head religious leaders and the other leaders talked the many people into asking for Barabbas to go free and for Jesus to be put to death. [21]The leader of the country said to them, "Which one of the two do you want me to let go free?" They said, "Barabbas." [22]Pilate said to them, "Then what am I to do with Jesus Who is called Christ?" They all said to him, "Nail Him to a cross!" [23]Then Pilate said, "Why, what bad thing has He done?" But they cried out all the more, "Nail Him to a cross!"

Nail Him to a cross!

[24]Pilate saw that he could do nothing. The people were making loud calls and there was much pushing around. He took water and washed his hands in front of the many people. He said, "I am not guilty of the blood of this good Man. This is your own doing."

²⁵Then all the people said, "Let His blood be on us and on our children!" ²⁶Pilate let Barabbas go free but he had men whip Jesus. Then he handed Him over to be nailed to a cross.

The Headband Made Of Thorns [Mark 15:15-21; John 19:1-5]

²⁷Then the soldiers of Pilate took Jesus into a large room. A big group of soldiers gathered around Him. ²⁸They took off His clothes and put a purple coat on Him. ²⁹They put a headband made of thorns on His head. They put a stick in His right hand. They got on their knees in front of Him and made fun of Him. They said, "Hello, King of the Jews!" ³⁰They spit on Him. They took a stick and hit Him on the head. ³¹After they had made fun of Him, they took the coat off and put His own clothes on Him. Then they led Him away to be nailed to a cross. ³²As they were on the way, they came to a man called Simon from the country of Cyrene. They made him carry the cross for Jesus.

Jesus On The Cross [Mark 15:22-26; Luke 23:26-38; John 19:17-22]

³³They came to a place called Golgotha. This name means the place of a skull. ³⁴They gave Him wine with something in it to take away the pain. After tasting it, He took no more. ³⁵When they had nailed Him to the cross, they divided His clothes by drawing names. *It happened as the early preacher said it would happen. He said, "They divided My clothes among them by drawing names to see who would get My coat." (Psalm 22:18) ³⁶Then they sat down and watched Him. ³⁷Over His head they put in writing what they had against Him, THIS IS JESUS THE KING OF THE JEWS.

The Two Robbers [Mark 15:27-32; Luke 23:39-43]

³⁸They nailed two robbers to crosses beside Him. One was on His right side. The other was on His left side. ³⁹Those who walked by shook their heads and laughed at Him. ⁴⁰They said, "You are the One Who could destroy the house of God and build it up again in three days. Now save Yourself. If You are the Son of God, come down from the cross."

⁴¹The head religious leaders and the teachers of the Law and the other leaders made fun of Him also. They said, ⁴²"He saved others but He cannot save Himself. If He is the King of the Jews, let Him come down from the cross. Then we will believe in Him. ⁴³He trusts God. Let God save Him now, if God cares for Him. He has said, 'I am the Son of God.' " ⁴⁴And the robbers who were nailed to crosses beside Him made fun of Him the same way also.

The Death Of Jesus [Mark 15:33-36; Luke 23:44-49; John 19:28-37]

⁴⁵From noon until three o'clock it was dark over all the land. ⁴⁶About three o'clock Jesus cried with a loud voice, "My God, My God, why have You left Me alone?" ⁴⁷When some of those who stood by heard that, they said, "This Man is calling for Elijah." ⁴⁸At once one of them ran and took a sponge and filled it with sour wine. He put it on a stick and gave it to Him to drink. ⁴⁹The others said, "Let Him alone. Let us see if Elijah will come and save Him." ⁵⁰Then Jesus gave another loud cry and gave up His spirit and died.

The Powerful Works At The Time Of His Death [Mark 15:37-39]

⁵¹At once the curtain in the house of God was torn in two from top to bottom. The earth shook and the rocks fell apart. ⁵²Graves were opened. Bodies of many of God's people who were dead were raised. ⁵³After Jesus was raised from the grave, these arose from their graves and went into Jerusalem, the Holy City. These were seen by many people.

The earth shook and the rocks fell apart.

⁵⁴The captain of the soldiers and those with him who were watching Jesus, saw all the things that were happening. They saw the earth shake and they were very much afraid. They said, "For sure, this Man was the Son of God."

For sure, this Man was the Son of God.

The Women At The Cross [Mark 15:40-41; John 19:25-27]

⁵⁵Many women were looking on from far away. These had followed Jesus from the country of Galilee. They had cared for Him. ⁵⁶Among them was Mary Magdalene and Mary the mother of James and Joseph and the mother of Zebedee's sons.

The Grave Of Jesus [Mark 15:42-47; Luke 23:50-56; John 19:38-42]

⁵⁷When it was evening, a rich man came from the city of Arimathea. His name was Joseph. He was a follower of Jesus also. ⁵⁸He went to Pilate and asked for the body of Jesus. Then Pilate said that the body should be given to him. ⁵⁹Joseph took the body and put clean linen cloth around it. ⁶⁰He laid it in his own new grave. This grave had been cut out in the side of a rock. He pushed a big stone over the door of the grave and went away. ⁶¹Mary Magdalene and the other Mary stayed there. They were sitting near the grave.

⁶²The next day, the day after Jesus was killed, the head religious leaders and the proud religious law-keepers gathered together in front of Pilate. ⁶³They said, "Sir, we remember what that Man Who fooled people said when He was living, 'After three days I am to rise from the dead.' ⁶⁴Speak the word to have the grave watched for three days. Then His followers cannot come at night and take Him away and say to the people, 'He has been raised from the dead.' The last mistake would be worse than the first." ⁶⁵Pilate said to them, "Take the soldiers. Go and watch the grave." ⁶⁶Then they went and made the soldiers stand by the grave. They put a lock on the big stone door.

Jesus Is Raised From The Dead [Mark 16:1-8; Luke 24:1-12; John 20:1-18]

28 The Day of Rest was over. The sun was coming up on the first day of the week. Mary Magdalene and the other Mary came to see the grave. ²At once the earth shook and an angel of the Lord came down from heaven. He came and pushed back the stone from the door and sat on it. ³His face was bright like lightning. His clothes were white as snow. ⁴The soldiers were shaking with fear and became as dead men.

⁵The angel said to the women, "Do not be afraid. I know you are looking for Jesus Who was nailed to the cross. ⁶He is not here! He has risen from the dead as He said He would. Come and see the place where the Lord lay. ⁷Run fast and tell His followers that He

is risen from the dead. He is going before you into the country of Galilee. You will see Him there as I have told you." ⁸They went away from the grave in a hurry. They were afraid and yet had much joy. They ran to tell the news to His followers.

Jesus Speaks To The Women

⁹As they went to tell the followers, Jesus met them and said hello to them. They came and held His feet and worshiped Him. ¹⁰Then Jesus said to them, "Do not be afraid. Go and tell My followers to go into the country of Galilee. They will see Me there."

The Jews Make Up A Story

¹¹While they were on their way, some of the soldiers who were to watch the grave came into the city. They told the head religious leaders everything that had happened. ¹²The soldiers gathered together with the other leaders and talked about what to do. The leaders gave much money to the soldiers. ¹³They said, "Tell the people, 'His followers came at night and took His body while we were sleeping.' ¹⁴We will see that you do not get into trouble over this if Pilate hears about it." ¹⁵They took the money and did as they were told. This story was told among the Jews and is still told today.

Jesus Sends His Followers To Teach [Mark 16:15-18; Luke 24:44-49; John 20:21-23]

¹⁶Then the eleven followers went into the country of Galilee. They went to the mountain where Jesus had told them to go. ¹⁷When they saw Jesus, they worshiped Him. But some did not believe. ¹⁸Jesus came and said to them, "All power has been given to Me in heaven and on earth. ¹⁹Go and make followers of all the nations. Baptize them in the name of the Father and of the Son and of the Holy Spirit. ²⁰Teach them to do all the things I have told you. And I am with you always, even to the end of the world."

All power has been given to Me in heaven and on earth.

John The Baptist Makes The Way Ready For The Coming Of Jesus [Matthew 3:1-12; Luke 3:1-18; John 1:15-28]

1 The Good News of Jesus Christ, the Son of God, ²begins with the words of the early preachers: "Listen! I will send My helper to carry the news ahead of you. He will make the way ready. ³His voice calls out in the desert, 'Make the way ready for the Lord. Make the road straight for Him!' " (Isaiah 40:3)

⁴John the Baptist preached in the desert. He preached that people should be baptized because they were sorry for their sins and turned from them. And they would be forgiven. ⁵People from over all the country of Judea and from Jerusalem came to him. They told of their sins and were baptized by John in the Jordan River.

⁶John wore clothes made of hair from camels. He had a leather belt around him. His food was locusts and wild honey. ⁷He preached, saying, "One is coming after me Who is greater than I. I am not good enough to get down and help Him take off His shoes. ⁸I have baptized you with water. But He will baptize you with the Holy Spirit."

The Baptism Of Jesus [Matthew 3:13-17; Luke 3:21-22; John 1:29-34]

⁹Jesus came to the Jordan River from the town of Nazareth in the country of Galilee. He was baptized by John. ¹⁰As soon as Jesus came up out of the water, He saw heaven open up. The Holy Spirit came down on Him like a dove. ¹¹A voice came from heaven and said, "You are My much-loved Son. I am very happy with You."

Jesus Was Tempted [Matthew 4:1-11; Luke 4:1-13]

¹²At once the Holy Spirit sent Jesus to a desert. ¹³He was tempted by Satan for forty days there. He was with wild animals but angels took care of Him.

Jesus Preaches In Galilee [Matthew 4:12-17; Luke 4:14-15]

The holy nation of God is near. Be sorry for your sins and turn from them.

[14]After John the Baptist was put into prison, Jesus came to the country of Galilee. He preached the Good News from God. [15]He said, "The time has come. The holy nation of God is near. Be sorry for your sins and turn from them. Believe the Good News."

Jesus Calls Simon And Andrew [Matthew 4:18-22; Luke 5:1-11]

[16]Jesus was walking by the Lake of Galilee. He saw Simon and his brother Andrew putting a net into the lake. They were fishermen. [17]Jesus said to them, "Follow Me. I will make you fish for men!" [18]At once they left their nets and followed Him.

Jesus Calls James And John

[19]Jesus went on a little farther. He saw James and his brother John who were sons of Zebedee. They were in a boat mending their nets. [20]Jesus called them and they left their father Zebedee. He was in the boat with men who were working for him.

Jesus Heals A Man With A Demon [Luke 4:31-37]

[21]Jesus and His followers went into the city of Capernaum on the Day of Rest. They went to the Jewish place of worship where Jesus taught the people. [22]The people were surprised and wondered about His teaching. He taught them as One Who had the right and the power to teach and not as the teachers of the Law.

[23]There was a man in the Jewish place of worship who had a demon. The demon cried out, [24]"What do You want of us, Jesus of Nazareth? Have You come to destroy us? I know Who You are. You are the Holy One of God." [25]Jesus spoke sharp words to the demon and said, "Do not talk! Come out of the man!" [26]The demon threw the man down and gave a loud cry. Then he came out of him. [27]The people were all surprised and wondered. They asked each other, "What is this? Is this a new teaching? He speaks with power even to the demons and they obey Him!" [28]At once the news about Jesus went through all the country around Galilee.

Peter's Mother-In-Law Healed [Matthew 8:14-15; Luke 4:38-39]

²⁹Jesus and His followers came out of the Jewish place of worship. Then they went to the house of Simon and Andrew. James and John went with them. ³⁰They told Jesus about Simon's mother-in-law who was in bed, very sick. ³¹He went and took her by the hand and raised her up. At once her sickness was gone. She got up and cared for them.

Jesus Heals In Galilee [Matthew 8:16-17; Luke 4:40-41]

³²In the evening as the sun went down, the people took all who were sick to Jesus. They took those who had demons to Him. ³³All the town gathered at the door. ³⁴Jesus healed those who were sick of many kinds of diseases. He put out many demons. Jesus would not allow the demons to speak because they knew Who He was.

Jesus Keeps On Preaching In Galilee [Matthew 4:23-25; Luke 4:42-44]

³⁵In the morning before the sun was up, Jesus went to a place where He could be alone. He prayed there. ³⁶Simon and the others looked for Jesus. ³⁷They found Him and said, "All the people are looking for You." ³⁸Jesus said to the followers, "Let us go to the towns near here so I can preach there also. That is why I came." ³⁹He went through the country of Galilee. He preached in their places of worship and put out demons.

Jesus Heals A Man With A Bad Skin Disease [Matthew 8:1-4; Luke 5:12-16]

⁴⁰A man came to Jesus with a bad skin disease. This man got down on his knees and begged Jesus, saying, "If You want to, You can heal me." ⁴¹Jesus put His hand on him with loving-pity. He said, "I want to. Be healed." ⁴²At once the disease was gone and the man was healed. ⁴³Jesus spoke strong words to the man before He sent him away. ⁴⁴He said to him, "Tell no one about this. Go and let the religious leader of the Jews see you. Give the gifts Moses has told you to give when a man is healed of a disease. Let the leaders know you have been healed." ⁴⁵But the man went out and talked about it everywhere. After this Jesus could not go

People came to Him
from everywhere.

into any town if people knew He was there. He had to stay in the desert. People came to Him from everywhere.

Jesus Heals A Man Who Was Let Down Through The Roof Of A House [Matthew 9:1-8; Luke 5:17-26]

2 After some days Jesus went back to the city of Capernaum. The news got around that He was home. ²Soon many people gathered there. There was no more room, not even at the door. He spoke the Word of God to them. ³Four men came to Jesus carrying a man who could not move his body. ⁴These men could not get near Jesus because of so many people. They made a hole in the roof of the house over where Jesus stood. Then they let down the bed with the sick man on it.

⁵When Jesus saw their faith, He said to the sick man, "Son, your sins are forgiven." ⁶Some teachers of the Law were sitting there. They thought to themselves, ⁷"Why does this Man talk like this? He is speaking as if He is God! Who can forgive sins? Only One can forgive sins and that is God!"

⁸At once Jesus knew the teachers of the Law were thinking this. He said to them, "Why do you think this in your hearts? ⁹Which is easier to say to the sick man, 'Your sins are forgiven,' or to say, 'Get up, take your bed, and start to walk?' ¹⁰I am doing this so you may know the Son of Man has power on earth to forgive sins." He said to the sick man who could not move his body, ¹¹"I say to you, 'Get up. Take your bed and go to your home.'" ¹²At once the sick man got up and took his bed and went away. Everybody saw him. They were all surprised and wondered about it. They thanked God, saying, "We have never seen anything like this!"

Jesus Calls Matthew [Matthew 9:9-13; Luke 5:27-32]

¹³Jesus walked along the lake shore again. Many people came together and He taught them. ¹⁴He walked farther and saw Levi (Matthew) the son of Alphaeus. Levi was sitting at his work gathering taxes. Jesus said to him, "Follow Me." Levi got up and followed Him.

Jesus Eats With Tax Gatherers And Sinners

¹⁵Jesus ate in Levi's house. Many men who gather taxes and others who were sinners came and sat down with Jesus and His followers. There were many following Him. ¹⁶The teachers of the Law and the proud religious law-keepers saw Jesus eat with men who gather taxes and others who were sinners. They said to His followers, "Why does He eat and drink with men who gather taxes and with sinners?" ¹⁷Jesus heard it and said to them, "People who are well do not need a doctor. Only those who are sick need a doctor. I have not come to call those who are right with God. I have come to call those who are sinners."

Jesus Teaches About Going Without Food So You Can Pray Better [*Matthew 9:14-17; Luke 5:33-35*]

¹⁸The followers of John and the proud religious law-keepers were not eating food so they could pray better. Some people came to Jesus and said, "Why do the followers of John and the proud religious law-keepers go without food so they can pray better, but Your followers do not?" ¹⁹Jesus said to them, "Can the friends at a wedding go without food when the man just married is with them? As long as they have him with them, they will not go without food. ²⁰The days will come when the man just married will be taken from them. Then they will not eat food so they can pray better. ²¹No man sews a piece of new cloth on an old coat. If it comes off, it will make the hole bigger. ²²No man puts new wine into old skin bags. The skin would break and the wine would run out. The bags would be no good. New wine must be put into new skin bags."

Jesus Teaches About The Day Of Rest [*Matthew 12:1-8; Luke 6:1-5*]

²³At that time Jesus walked through the grain fields on the Day of Rest. As they went, His followers began to take some of the grain. ²⁴The proud religious law-keepers said to Jesus, "Look! Why are they doing what the Law says should not be done on the Day of Rest?" ²⁵He said to them, "Have you not read what David did when he and his men were hungry? ²⁶He went into the house of God when Abiathar was head religious leader of the Jews. He ate the special bread used in the religious worship. The Law says only

the Jewish religious leaders may eat that. David gave some to those who were with him also." ²⁷Jesus said to them, "The Day of Rest was made for the good of man. Man was not made for the Day of Rest. ²⁸The Son of Man is Lord of the Day of Rest also."

Jesus Heals On The Day Of Rest [Matthew 12:9-14; Luke 6:6-11]

3 Jesus went into the Jewish place of worship again. A man was there with a dried-up hand. ²The proud religious law-keepers watched Jesus to see if He would heal the man on the Day of Rest. They wanted to have something to say against Jesus. ³Jesus said to the man with the dried-up hand, "Stand up." ⁴Then Jesus said to the proud religious law-keepers, "Does the Law say to do good on the Day of Rest or to do bad, to save life or to kill?" But they said nothing. ⁵Jesus looked around at them with anger. He was sad because of their hard hearts. Then He said to the man, "Put out your hand." He put it out and his hand was healed. It was as good as the other. ⁶The proud religious law-keepers went out and made plans with the followers of King Herod how they might kill Jesus.

Jesus Heals By The Shore Of The Lake [Matthew 12:15-21; Luke 6:17-19]

⁷Jesus went with His followers to the lake. Many people followed Him from the countries of Galilee and Judea. ⁸They followed from Jerusalem and from the country of Idumea. They came from the other side of the Jordan River and from the cities of Tyre and Sidon. Many people heard all that Jesus was doing and came to Him. ⁹He told His followers to have a small boat ready for Him because so many people might push Him down. ¹⁰He had healed so many that the sick people were pushing in on Him. They were trying to put their hands on Him. ¹¹When demons saw Him, they got down at His feet and cried out, "You are the Son of God!" ¹²He spoke strong words that the demons should tell no one Who He was.

Jesus Calls His Twelve Followers [Matthew 10:1-4; Luke 6:12-16]

¹³He went up on a mountain and called those He wanted. They followed Him. ¹⁴He picked out twelve followers to be with Him so

He might send them out to preach. ¹⁵They would have the right and the power to heal diseases and to put out demons. ¹⁶Jesus gave Simon another name, Peter. ¹⁷James and John were brothers. They were the sons of Zebedee. He named them Boanerges, which means, The Sons of Thunder. ¹⁸The others were Andrew, Philip, Bartholomew, Matthew, Thomas, James the son of Alphaeus, Thaddaeus, Simon the Canannite, ¹⁹and Judas Iscariot. Judas was the one who handed Jesus over to be killed.

The Family Of Jesus Holds Him Back

²⁰When Jesus came into a house, many people gathered around Him again. Jesus and His followers could not even eat. ²¹When His family heard of it, they went to take Him. They said, "He must be crazy."

A Nation That Cannot Stand [Matthew 12:22-37; Luke 11:14-23]

²²Teachers of the Law came down from Jerusalem. They said, "Jesus has Satan in Him. This Man puts out demons by the king of demons." ²³Jesus called them to Him and spoke to them in picture-stories. He said, "How can the devil put out the devil? ²⁴A nation cannot last if it is divided against itself. ²⁵A family cannot last if it is divided against itself. ²⁶If the devil fights against himself and is divided, he cannot last. He will come to an end. ²⁷No man can go into a strong man's house and take away his things, unless he ties up the strong man first. Only then can he take things from his house. ²⁸For sure, I tell you, all sins will be forgiven people, and bad things they speak against God. ²⁹But if anyone speaks bad things against the Holy Spirit, he will never be forgiven. He is guilty of a sin that lasts forever." ³⁰Jesus told them this because they said, "He has a demon."

A family cannot last if it is divided against itself.

The New Kind Of Family [Matthew 12:46-50; Luke 8:19-21]

³¹Then His mother and brothers came and stood outside. They sent for Jesus. ³²Many people were sitting around Him. They said, "Look! Your mother and brothers are outside looking for You." ³³He said to them, "Who is My mother or My brothers?" ³⁴He turned to those sitting around Him and said, "Look! My

Whoever does
what My Father wants
is My brother
and My sister
and My mother.

mother and My brothers! [35]Whoever does what My Father wants is My brother and My sister and My mother.''

The Picture-Story Of The Man Who Planted Seed [Matthew 13:1-52; Luke 8:4-18]

4 Jesus began to teach by the lake shore again. Many people gathered around Him. There were so many He had to get into a boat and sit down. The people were on the shore. [2]He taught them many things by using picture-stories. As He taught, He said, [3]''Listen! A man went out to plant seed. [4]As he planted the seed, some fell by the side of the road. Birds came and ate them. [5]Some seed fell among rocks. It came up at once because there was so little ground. [6]But it dried up when the sun was high in the sky because it had no root. [7]Some seed fell among thorns. The thorns grew and did not give the seed room to grow. This seed gave no grain. [8]Some seed fell on good ground. It came up and grew and gave much grain. Some gave thirty times as much grain. Some gave sixty times as much grain. Some gave one hundred times as much grain.'' [9]He said to them, ''You have ears, then listen!'' [10]Those who were with Jesus and the twelve followers came to Him when He was alone. They asked about the picture-story. [11]He said to them, ''You were given the secrets about the holy nation of God. Everything is told in picture-stories to those who are outside the holy nation of God. [12]They see, but do not know what it means. They hear, but do not understand. If they did, they might turn to God and have their sins forgiven.'' (Isaiah 6:9-10)

Jesus Tells About The Man Who Planted The Seed

[13]Jesus said to them, ''Do you not understand this picture-story? Then how will you understand any of the picture-stories? [14]What the man plants is the Word of God. [15]Those by the side of the road are the ones who hear the Word. As soon as they hear it, the devil comes and takes away the Word that is planted in their hearts. [16]The seed that fell among rocks is like people who receive the Word with joy when they hear it. [17]Their roots are not deep so they live only a short time. When sorrow and trouble come because of the Word, they give up and fall away. [18]The seed that was planted among thorns is like some people who listen to the

Word. ¹⁹But the cares of this life let thorns come up. A love for riches and always wanting other things let thorns grow. These things do not give the Word room to grow so it does not give grain. ²⁰The seed that fell on good ground is like people who hear the Word and understand it. They give much grain. Some give thirty times as much grain. Some give sixty times as much grain. Some give one hundred times as much grain.''

The seed that fell on good ground is like people who hear the Word and understand it.

The Picture-Story Of The Lamp

²¹He said to them, "Is a lamp to be put under a pail or under a bed? Should it not be put on a table? ²²Everything that is hidden will be brought into the light. Everything that is a secret will be made known. ²³You have ears, then listen!''

²⁴Jesus said to them, "Be careful what you listen to. The same amount you give will be given to you, and even more. ²⁵He who has, to him will be given. To him who does not have, even the little he has will be taken from him.''

The Picture-Story Of The Grain

²⁶He said, "The holy nation of God is like a man who plants seed in the ground. ²⁷He goes to sleep every night and gets up every day. The seed grows, but he does not know how. ²⁸The earth gives fruit by itself. The leaf comes first and then the young grain can be seen. And last, the grain is ready to gather. ²⁹As soon as the grain is ready, he cuts it. The time of gathering the grain has come.''

The Picture-Story Of The Mustard Seed

³⁰Jesus said, "In what way can we show what the holy nation of God is like? Or what picture-story can we use to help you understand? ³¹It is like a grain of mustard seed that is planted in the ground. It is the smallest of all seeds. ³²After it is put in the ground, it grows and becomes the largest of the spices. It puts out long branches so birds of the sky can live in it.'' ³³As they were able to understand, He spoke the Word to them by using many picture-stories. ³⁴Jesus helped His followers understand everything when He was alone with them.

The Wind And Waves Obey Jesus [Matthew 8:23-27; Luke 8:22-25]

35It was evening of that same day. Jesus said to them, "Let us go over to the other side." 36After sending the people away, they took Jesus with them in a boat. It was the same boat He used when He taught them. Other little boats went along with them. 37A bad wind storm came up. The waves were coming over the side of the boat. It was filling up with water. 38Jesus was in the back part of the boat sleeping on a pillow. They woke Him up, crying out, "Teacher, do You not care that we are about to die?" 39He got up and spoke sharp words to the wind. He said to the sea, "Be quiet! Be still." At once the wind stopped blowing. There were no more waves. 40He said to His followers, "Why are you so full of fear? Do you not have faith?" 41They were very much afraid and said to each other, "Who is this? Even the wind and waves obey Him!"

Demons Ask Jesus To Let Them Live In Pigs [Matthew 8:28-34; Luke 8:26-39]

5 Jesus and His followers came to the other side of the lake to the country of the Gerasenes. 2He got out of the boat. At once a man came to Him from among the graves. This man had a demon. 3He lived among the graves. No man could tie him, even with chains. 4Many times he had been tied with chains on his feet. He had broken the chains as well as the irons from his hands and legs. No man was strong enough to keep him tied. 5Night and day he was among the graves and in the mountains. He would cry out and cut himself with stones.

6When the man with the demon saw Jesus a long way off, he ran and worshiped Him. 7The man spoke with a loud voice and said, "What do You want with me, Jesus, Son of the Most High God? I ask You, in the name of God, do not hurt me!" 8At the same time, Jesus was saying, "Come out of the man, you demon!" 9Jesus asked the demon, "What is your name?" He said, "My name is Many for there are many of us." 10The demons asked Jesus not to send them out of the country. 11There were many pigs feeding on the mountain side. 12The demons asked Him saying, "Send us to the pigs that we may go into them." 13Then Jesus let them do what they wanted to do. So they went into the pigs. The pigs ran fast down the side of the mountain and into the lake and died. There were about 2000. ¹⁴The men who cared for the pigs ran fast to the town and out to the country telling what had been done. People came to see what had happened. ¹⁵They came to Jesus and saw the man who had had the demons. He was sitting with clothes on and in his right mind. The men were afraid. ¹⁶Those who had seen it told what had happened to the man who had had the demons. They told what had happened to the pigs. ¹⁷Then they asked Jesus to leave their country.

¹⁸Jesus got into the boat. The man who had had the demons asked to go with Him. ¹⁹Jesus would not let him go but said to him, "Go home to your own people. Tell them what great things the Lord has done for you. Tell them how He had pity on you." ²⁰The man went his way and told everyone in the land of Decapolis what great things Jesus had done for him. All the people were surprised and wondered.

Go home to your own people. Tell them what great things the Lord has done for you.

Two Were Healed Through Faith [*Matthew 9:18-26; Luke 8:40-56*]

²¹Then Jesus went over to the other side of the lake by boat. Many people gathered around Him. He stayed by the lake shore. ²²Jairus was one of the leaders of the Jewish place of worship. As Jairus came to Jesus, he got down at His feet. ²³He cried out to Jesus and said, "My little daughter is almost dead. Come and put your hand on her that she may be healed and live." ²⁴Jesus went with him. Many people followed and pushed around Jesus.

²⁵A woman had been sick for twelve years with a flow of blood. ²⁶She had suffered much because of having many doctors. She had spent all the money she had. She had received no help, but became worse. ²⁷She heard about Jesus and went among the people who were following Him. She touched His coat. ²⁸For she said to herself, "If I can only touch His coat, I will be healed." ²⁹At once the flow of blood stopped. She felt in her body that she was healed of her sickness.

³⁰At the same time Jesus knew that power had gone from Him. He turned and said to the people following Him, "Who touched

My coat?'' ³¹His followers said to Him, "You see the many people pushing on every side. Why do You ask, "Who touched My coat?" ³²He looked around to see who had done it. ³³The woman was filled with fear when she knew what had happened to her. She came and got down in front of Jesus and told Him the truth. ³⁴He said to her, "Daughter, your faith has healed you. Go in peace and be free from your sickness."

³⁵While Jesus spoke, men came from the house of the leader of the place of worship. They said, "Your daughter is dead. Why trouble the Teacher anymore?" ³⁶Jesus heard this. He said to the leader of the Jewish place of worship, "Do not be afraid, just believe." ³⁷He allowed no one to go with Him but Peter and James and John, the brother of James. ³⁸They came to the house where the leader of the place of worship lived. Jesus found many people making much noise and crying. ³⁹He went in and asked them, "Why is there so much noise and crying? The girl is not dead. She is sleeping."

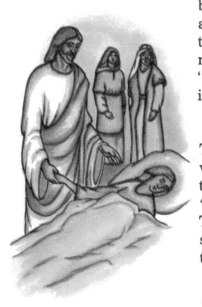

⁴⁰They laughed at Jesus. But He sent them all out of the room. Then He took the girl's father and mother and those who were with Him. They went into the room where the girl was. ⁴¹He took the girl by the hand and said, "Little girl, I say to you, get up!" ⁴²At once the girl got up and walked. She was twelve years old. They were very much surprised and wondered about it. ⁴³He spoke sharp words to them that they should not tell anyone. He told them to give her something to eat.

Jesus Visits His Own Town, Nazareth [Matthew 13:53-58]

6 Jesus went from the house of Jairus and came to His home town. His followers came after Him. ²On the Day of Rest He began to teach in the Jewish place of worship. Many people heard Him. They were surprised and wondered, saying, "Where did this Man get all this? What wisdom is this that has been given to Him? How can He do these powerful works with His hands? ³Is He not a Man Who makes things from wood? Is He not the Son of Mary and the brother of James and Joses and Judas and Simon? Do not His sisters live here with us?" The people were ashamed of Him and turned away from Him. ⁴Jesus said to them, "One who speaks for God is respected everywhere but in his own country and among his own family and in his own house."

⁵So Jesus could do no powerful works there. But He did put His hands on a few sick people and healed them. ⁶He wondered because they had no faith. But He went around to the towns and taught as He went.

Jesus Calls Twelve Followers And Sends Them Out [*Matthew 10:1-42; Luke 9:1-6*]

⁷Jesus called the twelve followers to Him and began to send them out two by two. He gave them power over demons. ⁸He told them to take nothing along with them but a walking stick. They were not to take a bag or food or money in their belts. ⁹They were to wear shoes. They were not to take two coats.

¹⁰He said to them, "Whatever house you go into, stay there until you leave that town. ¹¹Whoever does not take you in or listen to you, when you leave there, shake the dust off your feet. By doing that, you will speak against them. For sure, I tell you, it will be easier for the cities of Sodom and Gomorrha on the day men stand in front of God and are told they are guilty than for that city."

¹²Then they left. They preached that men should be sorry for their sins and turn from them. ¹³They put out many demons. They poured oil on many people that were sick and healed them.

They preached that men should be sorry for their sins and turn from them.

John The Baptist Is Put Into Prison [*Matthew 14:1-5; Luke 3:18-20*]

¹⁴King Herod heard about Jesus because everyone was talking about Him. Some people said, "John the Baptist has been raised from the dead. That is why he is doing such powerful works." ¹⁵Other people said, "He is Elijah." Others said, "He is one who speaks for God like one of the early preachers." ¹⁶When Herod heard this, he said, "It is John the Baptist, whose head I cut off. He has been raised from the dead." ¹⁷For Herod had sent men to take John and put him into prison. He did this because of his wife, Herodias. She had been the wife of his brother Philip. ¹⁸John the Baptist had said to Herod, "It is wrong for you to have your

brother's wife." [19]Herodias became angry with him. She wanted to have John the Baptist killed but she could not. [20]Herod was afraid of John. He knew he was a good man and right with God, and he kept John from being hurt or killed. He liked to listen to John preach. But when he did, he became troubled.

John The Baptist Is Killed [Matthew 14:6-12; Luke 9:7-9]

[21]Then Herodias found a way to have John killed. Herod gave a big supper on his birthday. He asked the leaders of the country and army captains and the leaders of Galilee to come. [22]The daughter of Herodias came in and danced before them. This made Herod and his friends happy. The king said to the girl, "Ask me for whatever you want and I will give it to you." [23]Then he made a promise to her, "Whatever you ask for, I will give it to you. I will give you even half of my nation." [24]She went to her mother and asked, "What should I ask for?" The mother answered, "I want the head of John the Baptist." [25]At once the girl went to Herod. She said, "I want you to give me the head of John the Baptist on a plate now."

[26]Herod was very sorry. He had to do it because of his promise and because of those who ate with him. [27]At once he sent one of his soldiers and told him to bring the head of John the Baptist. The soldier went to the prison and cut off John's head. [28]He took John's head in on a plate and gave it to the girl. The girl gave it to her mother. [29]John's followers heard this. They went and took his body and buried it.

The Feeding Of The Five Thousand [Matthew 14:13-21; Luke 9:10-17; John 6:1-14]

[30]The followers of Jesus came back to Him. They told Jesus all they had done and taught. [31]He said to them, "Come away from the people. Be by yourselves and rest." There were many people coming and going. They had had no time even to eat. [32]They went by themselves in a boat to a desert. [33]Many people saw them leave and knew who they were. People ran fast from all the cities and got there first. [34]When Jesus got out of the boat, He saw many people gathered together. He had loving-pity for them. They were like sheep without a shepherd. He began to teach them many things.

He had loving-pity for them. They were like sheep without a shepherd.

[35]The day was almost gone. The followers of Jesus came to Him. They said, "This is a desert. It is getting late. [36]Tell the people to go into the country and into the towns and buy food for themselves." [37]He said to them, "Give them something to eat." They said to Him, "Are we to go and buy many loaves of bread and give it to them?" [38]He said to them, "How many loaves of bread do you have here? Go and see." When they knew, they said, "Five loaves of bread and two fish." [39]Then He told them to have all the people sit down together in groups on the green grass. [40]They sat down in groups of fifty people and in groups of one hundred people. [41]Jesus took the five loaves of bread and two fish. He looked up to heaven and gave thanks. He broke the loaves in pieces and gave them to the followers to set before the people. He divided the two fish among them all. [42]They all ate and were filled. [43]After that the followers picked up twelve baskets full of pieces of bread and fish. [44]About five thousand men ate the bread.

Five loaves of bread and two fish.

About five thousand men ate the bread.

Jesus Walks On The Water [Matthew 14:22-33; John 6:15-21]

[45]At once Jesus had His followers get into the boat and go ahead of Him to the other side to the town of Bethsaida. He sent the people away. [46]When they were all gone, He went up to the mountain to pray. [47]It was evening. The boat was half way across the lake. Jesus was alone on the land. [48]He saw His followers were in trouble. The wind was against them. They were working very hard rowing the boat. About three o'clock in the morning Jesus came to them walking on the lake. He would have gone past them. [49]When the followers saw Him walking on the water, they thought it was a spirit and cried out with fear. [50]For they all saw Him and were afraid. At once Jesus talked to them. He said, "Take hope. It is I, do not be afraid." [51]He came over to them and got into the boat. The wind stopped. They were very much suprised and wondered about it. [52]They had not learned what they should have learned from the loaves because their hearts were hard.

People Are Healed At Gennesaret [Matthew 14:34-36]

[53]Then they crossed the lake and came to the land of Gennesaret and went to shore. [54]When Jesus got out of the boat, the people knew Him at once. [55]They ran through all the country bringing people who were sick on their beds to Jesus. [56]Wherever He went, they would lay the sick people in the streets in the center of town

once his ears were opened. His tongue was made loose and he spoke as other people. [36]Then Jesus told them they should tell no one. The more He told them this, the more they told what He had done. [37]They were very much surprised and wondered about it. They said, "He has done all things well. He makes those who could not hear so they can hear. He makes those who could not speak so they can speak."

The Feeding Of The Four Thousand [Matthew 15:32-39]

8 In those days many people were gathered together. They had nothing to eat. Jesus called His followers to Him and said, [2]"I pity these people because they have been with Me three days and have nothing to eat. [3]If I send them home without food, they may be too weak as they go. Many of them have come a long way."

[4]His followers said to Him, "Where can anyone get enough bread for them here in this desert?" [5]He asked them, "How many loaves of bread do you have?" They said, "Seven." [6]Then He told the people to sit down on the ground. Jesus took the seven loaves of bread and gave thanks to God. He broke the loaves and gave them to His followers to give to the people. The followers gave the bread to them. [7]They had a few small fish also. He gave thanks to God and told the followers to give the fish to them. [8]They all ate and were filled. They picked up seven baskets full of pieces of bread and fish after the people were finished eating. [9]About four thousand ate. Then Jesus sent the people away.

They all ate and were filled.

The Proud Religious Law-Keepers Ask For Something Special To See [Matthew 16:1-4]

[10]At once Jesus got into a boat with His followers and came to the country of Dalmanutha. [11]The proud religious law-keepers came and began to ask Him for something special to see from heaven. They wanted to trap Jesus. [12]He breathed deep within and said, "Why do the people of this day look for something special to see? For sure, I tell you, the people of this day will have nothing special to see from heaven." [13]Then He left them. He got into the boat and went to the other side of the lake.

Jesus Shows That The Teaching Of The Proud Religious Law-Keepers Is Wrong [Matthew 16:5-12]

¹⁴The followers had forgotten to take bread, only one loaf was in the boat. ¹⁵He said to them, "Look out! Have nothing to do with the yeast of the proud religious law-keepers and of Herod." ¹⁶They talked about it among themselves. They said, "He said this because we forgot to bring bread." ¹⁷Jesus knew what they were thinking. He said to them, "Why are you talking among yourselves about forgetting to bring bread? Do you not understand? Is it not plain to you? Are your hearts still hard? ¹⁸You have eyes, do you not see? You have ears, do you not hear? Do you not remember? ¹⁹When I divided the five loaves of bread among the five thousand, how many baskets full of pieces did you pick up?" They said, "Twelve." ²⁰"When I divided the seven loaves of bread among the four thousand, how many baskets full of pieces did you pick up?" They said, "Seven." ²¹Then He asked, "Why do you not understand yet?"

Jesus Heals A Blind Man

²²Then they came to the town of Bethsaida. Some people brought a blind man to Jesus. They asked if He would touch him. ²³He took the blind man by the hand out of town. Then He spit on the eyes of the blind man and put His hands on him. He asked, "Do you see anything?" ²⁴The blind man looked up and said, "I see some men. They look like trees, walking." ²⁵Jesus put His hands on the man's eyes again and told him to look up. Then he was healed and saw everything well. ²⁶Jesus sent him to his home and said, "Do not go into the town, *or tell it to anyone there."

Peter Says Jesus Is The Christ [Matthew 16:13-20; Luke 9:18-20]

²⁷Jesus and His followers went from there to the towns of Caesarea Philippi. As they went, He asked His followers, "Who do people say that I am?" ²⁸They answered, "Some say John the Baptist and some say Elijah and others say one of the early preachers." ²⁹He said to them, "But who do you say that I am?" Peter said, "You are the Christ." ³⁰He told them with strong words that they should tell no one about Him.

Jesus Tells Of His Death For The First Time [*Matthew 16:21-28; Luke 9:21-27*]

³¹He began to teach them that the Son of Man must suffer many things. He told them that the leaders and the religious leaders of the Jews and the teachers of the Law would have nothing to do with Him. He told them He would be killed and three days later He would be raised from the dead.

³²He had said this in plain words. Peter took Him away from the others and began to speak sharp words to Him. ³³Jesus turned around. He looked at His followers and spoke sharp words to Peter. He said, "Get behind Me, Satan! Your thoughts are not thoughts from God but from men."

Giving Up Self And One's Own Desires

³⁴Jesus called the people and His followers to Him. He said to them, "If anyone wants to be My follower, he must give up himself and his own desires. He must take up his cross and follow Me. ³⁵If anyone wants to keep his own life safe, he will lose it. If anyone gives up his life because of Me and because of the Good News, he will save it. ³⁶For what does a man have if he gets all the world and loses his own soul? ³⁷What can a man give to buy back his soul? ³⁸Whoever is ashamed of Me and My Words among the sinful people of this day, the Son of Man will be ashamed of him when He comes in the shining greatness of His Father and His holy angels."

A Look At What Jesus Will Be Like [*Matthew 17:1-13; Luke 9:28-36*]

9 Jesus said to them, "For sure I tell you, some standing here will not die until they see the holy nation of God come with power!"

²Six days later Jesus took Peter and James and John with Him. He led them up to a high mountain by themselves. Jesus was changed as they looked at Him. ³His clothes did shine. They were as white as snow. No one on earth could clean them so white. ⁴Moses and Elijah were seen talking to Jesus.

⁵Peter said to Jesus, "Teacher, it is good for us to be here. Let us make three altars. One will be for You and one for Moses and one for Elijah." ⁶Peter did not know what to say. They were very much afraid.

⁷A cloud came over them and a voice from the cloud said, "This is My much-loved Son. Listen to Him." ⁸At once they looked around but saw no one there but Jesus.

This is My much-loved Son. Listen to Him.

⁹They came down from the mountain. Then Jesus said with strong words that they should tell no one what they had seen. They should wait until the Son of Man had risen from the dead. ¹⁰So they kept those words to themselves, talking to each other about what He meant by being raised from the dead.

¹¹They asked Jesus, "Why do the teachers of the Law say that Elijah must come first?" ¹²He said to them, "For sure, Elijah will come first and get things ready. Is it not written that the Son of Man must suffer many things and that men will have nothing to do with Him? (Isaiah 53:3) ¹³But I say to you, Elijah has already come. They did to him whatever they wanted to do. It is written that they would."

A Boy With A Demon Is Healed [*Matthew 17:14-21; Luke 9:37-42*]

¹⁴When Jesus came back to His followers, He saw many people standing around them. The teachers of the Law were arguing with them. ¹⁵The people saw Jesus and were surprised and ran to say hello to Him. ¹⁶Jesus asked the teachers of the Law, "What are you arguing about with them?" ¹⁷One of the people said, "Teacher, I brought my son to You. He has a demon in him and cannot talk. ¹⁸Wherever the demon takes him, it throws him down. Spit runs from his mouth. He grinds his teeth. He is getting weaker. I asked Your followers to put the demon out but they could not."

¹⁹He said, "You people of this day have no faith. How long must I be with you? How long must I put up with you? Bring the boy to Me." ²⁰They brought the boy to Jesus. The demon saw Jesus and at once held the boy in his power. The boy fell to the

ground with spit running from his mouth. [21]Jesus asked the boy's father, "How long has he been like this?" The father said, "From the time he was a child. [22]Many times it throws him into the fire and into the water to kill him. If You can do anything to help us, take pity on us!" [23]Jesus said to him, "Why do you ask Me that? The one who has faith can do all things." [24]At once the father cried out. He said with tears in his eyes, "Lord, I have faith. Help my weak faith to be stronger!" [25]Jesus saw that many people were gathering together in a hurry. He spoke sharp words to the demon. He said, "Demon! You who cannot speak or hear, I say to you, come out of him! Do not ever go into him again." [26]The demon gave a cry. It threw the boy down and came out of him. The boy was so much like a dead man that people said, "He is dead!" [27]But Jesus took him by the hand and helped him and he stood up.

[28]When Jesus went into the house, His followers asked Him when He was alone, "Why could we not put out the demon?" [29]He said to them, "The only way this kind of demon is put out is by prayer and by going without food so you can pray better."

Jesus Tells Of His Death The Second Time [*Matthew 17:22-23; Luke 9:43-45*]

[30]From there Jesus and His followers went through the country of Galilee. He did not want anyone to know where He was. [31]He taught His followers, saying, "The Son of Man will be handed over to men. They will kill Him. Three days after He is killed, He will be raised from the dead." [32]They did not understand what He said and were afraid to ask Him.

Jesus Teaches About The Faith Of A Child [*Matthew 18:1-35; Luke 9:46-50*]

[33]They came to the city of Capernaum and were in the house. Jesus asked His followers, "What were you arguing about along the road?" [34]They did not answer. They had been arguing along the road about who was the greatest. [35]Jesus sat down and called the followers to Him. He said, "If anyone wants to be first, he must be last of all. He will be the one to care for all."

If anyone wants to be first, he must be last of all.

³⁶Jesus took a child and stood it among them. Then He took the child up in His arms and said to the followers, ³⁷"Whoever receives one of these little children in My name, receives Me. Whoever will receive Me, receives not Me, but Him Who sent Me."

Jesus Speaks Sharp Words Against The Followers

³⁸John said to Him, "Teacher, we saw someone putting out demons in Your name. We told him to stop because he was not following us." ³⁹Jesus said, "Do not stop him. No one who does a powerful work in My name can say anything bad about Me soon after. ⁴⁰The person who is not against us is for us. ⁴¹For sure, I tell you, whoever gives you a cup of water to drink in My name because you belong to Christ will not lose his pay from God. ⁴²Whoever is the reason for one of these little ones who believes in Me to sin, it would be better for him to have a large stone put around his neck and to be thrown into the sea. ⁴³If your hand is the reason you fall into sin, cut it off. It is better to go into life without a hand, than to have two hands and go into the fire of hell that cannot be put out. ⁴⁴*There is where their worm never dies and the fire cannot be put out. ⁴⁵If your foot is the reason you fall into sin, cut it off. It is better to go into life with only one foot, than to have two feet and go into the fire of hell that cannot be put out. ⁴⁶*There is where their worm never dies and the fire cannot be put out. ⁴⁷If your eye is the reason you fall into sin, take it out. It is better to go into the holy nation of God with only one eye, than to have two eyes and be thrown into the fire of hell. ⁴⁸There is where their worm never dies and the fire is never put out.

⁴⁹"Everyone will be made cleaner and stronger with fire. ⁵⁰Salt is good. But if salt loses its taste, how can it be made to taste like salt again? Have salt in yourselves and be at peace with each other."

Be at peace with each other.

Jesus Teaches About Divorce [Matthew 19:1-12]

10 Jesus went away from the city of Capernaum. He came into the country of Judea and to the other side of the Jordan River. Again the people gathered around Him. He began to teach them as He had been doing.

²The proud religious law-keepers came to Him. They tried to trap Him and asked, "Does the Law say a man can divorce his wife?" ³He said to them, "What did the Law of Moses say?" ⁴They said, "Moses allowed a man to divorce his wife, if he put it in writing and gave it to her." ⁵Jesus said to them, "Because of your hard hearts, Moses gave you this Law. ⁶From the beginning of the world, God made them man and woman. ⁷Because of this, a man is to leave his father and mother and is to live with his wife. ⁸The two will become one. So they are no longer two, but one. ⁹Let no man divide what God has put together."

Let no man divide what God has put together.

¹⁰In the house the followers asked Jesus about this again. ¹¹He said to them, "Whoever divorces his wife and marries another is not faithful to her and is guilty of a sex sin. ¹²If a woman divorces her husband and marries another, she is not faithful to her husband and is guilty of a sex sin."

Jesus Gives Thanks For Little Children [*Matthew 19:13-15; Luke 18:15-17*]

¹³They brought little children to Jesus that He might put His hand on them. The followers spoke sharp words to those who brought them. ¹⁴Jesus saw this and was angry with the followers. He said, "Let the little children come to Me. Do not stop them. The holy nation of God is made up of ones like these. ¹⁵For sure, I tell you, whoever does not receive the holy nation of God as a little child does not go into it." ¹⁶He took the children in His arms. He put His hands on them and prayed that good would come to them.

Jesus Teaches About Keeping The Law [*Matthew 19:16-30; Luke 18:18-30*]

¹⁷Jesus was going on His way. A man ran to Him and got down on his knees. He said, "Good Teacher, what must I do to have life that lasts forever?" ¹⁸Jesus said to him, "Why do you call Me good? There is only One Who is good. That is God. ¹⁹You know the Laws, 'Do not be guilty of sex sins in marriage. Do not kill another person. Do not take things from people in wrong ways. Do not steal. Do not lie. Respect your father and mother.' " ²⁰The man said to Jesus, "Teacher, I have obeyed all these Laws since I was a boy." ²¹Jesus looked at him with love and said, "There is

one thing for you to do yet. Go and sell everything you have and give the money to poor people. You will have riches in heaven. Then come and follow Me." ²²When the man heard these words, he was sad. He walked away with sorrow because he had many riches here on earth.

The Danger Of Riches

²³Jesus looked around Him. He said to His followers, "How hard it is for rich people to get into the holy nation of God!" ²⁴The followers were surprised and wondered about His words. But Jesus said to them again, "Children! How hard it is for those who put their trust in riches to get into the holy nation of God! ²⁵It is easier for a camel to go through the eye of a needle than for a rich man to go to heaven."

²⁶They were very surprised and wondered, saying to themselves, "Then who can be saved from the punishment of sin?" ²⁷Jesus looked at them and said, "This cannot be done by men but God can do anything."

²⁸Then Peter began to say to Him, "We have given up everything we had and have followed You." ²⁹Jesus said, "For sure, I tell you, there are those who have given up houses or brothers or sisters or father or mother or wife or children or lands because of Me, and the Good News. ³⁰They will get back one hundred times as much now at this time in houses and brothers and sisters and mothers and children and lands. Along with this, they will have very much trouble. And they will have life that lasts forever in the world to come. ³¹Many who are first will be last. Many who are last will be first."

Jesus Tells Of His Death The Third Time [*Matthew 20:17-19; Luke 18:31-34*]

³²They were on their way to Jerusalem. Jesus walked in front of them. Those who followed were surprised and afraid. Then Jesus took the twelve followers by themselves. He told them what would happen to Him. ³³He said, "Listen, we are going to Jerusalem. The Son of Man will be handed over to the religious leaders of the Jews and to the teachers of the Law. They will say that He must

be put to death. They will hand Him over to the people who are not Jews. ³⁴They will make fun of Him and will beat Him. They will spit on Him and will kill Him. But three days later He will be raised from the dead.''

James And John Ask Jesus Something Hard [Matthew 20:20-28]

³⁵James and John, the sons of Zebedee, came to Jesus. They said, ''Teacher, we would like to have You do for us whatever we ask You.'' ³⁶He said to them, ''What would you like to have Me do for you?'' ³⁷They said to Him, ''Let one of us sit by Your right side and the other by Your left side when You receive Your great honor in heaven.'' ³⁸Jesus said to them, ''You do not know what you ask. Can you take the suffering I am about to take? Can you be baptized with the baptism that I am baptized with?'' ³⁹They said to Him, ''Yes, we can.'' Jesus said to them, ''You will, for sure, suffer the way I will suffer. You will be baptized with the baptism that I am baptized with. ⁴⁰But to sit on My right side or on My left side is not for Me to give. It will be given to those for whom it has been made ready.'' ⁴¹The other ten followers heard it. They were angry with James and John. ⁴²Jesus called them to Him and said, ''You know that those who are made leaders over the nations show their power to the people. Important leaders use their power over the people. ⁴³It must not be that way with you. Whoever wants to be great among you, let him care for you. ⁴⁴Whoever wants to be first among you, must be the one who is owned and cares for all. ⁴⁵For the Son of Man did not come to be cared for. He came to care for others. He came to give His life so that many could be bought by His blood and be made free from sin.''

Healing Of The Blind Man [Matthew 20:29-34; Luke 18:35-43]

⁴⁶Then they came to the city of Jericho. When He was leaving the city with His followers and many people, a blind man was sitting by the road. He was asking people for food or money as they passed by. His name was Bartimaeus, the son of Timaeus. ⁴⁷He heard that Jesus of Nazareth was passing by. He began to speak with a loud voice, saying, ''Jesus, Son of David, take pity on me!'' ⁴⁸Many people spoke sharp words to the blind man telling him not to call out like that. But he spoke all the more. He said, ''Son of David, take pity on me.'' ⁴⁹Jesus stopped and told them

> For the Son of Man did not come to be cared for. He came to care for others.

to call the blind man. They called to him and said, "Take hope! Stand up, He is calling for you!" 50As he jumped up, he threw off his coat and came to Jesus. 51Jesus said to him, "What do you want Me to do for you?" The blind man said to Him, "Lord, I want to see!" 52Jesus said, "Go! Your faith has healed you." At once he could see and he followed Jesus down the road.

The Last Time Jesus Goes Into Jerusalem [Matthew 21:1-11; Luke 19:29-44; John 12:12-19]

11 Jesus and His followers were near Jerusalem at the Mountain of Olives. They were in the towns of Bethphage and Bethany. Jesus sent two of His followers on ahead. 2He said to them, "Go into the town over there. As soon as you get there, you will find a young donkey tied. No man has ever sat on it. Let the donkey loose and bring it here. 3If anyone asks you, 'Why are you doing that?' say, 'The Lord needs it. He will send it back again soon.' "

4The two followers went on their way. They found the young donkey tied by the door where two streets crossed. They took the rope off its neck. 5Some men were standing there. They said to the two followers, "Why are you taking the rope off that young donkey?" 6The two followers told them what Jesus had said and the men let them take the donkey. 7They brought it to Jesus and put their coats over it. Jesus sat on the donkey. 8Many people put their clothes down on the road. Others cut branches off the trees and put them down on the road. 9Those who went in front and those who followed spoke with loud voices, "Greatest One! Great and honored is He Who comes in the name of the Lord! 10Great is the coming holy nation of our father David. It will come in the name of the Lord, Greatest One in the highest heaven."

11Jesus came into Jerusalem and went into the house of God. He looked around at everything. Then He went with the twelve followers to the town of Bethany because it was late.

The Fig Tree With No Fruit

12They came from the town of Bethany the next morning. Jesus was hungry. 13Along the road He saw a fig tree with leaves on it. He went over to see if it had any fruit. He saw nothing but leaves.

It was not the right time for figs. [14]Jesus said to the tree, "Let no one ever again eat fruit from you." His followers heard Him say it.

Jesus Stops The Buying And The Selling In The House Of God
[Matthew 21:12-17; Luke 19:45-48; John 2:13-17]

[15]Then they came to Jerusalem. Jesus went into the house of God. He began to make the people leave who were selling and buying in the house of God. He turned over the tables of the men who changed money. He turned over the seats of those who sold doves. [16]He would not allow anyone to carry a pot or pan through the house of God. [17]He taught them saying, "Is it not written, 'My house is to be called a house of prayer for all the nations'? You have made it a place of robbers."

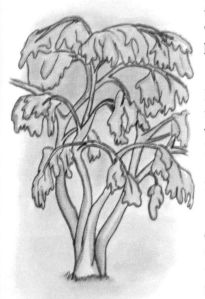

[18]The teachers of the Law and the religious leaders of the Jews heard it. They tried to find some way to put Jesus to death. But they were afraid of Him because all the people were surprised and wondered about His teaching. [19]When evening came, Jesus and His followers went out of the city.

The Fig Tree Dries Up [Matthew 21:18-22]

[20]In the morning they passed by the fig tree. They saw it was dried up from the roots. [21]Peter remembered what had happened the day before and said to Jesus, "Teacher, look! The fig tree which You spoke to has dried up!" [22]Jesus said to them, "Have faith in God. [23]For sure, I tell you, a person may say to this mountain, 'Move from here into the sea.' And if he does not doubt, but believes that what he says will be done, it will happen. [24]Because of this, I say to you, whatever you ask for when you pray, have faith that you will receive it. Then you will get it. [25]When you stand to pray, if you have anything against anyone, forgive him. Then your Father in heaven will forgive your sins also. [26]*If you do not forgive them their sins, your Father in heaven will not forgive your sins."

They Ask Jesus Who Gave Him The Right And The Power To Do These Things [Matthew 21:23-32; Luke 20:1-8]

[27]They came again to Jerusalem. Jesus was walking around in the house of God. The religious leaders and the teachers of the

Law and other leaders came to Him. [28]They asked, "How do You have the right and the power to do these things? Who gave You the right and the power to do them?" [29]Jesus said to them, "I will ask you one thing also. If you tell Me, then I will tell you by what right and power I do these things. [30]Was the baptism of John from heaven or from men? Tell Me." [31]They talked among themselves. They said, "If we say from heaven, He will say, 'Why did you not believe him?' [32]But how can we say, 'From men'?" They were afraid of the people because everyone believed that John was one who spoke for God. [33]So they said, "We do not know." Then Jesus said, "Then I will not tell you by what right and power I do these things."

The Picture-Story Of The Grape Field [Matthew 21:33-46; Luke 20:9-18]

12 Jesus began to teach them by using picture-stories, saying, "There was a man who planted grapes in a field. He put a fence around it and made a place for making wine. He built a high building to look over the field. Then he let farmers rent it and went into another country.

[2]"The time came for gathering the grapes. He sent his workman to the farmers to get some of the grapes. [3]The farmers took him and beat him. They sent him back with nothing. [4]The owner sent another workman. The farmers threw stones at him and hit him on the head and did other bad things to him. [5]Again the owner sent another workman. The farmers killed that one. Many other workmen were sent. They beat some and they killed others.

[6]"He had a much-loved son to send yet. So last of all he sent him to them, saying, 'They will respect my son.' [7]The farmers said to themselves, 'This is the one who will get everything when the owner dies. Let us kill him and we will get everything.' [8]They took him and killed him. They threw his body outside the field. [9]What will the owner of the field do? He will come and kill the farmers. He will give the field to other farmers.

[10]"Have you not read what the Holy Writings say? 'The Stone that was put aside by the workmen has become the most

gather. [39]They like to have the important seats in the places of worship and the important places at big suppers. [40]They take houses from poor women whose husbands have died. They cover up the bad they do by saying long prayers. They will be punished all the more."

The Woman Whose Husband Had Died Gave All She Had [Luke 21:1-4]

[41]Jesus sat near the money box in the house of God. He watched the people putting in money. Many of them were rich and gave much money. [42]A poor woman whose husband had died came by and gave two very small pieces of money.

[43]Jesus called His followers to Him. He said, "For sure, I tell you, this poor woman whose husband has died has given more money than all the others. [44]They all gave of that which was more than they needed for their own living. She is poor and yet she gave all she had, even what she needed for her own living."

Jesus Tells Of The House Of God [Matthew 24:1-51; Luke 21:5-36]

13 Jesus went out of the house of God. One of His followers said to Him, "Teacher, look at the big stones and these great buildings!" [2]Jesus said, "Do you see these great buildings? All these stones will be thrown down. Not one will be left standing on another."

Jesus Teaches On The Mountain Of Olives

[3]Jesus sat down on the Mountain of Olives at a place where He could see the house of God. Peter and James and John and Andrew came to Him. They asked without anyone else hearing, [4]"Tell us when this will be. What are we to look for when these things are to happen?"

What To Look For Before Jesus Returns

[5]Jesus began to say to them, "Be careful that no one leads you the wrong way. [6]Many people will come using My name. They will

say, 'I am Christ.' They will turn many to the wrong way. ⁷When you hear of wars and much talk about wars, do not be surprised. These things have to happen. But the end is not yet. ⁸Nations will have wars with other nations. Countries will fight against countries. The earth will shake and break apart in different places. There will be no food for people. There will be much trouble. These things are the beginning of much sorrow and pain.

It Will Be Hard For Those Who Believe

⁹"Watch out for yourselves. They will take you to the courts. In the places of worship they will beat you. You will be taken in front of the leaders of the people and in front of kings because of Me. You will be there to tell them about Me. ¹⁰The Good News must first be preached to all the nations.

The Good News must first be preached to all the nations.

¹¹"When you are put into their hands, do not be afraid of what you are to say or how you are to say it. Whatever is given to you to say at that time, say it. It will not be you who speaks, but the Holy Spirit. ¹²A brother will hand over a brother to death. A father will hand over his son. Children will turn against their parents and have them put to death. ¹³You will be hated by all people because of Me. But he who stays true to the end will be saved.

Days Of Trouble And Pain And Sorrow

¹⁴"You will see a very sinful man-made god standing in the house of God where it has no right to stand. Then those in the country of Judea should run to the mountains. It was spoken of by the early preacher Daniel. (Daniel 9:27; 12:11) The one who reads this should understand. ¹⁵He that is on the top of the house should not take the time to get anything out of his house. ¹⁶He that is in the field should not go back to get his coat. ¹⁷It will be hard for women who will soon be mothers. It will be hard for those feeding babies in those days! ¹⁸Pray that it will not be during the winter. ¹⁹In those days there will be much trouble and pain and sorrow. It has never been this bad from the beginning of time and never will be again. ²⁰If the Lord had not made those days short, no life would have been saved. Because of God's people whom He has chosen, He made the days short.

The False Religious Teachers

[21]"If anyone says to you, 'Look! Here is the Christ' or, 'There He is!' do not believe it. [22]Some will come who will say they are Christ. False preachers will come. These people will do special things for people to see. They will do surprising things, so that, if it can be, God's people will be led to believe something wrong. [23]Listen! I have told you about these things before they happen.

Jesus Will Come Again In His Greatness

[24]"After those days of much trouble and pain and sorrow are over, the sun will get dark. The moon will not give light. [25]The stars will fall from the sky. The powers in the heavens will be shaken. [26]Then they will see the Son of Man coming in the clouds with great power and shining greatness. [27]He will send His angels. They will gather together God's people from the four winds. They will come from one end of the earth to the other end of heaven.

The Picture-Story Of The Fig Tree

[28]"Now learn something from the fig tree. When the branch begins to grow and puts out its leaves, you know summer is near. [29]In the same way, when you see all these things happen, you know the Son of Man is near. He is even at the door. [30]For sure, I tell you, the people of this day will not pass away before all these things have happened.

No One Knows When Jesus Will Come Again

Heaven and earth will pass away, but My Words will not pass away.

[31]"Heaven and earth will pass away, but My Words will not pass away. [32]But no one knows the day or the hour. No! Not even the angels in heaven know. The Son does not know. Only the Father knows.

[33]"Be careful! Watch and pray. You do not know when it will happen. [34]The coming of the Son of Man is as a man who went from his house to a far country. He gave each of the workmen he owned some work to do. He told the one standing at the door to watch. [35]In the same way, you are to watch also! You do not know

when the Owner of the house will be coming. It may be in the evening or in the night or when the sun comes up or in the morning. ³⁶He may come when you are not looking for Him and find you sleeping. ³⁷What I say to you, I say to all. Watch!''

They Look For A Way To Put Jesus To Death [Matthew 26:1-5; Luke 22:1-6]

14 It was now two days before the supper of the special religious gathering to remember how the Jews left Egypt and the supper of bread without yeast. The religious leaders and the teachers of the Law tried to trap Jesus. They tried to take Him so they could put Him to death. ²These men said, ''This must not happen on the day of the special supper. The people would be against it and make much trouble.''

Mary Of Bethany Puts Special Perfume On Jesus [Matthew 26:6-13; John 12:1-11]

³Jesus was in the town of Bethany eating in the house of Simon. Simon was a man with a very bad skin disease. A woman came with a jar of special perfume. She had given much money for this. She broke the jar and poured the special perfume on the head of Jesus. ⁴Some of them were angry. They said, ''Why was this special perfume wasted? ⁵This perfume could have been sold for much money and given to poor people.'' They spoke against her.

⁶Jesus said, ''Let her alone. Why are you giving her trouble? She has done a good thing to Me. ⁷You will have poor people with you all the time. Whenever you want, you can do something good for them. You will not have Me all the time. ⁸She did what she could. She put this perfume on My body to make Me ready for the grave. ⁹For sure, I tell you, wherever this Good News is preached in all the world, this woman will be remembered for what she has done.''

Judas Hands Jesus Over To Be Killed [Matthew 26:14-16]

¹⁰Judas Iscariot was one of the twelve followers. He went to the head religious leaders of the Jews to talk about how he might hand

Jesus over to them. [11]When the leaders heard it, they were glad. They promised to give Judas money. Then he looked for a way to hand Jesus over.

Getting Ready For The Special Supper [*Matthew 26:17-19; Luke 22:7-13*]

[12]The first day of the supper of bread without yeast was the day to kill an animal. It was for the special religious gathering to remember how the Jews left Egypt. His followers said to Jesus, "What place do You want us to make ready for You to eat this special supper?" [13]Jesus sent two of His followers on ahead and said to them, "Go into the city. There a man will meet you carrying a jar of water. Follow him. [14]He will go into a house. You say to the owner of the house, 'The Teacher asks, "Where is the room you keep for friends, where I can eat this special supper with My followers?" ' [15]He will take you to a large room on the second floor with everything in it. Make it ready for us."

[16]The followers went from there and came into the city. They found everything as Jesus had said. They made things ready for the special supper.

The Last Special Supper [*Matthew 26:20-25; Luke 22:14-18; John 13:21-35*]

[17]In the evening He came with the twelve followers. [18]They sat at the table and ate. Jesus said, "For sure, I tell you, one of you will hand Me over to be killed. He is eating with Me." [19]They were very sad. They said to Him one after the other, "Is it I?" [20]He said to them, "It is one of the twelve followers. It is the one who is putting his hand with mine into the same dish. [21]The Son of Man is going away as it is written of Him. But it will be bad for that man who hands the Son of Man over to be killed! It would have been better if he had not been born!"

The First Lord's Supper [*Matthew 26:26-30; Luke 22:19-20*]

[22]As they were eating, Jesus took a loaf of bread. He gave thanks and broke it in pieces. He gave it to them and said, "Take, eat, this is My body." [23]Then He took the cup and gave thanks.

He gave it to them and they all drank from it. [24]He said to them, "This is My blood of the New Way of Worship which is given for many. [25]For sure, I tell you, that I will not drink of the fruit of the vine until that day when I drink it new in the holy nation of God." [26]After they sang a song, they went out to the Mountain of Olives.

Jesus Tells How Peter Will Lie About Him [*Matthew 26:31-35; Luke 22:31-34; John 13:36-38*]

[27]Jesus said to them, "All of you will be ashamed of Me and leave Me tonight. For it is written, 'I will kill the shepherd and the sheep of the flock will spread everywhere.' (Zechariah 13:7) [28]After I am raised from the dead, I will go before you into the country of Galilee." [29]Peter said to Him, "Even if all men are ashamed of You and leave You, I never will." [30]Jesus said to him, "For sure, I tell you, that today, even tonight, before a rooster crows two times, you will say three times you do not know Me." [31]Peter spoke with stronger words, "Even if I have to die with You, I will never say that I do not know You." All the followers said the same thing.

Jesus Prays In Gethsemane [*Matthew 26:36-46; Luke 22:39-46*]

[32]They came to a place called Gethsemane. Jesus said to His followers, "You sit here while I pray." [33]He took Peter and James and John with Him. He began to have much sorrow and a heavy heart. [34]He said to them, "My soul is very sad. My soul is so full of sorrow I am ready to die. You stay here and watch." [35]He went a little farther and got down with His face on the ground. He prayed that this time of suffering might pass from Him if it could. [36]He said, "Father, You can do all things. Take away what must happen to Me. Even so, not what I want, but what You want."

[37]Then Jesus came to the followers and found them sleeping. He said to Peter, "Simon, are you sleeping? Were you not able to watch one hour? [38]Watch and pray so that you will not be tempted. Man's spirit wants to do this, but the body does not have the power to do it."

[39]Again Jesus went away and prayed saying the same words. [40]He came back and found them sleeping again. Their eyes were

heavy. They did not know what to say to Him. 41He came the third time and said to them, "Are you still sleeping and resting? It is enough! Listen, the time has come when the Son of Man will be handed over to sinners. 42Get up and let us go. Look! The man who will hand Me over to the head religious leader is near."

Jesus Handed Over To Sinners [Matthew 26:47-56; Luke 22:47-51; John 18:1-11]

43At once, while Jesus was talking, Judas came. He was one of the twelve followers. He came with many other men who had swords and sticks. They came from the head religious leaders of the Jews and the teachers of the Law and the leaders of the people. 44The man who was going to hand Jesus over gave the men something to look for. He said, "The Man I kiss is the One. Take hold of Him and take Him away."

45At once Judas went straight to Jesus and said, "Teacher!" and kissed Him. 46Then they put their hands on Him and took Him.

47One of the followers of Jesus who stood watching took his sword. He hit the workman owned by the head religious leader and cut off his ear. 48Jesus said to them, "Have you come with swords and sticks to take Me as if I were a robber?   49I have been with you every day teaching in the house of God. You never took hold of Me. But this has happened as the Holy Writings said it would happen." 50Then all His followers left Him and ran away.

51A young man was following Him with only a piece of cloth around his body. They put their hands on the young man. 52Leaving the cloth behind, he ran away with no clothes on.

Jesus Stands In Front Of The Head Religious Leaders [Matthew 26:57-58; Luke 22:52-54; John 18:19-24]

53They led Jesus away to the head religious leader. All the religious leaders and other leaders and the teachers of the Law were gathered there. 54But Peter followed a long way behind as they went to the house of the head religious leader. He sat with the helpers and got warm by the fire.

Jesus Stands In Front Of The Court [*Matthew 26:59-68*]

⁵⁵The religious leaders and all the court were looking for something against Jesus. They wanted to find something so they could kill Him. But they could find nothing. ⁵⁶Many came and told false things about Him, but their words did not agree. ⁵⁷Some got up and said false things against Him. They said, ⁵⁸"We have heard Him say, 'I will destroy the house of God that was made with hands. In three days I will build another that is not made with hands.' " ⁵⁹Even these who spoke against Him were not able to agree.

⁶⁰The head religious leader stood up in front of the people. He asked Jesus, "Have You nothing to say? What about the things these men are saying against You?" ⁶¹Jesus said nothing. Again the head religious leader asked Him, "Are You the Christ, the Son of the Holy One?" ⁶²Jesus said, "I am! And you will see the Son of Man seated on the right side of the All-powerful God. You will see Him coming again in the clouds of the sky."

You will see Him
coming again
in the clouds of the sky.

⁶³Then the head religious leader tore his clothes apart. He said, "Do we need other people to speak against Him? ⁶⁴You have heard Him speak as if He were God! What do you think?" They all said He was guilty of death. ⁶⁵Some began to spit on Him. They covered Jesus' face. They hit Him. They said, "Tell us what is going to happen." Soldiers hit Him with their hands.

Peter Said He Did Not Know Jesus [*Matthew 26:69-75; Luke 22:55-62; John 18:15-18, 25-27*]

⁶⁶Peter was outside in the yard. One of the women helpers of the head religious leader came. ⁶⁷She saw Peter getting warm. She looked at him and said, "You were with Jesus of Nazareth." ⁶⁸Peter lied, saying, "I do not know Jesus and do not understand what you are talking about." As he went out, a rooster crowed.

⁶⁹The girl saw him again. She said to the people standing around, "This man is one of them." ⁷⁰He lied again saying that he did not know Jesus. Later, those who stood around said to Peter again, "For sure you are one of them. You are from the country of Galilee. You talk like they do." ⁷¹He began to say strong words

and to swear. He said, "I do not know the Man you are talking about!"

72At once a rooster crowed the second time. Peter remembered what Jesus had said to him, "Before a rooster crows two times, you will say three times you do not know Me." When he thought about it, he cried.

Jesus Before Pilate [*Matthew 27:1-2, 11-14; Luke 23:1-5; John 18:28-37*]

15 Early in the morning the head religious leaders of the Jews and other leaders and the teachers of the Law and all the court gathered together to talk about Jesus. Then they tied up Jesus and led Him away. They handed Him over to Pilate. 2Pilate asked Jesus, "Are You the King of the Jews?" He said to Pilate, "What you say is true."

3The religious leaders spoke many things against Him. Jesus did not say a word. 4Pilate asked Him again, "Have You nothing to say? Listen to the things they are saying against You!" 5Jesus did not say a word. Pilate was much surprised and wondered about it.

Jesus Or Barabbas Is To Go Free [*Matthew 27:15-26; Luke 23:17-25; John 18:38-40*]

6Each year at the special supper Pilate would let one person who was in prison go free. It would be the one the people asked for. 7The name of one of those in prison was Barabbas. He, together with others, had killed people while working against the leaders of the country. 8All the people went to Pilate and asked him to do as he had done before. 9Pilate said, "Do you want me to let the King of the Jews go free?" 10He knew the religious leaders had handed Jesus over to him because they were jealous. 11The religious leaders talked the people into thinking that Pilate should let Barabbas go free. 12Pilate said to them again, "What do you want me to do with the Man you call the King of the Jews?" 13They spoke with loud voices again, "Nail Him to a cross." 14Then Pilate said to them, "Why? What bad thing has He done?" They spoke with loud voices all the more, "Nail Him to a cross!"

The Headband Of Thorns [Matthew 27:27-32; John 19:1-5]

¹⁵Pilate wanted to please the people. He gave Barabbas to them and had Jesus beaten. Then he handed Him over to be nailed to a cross. ¹⁶The soldiers led Jesus away to a large room in the court. They called all the soldiers together. ¹⁷The soldiers put a purple coat on Him. They put a headband of thorns on His head, ¹⁸and said to Him, "Hello, King of the Jews!" ¹⁹They hit Him on the head with a stick and spit on Him. They got down on their knees and worshiped Him. ²⁰After they had made fun of Him, they took the purple coat off of Him and put His own clothes back on Him. Then they led Him away to be nailed to a cross.

²¹They came to a man called Simon who was coming from the country of Cyrene. He was the father of Alexander and Rufus. They made Simon carry the cross of Jesus.

Jesus On The Cross [Matthew 27:33-37; Luke 23:26-38; John 19:17-22]

²²They led Jesus to a place called Golgotha. This name means the place of the skull. ²³They gave Him wine with something in it to take away the pain, but He would not drink it. ²⁴When they had nailed Jesus to the cross, they divided His clothes by drawing names to see what each man should take. ²⁵It was about nine o'clock in the morning when they nailed Him to the cross. ²⁶Over Jesus' head they put in writing what they had against Him, THE KING OF THE JEWS.

The Two Robbers [Matthew 27:38-44; Luke 23:39-43]

²⁷They nailed two robbers on crosses beside Jesus. One was on His right side and the other was on His left side. ²⁸*It happened as the Holy Writings said it would happen, "They thought of Him as One Who broke the Law." (Isaiah 53:12)

²⁹Those who walked by shook their heads and laughed at Jesus. They said, "You were the One Who could destroy the house of God and build it again in three days. ³⁰Save Yourself and come down from the cross." ³¹The head religious leaders and the teachers of the Law made fun of Him also. They said to each

other, "He saved others but He cannot save Himself. ³²Let Christ, the King of the Jews, come down from the cross. We want to see it and then we will believe." Those who were on the crosses beside Jesus spoke bad things to Him.

The Death Of Jesus [*Matthew 27:45-50; Luke 23:44-49; John 19:28-37*]

³³From noon until three o'clock it was dark over all the land. ³⁴At three o'clock Jesus cried with a loud voice, "My God, My God, why have You left Me alone?"

³⁵When some of those who stood by heard that, they said, "Listen! He is calling for Elijah." ³⁶One of them ran and took a sponge and filled it with sour wine. He put it on a stick and gave it to Him to drink. He said, "Let Him alone. Let us see if Elijah will come and take Him down."

The Powerful Works At The Time Of His Death [*Matthew 27:51-54*]

³⁷Then Jesus gave a loud cry. He gave up His spirit and died. ³⁸The curtain in the house of God was torn in two from top to bottom.

³⁹The captain of the soldiers was looking at Jesus when He cried out. He saw Him die and said, "For sure, this Man was the Son of God."

The Women At The Cross [*Matthew 27:55-56; John 19:25-27*]

⁴⁰Women were looking on from far away. Among them was Mary Magdalene and Mary the mother of the younger James and of Joses, and Salome. ⁴¹These cared for Him when He was in the country of Galilee. There were many other women there who had followed Him to Jerusalem.

The Grave Of Jesus [*Matthew 27:57-66; Luke 23:50-56; John 19:38-42*]

⁴²It was the day to get ready for the Day of Rest and it was now evening. ⁴³Joseph, who was from the city of Arimathea, was an

important man in the court. He was looking for the holy nation of God. Without being afraid, he went to Pilate and asked for the body of Jesus. ⁴⁴Pilate was surprised and wondered if Jesus was dead so soon. He called the captain of the soldiers and asked if Jesus was already dead.

⁴⁵After the captain said that Jesus was dead, Pilate let Joseph take the body. ⁴⁶Joseph took the body of Jesus down from the cross. He put the linen cloth he had bought around the body. Then he laid the body in a grave which had been cut out in the side of a rock. He pushed a stone over to cover the door of the grave. ⁴⁷Mary Magdalene and Mary the mother of Joses saw where He was laid.

Jesus Is Raised From The Dead [*Matthew 28:1-10; Luke 24:1-12; John 20:1-18*]

16 The Day of Rest was over. Mary Magdalene and Mary the mother of James, and Salome bought spices. They wanted to put the spices on Jesus' body. ²Very early in the morning on the first day of the week, they came to the grave. The sun had come up. ³They said to themselves, "Who will roll the stone away from the door of the grave for us?" ⁴But when they looked, they saw the very large stone had been rolled away.

⁵They went into the grave. There they saw a young man with a long white coat sitting on the right side. They were afraid. ⁶He said, "Do not be afraid. You are looking for Jesus of Nazareth Who was nailed to a cross. He is risen! He is not here! Look, here is the place where they laid Him. ⁷Go and tell His followers and Peter that He is going ahead of you into the country of Galilee. You will see Him there as He told you." ⁸They ran from the grave shaking and were surprised. They did not say anything to anyone because they were afraid.

The Followers Of Jesus Do Not Believe He Was Raised From The Dead [*Luke 24:13-43; John 20:24-29*]

⁹*(It was early on the first day of the week when Jesus was raised from the dead. Mary Magdalene saw Him first. He had put

birth, he will be filled with the Holy Spirit. [16]Many of the Jews will be turned to the Lord their God by him. [17]He will be the one to go in the spirit and power of Elijah before Christ comes. He will turn the hearts of the fathers back to their children. He will teach those who do not obey to be right with God. He will get people ready for the Lord." (Malachi 4:5-6)

Zacharias Does Not Believe The Angel

[18]Zacharias said to the angel, "How can I know this for sure? I am old and my wife is old also." [19]The angel said to him, "My name is Gabriel. I stand near God. He sent me to talk to you and bring to you this good news. [20]Listen! You will not be able to talk until the day this happens. It is because you did not believe my words. What I said will happen at the right time."

[21]The people outside were waiting. They were surprised and wondered why Zacharias stayed so long in the house of God. [22]When he came out, he could not talk to them. They knew he had seen something special from God while he was in the house of God. He tried to talk to them with his hands but could say nothing. [23]When his days of working in the house of God were over, he went to his home.

The Lord Did What He Promised

[24]Some time later Elizabeth knew she was to become a mother. She kept herself hidden for five months. She said, [25]"This is what the Lord has done for me. He has looked on me and has taken away my shame from among men."

Gabriel Speaks To Mary

[26]Six months after Elizabeth knew she was to become a mother, Gabriel was sent from God to Nazareth. Nazareth was a town in the country of Galilee. [27]He went to a woman who had never had a man. Her name was Mary. She was promised in marriage to a man named Joseph. Joseph was of the family of David. [28]The angel came to her and said, "You are honored very much. You are a favored woman. The Lord is with you. *You are chosen from among many women."

²⁹When she saw the angel, she was troubled at his words. She thought about what had been said. ³⁰The angel said to her, "Mary, do not be afraid. You have found favor with God. ³¹Listen! You are to become a mother and have a Son. You are to give Him the name Jesus. ³²He will be great. He will be called the Son of the Most High. The Lord God will give Him the place where His early father David sat. ³³He will be King over the family of Jacob forever and His nation will have no end."

³⁴Mary said to the angel, "How can this happen? I have never had a man." ³⁵The angel said to her, "The Holy Spirit will come on you. The power of the Most High will cover you. The holy Child you give birth to will be called the Son of God.

³⁶"Listen, your cousin Elizabeth, as old as she is, is going to give birth to a child. She was not able to have children before, but now she is in her sixth month. ³⁷For God can do all things." God can do all things. ³⁸Then Mary said, "I am willing to be used of the Lord. Let it happen to me as you have said." Then the angel went away from her.

Mary Visits Elizabeth

³⁹At once Mary went from there to a town in the hill country of Judea. ⁴⁰She went to the house of Zacharias to see Elizabeth. ⁴¹When Elizabeth heard Mary speak, the baby moved in her body. At the same time Elizabeth was filled with the Holy Spirit.

⁴²Elizabeth spoke in a loud voice, "You are honored among women! Your Child is honored! ⁴³Why has this happened to me? Why has the mother of my Lord come to me? ⁴⁴As soon as I heard your voice, the baby in my body moved for joy. ⁴⁵You are happy because you believed. Everything will happen as the Lord told you it would happen."

Mary's Song Of Thanks

⁴⁶Then Mary said, "My heart sings with thanks for my Lord. ⁴⁷And my spirit is happy in God, the One Who saves from the My spirit punishment of sin. ⁴⁸The Lord has looked on me, the one He owns is happy in God. and the one who is not important. But from now on all people will

The loving-pity
of the Lord
is given to the people
of all times
who honor Him.

honor me. ⁴⁹He Who is powerful has done great things for me. His name is holy. ⁵⁰The loving-pity of the Lord is given to the people of all times who honor Him. ⁵¹He has done powerful works with His arm. He has divided from each other those who have pride in their hearts. ⁵²He has taken kings down from the place where they sit. He has put those who are in a place that is not important to a place that is important. ⁵³He has filled those who are hungry with good things. He has sent the rich people away with nothing. ⁵⁴He has helped the Jews who are the people He owns. This was done to remember His loving-pity. ⁵⁵He promised He would do this to our early fathers and to Abraham and to his family forever.'' ⁵⁶Mary stayed with Elizabeth about three months. Then she went to her own home.

The Birth Of John The Baptist

⁵⁷When the time came, Elizabeth gave birth to a son. ⁵⁸Her neighbors and family heard how the Lord had shown loving-pity to her. They were happy for her. ⁵⁹On the eighth day they did the religious act of the Jews on the child. They named him Zacharias, after his father. ⁶⁰But his mother said, "No! His name is John." ⁶¹They said to her, "No one in your family has that name."

⁶²Then they talked to his father with their hands to find out what he would name the child. ⁶³He asked for something to write on. He wrote, "His name is John." They were all surprised and wondered about it. ⁶⁴Zacharias was able to talk from that time on and he gave thanks to God.

⁶⁵All those who lived near them were afraid. The news of what had happened was told through all the hill country of Judea. ⁶⁶And all who heard those words remembered them and said, "What is this child going to be?" For the hand of the Lord was on him.

Zacharias' Song Of Thanks To God

⁶⁷Zacharias, the father of John, was filled with the Holy Spirit. He told what was going to happen, saying, ⁶⁸"Let us thank the Lord God of the Jews. He has bought His people and made them free. ⁶⁹He has raised up One from the family of David Who saves

people from the punishment of their sins. [70]His holy early preachers told us this long ago. [71]God told us that we should be saved from those who hate us and from all those who work against us. [72]He would show loving-pity to our early fathers. He would remember His holy promise. [73]God promised this to our early father Abraham. [74]He promised that we would be saved from those who hate us and that we might worship Him without being afraid. [75]We can be holy and right with God all the days of our life.

[76]"And you, my son, will be the one who speaks for the Most High. For you will go before the Lord to make the way ready for Him. [77]You will tell His people how to be saved from the punishment of sin by being forgiven of their sins. [78]Because the heart of our God is full of loving-pity for us, a light from heaven will shine on us. [79]It will give light to those who live in darkness and are under the shadow of death. It will lead our feet in the way of peace."

[80]The child grew and became strong in spirit. He lived in a desert until the day he started to preach to the Jews.

The Birth Of Jesus [*Matthew 1:18-25*]

2 In those days Caesar Augustus sent out word that the name of every person in the Roman nation must be written in the books of the nation. [2]This first writing took place while Quirinius was leader of Syria.

[3]So all the people went to their own cities to have their names written in the books of the nation. [4]Joseph went up from the town of Nazareth in the country of Galilee to the town of Bethlehem. It was known as the city of David. He went there because he was from the family of David. [5]Joseph went to have his and Mary's names written in the books of the nation. Mary was his promised wife and soon to become a mother.

[6]While they were there in the town of Bethlehem, the time came for Mary to give birth to her baby. [7]Her first son was born. She put cloth around Him and laid Him in a place where cattle are fed.

There was no room for them in the place where people stay for the night.

The Shepherds Learn Of The Birth Of Jesus

[8]In the same country there were shepherds in the fields. They were watching their flocks of sheep at night. [9]The angel of the Lord came to them. The shining greatness of the Lord shone around them. They were very much afraid. [10]The angel said to them, "Do not be afraid. Listen! I bring you good news of great joy which is for all people. [11]Today, One Who saves from the punishment of sin has been born in the city of David. He is Christ the Lord. [12]There will be something special for you to see. This is the way you will know Him. You will find the Baby with cloth around Him, lying in a place where cattle are fed."

[13]At once many angels from heaven were seen, along with the angel, giving thanks to God. They were saying, [14]"Greatness and honor to our God in the highest heaven and peace on earth among men who please Him."

The Shepherds Go To Bethlehem

[15]The angels went from the shepherds back to heaven. The shepherds said to each other, "Let us go to the town of Bethlehem and see what has happened. The Lord has told us about this." [16]They went fast and found Mary and Joseph. They found the Baby lying in a place where cattle are fed. [17]When they saw the Child, they told what the angel said about Him. [18]All who heard it were surprised at what the shepherds told them. [19]But Mary hid all these words in her heart. She thought about them much. [20]The shepherds went back full of joy. They thanked God for all they had heard and seen. It happened as the angel had told them.

Jesus Taken To The House Of God

[21]When eight days were over, they did the religious act of the Jews on the Child. He was named Jesus. This name was given to Him by the angel when Mary was told He was to be born. [22]When the days were over for her to be made pure as it was written in the Law of Moses, they took Jesus to Jerusalem to give Him to the

Lord. 23It is written in the Law of the Lord, "The first boy child born of a woman will be called holy to the Lord." 24They were to give a gift of two doves or two young birds on the altar in worship to the Lord. This was written in the Law of the Lord.

Simeon's Song Of Thanks

25There was a man in Jerusalem by the name of Simeon. He was a good man and very religious. He was looking for the time when the Jewish nation would be saved. The Holy Spirit was on him. 26The Holy Spirit made it known to Simeon that he would not die before he had seen God's Chosen One. 27He came into the house of God being led by the Holy Spirit. The parents took Jesus into the house of God. They came to do what the Jewish Law said must be done. 28Then Simeon took Jesus in his arms. He gave honor to Him and thanked God, saying,

29"Lord, now let me die in peace, as You have said. 30My eyes have seen the One Who will save men from the punishment of their sins. 31You have made Him ready in the sight of all nations. 32He will be a light to shine on the people who are not Jews. He will be the shining greatness of Your people the Jews." 33Joseph and the mother of Jesus were surprised and wondered about these words which were said about Jesus. 34Simeon honored them and said to Mary the mother of Jesus, "Listen! This Child will make many people fall and many people rise in the Jewish nation. He will be spoken against. 35A sword will cut through your soul. By this the thoughts of many hearts will be understood."

You have made Him
ready in the sight
of all nations.
He will be a light
to shine on the people
who are not Jews.

Anna Gives Thanks For Jesus

36Anna was a woman who spoke God's Word. She was the daughter of Phanuel of the family group of Asher. Anna was many years old. She had lived with her husband seven years after she was married. 37Her husband had died and she had lived without a husband eighty-four years. Yet she did not go away from the house of God. She worked for God day and night, praying and going without food so she could pray better. 38At that time she came and gave thanks to God. She told the people in Jerusalem about Jesus. They were looking for the One to save them from the punishment of their sins and to set them free.

They Return To Nazareth [Matthew 2:19-23]

³⁹When Joseph and Mary had done everything the Law said to do, they went back to their own town of Nazareth in the country of Galilee. ⁴⁰The Child grew and became strong in spirit. He was filled with wisdom and the loving-favor of God was on Him.

Jesus In The House Of God

⁴¹His parents went to Jerusalem every year for the special religious gathering to remember how the Jews left Egypt. ⁴²When He was twelve years old, they went up to Jerusalem as they had done before. ⁴³When the days of the special supper were over, they started back to their town. But the boy Jesus was still in Jerusalem. His parents did not know it. ⁴⁴They thought Jesus was with the others of the group. They walked for one day. Then they looked for Him among their family and friends.

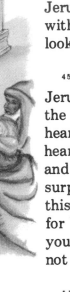

⁴⁵When they could not find Jesus, they turned back to Jerusalem to look for Him. ⁴⁶Three days later they found Him in the house of God. He was sitting among the teachers. He was hearing what they said and asking questions. ⁴⁷All those who heard Him were surprised and wondered about His understanding and at what He said. ⁴⁸When His parents saw Him, they were surprised. His mother said to Him, "My Son, why have You done this to us? Look! Your father and I have had much sorrow looking for You." ⁴⁹He said to them, "Why were you looking for Me? Do you not know that I must be in My Father's house?" ⁵⁰They did not understand the things He said to them.

⁵¹He went with them to the town of Nazareth and obeyed them. But His mother kept all these words in her heart. ⁵²Jesus grew strong in mind and body. He grew in favor with God and men.

He grew in favor with God and men.

John The Baptist Makes The Way Ready For Jesus [Matthew 3:1-12; Mark 1:1-8; John 1:15-28]

3 Tiberius Caesar had been leader for fifteen years. Pontius Pilate was leader of the country of Judea. Herod was the leader of the country of Galilee. His brother Philip was the leader of the countries of Ituraea and Trachonitis. Lysanias was the leader of the country of Abilene. ²Annas and Caiaphas were the head religious leaders.

The Word of God came to John the Baptist, the son of Zacharias. John was in the desert. ³He went into all the country around the Jordan River. He preached that people should be baptized because they were sorry for their sins and turned from them. And they would be forgiven. ⁴The early preacher Isaiah wrote these words: "His voice calls out in the desert. 'Make the way ready for the Lord. Make the road straight for Him! ⁵Every valley will be filled and every mountain and hill will be brought down. The turns in the road will be made straight and the rough places will be made smooth. ⁶And all men will see God saving people from the punishment of their sins.'" (Isaiah 40:3-5)

⁷John said to the people who came to be baptized by him, "You family of snakes! Who told you how to keep from the anger of God that is coming? ⁸Do something to let me see that you have turned from your sins. Do not begin to say to yourselves, 'We have Abraham as our father.' I tell you, God can make children for Abraham out of these stones. ⁹Even now the ax is on the root of the trees. Every tree that does not give good fruit is cut down and thrown into the fire." ¹⁰The people asked him, "Then what should we do?" ¹¹He answered them, "If you have two coats, give one to him who has none. If you have food, you must share some."

¹²Tax gatherers came to be baptized also. They asked him, "Teacher, what are we to do?" ¹³He said to them, "Do not take more money from people than you should." ¹⁴Also soldiers asked him, "What are we to do?" He answered them, "Take no money from anyone by using your own strength. Do not lie about anyone. Be happy with the pay you get."

Be happy with the pay you get.

¹⁵The people were looking for something to happen. They were thinking in their hearts about John the Baptist. They wondered if he might be the Christ. ¹⁶But John said to all of them, "I baptize you with water. There is One coming Who is greater than I. I am not good enough to get down and help Him take off His shoes. He will baptize you with the Holy Spirit and with fire. ¹⁷He comes ready to clean the grain. He will gather the grain and clean it all.

He will put the clean grain into a building. But He will burn that which is no good with a fire that cannot be put out."

John The Baptist Is Put Into Prison [Matthew 14:1-5; Mark 6:14-20]

18John spoke much more as he preached the Good News to the people. 19He had also spoken sharp words to Herod the leader because of Herodias. She was his brother Philip's wife. And John spoke to Herod about all the wrongs he had done. 20To all these, Herod added another sin by putting John into prison.

The Baptism Of Jesus [Matthew 3:13-17; Mark 1:9-11; John 1:29-34]

You are My much-loved Son. I am very happy with You.

21When all the people were being baptized, Jesus was baptized also. As He prayed, the heaven opened. 22The Holy Spirit came down on Him in a body like a dove. A voice came from heaven and said, "You are My much-loved Son. I am very happy with You."

The Family Of Jesus Through Mary [Matthew 1:1-17]

23Jesus was about thirty years old when He began His work. People thought Jesus was the son of Joseph, the son of Heli. 24Heli was the son of Matthat. Matthat was the son of Levi. Levi was the son of Melchi. Melchi was the son of Jannai. Jannai was the son of Joseph. 25Joseph was the son of Mattathias. Mattathias was the son of Amos. Amos was the son of Nahum. Nahum was the son of Esli. Esli was the son of Naggai. 26Naggai was the son of Maath. Maath was the son of Mattathias. Mattathias was the son of Semein. Semein was the son of Joseck. Joseck was the son of Juda. 27Juda was the son of Johanan. Johanan was the son of Rhesa. Rhesa was the son of Zerubbabel. Zerubbabel was the son of Salathiel. Salathiel was the son of Neri. 28Neri was the son of Melchi. Melchi was the son of Addi. Addi was the son of Cosam. Cosam was the son of Elmadam. Elmadam was the son of Er. 29Er was the son of Joshua. Joshua was the son of Eliezer. Eliezer was the son of Jorim. Jorim was the son of Matthat. Matthat was the son of Levi. 30Levi was the son of Simeon. Simeon was the son of Judah. Judah was the son of Joseph. Joseph was the son of

Janam. Janam was the son of Eliakim. ³¹Eliakim was the son of
Melea. Melea was the son of Menna. Menna was the son of
Mattatha. Mattatha was the son of Nathan. Nathan was the son
of David. ³²David was the son of Jesse. Jesse was the son of Obed.
Obed was the son of Boaz. Boaz was the son of Salmon. Salmon
was the son of Nahshon. ³³Nahshon was the son of Amminadab.
Amminadab was the son of Admin. Admin was the son of Hezron.
Hezron was the son of Perez. Perez was the son of Judah. ³⁴Judah
was the son of Jacob. Jacob was the son of Isaac. Isaac was the
son of Abraham. Abraham was the son of Terah. Terah was the
son of Nahor. ³⁵Nahor was the son of Serug. Serug was the son of
Ragau. Ragau was the son of Peleg. Peleg was the son of Eber.
Eber was the son of Shelah. ³⁶Shelah was the son of Cainan.
Cainan was the son of Arphaxad. Arphaxad was the son of Shem.
Shem was the son of Noah. Noah was the son of Lamech.
³⁷Lamech was the son of Methuselah. Methuselah was the son of
Enoch. Enoch was the son of Jared. Jared was the son of
Mahalaleel. Mahalaleel was the son of Cainan. ³⁸Cainan was the
son of Enos. Enos was the son of Seth. Seth was the son of Adam.
Adam was the son of God.

Jesus Was Tempted [*Matthew 4:1-11; Mark 1:12-13*]

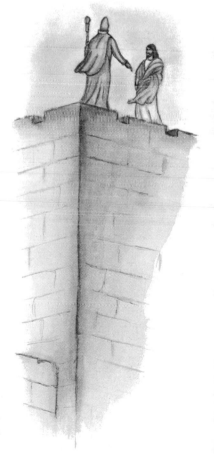

4 Jesus was full of the Holy Spirit when He returned from the
Jordan River. Then He was led by the Holy Spirit into a
desert. ²He was tempted by the devil for forty days and He ate
nothing during that time. After that He was hungry. ³The devil
said to Him, "If You are the Son of God, tell this stone to be made
into bread." ⁴Jesus said to him, "It is written, 'Man is not to live
by bread alone.' " (Deuteronomy 8:3) ⁵The devil took Jesus up on
a high mountain. He had Jesus look at all the nations of the world at
one time. ⁶The devil said to Jesus, "I will give You all this power
and greatness. It has been given to me. I can give it to anyone I
want to. ⁷If You will worship me, all this will be Yours." ⁸Jesus said
to the devil, "Get behind Me, Satan! For it is written, 'You must
worship the Lord your God. You must obey Him only.' "
(Deuteronomy 6:13) ⁹Then the devil took Jesus up to Jerusalem.
He had Jesus stand on the highest part of the house of God. The
devil said to Jesus, "If You are the Son of God, throw Yourself
down from here. ¹⁰For it is written, 'He has told His angels to care

for You and to keep You. ¹¹In their hands they will hold You up. Then Your foot will not hit against a stone.' '' (Psalm 91:11-12) ¹²Jesus said to the devil, "It is written, 'You must not tempt the Lord your God.' '' (Deuteronomy 6:16) ¹³When the devil finished tempting Jesus in every way, he went away from Jesus for awhile.

Jesus Preaches In Galilee [Matthew 4:12-17; Mark 1:14-15]

¹⁴Jesus went back to the country of Galilee in the power of the Holy Spirit. People talked about Him so much that He was well-known through all the country. ¹⁵Jesus taught in their places of worship and was honored by all people.

In Nazareth They Do Not Believe In Jesus

¹⁶Jesus came to the town of Nazareth where He had grown up. As He had done before, He went into the Jewish place of worship on the Day of Rest. Then He stood up to read. ¹⁷Someone handed Him the book of the early preacher Isaiah. He opened it and found the place where it was written, ¹⁸"The Spirit of the Lord is on Me. He has put His hand on Me to preach the Good News to poor people. He has sent Me to heal those with a sad heart. He has sent Me to tell those who are being held that they can go free. He has sent Me to make the blind to see and to free those who are held because of trouble. ¹⁹He sent Me to tell of the time when men can receive favor with the Lord." (Isaiah 61:1-2)

²⁰Jesus closed the book. Then He gave it back to the leader and sat down. All those in the Jewish place of worship kept their eyes on Him. ²¹Then He began to say to them, "The Holy Writings you have just heard have been completed today."

²²They all spoke well of Jesus and agreed with the words He spoke. They said, "Is not this the son of Joseph?" ²³He said to them, "I wonder if you will tell this old saying to Me, 'Doctor, heal Yourself. What You did in the city of Capernaum, do in Your own country!' '' ²⁴He said, "A man who speaks for God is not respected in his own country. ²⁵It is true that there were many women whose husbands had died in the Jewish land when Elijah lived. For three and a half years there was no rain and there was very little food in the land. ²⁶Elijah was sent to none of them, but

he was sent to a woman in the city of Zarephath in the land of Sidon. This woman's husband had died. 27There were many people in the Jewish land who had a very bad skin disease when the early preacher Elisha lived. None of them but Naaman was healed. He was from the country of Syria."

28All those in the Jewish place of worship were angry when they heard His words. 29They got up and took Jesus out of town to the top of a high hill. They wanted to throw Him over the side. 30But Jesus got away from among them and went on His way.

Jesus Heals A Man With A Demon [Mark 1:21-28]

31Jesus went down to the city of Capernaum in the country of Galilee. He taught them on the Days of Rest. 32The people were surprised and wondered about His teaching. His words had power. 33A man in the Jewish place of worship had a demon. He cried with a loud voice, 34"What do You want of us, Jesus of Nazareth? I know Who You are. You are the Holy One of God." 35Jesus spoke sharp words to the demon and said, "Do not talk! Come out of him!" When the demon had thrown the man down, he came out without hurting the man.

36The people were all surprised. They asked each other, "What kind of word is this? He speaks to the demons with power and they come out!" 37The news about Jesus went through all the country.

The news about Jesus went through all the country.

Peter's Mother-In-Law Healed [Matthew 8:14-15; Mark 1:29-31]

38Jesus went away from the Jewish place of worship and went into Simon's house. Simon's mother-in-law was in bed, very sick. They asked Jesus to help her. 39He stood by her and told the disease to leave. It went from her. At once she got up and cared for them.

Jesus Heals In Galilee [Matthew 8:16-17; Mark 1:32-34]

40As the sun went down, the people took all that were sick with many kinds of disease to Jesus. He put His hands on all of them and they were healed. 41Also demons came out of many people.

The demons cried out and said, "You are Christ, the Son of God." Jesus spoke strong words to them and would not let them speak. They knew He was the Christ.

Jesus Keeps On Preaching In Galilee [*Matthew 4:23-25; Mark 1:35-39*]

⁴²In the morning He went out to a desert. The people looked for Him. When they found Him, they were trying to keep Him from going away from them. ⁴³He said to them, "I must preach about the holy nation of God in other cities also. This is why I was sent." ⁴⁴And He kept on preaching in the Jewish places of worship in the country of Galilee.

Jesus Calls Simon And James And John [*Matthew 4:18-22; Mark 1:16-20*]

5 While Jesus was standing by the lake of Gennesaret, many people pushed to get near Him. They wanted to hear the Word of God. ²Jesus saw two boats on the shore. The fishermen were not there because they were washing their nets. ³Jesus got into a boat which belonged to Simon. Jesus asked him to push it out a little way from land. Then He sat down and taught the people from the boat.

⁴When He had finished speaking, He said to Simon, "Push out into the deep water. Let down your nets for some fish." ⁵Simon said to Him, "Teacher, we have worked all night and we have caught nothing. But because You told me to, I will let the net down." ⁶When they had done this, they caught so many fish, their net started to break. ⁷They called to their friends working in the other boat to come and help them. They came and both boats were so full of fish they began to sink. ⁸When Simon Peter saw it, he got down at the feet of Jesus. He said, "Go away from me, Lord, because I am a sinful man." ⁹He and all those with him were surprised and wondered about the many fish. ¹⁰James and John, the sons of Zebedee, were surprised also. They were working together with Simon. Then Jesus said to Simon, "Do not be afraid. From now on you will fish for men." ¹¹When they came to land with their boats, they left everything and followed Jesus.

Jesus Heals A Man With A Bad Skin Disease [Matthew 8:1-4; Mark 1:40-45]

[12]While Jesus was in one of the towns, a man came to Him with a bad skin disease over all his body. When he saw Jesus, he got down on his face in front of Him. He begged Him, saying, "Lord, if You are willing, You can heal me." [13]Jesus put His hand on him and said, "I will. Be healed." At once the disease went away from him. [14]Then Jesus told him to tell no one. He said, "Go and let the religious leader of the Jews see you. Give the gift on the altar in worship that Moses told you to give when a man is healed of a disease. This will show the leaders you have been healed." [15]The news about Jesus went out all the more. Many people came to hear Him and to be healed of their diseases. [16]Then He went away by Himself to pray in a desert.

He went away
by Himself
to pray in a desert.

Jesus Heals A Man Let Down Through The Roof Of A House [Matthew 9:1-8; Mark 2:1-12]

[17]On one of the days while Jesus was teaching, some proud religious law-keepers and teachers of the Law were sitting by Him. They had come from every town in the countries of Galilee and Judea and from Jerusalem. Jesus had the power of the Lord to heal. [18]Some men took a man who was not able to move his body to Jesus. He was carried on a bed. They looked for a way to take the man into the house where Jesus was. [19]But they could not find a way to take him in because of so many people. They made a hole in the roof over where Jesus stood. Then they let the bed with the sick man on it down in front of Jesus. [20]When Jesus saw their faith, He said to the man, "Friend, your sins are forgiven."

Friend,
your sins are forgiven.

[21]The teachers of the Law and the proud religious law-keepers thought to themselves, "Who is this Man Who speaks as if He is God? Who can forgive sins but God only?" [22]Jesus knew what they were thinking. He said to them, "Why do you think this way in your hearts? [23]Which is easier to say, 'Your sins are forgiven' or, 'Get up and walk'?

[24]"So that you may know the Son of Man has the right and the power on earth to forgive sins," He said to the man who could not move his body, "I say to you, get up. Take your bed and go to

your home.'' ²⁵At once the sick man got up in front of them. He took his bed and went to his home thanking God. ²⁶All those who were there were surprised and gave thanks to God, saying, "We have seen very special things today."

Jesus Calls Matthew [Matthew 9:9-13; Mark 2:13-17]

²⁷After this Jesus went out and saw a man who gathered taxes. His name was Levi (Matthew). Levi was sitting at his work. Jesus said to him, "Follow Me." ²⁸Levi got up, left everything and followed Jesus. ²⁹Levi made a big supper for Jesus in his house. Many men who gathered taxes and other people sat down with them. ³⁰The teachers of the Law and the proud religious law-keepers talked against the followers of Jesus. They said, "Why do You eat and drink with men who gather taxes and with sinners?" ³¹Jesus said to them, "People who are well do not need a doctor. Only those who are sick need a doctor. ³²I have not come to call good people. I have come to call sinners to be sorry for their sins and to turn from them."

Jesus Teaches About Going Without Food So You Can Pray Better [Matthew 9:14-17; Mark 2:18-22]

I have come to call sinners to be sorry for their sins and to turn from them.

³³They asked Jesus, "Why do the followers of John and of the proud religious law-keepers go without food so they can pray better, but Your followers keep on eating and drinking?" ³⁴Jesus answered them, "Can the friends at a wedding be sorry when the man just married is with them? ³⁵The days will come when the man just married will be taken from them. Then they will not eat food so they can pray better in those days."

The Picture Story Of The Cloth And The Bags

³⁶Then Jesus told them a picture-story. He said, "No one sews a piece of cloth from a new coat on an old coat. If he does, the new coat will have a hole. The new piece and the old coat will not be the same. ³⁷No man puts new wine into old skin bags. If they did, the skins would break and the wine would run out. The bags would be no good. ³⁸New wine must be put into new bags and both are kept safe. ³⁹No one wants new wine after drinking old wine. He says, 'The old wine is better.'"

Jesus Teaches About The Day Of Rest [Matthew 12:1-8; Mark 2:23-28]

6 On the next Day of Rest Jesus was walking through the grain fields. His followers picked grain. They rubbed it in their hands and ate it. 2Some of the proud religious law-keepers said to them, "Why are you doing what the Law says should not be done on the Day of Rest?" 3Jesus answered them, "Have you not read what David did when he and his men were hungry? 4He went into the house of God and ate the special bread used in the religious worship. He gave some to those who were with him also. The Law says only the religious leaders may eat that bread. 5The Son of Man is Lord of the Day of Rest also."

Jesus Heals On The Day Of Rest [Matthew 12:9-14; Mark 3:1-6]

6On another Day of Rest Jesus went into the Jewish place of worship and taught. A man with a dried-up hand was there. 7The teachers of the Law and the proud religious law-keepers watched to see if He would heal on the Day of Rest. They wanted to have something to say against Him. 8Jesus knew what they were thinking. He said to the man with the dried-up hand, "Stand up and come here." The man stood up and went to Jesus. 9Then Jesus said to them, "I will ask you one thing. Does the Law say to do good on the Day of Rest or to do bad? To save life or to kill?" 10Jesus looked around at them all and said to the man, "Put out your hand." He put it out and his hand was healed. It was as good as his other hand. 11The teachers of the Law and the proud religious law-keepers were filled with anger. They talked with each other about what they might do to Jesus.

Jesus Calls His Twelve Followers [Matthew 10:1-4; Mark 3:13-19]

12One day Jesus went up on a mountain to pray. He prayed all night to God. 13In the morning He called His followers to Him. He chose twelve of them and called them missionaries. 14There were Simon, whom He also named Peter, and his brother Andrew. There were James and John, Philip and Bartholomew, 15Matthew and Thomas. There were James the son of Alphaeus, and Simon the Canaanite. 16There were Judas, who was the brother of James, and Judas Iscariot who would hand Jesus over to be killed.

Jesus Heals Many People [Matthew 12:15-21; Mark 3:7-12]

¹⁷Then Jesus came down and stood on a plain with many of His followers. Many people came from all over the country of Judea and from Jerusalem and from the cities of Tyre and Sidon. They came to hear Him and to be healed of their diseases. ¹⁸Those who were troubled with demons came and were healed. ¹⁹All the people tried to put their hands on Jesus. Power came from Him and He healed them all.

Jesus Teaches On The Mountain [Matthew 5:1-7:29]

²⁰He looked at His followers and said, "Those of you who are poor are happy, because the holy nation of God is yours. ²¹Those of you who are hungry now are happy, because you will be filled. Those of you who have sorrow now are happy, because you will laugh. ²²You are happy when men hate you and do not want you around and put shame on you because you trust in Me. ²³Be glad in that day. Be full of joy for your pay is much in heaven. Their fathers did these things to the early preachers.

²⁴"It is bad for you who are rich. You are receiving all that you will get. ²⁵It is bad for you that are full. You will be hungry. It is bad for you who laugh now. You will have sorrow and you will cry. ²⁶It is bad for you when everyone speaks well of you. In the same way, their fathers spoke well of the false teachers.

Jesus Teaches What The Law Says About Love

²⁷"I say to you who hear Me, love those who work against you. Do good to those who hate you. ²⁸Respect and give thanks for those who try to bring bad to you. Pray for those who make it very hard for you. ²⁹Whoever hits you on one side of the face, turn so he can hit the other side also. Whoever takes your coat, give him your shirt also. ³⁰Give to any person who asks you for something. If a person takes something from you, do not ask for it back. ³¹Do for other people what you would like to have them do for you.

Do for other people what you would like to have them do for you.

³²"If you love those who love you, what pay can you expect from that? Sinners also love those who love them. ³³If you do good

to those who do good to you, what pay can you expect from that? Sinners also do good to those who do good to them. ³⁴If you let people use your things and expect to get something back, what pay can you expect from that? Even sinners let sinners use things and they expect to get something back. ³⁵But love those who hate you. Do good to them. Let them use your things and do not expect something back. Your pay will be much. You will be the children of the Most High. He is kind to those who are not thankful and to those who are full of sin.

Jesus Teaches About Finding Bad In Others

³⁶"You must have loving-kindness just as your Father has loving-kindness. ³⁷Do not say what is wrong in other people's lives. Then other people will not say what is wrong in your life. Do not say someone is guilty. Then other people will not say you are guilty. Forgive other people and other people will forgive you.

³⁸"Give, and it will be given to you. You will have more than enough. It can be pushed down and shaken together and it will still run over as it is given to you. The way you give to others is the way you will receive in return."

³⁹Jesus used a picture-story as He spoke to them. He said, "Can one blind man lead another blind man? Will they not fall into the ditch together? ⁴⁰The follower is not more important than his teacher. But everyone who learns well will be like his teacher.

Jesus Teaches About Saying What Is Wrong In Others

⁴¹"Why do you look at the small piece of wood in your brother's eye and do not see the big piece of wood in your own eye? ⁴²How can you say to your brother, 'Let me take that small piece of wood out of your eye,' when you do not see the big piece of wood in your own eye? You pretend to be someone you are not. First, take the big piece of wood out of your own eye. Then you can see better to take the small piece of wood out of your brother's eye.

Jesus Teaches About False Teachers

⁴³"A good tree cannot have bad fruit. A bad tree cannot have good fruit. ⁴⁴For every tree is known by its own fruit. Men do not

gather figs from thorns. They do not gather grapes from thistles. 45Good comes from a good man because of the riches he has in his heart. Sin comes from a sinful man because of the sin he has in his heart. The mouth speaks of what the heart is full of.

Jesus Teaches About Houses Built On Rock And Sand

46"And why do you call Me, 'Lord, Lord,' but do not do what I say? 47Whoever comes to Me and hears and does what I say, I will show you who he is like. 48He is like a man who built a house. He dug deep to put the building on rock. When the water came up and the river beat against the house, the building could not be shaken because it was built on rock. 49But he who hears and does not do what I say, is like a man who built a house on nothing but earth. The water beat against the house. At once it fell and was destroyed."

The Healing Of The Captain's Helper [Matthew 8:5-13]

7 When Jesus had finished teaching the people, He went back to Capernaum. 2A captain of the army owned a workman that he thought much of. This workman was very sick and was about to die. 3When the captain heard of Jesus, he sent some Jewish leaders to Him. They were to ask if He would come and heal this workman. 4They came to Jesus and begged Him, saying, "The man is respected and should have this done for him. 5He loves our nation and has built our Jewish place of worship."

6Jesus went with them. When He was not far from the house, the captain told some friends to tell this to Jesus, "Lord, do not take the time to come to my house, because I am not good enough. 7And I am not good enough to come to You. But just say the word and my workman will be healed. 8For I am a man who works for someone else also, and I have soldiers who work for me. I say to this man, 'Go!' and he goes. I say to another, 'Come!' and he comes. I say to my workman, 'Do this!' and he does it."

9Jesus was surprised when He heard this. He turned to the people following Him and said, "I tell you, I have not found so much faith even in the Jewish nation." [10]Those who had been sent went back to the captain's house and found the workman well again.

The Son Of A Woman Whose Husband Had Died Was Raised From The Dead

[11]The next day Jesus went to a city called Nain. His followers and many other people went with Him. [12]When they came near the city gate, a dead man was being carried out. He was the only son of a woman whose husband had died. Many people of the city were with her. [13]When the Lord saw her, He had loving-pity for her and said, "Do not cry." [14]He went and put His hand on the box in which the dead man was carried. The men who were carrying it, stopped. Jesus said, "Young man, I say to you, get up!" [15]The man who was dead sat up and began to talk. Then Jesus gave him to his mother. [16]Everyone was afraid and they gave thanks to God. They said, "A great Man Who speaks for God has come among us! God has cared for His people!" [17]The news about Jesus went through all the country of Judea and over all the land.

John The Baptist Asks About Jesus [Matthew 11:1-6]

[18]The followers of John the Baptist told him about all these things. [19]John called two of his followers and sent them to Jesus to ask, "Are You the One Who is to come? Or are we to look for another?" [20]The men came to Jesus and said, "John the Baptist sent us to ask You, 'Are You the One Who is to come? Or are we to look for another?'"

[21]At that time Jesus was healing many people of all kinds of sickness and disease and was putting out demons. Many that were blind were able to see. [22]Jesus said to John's followers, "Go back to John the Baptist and tell him what you have seen and heard. Tell him the blind are made to see. Those who could not walk, are walking. Those with a bad skin disease are healed. Those who could not hear, are hearing. The dead are raised to life and poor people have the Good News preached to them. [23]The person who is not ashamed of Me and does not turn away from Me is happy."

The person who is not ashamed of Me and does not turn away from Me is happy.

Jesus Tells About John The Baptist [*Matthew 11:7-19*]

24As John's followers were going away, Jesus began to tell the people about John the Baptist. He said, "Why did you go out to the desert? Did you go out to see a small tree moving in the wind? 25What did you go out to see? A man dressed in good clothes? Those who are dressed in good clothes are in the houses of kings. 26But what did you go to see? One who speaks for God? Yes, I tell you, he is more than one who speaks for God. 27This is the man the Holy Writings spoke of when they said, 'Look! I will send My helper to carry news ahead of You. He will make Your way ready for You!' (Malachi 3:1; Isaiah 40:3)

28"I tell you, of those born of women, there is no one greater than John the Baptist. The least in the holy nation of God is greater than he."

29All the people who heard Jesus and those who gathered taxes showed they knew God was right and were baptized by John. 30But the proud religious law-keepers and the men who knew the Law would not listen. They would not be baptized by John and they did not receive what God had for them.

Jesus Speaks Against The People Of This Day

31Then the Lord said, "What are the people of this day like? 32They are like children playing in front of stores. They call to their friends, 'We have played music for you, but you did not dance. We have had sorrow for you, but you did not have sorrow.' 33John the Baptist did not come eating bread or drinking wine and you say, 'He has a demon.' 34The Son of Man came eating and drinking and you say, 'Look! He likes food and wine. He is a friend of men who gather taxes and of sinners!' 35Wisdom is shown to be right by those who are wise."

Wisdom is shown to be right by those who are wise.

A Woman Puts Special Perfume On The Feet Of Jesus

36One of the proud religious law-keepers wanted Jesus to eat with him. Jesus went into his house and sat down to eat. 37There was a woman in the city who was a sinner. She knew Jesus was eating in the house of the proud religious law-keeper. She brought a jar of special perfume. ³⁸Then she stood behind Him by His feet and cried. Her tears wet His feet and she dried them with her hair. She kissed His feet and put the special perfume on them.

³⁹The proud religious law-keeper who had asked Jesus to eat with him saw this. He said to himself, "If this Man were One Who speaks for God, He would know who and what kind of a woman put her hands on Him. She is a sinner." ⁴⁰Jesus said to him, "I have something to say to you, Simon." And Simon said, "Teacher, say it."

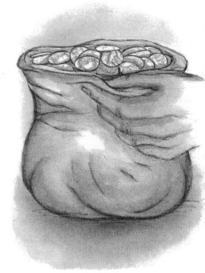

⁴¹"There were two men who owed a certain man some money. The one man owed 500 pieces of silver money. The other man owed 50 pieces of silver money. ⁴²Neither one of them had any money, so he told them they did not have to pay him back. Tell Me, which one would love him the most?" ⁴³Simon said, "I think it would be the one who owed the most." And Jesus said to him, "You have said the right thing."

⁴⁴He turned to the woman and said to Simon, "Do you see this woman? I came into your house and you gave Me no water to wash My feet. She washed My feet with her tears and dried them with the hairs of her head. ⁴⁵You gave me no kiss, but this woman has kissed my feet from the time I came in. ⁴⁶You did not put even oil on My head but this woman has put special perfume on My feet. ⁴⁷I tell you, her many sins are forgiven because she loves much. But the one who has little to be forgiven, loves only a little."

⁴⁸Then He said to the woman, "Your sins are forgiven." ⁴⁹Those who were eating with Him began to say to themselves, "Who is this Man Who even forgives sins?" ⁵⁰He said to the woman, "Your faith has saved you from the punishment of sin. Go in peace."

Jesus Teaches In Galilee

8 After this Jesus went to all the cities and towns preaching and telling the Good News about the holy nation of God. The twelve followers were with Him. ²Some women who had been

healed of demons and diseases were with Him. Mary Magdalene, who had had seven demons put out of her, was one of them. [3]Joanna, the wife of Chuza who was one of Herod's helpers, was another one. Susanna and many others also cared for Jesus by using what they had.

The Picture-Story Of The Man Who Planted Seed [Matthew 13:1-52; Mark 4:1-34]

[4]Many people came together from every town to Jesus. He told them a picture-story.

[5]"A man went out to plant seed. As he planted the seed, some fell by the side of the road. They were walked on and birds came and ate them. [6]Some seed fell between rocks. As soon as they started to grow, they dried up because they had no water. [7]Some seed fell among thorns. The thorns grew and did not give the seed room to grow. [8]Some seed fell on good ground. They grew and gave one hundred times as much grain." When Jesus had finished saying this, He cried out, "You have ears, then listen!"

[9]His followers asked Him what this picture-story meant. [10]Jesus said, "You were given the secrets about the holy nation of God. Others are told picture-stories. As they look, they do not see. As they hear, they do not understand.

Jesus Tells About The Man Who Planted Seed

[11]"This is what the picture-story means. The seed is the Word of God. [12]Those by the side of the road hear the Word. Then the devil comes and takes the Word from their hearts. He does not want them to believe and be saved from the punishment of sin. [13]Those which fell among rocks receive the Word with joy. These have no root. For awhile they believe, but when they are tempted they give up. [14]Those which fell among thorns hear the Word but go their own way. The cares of this life let the thorns grow. A love for money lets the thorns grow also. And the fun of this life lets the thorns grow. Their grain never becomes full-grown. [15]But those which fell on good ground have heard the Word. They keep it in a good and true heart and they keep on giving good grain.

The cares of this life let the thorns grow. A love for money lets the thorns grow also. And the fun of this life lets the thorns grow.

The Picture-Story Of The Lamp

16"No man lights a lamp and puts it under a pail or under a bed. He puts it on a table so all who come into the room may see it. 17Nothing is secret but what will be known. Anything that is hidden will be brought into the light. 18Be careful how you listen! Whoever has, to him will be given. Whoever does not have, even the little he has will be taken from him."

The New Kind Of Family [Matthew 12:46-50; Mark 3:31-35]

19The mother of Jesus and His brothers came to Him. They could not get near Him because of so many people. 20Someone said to Jesus, "Your mother and brothers are standing outside. They want to see You." 21Jesus said to them, "My mother and brothers are these who hear the Word of God and do it."

The Wind And Waves Obey Jesus [Matthew 8:23-27; Mark 4:35-41]

22On one of those days Jesus and His followers got into a boat. Jesus said to them, "Let us go over to the other side of the lake." Then they pushed out into the water. 23As they were going, Jesus fell asleep. A wind storm came over the lake. The boat was filling with water and they were in danger. 24The followers came to awake Jesus. They said, "Teacher! Teacher! We are going to die!" Then Jesus got up and spoke sharp words to the wind and the high waves. The wind stopped blowing and there were no more waves. 25He said to them, " Where is your faith?' The followers were surprised and afraid. They said to each other, "What kind of a man is He? He speaks to the wind and the waves and they obey Him."

Demons Ask Jesus To Let Them Live In Pigs [Matthew 8:28-34; Mark 5:1-20]

26They came to the land of the Gadarenes, which is on the other side of the country of Galilee. 27As Jesus stepped out on land, a man met Him who had come from the city. This man had demons in him. For a long time he had worn no clothes. He did not live in a house, but lived among the graves. 28When he saw Jesus, he got

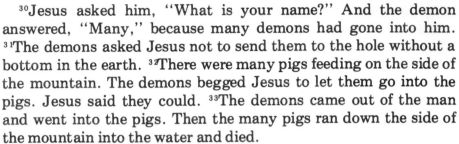

down in front of Him and cried with a loud voice, "What do You want with me, Jesus, Son of the Most High? I beg of You not to hurt me!" 29For Jesus had spoken to the demon to come out of the man. Many times the demon had taken hold of him. The man had to be tied with chains. But he would break the chains and be taken by the demon into the desert.

30Jesus asked him, "What is your name?" And the demon answered, "Many," because many demons had gone into him. 31The demons asked Jesus not to send them to the hole without a bottom in the earth. 32There were many pigs feeding on the side of the mountain. The demons begged Jesus to let them go into the pigs. Jesus said they could. 33The demons came out of the man and went into the pigs. Then the many pigs ran down the side of the mountain into the water and died.

34The men who cared for the pigs ran fast and told what had happened in the town and in the country. 35People came to see what had happened. They came to Jesus and saw the man from whom the demons had been sent. He was sitting at the feet of Jesus with clothes on and had the right use of his mind. The people were afraid. 36Those who had seen it told how the man who had had the demons was healed. 37Then all the people of the country of the Gadarenes begged Jesus to go away from them. They were very much afraid. Jesus got into the boat and went back to the other side.

38The man out of whom the demons had gone begged to go with Jesus. But Jesus sent him away and said, 39"Go back to your house and tell everything God has done for you." He went back and told all the people of the city what great things Jesus had done for him.

Two Were Healed Through Faith [*Matthew 9:18-26; Mark 5:21-43*]

40Many people were glad to see Jesus when He got back. They were waiting for Him. 41A man named Jairus was a leader of the Jewish place of worship. As he came to Jesus, he got down at His feet. He asked Jesus if He would come to his house. 42He had only one daughter and she was dying. This girl was about twelve years old. As Jesus went, the people pushed Him from every side.

43A woman had been sick for twelve years with a flow of blood. *(She had spent all the money she had on doctors.) But she could not be healed by anyone. 44She came behind Jesus and touched the bottom of His coat. At once the flow of blood stopped. 45Jesus said, "Who touched Me?" Everyone said that they had not touched Him. Peter said, "Teacher, so many people are pushing You from every side and You say, 'Who touched Me?' " 46Then Jesus said, "Someone touched Me because I know power has gone from Me." 47When the woman saw she could not hide it, she came shaking. She got down in front of Jesus. Then she told Jesus in front of all the people why she had touched Him. She told how she was healed at once. 48Jesus said to her, "Daughter, your faith has healed you. Go in peace."

Your faith has healed you. Go in peace.

49While Jesus was yet talking, a man came from the house of the leader of the place of worship. This man said to Jairus, "Your daughter is dead. Do not make the Teacher use anymore of His time." 50Jesus heard it and said to Jairus, "Do not be afraid, only believe. She will be made well."

51Jesus went into the house. He let only Peter and James and John and the father and mother of the girl go in with Him. 52Everyone was crying and full of sorrow because of her. Jesus said, "Do not cry. She is not dead, but is sleeping." 53Then they laughed at Jesus because they knew she was dead. 54Jesus sent them all out. He took the girl by the hand and said, "Child, get up!" 55Her spirit came back and she got up at once. Jesus told them to bring her food. 56Her parents were surprised and wondered about it. Then Jesus told them they should tell no one what had happened.

Jesus Sends His Twelve Followers Out [*Matthew 10:1-42; Mark 6:7-13*]

9 Jesus called His twelve followers to Him. He gave them the right and the power over all demons and to heal diseases. 2He sent them to preach about the holy nation of God and to heal the sick. 3Then He said to them, "Take nothing along for the trip. Do not take a walking stick or a bag or bread or money. Do not take two coats. 4Whatever house you go into, stay there until you are

He sent them to preach about the holy nation of God and to heal the sick.

ready to go on. 5If anyone will not take you in, as you leave that city, shake its dust off your feet. That will speak against them.''

6They went out, going from town to town. They preached the Good News and healed the sick everywhere.

John The Baptist Is Killed [Matthew 14:6-12; Mark 6:21-29]

7Now Herod the leader heard of all that had been done by Jesus. He was troubled because some people said that John the Baptist had been raised from the dead. 8Some people said that Elijah had come back. Others thought one of the early preachers had been raised from the dead. 9Then Herod said, ''I had John's head cut off. But who is this Man that I hear these things about?'' He wanted to see Jesus.

The Feeding Of The Five Thousand [Matthew 14:13-21; Mark 6:30-44; John 6:1-14]

10The twelve missionaries came back. They told Jesus what they had done. Jesus took them to a desert near the town of Bethsaida. There they could be alone. 11When the people knew where Jesus was, they followed Him. Jesus was happy to see them and talked to them about the holy nation of God. He healed all who were sick.

12When the day was about over, the twelve followers came to Jesus. They said, ''Send these many people away so they can go to the towns and country near here. There they can find a place to sleep and get food. We are here in a desert.'' 13But Jesus said to them, ''Give them something to eat.'' They said, ''We have only five loaves of bread and two fish. Are we to go and buy food for all these people?'' 14There were about five thousand men. Jesus said to His followers, ''Have them sit down in groups of fifty people.'' 15They did as He told them. They made all of the people sit down. 16As Jesus took the five loaves of bread and two fish, He looked up to heaven and gave thanks. He broke them in pieces and gave them to His followers to give to the people. 17They all ate and were filled. They picked up twelve baskets full of pieces of bread and fish after the people finished eating.

Peter Says Jesus Is The Christ [*Matthew 16:13-20; Mark 8:27-30*]

¹⁸While Jesus was praying alone, His followers were with Him. Jesus asked them, "Who do people say that I am?" ¹⁹They said, "John the Baptist, but some say Elijah. Others say that one of the early preachers has been raised from the dead." ²⁰Jesus said to them, "But who do you say that I am?" Peter said, "You are the Christ of God."

Jesus Tells Of His Death For The First Time [*Matthew 16:21-28; Mark 8:31-38*]

²¹Then Jesus spoke to them and told them to tell no one. ²²He said, "The Son of Man must suffer many things. The leaders and the religious leaders and the teachers of the Law will have nothing to do with Him. He must be killed and be raised from the dead three days later."

Giving Up Self And One's Own Desires

²³Then Jesus said to them all, "If anyone wants to follow Me, he must give up himself and his own desires. He must take up his cross every day and follow Me. ²⁴If anyone wants to keep his own life safe, he must lose it. If anyone gives up his life because of Me, he will save it. ²⁵For what does a man have if he gets all the world and loses or gives up his life? ²⁶Whoever is ashamed of Me and My Words, the Son of Man will be ashamed of him when He comes in His own shining greatness and of the Father's and of the holy angels. ²⁷I tell you the truth, some standing here will not die until they see the holy nation of God."

> If anyone wants to keep his own life safe, he must lose it. If anyone gives up his life because of Me, he will save it.

A Look At What Jesus Will Be Like [*Matthew 17:1-13; Mark 9:1-13*]

²⁸About eight days after Jesus had said these things, He took Peter and James and John with Him. They went up on a mountain to pray. ²⁹As Jesus prayed, He was changed in looks before them. His clothes became white and shining bright. ³⁰Two men talked with Jesus. They were Moses and Elijah. ³¹They looked like the shining greatness of heaven as they talked about His death in Jerusalem which was soon to happen.

³²But Peter and those with him had gone to sleep. When they woke up, they saw His shining greatness and the two men who stood with Him. ³³As the two men went from Jesus, Peter said to Him, "Teacher, it is good for us to be here. Let us build three altars. One will be for You. One will be for Moses. One will be for Elijah." He did not know what he was saying. ³⁴While he was talking, a cloud came over them. They were afraid as the cloud came in around them.

This is My Son, the One I have chosen. Listen to Him!

³⁵A voice came out of the cloud, saying, "This is My Son, the One I have chosen. Listen to Him!" ³⁶When the voice was gone, Jesus was standing there alone. From that time on, they kept these things to themselves. They told no one what they had seen.

A Boy With A Demon Is Healed [*Matthew 17:14-21; Mark 9:14-29*]

³⁷The next day they came down from the mountain and many people met Jesus. ³⁸A man from among the people cried out, "Teacher, I beg of You to look at my son. He is my only child. ³⁹See, a demon takes him and makes him cry out. It takes hold of him and makes him shake. Spit runs from his mouth. He has marks on his body from being hurt. The demon does not want to go from him. ⁴⁰I begged Your followers to put the demon out, but they could not."

⁴¹Then Jesus said, "You people of this day do not have faith. You turn from what is right! How long must I be with you? How long must I put up with you? Bring your son to Me." ⁴²While the boy was coming, the demon threw him down and made him lose the use of his mind for awhile. Jesus spoke sharp words to the demon. He healed the child and gave him back to his father.

Jesus Tells Of His Death The Second Time [*Matthew 17:22-23; Mark 9:30-32*]

⁴³They were all surprised at the great power of God. They all were thinking about the special things Jesus had done. And Jesus said to His followers, ⁴⁴"Remember these words. For the Son of Man will be given over into the hands of men." ⁴⁵They did not understand these words because it was hid from them. They did not know what Jesus meant and were afraid to ask Him.

Jesus Teaches About The Faith Of A Child [*Matthew 18:1-35; Mark 9:33-50*]

⁴⁶The followers argued among themselves about which of them would be the greatest. ⁴⁷Jesus knew what they were thinking. He put a child beside Him. ⁴⁸He said to the followers, "Whoever receives this child in My name, receives Me. Whoever receives Me, receives Him that sent Me. The one who is least among you is the one who is great."

The Sharp Words Against The Followers

⁴⁹John said, "Teacher, we saw someone putting out demons in Your name. We told him to stop because he was not following us." ⁵⁰Jesus said to him, "Do not stop him. He who is not against us is for us."

Jesus And His Followers Leave Galilee

⁵¹It was about time for Jesus to be taken up into heaven. He turned toward Jerusalem and was sure that nothing would stop Him from going. ⁵²He sent men on ahead of Him. They came to a town in Samaria. There they got things ready for Jesus. ⁵³The people did not want Him there because they knew He was on His way to Jerusalem. ⁵⁴James and John, His followers, saw this. They said, "Lord, do You want us to speak so fire will come down from heaven and burn them up as Elijah did?" ⁵⁵Jesus turned and spoke sharp words to them. *(He said, "You do not know what kind of spirit you have. ⁵⁶The Son of Man did not come to destroy men's lives. He came to save them from the punishment of sin." They went on their way to another town.)

The Testing Of Some Followers [*Matthew 8:18-22*]

⁵⁷As they were going on their way, a man said to Jesus, "Lord, I will follow You wherever You go." ⁵⁸Jesus said to him, "Foxes have holes. Birds of the sky have nests. The Son of Man has no place to put His head." ⁵⁹He said to another, "Follow Me." But the man said, "Lord, let me go first and bury my father." ⁶⁰Jesus said to him, "Let the people who are dead bury their own dead. You go and preach about the holy nation of God." ⁶¹And another

one said, "Lord, I will follow You, but first let me go and say good-by to those at home." 62Jesus said to him, "Anyone who puts his hand on a plow and looks back at the things behind is of no use in the holy nation of God."

Seventy Are Sent Out

The workmen are few. Pray that He will send workmen to gather His grain.

10 After this the Lord chose seventy others. He sent them out two together to every city and place where He would be going later. 2Jesus said to them, "There is much grain ready to gather. But the workmen are few. Pray then to the Lord Who is the Owner of the grain fields that He will send workmen to gather His grain. 3Go on your way. Listen! I send you out like lambs among wolves. 4Take no money. Do not take a bag or shoes. Speak to no one along the way. 5When you go into a house, say that you hope peace will come to them. 6If a man who loves peace lives there, your good wishes will come to him. If your good wishes are not received, they will come back to you. 7Stay in the same house. Eat and drink what they give you. The workman should have his pay. Do not move from house to house.

8"Whenever a city receives you, eat the things that are put before you there. 9Heal the sick. Say to them, 'The holy nation of God is near.' 10Whatever city does not receive you, go into its streets and say, 11"Even the dust of your city that is on our feet we are cleaning off against you. But understand this, the holy nation of God has come near you!' 12I tell you, on the day men stand in front of God, it will be easier for the city of Sodom than for that city.

13"It is bad for you, city of Chorazin! It is bad for you, town of Bethsaida! For if the powerful works which were done in you had been done in the cities of Tyre and Sidon they would have turned from their sins long ago. They would have shown their sorrow by putting on clothes made from hair and would have sat in ashes. 14It will be better for Tyre and Sidon on the day men stand in front of God and be told they are guilty than for you. 15And you, Capernaum, are you to be lifted up into heaven? You will be taken down to hell. 16Whoever listens to you, listens to Me. Whoever has nothing to do with you, has nothing to do with Me. Whoever has nothing to do with Me, has nothing to do with the One Who sent Me.''

The Seventy Came Back

17The seventy came back full of joy. They said, ''Lord, even the demons obeyed us when we used Your name.'' 18Jesus said to them, ''I saw Satan fall from heaven like lightning. 19Listen! I have given you power to walk on snakes. I have given you power over small animals with a sting of poison. I have given you power over all the power of the one who works against you. Nothing will hurt you. 20Even so, you should not be happy because the demons obey you but be happy because your names are written in heaven.''

The Joy Of The Holy Spirit

21At this time Jesus was full of the joy of the Holy Spirit. He said, ''I thank You, Father, Lord of heaven and earth. You have kept these things hid from the wise and from those who have much learning. You have shown them to little children. Yes, Father, it was what you wanted done.

22''Everything has been given to Me by My Father. No one knows the Son but the Father. No one knows the Father but the Son and the Son makes the Father known to those He chooses.''

23Then He turned to His followers and said without anyone else hearing, ''Happy are those who see what you see! 24I tell you, many early preachers and kings have wanted to see the things you are seeing, but they did not see them. They have wanted to hear the things you are hearing, but they did not hear them.''

Jesus Talks To The Man Who Knew The Law

25A man stood up who knew the Law and tried to trap Jesus. He said, ''Teacher, what must I do to have life that lasts forever?'' 26Jesus said to him, ''What is written in the Law? What does the Law say?'' 27The man said, ''You must love the Lord your God with all your heart. You must love Him with all your soul. You must love Him with all your strength. You must love Him with all

your mind. You must love your neighbor as you love yourself.'' ²⁸Jesus said to him, "You have said the right thing. Do this and you will have life.'' ²⁹The man tried to make himself look good. He asked Jesus, "Who is my neighbor?''

The Picture-Story Of The Good Samaritan

³⁰Jesus said, "A man was going down from Jerusalem to the city of Jericho. Robbers came out after him. They took his clothes off and beat him. Then they went away, leaving him almost dead. ³¹A religious leader was walking down that road and saw the man. But he went by on the other side. ³²In the same way, a man from the family group of Levi was walking down that road. When he saw the man who was hurt, he came near to him but kept on going on the other side of the road. ³³Then a man from the country of Samaria came by. He went up to the man. As he saw him, he had loving-pity on him. ³⁴He got down and put oil and wine on the places where he was hurt and put cloth around them. Then the man from Samaria put this man on his own donkey. He took him to a place where people stay for the night and cared for him. ³⁵The next day the man from Samaria was ready to leave. He gave the owner of that place two pieces of money to care for him. He said to him, 'Take care of this man. If you use more than this, I will give it to you when I come again.'

³⁶"Which of these three do you think was a neighbor to the man who was beaten by the robbers?'' ³⁷The man who knew the Law said, "The one who showed loving-pity on him.'' Then Jesus said, "Go and do the same.''

Mary And Martha Care For Jesus

³⁸As they went on their way, they came to a town where a woman named Martha lived. She cared for Jesus in her home. ³⁹Martha had a sister named Mary. Mary sat at the feet of Jesus and listened to all He said. ⁴⁰Martha was working hard getting the supper ready. She came to Jesus and said, "Do You see that my sister is not helping me? Tell her to help me.'' ⁴¹Jesus said to her, "Martha, Martha, you are worried and troubled about many things. ⁴²Only a few things are important, even just one. Mary has chosen the good thing. It will not be taken away from her.''

Jesus Teaches His Followers To Pray

11 Jesus had been praying. One of His followers said to Him, "Lord, teach us to pray as John the Baptist taught his followers." ²Jesus said to them, "When you pray, say, 'Our Father in heaven, Your name is holy. May Your holy nation come. *What You want done, may it be done on earth as it is in heaven. ³Give us the bread we need everyday. ⁴Forgive us our sins, as we forgive those who sin against us. Do not let us be tempted.' "

Forgive us our sins, as we forgive those who sin against us.

A Picture-Story About How To Ask

⁵Jesus said to them, "If any of you have a friend and go to him in the night and say, 'Friend, give me three loaves of bread. ⁶A friend of mine is on a trip and has stopped at my house. I have no food to give him.' ⁷The man inside the house will say, 'Do not trouble me. The door is shut. My children and I are in bed. I cannot get up and give you bread.' ⁸I say to you, he may not get up and give him bread because he is a friend. Yet, if he keeps on asking, he will get up and give him as much as he needs. ⁹I say to you, ask, and what you ask for will be given to you. Look, and what you are looking for you will find. Knock, and the door you are knocking on will be opened to you. ¹⁰For everyone who asks, will receive what he asks for. Everyone who looks, will find what he is looking for. Everyone who knocks, will have the door opened to him.

¹¹"Would any of you fathers give your son a stone if he asked for bread? Or would you give a snake if he asked for a fish? ¹²Or if he asked for an egg, would you give him a small animal with a sting of poison? ¹³You are sinful and you know how to give good things to your children. How much more will your Father in heaven give the Holy Spirit to those who ask Him?"

A Nation That Cannot Stand [*Matthew 12:22-37; Mark 3:22-30*]

¹⁴Jesus was putting a demon out of a man who could not speak. When the demon was gone, the man could speak. All the people were surprised and wondered about it. ¹⁵Some of them said, "He puts out demons through Satan, the king of demons." ¹⁶Others tried to trap Jesus. They asked for something special to see from

Jesus Speaks Sharp Words To The Men Who Knew The Law

45One of the men who knew the Law said to Jesus, "Teacher, You are making us look bad when You speak like this." 46Jesus said, "It is bad for you also, you men who know the Law! For you put heavy loads on the shoulders of men. But you will not even put your finger on one of these loads to help them. 47It is bad for you! For you make beautiful buildings for the graves of the early preachers your fathers killed. 48You are saying what your fathers did was good, because they killed the early preachers and you are making their graves.

49"For this reason the wisdom of God has said, 'I will send them early preachers and missionaries. Some they will kill and some they will make it very hard for.' 50The blood of all the early preachers from the beginning of the world is on the people of this day. 51It will be from the blood of Abel to the blood of Zacharias, the one who died between the altar and the house of God. For sure, I tell you, the people of this day will be guilty for this.

52"It is bad for you men who know the Law! For you have locked the door to the house of learning. You are not going in yourselves and you do not allow those to go in who are about to go in."

53As Jesus went away from there, the teachers of the Law and the proud religious law-keepers were very angry and tried to make Him say many things. 54They planned against Jesus and tried to trap Him with something He might say.

Jesus Teaches His Followers And Thousands Of Other People

12 At that time thousands of people gathered together. There were so many that they walked on each other. Jesus spoke to His twelve followers first, saying, "Look out! Have nothing to do with the yeast of the proud religious law-keepers which is pretending to be something it is not. 2For there is nothing covered up that will not be seen. There is nothing hidden that will not be known. 3What you have said in the dark will be heard in the light. What you have said in a low voice in a closed room will be spoken with a loud voice from the top of houses.

There is nothing hidden that will not be known.

[4]"I say to you, My friends, do not be afraid of those who kill the body and then can do no more. [5]I will tell you the one to be afraid of. Be afraid of Him Who has power to put you into hell after He has killed you. Yes, I say to you, be afraid of Him!

[6]"Are not five small birds sold for two small pieces of money? God does not forget even one of the birds. [7]God knows how many hairs you have on your head. Do not be afraid. You are worth more than many small birds.

[8]"Also, I tell you, everyone who makes Me known to men, the Son of Man will make him known to the angels of God. [9]But whoever acts as if he does not know Me and does not make Me known to men, he will not be spoken of to the angels of God.

The Sin That Cannot Be Forgiven

[10]"Whoever speaks a word against the Son of Man will be forgiven. Whoever speaks against the Holy Spirit will not be forgiven. [11]When they take you to the places of worship and to the courts and to the leaders of the country, do not be worried about what you should say or how to say it. [12]The Holy Spirit will tell you what you should say at that time."

[13]One of the people said to Jesus, "Teacher, tell my brother to divide the riches that our father left us." [14]Jesus said to him, "Friend, who has told Me to say who should get what?" [15]Then Jesus said to them all, "Watch yourselves! Keep from wanting all kinds of things you should not have. A man's life is not made up of things, even if he has many riches."

The Picture-Story Of The Rich Fool

[16]Then He told them a picture-story, saying, "The fields of a rich man gave much grain. [17]The rich man thought to himself, 'What will I do? I have no place to put the grain.' [18]Then he said, 'I know what I will do. I will take down my grain building and I will build a bigger one. I will put all my grain and other things I own into it. [19]And I will say to my soul, "Soul, you have many good things put away in your building. It will be all you need for many years to come. Now rest and eat and drink and have lots of

fun." ' ²⁰But God said to him, 'You fool! Tonight your soul will be taken from you. Then who will have all the things you have put away?' ²¹It is the same with a man who puts away riches for himself and does not have the riches of God."

Jesus Teaches About The Cares Of This Life

²²Jesus said to His followers, "Because of this, I say to you, do not worry about your life, what you are going to eat. Do not worry about your body, what you are going to wear. ²³Life is worth more than food. The body is worth more than clothes. ²⁴Look at the birds. They do not plant seeds. They do not gather grain. They have no grain buildings for keeping grain. Yet God feeds them. Are you not worth more than the birds?

²⁵"Which of you can make yourself a little taller by worrying? ²⁶If you cannot do that which is so little, why do you worry about other things? ²⁷Think how the flowers grow. They do not work or make cloth. Yet, I tell you, that King Solomon in all his greatness was not dressed as well as one of these flowers. ²⁸God puts these clothes on the grass of the field. The grass is in the field today and put into the fire tomorrow. How much more would He want to give you clothing? You have so little faith! ²⁹Do not give so much thought to what you will eat or drink. Do not be worried about it. ³⁰For all the nations of the world go after these things. Your Father knows you need these things. ³¹Instead, go after the holy nation of God. Then all these other things will be given to you. ³²Do not be afraid, little flock. Your Father wants to give you the holy nation of God. ³³Sell what you have and give the money to poor people. Have money-bags for yourselves that will never wear out. These money-bags are riches in heaven that will always be there. No robber can take them and no bugs can eat them there. ³⁴Your heart will be wherever your riches are.

Jesus Says To Watch And Be Ready For His Second Coming

³⁵"Be ready and dressed. Have your lights burning. ³⁶Be like men who are waiting for their owner to come home from a wedding supper. When he comes and knocks on the door, they will open it for him at once. ³⁷Those workmen are happy when their owner finds them watching when he comes. For sure, I tell you, he will

be dressed and ready to care for them. He will have them seated at the table. ³⁸The owner might come late at night or early in the morning. Those workmen are happy if their owner finds them watching whenever he comes. ³⁹But understand this, that if the owner of a house had known when the robber was coming, he would have been watching. He would not have allowed his house to be broken into. ⁴⁰You must be ready also. The Son of Man is coming at a time when you do not think He will come.''

Faithful Workmen And Workmen Who Are Not Faithful

⁴¹Peter said, "Lord, are You telling this picture-story to us or to all the people?'' ⁴²The Lord said, "Who is the faithful and wise workman his owner made boss over the others? He is the one who is to have food ready at the right time. ⁴³That workman is happy who is doing his work when the owner comes. ⁴⁴For sure, I tell you, he will make him boss over all he has.

⁴⁵"But what if that workman says to himself, 'The owner will not be coming soon,' and then beats the other workmen and eats and drinks and gets drunk? ⁴⁶The owner of that workman will come on a day and at an hour when he is not looking for him. He will cut him in pieces and will put him with those who do not believe.

⁴⁷"The workman who knew what the owner wanted done, but did not get ready for him, or did not do what he wanted done, will be beaten many times. ⁴⁸But the workman who did not know what his owner wanted done, but did things that would be reason to be beaten, will be beaten only a few times. The man who receives much will have to give much. If much is given to a man to take care of, men will expect to get more from him.

That workman is happy who is doing his work when the owner comes.

The man who receives much will have to give much.

Men Are Divided When They Follow Christ

⁴⁹"I have come to bring fire down to the earth. I wish it were already started! ⁵⁰I have a baptism to go through. How troubled I am until it is over! ⁵¹Do you think I came to bring peace on the earth? I tell you, no! I came to divide. ⁵²From now on there will be five in one house divided. Three will be against two and two will be against three. ⁵³The father will be against the son. The son will be

against the father. The mother will be against the daughter. The daughter will be against the mother. The mother-in-law will be against the daughter-in-law. The daughter-in-law will be against the mother-in-law."

54Then Jesus also said to the people, "When you see a cloud coming in the west, you say at once, 'It is going to rain.' And it does. 55When you see the wind blow from the south, you say, 'It will be a hot day.' And it is. 56You who pretend to be someone you are not, you know all about the sky and the earth. But why do you not know what is happening these days? 57Why do you not know for yourselves what is right? 58When a person says you are wrong and takes you to court, try to make it right with him as you go, or he will take you to the head of the court. Then he will take you to the police and you will be put into prison. 59I tell you, you will not be let out of prison until you have paid the last piece of money of the fine."

Everyone Should Be Sorry For Their Sins And Turn From Them

13 At this time some people came to Jesus. They told Him that Pilate had killed some people from the country of Galilee. It was while they were giving gifts of animals on the altar in worship to God. 2Pilate put their blood together with the blood of the animals. Jesus said to them, "What about these people from Galilee? Were they worse sinners than all the other people from Galilee because they suffered these things? 3No, I tell you. But unless you are sorry for your sins and turn from them, you too will all die. 4What about those eighteen men who were killed when the high building in Siloam fell on them? Do you think they were the worst sinners living in Jerusalem? 5No, I tell you. But unless you are sorry for your sins and turn from them, you too will all die."

The Picture-Story Of The Fig Tree Which Had No Fruit

6Then He told them this picture-story: "A man had a fig tree in his grape field. He looked for fruit on it but found none. 7He said to his workman, 'Look! For three years I have been coming here looking for fruit on this fig tree. I never find any. Cut it down. Why does it even waste the ground?' 8The workman said, 'Sir!

Leave it here one more year. I will dig around it and put plant food on it. 9It may be that it will give fruit next year. If it does not, then cut it down.' "

Jesus Heals On The Day Of Rest

10Jesus was teaching in one of the Jewish places of worship on the Day of Rest. 11A woman was there who had suffered for eighteen years because of a demon. She was not able to stand up straight. 12Jesus saw her and said, "Woman, you are now free from your trouble!" 13Then He put His hand on her. At once she stood up straight and gave thanks to God.

14The leader of the Jewish place of worship was angry because Jesus healed on the Day of Rest. The leader said to the people, "There are six days in which work should be done. Come on those days and get healed. Do not come to be healed on the Day of Rest." 15The Lord said to him, "You pretend to be someone you are not! Do not each of you let his cow or his donkey out and lead them to water on the Day of Rest? 16Should not this Jewish woman be made free from this trouble on the Day of Rest? She has been chained by Satan for eighteen years." 17When He said this, all those who were against Him were ashamed. All the many people were glad for the great things being done by Him.

The Picture-Stories Of The Mustard Seed And The Yeast
[Matthew 13:1-52;Mark 4:1-34]

18Then Jesus asked, "What is the holy nation of God like? What can I use to show you? 19It is like a mustard seed which a man took and planted in his field. It grew and became a tree. The birds of the sky stayed in its branches." 20Again Jesus said, "What can I use to show you what the holy nation of God is like? 21It is like yeast that a woman put into three pails of flour until it was all full of yeast."

Jesus Teaches On The Way To Jerusalem

22Jesus taught the people as He went through the cities and towns on His way to Jerusalem. 23Someone asked Jesus, "Lord, will only a few people be saved from the punishment of sin?" Jesus said to them, [24]"Work hard to go in through the narrow door. I tell you, many will try to go in but will not be able to go in. [25]The owner of the house will get up and shut the door. You who are on the outside will knock on the door and say, 'Lord, let us in.' Then He will say, 'I do not know you.' [26]Then you will say, 'We ate and drank with You when You taught in our streets.' [27]But He will say, 'I tell you, I do not know you. Go away from Me. You are sinful.'

[28]"There will be loud crying and grinding of teeth when you see Abraham and Isaac and Jacob and all the early preachers in the holy nation of God, but you will be put out. [29]Those who sit at the table in the holy nation of God will come from the east and west and from the north and south. [30]Listen! Some are last who will be first. Some are first who will be last."

Some are last who will be first. Some are first who will be last.

[31]That same day some of the proud religious law-keepers came to Jesus. They said, "Go away from here! Herod wants to kill You." [32]Jesus said to them, "Go and tell that fox, 'Look. I put out demons and heal the sick. I will do these things today and tomorrow. And the third day My work will be finished.' [33]But I must go on My way today and tomorrow and the day after. One who speaks for God cannot die except at Jerusalem.

Jesus Sorrows Over Jerusalem

[34]"Jerusalem, Jerusalem, you kill the early preachers and throw stones on those sent to you. How many times I wanted to gather your children around me, as a bird gathers her young under her wings, but you would not let Me. [35]Look! Your house is empty. And I tell you, you will not see Me again until the time comes when you will say, 'Great and honored is the One Who comes in the name of the Lord.' "

Another Man Healed On The Day Of Rest

14 On the Day of Rest Jesus went into the house of one of the leaders of the proud religious law-keepers to eat. They all watched Jesus to see what He would do. [2]A man who had very large arms and legs because of a sickness was put in front of

Jesus. ³Jesus asked the teachers of the Law and the proud religious law-keepers, "Does the Law say it is right to heal on the Day of Rest, or not?" ⁴They did not answer. Jesus took hold of the man and healed him and sent him away. ⁵Then Jesus said to the leaders, "If one of you had a cow or donkey that fell into a hole, would you not go at once and pull it out on the Day of Rest?" ⁶And they were not able to answer His questions.

Jesus Teaches About How To Live With Others

⁷Jesus had been watching those who were asked to come to supper. They were all trying to get the important seats. He told them a picture-story, saying, ⁸"When you are asked by someone to a wedding supper, do not take the important seat. Someone more important than you may have been asked to come also. ⁹The one who asked both of you to come may say to you, 'The important seat is for this man.' Then you will be ashamed as you take the last place. ¹⁰But when you are asked to come to the table, sit down on the last seat. Then the one who asked you may come and say to you, 'Friend, go to a more important place.' Then you will be shown respect in front of all who are at the table with you. ¹¹Whoever makes himself look more important than he is will find out how little he is worth. Whoever does not try to honor himself will be made important."

¹²Then Jesus said to the man who asked Him to eat in his house, "When you have a supper, do not ask your friends or your brothers or your family or your rich neighbors. They will ask you to come to their place for a supper. That way you will be paid back for what you have done. ¹³When you have a supper, ask poor people. Ask those who cannot walk and those who are blind. ¹⁴You will be happy if you do this. They cannot pay you back. You will get your pay when the people who are right with God are raised from the dead."

¹⁵When one of those eating at the table with Jesus heard this, he said, "Everyone is happy who will eat in the holy nation of God."

The Picture-Story Of The Big Supper [Matthew 22:1-14]

¹⁶Then Jesus said to the leader of the proud religious law-keepers, "There was a man who was giving a big supper. He asked

many people to come to eat. [17]When it was about time to eat, he sent one of the workmen he owned to tell those he had asked, saying, 'Come, everything is ready now.' [18]They all gave different reasons why they could not come. The first said, 'I have bought some land and I must go and see it. Do not expect me to come.' [19]Another one said, 'I have bought ten cows to use for working in my fields. I must go and try them out. Do not expect me to come.' [20]And another one said, 'I have just been married and I cannot come.'

[21]"The workman went back to his owner and told him these things. Then his owner became angry. He said to his workman, 'Hurry into the streets and narrow roads of the city and bring poor people here. Bring those whose bodies are diseased. Bring those who cannot walk and those who are blind.' [22]The workman came back and said, 'Sir, what you told me to do has been done. But there are still some empty places.' [23]Then the owner said to his workman, 'Go out along the roads leading away from the city and into the fields. Tell them they must come. Do this so my house will be filled. [24]I tell you, not one of those I had asked will eat of my supper.' "

Giving Up Things Of This Earth [Matthew 10:37-39]

[25]Many people followed Jesus. Then He turned around and said to them, [26]"If any man comes to Me and does not have much more love for Me than for his father and mother, wife and children, brothers and sisters, and even his own life, he cannot be My follower. [27]If he does not carry his cross and follow Me, he cannot be My follower.

If he does not carry his cross and follow Me, he cannot be My follower.

[28]"If one of you wanted to build a large building, you would sit down first and think of how much money it would take to build it. You would see if you had enough money to finish it, [29]or when the part on the ground that holds up the building is finished, you might see that you do not have enough money to finish it. Then all who would see it would make fun of you. [30]They would say, 'This man began to build and was not able to finish.'

[31]"What if a king is going to war with another king? Will he not sit down first and decide if he is able to go with 10,000 men against the other king who is coming with 20,000 men? [32]Or, he

will send a soldier to the other king while he is still a long way off. He will ask what can be done to have peace. [33]In the same way, whoever does not give up all that he has, cannot be My follower.

[34]"Salt is good. But if salt has lost its taste, how can it be made to taste like salt again? [35]It is no good for the field or the waste place. Men throw it away. You have ears, then listen!"

The Picture-Story Of The Lost Sheep

15 All the men who gathered taxes and sinners were coming to hear Jesus. [2]The proud religious law-keepers and the teachers of the Law began to speak against Him. They said, "This man receives sinners and eats with them."

[3]Then Jesus told them a picture-story, saying, [4]"What if one of you had one hundred sheep and you lost one of them? Would you not leave the ninety-nine in the country and go back and look for the one which was lost until you find it? [5]When you find it, you are happy as you carry it back on your shoulders. [6]Then you would go to your house and call your friends and neighbors. You would say to them, 'Be happy with me because I have found my sheep that was lost.' [7]I tell you, there will be more joy in heaven because of one sinner who is sorry for his sins and turns from them, than for ninety-nine people right with God who do not have sins to be sorry for.

The Picture-Story Of The Lost Piece Of Money

[8]"What if a woman has ten silver pieces of money and loses one of them? Does she not light a lamp and sweep the floor and look until she finds it? [9]When she finds it, she calls her friends and neighbors together. She says to them, 'Be happy with me. I have found the piece of money I had lost.' [10]I tell you, it is the same way among the angels of God. If one sinner is sorry for his sins and turns from them, the angels are very happy."

The Picture-Story Of The Foolish Son Who Spent All His Money

[11]And Jesus said, "There was a man who had two sons. [12]The younger son said to his father, 'Father, let me have the part of the

family riches that will be coming to me.' Then the father divided all that he owned between his two sons. ¹³Soon after that the younger son took all that had been given to him and went to another country far away. There he spent all he had on wild and foolish living. ¹⁴When all his money was spent, he was hungry. There was no food in the land. ¹⁵He went to work for a man in this far away country. His work was to feed pigs. ¹⁶He was so hungry he was ready to eat the outside part of the ears of the corn the pigs ate because no one gave him anything.

¹⁷"He began to think about what he had done. He said to himself, 'My father pays many men who work for him. They have all the food they want and more than enough. I am about dead because I am so hungry. ¹⁸I will get up and go to my father. I will say to him, "Father, I have sinned against heaven and against you. ¹⁹I am not good enough to be called your son. But may I be as one of the workmen you pay to work?" '

²⁰"The son got up and went to his father. While he was yet a long way off, his father saw him. The father was full of loving-pity for him. He ran and threw his arms around him and kissed him. ²¹The son said to him, 'Father, I have sinned against heaven and against you. I am not good enough to be called your son.' ²²But the father said to the workmen he owned, 'Hurry! Get the best coat and put it on him. Put a ring on his hand and shoes on his feet. ²³Bring the calf that is fat and kill it. Let us eat and be glad. ²⁴For my son was dead and now he is alive again. He was lost and now he is found. Let us eat and have a good time.'

²⁵"The older son was out in the field. As he was coming near the house, he heard music and dancing. ²⁶He called one of the helper boys and asked what was happening. ²⁷The helper boy answered, 'Your brother has come back and your father has killed the fat calf. Your brother is in the house and is well.' ²⁸The older brother was angry and would not go into the house. His father went outside and asked him to come in. ²⁹The older son said to his father, 'All these many years I have worked for you. I have always obeyed what you said. But you never gave me a young goat so I could have a supper and a good time with my friends. ³⁰But as soon as this son of yours came back, you kill the fat calf. And yet he wasted your money with bad women.'

³¹"The father said to him, 'My son, you are with me all the time. All that I have is yours. ³²It is right and good that we should have a good time and be glad. Your brother was dead and now he is alive again. He was lost and now he is found.' "

The Picture-Story Of The Boss Who Stole

16 Jesus said to His followers, "There was a rich man who put a boss over his houses and lands. Someone told him that his boss was not using his riches in a right way. ²The rich man sent for the boss and said, 'What is this I hear about you? Tell me what you have done with my things. You are not to be the boss of my houses and lands anymore.'

³"The boss said to himself, 'What will I do now? The owner of the houses and lands is taking my work away from me. I cannot dig in the ground for a living. I am too proud to ask for help. ⁴I know what I will do. I will make it so that when I lose this work I will be able to go to the homes of my friends.'

⁵"He sent for the people who owed the rich man. He asked the first one, 'How much do you owe the owner?' ⁶The first man said, 'One hundred barrels of oil.' The boss said to him, 'Take your bill. Sit down at once and change it to fifty.' ⁷He asked another one, 'How much do you owe?' He said, 'One hundred bags of wheat.' He said to him, 'Take your bill and change it to eighty.' ⁸Then the rich man said that this sinful boss had been wise to plan for himself for the days ahead. For the people of the world are wiser in their day than the children of light.

⁹"I tell you, make friends for yourselves by using the riches of the world that are so often used in wrong ways. So when riches are a thing of the past, friends may receive you into a home that will be forever. ¹⁰He that is faithful with little things is faithful with big things also. He that is not honest with little things is not honest with big things. ¹¹If you have not been faithful with riches of this world, who will trust you with true riches? ¹²If you have not been faithful in that which belongs to another person, who will give you things to have as your own? ¹³No workman can have two bosses. He will hate the one and love the other. Or, he will be

He that is faithful
with little things
is faithful
with big things also.

No workman
can have two bosses.

faithful to one and not faithful to the other. You cannot be faithful to God and to riches at the same time.''

Jesus Teaches That The Law Is Not Finished

[14]The proud religious law-keepers heard all these things. They loved money so they made fun of Jesus. [15]Jesus said to them, ''You are the kind of people who make yourselves look good before other people. God knows your hearts. What men think is good is hated in the eyes of God. [16]Until John came, you had the writings of the Law and of the early preachers. From that time until now the Good News of the holy nation of God has been preached. Everyone is pushing his way in. [17]But it is easier for heaven and earth to pass away than for one small part of a word in the Law to be of no more use.

[18]''Whoever divorces his wife and marries another woman is not faithful in marriage and is guilty of sex sins.

The Rich Man And The Man Who Begged For Food

[19]''There was a rich man who dressed in purple linen clothes everyday. He lived like a king would live with the best of food. [20]There was a poor man named Lazarus who had many bad sores. He was put by the door of the rich man. [21]He wanted the pieces of food that fell from the table of the rich man. Even dogs came and licked his sores.

[22]''The poor man who asked for food died. He was taken by the angels into the arms of Abraham. The rich man died also and was buried. [23]In hell the rich man was in much pain. He looked up and saw Abraham far away and Lazarus beside him. [24]He cried out and said, 'Father Abraham, take pity on me. Send Lazarus. Let him put the end of his finger in water and cool my tongue. I am in much pain in this fire.' [25]Abraham said, 'My son, do not forget that when you were living you had your good things. Lazarus had bad things. Now he is well cared for. You are in pain. [26]And more than all this, there is a big deep place between us. No one from here can go there even if he wanted to go. No one can come from there.'

²⁷"Then the rich man said, 'Father, then I beg you to send Lazarus to my father's house. ²⁸I have five brothers. Let him tell them of these things, or they will come to this place of much pain also.' ²⁹Abraham said, 'They have the Writings of Moses and of the early preachers. Let them hear what they say.' ³⁰But the rich man said, 'No, Father Abraham. If someone goes to them from the dead, they will be sorry for their sins and turn from them.' ³¹Abraham said to him, 'If they do not listen to Moses and to the early preachers, they will not listen even if someone is raised from the dead.' "

Jesus Teaches About Forgiving

17 Jesus said to His followers, "For sure, things will come that will make people sin. But it is bad for the person who makes someone else sin. ²It would be better for him to have a large rock put around his neck and be thrown into the sea, than that he should be the reason one of these little ones sin.

³"Watch yourselves! If your brother sins, speak sharp words to him. If he is sorry and turns from his sin, forgive him. ⁴What if he sins against you seven times in one day? If he comes to you and says he is sorry and turns from his sin, forgive him."

⁵The missionaries said to the Lord, "Give us more faith." ⁶The Lord said, "If your faith was as a mustard seed, you could say to this tree, 'Be pulled out of the ground and planted in the sea,' and it would obey you.

Jesus Teaches About Being Faithful

⁷"What if you owned a workman who was working in the field or taking care of sheep? Would you say to him when he came in from his work, 'Come and sit down to eat?' ⁸No, instead you would say, 'Get my supper ready. Dress yourself and care for me until I am through eating and drinking. Then you can eat and drink.' ⁹Does the workman get thanks for doing what he was told to do? I am sure he does not. ¹⁰It is the same with you also. When you do everything you have been told to do, you must say, 'We are not

Give us more faith.

any special workmen. We have done only what we should have done.' ''

Jesus Heals Ten Men With A Bad Skin Disease

¹¹Jesus went on His way to Jerusalem. He was passing between the countries of Samaria and Galilee. ¹²As He was going into one of the towns, ten men with a bad skin disease came to Him. They stood a little way off. ¹³They called to Him, "Jesus! Teacher! Take pity on us!" ¹⁴When Jesus saw them, He said, "Go and show yourselves to the religious leaders." As they went, they were healed. ¹⁵One of them turned back when he saw he was healed. He thanked God with a loud voice. ¹⁶He got down on his face at the feet of Jesus and thanked Him. He was from the country of Samaria. ¹⁷Jesus asked, "Were there not ten men who were healed? Where are the other nine? ¹⁸Is this stranger from another country the only one who turned back to give thanks to God?" ¹⁹Then Jesus said to him, "Get up and go on your way. Your trust in God has healed you."

Jesus Teaches About The Holy Nation Of God

²⁰The proud religious law-keepers asked when the holy nation of God would come. Jesus said to them, "The holy nation of God is not coming in such a way that can be seen with the eyes. ²¹It will not be said, 'Look, here it is!' or, 'There it is!' For the holy nation of God is in you."

Jesus Tells Of His Second Coming

²²Jesus said to His followers, "The time will come when you will wish you could see the Son of Man for one day. But you will not be able to. ²³They will say to you, 'He is here' or, 'He is there,' but do not follow them. ²⁴When the Son of Man comes, He will be as lightning that shines from one part of the sky to the other. ²⁵But before that, He must suffer many hard things. The people of this day will have nothing to do with Him.

As it was in the time of Noah, so will it be when the Son of Man comes back.

²⁶"As it was in the time of Noah, so will it be when the Son of Man comes back. ²⁷People ate and drank. They married and were given in marriage. They did these things until the day Noah went

into the large boat. Then the flood came and killed all the people on earth. ²⁸It was the same in the time of Lot. People ate and drank. They bought and sold. They planted and built. ²⁹But the day Lot left the city of Sodom, fire and sulphur came down from heaven like rain. It killed all the people of Sodom.

³⁰"It will be the same on the day when the Son of Man comes again. ³¹In that day the man who is on top of a house should not come down to take his things out of the house. In the same way, the man who is in the field should not go back to his house. ³²Remember Lot's wife!

³³"He who wants to keep his life will have it taken away from him. He who loses his life will have it given back to him. ³⁴I tell you, on that night there will be two men in the same bed. One of them will be taken. The other will be left. ³⁵Two women will be grinding grain together. One of them will be taken. The other will be left. ³⁶*Two men will be working in a field. One will be taken. The other will be left."

³⁷Then they asked Jesus, "Where will this happen?" He said to them, "Birds also gather where there is a dead body."

The Picture-Story Of The Woman Whose Husband Had Died

18 Jesus told them a picture-story to show that men should always pray and not give up. ²He said, "There was a man in one of the cities who was head of the court. His work was to say if a person was guilty or not. This man was not afraid of God. He did not respect any man. ³In that city there was a woman whose husband had died. She kept coming to him and saying, 'Help me! There is someone who is working against me.' ⁴For awhile he would not help her. Then he began to think, 'I am not afraid of God and I do not respect any man. ⁵But I will see that this woman whose husband has died gets her rights because I get tired of her coming all the time.' " ⁶Then the Lord said, "Listen to the words of the sinful man who is head of the court. ⁷Will not God make the things that are right come to His chosen people who cry day and night to Him? Will He wait a long time to help them? ⁸I tell you, He will be quick to help them. But when the Son of Man comes, will He find faith on the earth?"

When the Son of Man comes, will He find faith on the earth?

The Picture-Story Of The Proud Religious Law-Keepers And The Tax-Gatherers

[9]Jesus told another picture-story to some people who trusted in themselves and thought they were right with God. These people did not think well of other men. [10]Jesus said, "Two men went up to the house of God to pray. One of them was a proud religious law-keeper. The other was a man who gathered taxes. [11]The proud religious law-keeper stood and prayed to himself like this, 'God, I thank You that I am not like other men. I am not like those who steal. I am not like those who do things that are wrong. I am not like those who do sex sins. I am not like even this tax-gatherer. [12]I go without food two times a week so I can pray better. I give one-tenth part of the money I earn.' [13]But the man who gathered taxes stood a long way off. He would not even lift his eyes to heaven. But he hit himself on his chest and said, 'God, have pity on me! I am a sinner!' [14]I tell you, this man went back to his house forgiven, and not the other man. For whoever makes himself look more important than he is will find out how little he is worth. Whoever does not try to honor himself will be made important.

Jesus Gives Thanks For Little Children [*Matthew 19:13-15; Mark 10:13-16*]

[15]People took their little children to Jesus so He could put His hand on them. When His followers saw it, they spoke sharp words to the people. [16]Jesus called the followers to Him and said, "Let the little children come to Me. Do not try to stop them. The holy nation of God is made up of ones like these. [17]For sure, I tell you, whoever does not receive the holy nation of God as a child will not go into the holy nation."

Jesus Teaches About Keeping The Law [*Matthew 19:16-30; Mark 10:17-31*]

What must I do to have life that lasts forever?

[18]A leader of the people asked Jesus, "Good Teacher, what must I do to have life that lasts forever?" [19]Jesus said to him, "Why do you call Me good? There is only One Who is good. That is God. [20]You know the Laws. You must not do any sex sins. You must not kill another person. You must not steal. You must not tell a lie about someone else. Respect your father and your

mother." ²¹The leader said, "I have obeyed all these Laws since I was a boy."

²²When Jesus heard this, He said to the leader of the people, "There is still one thing you need to do. Sell everything you have. Give the money to poor people. Then you will have riches in heaven. Come and follow Me." ²³When the leader heard this, he was very sad because he had many riches. ²⁴When Jesus saw that he was very sad, He said, "It is hard for those with riches to go into the holy nation of God! ²⁵It is easier for a camel to go through the eye of a needle than for a rich man to go into the holy nation of God."

²⁶Those who heard this, said, "Then who can be saved from the punishment of sin?" ²⁷Jesus said, "God can do things men cannot do." ²⁸Then Peter said, "See, we have left everything and have followed You." ²⁹Jesus said to them, "For sure, I tell you, anyone who has left his house or parents or brothers or wife or children because of the holy nation of God ³⁰will receive much more now. In the time to come he will have life that lasts forever."

Jesus Tells Of His Death The Third Time [Matthew 20:17-19; Mark 10:32-34]

³¹Then Jesus took the twelve followers to one side and said, "Listen! We are going up to Jerusalem. All the things the early preachers wrote about the Son of Man are going to happen. ³²He will be given over to the people who are not Jews. He will be made fun of. He will be hurt. He will be spit on. ³³They will beat Him and kill Him. After three days He will be raised again."

³⁴The followers did not understand these words. The meaning of these words was hidden from them. They did not know what He said.

Healing Of The Blind Man [Matthew 20:29-34; Mark 10:46-52]

³⁵Jesus was coming near Jericho. A blind man was sitting by the side of the road, begging. ³⁶He heard many people going by and asked what was happening. ³⁷They told him that Jesus of Nazareth was going by. ³⁸Then he cried out and said, "Jesus, Son

of David, have pity on me." [39]The people spoke sharp words to him and told him not to call out. But he cried out all the more, "Son of David, have pity on me."

[40]Jesus stopped and told the people to bring the blind man to Him. When the man was near, Jesus asked, [41]"What do you want Me to do for you?" He answered, "Lord, I want to see." [42]Jesus said to him, "Then see! Your faith has healed you." [43]At once he could see. He followed Jesus and gave thanks to God. All the people gave thanks to God when they saw it.

The Changed Life Of Zaccheus

19 Jesus went on into the city of Jericho and was passing through it. [2]There was a rich man named Zaccheus. He was a leader of those who gathered taxes. [3]Zaccheus wanted to see Jesus but he could not because so many people were there and he was a short man. [4]He ran ahead and got up into a sycamore tree to see Him. Jesus was going by that way.

[5]When Jesus came to the place, He looked up and saw Zaccheus. He said, "Zaccheus, come down at once. I must stay in your house today." [6]At once he came down and was glad to have Jesus come to his house. [7]When the people saw it, they began to complain among themselves. They said, "He is going to stay with a man who is known to be a sinner."

[8]Zaccheus stood up and said to the Lord, "Lord, look! Half of what I own I will give to poor people. And if I have taken money from anyone in a wrong way, I will pay him back four times as much." [9]Jesus said to him, "Today, a person has been saved in this house. This man is a Jew also. [10]For the Son of Man came to look for and to save from the punishment of sin those who are lost."

The Picture-Story Of The Ten Workmen And The Money

[11]As they heard these things, Jesus told them a picture-story. Because He was near Jerusalem, they thought the holy nation of

God would come at once. ¹²So Jesus said, "A leader of a country went to another country far away. A nation was to be given to him. Then he would return home. ¹³He called ten of the workmen he owned. He gave them ten pieces of money and said to them, 'Put this money to use until I return.' ¹⁴But other men in his country hated him. They sent men after him to tell him they did not want him as their king. ¹⁵After he had been given the other nation, he returned as king. He asked for his workmen who had received the money to come to him. He wanted to know how much more they had after putting it to use. ¹⁶The first one came and said, 'Lord, the piece of money you gave me has made ten more pieces of money.' ¹⁷He said to him, 'You are a good workman. You have been faithful in using a little. Now you will be leader over ten cities.'

¹⁸"The second man came to him and said, 'Lord, the piece of money you gave me has made five more pieces of money.' ¹⁹He said to him, 'You are to be leader over five cities.'

²⁰"Another one came saying, 'Lord, look! Here is your piece of money. I have kept it hid in a piece of cloth. ²¹I was afraid of you. You are a hard man. You take what you have not put down. You gather where you have not planted.' ²²The king said to him, 'By the words from your own mouth I must say that you are guilty. You are a sinful workman. You knew I was a hard man. You knew I take what I have not put down. You knew I gather where I have not planted. ²³Why did you not put my money in the bank? Then when I came back I could have had my own money and what the bank paid for using it.'

²⁴"Then he said to those who were standing by, 'Take the piece of money from him and give it to the one who has ten pieces of money.' ²⁵And they said to him, 'Lord, he already has ten pieces of money.'"

²⁶Jesus said, "I tell you, he who has, to him will be given more. To him who does not have, even the little he has will be taken from him. ²⁷Bring here those who hated me and did not want me to be their king and kill them in front of me.'" ²⁸When He had finished the picture-story, He went on ahead of them up to Jerusalem.

The Last Time Jesus Goes Into Jerusalem [Matthew 21:1-11; Mark 11:1-11; John 12:12-19]

²⁹When Jesus was coming near the towns of Bethphage and Bethany by the Mountain of Olives, He sent two of His followers on ahead. ³⁰He said, "Go into the town ahead of you. There you will find a young donkey tied. No man has ever sat on it. Let it loose and bring it to Me. ³¹If anyone asks you, 'Why are you letting it loose?' say to him, 'Because the Lord needs it.'"

³²Those who were sent found everything as Jesus had told them. ³³As they were letting the young donkey loose, the owners said to them, "Why are you letting the young donkey loose?" ³⁴They answered, "The Lord needs it." ³⁵Then they brought it to Jesus. They put their coats on the donkey and they put Jesus on it.

³⁶As Jesus was going, they put their coats down on the road. ³⁷Jesus was near the city and ready to go down the Mountain of Olives. The many people who were following Him began to sing with loud voices and give thanks for all the powerful works they had seen. ³⁸They said, "Great and honored is the King Who comes in the name of the Lord. There is peace and greatness in the highest heaven."

³⁹Some of the proud religious law-keepers who were in among the people said to Jesus, "Teacher, speak sharp words to Your followers." ⁴⁰Jesus said to them, "I tell you that if these did not speak, the very stones would call out."

Jesus Cried As He Saw Jerusalem

⁴¹When Jesus came near the city, He cried as He saw it. ⁴²He said, "If you had only known on this great day the things that make peace! But now they are hidden from your eyes. ⁴³The time is coming when those who hate you will dig earth and throw it up around you making a wall. They will shut you in from every side. ⁴⁴They will destroy you and your children with you. There will not be one stone on another. It is because you did not know when God visited you."

Jesus Stops The Buying And Selling In The House Of God
[Matthew 21:12-17; Mark 11:15-19; John 2:13-17]

⁴⁵Jesus went into the house of God. He made those leave who were buying and selling there. ⁴⁶He said to them, "It is written, 'My house is a house of prayer.' 'But you have made it a place of robbers.'" (Isaiah 56:7; Jeremiah 7:11)

⁴⁷Jesus taught each day in the house of God. But the religious leaders and the teachers of the Law and other leaders of the people tried to think of some way they could kill Him. ⁴⁸They could not find a way because the people were always near Him listening to Him teach.

They Ask Jesus Who Gave Him The Power To Do These Things
[Matthew 21:23-32; Mark 11:27-33]

20 As He was teaching and preaching the Good News, the religious leaders and the teachers of the Law and the elders came. ²They said to Him, "Tell us, by what right and power are You doing these things? Who gave You the right and the power?" ³Jesus said to them, "I will ask you one question also. You answer Me. ⁴Was the baptism of John from heaven or from men?"

⁵They said to themselves, "If we say, 'From heaven,' He will say, 'Then why did you not believe Him?' ⁶But if we say, 'From men,' then all the people will throw stones at us because they believe John was one who spoke for God." ⁷They said that they did not know where John's baptism came from. ⁸Jesus said to them, "And I will not tell you where I get the right and the power to do these things."

The Picture-Story Of The Grape Field [Matthew 21:33-46; Mark 12:1-12]

⁹Jesus began to tell the people a picture-story, saying, "There was a man who planted a grape field. He rented it to farmers. Then he went to a country far away for a long time. ¹⁰At the time of gathering fruit he sent one of his workmen to the farmers to get some of the fruit. But the farmers beat him and sent him away

without fruit. ¹¹He sent another workman. The farmers beat him also. They made it very hard for him and sent him away without fruit. ¹²He sent a third workman. They hurt him and threw him out of the grape field.

¹³"Then the owner of the grape field said, 'What should I do? I will send my much-loved son. They might respect him.' ¹⁴The farmers saw the son. They said to themselves, 'This is the one who will get everything when the owner dies. Let us kill him, and we will get everything.' ¹⁵They put him out of the grape field and killed him. Now what will the owner of the grape field do to them? ¹⁶He will come and kill those farmers. Then he will rent the grape field to other farmers."

When they heard this, they said, "May this never be done!" ¹⁷Jesus looked at them and said, "What does this writing mean, 'The Stone that was put aside by the workman has become the most important Stone in the building?' (Psalm 118:22) ¹⁸Whoever falls on this Stone will be broken. And on the one it falls, it will make him like dust."(Isaiah 8:14-15)

They Try To Trap Jesus [Matthew 22:15-22; Mark 12:13-17]

¹⁹At this time the religious leaders and the teachers of the Law tried to take Jesus, but they were afraid of the people. These leaders knew Jesus had told this picture-story against them. ²⁰They watched Jesus and they sent men who pretended to be good people to watch Him. They wanted to trap Him in something He said. Then they could give Him over to the leader of the people who had the right and the power to say what to do with Him.

²¹These men who were sent asked Jesus, "Teacher, we know what You say and teach is right. We know You do not show more respect to one person than to another. We know You teach the truth about God. ²²Is it right for us to pay taxes to Caesar or not?" ²³Jesus knew they were trying to trap Him. He said, ²⁴"Show Me a piece of money. Whose picture is this? Whose name is on it?" And they said, "Caesar's." ²⁵Jesus said to them, "Pay to Caesar the things that belong to Caesar. Pay to God the things that belong to God." ²⁶They could find nothing wrong with what

He taught. They were surprised and wondered about what He told the people, so they said nothing more.

They Ask About Being Raised From The Dead [*Matthew 22:23-33; Mark 12:18-27*]

27Some people from the religious group who believe no one will be raised from the dead came to Jesus. They asked Him, 28"Teacher, Moses wrote to us in the Law, 'If a man's brother dies and leaves a wife but no children, then his brother must marry her. He should have children for his brother who died.' (Deuteronomy 25:5) 29There were seven brothers. The first had a wife but died without children. 30The second brother took her for his wife. He died without children. 31The third brother took her for his wife. In the same way all seven took her for a wife. They all died without children. 32Then the woman died also. 33When people are raised from the dead, whose wife will she be? All seven brothers had her for a wife."

34Jesus said to them, "People of this earth marry and are given in marriage. 35But those who have the right to have that life and are raised from the dead do not marry and are not given in marriage. 36They cannot die anymore. They are as the angels and are sons of God. They are children who have been raised from the dead. 37As for the dead being raised, even Moses spoke of that when he told of the burning bush. There he calls the Lord, the God of Abraham and the God of Isaac and the God of Jacob. 38For He is not the God of the dead. He is the God of the living. All live for Him."

39One of the teachers of the Law said, "Teacher, You have spoken well." 40After that they were afraid to ask Him anything.

Jesus Asks The Teachers Of The Law About The Christ [*Matthew 22:41-46; Mark 12:35-37*]

41Jesus said to them, "How do they say that Christ is the Son of David? 42For David himself said in the Book of Psalms, 'The Lord said to My Lord, "Sit at my right side 43until I make those who hate You a place to rest Your feet." ' (Psalm 110:1) 44David calls Him, 'Lord!' Then how can He be his son?"

False Teachers [*Matthew 23:1-36; Mark 12:38-40*]

⁴⁵All the people were listening. He said to His followers, ⁴⁶"Look out for the teachers of the Law. They like to walk around in long coats. They like to have people speak words of respect to them in the center of town where people gather. They like the important seats in the places of worship. They like the important places at big suppers. ⁴⁷They take houses from poor women whose husbands have died. They cover up their actions by making long prayers. They will be punished all the more."

A Woman Whose Husband Had Died Gave All She Had [*Mark 12:41-44*]

21 Jesus looked up and saw rich men putting their money into the money box in the house of God. ²He saw a poor woman whose husband had died. She put in two very small pieces of money. ³He said, "I tell you the truth, this poor woman has put in more than all of them. ⁴For they have put in a little of the money they had no need for. She is very poor and has put in all she had. She has put in what she needed for her own living."

Jesus Tells Of The House Of God [*Matthew 24:1-51; Mark 13:11-37*]

⁵Some people were talking about the house of God. They were saying that the stones were beautiful and that many gifts had been given. Jesus said, ⁶"As for these things you see, all these stones will be thrown down. Not one will be left on another." ⁷They asked Jesus, "Teacher, when will this take place? What are we to look for to show us these things are about to happen?" ⁸He said, "Be careful that no one leads you the wrong way. For many people will come in My name. They will say, 'I am the Christ.' The time is near. Do not follow them. ⁹When you hear of wars and fighting in different places, do not be afraid. These things have to happen first, but the end is not yet."

¹⁰Then Jesus said to them, "Nations will have wars with other nations. Countries will fight against countries. ¹¹The earth will shake and break apart in different places. There will be no food.

There will be bad diseases among many people. Very special things will be seen in the sky that will make people much afraid.

12"But before all this happens, men will take hold of you and make it very hard for you. They will give you over to the places of worship and to the prisons. They will bring you in front of kings and the leaders of the people. This will all be done to you because of Me. 13This will be a time for you to tell about Me. 14Do not think about what you will say ahead of time. 15For I will give you wisdom in what to say and I will help you say it. Those who are against you will not be able to stop you or say you are wrong.

16"You will be handed over by your parents and your brothers and your family and your friends. They will kill some of you. 17All men will hate you because of Me. 18Yet not one hair of your head will be lost. 19But stay true and your souls will have life.

Days Of Trouble And Pain And Sorrow

20"When you see armies all around Jerusalem, know that it will soon be destroyed. 21Those in the country of Judea must run to the mountains. Those in the city must leave at once. Those in the country must not go into the city. 22People will be punished in these hard days. All things will happen as it is written.

23"It will be hard for women who will soon be mothers. It will be hard for those feeding babies in those days. It will be very hard for the people in the land and anger will be brought down on them. 24People will be killed by the sword. They will be held in prison by all nations. Jerusalem will be walked over by the people who are not Jews until their time is finished.

Jesus Will Come Again In His Shining Greatness

25"There will be special things to look for in the sun and moon and stars. The nations of the earth will be troubled and will not know what to do. They will be troubled at the angry sea and waves. 26The hearts of men will give up because of being afraid of what is coming on the earth. The powers of the heavens will be shaken. 27Then they will see the Son of Man coming in the clouds with power and much greatness. 28When these things begin to

Then they will see the Son of Man coming in the clouds with power and much greatness.

happen, stand up and lift up your heads. You have been bought by the blood of Christ and will soon be free.''

The Picture-Story Of The Fig Tree

[29]Jesus told them a picture-story. He said, "Look at the fig tree and all the other trees. [30]When you see their leaves coming out, you know summer is near. [31]In the same way, when you see these things happening, you will know the holy nation of God is near. [32]For sure, I tell you, that the people of this day will not die before all these things happen.

No One Knows When Jesus Will Come Again

Heaven and earth will pass away, but My Words will not pass away.

[33]"Heaven and earth will pass away, but My Words will not pass away. [34]Watch yourselves! Do not let yourselves be loaded down with too much eating and strong drink. Do not be troubled with the cares of this life. If you do, that day will come on you without you knowing it. [35]It will come on all people over all the earth. [36]Be sure you watch. Pray all the time so that you may be able to keep from going through all these things that will happen and be able to stand in front of the Son of Man.''

[37]Everyday Jesus taught in the house of God. At night He went to the Mountain of Olives and stayed there. [38]Early in the morning all the people came to the house of God to hear Him.

They Look For A Way To Put Jesus To Death [Matthew 26:1-5; Mark 14:1-2]

22 The time for the supper of bread without yeast was near. It was the special religious gathering to remember how the Jews left Egypt. [2]The religious leaders and the teachers of the Law looked for a way to kill Jesus. But they were afraid of the people.

[3]Then Satan came into the heart of Judas who was called Iscariot. He was one of the twelve followers. [4]Judas went away and talked with the religious leaders and the leaders of the people. He talked about how he might hand Jesus over to them. [5]They were glad and promised to pay him money. [6]Judas promised to do

this and then looked for a way to hand Jesus over when there were no people around.

Getting Ready For The Special Supper [Matthew 26:17-19; Mark 14:12-16]

⁷The day of bread without yeast came. It was the day when the lamb had to be killed and given on the altar in worship in the house of God. It was the special religious gathering to remember how the Jews left Egypt. ⁸Jesus sent Peter and John and said, "Go and get this special supper ready for us that we may eat." ⁹They said to Him, "Where do You want us to get it ready?" ¹⁰He answered, "Listen, when you go into the city, you will meet a man carrying a jar of water. Follow him into the house where he goes. ¹¹Say to the owner of the house, 'The Teacher asks you, "Where is the room you keep for friends where I may eat this special supper with My followers?" ' ¹²He will take you to a large room on the second floor with everything in it. Make it ready for us."

¹³They went and found everything as Jesus had said. They got ready for the special supper.

The Last Special Supper [Matthew 26:20-25; Mark 14:17-21; John 13:21-35]

¹⁴When the time came, Jesus sat down with the twelve missionaries. ¹⁵He said to them, "I have wanted very much to eat this special supper with you to remember how the Jews left Egypt. I have wanted to eat this with you before I suffer. ¹⁶I say to you, I will not eat this special supper again until its true meaning is completed in the holy nation of God."

¹⁷Then Jesus took the cup and gave thanks. He said, "Take this and pass it to each one. ¹⁸I say to you that I will not drink of the fruit of the vine until the holy nation of God comes."

The First Lord's Supper [Matthew 26:26-30; Mark 14:22-26]

¹⁹Then Jesus took bread and gave thanks and broke it in pieces. He gave it to them, saying, "This is My body which is given for you. Do this to remember Me." ²⁰In the same way, after they had

finished the bread, He took the cup. He said, "This cup is My blood of the New Way of Worship which is given for you.

Jesus Tells Of The One Who Will Hand Him Over

21"Listen, the hand of the one who will give Me over to the leaders of the country is on the table with Me. 22The Son of Man will be taken this way because it has been in God's plan. But it is bad for that man who hands Him over!" 23They began to ask each other which of them would do this.

They Argue About Who Is The Greatest

24They started to argue among themselves about who was thought to be the greatest. 25Jesus said to them, "The kings of the nations show their power to the people. Those who have power over the people are given names of honor. 26But you will not be like that. Let the greatest among you be as the least. Let the leader be as the one who cares for others. 27Who is greater, the one who is eating at the table, or the one who is caring for him? Is it not the one who is eating at the table? But I am here with you as One Who cares for you.

Let the leader be as the one who cares for others.

28"You have stayed with Me through all the hard things that have come to Me. 29As My Father has given Me a holy nation, I will give you the right 30to eat and drink at My table in My holy nation. You will sit on the place where kings sit and say who is guilty in the twelve family groups of the Jewish nation."

Jesus Tells How Peter Will Lie About Him [Matthew 26:31-35; Mark 14:27-31; John 13:36-38]

31The Lord said, "Simon, Simon, listen! Satan has wanted to have you. He will divide you as wheat is divided from that which is no good. 32But I have prayed for you. I have prayed that your faith will be strong and that you will not give up. When you return, you must help to make your brothers strong." 33Peter said to Jesus, "Lord, I am ready to go to prison and to die with You!" 34Jesus said, "I tell you, Peter, a rooster will not crow today before you will say three times that you do not know Me."

The Followers Are Told Of Trouble To Come

³⁵Jesus said to them, "I sent you without money or bag or shoes. Did you need anything?" They said, "Nothing." ³⁶Then He said to them, "But now whoever has a money-bag and a bag for food should take it. Whoever does not have a sword should sell his coat and buy one. ³⁷I tell you, that what has been written about Me must happen. It says, 'He was among the wrong-doers.' What is told about Me must happen." (Isaiah 53:12)

³⁸They said, "Lord, look, we have two swords." He answered, "That is enough."

Jesus Prays In The Garden [Matthew 26:36-46; Mark 14:32-42]

³⁹Jesus came out of the room. Then He went to the Mountain of Olives as He had been doing. The followers went with Him. ⁴⁰When He got there, He said to them, "Pray that you will not be tempted." ⁴¹He walked away from them about as far as a stone can be thrown. There He got down with His face on the ground and prayed. ⁴²He said, "Father, if it can be done, take away what must happen to Me. Even so, not what I want, but what You want."

⁴³An angel from heaven came and gave Him strength. ⁴⁴His heart was much troubled and He prayed all the more. Water ran from His face like blood and fell to the ground.

⁴⁵When Jesus got up after praying, He went back to the followers. He found them sleeping because of so much sorrow. ⁴⁶He said to them, "Why are you sleeping? Get up and pray that you will not be tempted."

Jesus Is Handed Over To Sinners [Matthew 26:47-56; Mark 14:43-52; John 18:1-11]

⁴⁷While Jesus was speaking, Judas came walking ahead of many people. He was one of the twelve followers. He came near to Jesus to kiss Him. ⁴⁸But Jesus said to him, "Judas, are you handing over the Son of Man with a kiss?" ⁴⁹Those around Jesus saw what was going to happen and asked, "Lord, should we fight

with our swords?" ⁵⁰One of them hit a workman and cut off his right ear. This workman was owned by the head religious leader. ⁵¹Jesus said, "Stop! This is enough." And He put His hand on his ear and healed him.

Jesus Stands In Front Of The Religious Leaders [Matthew 26:57-58; Mark 14:53-54; John 18:19-24]

⁵²Jesus said to the religious leaders and the leaders of the house of God and the other leaders who came to Him, "Have you come with swords and sticks to take Me, as if I were a robber? ⁵³While I was with you everyday in the house of God, you never took hold of Me. But now is the time you are to come and you have come in the dark."

⁵⁴Then they led Jesus away to the house of the head religious leader. Peter followed a long way behind Him.

Peter Said He Did Not Know Jesus [Matthew 26:69-75; Mark 14:66-72; John 18:15-18, 25-27]

⁵⁵They built a fire in the yard and sat down. Peter sat down with them. ⁵⁶One of the women helpers saw Peter as he sat by the fire and looked right at him. She said, "This man was with Jesus also." ⁵⁷Peter lied and said, "Woman, I do not know Him." ⁵⁸After awhile another person saw him and said, "You are one of them also." Peter said, "No, sir, I am not." ⁵⁹About an hour later another person said the same thing, "For sure, this man was with Jesus also because he is from Galilee." ⁶⁰But Peter said, "Sir, I do not know what you are saying." And at once, while he was talking, a rooster crowed. ⁶¹The Lord turned and looked at Peter. He remembered the Lord had said, "Before a rooster crows, you will say three times that you do not know Me." ⁶²Peter went outside and cried with a troubled heart.

⁶³Those who watched Jesus so He could not get away made fun of Him and beat Him. ⁶⁴They covered His eyes with a cloth and asked Him, "Tell us who hit You?" ⁶⁵They said many other bad things against Jesus.

⁶⁶When it was morning the leaders of the people and the religious leaders and the teachers of the Law got together. They

took Jesus to the court of the religious leader. They said, [67]"Tell us if you are the Christ." He said to them, "If I tell you, you will not believe Me. [68]If I ask you something, you will not tell Me. [69]From now on, the Son of Man will be seated at the right hand of the All-powerful God." [70]They all said, "Then are You the Son of God?" He said, "You say that I am." [71]Then they said, "What other word do we need against Him? We have heard Him say this with His own mouth."

From now on the Son of Man will be seated at the right hand of the All-powerful God.

Jesus Stands In Front Of Pilate [*Matthew 27:1-2, 11-14; Mark 15:1-5; John 18:28-37*]

23 Then all the many people got up and took Jesus to Pilate. [2]They began to tell things against Him, saying, "We have found this Man leading the people of our nation in a wrong way. He has been telling them not to pay taxes to Caesar. He has been saying He is Christ, a King."

[3]Pilate asked Jesus, "Are You the King of the Jews?" He said, "What you said is true." [4]Then Pilate said to the religious leaders and to the people, "I find nothing wrong in this Man." [5]They became more angry. They said, "He makes trouble among the people. He has been teaching over all the country of Judea, starting in Galilee and now here."

Jesus Is Sent To Herod

[6]When Pilate heard the word, Galilee, he asked, "Is the Man from Galilee?" [7]As soon as Pilate knew Jesus belonged in the country where Herod was king, he sent Him to Herod. Herod was in Jerusalem at that time also.

[8]Herod was very glad when he saw Jesus because he had wanted to see Him for a long time. He had heard many things about Him and had hoped to see Him do some powerful work. [9]Herod talked to Jesus and asked many things. But Jesus said nothing. [10]The religious leaders and the teachers of the Law were standing there. They said many false things against Him.

[11]Then Herod and his soldiers were very bad to Jesus and made fun of Him. They put a beautiful coat on Him and sent Him back

to Pilate. [12]That day Pilate and Herod became friends. Before that they had worked against each other.

[13]Pilate called the religious leaders and the leaders of the people and the people together. [14]He said to them, "You brought this Man to me as one that leads the people in the wrong way. I have asked Him about these things in front of you. I do not find Him guilty of the things you say against Him. [15]Herod found nothing wrong with Him because he sent Him back to us. There is no reason to have Him put to death. [16]I will punish Him and let Him go free."

Jesus Or Barabbas Is To Go Free [Matthew 27:15-26; Mark 15:6-1; John 18:38-40]

[17]*Every year at the time of the special supper, Pilate would let one person who was in prison go free. [18]They all cried out together with a loud voice, "Take this Man away! Let Barabbas go free." [19]Barabbas had killed some people and had made trouble against the leaders of the country. He had been put into prison.

[20]Pilate wanted to let Jesus go free so he talked to them again. [21]But they cried out, "Nail Him to a cross! Nail Him to a cross!" [22]Pilate said to them the third time, "Why, what bad thing has He done? I have found no reason to put Him to death. I will punish Him and let Him go free."

[23]But they kept on crying out with loud voices saying that He must be nailed to a cross. Their loud voices got what they wanted. [24]Then Pilate said that it should be done as they wanted. [25]Pilate let the man go free who had made trouble against the leaders of the country and who had killed people. He gave Jesus over to them to do with as they wanted.

Jesus On The Cross [Matthew 27:33-37; Mark 15:22-26; John 19:17-22]

[26]They led Jesus away. A man named Simon was coming in from the country of Cyrene and they made him carry the cross following behind Jesus.

²⁷Many people followed Jesus. There were women who cried and had sorrow for Him. ²⁸Jesus turned to them and said, "Daughters of Jerusalem, do not cry for Me. Cry for yourselves and your children. ²⁹Listen! The days are coming when they will say, 'Those who have never had children are happy. Those whose bodies have never given birth are happy. Those who have never fed babies are happy.' ³⁰They will begin to say to the mountains, 'Fall on us.' They will say to the hills, 'Cover us.' ³¹If they do these things to a green tree, what will they do when it is dry?''

³²Two other men were led away with Jesus to be put to death also. These men had done things making them guilty of death. ³³When they came to the place called Calvary, they nailed Jesus to a cross. The other two men were nailed to crosses also. One was on the right side of Jesus and the other was on His left side. ³⁴Then Jesus said, "Father, forgive them. They do not know what they are doing." And they divided His clothes by drawing names.

³⁵The people stood around looking on. The leaders were there with them making fun of Jesus. They said, "He saved others, let Him save Himself if He is the Christ, the Chosen One of God!" ³⁶The soldiers made fun of Him also. They put sour wine in front of Him. ³⁷They said, "If You are the King of the Jews, save yourself." ³⁸These words were written in the Greek and Latin and Hebrew languages above His head: "THIS IS THE KING OF THE JEWS."

The Two Robbers [*Matthew 27:38-44; Mark 15:27-32*]

³⁹One of the men who was guilty of death who was on a cross beside Jesus spoke bad words to Him. He said, "If You are the Christ, save Yourself and us." ⁴⁰But the other man on a cross spoke sharp words to the one who made fun of Jesus. He said, "Are you not afraid of God? You are also guilty and will be punished. ⁴¹We are suffering and we should, because of the wrong we have done. But this Man has done nothing wrong." ⁴²And he said to Jesus, "Lord, remember me when You come into Your holy nation." ⁴³Jesus said to him, "For sure, I tell you, today you will be with Me in Paradise."

The Death Of Jesus [Matthew 27:45-50; Mark 15:33-36; John 19:28-37]

⁴⁴"It was dark over all the earth from noon until three o'clock. ⁴⁵The sun did not shine. In the house of God the curtain was torn in two pieces.

⁴⁶Then Jesus cried out with a loud voice, "Father, into Your hands I give My spirit." When He said this, He died.

⁴⁷When the soldier saw what had happened, he thanked God. He said, "For sure, He was a good man." ⁴⁸All the many people who came together to see the things that were done, went away beating themselves on their chests. ⁴⁹All His friends and the women who had come with Him from Galilee stood a long way off watching these things.

The Grave Of Jesus [Matthew 27:57-66; Mark 15:42-47; John 19:38-42]

⁵⁰There was a man named Joseph who belonged to the court. He was a good man and one who did right. ⁵¹This man did not agree with what the court did. He was from Arimathea, a city of the Jews. He was looking for the holy nation of God to come. ⁵²Joseph went to Pilate and asked for the body of Jesus.

⁵³Then he took it down and put it in linen cloth. It was laid in a grave which had been cut out in the side of a rock. This grave had never been used.

⁵⁴It was time to get ready for the Day of Rest which was about to begin. ⁵⁵The women who had come with Jesus from Galilee followed behind. They saw the grave and how His body was laid. ⁵⁶They went back and got some spices and perfumes ready. But they rested on the Day of Rest as the Law said to do.

Jesus Is Raised From The Dead [Matthew 28:1-10; Mark 16:1-8; John 20:1-18]

24 Early in the morning on the first day of the week, the women went to the grave taking the spices they had made ready. ²They found the stone had been pushed away from the grave.

[3]They went in but they did not find the body of the Lord Jesus.

[4]While they wondered about what had happened, they saw two men standing by them in shining clothes. [5]They were very much afraid and got down with their faces to the ground. The men said to them, "Why do you look for the living One among those who are dead? [6]He is not here. He is risen. Do you not remember what He said to you when He was yet in Galilee? [7]He said, 'The Son of Man must be given over into the hands of sinful men. He must be nailed to a cross. He will rise again three days later.' " [8]They remembered what He had said.

He is risen.

[9]When they came back from the grave, they told all these things to the eleven followers and to all the others. [10]They were Mary Magdalene and Joanna and Mary the mother of James. Other women who were with them told these things to the missionaries also. [11]Their words sounded like foolish talk. The missionaries did not believe them. [12]But Peter got up and ran to the grave. He got down to look in and saw only the linen clothes. Then he went away, surprised about what had happened.

The Followers Of Jesus Do Not Believe He Is Risen [*Mark 16:9-14; John 20:24-29*]

[13]That same day two of His followers were going to the town of Emmaus. It was about a two-hour walk from Jerusalem. [14]They talked of all these things that had happened. [15]While they were talking together, Jesus Himself came and walked along with them. [16]Something kept their eyes from seeing Who He was.

[17]He said to them, "What are you talking about as you walk?" They stood still and looked sad. [18]One of them, whose name was Cleopas, said to Him, "Are you the only one visiting Jerusalem who has not heard of the things that have happened here these days?" [19]Jesus said to them, "What things?" They answered, "The things about Jesus of Nazareth. He was the great One Who spoke for God. He did powerful works and spoke powerful words in the sight of God and the people. [20]And the religious leaders and the leaders of the people gave Him over to be killed and nailed Him to a cross. [21]We were hoping He was the One Who was going

to make the Jewish people free. But it was three days ago when these things happened.

22"Some of the women of our group have surprised us and made us wonder. They went to the grave early this morning. 23They did not find His body. They came back saying they had seen angels in a special dream who said that He was alive. 24Some of those who were with us went to the grave and found it as the women had said. But they did not see Him."

25Then Jesus said to them, "You foolish men. How slow you are to believe what the early preachers have said. 26Did not Christ have to go through these hard things to come into His shining greatness?" 27Jesus kept on telling them what Moses and all the early preachers had said about Him in the Holy Writings.

28When they came to the town where they were going, Jesus acted as if He were going farther. 29But they said to Him, "Stay with us. It will soon be evening. The day is about over." He went in to stay with them. 30As He sat at the table with them, He took the bread and gave thanks and broke it. Then He gave it to them.

Their eyes were opened and they knew Him. 31And their eyes were opened and they knew Him. Then He left them and could not be seen. 32They said to each other, "Were not our hearts filled with joy when He talked to us on the road about what the Holy Writings said?"

33Then they got up at once and went back to Jerusalem. They found the eleven followers together and others with them. 34They said, "For sure the Lord is risen and was seen by Simon." 35Then they told what had happened on the road and how they came to know Him when He broke the bread.

Jesus Is Seen By The Other Ten Followers

36As they talked, Jesus Himself stood among them. He said, "May you have peace." 37But they were afraid and full of fear. They thought they saw a spirit. 38Jesus said to them, "Why are you afraid? Why do you have doubts in your hearts? 39Look at My hands and My feet. Look! It is I, Myself! Touch Me and see for yourself. A spirit does not have flesh and bones as I have." 40When Jesus had said this, He showed them His hands and feet.

⁴¹They still wondered. It was hard for them to believe it and yet it made them happy. Then He said to them, "Do you have anything here to eat?" ⁴²They gave Jesus a piece of fish that had been cooked and some honey. ⁴³He took it and ate it in front of them.

Jesus Sends His Followers To Teach [*Matthew 28:16-20; Mark 16:15-18; John 20:21-23*]

⁴⁴Jesus said to them, "These are the things I told you while I was yet with you. All things written about Me in the Law of Moses and in the Books of the early preachers and in the Psalms must happen as they said they would happen." ⁴⁵Then He opened their minds to understand the Holy Writings. ⁴⁶He said to them, "It is written that Christ should suffer and be raised from the dead after three days. ⁴⁷It must be preached that men must be sorry for their sins and turn from them. Then they will be forgiven. This must be preached in His name to all nations beginning in Jerusalem. ⁴⁸You are to tell what you have seen. ⁴⁹Listen! I will send you what My Father promised. But you are to stay in Jerusalem until you have received power from above."

Jesus Goes To Be Beside His Father [*Mark 16:19-20*]

⁵⁰Jesus led them out as far as Bethany. Then He lifted up His hands and prayed that good would come to them. ⁵¹And while He was praying that good would come to them, He went from them *(and was taken up to heaven and ⁵²they worshiped Him.) Then they went back to Jerusalem with great joy. ⁵³They spent all their time in the house of God honoring and giving thanks to God.

Christ Lived Before The World Was Made

The Word (Christ) was in the beginning. The Word was with God. The Word was God.

He made all things.

Life began by Him.

1 The Word (Christ) was in the beginning. The Word was with God. The Word was God. ²He was with God in the beginning. ³He made all things. Nothing was made without Him making it. ⁴Life began by Him. His Life was the Light for men. ⁵The Light shines in the darkness. The darkness has never been able to put out the Light.

John the Baptist Tells Of The Coming Of Christ

⁶There was a man sent from God whose name was John. ⁷He came to tell what he knew about the Light so that all men might believe through him. ⁸John was not the Light, but he was sent to tell about the Light.

⁹This true Light, coming into the world, gives light to every man. ¹⁰He came into the world. The world was made by Him, but it did not know Him. ¹¹He came to His own, but His own did not receive Him. ¹²He gave the right and the power to become children of God to those who received Him. He gave this to those who put their trust in His name. ¹³These children of God were not born of blood and of flesh and of man's desires, but they were born of God. ¹⁴Christ became human flesh and lived among us. We saw His shining greatness. This greatness is given only to a much-loved Son from His Father. He was full of loving-favor and truth.

John The Baptist Makes The Way Ready For Jesus Christ
[Matthew 3:1-12; Mark 1:1-8; Luke 3:1-18]

¹⁵John told about Christ and said, "I have been telling you about this One. I said, 'He is coming after me. He is more important than I because He lived before me.'" ¹⁶From Him Who has so much we have all received loving-favor, one loving-favor after another. ¹⁷The Law was given through Moses, but loving-favor and truth came through Jesus Christ. ¹⁸The much-loved Son

is beside the Father. No man has ever seen God. But Christ has made God known to us.

¹⁹The Jews sent their religious leaders and men from the family group of Levi to ask John, "Who are you?" ²⁰He told them without holding back any words, "I am not the Christ!" ²¹They asked him, "Then who are you? Are you Elijah?" He said, "I am not!" Then they asked, "Are you the special One Who was to come to speak for God?" John said, "No." ²²Then they asked him, "Who are you? We must tell those who sent us. What do you say about yourself?"

²³John said, "I am the voice of one crying in the desert. 'Make the road straight for the Lord,' as the early preacher Isaiah said." (Isaiah 40:3)

²⁴Those who had been sent were from the proud religious law-keepers. ²⁵They asked John again, "Then why do you baptize if you are not the Christ or Elijah or that special One Who was to come to speak for God?" ²⁶John answered, "I baptize with water. But there is One standing among you Whom you do not know. ²⁷He is the One Who is coming after me. I am not good enough to get down and help Him take off His shoes." ²⁸All this happened when John was baptizing in the town of Bethany. He was on the other side of the Jordan River.

The Baptism Of Jesus [*Matthew 3:13-17; Mark 1:9-11; Luke 3:21-22*]

²⁹The next day John the Baptist saw Jesus coming to him. He said, "Look! The Lamb of God Who takes away the sin of the world! ³⁰I have been talking about Him. I said, 'One is coming after me Who is more important than I, because He lived before I was born.' ³¹I have not known Jesus but I have come to baptize with water so the Jews might know about Him."

³²Then John said, "I saw the Holy Spirit come down on Jesus as a dove from heaven. The Holy Spirit stayed on Him. ³³I did not know Him then. But God sent me to baptize with water. God said to me, 'The Holy Spirit will come down and stay on Him. He is the One Who baptizes with the Holy Spirit.' ³⁴I saw this happen. I am now saying that Jesus is the Son of God."

Jesus Calls Andrew And Peter

[35]The next day John the Baptist was standing with two of his own followers. [36]Jesus walked by. John looked at Him and said, "Look! The Lamb of God." [37]John's two followers heard him say this and followed Jesus.

[38]Jesus turned around and saw them following. He said to them, "What are you looking for?" They answered, "Teacher, where are you staying?" [39]He said to them, "Come and see." They followed Him and saw where He lived. They stayed with Him that day. It was about four o'clock in the afternoon.

[40]Andrew, Simon Peter's brother, was one of the two who had heard John's words and had followed Jesus. [41]The first thing he did was to find his brother Simon. He said to him, "We have found the Christ!" [42]Andrew took Simon to Jesus. When Jesus saw Simon, He said, "You are Simon, the son of John. Your name will be Cephas." The name Cephas means Peter, or a rock.

Jesus Calls Philip And Nathanael

[43]The next day Jesus wanted to go into the country of Galilee. He found Philip and said to him, "Follow Me." [44]Philip was from the town of Bethsaida. Andrew and Peter were from this town also. [45]Philip found Nathanael and said to him, "We have found the One Moses wrote about in the Law. He is the One the early preachers wrote about. He is Jesus of Nazareth, the Son of Joseph." [46]Nathanael said, "Can anything good come out of the town of Nazareth?" Philip said, "Come and see."

[47]Jesus saw Nathanael coming to Him and said, "Look! There is a true Jew. There is nothing false in him." [48]Nathanael said to Jesus, "How do You know me?" Jesus answered him, "Before Philip talked to you, I saw you under the fig tree." [49]Nathanael said to Him, "Teacher, You are the Son of God. You are the King of the Jews." [50]Jesus said to him, "Do you believe because I said I saw you under the fig tree? You will see greater things than that. [51]For sure, I tell you, you will see heaven opened and God's angels going up and coming down on the Son of Man."

The Powerful Work At The Wedding In The Town Of Cana

2 Three days later there was a wedding in the town of Cana in the country of Galilee. The mother of Jesus was there. ²Jesus and His followers were asked to come to the wedding. ³When the wine was all gone, the mother of Jesus said to Him, "They have no more wine." ⁴Jesus said to her, "Woman, what is that to you and to Me? It is not time for Me to work yet." ⁵His mother said to the helpers, "Do whatever He says."

⁶Six stone water jars were there. Each one held about one-half barrel of water. These water jars were used in the Jewish worship of washing. ⁷Jesus said to the helpers, "Fill the jars with water." They filled them to the top. ⁸Then He said, "Take some out and give it to the head man who is caring for the people." They took some to him. ⁹The head man tasted the water that had become wine. He did not know where it came from but the helpers who took it to him knew. He called the man who had just been married. ¹⁰The head man said to him, "Everyone puts out his best wine first. After people have had much to drink, he puts out the wine that is not so good. You have kept the good wine until now!"

¹¹This was the first powerful work Jesus did. It was done in the town of Cana in the country of Galilee where He showed His power. His followers put their trust in Him. ¹²After this He went down to the city of Capernaum. His mother and brothers and followers went with Him. They stayed there a few days.

Jesus Stops The Buying And The Selling In The House Of God
[Matthew 21:12-17; Mark 11:15-19; Luke 19:45-48]

¹³It was time for the special religious gathering to remember how the Jews left Egypt. Jesus went up to Jerusalem. ¹⁴He went into the house of God and found cattle and sheep and doves being sold. Men were sitting there changing money. ¹⁵Jesus made a whip of small ropes. He used it to make them all leave the house of God along with the sheep and cattle. He pushed their money off the tables and turned the tables over. ¹⁶He said to those who sold doves, "Take these things out of here! You must not make My Father's house a place for buying and selling!" ¹⁷Then His followers remembered that it was written in the Holy Writings, "I am jealous for the honor of Your house." (Psalm 69:9)

The Jews Ask For Something Special To See

¹⁸Then the Jews asked Him, "What can You do to show us You have the right and the power to do these things?" ¹⁹Jesus answered them, "Destroy this house of God and in three days I will build it again." ²⁰Then the Jews said, "It took forty-six years to build this house of God. Will You build it up in three days?" ²¹Jesus was speaking about His body as the house of God. ²²After Jesus had been raised from the dead, His followers remembered He said this. They believed the Holy Writings and what He had said.

²³Jesus was in Jerusalem at the time of the special religious gathering to remember how the Jews left Egypt. Many people put their trust in Him when they saw the powerful works He did. ²⁴But Jesus did not trust them because He knew all men. ²⁵He did not need anyone to tell Him about man. He knew what was in man.

Nicodemus Asks Jesus About Life

3 There was a man named Nicodemus. He was a proud religious law-keeper and a leader of the Jews. ²He came to Jesus at night and said, "Teacher, we know You have come from God to teach us. No one can do these powerful works You do unless God is with Him."

Jesus Tells Of The New Kind Of Birth

³Jesus said to him, "For sure, I tell you, unless a man is born again, he cannot see the holy nation of God." ⁴Nicodemus said to Him, "How can a man be born when he is old? How can he get into his mother's body and be born the second time?" ⁵Jesus answered, "For sure, I tell you, unless a man is born of water and of the Spirit of God, he cannot get into the holy nation of God. ⁶Whatever is born of the flesh is flesh. Whatever is born of the Spirit is spirit.

Unless a man is born again, he cannot see the holy nation of God.

⁷"Do not be surprised that I said to you, 'You must be born again.' ⁸The wind blows where it wants to and you hear its sound.

You do not know where it comes from or where it goes. It is the same with everyone who is born of the Spirit of God."

⁹Nicodemus said to Him, "How can this be?" ¹⁰Jesus said, "Are you a teacher among the Jews and do not know these things? ¹¹For sure, I tell you, We are talking about things We know. We tell of what We have seen. Yet you do not take Our words to be true. ¹²I tell you about things of the earth and you do not believe them. How will you believe if I tell you things about heaven?

¹³"No one has gone up into heaven except the One Who came down from heaven. That One is the Son of Man*Who is in heaven. ¹⁴As Moses lifted up the snake in the desert, so the Son of Man must be lifted up. ¹⁵Then whoever puts his trust in Him will have life that lasts forever. ¹⁶For God so loved the world that He gave His only Son. Whoever puts his trust in God's Son will not be lost but will have life that lasts forever. ¹⁷For God did not send His Son into the world to say it is guilty. He sent His Son so the world might be saved from the punishment of sin by Him. ¹⁸Whoever puts his trust in His Son is not guilty. Whoever does not put his trust in Him is guilty already. It is because he does not put his trust in the name of the only Son of God.

> For God
> so loved the world
> that He gave
> His only Son.

¹⁹"The Light has come into the world. And the Light is the test by which men are guilty or not. People love darkness more than the Light because the things they do are sinful. ²⁰Everyone who sins hates the Light. He stays away from the Light because his sin would be found out. ²¹The man who does what is right comes to the Light. What he does will be seen because he has done what God wanted him to do."

Jesus Preaches In The Country Of Judea

²²After this, Jesus and His followers came into the country of Judea. He stayed with them there and baptized people.

John The Baptist Tells More About Jesus

²³John was baptizing in the town of Aenon near Salim. There was much water there and people were coming to be baptized. ²⁴John had not been put into prison yet.

25Then some of the followers of John and a Jew started to argue about the religious washing of the Jewish worship. 26They came to John and said to him, "Teacher, the One with you on the other side of the Jordan River is baptizing also. He is the One you told of. Everyone is going to Him."

27John said, "A man can receive nothing unless it has been given to him from heaven. 28You heard the words that I said, 'I am not the Christ, but I have been sent before Him.' 29The man who has just been married has the bride. The friend of the man just married stands at his side and listens to him. He has joy when he hears the voice of the man just married. I am full of this joy. 30He must become more important. I must become less important.

31"He Who comes from above is above all. He who comes from the earth is of the earth and speaks of the earth. He Who comes from heaven is above all. 32He tells of what He has seen and heard. But no one believes what He says. 33Whoever receives His words proves that God is true. 34He was sent by God and He speaks God's Word. God gives Him all of His Spirit. 35The Father loves the Son and has given all things into His hand. 36He who puts his trust in the Son has life that lasts forever. He who does not put his trust in the Son will not have life, but the anger of God is on him."

A Woman Of Samaria At The Well

4 Jesus knew the proud religious law-keepers had heard He was making and baptizing more followers than John. 2Jesus did not baptize anyone Himself but His followers did. 3Then Jesus went from the country of Judea to the country of Galilee. 4He had to go through the country of Samaria. 5So He came to a town in Samaria called Sycar. It was near the piece of ground that Jacob gave to his son Joseph. 6Jacob's well was there. Jesus was tired from traveling so He sat down just as He was by the well. It was about noon.

7A woman of Samaria came to get water. Jesus said to her, "Give me a drink." 8His followers had gone into the town to buy food. 9The woman of Samaria said to Him, "You are a Jew. I am

of Samaria. Why do You ask me for a drink when the Jews have
nothing to do with the people of Samaria?''

¹⁰Jesus said to her, "You do not know what God has to give.
You do not know Who said to you, 'Give Me a drink.' If you knew,
you would have asked Him. He would have given you living
water." ¹¹The woman said to Him, "Sir, the well is deep. You have
nothing to get water with. Where will you get the living water?
¹²Are You greater than our early father Jacob? He gave us the
well. He and his children and his cattle drank from it.''

Jesus Tells Of The Living Water

¹³Jesus said to her, "Whoever drinks this water will be thirsty
again. ¹⁴Whoever drinks the water that I will give him will never
be thirsty. The water that I will give him will become in him a well
of life that lasts forever.''

¹⁵The woman said, "Sir, give me this water so I will never be
thirsty. Then I will not have to come all this way for water. '

The True Kind Of Worship

¹⁶Jesus said to her, "Go call your husband and come back.''
¹⁷The woman said, "I have no husband." Jesus said, "You told
the truth when you said, 'I have no husband.' ¹⁸You have had five
husbands. The one you have now is not your husband. You told
the truth.''

¹⁹The woman said to Him, "Sir, I think You are a person Who
speaks for God. ²⁰Our early fathers worshiped on this mountain.
You Jews say Jerusalem is the place where men should worship.''

²¹Jesus said to her, "Woman, believe Me. The time is coming
when you will not worship the Father on this mountain or in
Jerusalem. ²²You people do not know what you worship. We Jews
know what we worship. It is through the Jews that men are saved
from the punishment of their sins. ²³The time is coming, yes, it is
here now, when the true worshipers will worship the Father in
spirit and in truth. The Father wants that kind of worshipers.
²⁴God is Spirit. Those who worship Him must worship Him in
spirit and in truth.''

Whoever drinks
the water
that I will give him
will never be thirsty.

Jesus Is The One The Jews Are Looking For

²⁵The woman said to Him, "I know the Jews are looking for One Who is coming. He is called the Christ. When He comes, He will tell us everything." ²⁶Jesus said to her, "I am the Christ, the One talking with you!"

²⁷Right then the followers came back and were surprised and wondered about finding Him talking with a woman. But no one said, "What do You want?" or, "Why are You talking with her?"

²⁸The woman left her water jar and went into the town. She said to the men, ²⁹"Come and see a Man Who told me everything I ever did! Can this be the Christ?" ³⁰They went out of town and came to Him.

Jesus Tells Them Of A New Kind Of Food

Open your eyes and look at the fields. They are white now and waiting for the grain to be gathered in.

³¹During this time His followers were saying to Him, "Teacher, eat something." ³²He said, "I have food to eat that you do not know of." ³³The followers said to each other, "Has someone taken food to Him?" ³⁴Jesus said, "My food is to do what God wants Me to do and to finish His work. ³⁵Do you not say, 'It is four months yet until the time to gather grain?' Listen! I say to you, open your eyes and look at the fields. They are white now and waiting for the grain to be gathered in. ³⁶The one who gathers gets his pay. He gathers fruit that lasts forever. The one who plants and the one who gathers will have joy together. ³⁷These words are true, 'One man plants and another man gathers.' ³⁸I sent you to gather where you have not planted. Others have planted and you have come along to gather in their fruit."

The People In The Country of Samaria Believe In Jesus

³⁹Many people in that town of Samaria believed in Jesus because of what the woman said about Him. She said, "He told me everything I ever did." ⁴⁰So the people of Samaria came to Him. They asked Him to stay with them. Jesus stayed there two days. ⁴¹Many more people believed because of what He said. ⁴²They said to the woman, "Now we believe! It is no longer because of what you said about Jesus but we have heard Him

ourselves. We know, for sure, that He is the Christ, the One Who saves men of this world from the punishment of their sins.'

Jesus Goes To Galilee

⁴³Two days later He went from there and came to the country of Galilee. ⁴⁴Jesus Himself said that no one who speaks for God is respected in his own country. ⁴⁵When He came to Galilee, the people there were glad. They had seen all the things He did in Jerusalem. It was at the time of the special religious gathering to remember how the Jews left Egypt. They had been there also.

Jesus Heals The Dying Boy In The City Of Capernaum

⁴⁶Jesus came again to the town of Cana in the country of Galilee where He had made water into wine. A man who worked with the king had a son who was sick in the city of Capernaum. ⁴⁷This man went to Jesus. He had heard that Jesus had come from the country of Judea to Galilee. The man asked Jesus if He would go to Capernaum and heal his son who was dying. ⁴⁸Then Jesus said to him, "Unless you see special things and powerful works done, you will not believe." ⁴⁹The man said to Him, "Sir, come with me before my son dies." ⁵⁰Jesus said to him, "Go your way. Your son will live." The man put his trust in what Jesus said and left.

⁵¹As he was on his way home, the workmen he owned met him. They said to him, "Your son is living!" ⁵²He asked them what time his boy began to get well. They said to him, "Yesterday at one o'clock the sickness left." ⁵³The father knew it was the time Jesus had said to him, "Your son will live." He and everyone in his house put their trust in Jesus. ⁵⁴This was the second powerful work that Jesus did after He came from the country of Judea to the country of Galilee.

Jesus Heals The Man At The Pool Of Bethesda

5 Some time later, there was a religious gathering of the Jews. Jesus went up to Jerusalem. ²In Jerusalem there is a pool with five porches called Bethesda near the sheep gate. ³Inside these porches lay many sick people. Some were blind. Some could

not walk. Some could not move their bodies. 4*An angel of the Lord came at certain times and made the water move. All of them were waiting for it to move. Whoever got into the water first after it was moving was healed of whatever sickness he had.

5A man was there who had been sick for thirty-eight years. 6Jesus saw him lying there and knew the man had been sick a long time. Jesus said to him, "Would you like to be healed?" 7The sick man said, "Sir, I have no one to put me into the pool when the water is moving. While I am coming, another one gets in first." 8Jesus said to him, "Get up! Pick up your bed and walk." 9At once the man was healed and picked up his bed and walked. This happened on the Day of Rest.

10The Jews said to the man who had been healed, "This is the Day of Rest. It is against the Law for you to carry your bed." 11He said to them, "The Man Who healed me said to me, 'Pick up your bed and walk.' " 12Then the Jews asked him, "What man said to you, 'Pick up your bed and walk?' " 13The man who had been healed did not know Who He was. Jesus had gone away while many people were there.

14Later Jesus found the man who had been healed in the house of God. He said to him, "Listen! You have been healed. Stop sinning or something worse will come to you." 15The man went away and told the Jews that it was Jesus Who had healed him.

The Jews Want To Kill Jesus

16Because Jesus did these things on the Day of Rest, the Jews made it very hard for Him. 17Jesus said to them, "My Father is still working all the time so I am working also." 18The Jews tried all the more to kill Him, not only because He had worked on the Day of Rest, but because He had also called God His Own Father. This made Him the same as God.

Jesus Tells How He Works

19Then Jesus said to them, "For sure, I tell you, the Son can do nothing by Himself. He does what He sees the Father doing. Whatever the Father does, the Son does also. 20The Father loves the Son and shows the Son everything He does. The Father will show Him greater works than these. They will surprise you. ²¹The Father raises up the dead and makes them live. The Son also gives life to anyone He chooses. ²²The Father does not say who is guilty. He gives this to the Son to do. ²³He does this so that all men will honor the Son as they honor the Father. He who does not honor the Son does not honor the Father Who sent Him.

²⁴"For sure, I tell you, anyone who hears My Word and puts his trust in Him Who sent Me has life that lasts forever. He will not be guilty. He has already passed from death into life.

The Good People And The Sinful People Are Raised From The Dead

²⁵"For sure, I tell you, the time is coming. Yes, the time is here when the dead will hear the voice of the Son of God. Those who hear will live. ²⁶The Father has life in Himself. He has given power to the Son to have life in Himself. ²⁷God has given Him the right and the power to say if people are guilty, because He is the Son of Man. ²⁸Do not be surprised at this. The time is coming when all who are in their graves will hear His voice. ²⁹They will come out. Those who have done good will be raised again and will have new life. Those who have been sinful will be raised again and will be told they are guilty and will be punished.

Jesus Tells Of John And Of Himself

³⁰"I can do nothing by Myself. I say who is guilty only as My Father tells Me. That way, what I say is right, because I am not trying to do what I want to do. I am doing what the Father, Who sent Me, wants Me to do. ³¹If I tell about Myself, My words are worth nothing. ³²There is another One Who tells about Me. I know the words He says about Me are true.

³³"You sent to John the Baptist and he told you the truth. ³⁴I do not need words from men to say I am right. I say this that you might be saved from the punishment of sin. ³⁵John the Baptist was a burning and shining light. You were willing for awhile to be glad in his light. ³⁶I have something greater than John which tells of Me. I am doing works the Father has given Me to do and they are proving that the Father has sent Me. ³⁷The Father has told of

Anyone
who hears My Word
and puts his trust
in Him Who sent Me
has life
that lasts forever.

Me and has sent Me. You have never heard His voice. You have never seen Him. 38You do not have His word living in your hearts because you do not put your trust in the One He sent.

39"You do read the Holy Writings. You think you have life that lasts forever just because you read them. They do tell of Me. 40But you do not want to come to Me so you might have life. 41I do not take any honor from men. 42I know you and you do not have the love of God in your hearts. 43I have come in the name of My Father. You do not receive Me. If another person comes in his own name, you will receive him. 44How can you believe when you are always wanting honor from each other. And yet you do not look for the honor that comes from the only God.

45"Do not think that I will tell the Father you are guilty. The one who says you are guilty is Moses. You trust him. 46If you had believed Moses, you would believe Me. For Moses wrote about Me. 47If you do not believe what he wrote, how will you believe My Words?"

The Feeding Of The Five Thousand [Matthew 14:13-21; Mark 6:30-44; Luke 9:10-17]

6 After this Jesus went over to the other side of the lake of Galilee. It is sometimes called the lake of Tiberias. 2Many people followed Him. They saw the powerful works He did on those who were sick. 3Jesus went up on a mountain and sat down with His followers. 4The special religious supper to remember how the Jews left Egypt was soon.

5Jesus looked up and saw many people coming to Him. He said to Philip, "Where can we buy bread to feed these people?" 6He said this to see what Philip would say. Jesus knew what He would do. 7Philip said to Him, "The money we have is not enough to buy bread to give each one a little."

8One of His followers was Andrew, Simon Peter's brother. He said to Jesus, 9"There is a boy here who has five loaves of barley bread and two small fish. What is that for so many people?" 10Jesus said, "Have the people sit down." There was much grass in that place. About five thousand men sat down.

[11]Jesus took the loaves and gave thanks. Then He gave the bread to those who were sitting down. The fish were given out the same way. The people had as much as they wanted. [12]When they were filled, Jesus said to His followers, "Gather up the pieces that are left. None will be wasted." [13]The followers gathered the pieces together. Twelve baskets were filled with pieces of barley bread. These were left after all the people had eaten.

[14]The people saw the powerful work Jesus had done. They said, "It is true! This is the One Who speaks for God Who is to come into the world."

Jesus Walks On The Water [Matthew 14:22-33, Mark 6:45-52]

[15]Jesus knew they were about to come and take Him to make Him King, so He went to the mountain by Himself. [16]When evening had come, His followers went down to the lake. [17]They got into a boat and started to cross the lake to go to the city of Capernaum. By this time it was dark. Jesus had not come back to them yet. [18]A strong wind was making high waves on the lake. [19]They were about half way across the lake when they saw Jesus walking on the water. As He got near the boat, they were afraid. [20]But Jesus called to them, "It is I. Do not be afraid." [21]They were glad to take Him into the boat. At once they got to the other side where they wanted to go.

Jesus Teaches Many People

[22]The next day the people on the other side of the lake saw no other boat there but the one His followers had been in. The people knew Jesus had not gone with His followers in the boat because they had gone alone. [23]There were other boats from Tiberias that had come near the place where they had eaten the bread after the Lord had given thanks. [24]The people saw that Jesus and His followers were not there. They got into boats and went to the city of Capernaum looking for Jesus.

[25]The people found Him on the other side of the lake. They said to Him, "Teacher, when did You come here?" [26]Jesus said to them, "For sure, I tell you, you are not looking for Me because of the powerful works. You are looking for Me because you ate bread

and were filled. ²⁷Do not work for food that does not last. Work for food that lasts forever. The Son of Man will give you that kind of food. God the Father has shown He will do this.''

Jesus Teaches About Doing The Work Of God

²⁸Then the people said to Him, ''What are the works God wants us to do?'' ²⁹Jesus said to them, ''This is the work of God, that you put your trust in the One He has sent.'' ³⁰They said to Him, ''Can You show us some powerful work? Then we can see it and believe You. What will You do? ³¹Our early fathers ate bread that came from heaven in the desert. This happened as it is written, 'He gave them bread from heaven to eat.' '' (Exodus 16:15)

Jesus Is The Bread Of Life

³²Then Jesus said to the people, ''For sure, I tell you, it was not Moses that gave you bread from heaven. My Father gives you the true Bread from heaven. ³³The Bread of God is He Who comes down from heaven and gives life to the world.'' ³⁴They said to Him, ''Sir, give us this Bread all the time.''

³⁵Jesus said to them, ''I am the Bread of Life. He who comes to Me will never be hungry. He who puts his trust in Me will never be thirsty. ³⁶I said to you that you have seen Me and yet you do not put your trust in Me. ³⁷All whom My Father has given to Me will come to Me. I will never turn away anyone who comes to Me. ³⁸I came down from heaven. I did not come to do what I wanted to do. I came to do what My Father wanted Me to do. He is the One Who sent Me.

³⁹''The Father sent Me. He did not want Me to lose any of all those He gave Me. He wants Me to raise them to life on the last day. ⁴⁰He wants everyone who sees the Son to put his trust in Him and have life that lasts forever. I will raise that one up on the last day.''

The Jews Do Not Like The Words Of Jesus

⁴¹The Jews talked among themselves against Him. They did not like it because He said, ''I am the Bread that came down from

I am the Bread of Life. He who comes to Me will never be hungry. He who puts his trust in Me will never be thirsty.

heaven.'' ⁴²They asked each other, "Is not this Jesus, the son of Joseph? We know His father and mother. How can He say, 'I came down from heaven'?''

Jesus Keeps On Teaching About The Bread Of Life

⁴³Jesus said to them, "Do not talk among yourselves against Me. ⁴⁴The Father sent Me. No man can come to Me unless the Father gives him the desire to come to Me. Then I will raise him to life on the last day. ⁴⁵The early preachers wrote, 'They will all be taught of God.' (Isaiah 54:13) Everyone who listens to the Father and learns from Him comes to me. ⁴⁶No one has seen the Father. I am the only One Who has seen Him. ⁴⁷For sure, I tell you, he who puts his trust in Me has life that lasts forever. ⁴⁸I am the Bread of Life. ⁴⁹Your early fathers ate bread that came from heaven in the desert. They died. ⁵⁰But this is the Bread that comes down from heaven. The one who eats it never dies. ⁵¹I am the Living Bread that came down from heaven. If anyone eats this Bread, he will live forever. The Bread which I will give is My flesh. I will give this for the life of the world.'' ⁵²The Jews argued among themselves, saying, "How can this Man give us His flesh to eat?''

⁵³Jesus said to them, "For sure, I tell you, unless you eat the flesh of the Son of Man and drink His blood, you do not have life in you. ⁵⁴Whoever eats My flesh and drinks My blood has life that lasts forever. I will raise him up on the last day. ⁵⁵My flesh is true food and My blood is true drink. ⁵⁶Whoever eats My flesh and drinks My blood lives in Me and I live in him. ⁵⁷The living Father sent Me and I live because of Him. In the same way, the one who eats Me will live because of Me. ⁵⁸I am this Bread that came down from heaven. It is not like the bread that your early fathers ate and they died. Whoever eats this Bread will live forever.'' ⁵⁹Jesus said these things in the Jewish place of worship while He was teaching in the city of Capernaum.

The Troubled Followers Leave Jesus

⁶⁰After hearing this, many of His followers said, "This teaching is too hard! Who can listen to it?'' ⁶¹Jesus knew His followers talked against what He had said. He said to them, "Does this trouble you? ⁶²Then what would you say if you saw the Son of Man going up where He was before? ⁶³It is the Spirit that gives

life. The flesh is of no help. The words I speak to you are spirit and life. 64"But some of you do not believe." Jesus knew from the beginning who would not put their trust in Him. He knew who would hand Him over to the leaders of the country. 65He said, "That is why I told you no one can come to Me unless the Father allows it." 66From that time on, many of His followers turned back to their old ways of living. They would not go along with Him after that.

Peter Knows Who Jesus Is

67Then Jesus said to the twelve followers, "Will you leave Me also?" 68Simon Peter said to Him, "Lord, who else can we go to? You have words that give life that lasts forever. 69We believe and know You are the Christ. You are the Son of the Living God." 70Jesus said to them, "I chose you twelve as My followers. And one of you is a devil." 71He was speaking of Judas Iscariot, Simon's son, who was one of the twelve followers. He was ready to hand Jesus over to the leaders of the country.

You have words that give life that lasts forever.

The Brothers Of Jesus Argue With Him

7 Jesus did not stay in the country of Judea because the Jews were trying to kill Him. After this He went from place to place in the country of Galilee. 2A religious gathering of the Jews was near. This gathering was called the Supper of Tents. 3The brothers of Jesus said to Him, "Leave here and go to the country of Judea. Let your followers there see the things You do. 4If a person wants others to know what he is doing, he does things to be seen. Since You are doing such things, show Yourself to the world." 5Not even His brothers were putting their trust in Him.

6Jesus said to them, "My time has not yet come. But any time is good for you. 7The world cannot hate you but it hates Me. I speak against the world because of its sinful works. 8You go to the religious gathering. I am not going yet. My time has not yet come."

9Jesus told His brothers this and then stayed in the country of Galilee. 10His brothers went to the religious gathering. He went later by Himself so He would not be seen there.

The Jews Look For Jesus

[11]At the religious gathering the Jews were looking for Jesus. They were saying, "Where is He?" [12]There was much talk among the people about Him. Some said, "He is a good Man." Others said, "No, He leads the people in the wrong way." [13]No one spoke about Him in front of other people. They were afraid of the Jews.

Jesus Tells Where His Teaching Is From

[14]The religious gathering was half over when Jesus went to the house of God and taught. [15]The Jews were surprised and wondered, saying, "How can this Man know so much when He has never been to school?"

[16]Jesus said to them, "What I teach is not Mine. It is from God Who sent Me. [17]If anyone will do what God wants, he will know if My teaching is from God, or if I am speaking of Myself. [18]The man who speaks of himself is looking for greatness for himself. But He Who is looking for the greatness of the One Who sent Him is true. There is nothing false in Him. [19]Did not Moses give you the Law? And yet not one of you keeps the Law. Why do you try to kill me?"

[20]The people said, "You have a demon in You. Who is trying to kill You?"

[21]Jesus said to them, "I did one work and you are surprised. [22]Moses gave you the religious act of becoming a Jew. (Yet it was not from Moses but from the early fathers.) You do this religious act on a man on the Day of Rest. [23]Now if you can do that, why are you angry with Me for healing a man on the Day of Rest? [24]Do not say a person is guilty by what you see. Be sure you know when you say what is right or wrong."

[25]Some of the people of Jerusalem said, "Is not this the Man the Jews want to kill? [26]But look! This Man is speaking out in the open. They are saying nothing to Him. Do the leaders know this is the true Christ? [27]We know where this Man came from. When the Christ comes, no one will know where He comes from."

28Then Jesus spoke with a loud voice as He taught in the house of God. He said, "You know Me. You know where I came from. I have not come on My own. The One Who sent Me is true but you do not know Him. 29I know Him because I am from Him and He sent Me."

30Then they wanted to take Jesus but no one put his hands on Him. His time had not yet come. 31Many of the people believed in Him. They said, "When Christ comes, will He do more powerful works than this Man?"

32The proud religious law-keepers heard the people talking about Jesus. The religious leaders of the Jews and the proud religious law-keepers sent soldiers to take Him. 33Jesus said to them, "I will be with you a little while yet. Then I will go back to Him Who sent Me. 34You will look for Me but you will not find Me. Where I go, you cannot come."

35The Jews said to themselves, "Where can He go that we will not find Him? Will He go to our people who live among the Greeks and teach the Greeks? 36What does He mean when He says, 'You will look for Me but you will not find Me, and where I go, you cannot come'?"

If anyone is thirsty, let him come to Me and drink.

Jesus Promises To Give The Holy Spirit

Rivers of living water will flow from the heart of the one who puts his trust in Me.

37It was the last and great day of the religious gathering. Jesus stood up and spoke with a loud voice, "If anyone is thirsty, let him come to Me and drink. 38The Holy Writings say that rivers of living water will flow from the heart of the one who puts his trust in Me." 39Jesus said this about the Holy Spirit Who would come to those who put their trust in Him. The Holy Spirit had not yet been given. Jesus had not yet been raised to the place of honor.

The People Cannot Make Up Their Minds Who He Is

40When many of the people heard His words, they said, "For sure, this is the One Who speaks for God." 41Others said, "He is the Christ!" Some said, "The Christ would not come from the country of Galilee, would He? 42Do not the Holy Writings say that the Christ will come from the family of David? Will He not come from the town of Bethlehem where David lived?" ⁴³The people were divided in what they thought about Him. ⁴⁴Some of them wanted to take Him. But no one put their hands on Him.

⁴⁵The soldiers came back to the religious leaders of the Jews and to the proud religious law-keepers. They said to the soldiers, "Why did you not bring Him?" ⁴⁶The soldiers answered, "No man has ever spoken like this Man speaks." ⁴⁷The proud religious law-keepers said, "Have you been led the wrong way also? ⁴⁸Has anyone of the leaders or anyone from our group believed in Him? ⁴⁹As for all these people, they do not know the Law. They are guilty and will be punished by God."

⁵⁰(Nicodemus was one of the proud religious law-keepers. He had come to Jesus at another time.) Nicodemus said to them, ⁵¹"Our Law does not say a man is guilty before he has been in court and before we know what he has done." ⁵²They said to him, "Are you from the country of Galilee also? Look into the Word of God yourself. You will see that no one who speaks for God comes from Galilee." ⁵³ *Then everyone went home.

Jesus Speaks To The Teachers Of The Law And The Proud Religious Law-Keepers

8 *(Jesus went to the Mountain of Olives. ²Early in the morning He went back to the house of God and all the people came to Him. He sat down and taught them.

³The teachers of the Law and the proud religious law-keepers came to Him. They brought a woman who had been caught doing a sex sin. They made her stand in front of them all. ⁴Then they said to Jesus, "Teacher, this woman was caught in the act of doing a sex sin. ⁵Moses told us in the Law to throw stones and kill a woman like this. What do You say about it?

⁶They were trying to set a trap to find something against Him. Jesus got down and began to write in the dust with His finger. ⁷They kept on asking Him. Then He stood up and said, "Anyone of you who is without sin can throw the first stone at her." ⁸Again He got down and wrote in the dust. ⁹When they

heard what He said, they went away one by one, beginning with the older ones until they were all gone. Then Jesus was left alone with the woman.

[10]Jesus stood up and said to her, "Woman, where are those who spoke against you? Has no man said you are guilty?" [11]She said, "No one, Sir." Jesus said to her, "Neither do I say you are guilty. Go on your way and do not sin again.")

Jesus Teaches About The Light Of The World

[12]Jesus spoke to all the people, saying, "I am the Light of the world. Anyone who follows Me will not walk in darkness. He will have the Light of Life."

[13]The proud religious law-keepers said to Him, "You are talking about Yourself. What You say about Yourself is not true."

[14]Jesus said, "Even if I speak of Myself, what I am saying is true. I know where I came from and where I am going. You do not know where I came from or where I am going. [15]You say as a man would say if people are guilty or not guilty. I am not saying anyone is guilty. [16]But even if I did, it would be true. I am not alone. The Father Who sent Me is with Me. [17]It is written in your Law that when two men agree about something, it proves it is true. (Deuteronomy 19:15) [18]I speak for Myself and the Father Who sent Me speaks for Me."

[19]The proud religious law-keepers asked Him, "Where is Your Father?" Jesus said, "You do not know Me or My Father. If you had known Me, you would have known My Father also."

[20]Jesus spoke these words near the money box while He taught in the house of God. No one put his hands on Jesus because His time had not yet come.

Jesus Tells Of His Going Away

[21]Jesus spoke to the Jews again, saying, "I am going away. You will look for Me but you will die in your sins. Where I am going, you cannot come." [22]The Jews said, "Will He kill Himself because He said, 'Where I am going you cannot come'?"

²³He answered them, "You are from below. I am from above. You are of this world. I am not of this world. ²⁴That is why I said that you will die in your sins. If you do not believe that I am the Christ, you will die in your sins."

²⁵Then they said to Him, "Who are You?" Jesus answered, "The answer is the same as I told you from the beginning. ²⁶I have much to say about you. I must say if you are guilty. But He Who sent Me is true. I tell the world the things I have heard from Him."

²⁷They did not understand that Jesus was speaking to them about the Father. ²⁸Jesus said to them, "When you have lifted up the Son of Man, you will know that I am the Christ. I do nothing of Myself. I say these things as My Father has taught Me. ²⁹He that sent Me is with Me. The Father has not left Me alone. I always do what He wants Me to do." ³⁰As Jesus said these things, many people put their trust in Him. ³¹He said to the Jews who believed, "If you keep and obey My Word, then you are My followers for sure. ³²You will know the truth and the truth will make you free."

You will know the truth and the truth will make you free.

Jesus Teaches What It Means To Be Free

³³They said to Jesus, "We are children of Abraham. We have never been owned by anyone. What do you mean when You say, 'You will be free'?" ³⁴Jesus answered them, "For sure, I tell you, everyone who sins is like the man who is owned by someone and has to work without pay. Sin has a hold on him. ³⁵A man who has to work without pay does not belong in the house. But a son does belong in the house. ³⁶So if the Son makes you free, you will be free for sure.

So if the Son makes you free, you will be free for sure.

Jesus Asks The Jews About Their Father

³⁷"I know that you are the children of Abraham. But you want to kill Me because My Word is not in your hearts. ³⁸I speak of what I saw when I was with My Father. You do what you have seen your father do."

³⁹They said to Him, "Abraham is our father." Jesus said, "If you were children of Abraham, you would do what he did. ⁴⁰I am a

Man Who has told you the truth as I heard it from God. Now you are trying to kill Me. Abraham never did anything like that. ⁴¹You are doing the works of your father.'' They said to Him, ''We were born of parents who were faithful in marriage. We have one Father. He is God.''

⁴²Jesus said to them, ''If God were your father, you would love Me. I came from God. I did not come on My own, but God sent Me. ⁴³Why do you not understand what I say? It is because you do not want to hear My teaching. ⁴⁴The devil is your father. You are from him. You want to do the sinful things your father, the devil, wants you to do. He has been a killer from the beginning. The devil has nothing to do with the truth. There is no truth in him. It is expected of the devil to lie, for he is a liar and the father of lies. ⁴⁵I tell you the truth and that is why you do not put your trust in Me. ⁴⁶Which one of you can say I am guilty of sin? If I tell you the truth, why do you not believe Me? ⁴⁷Whoever is born of God listens to God's Word. You do not hear His Word because you are not born of God.''

The Jews Say Jesus Has A Demon

⁴⁸The Jews said to Jesus, ''Are we not right when we say You are from the country of Samaria, and You have a demon?'' ⁴⁹Jesus said, ''No, I do not have a demon. I honor My Father. You do not honor Me. ⁵⁰I am not looking for honor for Myself. There is One Who is looking for it. He says what is right from wrong. ⁵¹For sure, I tell you, if anyone keeps My Word, that one will never die.''

⁵²Then the Jews said to Him, ''Now we know You have a demon. Abraham died. The early preachers died. You say, 'If anyone keeps My Word, that one will never die.' ⁵³Are you greater than our father Abraham? He died and the early preachers died. Who do You think You are?'' ⁵⁴Jesus said, ''If I honor Myself, My honor would be worth nothing. My Father honors Me. You say He is your God. ⁵⁵You have never known Him, but I know Him. If I said I did not know Him, I would be a liar like you. But I do know the Father and obey His Word. ⁵⁶Your father Abraham was glad that he was to see My coming. He saw it and was happy.''

[57]The Jews said to Jesus, "You are not even fifty years old. How could you have seen Abraham?" [58]Jesus said to them, "For sure, I tell you, before Abraham was born, I was and am and always will be!"

[59]Then they picked up stones to throw at Him. *Jesus hid Himself and left the house of God.

Jesus Heals A Man Who Was Born Blind

9 As Jesus went on His way, He saw a man who had been born blind. [2]His followers asked Him, "Teacher, whose sin made this man to be born blind? Was it the sin of this man or the sin of his parents?" [3]Jesus answered, "The sin of this man or the sin of his parents did not make him to be born blind. He was born blind so the work of God would be seen in him. [4]We must keep on doing the work of Him Who sent Me while it is day. Night is coming when no man can work. [5]While I am in the world, I am the Light of the world."

[6]After Jesus had said this, He spit on the ground. He mixed it with dust and put that mud on the eyes of the blind man. [7]Then Jesus said to him, "Go and wash in the pool of Siloam." (Siloam means Sent.) The man went away and washed. When he came back, he could see.

[8]Neighbors and others had seen him begging. They said, "Is not this the man who sat and begged?" [9]Some said, "This is the one." Others said, "No, but he looks like him." But the man who had been blind said, "I am the man." [10]They said to him, "How were your eyes opened?" [11]He answered, "A Man called Jesus made mud and put it on my eyes. Then He said to me, 'Go and wash in the pool of Siloam.' I went and washed and I can see." [12]Then they asked him, "Where is He?" He answered, "I do not know."

The Proud Religious Law-Keepers Are Troubled About This Healing

[13]They took the man who had been born blind to the proud religious law-keepers. [14]It was the Day of Rest when Jesus had made mud and opened his eyes. [15]Again the proud religious law-

keepers asked the man who had been born blind how he had been made to see. He answered them, "Jesus put mud on my eyes. I washed and now I see!" [16]Some of the proud religious law-keepers said, "The Man Who did this is not from God because He worked on the Day of Rest." Others said, "How can a sinful man do powerful works?" They could not agree about Jesus. [17]They spoke again to the blind man, saying, "What do you say about Him since He opened your eyes?" He answered, "He is One Who speaks for God."

[18]The Jews did not believe this man had been blind and had been made to see. They called his parents [19]and asked them, "Is this your son? Do you say he was born blind? How does he see now?" [20]They answered, "We know this is our son and we know he was born blind. [21]But we do not know how it is that he can see now. We do not know who opened his eyes. He is old enough, ask him. He can tell you himself." [22]His parents said this because they were afraid of the Jews. The Jews had talked among themselves. They had agreed that the person who said that Jesus was the Christ would be put out of the Jewish place of worship. [23]That is why his parents said, "He is old enough, ask him."

[24]The proud religious law-keepers asked the man again, who had been blind, to come. They said to him, "Give thanks to God. We know this man is a sinner." [25]The man who had been blind said to them, "I do not know if He is a sinner or not. One thing I know. I was blind, but now I can see." [26]They asked him again, "What did He do to you? How did He open your eyes?" [27]He answered, "I have told you already. You did not listen. Why do you want to hear it again? Do you want to become His followers also?"

[28]The proud religious law-keepers became angry at him and said, "You are a follower of Jesus. We are followers of Moses. [29]We know God spoke to Moses. We do not know where this Man is from." [30]The man said to them, "This is strange! You do not know where He came from and yet He opened my eyes. [31]We know that God does not listen to sinners. We know if anyone loves and worships God, and does what He wants, God listens to him. [32]From the beginning of the world no one has ever heard of anyone opening the eyes of a man born blind. [33]If this

Man were not from God, He would not be able to do anything like this.''

³⁴"They said to him, "You were born in sin. Are you trying to teach us?'' Then they put him out of the place of worship.

Jesus Speaks Sharp Words To The Proud Religious Law-Keepers

³⁵Jesus heard that the proud religious law-keepers had put the man who had been healed out of the place of worship. He found the man and said to him, "Do you put your trust in the Son of God?'' ³⁶He said, "Who is He, Sir? Tell me so that I can put my trust in Him.'' ³⁷Jesus said to him, "You have seen Him. He is talking with you.'' ³⁸He said, "I do put my trust in You, Lord.'' Then he got down in front of Jesus and worshiped Him.

³⁹Jesus said, "I came into this world to say what is right from wrong. I came so those who do not see might see, and those who do see might be made blind.'' ⁴⁰Some of the proud religious law-keepers who were with Him heard this. They said to Him, "Are we blind also?'' ⁴¹Jesus said to them, "If you were blind, you would not be guilty of sin. But because you say, 'We see' you still are guilty of your sin.

The Shepherd And The Door

10 "For sure, I tell you, the man who goes into the sheep-pen some other way than through the door is one who steals and robs. ²The shepherd of the sheep goes in through the door. ³The one who watches the door opens it for him. The sheep listen to the voice of the shepherd. He calls his own sheep by name and he leads them out. ⁴When the shepherd walks ahead of them, they follow him because they know his voice. ⁵They will not follow someone they do not know because they do not know his voice. They will run away from him.'' ⁶Jesus told this picture-story to them. Yet they did not understand what He said.

Jesus Is The Door

⁷Again Jesus said to them, "For sure, I tell you, I am the Door of the sheep. ⁸All others who came ahead of Me are men who steal

and rob. The sheep did not obey them. ⁹I am the Door. Anyone who goes in through Me will be saved from the punishment of sin. He will go in and out and find food. ¹⁰The robber comes only to steal and to kill and to destroy. I came so they might have life, a great full life.

Jesus Teaches About The Good Shepherd

I am the Good Shepherd.

¹¹"I am the Good Shepherd. The Good Shepherd gives His life for the sheep. ¹²One who is hired to watch the sheep is not the shepherd. He does not own the sheep. He sees the wolf coming and leaves the sheep. He runs away while the wolf gets the sheep and makes them run everywhere. ¹³The hired man runs away because he is hired. He does not care about the sheep.

¹⁴"I am the Good Shepherd. I know My sheep and My sheep know Me. ¹⁵I know My Father as My Father knows Me. I give My life for the sheep. ¹⁶I have other sheep which are not from this sheep pen. I must bring them also. They will listen to My voice. Then there will be one flock with one shepherd.

¹⁷"For this reason My Father loves Me. It is because I give My life that I might take it back again. ¹⁸No one takes my life from Me. I give it by Myself. I have the right and the power to take it back again. My Father has given Me this right and power.

¹⁹Because of what He said, the Jews did not agree in their thinking. ²⁰Many of them said, "He has a demon and is crazy. Why listen to Him?" ²¹Others said, "A man who has a demon does not talk this way. Can a demon open the eyes of a blind man?"

Jesus Tells Who He Is

²²It was time for the religious gathering of remembering how the house of God was opened in Jerusalem. ²³It was winter and Jesus was there. He was walking in Solomon's porch in the house of God. ²⁴The Jews gathered around Him. They said, "How long are You going to keep us in doubt? If You are the Christ, tell us."

²⁵Jesus answered, "I told you and you do not believe. The works I do in My Father's name speak of Me. ²⁶You do not

believe because you are not My sheep. ²⁷My sheep hear My voice and I know them. They follow Me. ²⁸I give them life that lasts forever. They will never be punished. No one is able to take them out of My hand. ²⁹My Father Who gave them to Me is greater than all. No one is able to take them out of My Father's hand. ³⁰My Father and I are one!''

Jesus Talks To Angry Men

³¹Again the Jews picked up stones to throw at Him. ³²Jesus said to them, ''Many good things have I shown you from My Father. For which of these things are you going to throw stones at Me?'' ³³They said, ''We are not going to throw stones at You for any good work. It is because of the way You talk against God. It is because You make Yourself to be God when You are only a man.'' ³⁴Jesus said to them, ''Is it not written in your Law, 'I said, you are gods'? (Psalm 82:6) ³⁵The Holy Writings were given to them and God called them gods. (The Word of God cannot be put aside.) ³⁶But God has set Me apart for Himself. He sent Me into the world. Then how can you say that I am speaking against God because I said, 'I am the Son of God'? ³⁷If I am not doing the works of My Father, do not believe Me. ³⁸But if I do them, even if you do not believe Me, believe the works that I do. Then you will know the Father is in Me and I am in Him.'' ³⁹They tried again to take Him but He got out of their hands.

Jesus Goes To The Other Side Of The Jordan River

⁴⁰Jesus went away to the other side of the Jordan River to the place where John was baptizing people. Jesus stayed there. ⁴¹Many people came to Him and said, ''John did no powerful work, but what John said about this Man is true.'' ⁴²Many people put their trust in Jesus there.

Many people put their trust in Jesus there.

Jesus Hears About Lazarus

11 A man named Lazarus was sick. He lived in the town of Bethany with his sisters, Mary and Martha. ²This was the Mary who put perfume on the Lord and dried His feet with her hair. It was her brother Lazarus who was sick. ³The sisters sent word to Jesus, saying, "Lord, your friend is sick!" When Jesus heard this, He said, "This sickness will not end in death. It has happened so that it will bring honor to God. And the Son of God will be honored by it also."

Jesus Tells Of The Death Of Lazarus

5Jesus loved Martha and her sister and Lazarus. 6But when He heard that Lazarus was sick, He stayed where He was two more days. 7Then He said to His followers, "Let us go into the country of Judea again." 8The followers said to Him, "Teacher, the Jews tried to throw stones at You to kill You not long ago. Are You going there again?" 9Jesus said, "Are there not twelve hours in the day? If a man walks during the day, he will not fall. He sees the light of this world. 10If a man walks during the night, he will fall. The light is not in him."

11After Jesus had said this, He spoke again and said, "Our friend Lazarus is sleeping. I will go and wake him up." 12The followers said to Him, "If he is sleeping, he will get well." 13But Jesus meant Lazarus was dead. They thought He meant Lazarus was resting in sleep. 14Then Jesus said to them, "Lazarus is dead. 15Because of you I am glad I was not there so that you may believe. Come, let us go to him."

16Thomas, who was called the Twin, said to the other followers, "Let us go also so we may die with Jesus."

Jesus Tells That The Grave Will Not Hold The Dead

17When Jesus got there, He heard that Lazarus had been in the grave four days. 18The town of Bethany was about one-half hour walk from Jerusalem. 19Many Jews had come to Martha and Mary to give words of comfort about their brother.

20Martha heard that Jesus was coming and went to meet Him. Mary stayed in the house. 21Martha said to Jesus, "Lord, if You had been here, my brother would not have died. 22I know even now God will give You whatever You ask." 23Jesus said to her, "Your brother will rise again." 24Martha said to Him, "I know

I know even now God will give You whatever You ask.

that he will rise again when the dead are raised from the grave on the last day."

25 Jesus said to her, "I am the One Who raises the dead and gives them life. Anyone who puts his trust in Me will live again, even if he dies. 26 Anyone who lives and has put his trust in Me will never die. Do you believe this?" 27 She answered, "Yes, Lord, I believe that You are the Christ, the Son of God. You are the One Who was to come into the world."

Yes, Lord, I believe that You are the Christ, the Son of God.

Lazarus Is Raised From The Dead

28 After Martha said this, she went and called her sister Mary. She said without anyone else hearing, "The Teacher is here and has sent for you." 29 When Mary heard this, she got up and went to Him. 30 Jesus had not yet come into their town. He was still where Martha had met Him.

31 The Jews had been in the house comforting Mary. They saw her get up and hurry out. They followed her and said, "She is going to the grave to cry there." 32 Mary went to the place where Jesus was. When she saw Him, she got down at His feet. She said to Him, "Lord, if You had been here, my brother would not have died." 33 Jesus saw her crying. The Jews who came with her were crying also. His heart was very sad and He was troubled. 34 He said, "Where did you lay Lazarus?" They said, "Lord, come and see." 35 Then Jesus cried. 36 The Jews said, "See how much He loved Lazarus." 37 Some of them said, "This Man opened the eyes of the blind man. Could He not have kept this man from dying?"

38 Jesus went to the grave with a sad heart. The grave was a hole in the side of a rock. A stone covered the door. 39 Jesus said, "Take the stone away." The dead man's sister, Martha, said to Him, "Lord, by now his body has a bad smell. He has been dead four days." 40 Jesus said to her, "Did I not say that if you would believe, you would see the shining greatness of God?"

41 They took the stone away. Jesus looked up and said, "Father, I thank You for hearing Me. 42 I know You always hear Me. But I have said this for the people standing here, so they may believe You have sent Me."

⁴³When He had said this, He called with a loud voice, "Lazarus, come out!" ⁴⁴The man who had been dead came out. His hands and feet were tied in grave clothes. A white cloth was tied around his face. Jesus said to the people, "Take off the grave clothes and let him go!"

The Proud Religious Law-Keepers Try To Think Of A Way To Kill Jesus

⁴⁵Many of the Jews who had come to visit Mary and had seen what Jesus had done put their trust in Him. ⁴⁶Some of them went to the proud religious law-keepers and told them what Jesus had done. ⁴⁷The religious leaders of the Jews and the proud religious law-keepers gathered a court together. They said, "What will we do? This Man is doing many powerful works. ⁴⁸If we let Him keep doing these things, all men will put their trust in Him. The Romans will come and take away the house of God and our nation." ⁴⁹Caiaphas was the head religious leader that year. He said to them, "You know nothing about this. ⁵⁰Do you not see it is better for one man to die for the people than for the whole nation to be destroyed?"

⁵¹Caiaphas did not think of these words himself. He spoke what God had said would happen. He was telling before it happened that Jesus must die for the nation. ⁵²He must die not only for the nation, but also to bring together into one group the children of God who were living in many places.

⁵³From that day on they talked together about how they might kill Jesus. ⁵⁴For this reason Jesus did not walk out in the open among the Jews. He went to a town called Ephraim. It was near a desert. He stayed there with His followers.

The Proud Religious Law-Keepers Look For Jesus

⁵⁵The special religious gathering to remember how the Jews left Egypt was soon. Many people from around the country came up to Jerusalem. They came to wash themselves in their religious worship before the special supper. ⁵⁶They looked for Jesus. They stood together in the house of God and asked each other, "What do you think? Will He come to the special supper?" ⁵⁷The

religious leaders of the Jews and the proud religious law-keepers had said that if any man knew where Jesus was, he should tell them. They wanted to take Him.

Mary Of Bethany Puts Special Perfume On Jesus [Matthew 26:6-13; Mark 14:3-9]

12 It was six days before the special religious gathering to remember how the Jews left Egypt. Jesus came to Bethany where Lazarus lived. Jesus had raised Lazarus from the dead. ²They made supper for Him. Martha put the food on the table. Lazarus was at the table with Him.

³Mary took a jar of special perfume that cost much money and poured it on the feet of Jesus. She dried His feet with her hair. The house was filled with the smell of the special perfume.

⁴Judas Iscariot was one of the followers. He was about to hand Jesus over to the leaders of the country. He said, ⁵"Why was not this special perfume sold for much money and given to poor people?" ⁶He did not say this because he cared for poor people. He said this because he was a robber. He carried the bag of money and would steal some of it for himself. ⁷Jesus said, "Let her alone. She has kept it for the time when I will be buried. ⁸You will always have poor people with you. You will not always have Me."

The Jews Talk About Having Lazarus Killed

⁹Many Jews came to the place because they knew Jesus was there. They came not only to see Jesus, but to see Lazarus also. Jesus had raised Lazarus from the dead. ¹⁰The religious leaders of the Jews talked together about having Lazarus killed also. ¹¹Because of Lazarus, many Jews were leaving their own religion. They were putting their trust in Jesus.

The Last Time Jesus Goes Into Jerusalem [Matthew 21:1-11; Mark 11:1-11; Luke 19:29-44]

¹²The next day many people were in Jerusalem for the religious gathering. They heard Jesus was coming. ¹³They took branches

of trees and went to meet Him. They spoke with a loud voice, "Greatest One! Great and honored is He Who comes in the name of the Lord, the King of the Jews!" ¹⁴Jesus found a young donkey and sat on it. The Holy Writings say, ¹⁵"Do not be afraid, people of Jerusalem. Look! Your King comes sitting on a young donkey!" (Zechariah 9:9) ¹⁶His followers did not understand what this meant at first. When Jesus had gone back to heaven to receive great honor, they remembered these things were written about Him. They remembered they had done this to Him.

¹⁷The people who had been with Jesus when He had called Lazarus from the grave kept telling of this powerful work to others. They had seen Lazarus raised from the dead. ¹⁸Because of this the people went to meet Jesus. They had heard He had done this powerful work. ¹⁹The proud religious law-keepers said among themselves, "Look, we are losing followers. Everyone is following Jesus!"

The Greek People Want To See Jesus

²⁰Some Greek people had come to worship at the religious gathering. They were among the others who had come to worship. ²¹These Greek people came to Philip. He was from the city of Bethsaida in the country of Galilee. They said to him, "Sir, we want to see Jesus!" ²²Philip went and told Andrew. Then Andrew and Philip told Jesus.

The Law Of Life

²³Jesus said to them, "The hour is near for the Son of Man to be taken to heaven to receive great honor. ²⁴For sure, I tell you, unless a seed falls into the ground and dies, it will only be a seed. If it dies, it will give much grain. ²⁵Anyone who loves his life will lose it. Anyone who hates his life in this world will keep it forever. ²⁶If anyone wants to work for Me, he must follow Me. So where I am, the one who wants to work for Me will be there also. If anyone works for Me, My Father will honor him.

²⁷"Now My soul is troubled. Should I say, 'Father, save Me from this time of trouble and pain'? No, this is why I came to this time. ²⁸Father, honor Your name!"

The People Hear The Voice Of God

Then a voice from heaven came, saying, "I have already honored My name. I will honor it again!" 29The people heard the voice. Some who stood there said, "It was thunder." Others said, "An angel spoke to Him." 30Jesus said, "The voice did not come for Me, but it came to be a help to you.

Jesus Tells How He Will Die

31"Now this world is being told it is guilty. Now the leader of this world will be thrown out. 32And when I am lifted up from the earth, I will attract all people toward Me." 33He said this to tell the kind of death He was going to die.

> When I am lifted up from the earth, I will attract all people toward Me.

34The people said to Him, "The Law of Moses says that the Christ is to live forever. Why do you say, 'The Son of Man must be lifted up'? Who is this Son of Man?"

35Jesus said to them, "The Light will be with you for a little while yet. Go on your way while you have the Light so you will not be in the dark. When a man is walking in the dark, he does not know where he is going. 36While you have the Light, put your trust in the Light. Then you will be the sons of the Light." Jesus said these things and then went away. He hid Himself from them.

The People Do Not Believe

37Jesus had done many powerful works in front of them, but they did not put their trust in Him. 38This happened as the words of the early preacher Isaiah said it would happen. He had said, "Lord, has anyone believed our preaching? Has the Lord shown His power to anyone?" 39The reason they could not believe is written again in Isaiah. 40It says, "He has blinded their eyes and made their hearts hard. Then they would not see with their eyes. They would not understand with their heart. They would not turn to Me. I could not heal them." (Isaiah 6:9-10) 41This is what Isaiah said when he saw the shining greatness of Jesus and spoke of Him.

42Even among the leaders of the people there were many who believed in Jesus. But because of the proud religious law-keepers, they did not tell about it. If they had, they would have been put out of the Jewish place of worship. ⁴³They loved to have the respect from men more than honor from God.

Jesus And His Father Are One

I came to the world to be a Light.

⁴⁴Then Jesus spoke with a loud voice, "Anyone who puts his trust in Me, puts his trust not only in Me, but in Him Who sent Me. ⁴⁵Anyone who sees Me, sees Him Who sent Me. ⁴⁶I came to the world to be a Light. Anyone who puts his trust in Me will not be in darkness. ⁴⁷If anyone hears My Words but does not believe them, I do not say he is guilty. I did not come to say the world is guilty. I came to save the world from the punishment of sin. ⁴⁸Anyone who does not receive Me and does not receive My teaching has One Who will say he is guilty. The Word that I have spoken will say he is guilty on the last day. ⁴⁹I have not spoken by My own power. The Father Who sent Me has told Me what to say and speak. ⁵⁰I know that His Word is life that lasts forever. I speak the things the Father has told Me to speak."

Jesus Washes The Feet Of His Followers

13 It was before the special religious gathering to remember how the Jews left Egypt. Jesus knew the time had come for Him to leave this world and go to the Father. He had loved His own who were in the world. He loved them to the end. ²He and His followers were having supper. Satan had put the thought into the heart of Judas Iscariot of handing Jesus over to the leaders of the country. ³Jesus knew the Father had put everything into His hands. He knew He had come from God and was going back to God. ⁴Jesus got up from the supper and took off His coat. He picked up a cloth and put it around Him. ⁵Then He put water into a wash pan and began to wash the feet of His followers. He dried their feet with the cloth He had put around Himself.

Peter Speaks Out Against Jesus Washing His Feet

⁶Jesus came to Simon Peter. Peter said to Him, "Lord, are You going to wash my feet?" ⁷Jesus answered him, "You do not understand now what I am doing but you will later." ⁸Peter said

to Him, "I will never let You wash my feet." Jesus said, "Unless I wash you, you will not be a part of Me." 9Simon Peter said to Him, "Lord, do not wash only my feet, but wash my hands and my head also." 10Jesus said to him, "Anyone who has washed his body needs only to wash his feet. Then he is clean all over. You are all clean except one." 11Jesus knew who was going to hand Him over to the leaders. That is why He said, "You are all clean except one."

Jesus Tells Why He Washed Their Feet

12Jesus washed their feet and put on His coat. Then He sat down again and said to them, "Do you understand what I have done to you? 13You call Me Teacher and Lord. You are right because that is what I am. 14I am your Teacher and Lord. I have washed your feet. You should wash each other's feet also. 15I have done this to show you what should be done. You should do as I have done to you. 16For sure, I tell you, a workman who is owned by someone is not greater than his owner. One who is sent is not greater than the one who sent him. 17If you know these things, you will be happy if you do them.

18"I am not speaking about all of you. I know the ones I have chosen. What is written in the Holy Writings must happen. It says, 'The man who eats bread with Me has turned against Me.' (Psalm 41:9) 19I tell you this now before it happens. After it happens, you will believe that I am what I say I am, the Christ. 20For sure, I tell you, he who receives the one I send out, receives Me. He who receives Me, receives Him who sent Me."

The Last Special Supper — Jesus Tells Of The One Who Will Hand Him Over To The Leaders [Matthew 26:20-25; Mark 14:17-21; Luke 22:14-18]

21When Jesus had said this, He was troubled in heart. He told them in very plain words, saying, "For sure, I tell you, one of you is going to hand Me over to the leaders of the country."

22The followers began to look at each other. They did not know which one He was speaking of. 23One follower, whom Jesus loved, was beside Jesus. 24Simon Peter got this follower to look his way.

He wanted him to ask Jesus which one He was speaking of. [25]While close beside Jesus, he asked, "Lord, who is it?" [26]Jesus answered, "It is the one I give this piece of bread to after I have put it into the dish." Then He put the bread into the dish and gave it to Judas Iscariot, the son of Simon. [27]After Judas had eaten the piece of bread, Satan went into him. Jesus said to Judas, "What you are going to do, do in a hurry."

[28]No one at the supper knew why Jesus had said this to Judas. [29]They thought it was because Judas carried the bag of money, and Jesus had said that Judas should buy what they needed for the religious gathering. Or they thought Judas should give something to poor people. [30]As soon as Judas had taken the piece of bread, he went out. It was night.

Love — The Greatest Law

[31]After Judas went out, Jesus said, "The Son of Man is now honored and God has been honored in Him. [32]If God is honored in Him, God will also honor Him in Himself right now. [33]Little children, I will be with you only a little while. You will look for Me. I say to you what I said to the Jews, 'Where I am going, you cannot come!' [34]I give you a new Law. You are to love each other. You must love each other as I have loved you. [35]If you love each other, all men will know you are My followers."

Jesus Tells How Peter Will Lie About Him [Matthew 26:31-35; Mark 14:27-31; Luke 22:31-34]

[36]Simon Peter said to Jesus, "Lord, where are You going?" Jesus answered, "You cannot follow Me now where I am going. Later you will follow Me." [37]Peter said to Jesus, "Why can I not follow You now? I will die for You." [38]Jesus answered Peter, "Will you die for Me? For sure, I tell you, before a rooster crows, you will have said three times that you do not know Me."

Jesus Comforts His Followers

14 "Do not let your heart be troubled. You have put your trust in God, put your trust in Me also. [2]There are many rooms in My Father's house. If it were not so, I would have told you. I am going away to make a place for you. ³After I go and make a place for you, I will come back and take you with Me. Then you may be where I am. ⁴You know where I am going and you know how to get there.''

⁵Thomas said to Jesus, "Lord, we do not know where You are going. How can we know the way to get there?" ⁶Jesus said, "I am the Way and the Truth and the Life. No one can go to the Father except by Me. ⁷If you had known Me, you would know My Father also. From now on you know Him and have seen Him. '

> I am the Way and the Truth and the Life. No one can go to the Father except by Me.

Jesus And His Father Are One

⁸Philip said to Jesus, "Lord, show us the Father. That is all we ask.'' ⁹Jesus said to him, "Have I been with you all this time and you do not know Me yet? Whoever has seen Me, has seen the Father. How can you say, 'Show us the Father'? ¹⁰Do you not believe that I am in the Father and that the Father is in Me? What I say to you, I do not say by My own power. The Father Who lives in Me does His work through Me.

¹¹"Believe Me that I am in the Father and that the Father is in Me. Or else believe Me because of the things I do. ¹²For sure, I tell you, whoever puts his trust in Me can do the things I am doing. He will do even greater things than these because I am going to the Father. ¹³Whatever you ask in My name, I will do it so the shining greatness of the Father may be seen in the Son. ¹⁴Yes, if you ask anything in My name, I will do it.

Jesus Promises To Give The Holy Spirit

¹⁵"If you love Me, you will do what I say. ¹⁶Then I will ask My Father and He will give you another Helper. He will be with you forever. ¹⁷He is the Spirit of Truth. The world cannot receive Him. It does not see Him or know Him. You know Him because He lives with you and will be in you.

Jesus Tells Of His Death

¹⁸"I will not leave you without help as children without parents. I will come to you. ¹⁹In a little while the world will see Me no

more. You will see Me. Because I live, you will live also. ²⁰When that day comes, you will know that I am in My Father. You will know that you are in Me. You will know that I am in you. ²¹The one who loves Me is the one who has My teaching and obeys it. My Father will love whoever loves Me. I will love him and will show Myself to him.''

²²The other Judas (not Iscariot) said to Him, ''Why is it You are going to show Yourself to us followers and not to the world?'' ²³Jesus said, ''The one who loves Me will obey My teaching. My Father will love him. We will come to him and live with him. ²⁴The one who does not love Me does not obey My teaching. The teaching you are now hearing is not My teaching but it is from My Father Who sent Me.

²⁵''I have told you these things while I am still with you. ²⁶The Helper is the Holy Spirit. The Father will send Him in My place. He will teach you everything and help you remember everything I have told you.

Jesus Gives His Followers Peace

²⁷''I give you My peace and leave it with you. I do not give peace to you as the world gives. Do not let your hearts be troubled or afraid. ²⁸You heard Me say that I am going away. But I am coming back to you. If you love Me, you would be glad that I am going to the Father. The Father is greater than I. ²⁹I have told you this before it happens. Then when it does happen, you will believe.

³⁰''I will not talk much more with you. The leader of this world is coming. He has no power over Me. ³¹I am doing what the Father told Me to do so the world may know I love the Father. Come, let us be on our way.

The Vine And The Branches

15 ''I am the true Vine. My Father is the One Who cares for the Vine. ²He takes away any branch in Me that does not give fruit. Any branch that gives fruit, He cuts it back so it will give more fruit. ³You are made clean by the words I have spoken to you. ⁴Get your life from Me and I will live in you. No branch can give fruit by itself. It has to get life from the vine. You are able to give fruit only when you have life from Me. ⁵I am the Vine and you are the branches. Get your life from Me. Then I will live in you and you will give much fruit. You can do nothing without Me.

You can do nothing without Me.

⁶"If anyone does not get his life from Me, he is cut off like a branch and dries up. Such branches are gathered and thrown into the fire and they are burned. ⁷If you get your life from Me and My Words live in you, ask whatever you want. It will be done for you.

⁸"When you give much fruit, My Father is honored. This shows you are My followers. ⁹I have loved you just as My Father has loved Me. Stay in My love. ¹⁰If you obey My teaching, you will live in My love. In this way, I have obeyed My Father's teaching and live in His love. ¹¹I have told you these things so My joy may be in you and your joy may be full.

The Christian With Other Christians

¹²"This is what I tell you to do: Love each other just as I have loved you. ¹³No one can have greater love than to give his life for his friends. ¹⁴You are My friends if you do what I tell you. ¹⁵I do not call you workmen that I own anymore. A workman does not know what his owner is doing. I call you friends, because I have told you everything I have heard from My Father. ¹⁶You have not chosen Me. I have chosen you. I have set you apart for the work of bringing in fruit. Your fruit should last. And whatever you ask the Father in My name, He will give it to you.

The Christian And The World

¹⁷"This is what I tell you to do: Love each other. ¹⁸If the world hates you, you know it hated Me before it hated you. ¹⁹If you belonged to the world, the world would love you as its own. You do not belong to the world. I have chosen you out of the world and the world hates you. ²⁰Remember I said to you, 'A workman who is owned by someone is not greater than his owner.' If they made it very hard for Me, they will make it very hard for you also. If they obeyed My teachings, they will obey your teachings also.

²¹They will do all these things to you because you belong to Me. They do not know My Father Who sent Me.

²²"I have come and have spoken to them so they are guilty of sin. But now they have no reason to give for keeping their sin any longer. ²³Whoever hates Me, hates My Father also. ²⁴I have done things among them which no one else has done so they are guilty of sin. But now they have seen these things and have hated Me and My Father. ²⁵This happened as their Law said it would happen, 'They hated Me without a reason.'

He is the
Spirit of Truth.

²⁶"The Helper (Holy Spirit) will tell about Me when He comes. I will send Him to you from the Father. He is the Spirit of Truth and comes from the Father. ²⁷You will also tell of Me because you have been with Me from the beginning.

Jesus Tells His Followers It Will Be Very Hard For Them

16 "I have told you these things so you will not be ashamed of Me and leave Me. ²They will put you out of the places of worship. The time will come when anyone who kills you will think he is helping God. ³They will do these things to you because they do not know the Father or Me.

⁴"When these things happen, you will remember I told you they would happen. That is why I am telling you about these things now. I did not tell you these things before, because I was with you. ⁵But now I am going to Him Who sent Me. Yet none of you asks Me, 'Where are You going?'

The Three Kinds Of Work Of The Holy Spirit

⁶"Your hearts are full of sorrow because I am telling you these things. ⁷I tell you the truth. It is better for you that I go away. If I do not go, the Helper will not come to you. If I go, I will send Him to you. ⁸When the Helper comes, He will show the world the truth about sin. He will show the world about being right with God. And He will show the world what it is to be guilty. ⁹He will show the world about sin, because they do not put their trust in Me. ¹⁰He will show the world about being right with God, because

I go to My Father and you will see Me no more. [11]He will show the world what it is to be guilty because the leader of this world (Satan) is guilty.

The Holy Spirit Will Give Honor To The Son

[12]"I still have many things to say to you. You are not strong enough to understand them now. [13]The Holy Spirit is coming. He will lead you into all truth. He will not speak His Own words. He will speak what He hears. He will tell you of things to come. [14]He will honor Me. He will receive what is Mine and will tell it to you. [15]Everything the Father has is Mine. That is why I said to you, 'He will receive what is Mine and will tell it to you.'

Jesus Tells Of His Death

[16]"In a little while you will not see Me. Then in a little while you will see Me again." [17]Some of His followers said to each other, "What is He trying to tell us when He says, 'In a little while you will not see Me, and in a little while you will see Me again,' and 'Because I go to My Father'?" [18]So they said, "What is He trying to tell us by saying, 'A little while'? We do not know what He is talking about."

[19]Jesus knew they wanted to ask Him something. He said to them, "Are you asking each other why I said, 'In a little while you will not see Me, and in a little while you will see Me again'? [20]For sure, I tell you, you will cry and have sorrow, but the world will have joy. You will have sorrow, but your sorrow will turn into joy. [21]When a woman gives birth to a child, she has sorrow because her time has come. After the child is born, she forgets her pain. She is full of joy because a child has been born into the world. [22]You are sad now. I will see you again and then your hearts will be full of joy. No one can take your joy from you.

Asking And Receiving

[23]"When the time comes that you see Me again, you will ask Me no question. For sure, I tell you, My Father will give you whatever you ask in My name. [24]Until now you have not asked for anything in My name. Ask and you will receive. Then your joy will be full.

25"I have told you these things in picture-stories. The time is coming when I will not use picture-stories. I will talk about My Father in plain words. 26In that day you will ask in My name. I will not ask the Father for you 27because the Father loves you. He loves you because you love Me and believe that I came from the Father.

Jesus Tells Of His Going

28"I came from the Father and have come into the world. I am leaving the world and going to the Father." 29His followers said to Him, "Now You are talking in plain words. You are not using picture-stories. 30Now we are sure You know everything. You do not need anyone to tell You anything. Because of this we believe that You came from God."

31Jesus said to them, "Do you believe now? 32The time is coming, yes, it is already here when you will be going your own way. Everyone will go to his own house and leave Me alone. Yet I am not alone because the Father is with Me. 33I have told you these things so you may have peace in Me. In the world you will have much trouble. But take hope! I have power over the world!"

Jesus Prays For Himself

17 When Jesus had said these things, He looked up to heaven and said, "Father, the time has come! Honor Your Son so Your Son may honor You. 2You have given Him power over all men. He is to give life that lasts forever to all You have given to Him. 3This is life that lasts forever. It is to know You, the only true God, and to know Jesus Christ Whom You have sent. 4I honored You on earth. I did the work You gave Me to do. 5Now, Father, honor Me with the honor I had with You before the world was made.

Jesus Prays For His Followers

6"I have made Your name known to the people You have given Me from the world. They were Yours but You gave them to Me. They have obeyed Your Word. 7Now they know that everything

You have given Me came from You. ⁸I gave them the Word which You gave Me. They received it. They know I came from You and they believe You sent Me.

⁹"I pray for them. I do not pray for the world. I pray for those You gave Me. They are Yours. ¹⁰All that is Mine is Yours. All that is Yours is Mine. I have been honored through them. ¹¹I am no longer in the world. I am coming to You. But these are still in the world. Holy Father, keep those You have given to Me in the power of Your name. Then they will be one, even as We are One. ¹²While I have been with them in the world, I have kept them in the power of Your name. I have kept watch over those You gave Me. Not one of them has been lost except the one who is going to be destroyed, which is the son of death. The Holy Writings said it would happen. (Psalm 41:9; John 6:70) ¹³But now I come to You, Father. I say these things while I am in the world. In this way, My followers may have My joy in their hearts.

¹⁴"I have given Your Word to My followers. The world hated them because they do not belong to the world, even as I do not belong to the world. ¹⁵I do not ask You to take them out of the world. I ask You to keep them from the devil. ¹⁶My followers do not belong to the world just as I do not belong to the world. ¹⁷Make them holy for Yourself by the truth. Your Word is truth.

¹⁸"As You sent Me into the world so I have sent them into the world also. ¹⁹I set Myself apart to be holy for them. Then they may be made holy by the truth.

Jesus Prays For All Christians

²⁰"I do not pray for these followers only. I pray also for those who will put their trust in Me through the teaching they have heard. ²¹May they all be as one, Father, as You are in Me and I am in You. May they belong to Us. Then the world will believe that You sent Me. ²²I gave them the honor You gave Me that they may be one as We are One. ²³I am in them and You are in Me so they may be one and be made perfect. Then the world may know that You sent Me and that You love them as You love Me.

²⁴"Father, I want My followers You gave Me to be with Me where I am. Then they may see My shining greatness which You

I pray also for those who will put their trust in Me through the teaching they have heard.

gave Me because You loved Me before the world was made. ²⁵Holy Father, the world has not known You. I have known You. These have known You sent Me. ²⁶I have made Your name known to them and will make it known. So then the love You have for Me may be in them and I may be in them.''

Jesus Handed Over To Sinners [Matthew 26:47-56; Mark 14:43-52; Luke 22:47-51]

18 When Jesus had said these things, He went with His followers across the small river Kidron. He and His followers went to a garden there. ²Judas, who was handing Him over to the leaders, knew the place also. Jesus and His followers had met there many times. ³Judas led some soldiers and some men who had been sent by the head religious leaders of the Jews and the proud religious law-keepers to the garden. They carried lamps and sticks that were burning and swords.

⁴Jesus knew what was going to happen to Him. He went out and asked them, "Who are you looking for?" ⁵The soldiers answered Him, "Jesus of Nazareth." Jesus said, "I am Jesus." Judas, who was handing Him over, was with them also.

⁶When He said to them, "I am Jesus," they stepped back and fell to the ground. ⁷He asked them again, "Who are you looking for?" They said again, "Jesus of Nazareth." ⁸He said, "I have told you that I am Jesus. If you are looking for Me, let these men go their way." ⁹He said this so the words He spoke might happen, "I have not lost one of those You gave Me."

¹⁰Simon Peter had a sword. He took it and hit a workman who was owned by the head religious leader and cut off his right ear. The workman's name was Malchus. ¹¹Then Jesus said to Peter, "Put your sword back where it belongs. Am I not to go through what My Father has given Me to go through?"

Jesus Stands In Front Of Annas

¹²Then the soldiers and their captain and the men sent by the Jewish religious leaders took Jesus and tied Him. ¹³They took

Him to Annas first. He was the father-in-law of Caiaphas. Caiaphas was the head religious leader that year. [14]Caiaphas had talked to the Jews. He told them it would be a good thing if one man should die for the people.

Peter Lies About Jesus [Matthew 26:69-75; Mark 14:66-72; Luke 22:55-62]

[15]Simon Peter and another follower came behind Jesus. This other follower was known to the head religious leader. He went with Jesus to the head religious leader's house. [16]Peter stood outside at the gate. The other follower, who was known by the head religious leader, went out and talked to the young woman who watched the gate. Then he took Peter inside. [17]The young woman who watched the door said to Peter, "Are you not a follower of this Man?" He said, "I am not!" [18]The workmen who were owned by someone and the soldiers had made a fire because it was cold. They were getting warm by the fire. Peter was standing with them getting warm.

Jesus Stands In Front Of Caiaphas [Matthew 26:57-58; Mark 14:53-54; Luke 22:52-54]

[19]The head religious leader of the Jews asked Jesus about His followers. He asked Jesus about His teaching. [20]Jesus said, "I have spoken very plain words to the world. I have always taught in the Jewish place of worship and in the house of God. It is where the Jews go all the time. My words have not been said in secret. [21]Why do you ask Me? Ask those who have heard what I said to them. They know what I said."

[22]Then one of the soldiers standing there hit Jesus with his hand. He said, "Is that how You talk to the head religious leaders?" [23]Jesus said, "If I said anything wrong, tell Me what was wrong. If I said what was right, why did you hit Me?" [24]Then Annas sent Jesus to Caiaphas, the head religious leader. Jesus was still tied up.

[25]Simon Peter was standing there and getting warm. They said to him, "Are you not one of His followers also?" He lied and said he did not know Jesus and answered, "I am not!" [26]A workman

who was owned by the head religious leader was there. He was of the family of the man whose ear Peter cut off. The man said, "Did I not see you in the garden with Him?" ²⁷Again Peter lied and said he did not know Jesus. At once a rooster crowed.

Jesus Stands In Front Of Pilate [Matthew 27:1-2, 11-14; Mark 15:1-5; Luke 23:1-5]

²⁸They led Jesus from Caiaphas into the court room. It was early in the morning. They did not go inside because their Law said if they did they would become dirty with sin. Then they would not be able to eat the religious supper to remember how the Jews left Egypt. ²⁹So Pilate came out to them. He asked, "What have you to say against this Man?" ³⁰The Jews said, "If He had not done wrong, we would not have brought Him to you."

³¹Then Pilate said to them, "Take Him yourselves and give Him a trial by your Law." The Jews said to him, "It is against our Law to put anyone to death." ³²This happened as Jesus said it would happen. He had told what kind of death He would die.

³³Then Pilate went back into the court room. He called for Jesus and said to Him, "Are You the King of the Jews?" ³⁴Jesus said, "Do you ask Me this yourself, or did others say this to you about Me?" ³⁵Pilate said, "Do you think I am a Jew? Your own people and religious leaders have handed You over to me. What have You done?"

³⁶Jesus said, "My holy nation does not belong to this world. If My holy nation were of this world, My helpers would fight so I would not be handed over to the Jews. My holy nation is not of this world." ³⁷Pilate said to Him, "So You are a King?" Jesus said, "You are right when you say that I am a King. I was born for this reason. I came into the world for this reason. I came to speak about the truth. Everyone who is of the truth hears My voice."

Jesus Or Barabbas Is To Go Free [Matthew 27:15-26; Mark 15:6-14; Luke 23:17-25]

³⁸Pilate said to Jesus, "What is truth?" After Pilate said this, he went out again to the Jews. He said, "I do not find Him guilty.

³⁹But every year a man who is in prison is allowed to go free at the special religious gathering to remember how the Jews left Egypt. Do you want the King of the Jews to go free?" ⁴⁰Then they spoke with loud voices, "Not this Man, but Barabbas!" Now Barabbas was a robber.

The Headband Of Thorns [Matthew 27:27-32; Mark 15:15-21]

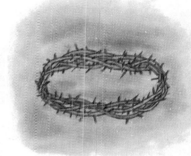

19 Then Pilate took Jesus and had Him beaten. ²The soldiers put a headband of thorns on His head. They put a purple coat on Him. ³Then they said, "Hello, King of the Jews!" and hit Him with their hands.

⁴Pilate went out again and said to the people, "See, I bring Him out to you so you will know I do not find Him guilty." ⁵Jesus came out. He had on the headband of thorns and a purple coat. Pilate said to the people, "Look! This is the Man!"

Pilate Tries To Let Jesus Go Free

⁶The religious leaders and the soldiers saw Him. They spoke with loud voices, "Nail Him to a cross! Nail Him to a cross!" Pilate said, "Take Him yourselves and nail Him to a cross. As for me, I do not find Him guilty." ⁷The Jews said to Pilate, "We have a Law that says He should die because He has said He is the Son of God."

⁸When Pilate heard them say this, he was more afraid. ⁹He went into the court room again. He said to Jesus, "Where do You come from?" Jesus did not say a word. ¹⁰Pilate said, "Will You not speak to me? Do You not know that I have the right and the power to nail You to a cross? I have the right and the power to let You go free also." Jesus said, "You would not have any right or power over Me if it were not given you from above. For this reason the one who handed Me over to you has the worse sin."

¹²When Pilate heard this, he wanted to let Jesus go free. But the Jews kept saying, "If you let this Man go free, you are not a friend of Caesar! Whoever makes himself as a king is working against Caesar." ¹³When Pilate heard this, he had Jesus brought in front of him. Pilate sat down at the place where men stand in

front of him if they are thought to be guilty. The place is called the Stone Floor.

¹⁴It was the day to get ready for the special religious gathering to remember how the Jews left Egypt. It was about noon. Pilate said to the Jews, "Look, your King!" ¹⁵They spoke with a loud voice, "Take Him away! Nail Him to a cross!" Pilate said to them, "Do you want me to nail your King to a cross?" The head religious leaders said, "We have no king but Caesar!" ¹⁶Then Pilate handed Him over to be nailed to a cross. They took Jesus and led Him away.

Jesus On The Cross [Matthew 27:33-37; Mark 15:22-26; Luke 23:26-38]

¹⁷Jesus carried His own cross to a hill called the Place of the Skull. ¹⁸There they nailed Him to the cross. With Him were two others. There was one on each side of Jesus. ¹⁹Then Pilate put a writing on the cross which said, JESUS OF NAZARETH, THE KING OF THE JEWS. ²⁰This was read by many of the Jews. The place where Jesus was nailed to the cross was near the city. The writing was written in the Hebrew and the Latin and the Greek languages. ²¹Then the head religious leaders of the Jews said to Pilate, "Do not write, 'The King of the Jews!' Write, 'He said, I am the King of the Jews.' " ²²Pilate said, "What I have written is to stay just as it is!"

They Divided His Clothes [Matthew 27:35; Mark 15:24]

²³The soldiers who nailed Jesus to the cross took His clothes and divided them in four parts, each soldier getting one part. But His coat which was not sewed was made in one piece. ²⁴They said to each other, "Let us not cut it up. Let us draw names to see whose it should be." This happened as the Holy Writings said it would happen, "They divided My clothes among them and they drew names for My coat." (Psalm 22:18) ²⁵This is what the soldiers did.

The Women At The Cross [Matthew 27:55-56; Mark 15:40-41]

The mother of Jesus and her sister Mary, the wife of Cleophas, were standing near the cross. Mary Magdalene was there also.

²⁶Jesus saw His mother and the follower whom He loved standing near. He said to His mother, "Woman, look at your son." ²⁷Then Jesus said to the follower, "Look at your mother." From that time the follower took her to his own house.

The Death Of Jesus [Matthew 27:45-50; Mark 15:33-36; Luke 23:44-49]

²⁸Jesus knew that everything was now finished. Everything happened as the Holy Writings said it would happen. He said, "I am thirsty." (Psalm 69:21) ²⁹There was a jar full of sour wine near. They filled a sponge and put it on a stick and put it to His mouth. ³⁰Jesus took the sour wine and said, "It is finished.' He put His head down and gave up His spirit and died.

It is finished

His Bones Were Not Broken

³¹This was the day before the special religious gathering to remember how the Jews left Egypt. The next day was the Day of Rest and the great day of the religious gathering. The Jews went to Pilate and asked to have the legs of the men broken. They wanted their bodies taken away so they would not be hanging on the crosses on the Day of Rest. ³²Then the soldiers came and broke the legs of the first man and of the other one who had been nailed to crosses beside Jesus. ³³They came to Jesus. They saw He was already dead so they did not break His legs. ³⁴But one of the soldiers pushed a spear into His side. Blood and water ran out.

³⁵The one who saw it is writing this and what he says is true. He knows he is telling the truth so you may believe. ³⁶These things happened as the Holy Writings said they would happen, "Not one of His bones will be broken." (Exodus 12:46) ³⁷And in another place the Holy Writings say, "They will look at Him Whose side they cut." (Zechariah 12:10)

The Grave Of Jesus [Matthew 27:57-66; Mark 15:42-47; Luke 23:50-56]

³⁸Joseph was from the town of Arimathea. He was a follower of Jesus but was afraid of the Jews. So he worshiped without anyone knowing it. He asked Pilate if he could take away the body of

Jesus. Pilate said he could. Then Joseph came and took it away. [39]Nicodemus came also. The first time he had come to Jesus had been at night. He brought with him a large box of spices. [40]Then they took the body of Jesus with the spices and put it in linen cloths. This was the way the Jews made a body ready for the grave.

[41]There was a garden near the place where He had been nailed to the cross. In the garden there was a new grave in the side of the rock. No one had ever been laid there. [42]This place was near by. Because it was the day the Jews got ready for the special religious gathering, they laid Jesus in it.

Jesus Is Raised From The Grave [*Matthew 28:1-10; Mark 16:1-8; Luke 24:1-12*]

20 It was the first day of the week. Mary Magdalene came to the grave early in the morning while it was still dark. She saw that the stone had been pushed away from the grave. [2]She ran to Simon Peter and the other follower whom Jesus loved. She said to them, "They have taken the Lord out of the grave. We do not know where they have put Him."

[3]Then Peter and the other follower went to the grave. [4]They ran but the other follower ran faster than Peter and came to the grave first. [5]He got down and looked in and saw the linen cloths but did not go in. [6]Then Simon Peter came and went into the grave. He saw the linen cloths lying there. [7]The white cloth that had been around the head of Jesus was not lying with the other linen cloths. It was rolled up and lying apart by itself. [8]Then the other follower, who had come first, went in also. He saw and believed. [9]They still did not understand what the Holy Writings meant when they said that He must rise again from the dead. [10]Then the followers went back again to their homes.

[11]Mary stood outside the grave crying. As she cried, she got down and looked inside the grave. [12]She saw two angels dressed in white clothes. They were sitting where the body of Jesus had lain. One angel was where His head had lain and one angel was where His feet had lain. [13]They said to her, "Woman, why are you

crying?" She said to them, "Because they have taken away my Lord. I do not know where they have put Him."

[14]After saying this, she turned around and saw Jesus standing there. But she did not know that it was Jesus. [15]He said to her, "Woman, why are you crying? Who are you looking for?" She thought He was the man who cared for the garden. She said to Him, "Sir, if you have taken Jesus from here, tell me where you have put Him. I will take Him away." [16]Jesus said to her, "Mary!" She turned around and said to Him, "Teacher!" [17]Jesus said to her, "Do not hold on to Me. I have not yet gone up to My Father. But go to My brothers. Tell them that I will go up to My Father and your Father, and to My God and your God!" [18]Mary Magdalene went and told the followers that she had seen the Lord. She told them the things He had said to her.

Jesus Was Seen By His Followers — Thomas Was Not There

[19]It was evening of the first day of the week. The followers had gathered together with the doors locked because they were afraid of the Jews. Jesus came and stood among them. He said, "May you have peace." [20]When He had said this, He showed them His hands and His side. When the followers saw the Lord, they were filled with joy.

Jesus Sends His Followers To Preach [Matthew 28:16-20; Mark 16:15-18; Luke 24:44-49]

[21]Then Jesus said to them again, "May you have peace. As the Father has sent Me, I also am sending you." [22]When Jesus had said this, He breathed on them. He said, "Receive the Holy Spirit. [23]If you say that people are free of sins, they are free of them. If you say that people are not free of sins, they still have them."

Thomas Does Not Believe Jesus Is Raised From The Dead [Mark 16:9-14; Luke 24:13-43]

[24]Thomas was not with them when Jesus came. He was one of the twelve followers and was called the Twin. [25]The other followers told him, "We have seen the Lord!" He said to them, "I will not

believe until I see the marks made by the nails in His hands. I will not believe until I put my finger into the marks of the nails. I will not believe until I put my hand into His side."

Jesus Was Seen Again By His Followers — Thomas Was There

²⁶Eight days later the followers were again inside a house. Thomas was with them. The doors were locked. Jesus came and stood among them. He said, "May you have peace!" ²⁷He said to Thomas, "Put your finger into My hands. Put your hand into My side. Do not doubt. Believe!" ²⁸Thomas said to Him, "My Lord and my God!" ²⁹Jesus said to him, "Thomas, because you have seen Me, you believe. Those are happy who have never seen Me and yet believe!"

³⁰Jesus did many other powerful works in front of His followers. They are not written in this book. ³¹But these are written so you may believe that Jesus is the Christ, the Son of God. When you put your trust in Him, you will have life that lasts forever through His name.

The Risen Christ Talks To His Followers

21 After this, Jesus again showed Himself to His followers at the lake of Tiberias. It happened like this: ²Simon Peter and Thomas who was called the Twin and Nathanael from the town of Cana in the country of Galilee and the sons of Zebedee and two other followers were all together. ³Simon Peter said to them, "I am going fishing." The others said, "We will go with you." They went out and got into a boat. That night they caught no fish.

⁴Early in the morning Jesus stood on the shore of the lake. The followers did not know it was Jesus. ⁵Then Jesus said to them, "Children, do you have any fish?" They said, "No." ⁶He said to them, "Put your net over the right side of the boat. Then you will catch some fish." They put out the net. They were not able to pull it in because it was so full of fish.

⁷Then the follower whom Jesus loved said to Peter, "It is the Lord!" When Peter heard it was the Lord, he put on his

fisherman's coat. (He had taken it off.) Then he jumped into the water. 8The other followers came in the boat. They were pulling the net with the fish. They were not far from land, only a little way out.

9When they came to land they saw fish and bread on a fire. 10Jesus said to them, "Bring some of the fish you have just caught." 11Simon Peter went out and pulled the net to land. There were 153 big fish. The net was not broken even with so many.

12Jesus said to them, "Come and eat." Not one of the followers would ask, "Who are You?" They knew it was the Lord. 13Jesus came and took bread and fish and gave it to them. 14This was the third time Jesus had shown Himself to His followers after He had risen from the dead.

The Risen Christ Talks To Peter

15When they were finished eating, Jesus said to Simon Peter, "Simon, son of John, do you love Me more than these?" Peter answered Jesus, "Yes, Lord, You know that I love You." Jesus said to him, "Feed My lambs."

16Jesus said to Peter the second time, "Simon, son of John, do you love Me?" He answered Jesus, "Yes, Lord, You know that I love You." Jesus said to him, "Take care of My sheep."

17Jesus said to Peter the third time, "Simon, son of John, do you love Me?" Peter felt bad because Jesus asked him the third time, "Do you love Me?" He answered Jesus, "Lord, You know everything. You know I love You." Jesus said to him, "Feed My sheep. 18For sure, I tell you, when you were young, you put on your belt and went wherever you wanted to go. When you get old, you will put out your hands and someone else will put on your belt and take you away where you do not want to go." 19He said this to tell Peter what kind of death he would die to honor God. After Jesus said this, He said to Peter, "Follow Me."

Follow Me.

20Peter turned around. He saw the follower whom Jesus loved, following. This one had been beside Jesus at the supper. This is the one who had asked Jesus, "Lord, who will hand You over?"

²¹Peter saw him and said to Jesus, "But Lord, what about this one?" ²²Jesus said, "If I want this one to wait until I come, what is that to you? You follow Me." ²³So the news spread among the followers that this follower would not die. But Jesus did not say to him that he would not die. He said, "If I want him to wait until I come, what is that to you?"

John Tells That He Wrote This Book

²⁴This is the follower who is telling of these things and who has written them. We know that his word is true. ²⁵There are many other things which Jesus did also. If they were all written down, I do not think the world itself could hold the books that would be written.

Luke Writes To Theophilus

1 Dear Theophilus, in my first writings I wrote about all the things Jesus did and taught from the beginning ²until the day He went to heaven. He spoke to the missionaries through the Holy Spirit. He told those whom He had chosen what they should do. ³After He had suffered much and then died, He showed Himself alive in many sure ways for forty days. He told them many things about the holy nation of God.

Jesus Speaks Before He Goes To Be With The Father

⁴As they were gathered together with Him, He told them, "Do not leave Jerusalem. Wait for what the Father has promised. You heard Me speak of this. ⁵For John the Baptist baptized with water but in a few days you will be baptized with the Holy Spirit."

⁶Those who were with Him asked, "Lord, is this the time for You to give the nation back to the Jews?" ⁷He said, "It is not for you to know the special days or the special times which the Father has put in His own power.

⁸"But you will receive power when the Holy Spirit comes into your life. You will tell about Me in the city of Jerusalem and over all the countries of Judea and Samaria and to the ends of the earth."

Jesus Goes To Be With The Father

⁹When Jesus had said this and while they were still looking at Him, He was taken up. A cloud carried Him away so they could not see Him. ¹⁰They were still looking up to heaven, watching Him go. All at once two men dressed in white stood beside them. ¹¹They said, "You men of the country of Galilee, why do you stand looking up into heaven? This same Jesus Who was taken from you

into heaven will return in the same way you saw Him go up into heaven."

Matthias Is Chosen To Take The Place Of Judas

¹²The followers went back to Jerusalem from the Mountain of Olives, which is close to Jerusalem. ¹³When they came into the city, they went up to a room on the second floor where they stayed. The followers were Peter and John, James and Andrew, Philip and Thomas, Bartholomew and Matthew, James the son of Alphaeus, Simon the Canaanite, and Judas the brother of James. ¹⁴These all agreed as they prayed together. The women and Mary the mother of Jesus and His brothers were there.

¹⁵On one of those days Peter got up in front of the followers. (There were about 120 people there.) He said, ¹⁶"Men and brothers, it happened as the Holy Writings said it would happen which the Holy Spirit spoke through David. They told about Judas who would hand Jesus over to those who wanted to take Him. ¹⁷Judas was one of our group and had a part in our work. ¹⁸This man bought a field with the money he received for his sin. And falling down head first, his body broke open and his insides ran out. ¹⁹All the people of Jerusalem knew about this. They called the place Field of Blood. ²⁰For it is written in the Book of Psalms, 'Let his place of living be empty and let no one live there,' and, 'Let another person take over his work.' (Psalm 69:25; 109:8)

²¹"The man to take the place of Judas should be one of these men who walked along with us when the Lord Jesus was with us. ²²He must have been with Jesus from the day He was baptized by John to the day He was taken up from us. So one of these should be added to our group who will tell others that he saw Jesus raised from the dead."

²³They brought two men in front of them. They were Joseph, also called Barsabbas Justus, and Matthias. ²⁴Then the followers prayed, saying, "Lord, You know the hearts of all men. Show us which of these two men You have chosen. ²⁵He is to take the place of Judas in this work and be a missionary. Judas lost his place and went where he belonged because of sin." ²⁶Then they drew names and the name of Matthias was chosen. He became one with the eleven missionaries.

The Holy Spirit Comes On The Followers Of Jesus

2 The followers of Jesus were all together in one place fifty days after the special religious gathering to remember how the Jews left Egypt. ²All at once there was a sound from heaven like a powerful wind. It filled the house where they were sitting. ³Then they saw tongues which were divided that looked like fire. These came down on each one of them. ⁴They were all filled with the Holy Spirit. Then they began to speak in other languages which the Holy Spirit made them able to speak.

⁵There were many religious Jews staying in Jerusalem. They were from every country of the world. ⁶When they heard this strange sound, they gathered together. They all listened! It was hard for them to believe they were hearing words in their own language. ⁷They were surprised and wondered about it. They said to each other, "Are not these Galileans who are speaking? ⁸How is it that each one of us can hear his own language? ⁹We are Parthians and Medes, Elamites and from the countries of Mesopotamia, Judea and Cappadocia, Pontus and in the countries of Asia, ¹⁰Phrygia and Pamphylia, Egypt and the parts of Libya near Cyrene. Some have come from the city of Rome. Some are Jews by birth and others have become Jews. ¹¹Some are also men of the countries of Crete and Arabia. They are speaking of the powerful works of God to all of us in our own language!" ¹²They were all surprised and wondered about this. They said to each other, "What can this mean?" ¹³But others laughed and made fun, saying, "These men are full of new wine."

Peter Preaches — What Joel Said Would Happen Has Happened

¹⁴Then Peter stood up with the eleven missionaries and spoke with a loud voice, "Men of the country of Judea and all of you who are living in Jerusalem, I want you to know what is happening. So listen to what I am going to say. ¹⁵These men are not drunk as you think. It is only nine o'clock in the morning. ¹⁶The early preacher Joel said this would happen. ¹⁷God says, 'In the last days I will send My Spirit on all men. Then your sons and daughters will

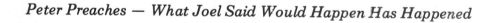

In the last days I will send My Spirit on all men.

speak God's Word. Your young men will see what God has given them to see. Your old men will dream dreams. ¹⁸Yes, on those I own, men and women, I will send My Spirit in those days. They will speak God's Word. ¹⁹I will show powerful works in the sky above. There will be things to see in the earth below like blood and fire and clouds of smoke. ²⁰The sun will turn dark and the moon will turn to blood before the day of the Lord. His coming will be a great and special day. ²¹It will be that whoever calls on the name of the Lord will be saved from the punishment of sin.' (Joel 2:28-32)

Peter Preaches — Jesus Shows Who He Is By What He Did

²²"Jewish men, listen to what I have to say! You knew Jesus of the town of Nazareth by the powerful works He did. God worked through Jesus while He was with you. You all know this. ²³Jesus was handed over to sinful men. God knew this and planned for it to happen. You had sinful men take Him and nail Him to a cross. ²⁴But God raised Him up. He allowed Him to be set free from the pain of death. Death could not hold its power over Him.

Peter Preaches — Jesus Shows Who He Is By What He Said

²⁵"David said this about Him, 'I can see the Lord before me all the time. He is at my right side so that I do not need to be troubled. ²⁶I am glad and my tongue is full of joy. My body rests in hope. ²⁷You will not leave my soul in death. You will not allow Your Holy One to be destroyed. ²⁸You have shown me the ways of life. I will be full of joy when I see Your face.' (Psalm 16)

²⁹"Brothers, I can tell you in plain words that our early father David not only died but was buried. We know where his grave is today. ³⁰He was one who spoke for God. He knew God had made a promise to him. From his family Christ would come and take His place as King. ³¹He knew this before and spoke of Christ being raised from the dead. Christ's soul would not be left in hell. His body would not be destroyed. ³²Jesus is this One! God has raised Him up and we have all seen Him.

³³"This Jesus has been lifted up to God's right side. The Holy Spirit was promised by the Father. God has given Him to us. That is what you are seeing and hearing now! ³⁴It was not David

who was taken up to heaven, because he said, 'The Lord said to my Lord, "Sit at My right side, [35]for those who hate You will be a place to rest Your feet." ' (Psalm 110:1) [36]The whole Jewish nation must know for sure that God has made this Jesus, Lord and Christ. He is the One you nailed to a cross!"

They Ask Peter What They Should Do

[37]When the Jews heard this, their hearts were troubled. They said to Peter and to the other missionaries, "Brothers, what should we do?" [38]Peter said to them, "Be sorry for your sins and turn from them and be baptized in the name of Jesus Christ, and your sins will be forgiven. You will receive the gift of the Holy Spirit. [39]This promise is to you and your children. It is to all people everywhere. It is to as many as the Lord our God will call."

Be sorry for your sins and turn from them and be baptized in the name of Jesus Christ, and your sins will be forgiven.

[40]He said many other things. He helped them understand that they should keep themselves from the sinful people of this day. [41]Those who believed what he said were baptized. There were about 3,000 more followers added that day.

The First Church

[42]They were faithful in listening to the teaching of the missionaries. They worshiped and prayed and ate the Lord's supper together. [43]Many powerful works were done by the missionaries. Surprise and fear came on them all. [44]All those who put their trust in Christ were together and shared what they owned. [45]As anyone had need, they sold what they owned and shared with everyone. [46]Day after day they went to the house of God together. In their houses they ate their food together. Their hearts were happy. [47]They gave thanks to God and all the people respected them. The Lord added to the group each day those who were being saved from the punishment of sin.

Peter And John Heal A Man At The Gate Of The House Of God

3 Peter and John were going to the house of God about three o'clock. It was the time for prayer. [2]Each day a certain man was carried to the Beautiful Gate of the house of God. This man had never been able to walk. He was there begging for money from those who were going in. ³He asked Peter and John for money when he saw them going in. ⁴Peter and John looked at him. Then Peter said, "Look at us!" ⁵The man who could not walk looked at them. He thought he would get something from them. ⁶Peter said, "I have no money, but what I have I will give you! In the name of Jesus Christ of Nazareth, get up and walk!" ⁷Peter took the man by the right hand and lifted him up. At once his feet and the bones in his legs became strong. ⁸He jumped up on his feet and walked. Then he went into the house of God with them. He gave thanks to God as he walked.

⁹All the people saw him walking and giving thanks to God. ¹⁰They knew it was the man who had been sitting and begging at the Beautiful Gate. They were surprised he was walking. ¹¹The man who was healed held on to Peter and John. All the people who were surprised gathered together around them in a place called Solomon's Porch.

Peter Preaches The Second Time

¹²When Peter saw this, he said to them, "Jewish men, why are you surprised at this? Why do you look at us as if we had made this man walk by our own power or holy lives? ¹³The God of our fathers, the God of Abraham and Isaac and Jacob, has done this. He has honored His Son Jesus. He is the One you handed over to Pilate. You turned your backs on Him after Pilate had decided to let Him go free. ¹⁴But you turned your backs against the Holy and Right One. Then you asked for a man who had killed someone to go free. ¹⁵You killed the very One Who made all life. But God raised Him from the dead. We saw Him alive. ¹⁶You see and know this man here. He has been made strong through faith in Jesus' name. Yes, it is faith in Christ that has made this man well and strong. This man is standing here in front of you all.

¹⁷"Brothers, I know you and your leaders did this without knowing what you were doing. ¹⁸In this way, God did what He said He would do through all the early preachers. He said that Christ must suffer many hard things. ¹⁹But you must be sorry for your sins and turn from them. You must turn to God and have

your sins taken away. Then many times your soul will receive new strength from the Lord. [20]He will send Jesus back to the world. He is the Christ Who long ago was chosen for you. [21]But for awhile He must stay in heaven until the time when all things are made right. God said these things would happen through His holy early preachers.

[22]"Moses said, 'The Lord God will raise up from among your brothers One Who speaks for God, as He raised me. You must listen to everything He says. [23]Everyone among the people who will not listen to that One Who speaks for God will be put to death.' (Deuteronomy 18:19) [24]All the early preachers who have spoken from Samuel until now have told of these days. [25]You are of the family of the early preachers and of the promise that God made with our early fathers. He said to Abraham, 'All the families of the earth will receive God's favor through your children.' [25]God has raised up His Son Jesus and has sent Him to you first to give God's favor to each of you who will turn away from his sinful ways."

Peter And John Are Put Into Prison

4 The religious leaders and the leader of the house of God and some of the religious group who believe no one will be raised from the dead came to Peter and John while they were talking to the people. [2]They were angry because Peter and John had been teaching the people and preaching that Jesus had been raised from the dead. [3]So they took them and put them into prison until the next day because it was evening. [4]But many of those who heard what Peter and John said put their trust in Christ. The group of followers was now about 5,000 men.

Peter Speaks To The Religious Leader's Court

[5]The next day the leaders of the court and the leaders of the people and the teachers of the Law came together in Jerusalem. [6]Annas the head religious leader was there. Caiaphas and John and Alexander were there also and all who were in the family of the head religious leader. [7]They put the missionaries in front of them and asked, "By what power or in whose name have you done this?"

⁸Then Peter, having been filled with the Holy Spirit, said, "You who are leaders of the people, ⁹are you asking us today about the good work we did to a man who needed help? Are you asking how he was healed? ¹⁰You and all the Jews must know that it was by the name of Jesus Christ of Nazareth, the One you nailed to a cross and God raised from the dead. It is through Him that this man stands in front of you well and strong. ¹¹Christ is the Stone that was put aside by you workmen. But He has become the most important Stone in the building. (Psalm 118:22) ¹²There is no way to be saved from the punishment of sin through anyone else. For there is no other name under heaven given to men by which we can be saved."

Peter And John Are Free To Go But Are Told Not To Preach

¹³They were surprised and wondered how easy it was for Peter and John to speak. They could tell they were men who had not gone to school. But they knew they had been with Jesus. ¹⁴They were not able to argue about what Peter and John had said because the man who had been healed was standing with them.

¹⁵The religious leaders told Peter and John to leave the court so the leaders could talk together. ¹⁶They said, "What should we do with these men? Everyone living in Jerusalem knows a powerful work has been done by them. We cannot say that it did not happen. ¹⁷Let us tell them with strong words that they must not speak again to anyone in this name. This will keep the news from going out among the people."

¹⁸Then they called them in and told them they must not speak or teach anymore in the name of Jesus. ¹⁹Peter and John said, "If it is right to listen to you more than to God, you decide about that. ²⁰For we must tell what we have seen and heard."

²¹After they had spoken more sharp words to them, they let them go. They could not beat them because the people were giving thanks to God for what had happened. ²²The man on whom this powerful work of healing had been done was more than forty years old.

The Prayer Of The Young Church

²³As soon as the missionaries were free to go, they went back to their own group. They told them everything the religious leaders had said. ²⁴When they heard it, they all prayed to God, saying, "Lord God, You made the heaven and the earth and the sea and everything that is in them. ²⁵You said through the Holy Spirit by the mouth of our early father David, 'Why are the nations so shaken up and the people planning foolish things? ²⁶The kings of the earth stood in a line ready to fight, and the leaders were all against the Lord and against His Christ.' (Psalm 2:1-2) ²⁷You know that Herod and Pilate and the Jews and the people who are not Jews gathered together here against Jesus. He was Your Holy Son and the One You had chosen ²⁸to do everything You planned and said would happen. ²⁹And now, Lord, listen to their sharp words. Make it easy for the workmen You own to preach Your Word with power. ³⁰May You heal and do powerful works and special things to see through the name of Jesus, Your Holy Son!"

The Christians Are Filled With The Holy Spirit

³¹When they had finished praying, the place where they were gathered was shaken. They were all filled with the Holy Spirit. It was easy for them to speak the Word of God.

The New Way Of Life

³²The many followers acted and thought the same way. None of them said that any of their things were their own, but they shared all things. ³³The missionaries told with much power how Jesus was raised from the dead. God's favor was on them all. ³⁴No one was in need. All who owned houses or pieces of land sold them and brought the money from what was sold. ³⁵They gave it to the missionaries. It was divided to each one as he had need.

³⁶Joseph was among them. The missionaries called him Barnabas. His name means Son of Comfort. He was from the family group of Levi and from the country of Cyprus. ³⁷He had some land which he sold and brought the money to the missionaries.

The Sin Of Ananias And Sapphira

5 A man by the name of Ananias and his wife, Sapphira, sold some land. ²He kept back part of the money for himself. His wife knew it also. The other part he took to the missionaries. ³Peter said to Ananias, "Why did you let Satan fill your heart? He made you lie to the Holy Spirit. You kept back part of the money you got from your land. ⁴Was not the land yours before you sold it? After it was sold, you could have done what you wanted to do with the money. Why did you allow your heart to do this? You have lied to God, not to men."

⁵When Ananias heard these words, he fell down dead. Much fear came on all those who heard what was done. ⁶The young men got up and covered his body and carried him out and buried him.

⁷About three hours later his wife came in. She did not know what had happened. ⁸Peter said to her, "Tell me, did you sell the land for this amount of money?" She said, "Yes." ⁹Then Peter said to her, "How could you two have talked together about lying to the Holy Spirit? Listen! Those who buried your husband are standing at the door and they will carry you out also." ¹⁰At once she fell down at his feet and died. When the young men came in, they found that she was dead. They took her out and buried her beside her husband. ¹¹Much fear came on all the church and on all who heard it.

The First Church Grows

¹²The missionaries did many powerful works among the people. They gathered together on Solomon's porch. ¹³No one from outside their own group came in with them because they were afraid. But those outside the church had respect for the followers. ¹⁴Many more men and women put their trust in Christ and were added to the group. ¹⁵They brought the sick people and laid them on the streets hoping that if Peter walked by, his shadow would fall on some of them. ¹⁶Many people went into Jerusalem from towns nearby. They took with them their sick people and all who were troubled with demons. All of them were healed.

The Missionaries Are Put Into Prison

¹⁷The head religious leader heard this. Some of the religious group who believe no one will be raised from the dead also heard of the people being healed. They became very jealous. ¹⁸They took hold of the missionaries and put them into prison. ¹⁹An angel of the Lord opened the doors of the prison in the night and let them out. The angel said to them, ²⁰"Go, stand where you have been standing in the house of God. Keep on telling the people about this new life."

²¹When Peter and John heard this, they went into the house of God early in the morning and began to teach. When the head religious leader and those with him had come, they gathered the men of the court and the leaders of the Jews together. Then they sent to have the missionaries brought to them from the prison. ²²When the soldiers got there, they did not find them in prison. They went back and told the court. ²³The soldiers said, "We found the door of the prison locked and the soldiers watching the doors. When we opened the door, we found no one inside."

²⁴When the religious leaders and the leader of the house of God heard this, they were much troubled as to what might happen. ²⁵Then someone came and told them. "The men you put into prison are now standing in the house of God and teaching the people." ²⁶The leader of the house of God took his men and got them. They did not hurt the missionaries because they were afraid the people would throw stones at them.

²⁷They brought the missionaries in and made them stand in front of the court. The head religious leader said, ²⁸"We told you not to teach about Christ! Look! You are spreading this teaching over all Jerusalem. Now you are making it look as if we are guilty of killing this Man."

The Missionaries Speak The Truth

²⁹Then Peter and the missionaries said, "We must obey God instead of men! ³⁰The God of our early fathers raised up Jesus, the One you killed and nailed to a cross. ³¹God raised this Man to His own right side as a leader and as the One Who saves from the punishment of sin. He makes it possible for the Jews to be sorry

Go, stand where you have been standing in the house of God. Keep on telling the people about this new life.

for their sins. Then they can turn from them and be forgiven. ³²We have seen these things and are telling about them. The Holy Spirit makes these things known also. God gives His Spirit to those who obey Him."

Gamaliel Speaks In Court

³³The religious leaders became angry when they heard this. They planned to kill the missionaries. ³⁴Gamaliel was a man of the religious leaders' court. He was a proud religious law-keeper and a teacher of the Law. He was respected by all the people. He stood up and said that the missionaries should be sent outside for a short time.

³⁵Then Gamaliel said to the court, "Jewish men, be careful what you plan to do with these men. ³⁶Remember that many years ago a man called Theudas made himself out to be someone great. He had about 400 followers. He was killed. His followers were divided and nothing came of his teaching. ³⁷After him, Judas of the country of Galilee gathered many followers. It was the time for every person to have his name written in the books of the nation. This Judas was killed also. All his followers were divided and went away. ³⁸I say to you now, stay away from these men and leave them alone. If this teaching and work is from men, it will come to nothing. ³⁹If it is from God, you will not be able to stop it. You may even find yourselves fighting against God."

⁴⁰The court agreed with Gamaliel. So they called the missionaries in and beat them. They told them they must not speak in the name of Jesus. Then they were sent away.

So the missionaries went away from the court happy that they could suffer shame because of His Name.

⁴¹So the missionaries went away from the court happy that they could suffer shame because of His Name. ⁴²Every day in the house of God and in the homes, they kept teaching and preaching about Jesus Christ.

Church Leaders Are Chosen

6 In those days the group of followers was getting larger. Greek-speaking Jews in the group complained against the Jews living in the country around Jerusalem. The Greek-speaking

Jews said that their women whose husbands had died were not taken care of when the food was given out each day. ²So the twelve missionaries called a meeting of the many followers and said. "It is not right that we should give up preaching the Word of God to hand out food. ³Brothers, choose from among you seven men who are respected and who are full of the Holy Spirit and wisdom. We will have them take care of this work. ⁴Then we will use all of our time to pray and to teach the Word of God."

⁵These words pleased all of them. They chose Stephen who was a man full of faith and full of the Holy Spirit. They also chose Philip, Prochorus, Nicanor, Timon, Parmenas and Nicholas of Antioch who had become a Jew. ⁶These men were taken to the missionaries. After praying, the missionaries laid their hands on them.

⁷The Word of God spread further. The group of followers became much larger in Jerusalem. Many of the religious leaders believed in the faith of the Christians.

Stephen Is Brought In Front Of The Religious Leaders' Court

⁸Stephen was a man full of faith and power. He did many great things among the people. ⁹But some men came from their place of worship who were known as the Free people. They started to argue with Stephen. These men were from the countries of Cyrene and Alexandria and Cilicia and Asia. ¹⁰Stephen spoke with wisdom and power given by the Holy Spirit. They were not able to say anything against what he said. ¹¹So they told other men to say, "We have heard him say things against Moses and God." ¹²In this way they got the people talking against Stephen. The leaders of the people and the teachers of the Law came and took him to the religious leader's court. ¹³The people were told to lie and say, "This man keeps on talking against this place of worship and the Law of Moses. ¹⁴We have heard him say, 'Jesus of Nazareth is going to pull down this place. He is going to change what Moses taught us.' "

¹⁵The men sitting in the religious leader's court were looking at Stephen. They all saw that his face looked like the face of an angel.

Stephen Speaks About The God Of Abraham

7 The head religious leader asked Stephen, "Are these things true?" ²Stephen said, "My brothers and fathers, listen to me. The great God showed Himself to our early father Abraham while he lived in the country of Mesopotamia. This was before he moved to the country of Haran. ³God said to him, 'Leave your family and this land where you were born. Go to a land that I will show you.' ⁴He went from the land of the Chaldeans and lived in Haran. After his father died, he came to this country where you now live. ⁵God did not give him any land to own, not even enough to put his feet on. But He promised that the land would be his and his children's after him. At that time he had no children. ⁶This is what God said, 'Your children's children will be living in a strange land. They will live there 400 years. They will be made to work without pay and will suffer many hard things. ⁷I will say to that nation that it is guilty for holding them and making them work without pay. After that they will go free. They will leave that country and worship Me in this place.'

⁸"He made a promise with Abraham. It was kept by a religious act of becoming a Jew. Abraham had a son, Isaac. On the eighth day Abraham took Isaac and had this religious act done to him. Isaac was the father of Jacob. Jacob was the father of our twelve early fathers.

⁹"The sons of Jacob sold Joseph to people from the country of Egypt because they were jealous of him. But God was with Joseph. ¹⁰He helped him in all his troubles. He gave him wisdom and favor with Pharaoh, the king of Egypt. This king made Joseph leader over Egypt and over all the king's house.

God was with Joseph.

¹¹"The time came when there was no food to eat in all the land of Egypt and Canaan. The people suffered much. Our early fathers were not able to get food. ¹²Then Jacob heard there was food in Egypt. He sent our early fathers there the first time.

¹³"The second time they went to the country of Egypt, Joseph made himself known to his brothers. The family of Joseph became

known to Pharaoh. ¹⁴Joseph asked his father Jacob and all his family to come. There were seventy-five people in the family. ¹⁵Jacob moved down to Egypt and died there. Our early fathers died there also. ¹⁶They were brought back to the city of Shechem where they were buried. Abraham paid money for the grave from the sons of Hamor in Shechem.

Stephen Speaks About The God Of Moses

¹⁷"The promise God had given Abraham was about to happen. At this time many more of our people were in the country of Egypt. ¹⁸Then another man became king in Egypt. He was a king who did not know Joseph. ¹⁹He was hard on our people and nation. He worked against our early fathers. He made them put their babies outside so they would die.

²⁰"At that time Moses was born. He was beautiful in God's sight. He was fed in his father's house for three months. ²¹Then he was put outside. Pharaoh's daughter took him and cared for him as her own son. ²²Moses was taught in all the wisdom of the Egyptians. He became a powerful man in words and in the things he did. ²³When he was forty years old, he thought he should visit his brothers, the Jews. ²⁴He saw one of the Jews being hurt. Moses helped the Jew and killed the man from Egypt. ²⁵He thought his people would understand. He thought they knew God would let them go free by his help. But the people did not understand.

²⁶"The next day Moses came to some Jews who were having a fight. He tried to get them to stop. Moses said to the Jews, 'Sirs, you are brothers. Why do you hurt each other?' ²⁷One was beating his neighbor. He pushed Moses away and said, 'Who made you a boss over us? Who said you could say who is guilty? ²⁸Do you want to kill me as you killed the man from Egypt yesterday?' ²⁹When Moses heard that, he went as fast as he could to the country of Midian where he was a stranger. While he was there, he became the father of two sons. ³⁰Forty years passed and Moses was near the Mountain of Sinai where no people live. There he saw an angel in the fire of a burning bush. ³¹He was surprised and wondered when he saw it. He went up close to see it better. Then

he heard the voice of the Lord speak to him. ³²'I am the God of your fathers, the God of Abraham and of Isaac and of Jacob.' Moses shook! He was so afraid he did not look at the bush.

³³"Then the Lord said to him, 'Take your shoes off your feet! The place where you are standing is holy ground. ³⁴I have seen My people suffer in the country of Egypt and I have heard their cries. I have come down to let them go free. So come now, I will send you back to Egypt.'

³⁵"The people had put Moses aside. They said, 'Who made you a leader over us? Who said you are the one to say what is right or wrong?' But God made this man a leader. Moses was the one who brought them out of the country of Egypt. This was done by the help of the angel who was in the burning bush. ³⁶This man led them. He did powerful works in the land of Egypt and at the Red Sea. For forty years he led them in the desert.

³⁷"Moses said to the Jews, 'God will give you one who speaks for Him like me from among your brothers.' ³⁸This is the man who was with the Jewish nation in the desert. The angel talked to him on the Mountain of Sinai. Moses told it to our early fathers. He also received the living Words of God to give to us.

³⁹"Our early fathers would not listen to him. They did not obey him. In their hearts they wanted to go back to the country of Egypt. ⁴⁰They said to Aaron, 'Make us gods to go before us. We do not know what has happened to this Moses who led us out of the land of Egypt.'

⁴¹"In those days they made a calf of gold. They put gifts down in front of their god in worship. They were happy with what they had made with their hands. ⁴²But God turned from them and let them worship the stars of heaven. This is written in the book of the early preachers, 'Nation of Jews, was it to Me you gave gifts of sheep and cattle on the altar for forty years in the desert? ⁴³No, you set up the tent to worship in to the god of Molock and the star of your god Rompha. You made gods to worship them. I will carry you away to the other side of the country of Babylon.' (Amos 5:25-27)

The Place Of Worship And The House Of God

44"'Our early fathers had the tent to worship in. They used it in the desert. God told Moses to make it like the plan which he had seen. 45This tent to worship in was received by our early fathers. They brought it here when they won the wars with the people who were not Jews. It was when Joshua was our leader. God made those people leave as our early fathers took the land. The tent was here until the time of David. 46David pleased God and wanted to build a house for worship for the God of Jacob. 47But Solomon was the one who built the house of God for Him. 48But the Most High does not live in buildings made by hands. The early preacher said, 49'Heaven is the place where I sit and the earth is the place where I rest My feet. What house will you build Me?' says the Lord. 'Or what is My place of rest? 50Did not My hands make all these things?' (Isaiah 66:1-2)

The Jews Are Hurt

51"'You have hard hearts and ears that will not listen to me! You are always working against the Holy Spirit. Your early fathers did. You do too. 52Which of the early preachers was not beaten and hurt by your early fathers? They killed those who told of the coming of the One Right with God. Now you have handed Him over and killed Him. 53You had the Law given to you by angels. Yet you have not kept it."

Stephen Is Killed

54The Jews and religious leaders listened to Stephen. Then they became angry and began to grind their teeth at him. 55He was filled with the Holy Spirit. As he looked up into heaven, he saw the shining greatness of God and Jesus standing at the right side of God. 56He said, "Look! I see heaven open and the Son of Man standing at the right side of God!" 57They cried out with loud voices. They put their hands over their ears and they all pushed on him. 58Then they took him out of the city and threw stones at him. The men who were throwing the stones laid their coats down in front of a young man named Saul. 59While they threw stones at Stephen, he prayed, "Lord Jesus, receive my spirit." 60After that he fell on his knees and cried out with a loud voice, "Lord, do not hold this sin against them." When he had said this, he died.

It Is Hard For The Christians In Jerusalem

8 Saul thought it was all right that Stephen was killed. On that day people started to work very hard against the church in Jerusalem. All the followers, except the missionaries, were made to leave. They went to parts of the countries of Judea and Samaria. ²Good men put Stephen in a grave. There was much sorrow because of him. ³During this time Saul was making it very hard for the church. He went into every house of the followers of Jesus and took men and women and put them into prison.

Philip Preaches In Samaria

⁴Those who had been made to go to other places preached the Word as they went. ⁵Philip went down to a city in Samaria and preached about Christ. ⁶The people all listened to what Philip said. As they listened, they watched him do powerful works. ⁷There were many people who had demons in their bodies. The demons cried with loud voices when they went out of the people. Many of the people could not move their bodies or arms and legs. They were all healed. ⁸There was much joy in that city.

Simon The Witchdoctor

⁹A man by the name of Simon had done witchcraft there. The people of Samaria were surprised at the things he did. He pretended that he was a great man. ¹⁰All the people watched and listened to him. They said, "This man must be that great power of God." ¹¹They kept running after him. For a long time he fooled them with his witchcraft.

¹²Philip told the Good News of the holy nation of God and of Jesus Christ. Both men and women put their trust in Christ and were baptized. ¹³Even Simon believed in Christ and was baptized. He went along with Philip everywhere. He was surprised when he saw the powerful works that were being done.

¹⁴The missionaries in Jerusalem heard that the people of Samaria had received the Word of God. They sent Peter and John

to them. [15]When Peter and John got there, they prayed that the new followers might receive the Holy Spirit. [16]He had not yet come on any of them. They had been baptized in the name of the Lord Jesus only. [17]They laid their hands on them and the followers received the Holy Spirit.

[18]When Simon saw that the Holy Spirit was given when the missionaries laid their hands on the people, he wanted to give money to the missionaries. [19]He said, "Let me also have this power. Then I can give the Holy Spirit to anyone I lay my hands on." [20]Peter said to him, "May your money be destroyed with you because you thought you could buy the gift of God with money! [21]You have no part or place in this work. Your heart is not right in God's sight. [22]You must be sorry for this sin of yours and turn from it. Pray to the Lord that He will forgive you for having such a thought in your heart. [23]I see that you are full of jealousy and chained by your sin." [24]Simon said, "Pray to the Lord for me that nothing you have said will come to me."

[25]Peter and John went back to Jerusalem after telling what they had seen and heard. They had preached the Word of the Lord also. On the way they preached the Good News in many other towns in the country of Samaria.

Philip And The Man From Ethiopia

[26]An angel of the Lord spoke to Philip saying, "Get up and go south. Take the road that goes down from Jerusalem to the country of Gaza. It goes through the desert." [27]Philip got up and went. A man from the country of Ethiopia had come to Jerusalem to worship. He had been made so he could not have children. He cared for all the riches that belonged to Candace who was Queen of the country of Ethiopia. [28]As he was going back home, he was sitting in his wagon reading the Book of the early preacher Isaiah. [29]The Holy Spirit said to Philip, "Go over to that wagon and get on it." [30]Philip ran up to him. He saw that the man from Ethiopia was reading from the writings of the early preacher Isaiah and said, "Do you understand what you are reading?" [31]The man from Ethiopia said, "How can I, unless someone teaches me?" Then he asked Philip to come up and sit beside him.

³²He was reading the part in the Holy Writings which says, "He was taken like a sheep to be put to death. A lamb does not make a sound while its wool is cut. So He made no sound. ³³No one listened to Him because of His shame. Who will tell the story of His day? For His life was taken away from the earth." (Isaiah 53:7-8)

³⁴The man from Ethiopia said to Philip, "Who is the early preacher talking about, himself, or someone else?" ³⁵So Philip started with this part of the Holy Writings and preached the Good News of Jesus to him.

³⁶As they went on their way, they came to some water. The man from Ethiopia said, "Look! Here is water. What is to stop me from being baptized?" ³⁷*Philip said, "If you believe with all your heart, you may." The man said, "I believe that Jesus Christ is the Son of God." ³⁸He stopped the wagon. Then both Philip and the man from Ethiopia went down into the water and Philip baptized him.

I believe that Jesus Christ is the Son of God.

³⁹When they came up out of the water, the Holy Spirit took Philip away. The man from Ethiopia did not see Philip again. He went on his way full of joy. ⁴⁰Philip found himself at the city of Azotus. Then Philip went through all the towns as far as the city of Caesarea preaching the Good News at each place.

Saul Becomes A Christian

9 Saul was still talking much about how he would like to kill the followers of the Lord. He went to the head religious leader. ²He asked for letters to be written to the Jewish places of worship in the city of Damascus. The letters were to say that if he found any men or women following the Way of Christ he might bring them to Jerusalem in chains.

³He went on his way until he came near the city of Damascus. All at once he saw a light from heaven shining around him. ⁴He fell to the ground. Then he heard a voice say, "Saul, Saul, why are you working so hard against Me?" ⁵Saul answered, "Who are You, Lord?" He said, "I am Jesus, the One Whom you are working against. You hurt yourself by trying to hurt Me." ⁶Saul

was shaken and surprised. Then he said, "What do you want me to do, Lord?" The Lord said to him, "Get up! Go into the city and you will be told what to do."

7Those with Saul were not able to say anything. They heard a voice but saw no one. 8Saul got up from the ground. When he opened his eyes, he saw nothing. They took him by the hand and led him into the city of Damascus. 9He could not see for three days. During that time he did not eat or drink.

10In Damascus there was a follower by the name of Ananias. The Lord showed him in a dream what He wanted him to see. He said, "Ananias!" And Ananias answered, "Yes, Lord, I am here." 11The Lord said, "Get up! Go over to Straight Street to Judas' house and ask for a man from the city of Tarsus. His name is Saul. You will find him praying there. 12Saul has seen a man called Ananias in a dream. He is to come and put his hands on Saul so he might see again."

13Ananias said, "But Lord, many people have told me about this man. He is the reason many of Your followers in Jerusalem have had to suffer much. 14He came here with the right and the power from the head religious leaders to put everyone in chains who call on Your name." 15The Lord said to him, "Go! This man is the one I have chosen to carry My name among the people who are not Jews and to their kings and to Jews. 16I will show him how much he will have to suffer because of Me."

Saul Is Baptized

17So Ananias went to that house. He put his hands on Saul and said, "Brother Saul, the Lord Jesus has sent me to you. You saw the Lord along the road as you came here. The Lord has sent me so you might be able to see again and be filled with the Holy Spirit." 18At once something like a covering fell from the eyes of Saul and he could see. He got up and was baptized. 19After that he ate some food and received strength. For some days he stayed with the followers in the city of Damascus.

Saul Preaches The Good News

20At once Saul began to preach in the Jewish places of worship that Jesus is the Son of God. 21All who heard him were surprised

and wondered. They said, "This is the man who beat and killed the followers in Jerusalem. He came here to tie the followers in chains and take them to the head religious leaders." ²²But Saul kept on growing in power. The Jews living in the city of Damascus wondered about Saul's preaching. He was proving that Jesus was the Christ.

²³After some days the Jews talked together and made plans how they might kill Saul. ²⁴He heard of their plans. Day and night they watched for him at the city gates to kill him. ²⁵So the followers helped him get away at night. They let him down over the wall in a basket.

Saul Comes To Jerusalem

²⁶When Saul had come to Jerusalem, he tried to join the followers. But they were afraid of him. They did not believe he was a true follower of Jesus. ²⁷Then Barnabas took him to the missionaries. He told them that Saul had seen the Lord on the road. He told them also how the Lord had spoken to Saul and how he had preached without fear in the city of Damascus in the name of Jesus. ²⁸After that he was with them going in and out of Jerusalem. ²⁹He preached without fear in the name of the Lord. He talked and argued with the Jews who spoke the Greek language. They kept trying to kill him. ³⁰When the followers heard this, they took him down to the city of Caesarea. From there they sent him to the city of Tarsus.

³¹Then the church through all the countries of Judea and Galilee and Samaria had peace for awhile. The church was made strong and it was given comfort by the Holy Spirit. It honored the Lord. More people were added to the church.

Aeneas Is Healed

³²When Peter was visiting all parts of the country, he came to the faithful followers who were living in the city of Lydda. ³³A man there named Aeneas could not move his body. He had been in bed eight years. ³⁴Peter said to him, "Aeneas, Jesus Christ heals you. Get up and roll up your bed." He got up at once. ³⁵All the people who lived in Lydda and in the city of Sharon saw Aeneas and they turned to the Lord.

Dorcas Is Raised From The Dead

[36]A woman who was a follower lived in the city of Joppa. Her name was Tabitha, or Dorcas. She did many good things and many acts of kindness. [37]One day she became sick and died. After they had washed her body, they laid her in a room on the second floor. [38]The city of Lydda was near Joppa. The followers heard that Peter was at Lydda and sent two men to ask him to come at once. [39]Peter went back with them. When he came, they took him to the room. All the women whose husbands had died were standing around crying. They were showing the clothes Dorcas had made while she was with them.

[40]Peter made them all leave the room. Then he got down on his knees and prayed. He turned to her body and said, "Tabitha, get up!" She opened her eyes and looked at Peter and sat up. [41]He took her by the hand and lifted her up. Then he called in the faithful followers and the women whose husbands had died. He gave her to them, a living person.

[42]News of this went through all Joppa. Many people put their trust in the Lord. [43]After this, Peter stayed in the city of Joppa many days in the house of Simon who worked with leather.

God Speaks To A Man Who Was Not A Jew

10 There was a man in the city of Caesarea by the name of Cornelius. He was a captain of an Italian group of the army. [2]He and his family were good people and honored God. He gave much money to the people and prayed always to God.

[3]One afternoon about three o'clock he saw in a dream what God wanted him to see. An angel of God came to him and said, "Cornelius." [4]He was afraid as he looked at the angel. He said, "What is it, Lord?" The angel said, "Your prayers and your gifts of money have gone up to God. He has remembered them. [5]Send some men to the city of Joppa and ask Simon Peter to come here. [6]He is living with Simon, the man who works with leather. His house is by the seashore. He will tell you what you must do." [7]The angel left him. Then Cornelius called two of the workmen he

owned and a religious soldier who took care of him. ⁸He told what had happened. Then he sent them to Joppa.

Peter's Dream

⁹The next day they went on their way. About noon they were coming near the town. At this time Peter went up on the roof to pray. ¹⁰He became very hungry and wanted something to eat. While they were getting food ready to eat, he saw in a dream things God wanted him to see. ¹¹He saw heaven opened and something like a large linen cloth being let down to earth by the four corners. ¹²On the cloth were all kinds of four-footed animals and snakes of the earth and birds of the sky. ¹³A voice came to him, "Get up, Peter, kill something and eat it." ¹⁴Peter said, "No, Lord! I have never eaten anything that our Law says is dirty." ¹⁵The voice said the second time, "What God has made clean you must not say is dirty." ¹⁶This happened three times. Then it was taken back to heaven.

Cornelius' Men Find Peter

¹⁷Peter thought about the meaning of the dream. The men that Cornelius had sent came. They were standing by the gate asking about Simon's house. ¹⁸They called to ask if Simon Peter was staying there.

¹⁹Peter was still thinking about the dream when the Holy Spirit said to him, "See, three men are looking for you. ²⁰Get up. Go down and go with them. Do not doubt if you should go, because I sent them." ²¹Peter went down to the men who had been sent by Cornelius. He said, "I am the one you are looking for. Why have you come?" ²²They said, "Cornelius sent us. He is a captain and a good man and he honors God. The whole Jewish nation can say this is true. An angel from God told him to send for you. He asks you to come to his house. He wants to hear what you have to say."

Peter Goes To Cornelius

²³Peter asked them to come in and stay with him for the night. The next day he went with them. Some of the brothers from the

city of Joppa went along. ²⁴The next day they came to the city of Caesarea. Cornelius was looking for them. He had gathered all his family and close friends at his house. ²⁵When Peter came, Cornelius got down at his feet and worshiped him. ²⁶But Peter raised him up and said, "Get up! I am just a man like you." ²⁷As Peter spoke with Cornelius, he went into the house and found a large group of people gathered together.

²⁸Peter said to them, "You know it is against our Law for a Jew to visit a person of another nation. But God has shown me I should not say that any man is dirty. ²⁹For this reason I came as soon as you sent for me. But I want to ask you why you sent for me?"

³⁰Cornelius said, "Four days ago at three o'clock in the afternoon I was praying here in my house. All at once, I saw a man standing in front of me. He had on bright clothes. ³¹He said to me, 'Cornelius, God has heard your prayers and has remembered your gifts of love. ³²You must send to the city of Joppa and ask Simon Peter to come here. He is staying at the house of Simon, the man who works with leather. His house is by the seashore.' ³³I sent for you at once. You have done well to come. We are all here and God is with us. We are ready to hear whatever the Lord has told you to say.'"

Peter Preached In Cornelius' House

³⁴Then Peter said, "I can see, for sure, that God does not respect one person more than another. ³⁵He is pleased with any man in any nation who honors Him and does what is right. ³⁶He has sent His Word to the Jews. He told them the Good News of peace through Jesus Christ. Jesus is Lord of all. ³⁷You know the story yourselves. It was told in all the country of Judea. It began in the country of Galilee after the preaching of John the Baptist. ³⁸God gave Jesus of Nazareth the Holy Spirit and power. He went around doing good and healing all who were troubled by the devil because God was with Him. ³⁹We have seen and heard everything He did in the land of the Jews and in Jerusalem. And yet they killed Him by nailing Him to a cross. ⁴⁰God raised Him to life on the third day and made Him to be seen. ⁴¹Not all the people saw Him but those who were chosen to see Him. We saw Him. We ate and drank with Him after He was raised from the dead. ⁴²He told

God raised Him to life on the third day.

us to preach to the people and tell them that God gave Christ the right to be the One Who says who is guilty of the living and the dead. ⁴³All the early preachers spoke of this. Everyone who puts his trust in Christ will have his sins forgiven through His name."

The Holy Spirit Comes To The Family Of Cornelius

⁴⁴While Peter was speaking, the Holy Spirit came on all who were hearing his words. ⁴⁵The Jewish followers who had come along with Peter were surprised and wondered because the gift of the Holy Spirit was also given to the people who were not Jews. ⁴⁶They heard them speak in special sounds and give thanks to God. Then Peter said, ⁴⁷"Will anyone say that these people may not be baptized? They have received the Holy Spirit just as we have." ⁴⁸He gave the word that they should be baptized in the name of the Lord. Then they asked Peter to stay with them for some days.

Peter Tells Why He Preached To The People Who Are Not Jews

11 The missionaries and followers who were in the country of Judea heard that the people who were not Jews also had received the Word of God. ²When Peter went up to Jerusalem, the Jewish followers argued with him. ³They said, "Why did you visit those people who are not Jews and eat with them?"

⁴Then Peter began to tell all that had happened from the beginning to the end. He said, ⁵"While I was praying in the city of Joppa, I saw in a dream something coming down from heaven. It was like a large linen cloth let down by the four corners until it came to me. ⁶As I looked at it, I saw four-footed animals and snakes of the earth and birds of the sky. ⁷I heard a voice saying to me, 'Get up, Peter, kill something and eat it.' ⁸But I said, 'No, Lord! Nothing that is dirty has ever gone into my mouth.' ⁹The voice from heaven said the second time, 'What God has made clean you must not say is dirty.' ¹⁰This happened three times and then it was taken up again into heaven.

¹¹"Three men had already come to the house where I was staying. They had been sent to me from the city of Caesarea.

¹²The Holy Spirit told me to go with them and not doubt about going. These six men also went with me to this man's house. ¹³He told us how he had seen an angel in his own home. The angel had stood in front of him and said, 'Send men to the city of Joppa to ask for Simon Peter. ¹⁴He will tell you and all your family how you can be saved from the punishment of sin.'

¹⁵"As I began to talk to them, the Holy Spirit came down on them just as He did on us at the beginning. ¹⁶Then I remembered the Lord had said, 'John baptized with water but you will be baptized with the Holy Spirit.' ¹⁷If God gave to them the same gift He gave to us when we put our trust in the Lord Jesus Christ, how could I stand against God?"

¹⁸When they heard these words, they said nothing more. They thanked God, saying, "Then God has given life also to the people who are not Jews. They have this new life by being sorry for their sins and turning from them."

God has given life also to the people who are not Jews.

The Followers Are Called Christians First In Antioch

¹⁹Those who went different places because of the trouble that started over Stephen had gone as far as the cities of Phoenicia and Cyprus and Antioch. They had preached the Word, but only to the Jews. ²⁰Some of the men from the cities of Cyprus and Cyrene returned to Antioch. They preached the Good News of Jesus Christ to the Greek people there. ²¹The Lord gave them power. Many people put their trust in the Lord and turned to Him.

²²The news of this came to the church in Jerusalem. They sent Barnabas to the city of Antioch. ²³When he got there and saw how good God had been to them, he was full of joy. He told them to be true and faithful to the Lord. ²⁴Barnabas was a good man and full of the Holy Spirit and faith. And many people became followers of the Lord.

²⁵From there Barnabas went on to the city of Tarsus to look for Saul. ²⁶When he found Saul, he brought him back with him to the city of Antioch. For a year they taught many people in the church. The followers were first called Christians in Antioch.

The Antioch Church Helps The Jerusalem Church

²⁷At that time some men who preached God's Word came to Antioch and told what was going to happen. They were from Jerusalem. ²⁸One of them was Agabus. The Holy Spirit told him to stand up and speak. He told them there would be very little food to eat over all the world. This happened when Claudius was leader of the country. ²⁹The Christians agreed that each one should give what money he could to help the Christians living in the country of Judea. ³⁰They did this and sent it to the church leaders with Barnabas and Saul.

The King Makes It Hard For The Church

12 At that time King Herod used his power to make it hard for the Christians in the church. ²He killed James, the brother of John, with a sword. ³When he saw that it made the Jews happy, he took hold of Peter also. This was during the special religious gathering to remember how the Jews left Egypt. ⁴Herod took Peter and put him into prison and had sixteen soldiers watch him. After the special religious gathering was over, he planned to bring Peter out to the people.

Peter Goes Free

⁵So Peter was held in prison. But the church kept praying to God for him. ⁶The night before Herod was to bring him out for his trial, Peter was sleeping between two soldiers. He was tied with two chains. Soldiers stood by the door and watched the prison.

⁷All at once an angel of the Lord was seen standing beside him. A light shone in the building. The angel hit Peter on the side and said, "Get up!" Then the chains fell off his hands. ⁸The angel said, "Put on your belt and shoes!" He did. The angel said to Peter, "Put on your coat and follow me." ⁹Peter followed him out. He was not sure what was happening as the angel helped him. He thought it was a dream.

¹⁰They passed one soldier, then another one. They came to the big iron door that leads to the city and it opened by itself and they

went through. As soon as they had gone up one street, the angel left him.

The Christians Find It Hard To Believe Peter Is Free

[11]As Peter began to see what was happening, he said to himself, "Now I am sure the Lord has sent His angel and has taken me out of the hands of Herod. He has taken me also from all the things the Jews wanted to do to me." [12]After thinking about all this, he went to Mary's house. She was the mother of John Mark. Many Christians were gathered there praying.

[13]When Peter knocked at the gate, a girl named Rhoda went to see who it was. [14]She knew Peter's voice, but in her joy she forgot to open the gate. She ran in and told them that Peter was standing outside the gate.

[15]They said to her, "You are crazy." But she said again that it was so. They kept saying, "It is his angel." [16]Peter kept knocking. When they opened the gate and saw him, they were surprised and wondered about it. [17]He raised his hand and told them not to talk but to listen to him. He told them how the Lord had brought him out of prison. He said, "Tell all these things to James and to the other Christian brothers." Then he went to another place.

The Death Of Herod

[18]In the morning the soldiers were very troubled about what had happened to Peter. [19]Herod looked for him but could not find him. He asked the soldiers who watched the prison about Peter. Herod said that the soldiers must be killed because Peter got away. Then Herod went down from the country of Judea to the city of Caesarea to stay for awhile.

[20]Herod was very angry with the people of the cities of Tyre and Sidon. They went to him and asked for peace to be made between them and the king. They asked this because their country got food from the king's country. The people made friends with Blastus, the king's helper. [21]A day was set aside. On that day Herod put on purple clothes a king wears. He sat on the place where kings sit

and spoke to the people. 22They all started to speak with a loud voice, "This is the voice of a god, not of a man." 23The angel of the Lord knocked him down because he did not give honor to God. He was eaten by worms and died.

24The Word of God was heard by many people and went into more places. 25Saul and Barnabas went back to Jerusalem after they had finished their work. They took John Mark with them.

The Word of God was heard by many people.

Saul And Barnabas Are Called To Be Missionaries

13 In the church in the city of Antioch there were preachers and teachers. They were Barnabas, Simeon Niger, Lucius of the country of Cyrene, Manaen of Herod's family, and Saul. 2While they were worshiping the Lord and eating no food so they could pray better, the Holy Spirit said, "Let Barnabas and Saul be given to Me for the work I have called them to."

Paul And Barnabas Go To Antioch

3These preachers and teachers went without food during that time and prayed. Then they laid their hands on Barnabas and Saul and sent them away. 4They were sent by the Holy Spirit to the city of Seleucia. From there they went by ship to the island of Cyprus. 5When they went to shore at the city of Salamis, they preached the Word of God in the Jewish place of worship. John Mark was with them as their helper.

6They went over the island of Cyprus as far as the city of Paphos. While there, they found a Jew who did witchcraft. He was a false preacher named Barjesus. 7Sergius Paulus was the leader of the country and a man who knew much. Barjesus was with Sergius Paulus. Sergius Paulus asked Barnabas and Saul to come to him so he might hear the Word of God. 8But Elymas (as he called himself), the man who did witchcraft, worked against Barnabas and Saul. He tried to keep the leader of the country from putting his trust in the Lord.

9Saul, whose other name was Paul, was full of the Holy Spirit. He looked at Elymas. 10Then Saul said, "You false preacher and trouble-maker! You son of the devil! You hate what is right! Will you always be turning people from the right ways of the Lord? ¹¹And now look! The hand of the Lord is on you. You will become blind. For a time you will not be able to see the sun." At once it became dark to Elymas, and he could not see. He asked people to take him by the hand to lead him from place to place.

¹²The leader of the country put his trust in the Lord because he saw what had happened. He was surprised and wondered about the teaching of the Lord. ¹³Paul and those with him went by ship from the city of Paphos to the city of Perga in the country of Pamphylia. John Mark did not go with them but went back to Jerusalem.

Paul Preaches In Antioch

¹⁴From Perga they went on to the city of Antioch in the country of Pisidia. On the Day of Rest they went into the Jewish place of worship and sat down. ¹⁵After the leaders had read from the Jewish Law and the writings of the early preachers, they sent to them saying, "Brothers, if you have any word of comfort and help for the people, say it now." ¹⁶Paul got up. He raised his hand and said, "Jewish men and you who honor God, listen! ¹⁷The God of the Jews chose our early fathers and made them a great people during the time they lived in the land of Egypt. With a strong hand He took them out from there. ¹⁸For about forty years He took care of them in the desert. ¹⁹He destroyed the people of seven nations in the land of Canaan. Then he divided the land and gave it to them as their own. ²⁰For about 450 years he let them have special leaders. They had these leaders until the time of Samuel.

²¹"Then they wanted a king. God gave them Saul who was the son of Kish from the family group of Benjamin. He was king forty years. ²²When God took Saul as king from them, He made David to be their king. He said, 'David, Jesse's son, will please My heart. He will do all I want done.'

²³"From this man's family, God gave to the Jews the One Who saves from the punishment of sin as He had promised. He is Jesus. ²⁴Before Jesus came, John had preached to all the Jews that they should be baptized because they were sorry for their sins and turned from them. ²⁵When John was near the end of his work,

he asked, 'Who do you think I am? I am not the Christ. No, but He is coming later and I am not good enough to get down and help Him take off His shoes!'

26"Men and brothers, sons of the family of Abraham, and all of you who honor God, listen! This news of being able to be saved from the punishment of sin has been sent to you. 27The people of Jerusalem and their leaders did not know Him. They did not understand the words from the early preachers. These words were read to them every Day of Rest. But they did the very thing the early preachers had said they would do by handing Him over to die. 28They could find no reason that He should die, but they asked Pilate to have Him killed. 29When everything was done that had been written about Him, they took Him down from the cross and laid Him in a grave. 30But God raised Him from the dead. 31For many days He was seen by those who came up with Him from Galilee to Jerusalem. These are the ones who tell the people about Him.

But God raised Him from the dead.

32"We bring you the Good News about the promise made to our early fathers. 33God has finished this for us who are their children. He did this by raising Jesus from the dead. It is written in the second Psalm, 'You are My Son. I have given you life today.' (Psalm 2:7) 34God proved that Jesus was His Son by raising Him from the dead. He will never die again. He has said, 'I will finish the promises made to David.' (Isaiah 55:3)

35"In another Psalm He says, 'You will not allow Your Holy One to go back to dust!' (Psalm 16:10) 36David was a good leader for the people of his day. He did what God wanted. Then he died and was put into a grave close to his father's grave. His body went back to dust. 37But God raised this One (Christ) to life. He did not go back to dust.

38"Men and brothers, listen to this. You may be forgiven of your sins by this One I am telling you about. 39Everyone who puts his trust in Christ will be made right with God. You will be made free from those things the Law of Moses could not make you free from. 40But look out! The writings of the early preachers tell of many things that you do not want to happen to you. 41"Listen, you who doubt and laugh at the truth will die. I will do a work during your days. It will be a work that you will not believe even if someone tells you about it.' " (Habakkuk 1:5)

42As Paul and Barnabas went out of the Jewish place of worship, the people asked them to talk about these things on the next Day of Rest. 43The people went from the place of worship. Many Jews and others who had become Jews followed Paul and Barnabas as they talked to the Jews. They told them to keep on trusting in the loving-favor of God.

Paul And Barnabas Go To The People Who Are Not Jews

44Almost all of the people of the town came to hear the Word of God on the next Day of Rest. 45The Jews were filled with jealousy when they saw so many people. They spoke against the things Paul said by saying he was wrong. They also spoke against God. 46Paul and Barnabas said to the people in plain words, "We must preach the Word of God to you first. But because you put it aside, you are not good enough for life that lasts forever. So we will go to the people who are not Jews. 47The Lord gave us a work to do. He said, 'You are to be a light to the people who are not Jews. You are to preach so that men over all the earth can be saved from the punishment of their sins.' " (Isaiah 49:6)

48The people who were not Jews were glad when they heard this. They were thankful for the Word of God. Those who were chosen for life that lasts forever believed. 49The Word of God was preached over all that land.

50The Jews worked on the feelings of the women who were religious and respected. They worked on the leading men of the city also. They worked against Paul and Barnabas and made them leave their city. 51But Paul and Barnabas shook off the dust from their feet against them and went to the city of Iconium. 52The missionaries were filled with joy and with the Holy Spirit.

Paul And Barnabas Preach In Iconium

14 In the city of Iconium, Paul and Barnabas went into the Jewish place of worship. They preached with power and many people became Christians. These people were Jews and Greeks.

²But the Jews who did not want to believe worked against those who were not Jews. They made them turn against the Christians. ³Paul and Barnabas stayed there a long time preaching with the strength the Lord gave. God helped them to do powerful works when they preached which showed He was with them. ⁴The people of the city were divided. Some were on the side of the Jews. Some were on the side of the missionaries. ⁵All the people and the leaders tried to hurt them and throw stones at them.

Paul And Barnabas Go To Lystra

⁶When Paul and Barnabas heard this, they got away and went to the cities of Lystra and Derbe in Lycaonia and to the country close by. ⁷They stayed there and kept on preaching the Good News. ⁸There was a man in Lystra who had never walked from the time he was born. ⁹This man listened as Paul spoke. Paul watched him. He saw that the man believed he could be healed. ¹⁰Calling to him with a loud voice, Paul said, "Stand up on your feet!" The man jumped up and walked around.

Paul And Barnabas Are Called Gods, Then Stoned

¹¹The people saw what Paul did. They called with loud voices in the language of the people of Lycaonia, "The gods have become like men and have come down to us." ¹²They said that Barnabas was Jupiter. Paul was called Mercury because he spoke more than Barnabas. ¹³The god of Jupiter was in a building near the gate leading into the city. The religious leader of that place brought cattle and flowers to the gate. He and many other people wanted to burn these as gifts in an act of worship to Paul and Barnabas.

¹⁴When Paul and Barnabas heard this, they ran among the people. They tore their clothes and cried out, ¹⁵"Why are you doing this? We are only men with feelings like yours. We preach the Good News that you should turn from these empty things to the living God. He made the heavens and the earth and the sea and everything in them. ¹⁶Long ago He allowed all people to live the way they wanted to. ¹⁷Even then God did not leave you without something to see of Him. He did good. He gave you rain from heaven and much food. He made you happy." ¹⁸Even with these words it was hard for Paul and Barnabas to keep the people from burning cattle in an act of worship to them.

[19]By this time some Jews from the cities of Antioch and Iconium came. They turned the minds of the people against Paul and Barnabas and told them to throw stones at Paul. After they threw stones at him, they dragged him out of the city thinking he was dead.

Paul And Barnabas Preach To The Christians On Their Return Trip To Antioch

[20]As the Christians gathered around Paul, he got up and went back into the city. The next day he went with Barnabas to Derbe. [21]In that city they preached the Good News and taught many people. Then they returned to the cities of Lystra and Iconium and Antioch. [22]In each city they helped the Christians to be strong and true to the faith. They told them, "We must suffer many hard things to get into the holy nation of God."

[23]In every church they chose leaders for them. They went without food during that time so they could pray better. Paul and Barnabas prayed for the leaders, giving them over to the Lord in Whom they believed.

[24]When they had gone through the city of Pisidia, they came to the city of Pamphylia. [25]Then they preached the Good News in the city of Perga. After this they went down to the city of Attalia. [26]From there they went by ship to the city of Antioch where they had been given to the Lord for His work. The work of this trip was done.

[27]When they got there, they called the church together. They told them everything God had done for them. They told how God had opened the door for the people who were not Jews to have faith. [28]They stayed there with the followers a long time.

God had opened the door for the people who were not Jews to have faith.

A Meeting Of Church Leaders In Jerusalem

15 Some men came down from the country of Judea and started to teach the Christians. They said, "Unless you go through the religious act of becoming a Jew as Moses taught, you cannot be saved from the punishment of sin." [2]Paul and Barnabas argued with them. Then Paul and Barnabas and some other men were chosen to go up to Jerusalem. They were to talk to the missionaries and church leaders about this teaching. ³The church sent them on their way. They went through the countries of Phoenicia and Samaria and told how those who were not Jews were turning to God. This made the Christians very happy.

⁴When they got to Jerusalem, the church and the missionaries and the church leaders were glad to see them. Paul and Barnabas told them what God had done through them.

⁵Some of the Christians there had been proud religious law-keepers. They got up and said, "Doing the religious act of becoming a Jew and keeping the Law of Moses are two things that must be done." ⁶The missionaries and church leaders got together to talk about this. ⁷After a long time of much talking, Peter got up and said to them, "Brothers, you know in the early days God was pleased to use me to preach the Good News to the people who are not Jews so they might put their trust in Christ. ⁸God knows the hearts of all men. He showed them they were to have His loving-favor by giving them the Holy Spirit the same as He gave to us. ⁹He has made no difference between them and us. They had their hearts made clean when they put their trust in Him also. ¹⁰Why do you test God by putting too heavy a load on the back of the followers? It was too heavy for our fathers or for us to carry. ¹¹We believe it is by the loving-favor of the Lord Jesus that we are saved. They are saved from the punishment of sin the same way."

¹²All those who were gathered together said nothing. They listened to Paul and Barnabas who told of the powerful works God had done through them among the people who are not Jews.

God's Call Is Also For The People Who Are Not Jews

¹³When they finished speaking, James said, "Brothers, listen to me. ¹⁴Simon Peter has told how God first visited the people who are not Jews. He was getting a people for Himself. ¹⁵This agrees with what the early preacher said, ¹⁶"After this I will come back and build again the building of David that fell down. Yes, I will build it again from the stones that fell down. I will set it up again. ¹⁷Then all the nations may look for the Lord, even all the people

who are not Jews who are called by My name. The Lord said this. He does all these things. [18]God has made all His works known from the beginning of time.' (Amos 9:11-12)

God has made all His works known from the beginning of time.

The People Who Are Not Jews Are Not Under The Law

[19]"So we should not trouble these people who are not Jews who are turning to God. [20]We should write to them that they should keep away from everything that is given to gods. They should keep away from sex sins and not eat blood or meat from animals that have been killed in ways against the Law. [21]For the Law of Moses has been read in every city from the early days. It has been read in the Jewish places of worship on every Day of Rest."

[22]Then the missionaries and the church leaders and the whole church chose some men from among them. They were to be sent to the city of Antioch with Paul and Barnabas. They chose Judas Barsabbas and Silas. These men were leaders among the Christians.

[23]They sent them with this letter: "The missionaries and church leaders and Christians say hello to the brothers who are not Jews in the cities of Antioch and Syria and Cilicia. [24]We have heard that some from our group have troubled you and have put doubt in your minds. They said that you must go through the religious act of becoming a Jew and you must keep the Law of Moses. We did not tell them to say these things. [25]All of us have wanted to send men to you with our much-loved Paul and Barnabas. [26]Their lives have been in danger for the name of our Lord Jesus Christ. [27]So now we send Judas and Silas to you. They will tell you the same things. [28]It pleased the Holy Spirit and us to ask you to do nothing more than these things that have to be done. [29]You are to keep away from everything that is given to gods. Do not eat blood or meat from animals that have been killed in ways against the Law. Keep away from sex sins. If you keep yourselves free from these things you will do well. Goodby."

The Missionaries Go Back To Antioch

[30]When the meeting was finished, they went to the city of Antioch. As soon as they gathered the people together, they gave

them the letter. ³¹When they read it, they were glad for the comfort and strength it brought them. ³²Judas and Silas were preachers also. They preached to the Christians and helped them to become stronger in the faith.

³³They were there for some time. Then they were sent back in peace to the missionaries who had sent them. ³⁴But Silas thought he should stay there. ³⁵Paul and Barnabas stayed in the city of Antioch. With the help of many others, they preached and taught the Word of God.

Paul Starts Out The Second Time

³⁶After awhile, Paul said to Barnabas, "Let us go back and visit the Christians in every city where we have preached the Word of God. Let us see how they are doing." ³⁷Barnabas wanted to take John Mark with them. ³⁸Paul did not think it was good to take him because he had left them while they were in the city of Pamphylia. He had not helped them in the work.

³⁹They argued so much that they left each other. Barnabas took John Mark with him and went by ship to the island of Cyprus. ⁴⁰Paul chose Silas. After the Christians asked for the Lord's favor to be on Paul and Silas, they went on their way. ⁴¹They went through the countries of Syria and Cilicia making the churches stronger in the faith.

Timothy Starts To Work With Paul

16 Paul went down to the cities of Derbe and Lystra. There was a follower there named Timothy. His mother was a Jewish Christian and his father was a Greek. ²The Christians in the city of Lystra and Iconium respected Timothy. ³Paul wanted Timothy to go with him as a missionary. He took him and had Timothy go through the religious act of becoming a Jew because of the Jews who were in those places. Everyone knew his father was a Greek.

⁴They went from city to city and told the Christians what the missionaries and the church leaders in Jerusalem had written for the Christians to do. ⁵The churches were made stronger in the faith. More people were added each day.

The churches were made stronger in the faith. More people were added each day.

Paul Is Called To Macedonia In A Dream

⁶They went through the countries of Phrygia and Galatia. The Holy Spirit kept them from preaching the Word of God in the countries of Asia. ⁷When they came to the city of Mysia, they tried to go on to the city of Bithynia but the Holy Spirit would not let them go. ⁸From Mysia they went down to the city of Troas.

⁹That night Paul had a dream. A man was standing in front of him crying out, "Come over to the country of Macedonia and help us!" ¹⁰After he had seen this, we agreed that God told us to go to Macedonia to tell them the Good News.

Lydia, The First Christian In Europe

¹¹We took a ship from the city of Troas to the city of Samothracia. The next day we went to the city of Neapolis. ¹²From there we went to the city of Philippi. This was an important city in the country of Macedonia. It was ruled by the leaders of the country of Rome. We stayed here for some days. ¹³On the Day of Rest we went outside the city to a place down by the river. We thought people would be gathering there for prayer. Some women came and we sat down and talked to them. ¹⁴One of the women who listened sold purple cloth. She was from the city of Thyatira. Her name was Lydia and she was a worshiper of God. The Lord opened her heart to hear what Paul said. ¹⁵When she and her family had been baptized, she said to us, "If you think I am faithful to the Lord, come and stay at my house." She kept on asking. Then we went with her.

Paul Heals A Girl With A Demon

¹⁶One day as we were going to the place to pray, we met a girl who was owned by someone. She could tell what was going to happen in the future by a demon she had. Her owner made much money from her power. ¹⁷She followed Paul and us crying out, "These are workmen who are owned by the Highest God. They are telling you how to be saved from the punishment of sin." ¹⁸She did this many days. Paul was troubled. Then he turned and said to the demon in her, "In the name of Jesus Christ, I speak to you. Come out of her!" At once it left her.

Paul And Silas In Jail

¹⁹The girl's owner saw that they could not make money with her anymore. Then they took hold of Paul and Silas and dragged them to the leaders. This happened in the center of town where people gather. ²⁰After they brought them in front of the leaders, they said, "These men are Jews and are making a lot of trouble in our city. ²¹They are teaching a religion that we Romans are not allowed to follow."

²²Many people had gathered around Paul and Silas. They were calling out things against them. The leaders had the clothes of Paul and Silas taken off and had them beaten with sticks. ²³After they had hit them many times, they put Paul and Silas into prison. The soldiers told the man who watched the prison to be sure to keep them from getting away. ²⁴Because of this, they were put into the inside room of the prison and their feet were put in pieces of wood that held them.

²⁵About midnight Paul and Silas were praying and singing songs of thanks to God. The other men in prison were listening to them. ²⁶All at once the earth started to shake. The stones under the prison shook and the doors opened. The chains fell off from everyone.

²⁷The man who watched the prison woke up. He saw the prison doors wide open and thought the men in prison had gotten away. At once he pulled out his sword to kill himself. ²⁸But Paul called to him, "Do not hurt yourself. We are all here!" ²⁹The man who watched the prison called for a light. Then he ran in and got down in front of Paul and Silas. He was shaking with fear. ³⁰As he took them outside, he said, "Sirs, what must I do to be saved?"

³¹They said, "Put your trust in the Lord Jesus Christ and you and your family will be saved from the punishment of sin."

³²Then Paul spoke the Word of God to him and his family. ³³It was late at night, but the man who watched the prison took Paul and Silas in and washed the places on their bodies where they were hurt. Right then he and his family were baptized. ³⁴He took Paul and Silas to his house and gave them food. He and all his family were full of joy for having put their trust in God.

Paul And Silas Are Allowed To Go Free

35 When it was day, the leaders sent a soldier to say, "Let these men go free." 36 The man who watched the prison told this to Paul. He said, "The leaders have sent word to let you go free. Come out now and go without any trouble."

37 Paul said, "No! They have beaten us in front of many people without a trial. We are Roman citizens and they have put us into prison. Now do they think they can send us away without anyone knowing? No! They must come themselves and take us out." 38 The soldiers told this to the leaders. Then the leaders were afraid when they heard that Paul and Silas were Roman citizens. 39 They went themselves and told Paul and Silas they were sorry. Then they took them out and asked them to leave their city. 40 Paul and Silas went to Lydia's house after they left the prison. They met with the Christians and gave them comfort. Then they went away from the city.

Paul And Silas Start A Church In Thessalonica

17 After Paul and Silas had gone through the cities of Amphipolis and Apollonia, they came to the city of Thessalonica. The Jews had a place of worship there. 2 Paul went in as he always did. They gathered together each Day of Rest for three weeks and he taught them from the Holy Writings. 3 He showed them that Christ had to suffer and rise again from the dead. He said, "I preach this Jesus to you. He is the Christ." 4 Some of them put their trust in Christ and followed Paul and Silas. There were many Greek people and some leading women who honored God among those who had become Christians.

He taught them from the Holy Writings.

The Jews Make It Hard For Paul And Silas

5 The Jews who did not put their trust in Christ became jealous. They took along some sinful men from the center of town where people gather and brought them out on the street. These angry men started all the people in the city to cry out with loud voices. They went to the house of Jason hoping to find Paul and Silas

there and bring them out to the people. ⁶But they did not find them there. Then they dragged Jason and some other Christians out in front of the leaders and cried out, "These men who have been making trouble over all the world have come here also. ⁷And Jason has taken them in. They say there is another King called Jesus. They are working against the laws made by Caesar."

⁸When the people and city leaders heard this, they were troubled. ⁹Then they made Jason and the others pay some money and let them go.

Paul And Silas Go To Berea

¹⁰At once the Christians sent Paul and Silas away at night to the city of Berea. When they got there, they went to the Jewish place of worship. ¹¹These Jews were more willing to understand than those in the city of Thessalonica. They were very glad to hear the Word of God, and they looked into the Holy Writings to see if those things were true. ¹²Many of them became Christians. Some of them were respected Greek women and men. ¹³The Jews of Thessalonica heard that Paul was preaching the Word of God in Berea. They went there and worked against the missionaries by talking to the people. ¹⁴At once the Christians sent Paul away to the seashore. But Silas and Timothy stayed there.

Paul Preaches On Mars' Hill In Athens

¹⁵Those who took Paul brought him to the city of Athens. Paul sent word with them that Silas and Timothy should come to him as soon as they could. Then they left. ¹⁶While Paul was waiting for Silas and Timothy in Athens, his spirit was troubled as he saw the whole city worshiping false gods. ¹⁷He talked to the Jews and other people who were worshiping in the Jewish place of worship. Every day he talked with people who gathered in the center of town.

¹⁸Some men from two different groups were arguing with Paul. The one group thought that men might as well get all the fun out of life that they can. The other group thought that wisdom alone makes men happy. Some of them said, "This man has lots of little things to talk about. They are not important. What is he trying to

say?'' Others said, ''He preaches about strange gods.'' It was because he preached of Jesus and of His being raised from the dead.

¹⁹Then they took him to Mars' Hill and said, ''We want to hear of this new teaching of yours. ²⁰Some of the things you are telling us are strange to our ears. We want to know what these things mean.'' ²¹The people of Athens and those visiting from far countries used all their time in talking or hearing some new thing.

We want to know what these things mean.

²²Then Paul stood up on Mars' Hill and said, ''Men of Athens, I see how very religious you are in every way. ²³As I was walking around and looking at the things you worship, I found an altar where you worship with the words written on it, TO THE GOD WHO IS NOT KNOWN. You are worshiping Him without knowing Him. He is the One I will tell you about.

²⁴''The God Who made the world and everything in it is the Lord of heaven and earth. He does not live in buildings made by hands. ²⁵No one needs to care for Him as if He needed anything. He is the One who gives life and breath and everything to everyone. ²⁶He made from one blood all nations who live on the earth. He set the times and places where they should live.

²⁷''They were to look for God. Then they might feel after Him and find Him because He is not far from each one of us. ²⁸It is in Him that we live and move and keep on living. Some of your own men have written, 'We are God's children.' ²⁹If we are God's children, we should not think of Him as being like gold or silver or stone. Such gods made of gold or silver or stone are planned by men and are made by them.

³⁰''God did not remember these times when people did not know better. But now He tells all men everywhere to be sorry for their sins and to turn from them. ³¹He has set a day when He will say in the right way if the people of the world are guilty. This will be done by Jesus Christ, the One He has chosen. God has proven this to all men by raising Jesus Christ from the dead.''

³²Some people laughed and made fun when they heard Paul speak of Christ being raised from the dead. Others said, ''We want to listen to you again about this.'' ³³So Paul went away from the

people. ³⁴Some people followed him and became Christians. One was Dionysius, a leader in the city. A woman named Damaris believed. And there were others also.

Paul Goes To Corinth

18 After that Paul went from the city of Athens and came to the city of Corinth. ²He met a Jew there named Aquila who was born in the country of Pontus. He had lived in the country of Italy a short time. His wife Priscilla was with him. Claudius, who was the leader of the country, had told all the Jews to leave Rome. Paul went to see Aquila and Priscilla. ³They made tents for a living. Paul did the same kind of work so he stayed with them and they worked together.

⁴Every Day of Rest he would go to the Jewish place of worship and teach both Jews and Greeks. ⁵Silas and Timothy came down from the country of Macedonia. Then Paul used all his time preaching to the Jews. He taught that Jesus was the Christ. ⁶But they worked against Paul and said bad things about him. He shook his clothes and said, "Whatever happens to you is your own doing. I am free from your guilt. From now on I will go to the people who are not Jews."

⁷Paul went from there and came to the house of a man named Titus Justus who worshiped God. His house was next to the Jewish place of worship. ⁸Crispus was the leader of the Jewish place of worship. He and his family believed in the Lord. Many of the people of the city of Corinth who heard Paul became Christians and were baptized.

⁹Paul saw the Lord in a dream one night. He said to Paul, "Do not be afraid. Keep speaking. Do not close your mouth. ¹⁰I am with you. No one will hurt you. I have many people in this city who belong to Me." ¹¹For a year and a half Paul stayed there and taught them the Word of God.

¹²Gallio was leader of the country of Greece. All the Jews worked against Paul and brought him in front of the court. ¹³They said, "This man is trying to get people to worship God against the Jewish Law." ¹⁴Paul was ready to speak, but Gallio said to the

Do not be afraid.

Jews, "If this were something bad or a wrong doing, I would listen to you. [15]But because it is about words and names and your own Law, you will have to take care of it yourselves. I do not want to say who is right or wrong in things like this." [16]And he sent them out of his court.

[17]Then all the Greek people took Sosthenes, the leader of the Jewish place of worship, and beat him in front of the court. But Gallio did not let this trouble him.

Paul Goes Back To Antioch

[18]Paul stayed in the city of Corinth many days longer. Then he said goodby and left the followers. He went by ship to the country of Syria with Priscilla and Aquila going with him. In the city of Cenchrea he had his hair cut short because of a promise he had made to God. [19]They came to the city of Ephesus. Priscilla and Aquila stayed there. Paul went to the Jewish place of worship and argued with the Jews. [20]They wanted him to stay longer but he would not. [21]As he left them, he said, *("I must go to the special supper at Jerusalem.) I will return again to you if God wants me to." Then he got on a ship and left the city of Ephesus. [22]He stopped in the city of Caesarea to say hello to the people in the church. Then he went down to the city of Antioch. [23]Paul stayed there for some time. Then he went from city to city through the countries of Galatia and Phrygia. In each place he helped the Christians become strong in the faith.

Aquila And Priscilla Help Apollos In Ephesus

[24]A Jew by the name of Apollos had come to the city of Ephesus. He was from the city of Alexandria. He could talk to people about the Holy Writings very well. [25]He had been taught in the way of the Lord. And with a strong desire in his heart, he taught about Jesus. What he said was true, but he knew only about the baptism of John.

[26]He began to speak without fear in the Jewish place of worship. Aquila and Priscilla heard him. They took him to their house and taught him much more about the things of God. [27]Apollos wanted to cross over to the country of Greece. The Christians wrote a

He showed
from the Holy Writings
that Jesus
was the Christ.

letter to the followers there asking them to be good to him. When he got there, he was much help to those who had put their trust in Christ. 28In front of everyone he proved with great power that the Jews were wrong. He showed from the Holy Writings that Jesus was the Christ.

Christians In Ephesus Are Filled With The Holy Spirit

19 While Apollos was in the city of Corinth, Paul went through the hill country to get to the city of Ephesus. He found a few followers there. 2He asked them, "Did you receive the Holy Spirit when you put your trust in Christ?" They said, "No, we have not even heard that there is a Holy Spirit." 3He asked them, "How were you baptized?" They answered, "The way John baptized." 4Paul said, "John baptized those who were sorry for their sins and turned from them. He told the people to put their trust in Jesus Who was coming later."

5The people there were baptized in the name of the Lord Jesus when they heard this. 6When Paul laid his hands on them, the Holy Spirit came on them. They started to talk in special sounds and to speak God's Word. 7There were about twelve men.

Paul Preaches In A Place Of Worship And In A School In Ephesus

8For three months Paul went into the Jewish place of worship and spoke without fear. He taught them things about the holy nation of God. 9Some let their hearts grow hard. They would not put their trust in Christ. These spoke against the Christian religion in front of other people. Then Paul took the followers away from the others. He taught them each day in the school of Tyrannus. 10He did this for two years. All the Jews and the Greeks in the countries of Asia heard the Word of the Lord.

Paul Does Powerful Works

11God used Paul to do powerful special works. 12Pieces of cloth and parts of his clothes that had been next to his body were put on sick people. Then they were healed of their diseases and demons came out of them.

¹³There were Jews who went from city to city trying to put demons out of people. Some of these tried to use the name of the Lord Jesus on those who had demons. They said, "I speak to you in the name of Jesus, the One Paul preaches about." ¹⁴A Jewish leader of the people by the name of Sceva had seven sons. These sons were trying to do this. ¹⁵The demon said, "I know Jesus. I know about Paul. But who are you?" ¹⁶Then the man with the demon jumped on the sons. He had power over them and beat them. They ran out of the house with no clothes on and they were hurt.

¹⁷All the Jews and Greeks living in the city of Ephesus heard about it. Because of this all the people became afraid. And the name of the Lord Jesus was held in great honor. ¹⁸Many Christians came and told of the wrong things they were doing. ¹⁹Many of those who did witchcraft gathered their books together and burned them in front of everyone. These books were worth 50,000 pieces of silver money. ²⁰The Word of the Lord became well-known.

²¹After this, Paul thought he would go through the countries of Macedonia and Greece. Then he would go to Jerusalem. He said, "After I have been there, I must go to the city of Rome also." ²²He sent two of his helpers, Timothy and Erastus, to Macedonia. Paul stayed in the countries of Asia awhile longer.

The Meeting Of The Silver Workmen In Ephesus

²³During that time there was much trouble about the Christians. ²⁴A man named Demetrius made small silver buildings for the worship of Diana. His workmen received much money for their work. ²⁵He called his workmen together and other men who made these small silver buildings. He said to them, "Men, you know we make much money from this work. ²⁶Now you hear that Paul has turned away many people in the city of Ephesus as well as in the countries of Asia. He tells them that gods made with hands are not gods. ²⁷It could be that our work will not be respected. Not only that, the house of worship for the god of Diana will be worth nothing and her greatness will be destroyed. All the countries of Asia and the world worship her."

[28]They became angry when they heard this and cried out, "Great is Diana of Ephesus." [29]The whole city was filled with loud cries. They caught Gaius and Aristarchus. These two men from the country of Macedonia were with Paul. They gathered around them at the meeting place in the city.

[30]Paul wanted to stand in front of all the people but his followers would not let him. [31]Some of the city leaders who were his friends told him not to go to the meeting. [32]All this time some were crying out one thing and some another. The meeting was all noise. Most of the people did not know why they had come together. [33]Then the Jews pushed Alexander to the front. Alexander held his hand up and was going to speak. [34]As soon as they saw he was a Jew, they cried out with a loud voice for two hours, "Great is Diana of Ephesus!"

[35]One of the city leaders stopped the noise. He spoke, "Men of Ephesus, everyone knows our city is where the god of Diana is kept. That is the stone god that fell from the sky. [36]Everyone knows this is true, so you must not cry out or do anything foolish. [37]The men you brought here do not rob houses of worship or talk against our god. [38]If Demetrius and his workmen have something against anyone, we have special days for courts. Let them go to court. [39]If you want anything else, it should be done in another meeting. [40]We are in danger of being asked about this trouble today. There is no good reason we can give for this meeting." [41]When he had said this, he told them to leave.

Paul Goes To Greece And Macedonia

20 When the noise had come to an end, Paul called the followers to him. He spoke words of comfort and then said goodby. He left to go to the country of Macedonia. [2]As he went through those parts of the country, he spoke words of comfort and help to the Christians. Then he went on to the country of Greece. [3]He stayed there three months. As he was about to get on a ship for the country of Syria, he learned that the Jews had made a plan to take him. He changed his plans and went back through the country of Macedonia. [4]Some men were going along with him. They were Sopater of the city of Berea, Aristarchus and Secundus of the city of Thessalonica, Gaius of the city of Derbe, and Timothy and Tychicus and Trophimus of the countries of Asia. ⁵They went on to the city of Troas and waited there for us. ⁶After the supper of bread without yeast we got on a ship in the city of Philippi. We met these men at Troas. It took five days to get there and we stayed one week.

Eutychus Falls From A Building While Paul Preaches

⁷On the first day of the week we met together to eat the Lord's supper. Paul talked to them. He thought he would leave the next day, so he kept on talking until twelve o'clock at night. ⁸There were many lights in the room on the third floor where we had our meeting. ⁹A young man named Eutychus sat in the window. As Paul kept on preaching, this man started to go to sleep. At last he went to sleep. He fell from the third floor to the ground and was picked up dead. ¹⁰Paul went down and stood over him. Then he took him in his arms and said, "Do not be worried. He is alive!" ¹¹Paul went up again to the meeting and ate with them. He talked with them until the sun came up. Then he left. ¹²They were happy they could take the young man home alive.

Paul Goes From The City Of Troas To Miletus

¹³We went on ahead by ship to the city of Assos. There we were to pick up Paul. He had planned it that way. He wanted to walk by land that far. ¹⁴We got to Assos and met him there. We picked him up and went on to the city of Mitylene. ¹⁵The next day we went by ship to a place beside the island of Chios. The next day we crossed over to the island of Samos. Then the next day we came to the city of Miletus. ¹⁶Paul planned to pass by the city of Ephesus so he would not lose more time in the country of Asia. He wanted to be in Jerusalem if he could be on the day to remember how the Holy Spirit came on the church.

Paul Meets With The Leaders Of The Church Of Ephesus

¹⁷From the city of Miletus he sent word to the city of Ephesus. He asked the leaders of the church to come to him. ¹⁸When they got there, he said to them, "From the first day that I came to the countries of Asia you have seen what my life has been like. ¹⁹I

worked for the Lord without pride. Because of the trouble the Jews gave me, I have had many tears. [20]I always told you everything that would be a help to you. I taught you in open meetings and from house to house. [21]I preached to the Jews and to the Greeks. I told them to turn from their sin to God and to put their trust in our Lord Jesus Christ.

[22]"As you see, I am on my way to Jerusalem. The Holy Spirit makes me go. I do not know what will happen to me there. [23]But in every city I have been, the Holy Spirit tells me that trouble and chains will be waiting for me there. [24]But I am not worried about this. I do not think of my life as worth much, but I do want to finish the work the Lord Jesus gave me to do. My work is to preach the Good News of God's loving-favor.

[25]"All of you have heard me preach the Good News. I am sure that none of you will ever see my face again. [26]I tell you this day that I am clean and free from the blood of all men. [27]I told you all the truth about God. [28]Keep a careful watch over yourselves and over the church. The Holy Spirit has made you its leaders. Feed and care for the church of God. He bought it with His own blood.

[29]"Yes, I know that when I am gone, hungry wolves will come in among you. They will try to destroy the church. [30]Also men from your own group will begin to teach things that are not true. They will get men to follow them. [31]I say again, keep watching! Remember that for three years I taught everyone of you night and day, even with tears.

[32]"And now, my brothers, I give you over to God and His word of love. It is able to make you strong and to give you what you are to have, along with all those who are set apart for God. [33]I have not tried to get anyone's money or clothes. [34]You all know that these hands worked for what I needed and for what those with me needed. [35]In every way I showed you that by working hard like this we can help those who are weak. We must remember what the Lord Jesus said, 'We are more happy when we give than when we receive.'"

[36]As he finished talking, he got down on his knees and prayed with them all. [37]They cried and put their arms around Paul and

kissed him. [38]What made them sad most of all was because he said that they would never see his face again. Then they went with him to the ship.

Paul Goes From Miletus To Tyre

21 After we left them, we got on a ship and came straight down to the island of Cos. The next day we came to the island of Rhodes and from there to the city of Patara. [2]There we found a ship that was going over to the country of Phoenicia. We got on it and went along. [3]We saw the island of Cyprus to our left but went on to the country of Syria. We came to land at the city of Tyre. The ship was to leave its load of freight there.

[4]We looked for the Christians and stayed with them seven days. The Christians had been told by the Holy Spirit to tell Paul not to go to Jerusalem. [5]When our time was up, we left there and went on our way. All of them with their wives and children went with us out of town. They got down on their knees on the shore and prayed. [6]After we said goodby, we got on the ship and they went back to their houses.

Paul Goes From Tyre To Jerusalem

[7]The same ship took us from the city of Tyre to the city of Ptolemais. We stayed with the Christians there one day. [8]The next day we left and came to the city of Caesarea. We went to the house of Philip and stayed with him. He was a preacher who goes from town to town and was one of the seven church leaders. [9]Philip had four daughters who were not married. They spoke the Word of God.

[10]While we were there a few days, a man who speaks for God named Agabus came down from the country of Judea. [11]He came to see us. Then he took Paul's belt and used it to tie his own feet and hands. He said, "This is what the Holy Spirit says, 'The Jews at Jerusalem will tie the man who owns this belt. Then they will hand him over to the people who are not Jews.'"

[12]When we heard this, we and all the people living there begged Paul not to go up to Jerusalem. [13]Then Paul said, "What do you

mean by crying and breaking my heart? I am ready to be put in chains in Jerusalem. I am also ready to die for the name of the Lord Jesus.'' [14]Paul would not listen to us. So we stopped begging him and said, "May whatever God wants be done."

Paul Is In Jerusalem

[15]After this, we got ready and started up to Jerusalem. [16]Some of the followers in the city of Caesarea went with us. They took us to Mnason's house. He was one of the first followers from the island of Cyprus. We stayed with him.

[17]When we got to Jerusalem, the Christians were glad to see us. [18]The next day we went with Paul to see James. All the church leaders came also. [19]After saying hello to them, Paul told of what God had done through his work for the people who were not Jews.

[20]When they heard this, they thanked the Lord. Then they said to him, "You see, brother, how many thousands of Christians there are among the Jews. They all obey the Law of Moses. [21]They have heard about you. They have heard you teach the Jews who live among people who are not Jews. They have heard you teach them to break away from the Law of Moses. They say you are telling them not to do the religious act of becoming a Jew and not to follow old religious ways of worship. [22]What should we do about it? They will hear that you have come. [23]You must do what we tell you. We have four men with us who have made a promise to God. [24]Take these four men and go through the religious worship of washing with them. You pay to have their hair cut off. Then everybody will know what they have heard about you is not true. They will know you are careful to obey the Law of Moses. [25]As for the people who are not Jews, we wrote to them. We said that they must keep away from everything that has been given to gods. They must not eat blood or meat from animals that have been killed in ways against the Law. They must keep away from sex sins.''

[26]The next day Paul took the men. He went through the religious worship of washing with them. They went into the house of God to tell when their religious worship of washing would be

finished. Then the gift for each one of them would be given as an act of worship.

[27]The seven days were almost finished. Jews from the countries of Asia saw Paul in the house of God. They made the people turn against him. Then they took hold of him. [28]They cried out, "You who are Jews, help us! This is the man who is teaching against our people and our Law and this house of God. Also he has brought Greek people into the house of God. This has made this holy place dirty." [29]They had seen him before in the city with Trophimus who was from the city of Ephesus. They thought Paul had brought him into the house of God also.

[30]All the people in the city were crying out with loud voices. The people pushed and moved together. They took Paul and dragged him out of the house of God. Then the doors were shut. [31]They were getting ready to kill him. The captain of the soldiers heard there was trouble over all Jerusalem. [32]At once the captain called his soldiers and they ran down to the people. When the people saw the captain and his soldiers, they stopped beating Paul.

Paul Is Tied With Chains

[33]The captain came and took hold of Paul. He told his soldiers to tie Paul with two chains. Then he asked who he was and what he had done. [34]Some of the people called out one thing and some another. The captain was not able to find out what had happened. He told his men to take Paul into the soldiers' building. [35]The people cried out so loud and pushed so hard that Paul had to be carried up the steps by the soldiers. [36]All the people kept pushing and calling out, "Kill him!"

[37]Paul was brought into the soldiers' building. He said to the captain, "May I say something to you?" The captain said, "Can you speak the Greek language? [38]Are you not the man from the country of Egypt who made trouble against our country? That man led 4,000 fighting men into the desert." [39]Paul said, "No! I am a Jew and a citizen of a large city. I am from Tarsus in the country of Cilicia. I ask you to let me speak to the people." [40]The captain told Paul to speak. So Paul stood on the steps and held up his hand. When there was no more noise, he spoke to them in the language of the Jews.

Paul Tells Of The Work He Did Before He Was A Christian

22 Paul said, "Brothers and fathers, listen to what I have to say to you." [2]When they heard him speak to them in their own language, they stopped making noise. Then he said,

[3]"I am a Jew. I was born in the city of Tarsus in the country of Cilicia. When I was a young man, I lived here in Jerusalem. I went to Gamaliel's school and learned all about the Law of our early fathers. I worked hard for God as you all do today.

[4]"I worked hard and killed men and women who believed as I believe today. I put them in chains and sent them to prison. [5]The head religious leader and the leaders of the people can tell you this is true. I got letters from them to take to our Jewish brothers in the city of Damascus. I was going there to put the Christians in chains and bring them to Jerusalem where they would be beaten.

The Change In Paul's Life On The Damascus Road

[6]"I was near the city of Damascus. All at once, about noon, I saw a bright light from heaven shining around me. [7]I fell to the ground. A voice said to me, 'Saul, Saul, why do you work so hard against Me?' [8]I said, 'Who are You, Lord?' He said to me, 'I am Jesus of Nazareth, the One you are working against.' [9]Those who were with me saw the light. But they did not hear Him speaking to me. [10]I asked, 'Lord, what should I do?' The Lord said to me, 'Get up! Go to Damascus. You will be told what to do there.'

[11]"I could not see because of the bright light. Those who were with me had to lead me by the hand until we came to Damascus. [12]Ananias lived there. He obeyed the Law and was respected by all the Jews. [13]He came and stood near me and said, 'Brother Saul, receive your sight.' At once I was able to see him. [14]Then Ananias said, 'The God of our fathers chose you to know what He wants done. He chose you to see Jesus Christ, the One Right with God, and to hear His voice. [15]You are to tell all men what you have seen

and heard. [16]What are you waiting for? Get up! Be baptized. Have your sins washed away by calling on His name.'

Paul Is Called To Work With The People Who Are Not Jews

[17]"I came back to Jerusalem. When I was praying in the house of God, I had a dream. [18]I saw Him as He said to me, 'Get out of Jerusalem! They will not listen to you when you tell them about Me!' [19]I said, 'Lord, they know I took Christians out of every Jewish place of worship. I had them beaten and put into prison. [20]Also when Stephen was killed, I stood there and watched them throw stones at him. Those who threw the stones had me watch their coats.' [21]The Lord said to me, 'Go! I will send you far away to the people who are not Jews.' " [22]They listened to him until he said that. Then they all cried out with loud voices, "Kill him! Take such a man from the earth! He should not live!" [23]They kept on calling out. Then they pulled off their coats and threw dust into the air.

Go!
I will send you
far away
to the people
who are not Jews.

Paul Tells Who He Is

[24]The captain told them to bring Paul into the soldiers' building. He told his soldiers to find out from Paul, by beating him, why the people were crying out against him. [25]As they tied him up, Paul said to the soldier, "Does the law say that you can beat a Roman citizen when no one has said he is guilty?"

[26]When the soldier heard this, he told it to the captain. He said, "Listen! What are you doing? This man is a Roman citizen." [27]The captain came and asked Paul, "Tell me, are you a Roman citizen?" Paul said, "Yes!" [28]The captain said, "I had to pay a lot of money to be a citizen." Paul said, "But I was born a Roman." [29]Those who were going to beat him left him at once. The captain was also afraid when he heard that Paul was a Roman citizen because he had him tied.

Paul Stands In Front Of The Religious Leaders' Court

[30]The next day they took off the ropes that were holding Paul. The captain wanted to know why the Jews wanted to kill him. So the captain told the head religious leaders to gather for their court. They brought Paul and put him in front of them.

Paul Speaks To The Religious Leaders' Court

23 Paul looked straight at the court and said, "Brother Jews, I have lived for God with a heart that has said I am not guilty to this day." ²Then Ananias, the head religious leader, told those standing near him to hit him on the mouth. ³Paul said, "God will hit you, you white-washed wall! Do you sit there and say I am guilty by the Law when you break the Law by having me hit?"

⁴Those standing near said, "Do you talk like that to God's head religious leader?" ⁵Paul said, "Brother Jews, I did not know that he was God's head religious leader. I know the Holy Writings say, 'You must not speak against the leader of your people.'" (Exodus 22:28)

⁶Paul saw that part of the court was made up of the religious group who believe no one is raised from the dead. The other part were proud religious law-keepers. Then he cried out, "Brother Jews, I am a proud religious law-keeper and from a family of proud religious law-keepers. I have been brought in front of this court because of the hope of being raised from the dead."

⁷When they heard this, both religious groups started to argue and the people of the court were divided in what they thought. ⁸The one religious group believes that no one is raised from the dead. Also, they do not believe in angels or spirits. But the other religious group, the proud religious law-keepers, believe that people are raised from the dead and that there are angels and spirits. ⁹The courtroom was filled with noise. Some of the teachers of the Law working with the proud religious law-keepers stood up and said, "We find nothing wrong with this man. What if an angel or spirit has spoken to him?"

¹⁰They argued all the more. Then the captain was afraid they would pull Paul to pieces. He told his men to get Paul out of there and take him back to the soldiers' building. ¹¹The next night the Lord came to Paul and said, "Paul, do not be afraid! You will tell about Me in the city of Rome the same as you have told about Me in Jerusalem."

The Plan To Kill Paul

¹²In the morning some of the Jews gathered together and made a plan to kill Paul. They promised each other that they would not eat or drink until they had killed him. ¹³There were more than forty of them who had made this promise. ¹⁴These people came to the head religious leader and to the leaders of the people and said, "We have made a promise not to eat any food until we have killed Paul. ¹⁵We ask you and the court to have the captain bring Paul down to you tomorrow. It will look as if you want to ask him some things. Before he gets near you, we will be waiting to kill him."

¹⁶Paul's nephew heard about the plan. He went to the soldiers' building and told Paul. ¹⁷Paul called one of the soldiers and said, "Take this young man to the captain. He has something to tell him." ¹⁸The soldiers brought the young man to the captain and said, "Paul asked me to bring this young man to you. He has something to tell you." ¹⁹The captain took him by the hand and they walked over where they could be alone. He said, "What is it that you have to tell me?" ²⁰The young man said, "The Jews have made a plan to ask you to bring Paul to the courtroom tomorrow. It would look as if they were going to ask him some things. ²¹Do not let them talk you into it. More than forty men are waiting in secret to kill him. They have promised each other not to eat or drink anything until they have killed him. They are all waiting for you to say the word." ²²The captain told the young man to go. He said, "Do not tell anyone you have told me this."

Paul Is Sent To Felix In Caesarea

²³Then the captain called two soldiers and said, "Get 200 men ready to go to the city of Caesarea by nine o'clock tonight. Also have seventy men ride on horses and 200 men carry spears. ²⁴Get horses ready for Paul to ride. Take him to Felix, the leader of the people."

²⁵He wrote a letter which said, ²⁶"Claudius Lysias says hello to Felix, the best leader of the people. ²⁷This man Paul was taken by the Jews. He was about to be killed by them. But I came along with my soldiers and kept him from being killed. I did this when I learned that he was a Roman citizen. ²⁸I wanted to know what

they had against him. So I took him to the religious leaders' court. ²⁹I learned they were holding him because of something about their Law. There was no reason for him to be killed or to be put into prison. ³⁰I was told that the Jews had a plan to kill this man. At once I sent him to you. I told the Jews who wanted to kill him to tell you what they have against him. Goodby.''

³¹The soldiers took Paul as they were told. They brought him during the night to Antipatris. ³²The next day they went back to their building in Jerusalem. The men riding horses went on with Paul. ³³When they came to the city of Caesarea, they gave the letter to the leader of the people. They also handed Paul over to him. ³⁴After he read the letter, he asked what part of the country Paul was from. He was told that Paul was from the city of Cilicia. ³⁵He said, ''I will listen to all of this when the men come who want to kill you.'' He had Paul kept in King Herod's building.

Paul Stands In Front Of Felix

24 Five days later Ananias came to the city of Caesarea. He was the head religious leader. Some other religious leaders and a man whose name was Tertullus came also. This man worked in courts and knew all about the laws. He told Felix what the Jews had against Paul. ²They brought in Paul. Then Tertullus started to tell what the Jews had against him, saying,

''Most respected Felix, because of you, we are living in peace. Wrong-doings have been made right in this nation. ³In every way and in every place, we thank you for all of this. ⁴We do not want to keep you here too long. I ask you to listen to our few words. You are known to be kind in this way. ⁵We have found this man to be a troublemaker among all the Jews in the world. He is a leader of a religious group called the Nazarenes. ⁶He even tried to make the house of God dirty by taking people into it who were not Jews. But we took hold of him. We could have said he was guilty by our Law. ⁷*But Lysias, the captain, came and took him out of our hands. ⁸He told those who wanted to kill him to tell you what they had against him. When you ask him these things, you will be able to learn everything we have against him.'' ⁹The Jews agreed to what he said against Paul.

Paul Speaks For Himself The First Time

[10]Then Felix, the leader of the people, told Paul to speak. Paul said, "I know that you have been a leader of this nation for many years. I am happy to be able to speak for myself. [11]Not more than twelve days ago I went up to Jerusalem to worship. You can find out about this yourself. [12]I did not argue with anyone in the house of God or in the Jewish places of worship or in the city. I was not making trouble. [13]They cannot prove any of these things they say against me.

[14]"I will say this, I worship the God of our fathers in the new Way. They say it is a false way. But I believe everything that has been written in the Law and by the early preachers. [15]I trust God for the same things they are looking for. I am looking for the dead to rise, both those right with God and the sinful. [16]I always try to live so my own heart tells me I am not guilty in front of God or man.

I worship the God of our fathers in the new Way.

[17]"After a few years I came to bring gifts of money to the people of my country (Jerusalem). [18]Some Jews from the countries of Asia found me in the house of God after I had gone through the worship of washing. There were no people around me and there was no noise or fighting. [19]They should be here if they have anything against me. [20]Or let these men tell what wrong they found in me as I stood in front of their court, [21]unless it was the words I cried out as I stood in front of them. I said, 'I have been brought in front of this court because of the hope of being raised from the dead.'"

Felix Waits For Lysias To Come

[22]Felix knew about the Christian religion. He stopped the court, saying, "When Lysias the captain comes down, I will decide about this." [23]He told the soldier to watch Paul, but to let him come and go as much as he wanted to. Paul's friends were to be able to come and care for him.

Paul Speaks For Himself The Second Time

[24]Some days later Felix came again. His Jewish wife Drusilla was with him. He sent for Paul and heard him talk about faith in

Christ Jesus. ²⁵Paul spoke about being right with God. He spoke about being the boss over our own desires. He spoke about standing in front of One Who will tell us if we are guilty. When Felix heard this, he became afraid and said, "Go now. I will send for you when it is a better time." ²⁶He was hoping that Paul would give him money so he could go free. For that reason he kept sending for Paul and talking to him.

²⁷After two years Porcius Festus became leader of the people instead of Felix. Felix wanted to please the Jews so he kept Paul in prison.

Paul Stands In Front Of Festus

25 Three days after Festus had become leader in the country, he went from the city of Caesarea to Jerusalem. ²The head religious leaders and the leaders of the Jews told Festus what they had against Paul. ³They asked Festus for a favor. They wanted Paul to be brought to Jerusalem because they had plans to kill him on the way. ⁴Festus told them that Paul was to be kept in the city of Caesarea and that he would be going there soon. ⁵Festus said, "If Paul has done anything wrong, let your leaders go along with me and say what they have against him."

⁶After staying with them about ten days, Festus went down to the city of Caesarea. The next day he sat in the courtroom and asked for Paul to be brought in. ⁷Paul came into the courtroom. The Jews who had come down from Jerusalem stood around him. They said many bad things against him. But they could not prove any of the things they said. ⁸Paul spoke for himself, saying, "I have done nothing wrong against the Law of the Jews or against the house of God or against Caesar."

⁹Festus was hoping to get the respect of the Jews. He asked Paul, "Will you go to the court in Jerusalem and let me say if you are guilty or not about these things?" ¹⁰Paul said, "I am standing in front of Caesar's court where I should be told I am right or wrong. I have done no wrong to the Jews. You know that. ¹¹If I have done wrong and should die, I am not trying to keep from dying. But if these things they say against me are not true, no one

can give me over to them. I ask to be taken to Caesar." [12]Festus talked to the leaders of the court. Then he said to Paul, "You have asked to be taken to Caesar. You will go to him."

Festus Tells King Agrippa About Paul

[13]After a few days, King Agrippa and his wife, Bernice, came down to the city of Caesarea. They went to Festus to say hello to him. [14]They stayed there a few days. Festus told them about Paul. He said, "There is a man here who was left in prison by Felix. [15]When I was at Jerusalem, the head religious leaders and the leaders of the people told me about him and asked me to say that he is guilty. [16]I told them it was against the Roman law to hand over a man to be put to death before he stood face to face with those who had something against him and could speak for himself. [17]When they came here, I took my seat in the courtroom at once. I had the man brought in. [18]When the others spoke, they had nothing against him that I thought they had. [19]They did not agree with him about their own religion, and they argued about someone called Jesus. He had died but Paul kept saying He was alive. [20]I did not know what to do. Then I asked him if he would go on trial about these things at Jerusalem. [21]But Paul asked to go on trial in front of Caesar. I said that he should be kept in prison until he could be sent to Caesar." [22]Agrippa said to Festus, "I would like to hear this man." Festus said, "Tomorrow you will hear him."

Paul Stands In Front Of King Agrippa

[23]The next day Agrippa and Bernice came into the courtroom. They were dressed to show their greatness as king and queen. Army leaders and leading men of the city came in with them. Festus had Paul brought in.

[24]Festus said, "King Agrippa and all of you who are here with us, you see this man. All of the Jews both here and at Jerusalem are saying that Paul should be put to death. [25]I have heard nothing against him that would be reason to put him to death. But he asked for a trial in front of Caesar. I have agreed to send Paul to him. [26]When I write to Caesar, I have nothing to say against him. For this reason, I brought him in front of you all and

in front of you, King Agrippa. After we ask him questions, I may have something to write about. ²⁷It is foolish for me to send a man up for trial without writing what is against him.''

Paul Speaks To King Agrippa

26 Agrippa said to Paul, ''You may now speak for yourself.'' Paul lifted his hand and started to talk, ²''King Agrippa, the Jews have said many things against me. I am happy to be able to tell you my side of the story. ³You know all about the Jewish ways and problems. So I ask you to listen to me until I have finished.

⁴''All the Jews know about my life from the time I was a boy until now. I lived among my own people in Jerusalem. ⁵If they would tell what they know, they would say that I lived the life of a proud religious law-keeper. I was in the group of proud religious law-keepers who tried to obey every law.

⁶''And now I am on trial here because I trust the promise God made to our fathers. ⁷This promise is what our twelve family groups of the Jewish nation hope to see happen. They worship God day and night. King Agrippa, it is because of this hope that they are saying things against me. ⁸Why do you think it is hard to believe that God raises people from the dead?

⁹''I used to think I should work hard against the name of Jesus of Nazareth. ¹⁰I did that in Jerusalem. I put many of the followers into prison. The head religious leaders gave me the right and the power to do it. Then when the followers were killed, I said it was all right. ¹¹I beat them and tried to make them speak against God in all the Jewish places of worship. In my fight against them, I kept going after them even into cities in other countries.

¹²''When I was going to Damascus to do this, I had the right and the power from the head religious leaders to make it hard for the followers. ¹³I was on the road at noon. King Agrippa, I saw a light from heaven brighter than the sun. It was shining around me and the men with me. ¹⁴We all fell to the ground. Then I heard a

voice speaking to me in the Jewish language, 'Saul, Saul, why are you working so hard against Me? You hurt yourself by trying to hurt Me.' 15I said, 'Who are You, Lord?' And He said, 'I am Jesus, the One you are working against. 16Get up. Stand on your feet. I have chosen you to work for Me. You will tell what you have seen and you will say what I want you to say. This is the reason I have allowed you to see Me. 17I will keep you safe from the Jews and from the people who are not Jews. I am sending you to these people. 18You are to open their eyes. You are to turn them from darkness to light. You are to turn them from the power of Satan to the power of God. In this way, they may have their sins forgiven. They may have what is given to them, along with all those who are set apart for God by having faith in Me.'

19"King Agrippa, I obeyed what I saw from heaven. 20First I told what I saw to those in the city of Damascus and then in Jerusalem. I told it through all the country of Judea. I even preached to the people who are not Jews that they should be sorry for their sins and turn from them to God. I told them they should do things to show they are sorry for their sins.

21"That is why the Jews took hold of me in the house of God and tried to kill me. 22God has helped me. To this day I have told these things to the people who are well-known and to those not known. I have told only what the early preachers and Moses said would happen. 23It was that Christ must suffer and be the first to rise from the dead. He would give light to the Jews and to the other nations."

24As Paul was speaking for himself, Festus cried out in a loud voice, "Paul, you are crazy! All your learning keeps you from thinking right!" 25Paul said, "Most respected Festus, I am not crazy. I am speaking the truth! 26The king knows about all this. I am free to speak to him in plain words. Nothing I have said is new to him. These things happened where everyone saw them. 27King Agrippa, do you believe the writings of the early preachers? I know that you believe them."

28Then Agrippa said to Paul, "In this short time you have almost proven to me that I should become a Christian!" 29Paul said, "My prayer to God is that you and all who hear me today

In this short time you have almost proven to me that I should become a Christian!

would be a Christian as I am, only not have these chains!'' [30]King Agrippa and Festus and Bernice and those who sat with them got up. [31]As they left the courtroom, they said to each other, ''This man has done nothing for which he should be kept in prison or be put to death.'' [32]Agrippa told Festus, ''This man could go free if he had not asked to be sent to Caesar.''

Paul Is Sent To Rome

27 It was decided that we should go to the country of Italy by ship. Then they put Paul and some other men in chains. Julius, a captain of Caesar's army, was to watch them. [2]We went on a ship that was from the city of Adramyttian. It was going to stop at the towns along the seashore of Asia. Aristarchus was with us. He was a man from the city of Thessalonica in the country of Macedonia. [3]The next day we stopped in the city of Sidon. Julius was kind to Paul. He let him visit friends who cared for him.

[4]After leaving Sidon we were blown by the wind along the south side of the island of Cyprus. The wind was against us. [5]We crossed the sea along the countries of Cilicia and Pamphylia and got to the city of Myra in the country of Lycia. [6]The captain found a ship from the city of Alexandria that was going to the country of Italy. He put us on it. [7]For many days the ship did not move fast. It was hard to get to the city of Cnidus. The wind would not let us go on. So we went along the south shore of the island of Crete and passed the end of the island called Salome. [8]The wind was against us, and we did not sail very fast. Then we came to a place called Fair Havens. It was near the city of Lasea.

[9]Much time had been lost. To keep going that late in the year would mean danger. Paul spoke with strong words, [10]''Sirs, it looks to me as if this ship and its freight will be lost. We are in danger of being lost also.''

[11]The captain of the soldiers listened to what the captain of the ship said and not to what Paul said. [12]It was not a good place to spend the winter. Most of those on the ship wanted to go on and try to get to Phoenix. The island of Crete was a good place to tie

up the ship. They wanted to spend the winter there. ¹³When a south wind started to blow, they thought their plan was right. They pulled up the anchor and went close to the shore of the island of Crete.

¹⁴Later a bad wind storm came down from the land. It was called a northeaster. ¹⁵The ship was stopped by the wind. After awhile we gave up and let it go with the wind. ¹⁶We went behind a small island called Claudia. It was hard work but we were able to make the ship's boat safe. ¹⁷They pulled it up and tied ropes around it and the ship. They were afraid of going on the Syrtis sands. So they took the sail down and let the ship go with the wind.

¹⁸The storm was so bad the high waves were beating against the ship. The next day the men threw some of the freight over into the sea. ¹⁹On the third day, with their own hands, they threw part of the sails and ropes into the sea. ²⁰We did not see the sun or stars for many days. A very bad storm kept beating against us. We lost all hope of being saved.

Paul Shows His Faith

²¹No one had eaten for a long time. Then Paul stood up and said to them, "Men, you should have listened to me and not left the island of Crete. You would not have had this trouble and loss. ²²But now I want you to take hope. No one will lose his life. Only the ship will be lost. ²³I belong to God and I work for Him. Last night an angel of God stood by me ²⁴and said, 'Do not be afraid, Paul. You must stand in front of Caesar. God has given you the lives of all the men on this ship.' ²⁵So take hope, men. I believe my God will do what He has told me. ²⁶But the ship will be lost on some island."

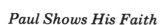

No one will lose his life.

I believe my God will do what He has told me.

²⁷It was now the fourteenth night. We were going with the wind on the Adriatic Sea. At midnight the sailors thought land was near. ²⁸They let down the lead weight and found the water was not very deep. After they had gone a little farther, they found there was not as much water. ²⁹They were afraid we might be thrown against the rocks on the shore. So they put out four anchors from the back of the ship. Then they waited for morning to come.

³⁰The sailors were thinking of leaving the ship. They let down a boat as if they were going to put out anchors from the front of the ship. ³¹But Paul said to the captain and the soldiers, "These men must stay on the ship or you cannot be safe!" ³²Then the soldiers cut the ropes and let the boat fall into the sea.

³³Just before the light of day came, Paul told all of them to eat. He said, "Today is the fourteenth day you have not eaten. ³⁴You must eat. It will give you strength. Not one of you will lose a hair from your head."

³⁵After he said this, he took some bread. He gave thanks to God in front of them all. He broke it in pieces and started to eat. ³⁶They all were comforted. Each one ate some food. ³⁷All together there were 276 of us on the ship. ³⁸After they had eaten, they threw the wheat into the sea so the ship would not be as heavy.

³⁹In the morning they could not see what land they were near. Later they could see a river. Near its mouth there was a shore of sand. They planned to run the ship onto the sand if they could. ⁴⁰The anchors were cut loose and left in the sea. Then they took the ropes off that were holding the rudder. When they put up the sail, the wind took the ship toward shore. ⁴¹But the ship hit a place where the water was low. It was made from where two seas meet. The front of the ship did not move but the back part broke in pieces by the high waves.

⁴²The soldiers planned to kill the men in chains. They were afraid they would swim to shore and get away, ⁴³but the captain wanted to save Paul. He kept them from their plan. Calling out to those who could swim, he told them to jump into the sea and swim to shore. ⁴⁴The others should use wood or anything from the ship. In this way, they all got to shore without getting hurt.

The Powerful Work Of Paul

28 After we were safe on the island, we knew that it was Malta. ²The people on the island were very kind to us. It was raining and cold. They made a fire so we could get warm. ³Paul had gathered some wood. As he laid it on the fire, a snake came out because of the heat. It held fast to Paul's hand. ⁴When the people of the island saw the snake holding to his hand, they said to each other, "This man is a killer. He was saved from the sea and yet it is not right for him to live." ⁵Paul shook off the snake into the fire. He was not hurt in any way. ⁶The people waited. They thought his hand would get large and he would fall over dead. After watching for a long time, they saw nothing happen to him. Then they changed their minds and said that Paul was a god.

The Father Of Publius Is Healed

⁷Publius was the head man of the island. He owned land around there. For three days he took us in and gave us everything we needed. ⁸The father of Publius was sick with a stomach sickness. Paul went to see him. He prayed and laid his hands on him and the man was healed. ⁹Because of this, other people of the island who were sick came to Paul and were healed. ¹⁰They had great respect for us. When we got into a ship to leave, they gave us everything we needed.

¹¹We had stayed on the island three months. Then we left on a ship that had stayed there during the winter. It was from the city of Alexandria. This ship was called the Twin Brothers. ¹²From there we went by ship around to the city of Rhegium. After a day a south wind started to blow. On the second day we came to the city of Puteoli. ¹⁴We found some Christians there, and they asked us to stay with them. We were there seven days and then went on to the city of Rome.

¹⁵When the Christians heard of our coming, they came to meet us. They came as far as the town of Appius and to a place to stay called the Three Stores. When Paul saw them, he thanked God and took courage.

He thanked God and took courage.

Paul Tells Why And How He Has Come

¹⁶When we got to Rome, Paul was allowed to live where he wanted to. But a soldier was always by his side to watch him. ¹⁷Three days later Paul asked the leaders of the Jews to come to him. When they had gathered together, he said, "Brothers, I have done nothing against our people or the way our early fathers lived.

And yet, I was tied with chains in Jerusalem and handed over to the Romans. ¹⁸I was put on trial, but they found no reason to put me to death. They would have let me go free. ¹⁹But the Jews did not like this. So I had to ask to be sent to Caesar. It was not because I had anything against my people. ²⁰The reason I have asked you to come is to tell you this. It is because of the hope of the Jewish nation that I am tied in these chains."

²¹They said to Paul, "We have had no letters from Judea about you. No Jew who has come here has ever said anything bad about you. ²²We would like to hear from you what you believe. As for this new religion, all we know is that everyone is talking against it."

²³They planned to meet him on a certain day. Many people came to the place where he stayed. He preached to them about the holy nation of God. He tried to get them to put their trust in Jesus Christ by preaching from the Law of Moses and from the writings of the early preachers. From morning until night he spoke to them. ²⁴Some of them believed his teaching. Others did not believe.

²⁵As they left, they did not agree with each other. Then Paul said, "The Holy Spirit spoke the truth to your early fathers through the early preacher Isaiah. ²⁶He said, 'Go to these people and say, "You will hear and never understand, you will look and never see, ²⁷because these people have hearts that have become fat. They do not hear well with their ears. They have closed their eyes so their eyes do not see and their ears do not hear and their minds do not understand and they do not turn to Me and let Me heal them." ' (Isaiah 6:9-10)

²⁸"I want you to know that the Good News of God of knowing how to be saved from the punishment of sin has been sent to the people who are not Jews. And they will listen to it!" ²⁹＊After he had said these things, the Jews went away and argued with each other.

³⁰Paul paid money to live in a house by himself for two years. He was happy for all who came to see him. ³¹He kept on preaching about the holy nation of God. He taught about the Lord Jesus Christ without fear. No one stopped him.

1 This letter is from Paul. I am a workman owned by Jesus Christ and a missionary chosen by God to preach His Good News. ²The Good News was promised long ago by God's early preachers in His Holy Writings. ³It tells of His Son, our Lord Jesus Christ, Who was born as a person in the flesh through the family of King David. ⁴The Holy Spirit proved by a powerful act that Jesus our Lord is the Son of God because He was raised from the dead. ⁵Jesus has given us His loving-favor and has made us His missionaries. We are to preach to the people of all nations that they should obey Him and put their trust in Him. ⁶You have been chosen to belong to Jesus Christ also. ⁷So I write to all of you in the city of Rome. God loves you and has chosen you to be set apart for Himself. May God our Father and the Lord Jesus Christ give you His loving-favor and peace.

Prayer Of Thanks

⁸First of all, I keep thanking my God, through Jesus Christ, for all of you. This is because the whole world knows of your faith in Christ. ⁹God knows how I work for Him. He knows how I preach with all my heart the Good News about His Son. He knows how I always pray for you. ¹⁰I pray that I might be able to visit you, if God wants me to. ¹¹I want to see you so I can share some special gift of the Holy Spirit with you. It will make you strong. ¹²Both of us need help. I can help make your faith strong and you can do the same for me. We need each other.

Sinful Man

¹³Christian brothers, many times I have wanted to visit you. Something has kept me from going until now. I have wanted to lead some of you to Christ also, as I have done in other places where they did not know God. ¹⁴I must help the people who have had a chance to hear the Good News and those who have not. I must help those with much learning and those who have never learned from books. ¹⁵So I want to preach the Good News to you who live in the city of Rome also.

¹⁶I am not ashamed of the Good News. It is the power of God. It is the way He saves men from the punishment of their sins if they put their trust in Him. It is for the Jew first and for all other people also. ¹⁷The Good News tells us we are made right with God by faith in Him. Then, by faith we live that new life through Him. The Holy Writings say, "A man right with God lives by faith." (Habakkuk 2:4)

A man right with God lives by faith.

The Sinful World

¹⁸We see the anger of God coming down from heaven against all the sins of men. These sinful men keep the truth from being known. ¹⁹Men know about God. He has made it plain to them. ²⁰Men cannot say they do not know about God. From the beginning of the world, men could see what God is like through the things He has made. This shows His power that lasts forever. It shows that He is God. ²¹They did know God, but they did not honor Him as God. They were not thankful to Him and thought only of foolish things. Their foolish minds became dark. ²²They said that they were wise, but they showed how foolish they were. ²³They gave honor to false gods that looked like people who can die and to birds and animals and snakes. This honor belongs to God Who can never die.

²⁴So God let them follow the desires of their sinful hearts. They did sinful things among themselves with their bodies. ²⁵They traded the truth of God for a lie. They worshiped and cared for what God made instead of worshiping the God Who made it. He is the One Who is to receive honor and thanks forever. Let it be so.

²⁶Because of this, God let them follow their sinful desires which lead to shame. Women used their bodies in ways God had not planned. ²⁷In the same way, men left the right use of women's bodies. They did sex sins with other men. They received for themselves the punishment that was coming to them for their sin.

²⁸Because they would not keep God in their thoughts anymore, He gave them up. Their minds were sinful and they wanted only to do things they should not do. ²⁹They are full of everything that is sinful and want things that belong to others. They hate people and are jealous. They kill other people. They fight and lie. They do not like other people and talk against them. ³⁰They talk about

people. They hate God. They are filled with pride and tell of all the good they do. They think of new ways to sin. They do not obey their parents. [31]They are not able to understand. They do not do what they say they will do. They have no love and no loving-pity. [32]They know God has said that all who do such things should die. But they keep on doing these things and are happy when others do them also.

All Men Are Sinners

2 So you can say nothing because you are guilty when you say someone else is guilty. While you say someone is guilty, you are doing the same things he does. [2]We know that God will say those who do such things are guilty. [3]Do you think God will punish others for doing wrong and let you keep sinning? [4]Do you forget about His loving-kindness to you? Do you forget how long He is waiting for you? You know that God is kind. He is trying to get you to be sorry for your sins and turn from them. [5]Because you are not sorry for your sins and will not turn from them, you will be punished even more on the day of God's anger. God will be right in saying you are guilty. [6]He will give to every man what he should get for the things he has done. [7]Those who keep on doing good and are looking for His greatness and honor will receive life that lasts forever. [8]Those who love only themselves and do not obey the truth, but do what is wrong, will be punished by God. His anger will be on them. [9]Every Jew and every person who is not a Jew who sins will suffer and have great sorrow. [10]But God will give His greatness and honor and peace to all those who obey the truth. Both Jews and those who are not Jews will receive this. [11]God does not show favor to one man more than to another.

God Does What Is Right To All Men

[12]Those who have sinned without having the Jewish Law will be lost without the Law being used. Those who have the Jewish Law and have sinned will be told they are guilty by the Law. [13]Just to hear the Jewish Law does not make a man right with God. The man right with God is the one who obeys the Law. [14]The people who are not Jews do not have the Jewish Law. When they do what the Law tells them to do, even if they do not have the Law, it shows they know what they should do. [15]They show that what the

Just to near the Jewish Law does not make a man right with God.

Law wants them to do is written in their hearts. Their own hearts tell them if they are guilty. ¹⁶There will be a day when God will say who is guilty because He knows the secret thoughts of men. He will do this through Jesus Christ. This is part of the Good News I preach.

¹⁷You are a Jew and think you are safe because of the Law. You tell others about how you know God. ¹⁸You know what He wants you to do. You understand how the Law works. You know right from wrong. ¹⁹You think you can lead a blind man. You think you can give light to those in darkness. ²⁰You think you can teach foolish people and children about God. You have in the Law the plan of truth and wisdom. ²¹You teach others. Why do you not teach yourselves? You tell others not to steal. Do you steal? ²²You say that no one should do sex sins. Do you do sex sins? You hate false gods. Do you rob the houses where they are kept? ²³You are proud of the Jewish Law. Do you take honor away from God when you do not obey the Law? ²⁴The Holy Writings say, "God's name is hated by the people who are not Jews because of you." (Isaiah 52:5)

²⁵Going through the religious act of becoming a Jew is worth something if you obey the Law. If you do not obey the Law, it is worth nothing to you. ²⁶If a person who is not a Jew, but has not gone through the act of becoming a Jew, and obeys the Jewish Law, God will think of him as a Jew. ²⁷You Jews have the Law but do not obey it. You have gone through the religious act also. At the same time those who are not Jews obey the Law even if they have not gone through the religious act of becoming a Jew. In this way, these people show you are guilty. ²⁸A man is not a Jew just because he goes through the religious act of becoming a Jew. ²⁹The true Jew is one whose heart is right with God. The religious act of becoming a Jew must be done in the heart. That is the work of the Holy Spirit. The Law does not do that kind of work. The true Jew gets his thanks from God, not from men.

Jews Are Sinners Also

3 Do the Jews have anything that those who are not Jews do not have? What good does it do to go through the religious act of becoming a Jew? ²Yes, the Jews have much more in every way. First of all, God gave the Jews His Law. [3]If some of them were not faithful, does it mean that God will not be faithful? [4]No, not at all! God is always true even if every man lies. The Holy Writings say, "Speak the truth and you will not be proven guilty." (Psalm 51:4)

[5]If our sins show how right God is, what can we say? Is it wrong for God to punish us for it? (I am speaking as men do.) [6]No, not at all! If it were wrong for God to punish us, how could He say what was right from wrong with the world? [7]If my lies honor God by showing how true He is, why am I still being punished as a sinner? [8]Why not say, "Let us sin that good will come from it." (Some people have said I talk like this!) They will be punished as they should be.

The Whole World Is Guilty Of Sin

[9]What about it then? Are we Jews better than the people who are not Jews? Not at all! I have already said that Jews and the people who are not Jews are all sinners. [10]The Holy Writings say, "There is not one person who is right with God. No, not even one! [11]There is not one who understands. There is not one who tries to find God." (Psalm 14:2) [12]Everyone has turned away from God. They have all done wrong. Not one of them does what is good. No, not even one! [13]Their mouth is like an open grave. They tell lies with their tongues. (Psalm 5:9; 140:3) Whatever they say is like the poison of snakes. [14]Their mouths speak bad things against God. They say bad things about other people. (Psalm 10:7) [15]They are quick to hurt and kill people. [16]Wherever they go, they destroy and make people suffer. [17]They know nothing about peace. (Isaiah 59:7-8) [18]They do not honor God with love and fear." (Psalm 36:1)

[19]Now we know that the Jewish Law speaks to those who live under the Law. No one can say that he does not know what sin is. Yes, every person in the world stands guilty in front of God. [20]No person will be made right with God by doing what the Jewish Law says. The Law shows us how sinful we are.

[21]But now God has made another way to make men right with Himself. It is not by the Jewish Law. The Law and the early preachers tell about it. [22]Men become right with God by putting their trust in Jesus Christ. God will accept men if they come this

There is not one person who is right with God. No, not even one!

Everyone has turned away from God.

For all men have sinned and have missed the shining greatness of God.

way. All men are the same to God. 23For all men have sinned and have missed the shining greatness of God. 24Anyone can be made right with God by the free gift of His loving-favor. It is Jesus Christ Who bought them with His blood and made them free from their sins. 25God gave Jesus Christ to the world. Men's sins can be forgiven through the blood of Christ when they put their trust in Him. God gave His Son Jesus Christ to show how right He is. Before this, God did not look on the sins that were done. 26But now God proves that He is right in saving men from sin. He shows that He is the One Who has no sin. God makes anyone right with Himself who puts his trust in Jesus.

27What then do we have to be proud of? Nothing at all! Why? Is it because men obey the Jewish Law? No! It is because men put their trust in Christ. 28This is what we have come to know. A man is made right with God by putting his trust in Christ. It is not by his doing what the Jewish Law says. 29Is God the God of the Jews only? Is He not the God of the people who are not Jews also? He is for sure. 30He is one God. He will make Jews and the people who are not Jews right with Himself if they put their trust in Christ. 31Does this mean that we do away with the Jewish Law when we put our trust in Christ? No, not at all. It means we know the Jewish Law is important.

Abraham Was Saved From Sin By His Trust In God

4 What about Abraham, our early father? What did he learn? 2If Abraham was made right with God by what he did, he would have had something to be proud of. But he could not be proud in front of God. 3The Holy Writings say, "Abraham put his trust in God and that made him right with God." (Genesis 15:6) 4If a man works, his pay is not a gift. It is something he has earned. 5If a man has not worked to be saved, but has put his trust in God Who saves men from the punishment of their sins, that man is made right with God because of his trust in God. 6David tells of this. He spoke of how happy the man is who puts his trust in God without working to be saved from the punishment of sin. 7"Those people are happy whose sinful acts are forgiven and whose sins are covered. 8Those people are happy whose sins the Lord will not remember." (Psalm 32:1-2)

⁹Is this happiness given to the Jews only? Or is it given also to the people who are not Jews? We say again, "Abraham put his trust in God and that made him right with God." (Genesis 15:6) ¹⁰When did this happen? Was it before or after Abraham went through the religious act of becoming a Jew? It was before. ¹¹He went through the religious act after he had put his trust in God. That religious act proved that his trust in God made him right with God even before he went through the religious act of becoming a Jew. In that way, it made him the early father of all those who believe. It showed that those who did not go through the religious act of becoming a Jew could be right with God. ¹²He is also the early father of all those who have gone through the religious act of becoming a Jew. It is not because they went through the act. It is because they put their trust in God the same as Abraham did before he went through the religious act of becoming a Jew. ¹³God promised to give the world to him and to all his family after him. He did not make this promise because Abraham obeyed the Jewish Law. He promised to give the world to Abraham because he put his trust in God. This made him right with God. ¹⁴If those who obey the Jewish Law are to get the world, then a person putting his trust in God means nothing. God's promise to Abraham would be worth nothing. ¹⁵God's anger comes on a man when he does not obey the Jewish Law. But if there were no Jewish Law, then no one could break it.

¹⁶So God's promise is given to us because we put our trust in Him. We can be sure of it. It is because of His loving-favor to us. It is for all the family of Abraham. It is for those who obey the Jewish Law. It is for those who put their trust in God as Abraham did. In this way, he is the father of all Christians. ¹⁷The Holy Writings say, "I have made you a father of many nations." This promise is good because of Who God is. He makes the dead live again. He speaks, and something is made out of nothing. ¹⁸Abraham believed he would be the father of many nations. He had no reason to hope for this, but he had been told, "Your children will become many nations." (Genesis 15:5) ¹⁹Abraham was about one hundred years old. His body was about dead, but his faith in God was not weak when he thought of his body. His faith was not weak when he thought of his wife Sarah being past the age of having children. ²⁰Abraham did not doubt God's

promise. His faith in God was strong, and he gave thanks to God. 21He was sure God was able to do what He had promised. 22Abraham put his trust in God and was made right with Him. 23The words, "He was made right with God," were not for Abraham only. 24They were for us also. God will make us right with Himself the same way He did Abraham, if we put our trust in God Who raised Jesus our Lord from the dead. 25Jesus died for our sins. He was raised from the dead to make us right with God.

The Joy Of Being Right With God

5 Now that we have been made right with God by putting our trust in Him, we have peace with Him. It is because of what our Lord Jesus Christ did for us. 2By putting our trust in God, He has given us His loving-favor and has received us. We are happy for the hope we have of sharing the shining greatness of God. 3We are glad for our troubles also. We know that troubles help us learn not to give up. 4When we have learned not to give up, it shows we have stood the test. When we have stood the test, it gives us hope. 5Hope never makes us ashamed because the love of God has come into our hearts through the Holy Spirit Who was given to us.

6We were weak and could not help ourselves. Then Christ came at the right time and gave His life for all sinners. 7No one is willing to die for another person, but for a good man someone might be willing to die. 8But God showed His love to us. While we were still sinners, Christ died for us. 9Now that we have been saved from the punishment of sin by the blood of Christ, He will save us from God's anger also. 10We hated God. But we were saved from the punishment of sin by the death of Christ. He has brought us back to God and we will be saved by His life. 11Not only that, we give thanks to God through our Lord Jesus Christ. Through Him we have been brought back to God.

Adam And Christ

12This is what happened: Sin came into the world by one man, Adam. Sin brought death with it. Death spread to all men because all have sinned. 13Sin was in the world before the Jewish Law was given. But sin is not held against a person when there is no Law.

¹⁴And yet death had power over men from the time of Adam until the time of Moses. Even the power of death was over those who had not sinned in the same way Adam sinned. Adam was like the One Who was to come.

¹⁵God's free gift is not like the sin of Adam. Many people died because of the sin of this one man, Adam. But the loving-favor of God came to many people also. This gift came also by one Man Jesus Christ, God's Son. ¹⁶The free gift of God is not like Adam's sin. God told Adam he was guilty because of his sin and through this one came sin and guilt. But the free gift makes men right with God. Through One, Christ, men's sins are forgiven. ¹⁷The power of death was over all men because of the sin of one man, Adam. But many people will receive His loving-favor and the gift of being made right with God. They will have power in life by Jesus Christ.

¹⁸Through Adam's sin, death and hell came to all men. But another Man, Christ, by His right act makes men free and gives them life. ¹⁹Adam did not obey God, and many people become sinners through him. Christ obeyed God and makes many people right with Himself.

God's Loving-Favor Is Greater Than The Jewish Law

²⁰Sin spread when the Jewish Law was given. But where sin spread, God's loving-favor spread all the more. ²¹Sin had power that ended in death. Now, God's loving-favor has power to make men right with Himself. It gives life that lasts forever. Our Lord Jesus Christ did this for us.

Being Right With God

6 What does this mean? Are we to keep on sinning so that God will give us more of His loving-favor? ²No, not at all! We are dead to sin. How then can we keep on living in sin? ³All of us were baptized to show we belong to Christ. We were baptized first of all to show His death. ⁴We were buried in baptism as Christ was buried in death. As Christ was raised from the dead by the great power of God, so we will have new life also. ⁵If we have become one with Christ in His death, we will be one with Him in being raised from the dead to new life.

As Christ was raised from the dead by the great power of God, so we will have new life also.

⁶We know that our old life, our old sinful self, was nailed to the cross with Christ. And so the power of sin that held us was destroyed. Sin is no longer our boss. ⁷When a man is dead, he is free from the power of sin. ⁸And if we have died with Christ, we believe we will live with Him also. ⁹We know that Christ was raised from the dead. He will never die again. Death has no more power over Him. ¹⁰He died once but now lives. He died to break the power of sin, and the life He now lives is for God. ¹¹You must do the same thing! Think of yourselves as dead to the power of sin. But now you have new life because of Jesus Christ our Lord. You are living this new life for God.

¹²So do not let sin have power over your body here on earth. You must not obey the body and let it do what it wants to do. ¹³Do not give any part of your body for sinful use. Instead, give yourself to God as a living person who has been raised from the dead. Give every part of your body to God to do what is right. ¹⁴Sin must not have power over you. You are not living by the Jewish Law. You have life because of God's loving-favor.

¹⁵What are we to do then? Are we to sin because we have God's loving-favor and are not living by the Jewish Law? No, not at all! ¹⁶Do you not know that when you give yourself as a workman to be owned by someone, that one becomes your owner? If you give yourself to sin, the end is death. If you give yourself to God, the end is being right with Him. ¹⁷At one time you were held by the power of sin. But now you obey with all your heart the teaching that was given to you. Thank God for this! ¹⁸You were made free from the power of sin. Being right with God has power over you now. ¹⁹I speak with words easy to understand because your human thinking is weak. At one time you gave yourselves over to the power of sin. You kept on sinning all the more. Now give yourselves over to being right with God. Set yourself apart for God-like living and to do His work.

You get what is coming to you when you sin. It is death! But God's free gift is life that lasts forever.

²⁰When sin had power over your life, you were not not right with God. ²¹What good did you get from the things you are ashamed of now? Those things bring death. ²²But now you are free from the power of sin. You have become a workman for God. Your life is set apart for God-like living. The end is life that lasts forever. ²³You get what is coming to you when you sin. It is death! But God's

free gift is life that lasts forever. It is given to us by our Lord Jesus Christ.

The Jewish Law Shows What Sin Is

7 Christian brothers, I am sure you understand what I am going to say. You know all about the Jewish Law. The Jewish Law has power over a man as long as he lives. ²A married woman is joined by law to her husband as long as he lives. But if he dies, she is free from the law that joined her to him. ³If she marries another man while her husband is still alive, she is sinning by not being faithful in marriage. If her husband dies, she is free from the law that joined her to him. After that she can marry someone else. She does not sin if she marries another man.

⁴My Christian brothers, that is the way it is with you. You were under the power of the Jewish Law. But now you are dead to it because you are joined to another. You are joined to Christ Who was raised from the dead. This is so we may be what God wants us to be. Our lives are to give fruit for Him. ⁵When we lived to please our bodies, those sinful desires were pulling at us all the time. We always wanted to do what the Jewish Law said not to do. Living that kind of life brings death, ⁶but now we are free from the Jewish Law. We are dead to sin that once held us in its power. No longer do we follow the Jewish Law which is the old way. We now follow the new way, the way of the Spirit.

The Jewish Law And Sin

⁷Then what are we saying? Is the Jewish Law sinful? No, not at all! But it was the Law that showed me what sin is. I did not know it was sin to follow wrong desires, but the Law said, "You must not follow wrong desires." ⁸The Jewish Law made me know how much I was sinning. It showed me how I had a desire for all kinds of things. For without the Law, sin is dead. ⁹I was once alive. That was when I did not know what the Law said I had to do. Then I found that I had broken the Law. I knew I was a sinner. Death was mine because of the Law. ¹⁰The Jewish Law was supposed to give me new life. Instead, it gave me death. ¹Sin

found a way to trap me by working through the Jewish Law. Then sin killed me by using the Law.

¹²The Jewish Law is holy. Each one of the Laws is holy and right and good. ¹³Then does it mean that the Jewish Law, which is good, brought death to me? No, not at all! It was sin that did it. Sin brought death to me by the Law that is good. In that way, sin was shown to be what it is. So because of the Law, sin becomes much more sinful.

The Two Kinds Of Men

¹⁴We know that the Jewish Law is right and good, but I am a person who does what is wrong and bad. I am not my own boss. Sin is my boss. ¹⁵I do not understand myself. I want to do what is right but I do not do it. Instead, I do the very thing I hate. ¹⁶When I do the thing I do not want to do, it shows me that the Law is right and good. ¹⁷So I am not doing it. Sin living in me is doing it. ¹⁸I know there is nothing good in me, that is, in my flesh. For I want to do good but I do not. ¹⁹I do not do the good I want to do. Instead, I am always doing the sinful things I do not want to do. ²⁰If I am always doing the very thing I do not want to do, it means I am no longer the one who does it. It is sin that lives in me. ²¹This has become my way of life: When I want to do what is right, I always do what is wrong. ²²My mind and heart agree with the Law of God. ²³But there is a different law at work deep inside of me that fights with my mind. This law of sin holds me in its power because sin is still in me. ²⁴There is no happiness in me! Who can set me free from my sinful old self? ²⁵God's Law has power over my mind, but sin still has power over my sinful old self. I thank God I can be free through Jesus Christ our Lord!

The Holy Spirit Makes Us Free

8 Now, because of this, those who belong to Christ will not suffer the punishment of sin. ²The power of the Holy Spirit has made me free from the power of sin and death. This power is mine because I belong to Christ Jesus. ³The Jewish Law could not make me free from the power of sin and death. It was weak because it had to work with weak human beings. But God sent

His own Son. He came to earth in a body of flesh which could be tempted to sin as we in our bodies can be. He gave Himself to take away sin. By doing that, He took away the power sin had over us. ⁴In that way, Jesus did for us what the Jewish Law said had to be done. We do not do what our sinful old selves tell us to do anymore. Now we do what the Holy Spirit wants us to do. ⁵Those who let their sinful old selves tell them what to do live under the power of their sinful old selves. But those who let the Holy Spirit tell them what to do are under His power. ⁶If your sinful old self is the boss over your mind, it leads to death. But if the Holy Spirit is the boss over your mind, it leads to life and peace. ⁷The mind that thinks only of ways to please the sinful old self is fighting against God. It is not able to obey God's Laws. It never can. ⁸Those who do what their sinful old selves want to do cannot please God.

⁹But you are not doing what your sinful old selves want you to do. You are doing what the Holy Spirit tells you to do, if you have God's Spirit living in you. No one belongs to Christ if he does not have Christ's Spirit in him. ¹⁰If Christ is in you, your spirit lives because you are right with God, and yet your body is dead because of sin. ¹¹The Holy Spirit raised Jesus from the dead. If the same Holy Spirit lives in you, He will give life to your bodies in the same way.

¹²So then, Christian brothers, we are not to do what our sinful old selves want us to do. ¹³If you do what your sinful old selves want you to do, you will die in sin. But if, through the power of the Holy Spirit, you destroy those actions to which the body can be led, you will have life. ¹⁴All those who are led by the Holy Spirit are sons of God. ¹⁵You should not act like people who are owned by someone. They are always afraid. Instead, the Holy Spirit makes us His sons, and we can call to Him, "My Father." ¹⁶For the Holy Spirit speaks to us and tells our spirit that we are children of God. ¹⁷If we are children of God, we will receive everything He has promised us. We will share with Christ all the things God has given to Him. But we must share His suffering if we are to share His shining greatness.

Another Picture Of The Future

¹⁸I am sure that our suffering now cannot be compared to the shining greatness that He is going to give us. ¹⁹Everything that

has been made in the world is waiting for the day when God will make His sons known. [20]Everything that has been made in the world is weak. It is not that the world wanted it to be that way. God allowed it to be that way. Yet there is hope. [21]Everything that has been made in the world will be set free from the power that can destroy. These will become free just as the children of God become free. [22]We know that everything on the earth cries out with pain the same as a woman giving birth to a child. [23]We also cry inside ourselves, even we who have received the Holy Spirit. The Holy Spirit is the first of God's gifts to us. We are waiting to become His complete sons when our bodies are made free. [24]We were saved with this hope ahead of us. Now hope means we are waiting for something we do not have. How can a man hope for something he already has? [25]But if we hope for something we do not yet see, we must learn how to wait for it.

[26]In the same way, the Holy Spirit helps us where we are weak. We do not know how to pray or what we should pray for, but the Holy Spirit prays to God for us with sounds that cannot be put into words. [27]God knows the hearts of men. He knows what the Holy Spirit is thinking. The Holy Spirit prays for those who belong to Christ the way God wants Him to pray.

God Gives Us His Greatness

We know that God makes all things work together for the good of those who love Him and are chosen to be a part of His plan.

[28]We know that God makes all things work together for the good of those who love Him and are chosen to be a part of His plan. [29]God knew from the beginning who would put their trust in Him. So He chose them and made them to be like His Son. Christ was first and all those who belong to God are His brothers. [30]He called to Himself also those He chose. Those He called, He made right with Himself. Then He shared His shining greatness with those He made right with Himself.

[31]What can we say about all these things? Since God is for us, who can be against us? [32]God did not keep His own Son for Himself but gave Him for us all. Then with His Son, will He not give us all things? [33]Who can say anything against the people God has chosen? It is God Who says they are right with Himself. [34]Who then can say we are guilty? It was Christ Jesus Who died. He was raised from the dead. He is on the right side of God

praying to Him for us. ³⁵Who can keep us away from the love of Christ? Can trouble or problems? Can suffering wrong from others or no food? Can it be because of no clothes or because of danger or war? ³⁶The Holy Writings say, "Because of belonging to Jesus, we are in danger of being killed all day long. We are thought of as sheep that are ready to be killed." (Psalm 44:22) ³⁷But we have power over all these things through Jesus Who loves us so much. ³⁸For I know that nothing can keep us from the love of God. Death cannot! Life cannot! Angels cannot! Leaders cannot! Any other power cannot! Hard things now or in the future cannot! ³⁹The world above or the world below cannot! Any other living thing cannot keep us away from the love of God which is ours through Christ Jesus our Lord.

The People God Chose For Himself

9 I am telling the truth because I belong to Christ. The Holy Spirit tells my heart that I am not lying. ²I have much sorrow. The pain in my heart never leaves. ³I could even wish that I might be kept from being with Christ if that would help my people to be saved from the punishment of sin. They are of my own flesh and blood. ⁴They are Jews and are the people God chose for Himself. He shared His shining greatness with them and gave them His Law and a way to worship. They have His promises. ⁵The early preachers came from this family. Christ Himself was born of flesh from this family and He is over all things. May God be honored and thanked forever. Let it be so.

⁶I am not saying that God did not keep His promises. Not all the Jews are people God chose for Himself. ⁷Not all of Abraham's family are children of God. God told Abraham, "Only the family of Isaac will be called your family." (Genesis 21:9-12) ⁸This means that children born to Abraham are not all children of God. Only those that are born because of God's promise to Abraham are His children. ⁹This was the promise God made: "About this time next year I will come, and Sarah will have a son." (Genesis 18:10) ¹⁰Not only this, but there was Rebecca also. Rebecca gave birth to two sons at the same time. Both of them were sons of Isaac. ¹¹Even before the two sons were born, we see God's plan of choosing. God could choose whom He wanted. It could not be

changed because of anything the older son tried to do about it. It was before either one had done anything good or bad. [12]Rebecca was told, "The older son will work for the younger son." [13]The Holy Writings say, "I loved Jacob, but hated Esau." (Malachi 1:2)

[14]What about it then? Can we say that God is not fair? No, not at all! [15]God said to Moses, "I will have loving-kindness and loving-pity for anyone I want to." (Exodus 33:19) [16]These good things from God are not given to someone because he wants them or works to get them. They are given because of His loving-kindness. [17]The Holy Writings say to Pharoah, "I made you leader for this reason: I used you to show My power. I used you to make My name known over all the world." (Exodus 9:16) [18]So God has loving-kindness for those He wants to. He makes some have hard hearts if He wants to.

[19]But you will ask me, "Why does God blame men for what they do? Who can go against what God wants?" [20]Who are you to talk back to God? A pot being made from clay does not talk to the man making it and say, "Why did you make me like this?" [21]The man making the pots has the right to use the clay as he wants to. He can make two pots from the same piece of clay. One can have an important use. The other one can be of little use. [22]It may be that God wants to show His power and His anger against sin. He waits a long time on some men who are ready to be destroyed. [23]God also wanted to show His shining greatness to those He has given His loving-kindness. He made them ready for His shining greatness from the beginning. [24]We are the ones He chose. He did not only choose Jews. He also chose some from among the people who are not Jews. [25]In the Book of Hosea He says, "Those who are not My people, I will call, 'My people.' Those who are not loved, I will call, 'My loved ones.'" (Hosea 2:23) [26]"And where it said, 'You are not my people,' they will be called sons of the living God." (Hosea 1:10) [27]Isaiah says this about the Jews, "Even if there are as many Jews as the sand by the sea, only a few of them will be saved from the punishment of sin. [28]For the Lord will do on earth what He says in His Word. He will work fast when He says what will happen here." (Isaiah 10:22-23) [29]Isaiah said also, "If God had not left some of the Jews, we would have all been

destroyed like the people who lived in the cities of Sodom and Gomorrah." (Isaiah 1:9)

The Jews And The Good News

[30]What are we to say about these things? The people who are not Jews were not made right with God by the Law. They were made right with God because they put their trust in Him. [31]The Jews tried to be right with God by obeying the Law, but they did not become right with God. [32]Why? Because they did not put their trust in God. They tried to be right with God by working for it. They tripped over the most important Stone (Christ). [33]The Holy Writings say, "Listen! I put in Jerusalem a Stone that people will trip over. It is a Rock that will make them fall. But the person who puts his trust in that Rock (Christ) will not be put to shame." (Isaiah 28:16)

The Jews Have Tried To Make Their Own Way

10 Christian brothers, the desire of my heart and my prayer to God is that the Jews might be saved from the punishment of sin. [2]I know about them. They have a strong desire for God, but they do not know what they should about Him. [3]They have not known how God makes men right with Himself. Instead, they have tried to make their own way. They have not become right with God because they have not done what God said to do. [4]For Christ has put an end to the Jewish Law, so everyone who has put his trust in Christ is made right with God.

[5]Moses writes that the man who obeys the Jewish Law has to live by it. [6]But when a man puts his trust in Christ, he is made right with God. You do not need to ask yourself, "Who will go up to heaven to bring Christ down?" [7]And you do not need to ask, "Who will go below and bring Christ up from the dead?" [8]This is what it says, "The Good News is near you. It is in your mouth and in your heart." (Deuteronomy 30:14) This Good News tells about putting your trust in Christ. This is what we preach to you. [9]If you say with your mouth that Jesus is Lord, and believe in your heart that God raised Him from the dead, you will be saved from the punishment of sin. [10]When we believe in our

If you say with your mouth that Jesus is Lord, and believe in your heart that God raised Him from the dead, you will be saved from the punishment of sin.

hearts, we are made right with God. We tell with our mouth how we were saved from the punishment of sin. [11]The Holy Writings say, "No one who puts his trust in Christ will ever be put to shame." (Isaiah 28:16) [12]There is no difference between the Jews and the people who are not Jews. They are all the same to the Lord. And He is Lord over all of them. He gives of His greatness to all who call on Him for help. [13]For everyone who calls on the name of the Lord will be saved from the punishment of sin.

[14]But how can they call on Him if they have not put their trust in Him? And how can they put their trust in Him if they have not heard of Him? And how can they hear of Him unless someone tells them? [15]And how can someone tell them if he is not sent? The Holy Writings say, "The feet of those who bring the Good News are beautiful." (Isaiah 52:7)

Faith comes to us by hearing the Good News. And the Good News comes by someone preaching it.

[16]But they have not all listened to the Good News. Isaiah says, "Lord, who believed what we told them?" (Isaiah 53:1) [17]So then, faith comes to us by hearing the Good News. And the Good News comes by someone preaching it. [18]And so I ask, "Did they not hear?" For sure they did. The Holy Writings say, "Their voice was heard over all the earth. The Good News was told to the ends of the earth." (Psalm 19:4) [19]Again I ask, "Did the Jews not understand?" First of all, Moses says, "I will make you jealous of those who are not a nation. I will make you angry with a foolish nation of people who do not understand." (Deuteronomy 32:21) [20]Isaiah says even stronger words, "I have been found by men who did not look for Me. I have shown Myself to those who were not asking for Me." (Isaiah 65:1) [21]This is what God says about the Jews, "All day long I held out my hand to a people who would not obey Me and who worked against Me." (Isaiah 65:2)

God's Loving-Kindness For The Jews

11 I ask then, "Has God put His people, the Jews, aside?" No, not at all! I myself am a Jew. Abraham was my early father. I am from the family group of Benjamin. [2]God has not put His people aside. He chose them from the beginning. Do you know what the Holy Writings say about Elijah? Do you know what Elijah said to God against the Jews? [3]He said, "Lord, they have killed Your early preachers. They have destroyed the places where

You are worshiped. I am the only one left. They are trying to kill me." ⁴But what did God say to him? God said, "I still have 7,000 men. None of them have worshiped the false god Baal." ⁵It is the same now. A few of the Jews are being chosen because of God's loving-favor. ⁶If they are saved from the punishment of sin because of God's loving-favor, it is nothing men have done to earn it. If men had earned it, then His loving-favor would not be a free gift. ⁷This is the way it was. Many Jews did not get what they were looking for. Only those God chose received it. The hearts of the others were made hard. They could not understand it. ⁸The Holy Writings say this about them, "God gave them hearts and minds that want to sleep. He gave them eyes that could not see. To this very day He gave them ears that could not hear." (Isaiah 29:10) ⁹David said, "Let their table of food become a trap to hold them. Let it be a hole into which they fall and will suffer. ¹⁰Let their eyes be closed so they cannot see. Keep their backs from being straight always because of their troubles." (Psalm 69:23)

¹¹I ask then, "Did the Jews fall so they would be lost forever?" No, not at all! It means the people who are not Jews are able to be saved from the punishment of sin because the Jews sinned by not putting their trust in Christ. This made the Jews jealous of those who are not Jews. ¹²The world received good things from God because of the sin of the Jews. Because the Jews did not receive God's free gift, the people who are not Jews received good things from Him. Think how much more the world will receive when the Jews finish God's plan by putting their trust in Christ!

¹³I am speaking to you people who are not Jews. As long as I am a missionary to you, I want you to know how important my job is. ¹⁴I do this so it will make my own people, the Jews, jealous. Then it may be that some will be saved from the punishment of sin. ¹⁵Because the Jews have been put aside, many other people in the world have been saved from the punishment of sin. Think what it will be like when they are also gathered in. It will be like the dead coming back to life!

¹⁶If the first loaf is holy, all the bread is holy. If the root is holy, all the branches are holy.

¹⁷But some of the branches (who are the Jews) were broken off. You who are not Jews were put in the place where the branches

had been broken off. Now you are sharing the rich root of the olive tree. ¹⁸Do not be proud. Do not think you are better than the branches that were broken off. If you are proud, remember that you do not hold the root. It is the root that holds you. ¹⁹You may say, "Branches were broken off to make room for me." ²⁰It is true. They were broken off because they did not put their trust in Christ. And you are there only because of your faith. Do not be proud. Instead, be afraid. ²¹God did not keep the first branches (who are the Jews) on the tree. Then watch, or He will not keep you on the tree. ²²We see how kind God is. It shows how hard He is also. He is hard on those who fall away. But He is kind to you if you keep on trusting Him. If you do not, He will cut you off. ²³If the Jews would put their trust in Christ, God would put them back into the tree. He has power to do that. ²⁴You people who are not Jews were cut off from a wild olive tree. Instead of being there, you were put into a garden olive tree which is not the right place for you to grow. It would be easy for God to put the Jews back onto their own olive tree because they are the branches that belong there.

God's Loving-Kindness To All

²⁵Christian brothers, I want you to understand this truth which is no longer a secret. It will keep you from thinking you are so wise. Some Jews have become hard until the right amount of people who are not Jews come to God. ²⁶Then all the Jews will be saved, as the Holy Writings say, "The One Who saves from the punishment of sin will come out of Jerusalem. He will turn the Jews from doing sinful things." (Isaiah 59:20-21) ²⁷"And this is My promise to them when I take away their sins." (Isaiah 27:9)

²⁸The Jews are fighting against the Good News. Because they hate the Good News, it has helped you who are not Jews. But God still loves the Jews because He has chosen them and because of His promise to their early fathers. ²⁹God does not change His mind when He chooses men and gives them His gifts. ³⁰At one time you did not obey God. But when the Jews did not receive God's gift, you did. It was because they did not obey. ³¹The Jews will not obey now. God's loving-kindness to you will some day turn them to Him. Then the Jews may have His loving-kindness also. ³²God has said that all men have broken His Law. But He will show loving-kindness on all of them.

³³God's riches are so great! The things He knows and His wisdom are so deep! No one can understand His thoughts. No one can understand His ways. ³⁴The Holy Writings say, "Who knows the mind of the Lord? Who is able to tell Him what to do?" (Isaiah 40:13-14) ³⁵"Who has given Him everything, for what can be paid back to Him?" (Job 35:7; 41:11) ³⁶Everything comes from Him. His power keeps all things together. All things are made for Him. May He be honored forever. Let it be so.

Our Bodies Are To Be A Living Gift

12 Christian brothers, I ask you from my heart to give your bodies to God because of His loving-kindness to us. Let your bodies be a living and holy gift given to God. He is pleased with this kind of gift. This is the true worship that you should give Him. ²Do not act like the sinful people of the world. Let God change your life. First of all, let Him give you a new mind. Then you will know what God wants you to do. And the things you do will be good and pleasing and perfect.

God's Church And The Gifts He Uses

³God has given me His loving-favor. This helps me write these things to you. I ask each one of you not to think more of himself than he should think. Instead, think in the right way toward yourself by the faith God has given you. ⁴Our bodies are made up of many parts. None of these parts have the same use. ⁵There are many people who belong to Christ. And yet, we are one body which is Christ's. We are all different but we depend on each other. ⁶We all have different gifts that God has given to us by His loving-favor. We are to use them. If someone has the gift of preaching the Good News, he should preach. He should use the faith God has given him. ⁷If someone has the gift of helping others, then he should help. If someone has the gift of teaching, he should teach. ⁸If someone has the gift of speaking words of comfort and help, he should speak. If someone has the gift of sharing what he has, he should give from a willing heart. If someone has the gift of leading other people, he should lead them. If someone has the gift of showing kindness to others, he should be happy as he does it.

Let your bodies be a living and holy gift given to God.

Ways Christians Can Help Other Christians

⁹Be sure your love is true love. Hate what is sinful. Hold on to whatever is good. ¹⁰Love each other as Christian brothers. Show respect for each other. ¹¹Do not be lazy but always work hard. Work for the Lord with a heart full of love for Him. ¹²Be happy in your hope. Do not give up when trouble comes. Do not let anything stop you from praying. ¹³Share what you have with Christian brothers who are in need. Give meals and a place to stay to those who need it. ¹⁴Pray and give thanks for those who make trouble for you. Yes, pray for them instead of talking against them. ¹⁵Be happy with those who are happy. Be sad with those who are sad. ¹⁶Live in peace with each other. Do not act or think with pride. Be happy to be with poor people. Keep yourself from thinking you are so wise. ¹⁷When someone does something bad to you, do not pay him back with something bad. Try to do what all men know is right and good. ¹⁸As much as you can, live in peace with all men. ¹⁹Christian brothers, never pay back someone for the bad he has done to you. Let the anger of God take care of the other person. The Holy Writings say, "I will pay back to them what they should get, says the Lord." (Deuteronomy 32:35) ²⁰"If the one who hates you is hungry, feed him. If he is thirsty, give him water. If you do that, you will be making him more ashamed of himself." (Proverbs 25:21-22) ²¹Do not let sin have power over you. Let good have power over sin!

Obey The Leaders Of The Land

13 Every person must obey the leaders of the land. There is no power given but from God, and all leaders are allowed by God. ²The person who does not obey the leaders of the land is working against what God has done. Anyone who does that will be punished.

³Those who do right do not have to be afraid of the leaders. Those who do wrong are afraid of them. Do you want to be free from fear of them? Then do what is right. You will be respected instead. ⁴Leaders are God's workmen to help you. If you do wrong, you should be afraid. They have the power to punish you. They work for God. They do what God wants done to those who do wrong.

⁵You must obey the leaders of the land, not only to keep from God's anger, but so your own heart will have peace. ⁶It is right for you to pay taxes because the leaders of the land are workmen for God who care for these things. ⁷Pay taxes to whom taxes are to be paid. Be afraid of those you should fear. Respect those you should respect.

How A Christian Should Live With His Neighbor

⁸Do not owe anyone anything, but love each other. Whoever loves his neighbor has done what the Law says to do. ⁹The Law says, "You must not do any sex sin. You must not kill another person. You must not steal. You must not tell a lie about another person. You must not want something someone else has." The Law also says that these and many other Laws are brought together in one Law, "You must love your neighbor as yourself." ¹⁰Anyone who loves his neighbor will do no wrong to him. You keep the Law with love.

¹¹There is another reason for doing what is right. You know what time it is. It is time for you to wake up from your sleep. The time when we will be taken up to be with Christ is not as far off as when we first put our trust in Him. ¹²Night is almost gone. Day is almost here. We must stop doing the sinful things that are done in the dark. We must put on all the things God gives us to fight with for the day. ¹³We must act all the time as if it were day. Keep away from wild parties and do not be drunk. Keep yourself free from sex sins and bad actions. Do not fight or be jealous. ¹⁴Let every part of you belong to the Lord Jesus Christ. Do not allow your weak thoughts to lead you into sinful actions.

Let every part of you
belong to
the Lord Jesus Christ.
Do not allow
your weak thoughts
to lead you
into sinful actions.

Help Weak Christians

14 If there is someone whose faith is weak, be kind and receive him. Do not argue about what he thinks. ²One man believes he may eat everything. Another man with weak faith eats only vegetables. ³The man who eats everything should not think he is better than the one who eats only vegetables. The man who eats only vegetables should not say the other man is wrong, because God has received him. ⁴Who are you to tell another person's workman if he is right or wrong? It is to his owner that he does good or bad. The Lord is able to help him.

⁵One man thinks one day is more important than another. Another man thinks every day is the same. Every man must be sure in his own mind. ⁶The man who worships on a special day does it to honor the Lord. The man who eats meat does it to honor the Lord. He gives thanks to God for what he eats. The other man does not eat meat. In this way, he honors the Lord. He gives thanks to God also.

⁷No one lives for himself alone. No one dies for himself alone. ⁸If we live, it is for the Lord. If we die, it is for the Lord. If we live or die, we belong to the Lord. ⁹Christ died and lived again. This is why He is the Lord of the living and of the dead. ¹⁰Why do you try to say your Christian brother is right or wrong? Why do you hate your Christian brother? We will all stand in front of the place where Christ sits when He will say if we are guilty or not. ¹¹The Holy Writings say, "As I live, says the Lord, every knee will get down in front of Me. And every tongue will say that I am God." ¹²Everyone of us will give an answer to God about himself.

¹³So you should stop saying that you think other people are wrong. Instead, decide to live so that your Christian brother will not have a reason to trip or fall into sin because of you. ¹⁴Christ has made me know that everything in itself is clean. But if a person thinks something is not clean, then to him it is not clean. ¹⁵If your Christian brother is hurt because of some foods you eat, then you are no longer living by love. Do not destroy the man for whom Christ died by the food you eat. ¹⁶Do not let what is good for you be talked about as bad. ¹⁷For the holy nation of God is not food and drink. It is being right with God. It is peace and joy given by the Holy Spirit. ¹⁸If you follow Christ in these things, God will be happy with you. Men will think well of you also.

¹⁹Work for the things that make peace and help each other become stronger Christians. ²⁰Do not destroy what God has done just because of some food. All food is good to eat. But it is wrong to eat anything that will make someone fall into sin. ²¹Do not eat meat or drink wine or do anything else if it would make your Christian brother fall into sin. ²²Keep the faith you have between

yourself and God. A man is happy if he knows he is doing right. [23]But if he has doubts about the food he eats, God says he is guilty when he eats it. It is because he is eating without faith. Anything that is not done in faith is sin.

Live To Please Your Neighbor

15 We who have strong faith should help those who are weak. We should not live to please ourselves. [2]Each of us should live to please his neighbor. This will help him grow in faith. [3]Even Christ did not please Himself. The Holy Writings say,"The sharp words spoken against you fell on Me." (Psalm 69:9) [4]Everything that was written in the Holy Writings long ago was written to teach us. By not giving up, God's Word gives us strength and hope. [5]Now the God Who helps you not to give up and gives you strength will help you think so you can please each other as Christ Jesus did. [6]Then all of you together can thank the God and Father of our Lord Jesus Christ.

The Good News Is For The People Who Are Not Jews

[7]Receive each other as Christ received you. This will honor God. [8]Christ came to help the Jews. This proved that God had told the truth to their early fathers. This proved that God would do what He promised. [9]This was done so the people who are not Jews can thank God for His loving-kindness. The Holy Writings say, "This is why I will give thanks to you among the people who are not Jews. I will sing to Your name." (Psalm 18:49) [10]It says also, "You who are not Jews, be happy with His people, the Jews." (Deuteronomy 32:43) [11]And, "Honor and give thanks to the Lord, you who are not Jews. Let everyone honor Him." (Psalm 117:1) [12]And Isaiah says, "There will be One from the family of Jesse Who will be a leader over the people who are not Jews. Their hope will be in Him." (Isaiah 11:10) [13]Our hope comes from God. May He fill you with joy and peace because of your trust in Him. May your hope grow stronger by the power of the Holy Spirit.

[14]I am sure you are wise in all things and full of much good. You are able to help and teach each other. [15]I have written to you with

strong words about some things. I have written so you would remember. God helped me write like this. [16]I am able to write these things because God made me a missionary to the people who are not Jews. I work as a workman for Jesus Christ. I preach the Good News of God so the people who are not Jews may be as a gift to God. The Holy Spirit will set them apart so God will be pleased with them. [17]I have reason to be proud of my work for God. It is because I belong to Christ Jesus. [18]I can only speak of what Christ has done through me. I have helped the people who are not Jews to obey Him. I have done it by words and by living with them. [19]God showed them His power through me. The Holy Spirit did powerful works through me in front of them. From Jerusalem to the country of Illyricum I have preached the Good News of Christ. [20]It is my desire to preach the Good News where it has never been preached. I want to preach only where Christ is not known. [21]The Holy Writings say, "Those who have never known about Him will see. And those who have never heard about Him will understand." (Isaiah 52:15)

Paul Hopes To Visit The Christians In Rome

[22]This is why I have been kept many times from coming to you. [23]But now I am finished with my work here. I have been wanting to come and visit you for many years. [24]I hope I can now. I am making plans to go the country of Spain. On my way there I will stop and visit you. After I have had the joy of visiting you for awhile, you can help me on my way again. [25]But now I am going to Jerusalem to hand the Christians the gift of money. [26]The churches in the countries of Macedonia and Greece have decided to give money to help some of the poor Christians in Jerusalem. [27]They wanted to do it. They should help them in this way because they owe much to the Christians in Jerusalem. The Jews shared the Good News with the people who are not Jews. For this reason, they should share what they can with the Jews. [28]I will hand this gift of money to them. Then I will stop to see you on my way to the country of Spain. [29]I know that when I come to you, Christ will give me much good to share with you.

[30]I ask you from my heart, Christian brothers, to pray much for me. I ask this in the name of our Lord Jesus Christ. [31]Pray that God will keep me safe from the people in the country of Judea who

are not Christians. Pray also that the work I am to do for the Christians in Jerusalem will help them. 32Then I will be coming to you if God wants me to come. I will be full of joy, and together we can have some rest. 33May our God Who gives us peace, be with you all. Let it be so.

Paul Says Hello To Many Friends

16 I want to let you know about our Christian sister Phoebe. She is a helper in the church in the city of Cenchrea. 2The Christians should receive her as a sister who belongs to the Lord. Help her any way you can. She has helped many people and has helped me also.

3Say hello to Prisca and Aquila. They worked with me for Christ. 4They almost died for me. I am thankful for them. All the churches that were started smong the people who are not Jews are thankful for them also. 5Say hello to the church that worships in their house. Say hello to Epaenetus, my much-loved friend. He was the first Christian in the countries of Asia. 6Say hello to Mary. She worked hard for you. 7Say hello to Andronicus and Junias. They are from my family and were in prison with me. They put their trust in Christ before I did. They have been respected missionaries. 8Say hello to Ampliatus. He is a much-loved Christian brother. 9Say hello to Urbanus. He worked with us for Christ. Say hello to Stachys, my much-loved friend. 10Say hello to Apelles. He proved he was faithful to Christ. Say hello to all the family of Aristobulus. 11Say hello to Herodian. He is one of my family. Say hello to the Christians in the family of Narcissus. 12Say hello to Tryphaena and Tryphosa and Persis. They are all much-loved workmen for the Lord. 13Say hello to Rufus and his mother. She was like a mother to me. Rufus is a good Christian. 14Say hello to Asyncritus and Phlegon and Hermes and Patrobas and Hermas and all the Christians with them. 15Say hello to Philologus and Julia and Nereus and his sister and Olympas and all the Christians with them. 16Say hello to each other with a kiss of holy love. All the churches here say hello to you.

17I ask you, Christian brothers, watch out for those who make trouble and start fights. Keep your eye on those who work against the teaching you received. Keep away from them. [18]Men like that are not working for our Lord Jesus Christ. They are chained to their own desires. With soft words they say things people want to hear. People are fooled by them. [19]Everyone knows you have obeyed the teaching you received. I am happy with you because of this. But I want you to be wise about good things and pure about sinful things. [20]God, Who is our peace, will soon crush Satan under your feet. May the loving-favor of our Lord Jesus be yours.

[21]Timothy, my helper, says hello to you. Lucius and Jason and Sosipater from my family say hello also. [22]I, Tertius, who am writing this letter for Paul, say hello to you as a Christian brother. [23]Gaius is the man taking care of me. The church meets here in his house. He says hello to you. Erastus, the man who takes care of the money for the city, says hello and Quartus does also. He is a Christian brother. [24]*May you have loving-favor from our Lord Jesus Christ. Let it be so.

[25]We give honor to God. He is able to make you strong as I preach from the Holy Writings about Jesus Christ. It was a secret hidden from the beginning of the world. [26]But now it is for us to know. The early preachers wrote about it. God says it is to be preached to all the people of the world so men can put their trust in God and obey Him.

[27]May God, Who only is wise, be honored forever through our Lord Jesus Christ. Let it be so.

1 This letter is from Paul. I have been chosen by God to be a missionary of Jesus Christ. Sosthenes, a Christian brother, writes also. ²I write to God's church in the city of Corinth. I write to those who belong to Christ Jesus and to those who are set apart by Him and made holy. I write to all the Christians everywhere who call on the name of Jesus Christ. He is our Lord and their Lord also. ³May you have loving-favor and peace from God our Father and from the Lord Jesus Christ.

Paul Gives Thanks For Their Faith

⁴I am thankful to God all the time for you. I am thankful for the loving-favor God has given to you because you belong to Christ Jesus. ⁵He has made your lives rich in every way. Now you have power to speak for Him. He gave you good understanding. ⁶This shows that what I told you about Christ and what He could do for you has been done in your lives. ⁷You have the gifts of the Holy Spirit that you need while you wait for the Lord Jesus Christ to come again. ⁸Christ will keep you strong until He comes again. No blame will be held against you. ⁹God is faithful. He chose you to be joined together with His Son, Jesus Christ our Lord.

God is faithful.

The Church In Corinth Is Divided

¹⁰Christian brothers, I ask you with all my heart in the name of the Lord Jesus Christ to agree among yourselves. Do not be divided into little groups. Think and act as if you all had the same mind. ¹¹My Christian brothers, I have heard from some of Chloe's family that you are arguing among yourselves. ¹²I hear that some of you are saying, "I am a follower of Paul," and "I am a follower of Apollos," and "I am a follower of Peter," and "I am a follower of Christ." ¹³Has Christ been divided? Was Paul put on a cross to die for your sins? Were you baptized in the name of Paul? ¹⁴I am thankful to God that I baptized Crispus and Gaius only. ¹⁵No one can say that you were baptized in the name of Paul. ¹⁶I remember I did baptize the family of Stephanas, but I do not remember baptizing any others. ¹⁷Christ did not send me to baptize. He sent

me to preach the Good News. I did not use big sounding words when I preached. If I had, the power of the cross of Christ would be taken away.

[18]Preaching about the cross sounds foolish to those who are dying in sin. But it is the power of God to those of us who are being saved from the punishment of sin. [19]The Holy Writings say, "I will destroy the wisdom of the wise people. I will put aside the learning of those who think they know a lot." [20]Where is the man who is wise? Where is the man who thinks he knows a lot? Where is the man who thinks he has all the answers? God has made the wisdom of this world look foolish. [21]In His wisdom, He did not allow man to come to know Him through the wisdom of this world. It pleased God to save men from the punishment of their sins through preaching the Good News. This preaching sounds foolish. [22]The Jews are looking for something special to see. The Greek people are looking for the answer in wisdom. [23]But we preach that Christ died on a cross to save them from their sins. These words are hard for the Jews to listen to. The Greek people think it is foolish. [24]Christ is the power and wisdom of God to those who are chosen to be saved from the punishment of sin for both Jews and Greeks. [25]God's plan looked foolish to men, but it is wiser than the best plans of men. God's plan which may look weak is stronger than the strongest plans of men.

God's Wisdom—Human Wisdom

[26]Christian brothers, think who you were when the Lord called you. Not many of you were wise or powerful or born into the family of leaders of a country. [27]But God has chosen what the world calls foolish to shame the wise. He has chosen what the world calls weak to shame what is strong. [28]God has chosen what is weak and foolish of the world, what is hated and not known, to destroy the things the world trusts in. [29]In that way, no man can be proud as he stands in front of God. [30]God Himself made the way so you can have new life through Christ Jesus. God gave us Christ to be our wisdom. Christ made us right with God and set us apart for God and made us holy. Christ bought us with His blood and made us free from our sins. [31]It is as the Holy Writings say, "If anyone is going to be proud of anything, he should be proud of the Lord."

Paul Received The Good News From God

2 Christian brothers, when I came to you, I did not preach the secrets of God with big sounding words or make it sound as if I were so wise. ²I made up my mind that while I was with you I would speak of nothing except Jesus Christ and of His death on the cross. ³When I was with you, I was weak. I was afraid and I shook. ⁴What I had to say when I preached was not in big sounding words of man's wisdom. But it was given in the power of the Holy Spirit. ⁵In this way, you do not have faith in Christ because of the wisdom of men. You have faith in Christ because of the power of God.

True Wisdom Comes From God

⁶We speak wisdom to full-grown Christians. This wisdom is not from this world or from the leaders of today. They die and their wisdom dies with them. ⁷What we preach is God's wisdom. It was a secret until now. God planned for us to have this honor before the world began. ⁸None of the world leaders understood this wisdom. If they had, they would not have put Christ up on a cross to die. He is the Lord of shining greatness. ⁹The Holy Writings say, "No eye has ever seen or nó ear has ever heard or no mind has ever thought of the wonderful things God has made ready for those who love Him." (Isaiah 64:4; 65:17) ¹⁰God has shown these things to us through His Holy Spirit. It is the Holy Spirit Who looks into all things, even the secrets of God, and shows them to us. ¹¹Who can know the things about a man, except a man's own spirit that is in him? It is the same with God. Who can understand Him except the Holy Spirit? ¹²We have not received the spirit of the world. God has given us His Holy Spirit that we may know about the things given to us by Him. ¹³We speak about these things also. We do not use words of man's wisdom. We use words given to us by the Holy Spirit. We use these words to tell what the Holy Spirit wants to say to those who put their trust in Him. ¹⁴But the person who is not a Christian does not understand these words from the Holy Spirit. He thinks they are foolish. He cannot understand them because he does not have the Holy Spirit to help

him understand. ¹⁵The full-grown Christian understands all things, and yet he is not understood. ¹⁶For who has the thoughts of the Lord? Who can tell Him what to do? But we have the thoughts of Christ.

3 Christian brothers, I could not speak to you as to full-grown Christians. I spoke to you as men who have not obeyed the things you have been taught. I spoke to you as if you were baby Christians. ²My teaching was as if I were giving you milk to drink. I could not give you meat because you were not ready for it. Even yet you are not able to have anything but milk. ³You still live as men who are not Christians. When you are jealous and fight with each other, you are still living in sin and acting like sinful men in the world. ⁴When one says, "I am a follower of Paul," and another says, "I am a follower of Apollos," does not this sound like the talk of baby Christians? ⁵Who is Apollos? Who is Paul? We are only workmen owned by God. He gave us gifts to preach His Word. And because of that, you put your trust in Christ. ⁶I planted the seed. Apollos watered it, but it was God Who kept it growing. ⁷This shows that the one who plants or the one who waters is not the important one. God is the important One. He makes it grow. ⁸The one who plants and the one who waters are alike. Each one will get his own pay. ⁹For we work together with God. You are God's field.

You are God's building also. ¹⁰Through God's loving-favor to me, I laid the stones on which the building was to be built. I did it like one who knew what he was doing. Now another person is building on it. Each person who builds must be careful how he builds on it. ¹¹Jesus Christ is the Stone on which other stones for the building must be laid. It can be only Christ. ¹²Now if a man builds on the Stone with gold or silver or beautiful stones, or if he builds with wood or grass or straw, ¹³Each man's work will become known. There will be a day when it will be tested by fire. The fire will show what kind of work it is. ¹⁴If a man builds on work that lasts, he will receive his pay. ¹⁵If his work is burned up, he will lose it. Yet he himself will be saved as if he were going through a fire.

¹⁶Do you not know that you are a house of God and that the Holy Spirit lives in you? ¹⁷If any man destroys the house of God,

God will destroy him. God's house is holy. You are the place where He lives.

[18]Do not fool yourself. If anyone thinks he knows a lot about the things of this world, he had better become a fool. Then he may become wise. [19]The wisdom of this world is foolish to God. The Holy Writings say, "He is the One Who gets them in a trap when they use their own wisdom." (Job 5:13) [20]They also say, "The Lord knows how the wise man thinks. His thinking is worth nothing." (Psalm 94:11) [21]As a Christian, do not be proud of men and of what they can do. All things belong to you. [22]Paul and Apollos and Peter belong to you. The world and life and death belong to you. Things now and things to come belong to you. [23]You belong to Christ, and Christ belongs to God.

4 Think of us as workmen who are owned by Christ. It is our job to share the secrets of God. [2]A workman must be faithful to his owner. This is expected of him. [3]It is not the most important thing to me what you or any other people think about me. Even what I think of myself does not mean much. [4]As for me, my heart tells me I am not guilty of anything. But that does not prove I am free from guilt. It is the Lord Who looks into my life and says what is wrong. [5]Do not be quick to say who is right or wrong. Wait until the Lord comes. He will bring into the light the things that are hidden in men's hearts. He will show why men have done these things. Every man will receive from God the thanks he should have.

[6]Christian brothers, I have used Apollos and myself to show you what I am talking about. This is to help you so you will not think more of men than what God's Word will allow. Never think more of one of God's workmen than another. [7]Who made you better than your brother? Or what do you have that has not been given to you? If God has given you everything, why do you have pride? Why do you act as if He did not give it to you? [8]You are full. You are rich. You live like kings and we do not. I wish you were kings and we could be leaders with you. [9]I think that God has made a show of us missionaries. We are the last and the least among men. We are like men waiting to be put to death. The whole world, men and angels alike, are watching us. [10]We are

thought of as fools because of Christ. But you are thought of as wise Christians! We are weak. You are strong. People respect you. They have no respect for us. [11]To this hour we are hungry and thirsty, and our clothes are worn out. People hurt us. We have no homes. [12]We work with our hands to make a living. We speak kind words to those who speak against us. When people hurt us, we say nothing. [13]When people say bad things about us, we answer with kind words. People think of us as dirt that is worth nothing and as the worst thing on earth to this very day.

We speak kind words to those who speak against us.

Follow Paul's Way Of Life

[14]I do not write these things to shame you. I am doing this to help you know what you should do. You are my much-loved children. [15]You may have 10,000 Christian teachers. But remember, I am the only father you have. You became Christians when I preached the Good News to you. [16]So I ask you with all my heart to follow the way I live. [17]For this reason I have sent Timothy to you. He is my much-loved child and a faithful Christian. He will tell you how I act as a Christian. This is the kind of life I teach in the churches wherever I go.

[18]Some of you are full of pride. You think that I am not coming to visit you. [19]If the Lord wants me to, I will come soon. I will find out when I come if these proud people have God's power, or if they just use a lot of big words. [20]The holy nation of God is not made up of words. It is made up of power. [21]What do you want? Do you want me to come with a stick to whip you? Or do you want me to come with love and a gentle spirit?

Sin In The Church

5 Someone has told me about a sex sin among you. It is so bad that even the people who do not know God would not do it. I have been told that one of the men is living with his father's wife as if she were his wife. [2]Instead of being sorry, you are proud of yourselves. The man who is living like that should be sent away from you. [3]I am far from you. Even if I am not there, my spirit is with you. I have already said that the man is guilty of this sin. I am saying this as if I were there with you. [4]Call a meeting of the church. I will be with you in spirit. In the name of the Lord Jesus

Christ, and by His power, 5hand this person over to the devil. His body is to be destroyed so his spirit may be saved on the day the Lord comes again.

6It is not good for you to be proud of the way things are going in your church. You know a little yeast makes the whole loaf of bread rise. 7Clean out the old yeast. Then you will be new bread with none of the old yeast in you. The Jews killed lambs when they left Egypt. Christ is our lamb. He has already been killed as a gift on the altar to God for us. 8Bread with yeast in it is like being full of sin and hate. Let us eat this supper together with bread that has no yeast in it. This bread is pure and true.

9I told you in my letter not to keep on being with people who do any kind of sex sins. 10I was not talking about people doing sex sins who are bad people of this world. I was not talking about people of this world who always want to get more or those who get things in a wrong way or those who worship false gods. To get away from people like that you would have to leave this world! 11What I wrote was that you should not keep on being with a person who calls himself a Christian if he does any kind of sex sins. You should not even eat with a person who says he is a Christian but always wants to get more of everything or uses bad language or who gets drunk or gets things in a wrong way. 12It is not for me to say if those outside the church are guilty. You are to say if those who belong to the church are guilty. 13God will say if those outside the church are guilty. So you must put that sinful person out of your church.

Going To Court Against Christians

6 Why do you go to court when you have something against another Christian? You are asking people who are not Christians to say who is guilty. You should go to those who belong to Christ and ask them. 2Did you not know that those who belong to Christ will someday say who is guilty in this world? If you are to say the people of the world are guilty, are you not able to do this in small things? 3Did you not know that we are to say if angels are guilty? So you should be able to take care of your problem here in this world without any trouble.

⁴When you have things to decide about this life, why do you go to men in courts who are not even Christians? ⁵You should be ashamed! Is it true that there is not one person wise enough in your church to decide who is right when people argue? ⁶Instead, one Christian takes another Christian to court. And that court is made up of people who are not Christians! ⁷This shows you are wrong when you have to go to court against each other. Would it not be better to let someone do something against you that is wrong? Would it not be better to let them rob you? ⁸Instead, you rob and do wrong to other Christians.

The Body Is To Be Holy

⁹Do you not know that sinful men will have no place in the holy nation of God? Do not be fooled. A person who does sex sins, or who worships false gods, or who is not faithful in marriage, or men who act like women, or people who do sex sins with their own sex, will have no place in the holy nation of God. ¹⁰Also those who steal, or those who always want to get more of everything, or who get drunk, or who say bad things about others, or take things that are not theirs, will have no place in the holy nation of God. ¹¹Some of you were like that. But now your sins are washed away. You were set apart for God-like living to do His work. You were made right with God through our Lord Jesus Christ by the Spirit of our God.

¹²I am allowed to do all things, but not everything is good for me to do! Even if I am free to do all things, I will not do them if I think it would be hard for me to stop when I know I should. ¹³Food was meant for the stomach. The stomach needs food, but God will bring to an end both food and the stomach. The body was not meant for sex sins. It was meant to work for the Lord. The Lord is for our body. ¹⁴God raised the Lord from death. He will raise us from death by His power also.

The Body Belongs To The Lord

¹⁵Do you not know that your bodies are a part of Christ Himself? Am I to take a part of Christ and make it a part of a woman who sells the use of her body? No! Never! ¹⁶Do you not know that a man who joins himself to a woman who sells the use of

her body becomes a part of her? The Holy Writings say, "The two will become one." [17]But if you join yourself to the Lord, you are one with Him in spirit.

[18]Have nothing to do with sex sins! Any other sin that a man does, does not hurt his own body. But the man who does a sex sin sins against his own body. [19]Do you not know that your body is a house of God where the Holy Spirit lives? God gave you His Holy Spirit. Now you belong to God. You do not belong to yourselves. [20]God bought you with a great price. So honor God with your body. You belong to Him.

> Do you not know that your body is a house of God where the Holy Spirit lives?

How A Husband And Wife Should Live

7 You asked me some questions in your letter. This is my answer. It is good if a man does not get married. [2]But because of being tempted to sex sins, each man should get married and have his own wife. Each woman should get married and have her own husband. [3]The husband should please his wife as a husband. The wife should please her husband as a wife. [4]The wife is not the boss of her own body. It belongs to the husband. And in the same way, the husband is not the boss of his own body. It belongs to the wife.

[5]Do not keep from each other that which belongs to each other in marriage unless you agree for awhile so you can use your time to pray. Then come together again or the devil will tempt you to do that which you know you should not do.

[6]This is what I think. I am not saying you must do it. [7]I wish everyone were as I am, but each has his own gift from God. One has one gift. Another has another gift.

[8]This is what I say to those who are not married and to women whose husbands have died. It is good if you do not get married. I am not married. [9]But if you are not able to keep from doing that which you know is wrong, get married. It is better to get married than to have such strong sex desires.

[10]I have this to say to those who are married. These words are from the Lord. A wife should not leave her husband, [11]but if she

does leave him, she should not get married to another man. It would be better for her to go back to her husband. The husband should not divorce his wife. [12]I have this to say. These words are not from the Lord. If a Christian husband has a wife who is not a Christian, and she wants to live with him, he must not divorce her. [13]If a Christian wife has a husband who is not a Christian, and he wants to live with her, she must not divorce him. [14]The husband who is not a Christian is set apart from the sin of the world because of his Christian wife. The wife who is not a Christian is set apart from the sin of the world because of her Christian husband. In this way, the lives of the children are not dirty from sin, they are clean. [15]If the one who is not a Christian wants to leave, let that one go. The Christian husband or wife should not try to make the other one stay. God wants you to live in peace. [16]Christian wife, how do you know you will not help your husband to become a Christian? Or Christian husband, how do you know you will not help your wife to become a Christian?

Stay As You Were When God Chose You

[17]Everyone should live the life the Lord gave to him. He should live as he was when he became a Christian. This is what I teach in all the churches. [18]If a man became a Christian after he had gone through the religious act of becoming a Jew, he should do nothing about it. If a man became a Christian before, he should not go through the religious act of becoming a Jew. [19]If it is done or not done, it means nothing. What is important is to obey God's Word. [20]Everyone should stay the same way he was when he became a Christian. [21]Were you a workman who was owned by someone when you became a Christian? Do not worry about it. But if you are able to become free, do that. [22]A workman who is owned by someone and who has become a Christian is the Lord's free man. A free man who has become a Christian is a workman owned by Christ. [23]He paid a great price for you when He bought you. Do not let yourselves become workmen owned by men. [24]Christian brothers, each one should stay as he was when he became a Christian.

[25]I have no word from the Lord about women or men who have never been married. I will tell you what I think. You can trust me because the Lord has given me His loving-kindness. [26]I think,

because of the troubles that are coming, it is a good thing for a person not to get married. ²⁷Are you married to a wife? Do not try to get a divorce. If you are not married, do not look for a wife. ²⁸If you do get married, you have not sinned. If a woman who is not married gets married, it is no sin. But being married will add problems. I would like to have you free from such problems.

²⁹I mean this, Christian brothers. The time is very short. A married man should use his time as if he did not have a wife. ³⁰Those who have sorrow should keep on working as if they had no sorrow. Those who have joy should keep on working as if there was no time for joy. Those who buy should have no time to get joy from what they have. ³¹While you live in this world, live as if the world has no hold on you. The way of this world will soon be gone.

³²I want you to be free from the cares of this world. The man who is not married can spend his time working for the Lord and pleasing Him. ³³The man who is married cares for the things of the world. He wants to please his wife. ³⁴Married women and women who have never been married are different. The woman who has never been married can spend her time working for the Lord. She wants to please the Lord with her body and spirit. The woman who is married cares for the things of the world. She wants to please her husband. ³⁵I am saying these things to help you. I am not trying to keep you from getting married. I want you to do what is best. You should work for Him without other things taking your time.

³⁶If a man and woman expect to get married, and he thinks his desires to marry her are getting too strong, and she is getting older, they should get married. It is no sin. ³⁷But if a man has the power to keep from getting married and knows in his mind that he should not, he is wise if he does not get married. ³⁸The man who gets married does well, but the man who does not get married does better.

³⁹A wife is not free as long as her husband lives. If her husband dies, she is free to marry anyone she wants, if he is a Christian. ⁴⁰I think she will be much more happy if she does not get married again. This is what I think. I believe it is what the Holy Spirit is saying.

Food Given To False Gods

8 I want to write about food that has been given as a gift in worship to a false god. We all know something about it. Knowing about it makes one feel important. But love makes one strong. ²The person who thinks he knows all the answers still has a lot to learn. ³But if he loves God, he is known by God also.

⁴What about food that has been given as a gift to a false god in worship? Is it right? We know that a false god is not a god at all. There is only one God! There is no other. ⁵Men have thought there are many such gods and lords in the sky and on the earth. ⁶But we know there is only one God. He is the Father. All things are from Him. He made us for Himself. There is one Lord. He is Jesus Christ. He made all things. He keeps us alive.

There is only one God! There is no other.

⁷Not all men know this. They have given food as a gift in worship to a god as if the god were alive. Some men have done this all their lives. If they eat such food, their hearts tell them it is wrong. ⁸Food will not bring us near to God. We are no worse if we do not eat it, or we are no better if we eat it. ⁹Since you are free to do as you please, be careful that this does not hurt a weak Christian. ¹⁰A Christian who is weak may see you eat food in a place where it has been given as a gift to false gods in worship. Since he sees you eat it, he will eat it also. ¹¹You may make the weak Christian fall into sin by what you have done. Remember, he is a Christian brother for whom Christ died. ¹²When you sin against a weak Christian by making him do what is wrong, you sin against Christ. ¹³So then, if eating meat makes my Christian brother trip and fall, I will never eat it again. I do not want to make my Christian brother sin.

A Missionary's Rights

9 Am I not a missionary? Am I not free? Have I not seen Jesus our Lord? Are you not Christians because of the work I have done for the Lord? ²Other people may not think of me as a

missionary, but you do. It proves I am a missionary because you are Christians now. ³When people ask questions about me, I say this: ⁴Do we not have the right to have food and drink when we are working for the Lord? ⁵Do we not have the right to take a Christian wife along with us? The other missionaries do. The Lord's brothers do and Peter does. ⁶Are Barnabas and I the only ones who should keep working for a living so we can preach?

⁷Have you ever heard of a soldier who goes to war and pays for what he needs himself? Have you ever heard of a man planting a field of grapes and not eating some of the fruit? Have you ever heard of a farmer who feeds cattle and does not drink some of the milk? ⁸These things are not just what men think are right to do. God's Law speaks about this. ⁹God gave Moses the Law. It says. "When the cow is made to walk on the grain to break it open, do not stop it from eating some." (Deuteronomy 25:4) Does God care about the cow? ¹⁰Did not God speak about this because of us. For sure, this was written for us. The man who gets the fields ready and the man who gathers in the grain should expect some of the grain. ¹¹We have planted God's Word among you. Is it too much to expect you to give us what we need to live each day? ¹²If other people have the right to expect this from you, do we not have more right? But we have not asked this of you. We have suffered many things. We did this so the Good News of Christ would not be held back.

¹³You must know that those who work in the house of God get their food there. Those who work at the altar in the house of God get a part of the food that is given there. ¹⁴The Lord has said also that those who preach the Good News should get their living from those who hear it.

¹⁵I have not used any of these things. I am not writing now to get anything. I would rather die than lose the joy of preaching to you without you paying me. ¹⁶I cannot be proud because I preach the Good News. I have been told to do it. It would be bad for me if I do not preach the Good News. ¹⁷If I do this because I want to, I will get my pay. If I do not want to do it, I am still expected to do it. ¹⁸Then what is my pay? It is when I preach the Good News without you paying me. I do not ask you to pay me as I could.

Learning To Get Along

¹⁹No man has any hold on me, but I have made myself a workman owned by all. I do this so I might lead more people to Christ. ²⁰I became as a Jew to the Jews so I might lead them to Christ. There are some who live by obeying the Jewish Law. I became as one who lives by obeying the Jewish Law so I might lead them to Christ. ²¹There are some who live by not obeying the Jewish Law. I became as one who lives by not obeying the Jewish Law so I might lead them to Christ. This does not mean that I do not obey God's Law. I obey the teachings of Christ. ²²Some are weak. I have become weak so I might lead them to Christ. I have become like every person so in every way I might lead some to Christ. ²³Everything I do, I do to get the Good News to men. I want to have a part in this work.

Live A Life That Pleases Christ

²⁴You know that only one person gets a prize for being in a race even if many people run. You must run so you will win the prize. ²⁵Everyone who runs in a race does many things so his body will be strong. He does it to get a prize that will soon be worth nothing, but we work for a prize that will last forever. ²⁶In the same way, I run straight for the place at the end of the race. I fight to win. I do not beat the air. ²⁷I keep working over my body. I make it obey me. I do this because I am afraid that after I have preached the Good News to others, I myself might be put aside.

The Danger Of Worshiping False Gods

10 Christian brothers, I want you to know what happened to our early fathers. They all walked from the country of Egypt under the cloud that showed them the way, and they all passed through the waters of the Red Sea. ²They were all baptized in the cloud and in the sea as they followed Moses. ³All of them ate the same holy food. ⁴They all drank the same holy drink. They drank from a holy Rock that went along with them. That holy Rock was Christ. ⁵Even then most of them did not please God. He destroyed them in the desert.

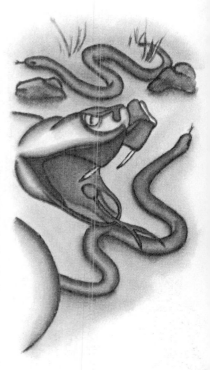

6These things show us something. They teach us not to want things that are bad for us like those people did. 7We must not worship false gods as some of them did. The Holy Writings tell us, "The people sat down to eat and drink. Then they got up to play." (Exodus 32:6) 8We must not do sex sins as some them did. In one day 23,000 died. 9We must not test the Lord as some of them did. They were destroyed by snakes. 10We must not complain against God as some of them did. That is why they were destroyed.

11All these things happened to show us something. They were written to teach us that the end of the world is near. 12So watch yourself! The person who thinks he can stand against sin had better watch that he does not fall into sin. 13You have never been tempted to sin in any different way than other people. God is faithful. He will not allow you to be tempted more than you can take. But when you are tempted, He will make a way for you to keep from falling into sin.

Teaching About The Lord's Supper

14My dear friends, keep away from the worship of false gods. 15I am speaking to you who are able to understand. See if what I am saying is true. 16When we give thanks for the fruit of the vine at the Lord's supper, are we not sharing in the blood of Christ? The bread we eat at the Lord's supper, are we not sharing in the body of Christ? 17There is one bread, and many of us Christians make up the body of Christ. All of us eat from that bread.

18Look at the Jews. They ate the animals that were brought to God as gifts in worship and put on the altar. Did this not show they were sharing with God? 19What do I mean? Am I saying that a false god or the food brought to it in worship is worth anything? 20No, not at all! I am saying that the people who do not know God bring gifts of animals in worship. But they have given them to demons, not to God. You do not want to have any share with demons. 21You cannot drink from the cup of the Lord and from the cup of demons. You cannot eat at the Lord's table and at the demon's table. 22Are we trying to make the Lord jealous? Do we think we are stronger than the Lord?

23We are allowed to do anything, but not everything is good for us to do. We are allowed to do anything, but not all things help us grow strong as Christians. ²⁴Do not work only for your own good. Think of what you can do for others. ²⁵Eat any meat that is sold in the stores. Ask no questions about it. Then your heart will not say it is wrong. ²⁶The Holy Writings say, "The earth and everything in it belongs to the Lord." ²⁷If a person who is not a Christian wants you to eat with him, and you want to go, eat anything that is on the table. Ask no questions about the food. Then your heart will not say it is wrong. ²⁸But if someone says, "This meat has been given as a gift to false gods in worship," do not eat it. In that way, it will not hurt the faith of the one who told you and his heart will have peace. ²⁹How the other person feels is important. We are not free to do things that will hurt another person. ³⁰If I can give thanks to God for my food, why should anyone say that I am wrong about eating food I can give thanks for? ³¹So if you eat or drink or whatever you do, do everything to honor God. ³²Do nothing that would make trouble for a Greek or for a Jew or for the church of God. ³³I want to please everyone in all that I do. I am not thinking of myself. I want to do what is best for them so they may be saved from the punishment of sin.

So if you eat or drink or whatever you do, do everything to honor God.

11 Follow my way of thinking as I follow Christ.

How Christian Women Should Live

²I think you have done well because you always remember me and have followed the things I taught you. ³I want you to know that Christ is the head of every man. The husband is the head of his wife. God is the head of Christ. ⁴If any man prays or preaches with his head covered, he does not give honor to Christ. ⁵Every woman who prays or preaches without her head covered does not respect her head. It is the same as if she had her hair cut off. ⁶If a woman does not cover her head, she might as well cut off her hair also. If a woman is ashamed to have her hair cut off, she should cover her head. ⁷Man is made like God and His shining greatness. For this reason a man should not have his head covered when he prays or preaches, but the woman respects the man. ⁸Man was not made from woman. Woman was made from man, ⁹and man was not made for woman. Woman was made for man. ¹⁰For this reason a woman should have a covering on her head. This shows she respects man. This is for the angels to see also. ¹¹In God's plan

women need men and men need women. ¹²Woman was made from man, but man is born of woman. God made all things.

¹³Think this over yourselves. Does it look right for a woman to pray with no covering on her head? ¹⁴Have we not already learned that it is a shame for a man to have long hair? ¹⁵But a woman can be proud to have long hair. Her hair is given to her for a covering. ¹⁶If anyone wants to argue about this, my answer is that this is what we teach, and all the churches agree with me.

How The Lord's Supper Should Be Eaten

¹⁷While writing about these things, let me tell you what I think. Nothing good is coming from your meeting together. ¹⁸First of all, I hear that when you meet together in the church you are divided into groups and you argue. I almost believe this is true. ¹⁹For there must be different groups among you. In that way, those who are right will be seen from those who are wrong. ²⁰When you gather together for your meetings, it is not to eat the Lord's supper. ²¹Each one is in a hurry to eat his own food first. He does not wait for others. In this way, one does not get enough food and drink. Others get too much and get drunk. ²²You have your own homes to eat and drink in. Or do you hate the church of God and shame those who are poor? What am I to say to you? Am I to say you are right? No! I cannot say you are right in this.

The Meaning Of The Lord's Supper

²³I have given you the teaching I received from the Lord. The night Jesus was handed over to the soldiers, He took bread. ²⁴When He had given thanks, He broke it and said, "Take this bread and eat it. This is My body which is broken for you. Do this to remember Me."

²⁵In the same way after supper, He took the cup. He said, "This cup is the New Way of Worship made between God and you by My blood. Whenever you drink it, do it to remember Me."

²⁶Every time you eat this bread and drink from this cup you are telling of the Lord's death until He comes again. ²⁷Anyone who eats the bread or drinks from the cup, if his spirit is not right with

the Lord, will be guilty of sinning against the body and the blood of the Lord. [28]This is why a man should look into his own heart and life before eating the bread and drinking from the cup. [29]Anyone who eats the bread and drinks from the cup, if his spirit is not right with the Lord, will be guilty as he eats and drinks. He does not understand the meaning of the Lord's body. [30]This is why some of you are sick and weak, and some have died. [31]But if we would look into our own lives and see if we are guilty, then God would not have to say we are guilty. [32]When we are guilty, we are punished by the Lord so we will not be told we are guilty with the rest of the world.

[33]Christian brothers, when you come together to eat, wait for each other. [34]If anyone is hungry, he should eat at home. Then he will not be guilty as you meet together. I will talk about the other things when I come.

The Gifts Of The Holy Spirit

12 Christian brothers, I want you to know about the gifts of the Holy Spirit. You need to understand the truth about this. [2]You know that before you were Christians you were led to worship false gods. None of these gods could speak. [3]So I tell you that no one speaking by the help of the Holy Spirit can say that he hates Jesus. No one can say, "Jesus is Lord," except by the help of the Holy Spirit.

Jesus is Lord.

The Kinds Of Gifts

[4]There are different kinds of gifts. But it is the same Holy Spirit Who gives them. [5]There are different kinds of work to be done for Him. But the work is for the same Lord. [6]There are different ways of doing His work. But it is the same God who uses all these ways in all people. [7]The Holy Spirit works in each person in one way or another for the good of all. [8]One person is given the gift of teaching words of wisdom. Another person is given the gift of teaching what he has learned and knows. These gifts are by the same Holy Spirit. [9]One person receives the gift of faith. Another person receives the gifts of healing. These gifts are given by the same Holy Spirit. [10]One person is given the gift of doing powerful works. Another person is given the gift of speaking God's Word. Another person is given the gift of telling the difference between

The Holy Spirit works in each person in one way or another for the good of all.

the Holy Spirit and false spirits. Another person is given the gift of speaking in special sounds. Another person is given the gift of telling what these special sounds mean. ¹¹But it is the same Holy Spirit, the Spirit of God, Who does all these things. He gives to each person as He wants to give.

Our Body Is Like The Body of Christ

¹²Our own body has many parts. When all these many parts are put together, they are only one body. The body of Christ is like this. ¹³It is the same way with us. Jews or those who are not Jews, men who are owned by someone or men who are free to do what they want to do, have all been baptized into the one body by the same Holy Spirit. We have all received the one Spirit.

¹⁴The body is not one part, but many parts. ¹⁵If the foot should say, "I am not a part of the body because I am not a hand," that would not stop it from being a part of the body. ¹⁶If the ear should say, "I am not a part of the body because I am not an eye," that would not stop it from being a part of the body. ¹⁷If the whole body were an eye how would it hear? If the whole body were an ear, how would it smell? ¹⁸But God has put all the parts into the body just as He wants to have them. ¹⁹If all the parts were the same, it could not be a body. ²⁰But now there are many parts, but one body.

²¹The eye cannot say to the hand, "I do not need you." Or the head cannot say to the feet, "I do not need you." ²²Some of the parts we think are weak and not important are very important. ²³We take good care of and cover with clothes the parts of the body that look less important. The parts which do not look beautiful have an important work to do. ²⁴The parts that can be seen do not need as much care. God has made the body so more care is given to the parts that need it most. ²⁵This is so the body will not be divided into parts. All the parts care for each other. ²⁶If one part of the body suffers, all the other parts suffer with it. If one part is given special care, the other parts are happy.

If one part of the body suffers, all the other parts suffer with it.

The Body Of Christ

²⁷You are all a part of the body of Christ. ²⁸God has chosen different ones in the church to do His work. First, there are

missionaries. Second, there are preachers or those who speak for God. And third, there are teachers. He has also chosen those who do powerful works and those who have the gifts of healing. And He has chosen those who help others who are in need and those who are able to lead others in work and those who speak in special sounds. ²⁹Are they all missionaries? No. Are they all preachers or those who speak for God? No. Do they all do powerful works? No. ³⁰Do they all have the gifts of healing? No. Do they all speak in special sounds? No. Are they all able to tell what the special sounds mean? No. ³¹But from your heart you should want the best gifts. Now I will show you even a better way.

Love — The Greatest Of All

13 I may be able to speak the languages of men and even of angels, but if I do not have love, it will sound like noise. ²If I have the gift of speaking God's Word and if I understand all secrets, but do not have love, I am nothing. If I know all things and if I have the gift of faith so I can move mountains, but do not have love, I am nothing. ³If I give everything I have to feed poor people and if I give my body to be burned, but do not have love, it will not help me.

⁴Love does not give up. Love is kind. Love is not jealous. Love does not put itself up as being important. Love has no pride. ⁵Love does not do the wrong thing. Love never thinks of itself. Love does not get angry. Love does not remember the suffering that comes from being hurt by someone. ⁶Love is not happy with sin. Love is happy with the truth. ⁷Love takes everything that comes without giving up. Love believes all things. Love hopes for all things. Love keeps on in all things.

⁸Love never comes to an end. The gift of speaking God's Word will come to an end. The gift of speaking in special sounds will be stopped. The gift of understanding will come to an end. ⁹For we only know a part now, and we speak only a part. ¹⁰When everything is perfect, then we will not need these gifts that are not perfect.

¹¹When I was a child, I spoke like a child. I thought like a child. I understood like a child. Now I am a man. I do not act like a child

anymore. [12]Now that which we see is as if we were looking in a broken mirror. But then we will see everything. Now I know only a part. But then I will know everything in a perfect way. That is how God knows me right now. [13]And now we have these three: faith and hope and love, but the greatest of these is love.

Faith and hope and love, but the greatest of these is love.

Speaking In Special Sounds Is Not The Greatest Gift

14 You should want to have this love. You should want the gifts of the Holy Spirit and most of all to be able to speak God's Word. [2]The man who speaks in special sounds speaks to God. He is not speaking to men. No one understands. He is speaking secret things through the power of the Holy Spirit. [3]The man who speaks God's Word speaks to men. It helps them to learn and understand. It gives them comfort. [4]The man who speaks in special sounds receives strength. The man who speaks God's Word gives strength to the church. [5]I wish all of you spoke in special sounds. But more than that, I wish all of you spoke God's Word. The one who speaks God's Word has a more important gift than the one who speaks in special sounds. But if he can tell what he is speaking, the church will be helped. [6]Christian brothers, if I come to you speaking in special sounds, what good is it to you? But if I tell you something God has shown me or something I have learned or what God's Word says will happen in the future or teach you God's Word, it will be for your good.

[7]There are things on which people play music. If strange sounds are made on these, how will others know which one is played. [8]If a horn does not make a good sound, how will men know they are to get ready to fight? [9]It is the same if you speak to a person in special sounds. How will he know what you say? Your sounds will be lost in the air. [10]There are many languages in the world. All of them have meaning to the people who understand them. [11]But if I do not understand the language someone uses to speak to me, the man who speaks is a stranger to me. I am a stranger to him. [12]Since you want gifts from the Holy Spirit, ask Him for those that will help the whole church. [13]So the man who speaks in special sounds should pray for the gift to be able to tell what they mean.

¹⁴If I pray in special sounds, my spirit is doing the praying. My mind does not understand. ¹⁵What should I do? I will pray with my spirit and I will pray with my mind also. I will sing with my spirit and I will sing with my mind also. ¹⁶If you honor and give thanks to God with your spirit in sounds nobody understands, how can others honor and give thanks also if they do not know what you are saying? ¹⁷You are honoring and giving thanks to God, but it is not helping other people.

¹⁸I thank God that I speak in special sounds more than all of you. ¹⁹But in a meeting of the church, it is better if I say five words that others can understand and be helped by than 10,000 words in special sounds.

Be full-grown, but be like children in not knowing how to sin.

²⁰Christian brothers, do not be like children in your thinking. Be full-grown, but be like children in not knowing how to sin. ²¹God says in the Holy Writings, "I will speak to My people. I will speak through men from other lands in other languages. Even then My people will not listen to Me." (Isaiah 28:11-12) ²²So then speaking in special sounds is for those who do not believe. It is not for those who believe. But speaking God's Word is for those who believe. It is not for those who do not believe.

²³If some people who are not Christians come to your church meeting while all the people are speaking in special sounds, they will think you are crazy. ²⁴But if a man who is not a Christian comes to your church meeting while you are all speaking God's Word, he will understand that he is a sinner by what he hears. He will know he is guilty. ²⁵The secrets of his heart will be brought into the open. He will get on his knees and worship God. He will say, "For sure, God is here with you!"

²⁶What am I saying, Christian brothers? When you meet together for worship, some of you have a song to sing. Some of you want to teach and some have special words from God. Some of you speak in special sounds and some of you tell what they mean. Everything should be done to help those who are meeting together to grow strong as Christians. ²⁷No more than two or three people should speak in special sounds. Only one should speak at a time. Someone must tell the meaning of the special sounds. ²⁸If no one is there who can tell the meaning of the special sounds, he should

not speak in the church. He should speak only to himself and to God. 29Two or three should speak God's Word. The other people should listen and decide if they are speaking right. 30If someone sitting in the meeting gets some special word from God, the one who is speaking should stop. 31All of you can speak God's Word, but only one person at a time. In that way, all of you can learn and be helped. 32Men who speak God's Word are able to stop when they should. 33God does not want everyone speaking at the same time in church meetings. He wants peace. All the churches of God's people worship this way.

34Women should not be allowed to speak in church meetings. They are to obey this teaching. The Jewish Law says this also. 35If they want to find out about something, they should ask their husbands at home. It is a shame for a woman to speak in a church meeting.

36Did the Word of God come from you Christians in the city of Corinth? Or are you the only people who received it? 37Some of you may think you have the gift of speaking God's Word or some other gift from the Holy Spirit. If you do, you should know that what I am writing to you is what God has told us we must obey. 38If any man does not listen to this, have nothing to do with him.

39So then, my Christian brothers, you should want to speak God's Word. Do not stop anyone from speaking in special sounds. 40All things should be done in the right way, one after the other.

Jesus Christ Was Raised From The Dead

15 Christian brothers, I want to tell the Good News to you again. It is the same as I preached to you before. You received it and your faith has been made strong by it. 2This is what I preached to you. You are saved from the punishment of sin by the Good News if you keep hold of it, unless your faith was worth nothing.

3First of all, I taught you what I had received. It was this: Christ died for our sins as the Holy Writings said He would. (Isaiah 53:5-12) 4Christ was buried. He was raised from the dead three days later as the Holy Writings said He would. (Psalm 16:9-10) ⁵Christ was seen by Peter. After that, the twelve followers saw Him. ⁶After that, more than 500 of His followers saw Him at one time. Most of them are still here, but some have died. ⁷After that, James saw Christ. Then all the missionaries saw Him. ⁸Last of all, Christ showed Himself to me as if I had been born too late. ⁹For I am the least important of all the missionaries. I should not be called a missionary because I made it so hard for God's church. ¹⁰I am different now. It is all because of what God did for me by His loving-favor. His loving-favor was not wasted. I worked harder than all the other missionaries. But it was not I who worked. It was God's loving-favor working through me. ¹¹It makes no difference how you heard the Good News. It could have been through the other missionaries or through me. The important thing is this: We preached the Good News to you and you believed it.

We Will Be Raised From The Dead Also

¹²We preached to you that Christ has been raised from the dead. But some of you say that people are not raised from the dead. Why do you say this? ¹³If the dead are not raised, then Christ was not raised from the dead. ¹⁴If Christ was not raised from the dead, then what we preach to you is worth nothing. Your faith in Christ is worth nothing. ¹⁵That makes us all liars because we said that God raised Christ from the dead. But God did not raise Christ from the dead if the dead do not come to life again. ¹⁶If the dead are not raised, then not even Christ was raised from the dead. ¹⁷If Christ was not raised from the dead, your faith is worth nothing and you are still living in your sins. ¹⁸Then the Christians who have already died are lost in sin. ¹⁹If we have hope in Christ in this life only, we are more sad than anyone else.

²⁰But it is true! Christ has been raised from the dead! He was the first One to be raised from the dead and all those who are in graves will follow. ²¹Death came because of a man, Adam. Being raised from the dead also came because of a Man, Christ. ²²All men will die as Adam died. But all those who belong to Christ will be raised to new life. ²³This is the way it is: Christ was raised from the dead first. Then all those who belong to Christ will be raised from the dead when He comes again. ²⁴Next, at the end of the

More than 500 of His followers saw Him at one time.

All those who belong to Christ will be raised to new life.

world, Christ will give His holy nation over to God the Father. Christ will have destroyed every nation and power. ²⁵Christ must be King until He has destroyed all those who hate Him and work against Him. ²⁶The last thing that will be destroyed is death. ²⁷The Holy Writings say that God has put all things under Christ's feet except Himself. ²⁸When Christ is over all things, He will put Himself under God Who put all things under Christ. And God will be over all things.

²⁹What good will it do people if they are baptized for the dead? If the dead are not raised, why are people baptized for them? ³⁰Why are we also in danger every hour? ³¹I say this, Christian brothers, I have joy in what Jesus Christ our Lord has done for you. That is why I face death every day. ³²As men look at it, what good has it done for me in the city of Ephesus to fight with men who act like wild animals? If the dead are not raised, we might as well be like those who say, "Let us eat and drink, for tomorrow we die."

³³Do not let anyone fool you. Bad people can make those who want to live good become bad. ³⁴Keep your minds awake! Stop sinning. Some do not know God at all. I say this to your shame.

The Body That Will Be Raised

³⁵Someone will say, "How are the dead raised? What kind of bodies will they have?" ³⁶What a foolish question! When you plant a seed, it must die before it starts new life. ³⁷When you put it into the earth, you are not planting the body into which it will become. You put in only a seed. ³⁸It is God Who gives it a body just as He wants it to have. Each kind of seed becomes a different kind of body.

³⁹All flesh is not the same. Men have one kind of flesh. Animals have another kind. Fish have another kind, and birds have another kind. ⁴⁰There are bodies in the heavens. There are bodies on earth. Their greatness is not the same. ⁴¹The sun has its greatness. The moon has its greatness. Stars have their greatness. One star is different from another star in greatness.

⁴²It is the same with people who are raised from the dead. The body will turn back into dust when it is put into a grave. When the

body is raised from the grave, it will never die. 43It has no greatness when it is put into a grave, but it is raised with shining greatness. It is weak when it is put into a grave, but it is raised with power. 44It is a human body when it dies, but it is a God-like body when it is raised from the dead. There are human bodies and there are God-like bodies. 45The Holy Writings say, "The first man, Adam, became a living soul." But the last Adam (Christ) is a life-giving Spirit.

46We have these human bodies first. Then we are given God-like bodies that are ready for heaven. 47Adam was the first man. He was made from the dust of the earth. Christ was the second man. He came down from heaven. 48All men of the earth are made like Adam. But those who belong to Christ will have a body like the body of Christ Who came from heaven. 49Now, our bodies are like Adam's body. But in heaven, our bodies will be like the body of Christ.

50Christian brothers, our bodies which are made of flesh and blood will not go into the holy nation of God. That which dies can have no part in that which will never die. 51For sure, I am telling you a secret. We will not all die, but we will all be changed. 52In a very short time, no longer than it takes for the eye to close and open, the Christians who have died will be raised. It will happen when the horn sounds. The dead will be raised never to die again. Then the rest of us who are alive will be changed. 53Our human bodies made from dust must be changed into a body that cannot be destroyed. Our human bodies that can die must be changed into bodies that will never die. 54When this that can be destroyed has been changed into that which cannot be destroyed, and when this that does die has been changed into that which cannot die, then it will happen as the Holy Writings said it would happen. They said, "Death has no more power over life." (Isaiah 25:8) 55O death, where is your power? O death, where are your pains? 56The pain in death is sin. Sin has power over those under the Law. 57But God is the One Who gives us power over sin through Jesus Christ our Lord. We give thanks to Him for this.

Death has no more power over life.

58So then, Christian brothers, because of all this, be strong. Do not allow anyone to change your mind. Always do your work well for the Lord. You know that whatever you do for Him will not be wasted.

Gifts For The Poor

16 I want to tell you what to do about the money you are gathering for the Christians. Do the same as I told the churches in the country of Galatia to do. ²On the first day of every week each of you should put aside some of your money. Give a certain part of what you have earned. Keep it there because I do not want money gathered when I come. ³When I get there, I will give letters to the men you want to send. They will take your gift to Jerusalem. ⁴If I can go, they can go with me.

Plans For A Visit

⁵I want to visit you after I have gone through the country of Macedonia for I am going through there. ⁶I may be staying with you and even spend the winter with you. Then you can send me on my way to the next place. ⁷I do not want to stop now. I want to spend some time with you when I can stay longer, if that is what the Lord wants. ⁸I will stay in the city of Ephesus until the special day to remember how the Holy Spirit came on the church. ⁹A wide door has been opened to me here to preach the Good News. But there are many who work against me.

¹⁰If Timothy comes, receive him and help him so he will not be afraid. He is working for the Lord as I am. ¹¹Everyone should respect him. Send him on his way to me in peace. I expect to see him and some of the other Christians soon. ¹²I wanted brother Apollos to go with the other Christians to visit you. But he is not sure he should go now. He will come when he can.

¹³Watch and keep awake! Stand true to the Lord. Keep on acting like men and be strong. ¹⁴Everything you do should be done in love.

¹⁵You know that the family of Stephanas were the first Christians in the country of Greece. They are working for the Lord in helping His people. ¹⁶I ask you to listen to leaders like these and

work with them as well as others like them. [17]I am happy that Stephanas and Fortunatus and Achaicus came here. They have helped me and you would have also if you had been here. [18]They have made me happy. They would have made you happy also. Show them you are thankful for their help.

[19]The churches in the countries of Asia say hello. Aquila and Priscilla and the Christians who meet in their house say hello with Christian love. [20]All the Christians here say hello to you. Say hello to each other with a kiss of holy love. [21]I, Paul, am writing the last part of this letter with my own hand. [22]If anyone does not love the Lord, let him be kept from being with Christ. The Lord is coming soon! [23]May you have the loving-favor of our Lord Jesus. [24]I love you all through Christ Jesus. Let it be so.

1 This letter is from Paul. I have been chosen by God to be a missionary for Jesus Christ. Timothy is here with me and is writing to you also. We are writing to God's church in the city of Corinth and to all of God's people in the country of Greece. ²May you have loving-favor and peace from God our Father and the Lord Jesus Christ.

³We give thanks to the God and Father of our Lord Jesus Christ. He is our Father Who shows us loving-kindness and our God Who gives us comfort. ⁴He gives us comfort in all our troubles. Then we can comfort other people who have the same troubles. We give the same kind of comfort God gives us. ⁵As we have suffered much for Christ and have shared in His pain, we also share His great comfort.

⁶But if we are in trouble, it is for your good. And it is so you will be saved from the punishment of sin. If God comforts us, it is for your good also. You too will be given strength not to give up when you have the same kind of trouble we have. ⁷Our hope for you is the same all the time. We know you are sharing our troubles. And so you will share the comfort we receive.

⁸We want you to know, Christian brothers, of the trouble we had in the countries of Asia. The load was so heavy we did not have the strength to keep going. At times we did not think we could live. ⁹We thought we would die. This happened so we would not put our trust in ourselves, but in God Who raises the dead. ¹⁰Yes, God kept us from what looked like sure death and He is keeping us. As we trust Him, He will keep us in the future. ¹¹You also help us by praying for us. Many people thank God for His favor to us. This is an answer to the prayers of many people.

Paul Wants To Visit Corinth

¹²I am happy to say this. Whatever we did in this world, and for sure when we were with you, we were honest and had pure desires. We did not trust in human wisdom. Our power came from God's

loving-favor. [13]We write to you only what we know you can understand. I hope you will understand everything. [14]When the Lord Jesus comes again, you can be as proud of us as we will be proud of you. Right now you do not understand us very well.

[15]It was because of this, I wanted to visit you first. In that way, you would be helped two times. [16]I wanted to stop to visit you on my way to the country of Macedonia. I would stop again as I came from there. Then you could help me on my way to the country of Judea. [17]Yes, I changed my mind. Does that show that I change my mind a lot? Do I plan things as people of the world who say yes when they mean no? You know I am not like that! [18]As God is true, my yes means yes. I am not the kind of person who says one thing and means another. [19]Timothy and Silvanus and I have preached to you about Jesus Christ, the Son of God. In Him there is no yes and no. In Him is yes. [20]Jesus says yes to all of God's many promises. It is through Jesus that we say, ''Let it be so,'' when we give thanks to God. [21]God is the One Who makes our faith and your faith strong in Christ. He has set us apart for Himself. [22]He has put His mark on us to show we belong to Him. His Spirit is in our hearts to prove this.

[23]I call on God to look into my heart. The reason I did not come to the city of Corinth was because I did not want my strong words to hurt you. [24]We are not the boss of your faith but we are working with you to make you happy. Your faith is strong.

2 As I thought about it, I decided I would not come to you again. It would only make you sad. [2]If I make you sad, who is going to make me happy? How can you make me happy if I make you sad? [3]That is why I wrote that letter to you. I did not want to visit you and be made sad by the very ones who should be making me happy. I am sure when I am happy, you are happy also. [4]I wrote you with a troubled heart. Tears were coming from my eyes. I did not want to make you sad. I wanted you to know how much I loved you.

Forgiving A Christian

[5]If someone among you has brought sorrow, he has not made me as sad as he has all of you. I say this so I may not make it hard

for you. 6Most of you have punished him. That is enough for such a person. 7Now you should forgive him and comfort him. If you do not, he will be so sad that he will want to give up. 8I ask you to show him you do love him. 9This is why I wrote to you. I wanted to test you to see if you were willing to obey in all things. 10If you forgive a man, I forgive him also. If I have forgiven anything, I have done it because of you. Christ sees me as I forgive. 11We forgive so that Satan will not win. We know how he works!

12When I arrived in the city of Troas, the Lord opened the door for me to preach the Good News of Christ. 13I was worried because I could not find our brother Titus. After saying good-by, I went on my way to the country of Macedonia. 14We thank God for the power Christ has given us. He leads us and makes us win in everything. He speaks through us wherever we go. The Good News is like a sweet smell to those who hear it. 15We are a sweet smell of Christ that reaches up to God. It reaches out to those who are being saved from the punishment of sin and to those who are still lost in sin. 16It is the smell of death to those who are lost in sin. It is the smell of life to those who are being saved from the punishment of sin. Who is able for such a work? 17We are not like others. They preach God's Word to make money. We are men of truth and have been sent by God. We speak God's Word with Christ's power. All the time God sees us.

We thank God for the power Christ has given us.

You Corinthians Prove What We Are

3 Are we making it sound as if we think we are so important? Other people write letters about themselves. Do we need to write such a letter to you? 2You are our letter. You are written in our hearts. You are known and read by all men. 3You are as a letter from Christ written by us. You are not written as other letters are written with ink on pieces of stone. You are written in human hearts by the Spirit of the living God.

4We can say these things because of our faith in God through Christ. 5We know we are not able in ourselves to do any of this work. God makes us able to do these things. 6God is the One Who made us preachers of a New Way of Worship. This New Way of Worship is not of the Law. It is of the Holy Spirit. The Law brings death, but the Holy Spirit gives life.

7The Law of Moses was written on stone and it brought death. But God's shining greatness was seen when it was given. When Moses took it to the Jews, they could not look at his face because of the bright light. But that bright light in his face began to pass away. 8The new way of life through the Holy Spirit comes with much more shining greatness. 9If the Law of Moses, that leads to death, came in shining greatness, how much greater and brighter is the light that makes us right with God? 10The Law of Moses came with shining greatness long ago. But that light is no longer bright. The shining greatness of the New Way of Worship that brings us life is so much brighter. 11The shining light that came with the Law of Moses soon passed away. But the new way of life is much brighter. It will never pass away.

12We speak without fear because our trust is in Christ. 13We are not like Moses. He put a covering over his face so the Jews would not see that the bright light was passing away. 14Their minds were not able to understand. Even to this day when the Jewish Law is read, there is a covering over their minds. They do not see that Christ is the only One Who can take the covering away. 15Yes, to this very day, there is a covering over their hearts whenever the Law of Moses is read. 16But whenever a man turns to the Lord, the covering is taken away. 17The heart is free where the Spirit of the Lord is. The Lord is the Spirit. 18All of us, with no covering on our faces, show the shining greatness of the Lord as in a mirror. All the time we are being changed to look like Him, with more and more of His shining greatness. This change is from the Lord Who is the Spirit.

Paul Is Faithful In Preaching The Good News

4 Through God's loving-kindness, He has given us this job to do. So we do not give up. 2We have put away all things that are done in secret and in shame. We do not play with the Word of God or use it in a false way. Because we are telling the truth, we want mens' hearts to listen to us. God knows our desires. 3If the Good News we preach is hidden, it is hidden to those who are lost in sin. 4The eyes of those who do not believe are made blind by Satan who is the god of this world. He does not want the light of the Good News to shine in their hearts. This Good News shines as

the shining greatness of Christ. Christ is as God is. ⁵We do not preach about ourselves. We preach Christ Jesus the Lord. We are your workmen because of Jesus. ⁶It was God Who said, "The light will shine in darkness." (Genesis 1:3) He is the One Who made His light shine in our hearts. This brings us the light of knowing God's shining greatness which is seen in Christ's face.

⁷We have this light from God in our human bodies. This shows that the power is from God. It is not from ourselves. ⁸We are pressed on every side, but we still have room to move. We are often in much trouble, but we never give up. ⁹People make it very hard for us, but we are not left alone. We are knocked down, but we are not destroyed. ¹⁰We carry marks on our bodies that show the death of Jesus. This is how Jesus makes His life seen in our bodies. ¹¹Every day of our life we face death because of Jesus. In this way, His life is seen in our bodies. ¹²Death is working in us because we work for the Lord, but His life is working in you.

¹³The Holy Writings say, "I believed, so I spoke." (Psalm 116:10) We have the same kind of faith as David had. We also believe, so we speak. ¹⁴We know that God raised the Lord Jesus from the dead. He will raise us up also. God will take us to Himself and He will take you. ¹⁵These things happened for your good. As more people receive God's favor, they will give thanks for the shining greatness of God.

Life Now — Life In Heaven

¹⁶This is the reason we do not give up. Our human body is wearing out. But our spirits are getting stronger every day. ¹⁷The little troubles we suffer now for a short time are making us ready for the great things God is going to give us forever. ¹⁸We do not look at the things that can be seen. We look at the things that cannot be seen. The things that can be seen will come to an end. But the things that cannot be seen will last forever.

This is the reason we do not give up. Our human body is wearing out. But our spirits are getting stronger every day.

Our Weak Human Bodies

5 Our body is like a house which we live in here on earth. When it is destroyed, we know that God has another body for us in heaven. The new one will not be made by human hands as a house is made. This body will last forever. ²Right now we cry inside ourselves because we wish we could have our new body which we will have in heaven. ³We will not be without a body. We will live in a new body. ⁴While we are in this body, we cry inside ourselves because things are hard for us. It is not that we want to die. Instead, we want to live in our new bodies. We want this dying body to be changed into a living body that lasts forever. ⁵It is God Who has made us ready for this change. He has given us His Spirit to show us what He has for us.

⁶We are sure of this. We know that while we are at home in this body we are not with the Lord. ⁷Our life is lived by faith. We do not live by what we see in front of us. ⁸We are sure we will be glad to be free of these bodies. It will be good to be at home with the Lord. ⁹So if we stay here on earth or go home to Him, we always want to please Him. ¹⁰For all of us must stand in front of Christ when He says who is guilty or not guilty. Each one will receive pay for what he has done. He will be paid for the good or the bad done while he lived in this body.

¹¹Because of this, we know the fear of God. So we try to get men to put their trust in Christ. God knows us. I hope that your hearts know me well also. ¹²We do not want to sound as if we think we are so important. Instead, we are making it easy for you to be proud of us. In that way, you will be able to tell them about us. They always talk about the way people look, but do not care about their hearts. ¹³Are we crazy to talk like this? It is all because of what God has done. If we are using our minds well, it is for you. ¹⁴For the love of Christ puts us into action. We are sure that Christ died for everyone. So, because of that, everyone has a part in His death. ¹⁵Christ died for everyone so that they would live for Him. They should not live to please themselves but for Christ Who died on a cross and was raised from the dead for them.

¹⁶So from now on, we do not think about what people are like by looking at them. We even thought about Christ that way one time. But we do not think of Him that way anymore. ¹⁷For if a man belongs to Christ, he is a new person. The old life is gone. New life has begun. ¹⁸All this comes from God. He is the One Who brought us to Himself when we hated Him. He did this through Christ. Then He gave us the work of bringing others to

If a man belongs to Christ he is a new person. New life has begun.

Him.   [19]God was in Christ. He was working through Christ to bring the whole world back to Himself. God no longer held men's sins against them. And He gave us the work of telling and showing men this.

[20]We are Christ's missionaries. God is speaking to you through us. We are speaking for Christ and we ask you from our hearts to turn from your sins and come to God.   [21]Christ never sinned but God put our sin on Him. Then we are made right with God because of what Christ has done for us.

Our Job To Do

6 We are working together with God. We ask you from our hearts not to receive God's loving-favor and then waste it. [2]The Holy Writings say, "I heard you at the right time. I helped you on that day to be saved from the punishment of sin. Now is the right time! Listen! Now is the day to be saved." (Isaiah 49:8) [3]We do not want to put anything in the way that would keep people from God. We do not want to be blamed. [4]Everything we do shows we are God's workmen. We have had to wait and suffer. We have needed things. We have been in many hard places and have had many troubles. [5]We have been beaten. We have been put into prison. We have been in fights. We have worked hard. We have stayed awake watching. We have gone without food. [6]We have been pure. We have known what to do. We have suffered long. We have been kind. The Holy Spirit has worked in us. We have had true love. [7]We have spoken the truth. We have God's power. We have the right kind of sword in the right hand and the right kind of covering in the left hand to fight with. [8]Some men respect us and some do not. Some men speak bad against us and some thank us. They say we lie, but we speak the truth. [9]Some men act as if they do not know us. And yet we are known by everyone. They act as if we were dead, but we are alive. They try to hurt and destroy us, but they are not able to kill us. [10]We are full of sorrow and yet we are always happy. We are poor and yet we make many people rich. We have nothing and yet we have everything.

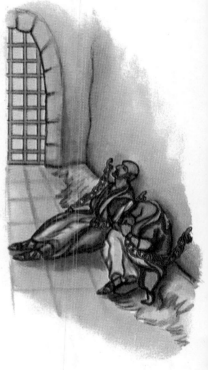

[11]We have spoken to you who are in the city of Corinth with plain words. Our hearts are wide open. [12]Our hearts are not closed

to you. But you have closed your hearts to us. [13]I am speaking to you now as if you were my own children. Open your hearts wide to us! That will pay us back for what we have done for you.

Do not be joined together with those who do not belong to Christ.

[14]Do not be joined together with those who do not belong to Christ. How can that which is good get along with that which is bad? How can light be in the same place with darkness? [15]How can Christ get along with the devil? How can one who has put his trust in Christ get along with one who has not put his trust in Christ? [16]How can the house of God get along with false gods? We are the house of the living God. God has said, "I will live in them and will walk among them. I will be their God and they will be my people." (Leviticus 26:12) [17]The Lord has said, "So come out from among them. Do not be joined to them. Touch nothing that is sinful. And I will receive you. [18]I will be a Father to you. You will be My sons and daughters, says the All-powerful God." (Isaiah 52:11)

7 Since we have these great promises, dear friends, let us turn away from every sin of the body or of the spirit. Let us honor God with love and fear by giving ourselves to Him in every way.

His Love For The Corinthians

[2]Receive us into your hearts. We have done no wrong to anyone. We have not led anyone in the wrong way. We have not used anyone for our good. [3]I do not say this to tell you that you are wrong. As I have said before, you have a place in our hearts and always will. If we live or die, we will be together. [4]I trust you and am proud of you. You give me much comfort and joy even when I suffer.

[5]When we arrived in the country of Macedonia, we had no rest. We had all kinds of trouble. There was fighting all around us. Our hearts were afraid. [6]But God gives comfort to those whose hearts are heavy. He gave us comfort when Titus came. [7]Not only did his coming comfort us, but the comfort you had given him made me happy also. He told us how much you wanted to see us. He said that you were sad because of my trouble and that you wanted to help me. This made me happy.

8I am not sorry now if my letter made you sad. I know it made you sad, but it was only for awhile. 9I am happy now. It is not because you were hurt by my letter, but because it turned you from sin to God. God used it and you were not hurt by what we did. 10The sorrow that God uses makes people sorry for their sin and leads them to turn from sin so they can be saved from the punishment of sin. We should be happy for that kind of sorrow, but the sorrow of this world brings death. 11See how this sorrow God allowed you to have has worked in you. You had a desire to be free of that sin I wrote about. You were angry about it. You were afraid. You wanted to do something about it. In every way you did what you could to make it right. 12I sent this. It was not written only because of the man who did the wrong or because of the one who suffered. 13All this has given us comfort. More than this, we are happy for the joy Titus has. His spirit has been made stronger by all of you. 14I told him how proud I was of you. You did not make me ashamed. What we said to Titus proved to be true. 15He loves you all the more. He remembers how all of you were ready to obey and how you respected him. 16I am happy that I can have complete trust in you.

The Christian Way To Give

8 Christian brothers, we want you to know how the loving-favor of God has been shown in the churches in the country of Macedonia. 2They have been put to the test by much trouble, but they have much joy. They have given much even though they were very poor. 3They gave as much as they could because they wanted to. 4They asked from their hearts if they could help the Christians in Jerusalem. 5It was more than we expected. They gave themselves to the Lord first. Then they gave themselves to us to be used as the Lord wanted. 6We asked Titus to keep on helping you finish this act of love. He was the one to begin this. 7You are rich in everything. You have faith. You can preach. You have much learning. You have a strong desire to help. And you have love for us. Now do what you should about giving also.

8I am not saying that you must do this, but I have told you how others have helped. This is a way to prove how true your love is. 9You know of the loving-favor shown by our Lord Jesus Christ.

He was very rich, but He became very poor for your good. In that way, because He became poor, you might become rich.

[10]This is what I think. You had better finish what you started a year ago. You were the first to want to give a gift of money. [11]Now do it with the same strong desires you had when you started. [12]If a man is ready and willing to give, he should give of what he has, not of what he does not have. [13]This does not mean that others do not have to give and you have to give much. You should share alike. [14]You have more than you need now. When you have need, then they can help you. You should share alike. [15]The Holy Writings say, "The man who gathered much did not have too much. The man who did not gather much had enough." (Exodus 16:18)

Titus Will Be Coming

[16]I thank God that He gave Titus the same desire to help you. [17]He was glad when we asked him to help you. He decided himself to go to you. [18]We are sending the Christian brother along. He is respected in the churches for his preaching. [19]Not only that, but he has been asked by the churches to travel with me to Jerusalem. He will help in giving them the gift. The Lord will be honored by it because it shows how we want to help each other.

[20]We want everyone to trust us with the way we take this large gift of money to them. [21]We want to do the right thing. We want God and men to know we are honest. [22]We are sending another Christian brother with them. We have tested him many times. His faith has proven to be true. He wants very much to help because he trusts you. [23]Titus works with me to help you. The other two Christian brothers have been sent by the churches. Their lives honor Christ. [24]Show these men you love them and let the churches see your love. Show them the reason I am proud of you.

Giving To Help Other Christians

9 I do not need to write to you about helping those who belong to Christ. [2]I know you want to do it. I have told the people in the country of Macedonia that you were ready to send money last year. Your desire has started most of them to give. ³I am sending these Christian brothers so the words I said about you will prove to be true and you will be ready to help. ⁴What if some of the people of the country of Macedonia came with me and found you were not ready to send your gift of money? We would all be ashamed since we have talked of you so much. ⁵That is why I asked these men to go ahead of me. They can see that the gift you promised is ready. In that way, it will be a true gift and not something you were made to do.

⁶Remember, the man who plants only a few seeds will not have much grain to gather. The man who plants many seeds will have much grain to gather. ⁷Each man should give as he has decided in his heart. He should not give, wishing he could keep it. Or he should not give if he feels he has to give. God loves a man who gives because he wants to give. ⁸God can give you all you need. He will give you more than enough. You will have everything you need for yourselves. And you will have enough left over to give when there is a need. ⁹The Holy Writings say, "He has given much to the poor. His acts of love last forever." (Psalm 112:9) ¹⁰It is God Who gives seed to the man to plant. He also gives the bread to eat. Then we know He will give you more seed to plant and make it grow so you will have more to give away. ¹¹God will give you enough so you can always give to others. Then many will give thanks to God for sending gifts through us. ¹²This gift you give not only helps those in need, it makes them give thanks to God also. ¹³You are proving by this act of love what you are. They will give thanks to God for your gift to them and to others. This proves you obey the Good News of Christ. ¹⁴They will pray for you with great love because God has given you His loving-favor. ¹⁵Thank God for His great Gift.

Paul Proves He Is A Missionary

10 I, Paul, ask you this myself. I do it through Christ Who is so gentle and kind. Some people say that I am gentle and quiet when I am with you, but that I have no fear and that my language is strong when I am away from you. ²Do not make me speak strong words to you when I come. Some people think we want the things of the world because of what we do and say. I have decided to talk to these people if I have to. ³It is true, we live in a body of flesh. But we do not fight like people of the world. ⁴We do not use those things to fight with that the world uses. We use the things God gives to fight with and they have power. Those things God gives to fight with destroy the strong places of the devil. ⁵We break down every thought and proud thing that puts itself up against the wisdom of God. We take hold of every thought and make it obey Christ. ⁶We are ready to punish those who will not obey as soon as you obey in everything.

⁷You are seeing things only as men see them. If anyone feels sure he belongs to Christ, he should remember that we belong to Christ also. ⁸I am not ashamed if I say this of myself. The Lord gave me the right and the power to help you become stronger, not to break you down. ⁹I do not want you to think I am trying to make you afraid with my letters. ¹⁰They say, "His letters are strong and they make us think. When he is here with us, he is weak and he is hard to listen to." ¹¹What we say in our letters we will do when we get there. They should understand this. ¹²We do not compare ourselves with those who think they are very good. They compare themselves with themselves. They decide what they think is good or bad and compare themselves with those ideas. They are foolish. ¹³But we will not talk with pride more than God allows us to. We will follow the plan of the work He has given us to do and you are a part of that work. ¹⁴We did not go farther than we were supposed to go when we came to you. But we did come to you with the Good News of Christ. ¹⁵We take no pride in the work others have done there. But we hope your faith will keep growing because of help from others. Then we will grow because of you. ¹⁶We hope to preach the Good News in the countries on the other side of you. Then we would take no pride in work done by another person in another country. ¹⁷If anyone wants to be proud, he should be proud of what the Lord has done. ¹⁸It is not what a man thinks and says of himself that is important. It is what God thinks of him.

If anyone wants to be proud, he should be proud of what the Lord has done.

Paul — The True Missionary

11 I wish you would listen to a little foolish talk from me. Now listen. ²I am jealous for you with a God-like jealousy. I have given you, as a woman who has never had a man, to one Husband,

Who is Christ. ³Eve was fooled by the snake in the garden of Eden. In the same way, I am afraid that you will be fooled and led away from your pure love for Christ. ⁴You listen when someone comes and preaches a different Jesus than the One we preached. You believe what you hear about a different spirit and different good news than that which we preached.

⁵I do not think I am less than those special missionaries who are coming to you. ⁶Even if it is hard for me to speak, I know what I am talking about. You know this by now. ⁷Did I do wrong? I did not ask you for anything when I preached the Good News to you. I made myself poor so you would be made rich. ⁸I did take money from other churches. I used it while I worked with you so you would not have to pay me. ⁹Some of the time I had no money when I was with you. But I did not ask you for money. The Christians from the country of Macedonia brought me what I needed. I did not ask you and I will not ask you for anything. ¹⁰As sure as the truth of Christ is in me, I will not stop telling those in the country of Greece that I am proud of this. ¹¹Does it mean I do not love you? God knows I do.

¹²What I am doing now, I will keep on doing. I will do it to stop those who say they work as we do. ¹³Those men are false missionaries. They lie about their work. But they make themselves look like true missionaries of Christ. ¹⁴It is no surprise! The devil makes himself look like an angel of light. ¹⁵And so it is no surprise if his workmen also make themselves look like preachers of the Good News. They and their work will come to the same end.

What Paul Suffered As A Missionary

¹⁶Let me say it again. Do not think of me as a fool. But if you do, then let this foolish man speak a little about himself. ¹⁷The Lord has not told me to talk about myself. I am foolish when I do talk about myself like this. ¹⁸Since the other men tell you all about themselves, I will talk about myself also. ¹⁹You are so wise! You put up with fools! ²⁰You listen to anyone who tells you what to do or makes money off of you or sets a trap for you. You will listen to anyone who makes himself bigger than you or hits you in the face. ²¹I am ashamed to say that I am weak! But I do not do as they do.

Whatever they say about themselves, I can say about myself also. (I know what I am saying sounds foolish.)

²²Are they Jews? So am I. Are they from the family of Israel? So am I. Are they from the family of Abraham? So am I. ²³Do they work for Christ? I have worked for Him much more than they have. (I speak as if I am crazy.) I have done much more work. I have been in prison more times. I cannot remember how many times I have been whipped. Many times I have been in danger of death. ²⁴Five different times the Jews whipped me across my back thirty-nine times. ²⁵Three times they beat me with sticks. One time they threw stones at me. Three times I was on ships that were wrecked. I spent a day and a night in the water. ²⁶I have made many hard trips. I have been in danger from high water on rivers. I have been in danger from robbers. I have been in danger from the Jews. I have been in danger from people who do not know God. I have been in danger in cities and in the desert. I have been in danger on the sea. I have been in danger among people who say they belong to Christ but do not. ²⁷I have worked very hard and have been tired and have had pain. I have gone many times without sleep. I have been hungry and thirsty. I have gone without food and clothes. I have been out in the cold. ²⁸More than all these things that have happened to my body, the care of all the churches is heavy on me. ²⁹When someone is weak, I feel weak also. When someone is led into sin, I have a strong desire to help him. ³⁰If I must talk about myself, I will do it about the things that show how weak I am. ³¹The God and Father of our Lord Jesus Christ is to be honored and thanked forever. He knows I am telling the truth. ³²In the city of Damascus the leader of the people under King Aretas put soldiers at the gates to take me. ³³But I was let down in a basket through a window in the wall and I got away.

Paul Sees Something True In A Special Dream

12 I have to talk about myself, even if it does no good. But I will keep on telling about some things I saw in a special dream and that which the Lord has shown me. ²I know a man who belongs to Christ. Fourteen years ago he was taken up to the highest heaven. (I do not know if his body was taken up or just his spirit. Only God knows.) ³I say it again, I know this man was taken up. But I do not know if his body or just his spirit was taken up. Only God knows. ⁴When he was in the highest heaven, he heard things that cannot be told with words. No man is allowed to tell them. ⁵I will be proud about this man, but I will not be proud about myself except to say things which show how weak I am. ⁶Even if I talk about myself, I would not be a fool because it is the truth. But I will say no more because I want no one to think better of me than he does when he sees or hears me.

⁷The things God showed me were so great. But to keep me from being too full of pride because of seeing these things, I have been given trouble in my body. It was sent from Satan to hurt me. It keeps me from being proud. ⁸I asked the Lord three times to take it away from me. ⁹He answered me, "I am all you need. I give you my loving-favor. My power works best in weak people." I am happy to be weak and have troubles so I can have Christ's power in me. ¹⁰I receive joy when I am weak. I receive joy when people talk against me and make it hard for me and try to hurt me and make trouble for me. I receive joy when all these things come to me because of Christ. For when I am weak, then I am strong.

I am all you need.

¹¹I have been making a fool of myself talking like this. But you made me do it. You should be telling what I have done. Even if I am nothing at all, I am not less important than those false missionaries of yours. ¹²When I was with you, I proved to you that I was a true missionary. I did powerful works and there were special things to see. These things were done in the strength and power from God. ¹³What makes you feel less important than the other churches? Is it because I did not let you give me food and clothing? Forgive me for this wrong!

¹⁴This is the third time I am ready to come to you. I want nothing from you. I want you, not your money. You are my children. Children should not have to help care for their parents. Parents should help their children. ¹⁵I am glad to give anything I have, even myself, to help you. When I love you more, it looks as if you love me less.

¹⁶It is true that I was not a heavy load to you. But some say I set a trap for you. ¹⁷How could I have done that? Did I get

anything from you through the men I sent to you? ¹⁸I asked Titus and the other Christian brother to visit you. Did Titus get anything from you? Did we not do things that showed we had the same desires and followed the same plan?

¹⁹It may look to you as if we had been trying to make everything look right for ourselves all this time. God knows and so does Christ that all this is done to help you. ²⁰I am afraid that when I visit you I will not find you as I would like you to be. And you will not find me as you would like me to be. I am afraid I will find you fighting and jealous and angry and arguing and talking about each other and thinking of yourselves as being too important and making trouble. ²¹I am afraid when I get there God will take all the pride away from me that I had for you. I will not be happy about many who have lived in sin and done sex sins and have had a desire for such things and have not been sorry for their sins and turned from them.

13 This is my third visit to you. The Holy Writings tell us that when people think someone has done wrong, it must be proven by two or three people who saw the wrong being done. ²During my second visit I talked to you who have been sinning and to all the others. While I am away, I tell you this again. The next time I come I will be hard on those who sin. ³Since you want to know, I will prove to you that Christ speaks through me. Christ is not weak when He works in your hearts. He uses His power in you. ⁴Christ's weak human body died on a cross. It is by God's power that Christ lives today. We are weak. We are as He was. But we will be alive with Christ through the power God has for us.

⁵Put yourselves through a test. See if you belong to Christ. Then you will know you belong to Christ, unless you do not pass the test. ⁶I trust you see that we belong to Him and have passed the test. ⁷We pray to God that you do no wrong. We do not pray this to show that our teaching is so great, but that you will keep on doing what is right, even if it looks as if we have done much wrong. ⁸We cannot work against the truth of God. We only work for it. ⁹We are glad when we are weak and you are strong. We pray that you will become strong Christians. ¹⁰This is why I am writing these things while I am away from you. Then when I get

there, I will not have to use strong words or punish you to show you that the Lord gives me this power. This power is to be used to make you stronger Christians, not to make you weak by hurting your faith.

¹¹Last of all, Christian brothers, good-by. Do that which makes you complete. Be comforted. Work to get along with others. Live in peace. The God of love and peace will be with you. ¹²Say hello to each other with a kiss of holy love. ¹³All those here who belong to Christ say hello. ¹⁴May you have loving-favor from our Lord Jesus Christ. May you have the love of God. May you be joined together by the Holy Spirit.

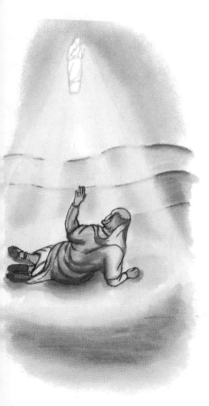

1 This letter is from Paul. I am a missionary sent by Jesus Christ and God the Father Who raised Jesus from the dead. I am not sent by men or by any one man. ²All the Christians join me in writing to you who are in the churches in the country of Galatia. ³May you have loving-favor and peace from God our Father and from the Lord Jesus Christ. ⁴He gave Himself to die for our sins. He did this so we could be saved from this sinful world. This is what God wanted Him to do. ⁵May He have all the honor forever. Let it be so.

He gave Himself to die for our sins.

Men Must Not Change The Good News

⁶I am surprised you are leaving Christ so soon. You were chosen through His loving-favor. But now you are turning and listening to another kind of good news. ⁷No! There is not another kind of good news. There are some who would like to lead you in the wrong way. They want to change the Good News about Christ. ⁸Even if we or an angel from heaven should preach another kind of good news to you that is not the one we preached, let him be kept from being with Christ. ⁹As we said before, I will say it again. If any man is preaching another good news to you which is not the one you have received, let him be kept from being with Christ.

This Good News Is From God

¹⁰Do you think I am trying to get the favor of men, or of God? If I were still trying to please men, I would not be a workman owned by Christ.

¹¹Christian brothers, I want you to know the Good News I preached to you was not made by man. ¹²I did not receive it from man. No one taught it to me. I received it from Jesus Christ as He showed it to me.

¹³You have heard of my old life when I followed the Jewish religion. I made it as hard as I could for the Christians and did

everything I could to destroy the Christian church. [14]I had learned more about the Jewish religion than many of the Jews my age. I had a much stronger desire than they to follow the ways of our early fathers. [15]But God chose me before I was born. By His loving-favor He called me to work for Him. [16]His Son was to be seen in me. He did this so I could preach about Christ to the people who are not Jews. When this happened, I did not talk to men. [17]I did not even go to Jerusalem to talk to those who were missionaries before me. Instead, I went to the country of Arabia. Later I returned to the city of Damascus.

[18]Three years later I went to Jerusalem to meet Peter. I stayed with him fifteen days. [19]I did not see any of the other missionaries except James, the Lord's brother. [20]I am writing the truth. God knows I am not lying.

[21]I went from Jerusalem to the countries of Syria and Cilicia. [22]None of the Christians in the churches in the country of Judea had ever seen me. [23]The only thing they heard was, "The one who tried to destroy the Christian church is now preaching the Good News!" [24]And they gave thanks to God because of me.

The Church Leaders In Jerusalem Say Paul Is A True Missionary

2 Fourteen years later I went again to Jerusalem. This time I took Barnabas. Titus went with us also. [2]God showed me in a special way I should go. I spoke to them about the Good News that I preach among the people who are not Jews. First of all, I talked alone to the important church leaders. I wanted them to know what I was preaching. I did not want that which I was doing or would be doing to be wasted.

[3]Titus was with me. Even being a Greek, he did not have to go through the religious act of becoming a Jew. [4]Some men who called themselves Christians asked about this. They got into our meeting without being asked. They came there to find out how free we are who belong to Christ. They tried to get us to be chained to the Jewish Law. [5]But we did not listen to them or do what they wanted us to do so the truth of the Good News might be yours.

⁶Those who seemed to be important church leaders did not help me. They did not teach me anything new. What they were, I do not care. God looks on us all as being the same. ⁷Anyway, they saw how I had been given the work of preaching the Good News to the people who are not Jews, as Peter had been given the work of preaching the Good News to the Jews. ⁸For God helped Peter work with the Jews. He also helped me work with those who are not Jews. ⁹James and Peter and John were thought of as being the head church leaders. They could see that God's loving-favor had been given to me. Barnabas and I were joined together with them by shaking hands. Then we were sent off to work with the people who are not Jews. They were to work with the Jews. ¹⁰They asked us to do only one thing. We were to remember to help poor people. I think this is important also.

¹¹But when Peter came to Antioch, I had to stand up against him because he was guilty. ¹²Peter had been eating with the people who are not Jews. But after some men came who had been with James, he kept away from them. He was afraid of those who believe in the religious act of becoming a Jew. ¹³Then the rest of the Jews followed him because they were afraid to do what they knew they should do. Even Barnabas was fooled by those who pretended to be someone they were not. ¹⁴When I saw they were not honest about the truth of the Good News, I spoke to Peter in front of them all. I said, "If you are Jew, but live like the people who are not Jews, why do you make the people who are not Jews live like the Jews?" ¹⁵You and I were born Jews. We were not sinners from among the people who are not Jews. ¹⁶Even so, we know we cannot become right with God by obeying the Jewish Law. A man is made right with God by putting his trust in Jesus Christ. For that reason, we have put our trust in Jesus Christ also. We have been made right with God because of our faith in Christ and not by obeying the Jewish Law. No man can be made right with God by obeying the Jewish Law. ¹⁷As we try to become right with God by what Christ has done for us, what if we find we are sinners also? Does that mean Christ makes us sinners? No! Never! ¹⁸But if I work toward being made right with God by keeping the Jewish Law, then I make myself a sinner. ¹⁹The Jewish Law has no power over me. I am dead to the Law. Now I can live for God. ²⁰I have been put up on the cross to die with Christ. I no longer live. Christ lives in me. The life I now live in

A man is made right with God by putting his trust in Jesus Christ.

this body, I live by putting my trust in the Son of God. He was the One Who loved me and gave Himself for me. ²¹I say that we are not to put aside the loving-favor of God. If we could be made right with God by keeping the Jewish Law, then Christ died for nothing.

3 You foolish Galatians! What strange powers are trying to lead you from the way of faith in Christ? We made it plain for you to see that Jesus Christ was put on a cross to die. ²There is one thing I want to know. Did you receive the Holy Spirit by keeping the Jewish Law? Or did you receive Him by hearing about Christ? ³How foolish can you be? You started the Christian life by the Holy Spirit. Do you think you are going to become better Christians by your old way of worship? ⁴You suffered so much because of the Good News you received. Was this all of no use? ⁵He gave you the Holy Spirit and did powerful works among you. Does He do it because you do what the Jewish Law says or because you hear and believe the truth?

⁶It was the same with Abraham. He put his trust in God. This made Abraham right with God. ⁷Be sure to remember that all men who put their trust in God are the sons of Abraham. ⁸The Holy Writings said long ago that God would save the people who are not Jews from the punishment of sin also. Before this time the Holy Writings gave the Good News to Abraham in these words, "All nations will be happy because of you." (Genesis 12:3) ⁹So then, all those who have faith will be happy, along with Abraham who had faith.

¹⁰All those who expect the Jewish Law to save them from the punishment of sin will be punished. Because it is written, "Everyone who does not keep on doing all the things written in the Book of the Law will be punished." (Deuteronomy 26:27) ¹¹No one is made right with God by doing what the Jewish Law says. For, "The man right with God will live by faith." (Habakkuk 2:4) ¹²The Jewish Law does not use faith. It says, "You must obey all the Jewish Law or you will die." (Leviticus 18:5) ¹³Christ bought us with His blood and made us free from the Jewish Law. In that way, the Law could not punish us. Christ did this by carrying the load and by being punished instead of us. It is

written, "Anyone who hangs on a cross is hated and punished." (Deuteronomy 21:23) [14]Because of the price Christ Jesus paid, the good things that came to Abraham might come to the people who are not Jews. And by putting our trust in Christ, we receive the Holy Spirit He has promised.

[15]Christian brothers, let me show you what this means. If two men agree to something and sign their names on a paper promising to stay true to what they agree, it cannot be changed. [16]Now the promise was made to Abraham and to his son. He does not say, "And to sons," speaking of many. But instead, "And to your Son," which means Christ. [17]This is what I am saying: The Jewish Law which came 430 years later could not change the promise. The promise had already been made by God. The Law could not put that promise aside. [18]If it had been possible to be saved from the punishment of sin by obeying the Jewish Law, the promise God gave Abraham would be worth nothing. But since it is not possible to be saved by obeying the Jewish Law, the promise God gave Abraham is worth everything.

[19]Then why do we have the Jewish Law? It was given because of sin. It was to be used until Christ came. The promise had been made looking toward Christ. The Law was given by angels through Moses who stood between God and man. [20]But when the promise was given to Abraham, God gave it without anyone standing between them. [21]Is the Jewish Law against the promise of God? No! Never! If it had been possible to be saved from the punishment of sin by obeying the Jewish Law, then being right with God would have come by obeying the Jewish Law. [22]But the Holy Writings say that all men are guilty of sin. Then that which was promised might be given to those who put their trust in Christ. It will be because their faith is in Him.

[23]Before it was possible to be saved from the punishment of sin by putting our trust in Christ, we were held under the Jewish Law. It was as if we were being kept in prison. We were kept this way until Christ came. [24]The Jewish Law was used to lead us to Christ. It was our teacher, and so we were made right with God by putting our trust in Christ. [25]Now that our faith is in Christ, we do not need the Jewish Law to lead us. [26]You are now children of God because you have put your trust in Christ Jesus. [27]All of you

The Jewish Law was used to lead us to Christ.

who have been baptized to show you belong to Christ have become like Christ. ²⁸God does not see you as a Jew or as a Greek. He does not see you as a person sold to work or as a person free to work. He does not see you as a man or as a woman. You are all one in Christ. ²⁹If you belong to Christ, then you have become the true children of Abraham. What God promised to him is now yours.

Sons Of God

4 Let me say this another way. A young child who will get all the riches of his family is not different from a workman who is owned by the family. And yet the young child owns everything. ²While he is young, he is cared for by men his father trusts. These men tell the child what he can and cannot do. The child cannot do what he wants to do until he has become a certain age. ³We were as children also held by the Jewish Law. We obeyed the Law in our religious worship. ⁴But at the right time, God sent His Son. A woman gave birth to Him under the Jewish Law. ⁵This all happened so He could buy with His blood and make free all those who were held by the Jewish Law. Then we might become the sons of God. ⁶Because you are the sons of God, He has sent the Spirit of His Son into our hearts. The Spirit cries, "Father!" ⁷So now you are no longer a workman who is owned by someone. You are a son. If you are a son, then you will receive what God has promised through Christ.

⁸During the time when you did not know God, you worshiped false gods. ⁹But now that you know God, or should I say that you are known by God, why do you turn back again to the weak old Law? Why do you want to do those religious acts of worship that will keep you from being free? Why do you want to be held under the power of the Jewish Law again? ¹⁰You do special things on certain days and months and years and times of the year. ¹¹I am afraid my work with you was wasted.

Living By The Law Or Being Free

¹²I ask you, Christian brothers, stay free from the Law as I am. Even if I am a Jew, I became free from the Law, just as you who are not Jews. You did no wrong to me. ¹³You know I preached the

Good News to you the first time because of my sickness. [14]Even though I was hard to look at because of my sickness, you did not turn away from me. You took me in as an angel from God. You took me in as you would have taken in Christ Jesus Himself. [15]What has become of the happiness you once had? You would have taken out your own eyes if you could have and given them to me. [16]Do you hate me because I have told you the truth? [17]Those false teachers are trying to turn your eyes toward them. They do not want you to follow my teaching. What they are doing is not good. [18]It is good when people help you if they do not hope to get something from it. They should help you all the time, not only when I am with you. [19]My children, I am suffering birth pains for you again. I will suffer until Christ's life is in your life. [20]I wish I could be with you now. I wish I could speak to you in a more gentle voice, but I am troubled about you.

It is good when people help you if they do not hope to get something from it.

[21]Listen! If you want to be under the Jewish Law, why do you not listen to what it says? [22]The Holy Writings say that Abraham had two sons. One was born from a workwoman (Hagar) who was owned by someone. She had to do what she was told. The other son was born from a woman (Sarah) who was free to work and live as she desired. (Genesis 16:15; 21:2-9) [23]The son born from the workwoman who was owned by someone was like any other birth. The son born from the free woman was different. That son had been promised by God. [24]Think of it like this: These two women show God's two ways of working with His people. The children born from Hagar are under the Jewish Law given on the Mountain of Sinai. They will be workmen who are owned by someone and will always be told what to do! [25]Hagar is known as the Mountain of Sinai in the country of Arabia. She is as Jerusalem is today, because she and her children are not free to do what they want to do. [26]But the Jerusalem of heaven is the free woman, and she is our mother. [27]The Holy Writings say, "Woman, be happy, you who have had no children. Cry for joy, you who have never had the pains of having a child, for you will have many children. Yes, you will have more children than the one who has a husband." (Isaiah 54:1) [28]Christian brothers, we are like Isaac. We are the children God promised. [29]At that time the son born as other children are born made it very hard for the son born by the Holy Spirit. It is the same way now. [30]But what do the Holy Writings say? They say, "Put the workwoman who is owned by someone

and her son out of your home. The son of that workwoman will never get any of the riches of the family. It will all be given to the son of the free woman." (Genesis 21:10) ³¹Christian brothers, we are not children of the workwoman who was owned by someone (Hagar). We are children of the free woman (Sarah).

Christ Made Us Free

5 Christ made us free. Stay that way. Do not get chained all over again in the Jewish Law and its kind of religious worship.

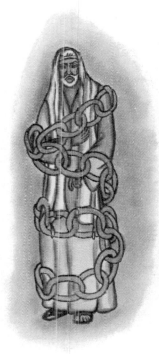

²Listen to me! I, Paul, tell you that if you have the religious act of becoming a Jew done on you, Christ will be of no use to you at all. ³I say it again. Every man who has the religious act of becoming a Jew done on him must obey every Jewish Law. ⁴If you expect to be made right with God by obeying the Jewish Law, then you have turned away from Christ and His loving-favor. ⁵We are waiting for the hope of being made right with God. This will come through the Holy Spirit and by faith. ⁶If we belong to Jesus Christ, it means nothing to have or not to have gone through the religious act of becoming a Jew. But faith working through love is important.

⁷You were doing well. Who stopped you from obeying the truth? ⁸Whatever he used did not come from the One Who chose you to have life. ⁹It only takes a little yeast to make the whole loaf of bread rise. ¹⁰I feel I can trust you because of what the Lord has done in your life. I believe you will not follow another way. Whoever is trying to lead you in the wrong way will suffer for it. ¹¹Christian brothers, if I would still preach that people must go through the religious act of becoming a Jew to be a Christian, I would not be suffering from those who are making it hard for me. If I preached like that, the Jews would have no reason to be against the cross of Christ. ¹²I wish those who are so willing to cut your bodies would complete the job by cutting themselves off from you.

¹³Christian brothers, you were chosen to be free. Be careful that you do not please your old selves by sinning because you are free.

Live this free life by loving and helping others. ¹⁴You obey the whole Jewish Law when you do this one thing, "Love your neighbor as you love yourself." (Leviticus 19:18) ¹⁵But if you hurt and make it very hard for each other, watch out or you may be destroyed by each other.

Let the Holy Spirit lead you in each step.

¹⁶I say this to you: Let the Holy Spirit lead you in each step. Then you will not please your sinful old selves. ¹⁷The things our old selves want to do are against what the Holy Spirit wants. The Holy Spirit does not agree with what our sinful old selves want. These two are against each other. So you cannot do what you want to do. ¹⁸If you let the Holy Spirit lead you, the Jewish Law no longer has power over you. ¹⁹The things your sinful old self wants to do are: sex sins, sinful desires, wild living, ²⁰worshiping false gods, witchcraft, hating, fighting, being jealous, being angry, arguing, dividing into little groups and thinking the other groups are wrong, false teaching, ²¹wanting something someone else has, killing other people, using strong drink, wild parties, and all things like these. I told you before and I am telling you again that those who do these things will have no place in the holy nation of God. ²²But the fruit that comes from having the Holy Spirit in our lives is: love, joy, peace, not giving up, being kind, being good, having faith, ²³being gentle, and being the boss over our own desires. The Jewish Law is not against these things. ²⁴Those of us who belong to Christ have nailed our sinful old selves on His cross. Our sinful desires are now dead.

²⁵If the Holy Spirit is living in us, let us be led by Him in all things. ²⁶Let us not become proud in ways in which we should not. We must not make hard feelings among ourselves as Christians or make anyone jealous.

Help Other Christians

6 Christian brothers, if a person is found doing some sin, you who are stronger Christians should lead that one back into the right way. Do not be proud as you do it. Watch yourself, because you may be tempted also. ²Help each other in troubles and problems. This is the kind of law Christ asks us to obey. ³If anyone thinks he is important when he is nothing, he is fooling himself. ⁴Everyone should look at himself and see how he does his own work. Then he can be happy in what he has done. He should not compare himself with his neighbor. ⁵Everyone must do his own work.

⁶He who is taught God's Word should share the good things he has with his teacher. ⁷Do not be fooled. You cannot fool God. A man will get back whatever he plants! ⁸If a man does things to please his sinful old self, his soul will be lost. If a man does things to please the Holy Spirit, he will have life that lasts forever. ⁹Do not let yourselves get tired of doing good. If we do not give up, we will get what is coming to us at the right time. ¹⁰Because of this, we should do good to everyone. For sure, we should do good to those who belong to Christ.

The Christian's Pride Should Be In The Cross

¹¹See what big letters I make when I write to you with my own hand. ¹²Those men who say you must go through the religious act of becoming a Jew are doing it because they want to make a good show in front of the world. They do this so they will not have to suffer because of following the way of the cross of Christ. ¹³Those who have gone through the religious act of becoming a Jew do not even keep the Jewish Law themselves. But they want you to go through that religious act so they can be proud that you are their followers. ¹⁴I do not want to be proud of anything except in the cross of our Lord Jesus Christ. Because of the cross, the ways of this world are dead to me, and I am dead to them. ¹⁵If a person does or does not go through the religious act of becoming a Jew, it is worth nothing. The important thing is to become a new person. ¹⁶Those who follow this way will have God's peace and loving-kindness. They are the people of God.

¹⁷Let no one make trouble for me from now on. For I have on my body the whip marks of one who has been a workman owned by Jesus. ¹⁸Christian brothers, may the loving-favor of our Lord Jesus Christ be with your spirit. Let it be so.

1 This letter is from Paul. I am a missionary for Jesus Christ. God wanted me to work for Him. This letter is to those who belong to Christ in the city of Ephesus and to you who are faithful followers of Christ Jesus. [2]May you have loving-favor and peace from God our Father and from our Lord Jesus Christ.

[3]Let us honor and thank the God and Father of our Lord Jesus Christ. He has already given us a taste of what heaven is like. [4]Even before the world was made, God chose us for Himself because of His love. He planned that we should be holy and without blame as He sees us. [5]God already planned to have us as His own children. This was done by Jesus Christ. In His plan God wanted this done. [6]We thank God for His loving-favor to us. He gave this loving-favor to us through His much-loved Son. [7]Because of the blood of Christ, we are bought and made free from the punishment of sin. And because of His blood, our sins are forgiven. His loving-favor to us is so rich. [8]He was so willing to give all of this to us. He did this with wisdom and understanding. [9]God told us the secret of what He wanted to do. It is this: In loving thought He planned long ago to send Christ into the world. [10]The plan was for Christ to gather us all together at the right time. If we are in heaven or still on earth, He will bring us together and will be head over all. [11]We were already chosen to be God's own children by Christ. This was done just like the plan He had. [12]We who were the first to put our trust in Christ should thank Him for His greatness. [13]The truth is the Good News. When you heard the truth, you put your trust in Christ. Then God marked you by giving you His Holy Spirit as a promise. [14]The Holy Spirit was given to us as a promise that we will receive everything God has for us. God's Spirit will be with us until God finishes His work of making us complete. God does this to show His shining greatness.

Because of the blood of Christ, we are bought and made free from the punishment of sin. And because of His blood, our sins are forgiven. His loving-favor to us is so rich.

The truth is the Good News.

Paul's Prayer For The Christians In Ephesus

[15]I have heard of your faith in the Lord Jesus and your love for all Christians. [16]Since then, I have always given thanks for you

and pray for you. ¹⁷I pray that the great God and Father of our Lord Jesus Christ may give you the wisdom of His Spirit. Then you will be able to understand the secrets about Him as you know Him better. ¹⁸I pray that your hearts will be able to understand. I pray that you will know about the hope given by God's call. I pray that you will see how great the things are that He has promised to those who belong to Him. ¹⁹I pray that you will know how great His power is for those who have put their trust in Him. ²⁰It is the same power that raised Christ from the dead. This same power put Christ at God's right side in heaven. ²¹This place was given to Christ. It is much greater than any king or leader can have. No one else can have this place of honor and power. No one in this world or in the world to come can have such honor and power. ²²God has put all things under Christ's power and has made Him to be the head leader over all things of the church. ²³The church is the body of Christ. It is filled by Him Who fills all things everywhere with Himself.

God Saved Us From Sin

2 At one time you were dead because of your sins. ²You followed the sinful ways of the world and obeyed the leader of the power of darkness. He is the devil who is now working in the people who do not obey God. ³At one time all of us lived to please our old selves. We gave in to what our bodies and minds wanted. We were sinful from birth like all other people and would suffer from the anger of God.

⁴But God had so much loving-kindness. He loved us with such a great love. ⁵Even when we were dead because of our sins, He made us alive by what Christ did for us. You have been saved from the punishment of sin by His loving-favor. ⁶God raised us up from death when He raised up Christ Jesus. He has given us a place with Christ in the heavens. ⁷He did this to show us through all the time to come the great riches of His loving-favor. He has shown us His kindness through Christ Jesus.

⁸For by His loving-favor you have been saved from the punishment of sin through faith. It is not by anything you have done. It is a gift of God. ⁹It is not given to you because you

worked for it. If you could work for it, you would be proud. ¹⁰We are His work. He has made us to belong to Christ Jesus so we can work for Him. He planned that we should do this.

Followers Now Become The Body Of Christ

¹¹Do not forget that at one time you did not know God. The Jews, who had gone through the religious act of becoming a Jew by man's hands, said you were people who do not know God. ¹²You were living without Christ then. The Jewish people who belonged to God had nothing to do with you. The promises He gave to them were not for you. You had nothing in this world to hope for. You were without God.

¹³But now you belong to Christ Jesus. At one time you were far away from God. Now you have been brought close to Him. Christ did this for you when He gave His blood on the cross. ¹⁴We have peace because of Christ. He has made the Jews and those who are not Jews one people. He broke down the wall that divided them. ¹⁵He stopped the fighting between them by His death on the cross. He put an end to the Jewish Law. Then He made of the two peoples one new kind of people like Himself. In this way, He made peace. ¹⁶He brought both groups together to God. Christ finished the fighting between them by His death on the cross. ¹⁷Then Christ came and preached the Good News of peace to you who were far away from God. And He preached it to us who were near God. ¹⁸Now all of us can go to the Father through Christ by way of the one Holy Spirit. ¹⁹From now on you are not strangers and people who are not citizens. You are citizens together with those who belong to God. You belong in God's family. ²⁰This family is the part on which the building stands. It is built on the teachings of the missionaries and the early preachers. Jesus Christ Himself is the cornerstone, which is the most important part of the building. ²¹Christ keeps this building together and it is growing into a holy building for the Lord. ²²You are also being put together as a part of this building because God lives in you by His Spirit.

3 I, Paul, am in prison because I am a missionary for Jesus Christ to you who are not Jews. ²I am sure you have heard that God trusted me with His loving-favor. ³I wrote a little about this to you before. In a special way, God showed me His secret plan. ⁴When you read this, you will understand how I know about the things that are not easy to understand about Christ. ⁵Long ago men did not know these things. But now it has been shown to His missionaries and to the early preachers by the Holy Spirit. ⁶Let me tell you that the Good News is for the people who are not Jews also. They are able to have life that lasts forever. They are to be a part of His church and family, together with the Jews. And together they are to receive all that God has promised through Christ.

⁷God asked me to preach this Good News. He gave me the gift of His loving-favor. He gave me His power to preach it. ⁸Of all those who belong to Christ, I am the least important. But this loving-favor was given to me to preach to the people who are not Jews. I was to tell them of the great riches in Christ which do not come to an end. ⁹I was to make all men understand the meaning of this secret. God kept this secret to Himself from the beginning of the world. And He is the One Who made all things. ¹⁰This was done so the great wisdom of God might be shown now to the leaders and powers in the heavenly places. It is being done through the church. ¹¹This was the plan God had for all time. He did this through Christ Jesus our Lord. ¹²We can come to God without fear because we have put our trust in Christ. ¹³So I ask you not to lose heart because of my suffering for you. It is to help you.

> We can come to God without fear because we have put our trust in Christ.

Paul's Prayer For The Church

¹⁴For this reason, I get down on my knees and pray to the Father. ¹⁵It is from Him that every family in heaven and on earth has its name. ¹⁶I pray that because of the riches of His shining greatness, He will make you strong with power in your hearts through the Holy Spirit. ¹⁷I pray that Christ may live in your hearts by faith. I pray that you will be filled with love. ¹⁸I pray that you will be able to understand how wide and how long and how high and how deep His love is. ¹⁹I pray that you will know the love of Christ. His love goes beyond anything we can understand. I pray that you will be filled with God Himself.

²⁰God is able to do much more than we ask or think through His power working in us. ²¹May we see His shining greatness in the church. May all people in all time honor Christ Jesus. Let it be so.

> God is able to do much more than we ask or think through His power working in us.

Full-grown Christians

4 I am being held in prison because of working for the Lord. I ask you from my heart to live and work the way the Lord expected you to live and work. ²Live and work without pride. Be gentle and kind. Do not be hard on others. Let love keep you from doing that. ³Work hard to live together as one by the help of the Holy Spirit. Then there will be peace. ⁴There is one body and one Spirit. There is one hope in which you were called. ⁵There is one Lord and one faith and one baptism. ⁶There is one God. He is the Father of us all. He is over us all. He is the One working through us all. He is the One living in us all.

⁷Loving-favor has been given to each one of us. We can see how great it is by the gift of Christ. ⁸The Holy Writings say, "When Christ went up to heaven, He took those who were held with Him. He gave gifts to men." (Psalm 68:18) ⁹When they say, "He went up," what does it mean but that He had first gone down to the deep parts of the earth. ¹⁰Christ Who went down into the deep also went up far above the heavens. He did this to fill all the world with Himself.

¹¹Christ gave gifts to men. He gave to some the gift to be missionaries, some to be preachers, others to be preachers who go from town to town. He gave others the gift to be church leaders and teachers. ¹²These gifts help His people work well for Him. And then the church which is the body of Christ will be made strong. ¹³All of us are to be as one in the faith and in knowing the Son of God. We are to be full-grown Christians standing as high and complete as Christ is Himself. ¹⁴Then we will not be as children any longer. Children are like boats thrown up and down on big waves. They are blown with the wind. False teaching is like the wind. False teachers try everything possible to make people believe a lie, ¹⁵but we are to hold to the truth with love in our hearts. We are to grow up and be more like Christ. He is the leader of the church. ¹⁶Christ has put each part of the church in its right place. Each part helps other parts. This is what is needed to keep the whole body together. In this way, the whole body grows strong in love.

We are to grow up and be more like Christ.

The Old And The New Life

[17]I tell you this in the name of the Lord: You must not live any longer like the people of the world who do not know God. Their thoughts are foolish. [18]Their minds are in darkness. They are strangers to the life of God. This is because they have closed their minds to Him and have turned their hearts away from Him. [19]They do not care anymore about what is right or wrong. They have turned themselves over to the sinful ways of the world and are always wanting to do every kind of sinful act they can think of.

[20]But you did not learn anything like this from Christ. [21]If you have heard of Him and have learned from Him, [22]put away the old person you used to be. Have nothing to do with your old sinful life. It was sinful because of being fooled into following bad desires. [23]Let your minds and hearts be made new. [24]You must become a new person and be God-like. Then you will be made right with God and have a true holy life.

[25]So stop lying to each other. Tell the truth to your neighbor. We all belong to the same body. [26]If you are angry, do not let it become sin. Get over your anger before the day is finished. [27]Do not let the devil start working in your life. [28]Anyone who steals must stop it! He must work with his hands so he will have what he needs and can give to those who need help. [29]Watch your talk! No bad words should be coming from your mouth. Say what is good. Your words should help others grow as Christians. [30]Do not make God's Holy Spirit have sorrow for the way you live. The Holy Spirit has put a mark on you for the day you will be set free. [31]Put out of your life all these things: bad feelings about other people, anger, temper, loud talk, bad talk which hurts other people, and bad feelings which hurt other people. [32]You must be kind to each other. Think of the other person. Forgive other people just as God forgave you because of Christ's death on the cross.

5 Do as God would do. Much-loved children want to do as their fathers do. [2]Live with love as Christ loved you. He gave Himself for us, a gift on the altar to God which was as a sweet smell to God.

³Do not let sex sins or anything sinful be even talked about among those who belong to Christ. Do not always want everything. ⁴Do not be guilty of telling bad stories and of foolish talk. These things are not for you to do. Instead, you are to give thanks for what God has done for you. ⁵Be sure of this! No person who does sex sins or who is not pure will have any part in the holy nation of Christ and of God. The same is true for the person who always wants what other people have. This becomes a god to him. ⁶Do not let anyone lead you in the wrong way with foolish talk. The anger of God comes on such people because they choose not to obey Him. ⁷Have nothing to do with them. ⁸At one time you lived in darkness. Now you are living in the light that comes from the Lord. Live as children who have the light of the Lord in them. ⁹This light gives us truth. It makes us right with God and makes us good. ¹⁰Learn how to please the Lord. ¹¹Have nothing to do with the bad things done in darkness. Instead, show that these things are wrong. ¹²It is a shame even to talk about these things done in secret. ¹³All things can be seen when they are in the light. Everything that can be seen is in the light. ¹⁴The Holy Writings say, "Wake up, you who are sleeping. Rise from the dead and Christ will give you light." (Isaiah 60:1)

Be Filled With The Spirit Of God

¹⁵So be careful how you live. Live as men who are wise and not foolish. ¹⁶Make the best use of your time. These are sinful days. ¹⁷Do not be foolish. Understand what the Lord wants you to do. ¹⁸Do not get drunk with wine. That leads to wild living. Instead, be filled with the Holy Spirit. ¹⁹Tell of your joy to each other by singing the Songs of David and church songs. Sing in your heart to the Lord. ²⁰Always give thanks for all things to God the Father in the name of our Lord Jesus Christ.

Always give thanks for all things.

How Wives Must Live

²¹Be willing to help and care for each other because of Christ. By doing this, you honor Christ. ²²Wives, obey your own husbands. In doing this, you obey the Lord. ²³For a husband is the head of his wife as Christ is the head of the church. It is His body (the church) that He saves. ²⁴As the church is to obey Christ, wives are to obey their own husbands in everything.

How Husbands Must Live

²⁵Husbands, love your wives. You must love them as Christ loved the church. He gave His life for it. ²⁶Christ did this so He could set the church apart for Himself. He made it clean by the washing of water with the Word. ²⁷Christ did this so the church might stand before Him in shining greatness. There is to be no sin of any kind in it. It is to be holy and without blame. ²⁸So men should love their wives as they love their own bodies. He who loves his wife loves himself. ²⁹No man hates himself. He takes care of his own body. That is the way Christ does. He cares for His body which is the church. ³⁰We are all a part of His body, the church. ³¹For this reason, a man must leave his father and mother when he gets married and be joined to his wife. The two become one. ³²This is very hard to understand, but it shows that the church is the body of Christ. ³³So every man must love his wife as he loves himself. Every wife must respect her husband.

How Children Must Live

6 Children, as Christians, obey your parents. This is the right thing to do. ²Respect your father and mother. This is the first Jewish Law given that had a promise. ³The promise is this: If you respect your father and mother, you will live a long time and your life will be full of many good things.

⁴Fathers, do not be too hard on your children so they will become angry. Teach them in their growing years with Christian teaching.

⁵You workmen who are owned by someone must obey your owners. Work for them as hard as you can. Work for them the same as if you were working for Christ. ⁶Do not work hard only when your owner sees you. You would be doing this just to please men. Work as you would work for Christ. Do what God wants you to do with all your heart. ⁷Be happy as you work. Do your work as for the Lord, not for men. ⁸Remember this, whatever good thing you do, the Lord will pay you for it. It is the same to the Lord if you are a workman owned by someone or if you work for pay.

Children, as Christians, obey your parents. This is the right thing to do.

⁹Owners, do the right thing for those who work for you. Stop saying that you are going to be hard on them. Remember that your Owner and their Owner is in heaven. God does not respect one person more than another.

Things God Gives The Christian To Fight With

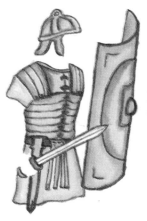

¹⁰This is the last thing I want to say: Be strong with the Lord's strength. ¹¹Put on the things God gives you to fight with. Then you will not fall into the traps of the devil. ¹²Our fight is not with people. It is against the leaders and the powers and the spirits of darkness in this world. It is against the demon world that works in the heavens. ¹³Because of this, put on all the things God gives you to fight with. Then you will be able to stand in that sinful day. When it is all over, you will still be standing. ¹⁴So stand up and do not be moved. Wear a belt of truth around your body. Wear a piece of iron over your chest which is being right with God. ¹⁵Wear shoes on your feet which are the Good News of peace. ¹⁶Most important of all, you need a covering of faith in front of you. This is to put out the fire-arrows of the devil. ¹⁷The covering for your head is that you have been saved from the punishment of sin. Take the sword of the Spirit which is the Word of God.

How And What To Pray For

Remember to pray for all Christians.

¹⁸You must pray at all times as the Holy Spirit leads you to pray. Pray for the things that are needed. You must watch and keep on praying. Remember to pray for all Christians. ¹⁹Pray for me also. Pray that I might open my mouth without fear. Pray that I will use the right words to preach that which is hard to understand in the Good News. ²⁰This is the reason I was sent out. But now I am in chains for preaching the Good News. I want to keep on speaking for Christ without fear the way I should.

²¹Tychicus will tell you how I am getting along. He is a much-loved brother and a faithful preacher. ²²I have sent him to you because I want him to tell you about us. He will comfort you.

²³May all the Christian brothers have peace and love with faith from God the Father and the Lord Jesus Christ. ²⁴May God give loving-favor to all who love our Lord Jesus Christ with a love that never gets weak.

1 This letter is from Paul and Timothy. We are workmen owned by Jesus Christ. This letter is to all who belong to Christ Jesus who are living in the city of Philippi and to the church leaders and their helpers also. ²May you have loving-favor and peace from God our Father and the Lord Jesus Christ.

Paul Gives Thanks For The True Christians

³I thank God for you whenever I think of you. ⁴I always have joy as I pray for all of you. ⁵It is because you have told others the Good News from the first day you heard it until now. ⁶I am sure that God Who began the good work in you will keep on working in you until the day Jesus Christ comes again. ⁷It is right for me to feel like this about all of you. It is because you are very dear to me. While I was in prison and when I was proving that the Good News is true, you all shared God's loving-favor with me. ⁸God knows what I am saying. He knows how much I love you all with a love that comes from Jesus Christ. ⁹And this is my prayer: I pray that your love will grow more and more. I pray that you will have better understanding and be wise in all things. ¹⁰I pray that you will know what is the very best. I pray that you will be true and without blame until the day Christ comes again. ¹¹And I pray that you will be filled with the fruits of right living. These come from Jesus Christ, with honor and thanks to God.

Paul's Being In Prison Has Turned Out To Be A Good Thing

¹²Christian brothers, I want you to know that what has happened to me has helped spread the Good News. ¹³Everyone around here knows why I am in prison. It is because I preached about Jesus Christ. All the soldiers who work for the leader of the country know why I am here. ¹⁴Because of this, most of my Christian brothers have had their faith in the Lord made stronger. They have more power to preach the Word of God without fear.

¹⁵Some are preaching because they are jealous and want to make trouble. Others are doing it for the right reason. ¹⁶These do

> I am sure
> that God Who began
> the good work in you
> will keep on working
> in you until the day
> Jesus Christ comes again.

it because of love. They know that I am put here to prove the Good News is true.   17The others preach about Christ for what they get out of it. Their hearts are not right. They want to make me suffer while I am in prison.   18What difference does it make if they pretend or if they are true? I am happy, yes, and I will keep on being happy that Christ is preached.

19Because of your prayers and the help the Holy Spirit gives me, all of this will turn out for good.   20I hope very much that I will have no reason to be ashamed. I hope to honor Christ with my body if it be by my life or by my death. I want to honor Him without fear, now and always.   21To me, living means having Christ. To die means that I would have more of Him.   22If I keep on living here in this body, it means that I can lead more people to Christ. I do not know which is better.   23There is a strong pull from both sides. I have a desire to leave this world to be with Christ, which is much better.   24But it is more important for you that I stay.   25I am sure I will live to help you grow and be happy in your faith.   26This will give you reason to give more thanks to Christ Jesus when I come to visit you again.

Fight For The Faith

Live your lives as the Good News of Christ says you should.

27Live your lives as the Good News of Christ says you should. If I come to you or not, I want to hear that you are standing true as one. I want to hear that you are working together as one, preaching the Good News.   28Do not be afraid of those who hate you. Their hate for you proves they will be destroyed. It proves you have life from God that lasts forever.   29You are not only to put your trust in Him, but you are to suffer for Him also.   30You know what the fight is like. Now it is time for you to have a part in it as I have.

A Christian Should Not Be Proud

Are you strong because you belong to Christ?

2 Are you strong because you belong to Christ? Does His love comfort you? Do you have joy by being as one in sharing the Holy Spirit? Do you have loving-kindness and pity for each other? 2Then give me true joy by thinking the same thoughts. Keep

Keep having the same love.

having the same love. Be as one in thoughts and actions. 3Nothing should be done because of pride or thinking about yourself. Think of other people as more important than yourself. ⁴Do not always be thinking about your own plans only. Be happy to know what other people are doing.

Christ Was Not Proud

⁵Think as Christ Jesus thought. ⁶Jesus has always been as God is. But He did not hold to His rights as God. ⁷He put aside everything that belonged to Him and made Himself the same as a workman who is owned by someone. He became human by being born as a man. ⁸After He became a man, He gave up His important place and obeyed by dying on a cross. ⁹Because of this, God lifted Jesus high above everything else. He gave Him a name that is greater than any other name. ¹⁰So when the name of Jesus is spoken, everyone in heaven and on earth and under the earth will get down on his knees in front of Him. ¹¹And everyone will say with his tongue that Jesus Christ is Lord. Everyone will give honor to God the Father.

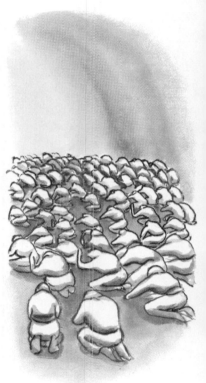

¹²My Christian friends, you have obeyed me when I was with you. You have obeyed even more when I have been away. You must keep on working to show you have been saved from the punishment of sin. Be afraid that you may not please God. ¹³He is working in you. God is helping you obey Him. God is doing what He wants done in you. ¹⁴Be glad you can do the things you should be doing. Do all things without arguing and talking about how you wish you did not have to do them. ¹⁵In that way, you can prove yourselves to be without blame. You are God's children and no one can talk against you, even in a sin-loving and sin-sick world. You are to shine as lights among the sinful people of this world. ¹⁶Take a strong hold on the Word of Life. Then when Christ comes again, I will be happy that I did not work with you for nothing. ¹⁷Even if I give my life as a gift on the altar to God for you, I am glad and share this joy with you. ¹⁸You must be happy and share your joy with me also.

Timothy Is Being Sent To You

¹⁹I hope by the help of the Lord Jesus that I can send Timothy to you soon. It will comfort me when he brings news about you. ²⁰I have no one else who is as interested in you as Timothy. ²¹Everyone else thinks of himself instead of Jesus Christ. ²²You

know how Timothy proved to be such a true friend to me when we preached the Good News. He was like a son helping his father. ²³I hope to send Timothy as soon as I know what they are going to do to me. ²⁴I hope by the help of the Lord that I can come soon also.

²⁵I thought it was right that I send Epaphroditus back to you. You helped me by sending him to me. We have worked together like brothers. He was like a soldier fighting beside me. ²⁶He has been wanting to see all of you and was troubled because you heard he was sick. ²⁷It is true, he was sick. Yes, he almost died, but God showed loving-kindness to him and to me. If he had died, I would have had even more sorrow. ²⁸This is all the more reason I have sent him to you. When you see him, you will be glad and I will have less sorrow. ²⁹Take him into your church with joy. Show respect for men like him. ³⁰He came close to death while working for Christ. He almost died doing things for me that you could not do.

It Is Christ Only — Not The Things You Do

Be happy because you belong to Christ.

3 So now, my Christian brothers, be happy because you belong to Christ. It is not hard for me to write the same things to you. It is good for you. ²Watch out for false teachers. Watch out for sinful men. They want you to depend on the religious act of becoming a Jew for your hope. ³The act of becoming a Jew has nothing to do with us becoming Christians. We worship God through His Spirit and are proud of Jesus Christ. We have no faith in what we ourselves can do. ⁴I could have reason to trust in the flesh. If anyone could feel that the flesh could do something for him, I could. ⁵I went through the religious act of becoming a Jew when I was eight days old. I was born a Jew and came from the family group of Benjamin. I was a Jewish son of Jewish parents. I belonged to the group of the proud religious law-keepers. ⁶I followed my religion with all my heart and did everything I could to make it very hard for the church. No one could say anything against the way I obeyed the Jewish Law.

Christ Must Be Lord Of Our Lives

⁷But I gave up those things that were so important to me for Christ. ⁸Even more than that, I think of everything as worth

nothing. It is so much better to know Christ Jesus my Lord. I have lost everything for Him. And I think of these things as worth nothing so that I can have Christ. 9I want to be as one with Him. I could not be right with God by what the Law said I must do. I was made right with God by faith in Christ. 10I want to know Him. I want to have the same power in my life that raised Jesus from the dead. I want to understand and have a share in His sufferings and be like Christ in His death. 11Then I may be raised up from among the dead.

12I do not say that I have received this or have already become perfect. But I keep going on to make that life my own as Christ Jesus made me His own. 13No, Christian brothers, I do not have that life yet. But I do one thing. I forget everything that is behind me and look forward to that which is ahead of me. 14My eyes are on the prize. I want to win the race and get the prize of God's call from heaven through Christ Jesus. 15All of us who are full-grown Christians should think this way. If you do not think this way, God will show it to you. 16So let us keep on obeying the same truth we have already been following.

17Christian brothers, live your lives as I have lived mine. Watch those who live as I have taught you to live. 18There are many whose lives show they hate the cross of Christ. I have told you this before. Now I tell you again with tears in my eyes. 19Their god is their stomach. They take pride in things they should be ashamed of. All they think about are the things of this world. In the end they will be destroyed. 20But we are citizens of heaven. Christ, the One Who saves from the punishment of sin, will be coming down from heaven again. We are waiting for Him to return. 21He will change these bodies of ours of the earth and make them new. He will make them like His body of shining greatness. He has the power to do this because He can make all things obey Him.

4 So, my dear Christian brothers, you are my joy and prize. I want to see you. Keep on staying true to the Lord, my dear friends.

2I ask Euodias and Syntyche to agree as Christians should. 3My true helper, I ask you also to help these women who have worked with me so much in preaching the Good News to others. Clement helped also. There are others who worked with me. Their names are in the book of life.

Again I say, be full of joy!

4Be full of joy always because you belong to the Lord. Again I say, be full of joy! 5Let all people see how gentle you are. The Lord is coming again soon. 6Do not worry. Learn to pray about everything. Give thanks to God as you ask Him for what you need. 7The peace of God is much greater than the human mind can understand. This peace will keep your hearts and minds through Christ Jesus.

8Christian brothers, keep your minds thinking about whatever is true, whatever is respected, whatever is right, whatever is pure, whatever can be loved, and whatever is well thought of. If there is anything good and worth giving thanks for, think about these things. 9Keep on doing all the things you learned and received and heard from me. Do the things you saw me do. Then the God Who gives peace will be with you.

10The Lord gives me a reason to be full of joy. It is because you are able to care for me again. I know you wanted to before but you did not have a way to help me. 11I am not saying I need anything. I have learned to be happy with whatever I have. 12I know how to get along with very little and how to live when I have much. I have learned the secret of being happy at all times. If I am full of food and have all I need, I am happy. If I am hungry and need more, I am happy. 13I can do all things because Christ gives me the strength.

It was kind of you to help me when I was in trouble.

14It was kind of you to help me when I was in trouble. 15You Philippians also know that when I first preached the Good News, you were the only church that helped me. It was when I left for the country of Macedonia. 16Even while I was in the city of Thessalonica you helped me more than once. 17It is not that I want to receive the gift. I want you to get the pay that is coming to you later. 18I have everything I need and more than enough. I am taken care of because Epaphroditus brought your gift. It is a sweet gift. It is a gift that cost you something. It is the kind of gift God is so pleased with. 19And my God will give you everything you need because of His great riches in Christ Jesus. 20Now may our God and Father be honored forever. Let it be so.

21Say hello to all those who belong to Christ Jesus. The Christian brothers here with me say hello to you. 22All those who belong to Christ say hello, and most of all, those who live in Caesar's house. 23May your spirit have the loving-favor of the Lord Jesus Christ.

Paul Gives Thanks For The Christians In Colossae

1 This letter is from Paul, a missionary for Jesus Christ. God wanted me to work for Him. This letter is from brother Timothy also. ²I am writing to you who belong to Christ in the city of Colossae. May all the Christian brothers there have loving-favor and peace from God our Father.

³We always pray and give thanks to God for you. He is the Father of our Lord Jesus Christ. ⁴We give thanks to God for you because we heard of your faith in Christ Jesus. We thank God for your love for all those who belong to Christ. ⁵We thank God for the hope that is being kept for you in heaven. You first heard about this hope through the Good News which is the Word of Truth. ⁶The Good News came to you the same as it is now going out to all the world. Lives are being changed, just as your life was changed the day you heard the Good News. You understood the truth about God's loving-kindness. ⁷You heard the Good News through our much-loved brother Epaphras who is taking my place. He is a faithful workman owned by Christ. ⁸He told us that the Holy Spirit had given you much love.

⁹This is why I have never stopped praying for you since I heard about you. I ask God that you may know what He wants you to do. I ask God to fill you with the wisdom and understanding the Holy Spirit gives. ¹⁰Then your lives will please the Lord. You will do every kind of good work, and you will know more about God. ¹¹I pray that God's great power will make you strong, and that you will have joy as you wait and do not give up. ¹²I pray that you will be giving thanks to the Father. He has made it so you could share the good things given to those who belong to Christ who are in the light. ¹³God took us out of a life of darkness. He has put us into the holy nation of His much-loved Son. ¹⁴We have been bought by His blood and made free. Our sins are forgiven through Him.

¹⁵Christ is as God is. God cannot be seen. Christ lived before anything was made. ¹⁶Christ made everything in the heavens and

We thank God for your love for all those who belong to Christ.

Christ is as God is. God cannot be seen. Christ lived before anything was made.

on the earth. He made everything that is seen and things that are not seen. He made all the powers of heaven. Everything was made by Him and for Him. ¹⁷Christ was before all things. All things are held together by Him. ¹⁸Christ is the head of the church which is His body. He is the beginning of all things. He is the first to be raised from the dead. He is to have first place in everything. ¹⁹God the Father was pleased to have everything made perfect by Christ, His Son. ²⁰Everything in heaven and on earth can come to God because of Christ's death on the cross. Christ's blood has made peace. ²¹At one time you were strangers to God and your minds were at war with Him. Your thoughts and actions were wrong. ²²But Christ has brought you back to God by His death on the cross. In this way, Christ can bring you to God, holy and pure and without blame. ²³This is for you if you keep the faith. You must not change from what you believe now. You must not leave the hope of the Good News you received. The Good News was preached to you and to all the world. And I, Paul, am one of Christ's missionaries.

Christ was
before all things.

Christ is the head
of the church.

Paul Is Sent By God To Preach

²⁴Now I am full of joy to be suffering for you. In my own body I am doing my share of what has to be done to make Christ's sufferings complete. This is for His body which is the Church. ²⁵I became a preacher in His church for your good. In the plan of God I am to preach the Good News. ²⁶This great secret was hidden to the people of times past, but it is now made known to those who belong to Christ. ²⁷God wants these great riches of the hidden truth to be made known to the people who are not Jews. The secret is this: Christ in you brings hope of all the great things to come. ²⁸We preach Christ. We tell every man how he must live. We use wisdom in teaching every man. We do this so every man will be complete in Christ. ²⁹This is the reason I am working. God's great power is working in me.

The Christian Is Complete In Christ

2 I want you to know how hard I have worked for you and for the Christians in the city of Laodicea and for those who have never seen me. ²May their hearts be given comfort. May they be brought close together in Christian love. May they be rich in understanding and know God's secret. It is Christ Himself. ³In Christ are hidden all the riches of wisdom and understanding. ⁴I tell you this so no one will try to change your mind with big sounding talk. ⁵Even if I am far away from you in body, I am with you in spirit. I am happy to learn how well you are getting along. It is good to hear that your faith is so strong in Christ.

As you have put your trust in Christ Jesus the Lord to save you from the punishment of sin, now let Him lead you in every step.

⁶As you have put your trust in Christ Jesus the Lord to save you from the punishment of sin, now let Him lead you in every step. ⁷Have your roots planted deep in Christ. Grow in Him. Get your strength from Him. Let Him make you strong in the faith as you have been taught. Your life should be full of thanks to Him.

Wisdom Of The World Is Empty

⁸Be careful that no one changes your mind and faith by much learning and big sounding ideas. Those things are what men dream up. They are always trying to make new religions. These leave out Christ. ⁹For Christ is not only God-like, He is God in human flesh. ¹⁰When you have Christ, you are complete. He is the head over all leaders and powers. ¹¹When you became a Christian, you were set free from the sinful things of the world. This was not done by human hands. You were set free from the sins of your old self by what was done in Christ's body. ¹²When you were baptized, you were buried as Christ was buried. When you were raised up in baptism, you were raised as Christ was raised. You were raised to a new life by putting your trust in God. It was God Who raised Jesus from the dead. ¹³When you were dead in your sins, you were not set free from the sinful things of the world. But God forgave your sins and gave you new life through Christ. ¹⁴We had broken the Law many ways. Those sins were held against us by the Law. That Law had writings which said we were sinners. But now He has destroyed that writing by nailing it to the cross. ¹⁵God took away the power of the leaders of this world and the powers of darkness. He showed them to the world. The battle was won over them through Christ.

For Christ is not only God-like, He is God in human flesh.

Watch For Those Who Want To Keep The Law

¹⁶Do not let anyone tell you what you should or should not eat or drink. They have no right to say if it is right or wrong to eat

certain foods or if you are to go to religious suppers. They have no right to say what you are to do at the time of the new moon or on the Day of Rest. [17]These things are a picture of what is coming. The important thing is Christ Himself. [18]Do not let anyone rob you of your prize. They will try to get you down on your knees to worship angels. They think this shows you are not proud. They say they were told to do this in a dream. These people are proud because of their sinful minds. [19]Such people are not a part of Christ. Christ is the Head. We Christians make up His body. We are joined together as a body is held together. Our strength to grow comes from Christ.

[20]You have died with Christ and become dead to those old ways. Then why do you follow the old ways of worship? Why do you obey man-made rules? [21]These rules say, "You must not put your hand on this." "Do not put this into your mouth." "You must not put your finger on that." [22]All these things come to an end when they are used. You are following only man-made rules. [23]It looks as if it is wise to follow these rules in an act of worship, because they are hard on the body. It looks as if they are done without pride, but they are worth nothing. They do not take away a man's desire to sin.

The New Life Lived By The Power Of Christ

3 If then you have been raised with Christ, keep looking for the good things of heaven. This is where Christ is seated on the right side of God. [2]Keep your minds thinking about things in heaven. Do not think about things on the earth. [3]You are dead to the things of this world. Your new life is now hidden in God through Christ. [4]Christ is our life. When He comes again, you will also be with Him to share His shining greatness.

Keep your minds thinking about things in heaven. Do not think about things on the earth.

The Old Person Put Aside

[5]Destroy the desires to sin that are in you. These desires are: sex sins, anything that is not clean, a desire for sex sins, and wanting something someone else has. This is worshiping a god. [6]It is because of these sins that the anger of God comes down on those who do not obey Him. [7]You used to do these sins when you

lived that kind of life.   ⁸Put out of your life these things also: anger, bad temper, bad feeling toward others, talk that hurts people, speaking against God, and dirty talk. ⁹Do not lie to each other. You have put out of your life your old ways. ¹⁰You have now become a new person and are always learning more about Christ. You are being made more like Christ. He is the One Who made you. ¹¹There is no difference in men in this new life. Greeks and Jews are the same. The man who has gone through the religious act of becoming a Jew and the one who has not are the same. There is no difference between nations. Men who are sold to work and those who are free are the same. Christ is everything. He is in all of us.

¹²God has chosen you. You are holy and loved by Him. Because of this, your new life should be full of loving-pity. You should be kind to others and have no pride. Be gentle and be willing to wait for others. ¹³Try to understand other people. Forgive each other. If you have something against someone, forgive him. That is the way the Lord forgave you. ¹⁴And to all these things, you must add love. Love holds everything and everybody together and makes all these good things perfect. ¹⁵Let the peace of Christ have power over your hearts. You were chosen as a part of His body. Always be thankful.

¹⁶Let the teaching of Christ and His words keep on living in you. These make your lives rich and full of wisdom. Keep on teaching and helping each other. Sing the Songs of David and the church songs and the songs of heaven with hearts full of thanks to God. ¹⁷Whatever you say or do, do it in the name of the Lord Jesus. Give thanks to God the Father through the Lord Jesus.

How Families Should Live

¹⁸Wives, obey your husbands. This is what the Lord wants you to do. ¹⁹Husbands, love your wives. Do not hold hard feelings against them. ²⁰Children, obey your parents in everything. The Lord is pleased when you do. ²¹Fathers, do not be so hard on your children that they will give up trying to do what is right.

²²You who are workmen who are owned by someone, obey your owners. Work hard for them all the time, not just when they are

watching you. Work for them as you would for the Lord because you honor God. 23Whatever work you do, do it with all your heart. Do it for the Lord and not for men. 24Remember that you will get your pay from the Lord. He will give you what you should receive. You are working for the Lord Christ. 25If anyone does wrong, he will suffer for it. God does not respect one person more than another.

4 Owners, give your workmen what is right. Do the same for all. Remember that your Owner is in heaven.

Some Things To Do

2You must keep praying. Keep watching! Be thankful always. 3As you pray, be sure to pray for us also. Pray that God will open the door for us to preach the Word. We want to tell the secret of Christ. And this is the reason I am in prison. 4Pray that I will be able to preach so everyone can understand. This is the way I should speak. 5Be wise in the way you live around those who are not Christians. Make good use of your time. 6Speak with them in such a way they will want to listen to you. Do not let your talk sound foolish. Know how to give the right answer to anyone.

Make good use of your time.

Paul's Helpers Say Hello

7Tychicus will tell you how I am getting along. He is a much-loved brother and faithful helper. Both of us are owned by the Lord. 8This is the reason I have sent him to you. It is so you can know about us. He can also bring joy to your hearts. 9Onesimus is going with Tychicus. He is one of your own people. He is faithful and we love him very much. They will tell you about everything here.

10One of the men here in prison with me is Aristarchus. He says hello. Mark, the cousin of Barnabas, says hello. (You have heard before that if he comes to you, you are to receive him and make him happy.) 11Jesus Justus says hello also. These are the only Jewish workers helping me teach about the holy nation of God. What a help they have been to me!

¹²Epaphras says hello. He is one of your people and a workman owned by Jesus Christ. As he prays for you, he asks God to help you to be strong and to make you perfect. He prays that you will know what God wants you to do in all things. ¹³I can tell you for sure that he works hard for you and for the Christians in the cities of Laodicea and Hierapolis. ¹⁴Luke, the dear doctor, and Demas say hello. ¹⁵Say hello to all the Christians in the city of Laodicea. Say hello to Nympha and the Christians who gather for church in her house.

¹⁶When this letter has been read to you, have it read in the church in the city of Laodicea also. Be sure you read the letter that is coming from Laodicea. ¹⁷Tell Archippus to be sure to finish the work the Lord called him to do.

¹⁸I, Paul, am writing this last part with my own hand. Do not forget that I am in prison. May you have God's loving-favor.

Paul Gives Thanks For Their Faith

1 This letter is from Paul and Silas and Timothy. It is to you, the church, in the city of Thessalonica. You belong to God the Father and the Lord Jesus Christ. May you have His loving favor and His peace.

²We thank God for you all the time and pray for you. ³While praying to God our Father, we always remember your work of faith and your acts of love and your hope that never gives up in our Lord Jesus Christ. ⁴Christian brothers, we know God loves you and that He has chosen you. ⁵The Good News did not come to you by word only, but with power and through the Holy Spirit. You knew it was true. You also knew how we lived among you. It was for your good. ⁶You followed our way of life and the life of the Lord. You suffered from others because of listening to us. But you had the joy that came from the Holy Spirit. ⁷Because of your good lives, you are showing all the Christians in the countries of Macedonia and Greece how to live. ⁸The Word of the Lord has been spoken by you in the countries of Macedonia and Greece. People everywhere know of your faith in God without our telling them. ⁹The people themselves tell us how you received us when we came to you. They talk of how you turned to God from worshiping false gods. Now you worship the true and living God. ¹⁰They tell us how you are waiting for His Son Jesus to come down from heaven. God raised Him from the dead. It is Jesus Who will save us from the anger of God that is coming.

2 Christian brothers, you know that my visit with you was not wasted. ²Just before we came to you, we had been in the city of Philippi. You know how they worked against us and made us suffer. But God helped us preach the Good News to you without fear, even while many people hated us and made it hard for us. ³You remember what we said to you was true. We had no wrong desire in teaching you. We did not try to fool you. ⁴God has allowed us to be trusted with the Good News. Because of this, we preach it to please God, not man. God tests and proves our hearts. [5]You know we never used smooth-sounding words. God knows we never tried to get money from you by preaching. [6]We never looked for thanks from men, not from you or from anyone else. But because we were missionaries of Christ, we could have asked you to do much for us. [7]Instead, we were gentle when we came to you. We were like a mother caring for her children. [8]We had such a strong desire to help you that we were happy to give you the Good News. Because we loved you so much, we were ready to give you our own lives also. [9]You remember, Christian brothers, we worked night and day for our food and clothes while we preached the Good News to you. We did not want to make it hard for you. [10]You know, and so does God, how pure and right and without blame we were among you who believe. [11]As a father helps his children, you know how we wanted to help you and give you comfort. We told you with strong words [12]that you should live to please God. He is the One Who chose you to come into His holy nation and to share His shining greatness.

You should live to please God.

[13]We always thank God that when you heard the Word of God from us, you believed it. You did not receive it as from men, but you received it as the Word of God. That is what it is. It is at work in the lives of you who believe. [14]Christian brothers, you became just like the churches in the country of Judea. You had to suffer from the men in your country as those churches had to suffer from the Jews. [15]It was the Jews who killed the Lord Jesus and the early preachers. The Jews made it hard for us and made us leave. They do not please God and are working against all men. [16]They tried to keep us from preaching the Good News to the people who are not Jews. The Jews do not want them saved from the punishment of sin. The lives of the Jews are full of more sin all the time. But now God's anger has come to them at last.

[17]Christian brothers, because we have not been able to be with you, our hearts have been with you. We have wanted very much to see you. [18]We wanted to come to you. I, Paul, have tried to come to you more than once but Satan kept us from coming. [19]Who is our hope or joy or prize of happiness? It is you, when you stand in front of our Lord Jesus Christ when He comes again. [20]You are our pride and joy.

3 When we could wait no longer, we decided it was best to stay in the city of Athens alone. ²And we sent Timothy to you. He works with us for God, teaching the Good News of Christ. We sent him to give strength and comfort to your faith. ³We do not want anyone to give up because of troubles. You know that we can expect troubles. ⁴Even when we were with you, we told you that much trouble would come to us. It has come as you can see. ⁵For this reason, I could wait no longer. I sent Timothy to find out about your faith. I was afraid the devil had tempted you. Then our work with you would be wasted.

⁶But Timothy has come to us from you. He brought good news about your faith and love. It is good to know that you think well of us and that you would like to see us. We would like to see you also. ⁷Christian brothers, word about your faith has made us happy even while we are suffering and are in much trouble. ⁸It is life to us to know that your faith in the Lord is strong. ⁹How can we give God enough thanks for you for all the joy you give us? ¹⁰We keep on praying night and day that we may see you again. We want to help your faith to be complete. ¹¹May our God and Father Himself and the Lord Jesus Christ take us on our way to you. ¹²May the Lord make you grow in love for each other and for everyone. We have this kind of love for you. ¹³May our God and Father make your hearts strong and without blame. May your hearts be without sin in God's sight when our Lord Jesus comes again with all those who belong to Him.

Paul Tells Them To Live Holy Lives

4 Christian brothers, we ask you, because of the Lord Jesus, to keep on living in a way that will please God. I have already told you how to grow in the Christian life. ²The Lord Jesus gave us the right and the power to tell you what to do. ³God wants you to be holy. You must keep away from sex sins. ⁴God wants each of you to use his body in the right way by keeping it holy and by respecting it. ⁵You should not use it to please your own desires like the people who do not know God. ⁶No man should do wrong to his Christian brother in anything. The Lord will punish a

God wants you
to be holy.
You must keep away
from sex sins.

For God has not called us to live in sin. He has called us to live a holy life.

person who does. I have told you this before. 7For God has not called us to live in sin. He has called us to live a holy life. 8The one who turns away from this teaching does not turn away from man, but from God. It is God Who has given us His Holy Spirit.

9You do not need anyone to write to you about loving your Christian brothers. God has taught you to love each other. 10You love all the Christians in all the country of Macedonia. But we ask you to love them even more. 11Do your best to live a quiet life. Learn to do your own work well. We told you about this before. 12By doing this, you will be respected by those who are not Christians. Then you will not be in need and others will not have to help you.

The Lord Is Coming Again

13Christian brothers, we want you to know for sure about those who have died. You have no reason to have sorrow as those who have no hope. 14We believe that Jesus died and then came to life again. Because we believe this, we know that God will bring to life again all those who belong to Jesus. 15We tell you this as it came from the Lord. Those of us who are alive when the Lord comes again will not go ahead of those who have died. 16For the Lord Himself will come down from heaven with a loud call. The head angel will speak with a loud voice. God's horn will give its sounds. First, those who belong to Christ will come out of their graves to meet the Lord. 17Then, those of us who are still living here on earth will be gathered together with them in the clouds. We will meet the Lord in the sky and be with Him forever. 18Because of this, comfort each other with these words.

Watch For The Lord To Come Again

5 You do not need anyone to write to tell you when and at what kind of times these things will happen. 2You know for sure that the day the Lord comes back to earth will be as a robber coming in the night. 3When they say, "Everything is fine and safe," then all at once they will be destroyed. It will be like pain that comes on a woman when a child is born. They will not be able to get away from it. 4But you are not in darkness, Christian

brothers. That day will not surprise you as a robber would. [5]For you are children of the light and of the day. We are not of darkness or of night. [6]Keep awake! Do not sleep like others. Watch and keep your minds awake to what is happening. [7]People sleep at night. Those who get drunk do it at night. [8]Because we are men of the day, let us keep our minds awake. Let us cover our chests with faith and love. Let us cover our heads with the hope of being saved. [9]God planned to save us from the punishment of sin through our Lord Jesus Christ. He did not plan for us to suffer from His anger. [10]He died for us so that, dead or alive, we will be with Him. [11]So comfort each other and make each other strong as you are already doing.

Christian Living

[12]We ask you, Christian brothers, to respect those who work among you. The Lord has placed them over you and they are your teachers. [13]You must think much of them and love them because of their work. Live in peace with each other.

[14]We ask you, Christian brothers, speak to those who do not want to work. Comfort those who feel they cannot keep going on. Help the weak. Understand and be willing to wait for all men. [15]Do not let anyone pay back for the bad he received. But look for ways to do good to each other and to all people

> Comfort those who feel they cannot keep going on.

[16]Be full of joy all the time. [17]Never stop praying. [18]In everything give thanks. This is what God wants you to do because of Christ Jesus. [19]Do not try to stop the work of the Holy Spirit. [20]Do not laugh at those who speak for God. [21]Test everything and do not let good things get away from you. [22]Keep away from everything that even looks like sin.

> In everything give thanks.

[23]May the God of peace set you apart for Himself. May every part of you be set apart for God. May your spirit and your soul and your body be kept complete. May you be without blame when our Lord Jesus Christ comes again. [24]The One Who called you is faithful and will do what He promised. [25]Christian brothers, pray for us. [26]Say hello to all the Christians with a kiss of holy love. [27]I tell you to have this letter read to all the Christians. [28]May you have loving-favor from our Lord Jesus Christ

> May the God of peace set you apart for Himself.

1 This letter is from Paul and Silas and Timothy. It is to the church in the city of Thessalonica that belongs to God the Father and the Lord Jesus Christ. ²May you have loving-favor and peace from God the Father and the Lord Jesus Christ.

³We must give thanks to God for you always, Christian brothers. It is the right thing to do because your faith is growing so much. Your love for each other is stronger all the time. ⁴We are proud of you and tell the other churches about you. We tell them how your faith stays so strong even when people make it very hard for you and make you suffer. ⁵God wants you to prove yourselves to be worth being in His holy nation by suffering for Him. ⁶He does what is right and will allow trouble to come to those who are making it hard for you. ⁷He will help you and us who are suffering. This will happen when the Lord Jesus comes down from heaven with His powerful angels in a bright fire. ⁸He will punish those who do not know God and those who do not obey the Good News of our Lord Jesus Christ. ⁹They will be punished forever and taken away from the Lord and from the shining greatness of His power. ¹⁰On the day He comes, His shining greatness will be seen in those who belong to Him. On that day, He will receive honor from all those who put their trust in Him. You believed what we had to say to you. ¹¹For this reason, we always pray for you. We pray that our God will make you worth being chosen. We pray that His power will help you do the good things you want to do. We pray that your work of faith will be complete. ¹²In this way, the name of the Lord Jesus Christ will be honored by you and you will be honored by Him. It is through the loving-favor of our God and of the Lord Jesus Christ.

Some People Will Believe A Lie

2 Our Lord Jesus Christ is coming again. We will be gathered together to meet Him. But we ask you, Christian brothers, ²do not be troubled in mind or worried by the talk you hear. Some say that the Lord has already come. People may say that I wrote this in a letter or that a spirit told them. ³Do not let anyone fool you. For the Lord will not come again until many people turn away from God. Then the leader of those who break the law will come. He is the man of sin. ⁴He works against and puts himself above every kind of god that is worshiped. He will take his seat in the house of God and say that he himself is God. ⁵Do you not remember that while I was with you, I told you this? ⁶You know the power that is keeping the man of sin back now. The man of sin will come only when his time is ready. ⁷For the secret power of breaking the law is already at work in the world. But that secret power can only do so much until the One Who keeps back the man of sin is taken out of the way. ⁸Then this man of sin will come. The Lord Jesus will kill him with the breath of His mouth. The coming of Christ will put an end to him. ⁹Satan will use this man of sin. He will have Satan's power. He will do strange things and many powerful works that will be false. ¹⁰Those who are lost in sin will be fooled by the things he can do. They are lost in sin because they did not love the truth that would save them. ¹¹For this reason, God will allow them to follow false teaching so they will believe a lie. ¹²They will all be guilty as they stand in front of God because they wanted to do what was wrong.

You Belong To Those Who Believe The Truth

¹³Christian brothers, the Lord loves you. We always thank God for you. It is because God has chosen you from the beginning to save you from the punishment of sin. He chose to make you holy by the Holy Spirit and to give you faith to believe the truth. ¹⁴It was by our preaching the Good News that you were chosen. He chose you to share the shining greatness of our Lord Jesus Christ. ¹⁵So then, Christian brothers, keep a strong hold on what we have taught you by what we have said and by what we have written.

¹⁶Our Lord Jesus Christ and God our Father loves us. Through His loving-favor He gives us comfort and hope that lasts forever. ¹⁷May He give your hearts comfort and strength to say and do every good thing.

Christian Brothers, Pray For Us

3 My last words to you, Christian brothers, are that you pray for us. Pray that the Word of the Lord will go out over all the land and prove its power just as it did with you. [2]Pray that we will be kept from sinful men, because not all men are Christians. [3]But the Lord is faithful. He will give you strength and keep you safe from the devil. [4]We have faith in the Lord for you. We believe you are doing and will keep on doing the things we told you. [5]May the Lord lead your hearts into the love of God. May He help you as you wait for Christ.

The Lord is faithful.

[6]Now this is what we tell you to do, Christian brothers. In the name of the Lord Jesus, keep away from any Christian who is lazy and who does not do what we taught you. [7]You know you should follow the way of life we lived when we were with you. We worked hard while we were there. [8]We did not eat anyone's food without paying for it. We worked hard night and day so none of you would have to give us anything. [9]We could have asked you to give us food. But we did not so that you might follow our way of living. [10]When we were with you, we told you that if a man does not work, he should not eat. [11]We hear that some are not working. But they are spending their time trying to see what others are doing. [12]Our words to such people are that they should be quiet and go to work. They should eat their own food. In the name of the Lord Jesus Christ we say this. [13]But you, Christian brothers, do not get tired of doing good. [14]If anyone does not want to listen to what we say in this letter, remember who he is and stay away from him. In that way, he will be put to shame. [15]Do not think of him as one who hates you. But talk to him as a Christian brother.

[16]May the Lord of peace give you His peace at all times. The Lord be with you all. [17]I, Paul, write this last part with my own hand. It is the way I finish all my letters. [18]May all of you have loving-favor from our Lord Jesus Christ.

1 This letter is from Paul, a missionary of Jesus Christ. I am sent by God, the One Who saves, and by our Lord Jesus Christ Who is our hope. ²I write to you, Timothy. You are my son in the Christian faith. May God the Father and Jesus Christ our Lord give you His loving-favor and loving-kindness and peace.

Watch For False Teachers

³When I left for the country of Macedonia, I asked you to stay in the city of Ephesus. I wanted you to stay there so you could tell those who are teaching what is not true to stop. ⁴They should not listen to stories that are not true. It is foolish for them to try to learn more about their early fathers. These only bring more questions to their minds and do not make their faith in God stronger. ⁵We want to see our teaching help you have a true love that comes from a pure heart. Such love comes from a heart that says we are not guilty and from a faith that does not pretend. ⁶But some have turned away from these things. They have turned to foolish talking. ⁷Some of them want to be teachers of the Jewish Law. But they do not know what they are talking about even if they act as if they do.

The Law Is Good

⁸We know the Jewish Law is good when it is used the way God meant it to be used. ⁹We must remember the Law is not for the person who is right with God. It is for those who do not obey anybody or anything. It is for the sinners who hate God and speak against Him. It is for those who kill their fathers and mothers and for those who kill other people. ¹⁰It is for those who do sex sins and for people who do sex sins with their own sex. It is for people who steal other people and for those who lie and for those who promise not to lie, but do. It is for everything that is against right teaching. ¹¹The great Good News of our honored God is right teaching. God has trusted me to preach this Good News.

The great Good News of our honored God is right teaching.

Paul Gives Thanks To God

¹²I thank Christ Jesus our Lord for the power and strength He has given me. He trusted me and gave me His work to do. ¹³Before He chose me, I talked bad about Christ. I made His followers suffer. I hurt them every way I could. But God had loving-kindness for me. I did not understand what I was doing for I was not a Christian then. ¹⁴Then our Lord gave me much of His loving-favor and faith and love which are found in Christ Jesus.

¹⁵What I say is true and all the world should receive it. Christ Jesus came into the world to save sinners from their sin and I am the worst sinner. ¹⁶And yet God had loving-kindness for me. Jesus Christ used me to show how long He will wait for even the worst sinners. In that way, others will know they can have life that lasts forever also. ¹⁷We give honor and thanks to the King Who lives forever. He is the One Who never dies and Who is never seen. He is the One Who knows all things. He is the only God. Let it be so.

The Good Fight Of Faith

¹⁸Timothy, my son, here is my word to you. Fight well for the Lord! God's preachers told us you would. ¹⁹Keep a strong hold on your faith in Christ. May your heart always say you are right. Some people have not listened to what their hearts say. They have done what they knew was wrong. Because of this, their faith in Christ was wrecked. ²⁰This happened to Hymenaeus and Alexander. I gave them over to Satan to teach them not to speak against God.

2 First of all, I ask you to pray much for all men and to give thanks for them. ²Pray for kings and all others who are in power over us so we might live quiet God-like lives in peace. ³It is good when you pray like this. It pleases God Who is the One Who saves. ⁴He wants all people to be saved from the punishment of sin. He wants them to come to know the truth. ⁵There is one God. There is one Man standing between God and men. That Man is Christ Jesus. ⁶He gave His life for all men so they could go free and not be held by the power of sin. God made this known to the world at the right time. ⁷This is why I was chosen to be a teacher and a missionary. I am to teach faith and truth to the people who do not know God. I am not lying but telling the truth.

Women In The Church

⁸I want men everywhere to pray. They should lift up holy hands as they pray. They should not be angry or argue. ⁹Christian women should not be dressed in the kind of clothes and their hair should not be combed in a way that will make people look at them. They should not wear much gold or pearls or clothes that cost much money. ¹⁰Instead of these things, Christian women should be known for doing good things and living good lives.

¹¹Women should be quiet when they learn. They should listen to what men have to say. ¹²I never let women teach men or be leaders over men. They should be quiet. ¹³Adam was made first, then Eve. ¹⁴Adam was not fooled by Satan. But it was the woman who was fooled and sinned. ¹⁵God will keep them safe when their children are born if they put their trust in Him and live loving and good lives.

What A Church Leader Must Be Like

3 It is true that if a man wants to be a church leader, he wants to do a good work. ²A church leader must be a good man. His life must be so no one can say anything against him. He must have only one wife and must be respected for his good living. He must be willing to take people into his home. He must be willing to learn and able to teach the Word of God. ³He must not get drunk or want to fight. Instead, he must be gentle. He must not have a love for money. ⁴He should be a good leader in his own home. His children must obey and respect him. ⁵If a man cannot be a good leader in his own home, how can he lead the church? ⁶A church leader must not be a new Christian. A new Christian might become proud and fall into sin which is brought on by the devil. ⁷A church leader must be respected by people who are not Christians so nothing can be said against him. In that way, he will not be trapped by the devil.

I want
men everywhere
to pray.

What The Church Helpers Must Be Like

⁸Church helpers must also be good men and act so people will respect them. They must speak the truth. They must not get drunk. They must not have a love for money. ⁹They must have their faith in Christ and be His followers with a heart that says they are right. ¹⁰They must first be tested to see if they are ready for the work as church helpers. Then if they do well, they may be chosen as church helpers. ¹¹The wives of church helpers must be careful how they act. They must not carry stories from one person to another. They must be wise and faithful in all they do. ¹²Church helpers must have only one wife. They must lead their home well and their children must obey them. ¹³Those who work well as church helpers will be respected by others and their own faith in Christ Jesus will grow.

Why Paul Writes To Timothy

¹⁴I hope to come to you soon. I am writing these things ¹⁵because it may be awhile before I get there. I wanted you to know how you should act among people in the church which is the house of the living God. The church holds up the truth. ¹⁶It is important to know the secret of God-like living, which is: Christ came to earth as a Man. He was pure in His Spirit. He was seen by angels. The nations heard about Him. Men everywhere put their trust in Him. He was taken up into heaven.

False Teaching In The Last Days

4 The Holy Spirit tells us in plain words that in the last days some people will turn away from the faith. They will listen to what is said about spirits and follow the teaching about demons. ²Those who teach this tell it as the truth when they know it is a lie. They do it so much that their own hearts no longer say it is wrong. ³They will say, "Do not get married. Do not eat some kinds of food." But God gave these things to Christians who know the truth. We are to thank God for them. ⁴Everything God made is good. We should not put anything aside if we can take it and thank God for it. ⁵It is made holy by the Word of God and prayer.

Christians Are To Grow

⁶If you keep telling these things to the Christians, you will be a good worker for Jesus Christ. You will feed your own soul on these words of faith and on this good teaching which you have followed. ⁷Have nothing to do with foolish stories old women tell. Keep yourself growing in God-like living. ⁸Growing strong in body is all right but growing in God-like living is more important. It will not only help you in this life now but in the next life also. ⁹These words are true and they can be trusted. ¹⁰Because of this, we work hard and do our best because our hope is in the living God, the One Who would save all men. He saves those who believe in Him.

> Growing strong in body is all right but growing in God-like living is more important.

Paul's Helpful Words To Young Timothy

¹¹Tell people that this is what they must do. ¹²Let no one show little respect for you because you are young. Show other Christians how to live by your life. They should be able to follow you in the way you talk and in what you do. Show them how to live in faith and in love and in holy living. ¹³Until I come, read and preach and teach the Word of God to the church. ¹⁴Be sure to use the gift God gave you. The leaders saw this in you when they laid their hands on you and said what you should do. ¹⁵Think about all this. Work at it so everyone may see you are growing as a Christian. ¹⁶Watch yourself how you act and what you teach. Stay true to what is right. If you do, you and those who hear you will be saved from the punishment of sin.

Teaching About Women Whose Husbands Have Died

5 Do not speak sharp words to an older man. Talk with him as if he were a father. Talk to younger men as brothers. ²Talk to older women as mothers. Talk to younger women as sisters, keeping yourself pure. ³Help women whose husbands have died. ⁴If a woman whose husband has died has children or grandchildren, they are the ones to care for her. In that way, they can pay back to their parents the kindness that has been shown to them. God is pleased when this is done. ⁵Women whose husbands have died are alone in this world. Their trust is in the Lord. They pray day and night. ⁶But the one who lives only for the joy she can receive from this world is the same as dead even if she is alive.

7Teach these things so they will do what is right. 8Anyone who does not take care of his family and those in his house has turned away from the faith. He is worse than a person who has never put his trust in Christ. 9A woman over sixty years old whose husband has died may receive help from the church. To receive this help, she must have been the wife of one man. 10She must be known for doing good things for people and for being a good mother. She must be known for taking strangers into her home and for washing the feet of Christians. She must be known for helping those who suffer and for showing kindness.

11Do not write the names of younger women whose husbands have died together with the names of others who need help. They will turn away from Christ because of wanting to get married again. 12Then they would be thought of as guilty of breaking their first promise. 13They will waste their time. They will go from house to house carrying stories. They will find fault with people and say things they should not talk about. 14I think it is best for younger women whose husbands have died to get married. They should have children and care for their own homes. Then no one can speak against them. 15Some of these women have already turned away to follow Satan. 16If you have any women whose husbands have died in your family, you must care for them. The church should not have to help them. The church can help women whose husbands have died who are all alone in this world and have no one else to help them.

Teaching About Leaders

17Older leaders who do their work well should be given twice as much pay, and for sure, those who work hard preaching and teaching. 18The Holy Writings say, "When a cow is walking on the grain to break it open, do not stop it from eating some" (Deuteronomy 25:4), and "A person who works should be paid." (Matthew 10:10)

19Do not listen to what someone says against a church leader unless two or three persons say the same thing. 20Show those who keep on sinning where they are wrong in front of the whole church. Then others will be afraid of sinning. 21I tell you from my heart that you must follow these rules without deciding before the truth is known. God and Jesus Christ and the chosen angels know what I am saying. Show favors to no one. ²²Do not be in a hurry about choosing a church leader. You do not want to have any part in other men's sins. Keep yourself pure.

²³Do not drink water only. Use a little wine because of your stomach and because you are sick so often.

²⁴The sins of some men can be seen. Their sins go before them and make them guilty. The sins of other men will be seen later. ²⁵In the same way, good works are easy to see now. But some that are not easy to be seen cannot always be hid.

Teaching About Christians Who Were Sold To Work

6 All you Christians who are owned by someone must respect your owners and work hard for them. Do not let the name of God and our teaching be spoken against because of poor work. ²Those who have Christian owners must respect their owners because they are Christian brothers. They should work hard for them because much-loved Christian brothers are being helped by their work. Teach and preach these things.

Live Like God Wants You To Live

³Someone may teach something else. He may not agree with the teaching of our Lord Jesus Christ. He may not teach you to live God-like lives. ⁴Such a person is full of pride and knows nothing. He wastes time on questions and argues about things that are not important. This makes those he teaches jealous and they want to fight. They talk bad and have bad ideas about others. ⁵Men who are not able to use their minds in the right way because of sin argue all the time. They do not have the truth. They think religion is a way to get much for themselves.

⁶A God-like life gives us much when we are happy for what we have. ⁷We came into this world with nothing. For sure, when we die, we will take nothing with us. ⁸If we have food and clothing, let us be happy. ⁹But men who want lots of money are tempted. They are trapped into doing all kinds of foolish things and things

which hurt them. These things drag them into sin and will destroy them. [10]The love of money is the beginning of all kinds of sin. Some people have turned from the faith because of their love for money. They have made much pain for themselves because of this.

Fight The Good Fight Of Faith

But you, man of God,
turn away from
all these sinful things.

Fight the good fight
of faith.
Take hold of the life
that lasts forever.

[11]But you, man of God, turn away from all these sinful things. Work at being right with God. Live a God-like life. Have faith and love. Be willing to wait. Have a kind heart. [12]Fight the good fight of faith. Take hold of the life that lasts forever. You were chosen to receive it. You have spoken well about this life in front of many people.

[13]I tell you this in front of God Who gives life to all people and in front of Jesus Christ Who spoke well in front of Pontius Pilate. [14]You must do all our Lord Jesus Christ said so no one can speak against you. Do this until He comes again. [15]At the right time, we will be shown that God is the One Who has all power. He is the King of kings and Lord of lords. [16]He can never die. He lives in a light so bright that no man can go near Him. No man has ever seen God or can see Him. Honor and power belong to Him forever. Let it be so.

Paul's Last Words To Timothy

[17]Tell those who are rich in this world not to be proud and not to trust in their money. Money cannot be trusted. They should put their trust in God. He gives us all we need for our happiness. [18]Tell them to do good and be rich in good works. They should give much to those in need and be ready to share. [19]Then they will be gathering together riches for themselves. These good things are what they will build on for the future. Then they will have the only true life!

[20]Timothy, keep safe what God has trusted you with. Turn away from foolish talk. Do not argue with those who think they know so much. They know less than they think they do. [21]Some people have gone after much learning. It has proved to be false and they have turned away from the faith. May you have God's loving-favor.

1 This letter is from Paul, a missionary of Jesus Christ. God has sent me to tell that He has promised life that lasts forever through Christ Jesus. ²I am writing to you, Timothy. You are my much-loved son. May God the Father and Christ Jesus our Lord give you His loving-favor and loving-kindness and peace.

Timothy's Special Gift

³I thank God for you. I pray for you night and day. I am working for God the way my early fathers worked. My heart says I am free from sin. ⁴When I remember your tears, it makes me want to see you. That would fill me with joy. ⁵I remember your true faith. It is the same faith your grandmother Lois had and your mother Eunice had. I am sure you have that same faith also.

⁶For this reason, I ask you to keep using the gift God gave you. It came to you when I laid my hands on you and prayed that God would use you. ⁷For God did not give us a spirit of fear. He gave us a spirit of power and of love and of a good mind. ⁸Do not be ashamed to tell others about what our Lord said, or of me here in prison. I am here because of Jesus Christ. Be ready to suffer for preaching the Good News and God will give you the strength you need. ⁹He is the One Who saved us from the punishment of sin. He is the One Who chose us to do His work. It is not because of anything we have done. But it was His plan from the beginning that He would give us His loving-favor through Christ Jesus. ¹⁰We know about it now because of the coming of Jesus Christ, the One Who saves. He put a stop to the power of death and brought life that never dies which is seen through the Good News. ¹¹I have been chosen to be a missionary and a preacher and a teacher of this Good News. ¹²For this reason, I am suffering. But I am not ashamed. I know the One in Whom I have put my trust. I am sure He is able to keep safe that which I have trusted to Him until the day He comes again. ¹³Keep all the things I taught you. They were given to you in the faith and love of Jesus Christ. ¹⁴Keep

I know the One in Whom
I have put my trust.
I am sure He is able
to keep safe that which
I have trusted to Him
until the day
He comes again.

safe that which He has trusted you with by the Holy Spirit Who lives in us.

Onesiphorus Was Faithful

[15]I am sure you have heard that all the Christians in the countries of Asia have turned away from me. Phygelus and Hermogenes turned away also. [16]Onesiphorus was not ashamed of me in prison. He came often to comfort me. May the Lord show loving-kindness to his family. [17]When he came to Rome, he looked everywhere until he found me. [18]You know what a help he was to me in Ephesus. When the Lord comes again, may He show loving-kindness to Onesiphorus.

Be A Good Soldier

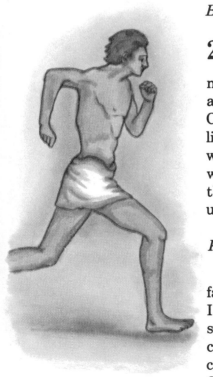

2 So you, my son, be strong in the loving-favor of Christ Jesus. [2]What you have heard me say in front of many people, you must teach to faithful men. Then they will be able to teach others also. [3]Take your share of suffering as a good soldier of Jesus Christ. [4]No soldier fighting in a war can take time to make a living. He must please the one who made him a soldier. [5]Anyone who runs in a race must follow the rules to get the prize. [6]A hardworking farmer should receive first some of what he gathers from the field. [7]Think about these things and the Lord will help you understand them.

Paul Is In Chains — The Good News Is Free

[8]Remember this! Jesus Christ, Who was born from the early family of David, was raised from the dead! This is the Good News I preach. [9]I suffer much and am in prison as one who has done something very bad. I am in chains, but the Word of God is not chained. [10]I suffer all things so the people that God has chosen can be saved from the punishment of their sin through Jesus Christ. Then they will have God's shining greatness that lasts forever. [11]These things are true. If we die with Him, we will live with Him also. [12]If we suffer and stay true to Him, then we will be a leader with Him. If we say we do not know Him, He will say He does not know us. [13]If we have no faith, He will still be faithful for He cannot go against what He is.

Foolish Talk

[14]Tell your people about these things again. In the name of the Lord, tell them not to argue over words that are not important. It helps no one and it hurts the faith of those who are listening. [15]Do your best to know that God is pleased with you. Be as a workman who has nothing to be ashamed of. Teach the words of truth in the right way. [16]Do not listen to foolish talk about things that mean nothing. It only leads people farther away from God. [17]Such talk will spread like cancer. Hymenaeus and Philetus are like this. [18]They have turned from the truth. They say the dead have already been raised. The faith of some people has been made weak because of such foolish talk. [19]But the truth of God cannot be changed. It says, "The Lord knows those who are His." And, "Everyone who says he is a Christian must turn away from sin!"

[20]In a big house there are not only things made of gold and silver, but also of wood and clay. Some are of more use than others. Some are used every day. [21]If a man lives a clean life, he will be like a dish made of gold. He will be respected and set apart for good use by the owner of the house.

[22]Turn away from the sinful things young people want to do. Go after what is right. Have a desire for faith and love and peace. Do this with those who pray to God from a clean heart. [23]Let me say it again. Have nothing to do with foolish talk and those who want to argue. It can only lead to trouble. [24]A workman owned by God must not make trouble. He must be kind to everyone. He must be able to teach. He must be willing to suffer when hurt for doing good. [25]Be gentle when you try to teach those who are against what you say. God may change their hearts so they will turn to the truth. [26]Then they will know they had been held in a trap by the devil to do what he wanted them to do. But now they are able to get out of it.

Things That Will Happen In The Last Days

3 You must understand that in the last days there will come times of much trouble. [2]People will love themselves and money. They will have pride and tell of all the things they have

The Lord knows those who are His.

Everyone who says he is a Christian must turn away from sin!

Go after what is right.

done. They will speak against God. Children and young people will not obey their parents. People will not be thankful and they will not be holy. ³They will not love each other. No one can get along with them. They will tell lies about others. They will not be able to keep from doing things they know they should not do. They will be wild and want to beat and hurt those who are good. ⁴They will not stay true to their friends. They will act without thinking. They will think too much of themselves. They will love fun instead of loving God. ⁵They will do things to make it look as if they are Christians. But they will not receive the power that is for a Christian. Keep away from such people.

⁶These are the kind of people who go from house to house. They talk to foolish women who are loaded down with sins and all kinds of sinful desires. ⁷Such women are always listening to new teaching. But they are never able to understand the truth. ⁸Jannes and Jambres fought against Moses. So do these teachers fight against the truth today. Their minds think only of sinful things. They have turned against the Christian teaching. ⁹They will not get very far. Their foolish teaching will be seen by everyone. That was the way it was with the two who worked against Moses.

Teach The Truth

¹⁰But you know what I teach and how I live. You know what I want to do. You know about my faith and my love. You know how long I am willing to wait for something. You know how I keep on working for God even when it is hard for me. ¹¹You know about all the troubles and hard times I have had. You have seen how I suffered in the cities of Antioch and Iconium and Lystra. Yet the Lord brought me out of all those troubles. ¹²Yes! All who want to live a God-like life who belong to Christ Jesus will suffer from others. ¹³Sinful men and false teachers will go from bad to worse. They will lead others the wrong way and will be led the wrong way themselves.

Hold on to what you have learned and know to be true.

¹⁴But as for you, hold on to what you have learned and know to be true. Remember where you learned them. ¹⁵You have known the Holy Writings since you were a child. They are able to give you wisdom that leads to being saved from the punishment of sin

by putting your trust in Christ Jesus. ¹⁶All the Holy Writings are God-given and are made alive by Him. Man is helped when he is taught God's Word. It shows what is wrong. It changes the way of a man's life. It shows him how to be right with God. ¹⁷It gives the man who belongs to God everything he needs to work well for Him.

All the Holy Writings are God-given and are made alive by Him.

Paul's Work Is Finished — Timothy Must Carry On

4 These words are from my heart to you. I say this in front of God and Jesus Christ. Some day He will say who is guilty and who is not of those who are living and of those who are dead. It will be when Christ comes to bring His holy nation. ²Preach the Word of God. Preach it when it is easy and people want to listen and when it is hard and people do not want to listen. Preach it all the time. Use the Word of God to show people they are wrong. Use the Word of God to help them do right. You must be willing to wait for people to understand what you teach as you teach them.

³The time will come when people will not listen to the truth. They will look for teachers who will tell them only what they want to hear. ⁴They will not listen to the truth. Instead, they will listen to stories made up by men. ⁵You must watch for all these things. Do not be afraid to suffer for our Lord. Preach the Good News from place to place. Do all the work you are to do.

⁶It will soon be time for me to leave this life. ⁷I have fought a good fight. I have finished the work I was to do. I have kept the faith. ⁸There is a prize which comes from being right with God. The Lord, the One Who will say who is guilty, will give it to me on that great day when He comes again. I will not be the only one to receive a prize. All those who love to think of His coming and are looking for Him will receive one also.

Paul Sends Word To Timothy About Some Friends

⁹Come to me here as soon as you can. ¹⁰Demas left me. He loved the things of this world and has gone to the city of Thessalonica. Crescens has gone to the city of Galatia. Titus has gone to the city

of Dalmatia. ¹¹Luke is the only one with me here. Bring Mark when you come. He is a help to me in this work. ¹²I sent Tychicus to the city of Ephesus. ¹³When you come, bring the coat I left with Carpus in the city of Troas. Bring the books and for sure do not forget the writings written on sheepskin. ¹⁴Alexander, the man who makes things out of copper, has worked hard against me. The Lord will give him the pay that is coming to him. ¹⁵Watch him! He fought against every word we preached.

¹⁶At my first trial no one helped me. Everyone left me. I hope this will not be held against them. ¹⁷But the Lord was with me. He gave me power to preach the Good News so all the people who do not know God might hear. I was taken from the mouth of the lion. ¹⁸The Lord will look after me and will keep me from every sinful plan they have. He will bring me safe into His holy nation of heaven. May He have all the shining greatness forever. Let it be so.

¹⁹Say hello to Prisca and Aquila for me and to all the family of Onesiphorus. ²⁰Erastus stayed in the city of Corinth. I left Trophimus sick in the city of Miletus. ²¹Try to come before winter. Eubulus, Pudens, Linus, Claudia, and all the Christian brothers say hello to you. ²²May the Lord Jesus Christ be with your spirit. May you have God's loving-favor.

1 This letter is from Paul, a workman owned by God. And I am a missionary of Jesus Christ. I have been sent to those God has chosen for Himself. I am to teach them the truth that leads to God-like living. ²This truth also gives hope of life that lasts forever. God promised this before the world began. He cannot lie. ³He made this known at the right time through His Word. God, the One Who saves, told me I should preach it. ⁴I am writing to you, Titus. You are my true son in the faith which we both have. May you have loving-favor and peace from God the Father and Jesus Christ, the One Who saves.

What A Church Leader Must Be Like

⁵I left you on the island of Crete so you could do some things that needed to be done. I asked you to choose church leaders in every city. ⁶Their lives must be so that no one can talk against them. They must have only one wife. Their children must be Christians and known to be good. They must obey their parents. They must not be wild. ⁷A church leader is God's workman. His life must be so that no one can say anything against him. He should not try to please himself and not be quick to get angry over little things. He must not get drunk or want to fight. He must not always want more money for himself. ⁸He must like to take people into his home. He must love what is good. He must be able to think well and do all things in the right way. He must live a holy life and be the boss over his own desires. ⁹He must hold to the words of truth which he was taught. He must be able to teach the truth and show those who are against the truth that they are wrong.

False Teachers

¹⁰There are many men who will not listen or will not obey the truth. Their teaching is foolish and they lead people to believe a lie. Some Jews believe their lies. ¹¹This must be stopped. It turns whole families from the truth. They teach these things to make money. ¹²One of their own teachers said, "People of the island of

Crete always lie. They are like wild animals. They are lazy. All they want to do is eat." ¹³This is true of them. Speak sharp words to them because it is true. Lead them into the right way so they will have strong faith. ¹⁴Do not let them listen to Jewish stories made up by men. Do not let them listen to man-made rules which lead them away from the truth. ¹⁵All things are pure to the man with a pure heart. But to sinful people nothing is pure. Both their minds and their hearts are bad. ¹⁶They say they know God, but by the way they act, they show that they do not. They are sinful people. They will not obey and are of no use for any good work.

Right Teaching

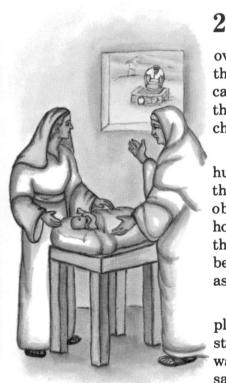

2 You must teach what is right and true. ²Older men are to be quiet and to be careful how they act. They are to be the boss over their own desires. Their faith and love are to stay strong and they are not to give up. ³Teach older women to be quiet and to be careful how they act also. They are not to go around speaking bad things about others or things that are not true. They are not to be chained by strong drink. They should teach what is good.

⁴Older women are to teach the young women to love their husbands and children. ⁵They are to teach them to think before they act, to be pure, to be workers at home, to be kind, and to obey their own husbands. In this way, the Word of God is honored. ⁶Also teach young men to be wise. ⁷In all things show them how to live by your life and by right teaching. ⁸You should be wise in what you say. Then the one who is against you will be ashamed and will not be able to say anything bad about you.

⁹Those who are owned by some one must obey their owners and please them in everything. They must not argue. ¹⁰They must not steal from their owners but prove they can be trusted in every way. In this way, their lives will honor the teaching of God Who saves us.

We are to live God-like lives in this world.

¹¹God's free gift of being saved is being given to everyone. ¹²We are taught to have nothing to do with that which is against God. We are to have nothing to do with the desires of this world. We are to be wise and to be right with God. We are to live God-like lives in this world. ¹³We are to be looking for the great hope and the

coming of our great God and the One Who saves, Christ Jesus. [14]He gave Himself for us. He did this by buying us with His blood and making us free from all sin. He gave Himself so His people could be clean and want to do good. [15]Teach all these things and give words of help. Show them if they are wrong. You have the right and the power to do this. Do not let anyone think little of you.

The Work Of A Leader

3 Teach your people to obey the leaders of their country. They should be ready to do any good work. [2]They must not speak bad of anyone, and they must not argue. They should be gentle and kind to all people.

God Saved Us From All These Things

[3]There was a time when we were foolish and did not obey. We were fooled in many ways. Strong desires held us in their power. We wanted only to please ourselves. We wanted what others had and were angry when we could not have them. We hated others and they hated us.

[4]But God, the One Who saves, showed how kind He was and how He loved us [5]by saving us from the punishment of sin. It was not because we worked to be right with God. It was because of His loving-kindness that He washed our sins away. At the same time He gave us new life when the Holy Spirit came into our lives. [6]God gave the Holy Spirit to fill our lives through Jesus Christ, the One Who saves. [7]Because of this, we are made right with God by His loving-favor. Now we can have life that lasts forever as He has promised.

[8]What I have told you is true. Teach these things all the time so those who have put their trust in God will be careful to do good things. These things are good and will help all men.

Paul's Last Words To Titus

[9]Do not argue with people about foolish questions and about the Jewish Law. Do not spend time talking about all of your early

But God,
the One Who saves,
showed
how kind He was
and how He loved us
by saving us from
the punishment of sin.

fathers. This does not help anyone and it is of no use. ¹⁰Talk once or twice to a person who tries to divide people into groups against each other. If he does not stop, have nothing to do with him. ¹¹You can be sure he is going the wrong way. He is sinning and he knows it.

¹²I will send Artemas or Tychicus to you. As soon as one of them gets there, try to come to me in the city of Nicopolis. I have decided to spend the winter there. ¹³Zenas, the man who knows the law, and Apollos are going on a trip. Do everything you can to help them. ¹⁴Our people must learn to work hard. They must work for what they need and be able to give to others who need help. Then their lives will not be wasted. ¹⁵All those with me here say hello to you. Say hello to my Christian friends there. May you have God's loving-favor.

1 This letter is from Paul. I am in prison because of Jesus Christ. Brother Timothy is also writing to you, Philemon. You are a much-loved workman together with us. ²We are also writing to the church that meets in your home. This letter is also for our Christian sister Apphia and it is for Archippus who is a soldier together with us. ³May God our Father and the Lord Jesus Christ give you His loving-favor and peace.

⁴I always thank God when I speak of you in my prayers. ⁵It is because I hear of your love and trust in the Lord Jesus and in all the Christians. ⁶I pray that our faith together will help you know all the good things you have through Christ Jesus. ⁷Your love has given me much joy and comfort. The hearts of the Christians have been made happy by you, Christian brother.

⁸So now, through Christ, I am free to tell you what you must do. ⁹But because I love you, I will only ask you. I am Paul, an old man, here in prison because of Jesus Christ. ¹⁰I am asking you for my son, Onesimus. He has become my son in the Christian life while I have been here in prison. ¹¹At one time he was of no use to you. But now he is of use to you and to me. ¹²I am sending him back to you. It is like sending you my own heart. ¹³I would like to keep him with me. He could have helped me in your place while I am in prison for preaching the Good News. ¹⁴But I did not want to keep him without word from you. I did not want you to be kind to me because you had to but because you wanted to. ¹⁵He ran away from you for awhile. But now he is yours forever. ¹⁶Do not think of him any longer as a workman you own. He is more than that to you. He is a much-loved Christian brother to you and to me.

¹⁷If you think of me as a true friend, take him back as you would take me. ¹⁸If he has done anything wrong or owes you anything, send me the bill. ¹⁹I will pay it. I, Paul, am writing this with my own hand. I will not talk about how much you owe me because you owe me your life. ²⁰Yes, Christian brother, I want you to be of use

to me as a Christian. Give my heart new joy in Christ. 21I write this letter knowing you will do what I ask and even more.

22Please have a room ready for me. I trust God will answer your prayers and let me come to you soon. 23Epaphras says hello. He is a brother in Christ in prison with me. 24Mark and Aristarchus and Demas and Luke who are workers with me say hello. 25May the loving-favor of the Lord Jesus Christ be with your spirit.

God Speaks Through His Son

1 Long ago God spoke to our early fathers in many different ways. He spoke through the early preachers. ²But in these last days He has spoken to us through His Son. God gave His Son everything. It was by His Son that God made the world. ³The Son shines with the shining greatness of the Father. The Son is as God is in every way. It is the Son Who holds up the whole world by the power of His Word. The Son gave His own life so we could be clean from all sin. After He had done that, He sat down on the right side of God in heaven.

The Son Was Greater Than The Angels

⁴The Son of God was made greater and better than the angels. God gave Him a greater name than theirs. ⁵God did not say to any of His angels, "You are My Son. Today I have become your Father." (Psalm 2:7) And He did not say to any angel, "I will be a Father to him. He will be a son to Me." (II Samuel 7:14) ⁶But when God brought His first-born Son, Jesus, into the world, He said, "Let all the angels of God worship Him." ⁷He said this about the angels, "He makes His angels to be winds. He makes those who work for Him a burning fire." (Psalm 104:4) ⁸But about His Son, He says, "O God, Your place of power will last forever. Whatever You say in Your nation is right and good. ⁹You have loved what is right. You have hated what is wrong. That is why God, Your God, has chosen You. He has poured over You the oil of joy more than over anyone else." (Psalm 45:6-7) ¹⁰He said also, "Lord, You made the earth in the beginning. You made the heavens with Your hands. ¹¹They will be destroyed but You will always be here. They will all become old just as clothes become old. ¹²You will roll up the heavens like a coat. They will be changed. But You are always the same. You will never grow old." (Psalm 102:25-27) ¹³God never said to any angel, "Sit at My right side, until I make those who hate You a place to rest Your feet." (Psalm 110:1) ¹⁴Are not all the angels spirits who work for God?

They are sent out to help those who are to be saved from the punishment of sin.

Do Not Wait To Be Saved From The Punishment Of Sin

2 That is why we must listen all the more to the truths we have been told. If we do not, we may slip away from them. ²These truths given by the angels proved to be true. People were punished when they did not obey them. ³God was so good to make a way for us to be saved from the punishment of sin. What makes us think we will not go to hell if we do not take the way to heaven that He has made for us. The Lord was the first to tell us of this. Then those who heard Him told it later. ⁴God proved what they said was true by showing us special things to see and by doing powerful works. He gave the gifts of the Holy Spirit as He wanted to.

Jesus, The Way To Heaven

⁵God did not make angels to be the leaders of that world to come which we have been speaking about. ⁶Instead, the Holy Writings say, "What is man that You think of him and the son of man that You should remember him?" (Psalm 8:4) ⁷"You made him so he took a place that was not as important as the angels for a little while. You gave him the prize of honor and shining greatness. *You made him the head over everything You have made. ⁸You have put everything under his feet." (Psalm 8:4-6) There is nothing that does not obey him, but we do not see all things obey him yet. ⁹But we do see Jesus. For a little while He took a place that was not as important as the angels. But God had loving-favor for everyone. He had Jesus suffer death on a cross for all of us. Then, because of Christ's death on a cross, God gave Him the prize of honor and shining greatness.

¹⁰God made all things. He made all things for Himself. It was right for God to make Jesus a perfect Leader by having Him suffer for men's sins. In this way, He is bringing many men to share His shining greatness. ¹¹Jesus makes men holy. He takes away their sins. Both Jesus and the ones being made holy have the same Father. That is why Jesus is not ashamed to call them

His brothers. ¹²Jesus is saying to His Father, "I will tell My brothers Your names. I will sing songs of thanks for You among the people." (Psalm 22:22) ¹³And again He says, "I will put My trust in God." At another time He said, "Here I am with the children God gave Me." (Isaiah 8:17-18)

¹⁴It is true that we share the same Father with Jesus. And it is true that we share the same kind of flesh and blood because Jesus became a man like us. He died as we must die. Through His death He destroyed the power of the devil who has the power of death. ¹⁵Jesus did this to make us free from the fear of death. We no longer need to be chained to this fear. ¹⁶Jesus did not come to help angels. Instead, He came to help men who are of Abraham's family. ¹⁷So Jesus had to become like His brothers in every way. He had to be one of us to be our Religious Leader to go between God and us. He had loving-pity on us and He was faithful. He gave Himself as a gift to die on a cross for our sins so that God would not hold these sins against us any longer. ¹⁸Because Jesus was tempted as we are and suffered as we do, He understands us and He is able to help us when we are tempted.

Because Jesus was tempted as we are and suffered as we do, He understands us and He is able to help us when we are tempted.

Jesus Was Greater Than Moses

3 Christian brothers, you have been chosen and set apart by God. So let us think about Jesus. He is the One God sent and He is the Religious Leader of our Christian faith. ²Jesus was faithful in God's house just as Moses was faithful in all of God's house. ³The man who builds a house gets more honor than the house. That is why Jesus gets more honor than Moses. ⁴Every house is built by someone. And God is the One Who has built everything. ⁵Moses was a faithful workman owned by God in God's house. He spoke of the things that would be told about later on. ⁶But Christ was faithful as a Son Who is Head of God's house. We are of God's house if we keep our trust in the Lord until the end. This is our hope. ⁷The Holy Spirit says, "If you hear His voice today, ⁸do not let your hearts become hard as your early fathers did when they turned against Me. It was at that time in the desert when they put Me to the test. ⁹Your early fathers tempted Me and tried Me. They saw the work I did for forty years. ¹⁰For this reason, I was angry with the people of this day.

And I said to them, 'They always think wrong thoughts. They have never understood what I have tried to do for them.' [11]I was angry with them and said to Myself, 'They will never go into My rest.' " (Psalm 95:7-11)

[12]Christian brothers, be careful that not one of you has a heart so bad that it will not believe and will turn away from the living **Help each other.** God. [13]Help each other. Speak day after day to each other while it is still today so your heart will not become hard by being fooled by sin. [14]For we belong to Christ if we keep on trusting Him to the end just as we trusted Him at first. [15]The Holy Writings say, "If you hear His voice today, do not let your hearts become hard as your early fathers did when they turned against Me." (Psalm 95:7-8)

[16]Who heard God's voice and turned against Him? Did not all those who were led out of the country of Egypt by Moses? [17]Who made God angry for forty years? Was it not those people who had sinned in the desert? Was it not those who died and were buried there? [18]Who did He say could never go into His rest? Was it not those who did not obey Him? [19]So we can see that they were not able to go into His rest because they did not put their trust in Him.

The Christian's Rest

4 The same promise of going into God's rest is still for us. But we should be afraid that some of us may not be able to go in. [2]We have heard the Good News even as they did, but it did them no good because it was not mixed with faith. [3]We who have put our trust in God go into His rest. God said this of our early fathers, "I was angry and said, 'They will not go into My rest.' " (Psalm 95:11) And yet God's work was finished after He made the world.

God's Rest

[4]In the Holy Writings He said this about the seventh day when He made the whole world, "God rested on the seventh day from all He had made." (Genesis 2:2) [5]But God said this about those who turned against Him, "They will not go into My rest." (Psalm

95:11) ⁶Those who heard the Good News first did not go into His rest. It was because they had not obeyed Him. But the promise is still good and some are going into His rest. ⁷God has again set a certain day for people to go into His rest. He says through David many years later as He had said before, "If you hear His voice today, do not let your hearts become hard." (Psalm 95:7-8)

⁸If Joshua had led those people into God's rest, He would not have told of another day after that. ⁹And so God's people have a complete rest waiting for them. ¹⁰The man who goes into God's rest, rests from his own work the same as God rested from His work. ¹¹Let us do our best to go into that rest or we will be like the people who did not go in.

¹²God's Word is living and powerful. It is sharper than a sword that cuts both ways. It cuts straight into where the soul and spirit meet and it divides them. It cuts into the joints and bones. It tells what the heart is thinking about and what it wants to do. ¹³No one can hide from God. His eyes see everything we do. We must give an answer to God for what we have done.

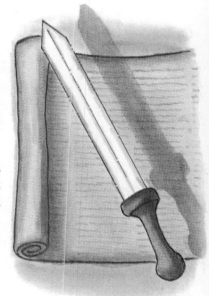

Jesus — Our Great Religious Leader

¹⁴We have a great Religious Leader Who has made the way for man to go to God. He is Jesus, the Son of God, Who has gone to heaven to be with God. Let us keep our trust in Jesus Christ. ¹⁵Our Religious Leader understands how weak we are. Christ was tempted in every way we are tempted, but He did not sin. ¹⁶Let us go with complete trust to the very place of God's loving-favor. We will receive His loving-kindness and have His loving-favor to help us whenever we need it.

Christ was tempted in every way we are tempted, but He did not sin.

The Job Of A Religious Leader

5 Every Jewish religious leader is chosen from among men. He is a helper standing between God and men. He gives gifts on the altar in worship to God from the people. He gives blood from animals for the sins of the people. ²A Jewish religious leader is weak in many ways because he is just a man himself. He knows how to be gentle with those who know little. He knows how to help those who are doing wrong. ³Because he is weak himself, he must give gifts to God for his own sins as well as for the sins of the people. ⁴A Jewish religious leader does not choose this honor for himself. God chooses a man for this work. Aaron was chosen this way.

Christ Is Our Religious Leader Who Has Made The Way For Man To Go To God

⁵It is the same way with Christ. He did not choose the honor of being a Religious Leader Who has made the way for man to go to God. Instead, God said to Christ, "You are My Son. Today I have become Your Father." (Psalm 2:7) ⁶God says in another part of His Word, "You will be a Religious Leader forever. You will be like Melchizedek." (Psalm 110:4) ⁷During the time Jesus lived on earth, He prayed and asked God with loud cries and tears. Jesus' prayer was to God Who was able to save Him from death. God heard Christ because Christ honored God. ⁸Even being God's Son, He learned to obey by the things He suffered. ⁹And having been made perfect, He planned and made it possible for all those who obey Him to be saved from the punishment of sin. ¹⁰In God's plan He was to be a Religious Leader Who made the way for man to go to God. He was like Melchizedek.

Do Not Fall Back Into Sin

¹¹There is much we could say about this, but it is hard to make you understand. It is because you do not want to hear well. ¹²By now you should be teachers. Instead, you need someone to teach you again the first things you need to know from God's Word. You still need milk instead of solid food. ¹³Anyone who lives on milk cannot understand the teaching about being right with God. He is a baby. ¹⁴Solid food is for full-grown men. They have learned to use their minds to tell the difference between good and bad.

Going Ahead

6 So let us leave the first things you need to know about Christ. Let us go on to the teaching that full-grown Christians should understand. We do not need to teach these first truths again. You already know that you must be sorry for your sins and turn from them. You know that you must have faith in God. ²You know about being baptized and about putting hands on people. You know about being raised from the dead and about being punished forever. ³We will go on, if God lets us.

⁴There are those who have known the truth. They have received the gift from heaven. They have shared the Holy Spirit. ⁵They know how good the Word of God is. They know of the powers of the world to come. ⁶But if they turn away, they cannot be sorry for their sins and turn from them again. It is because they are nailing the Son of God on a cross again. They are holding Him up in shame in front of all people. ⁷It is the same with a piece of ground that has had many rains fall on it. God makes it possible for that ground to give good fruits and vegetables. ⁸But if it gives nothing but weeds, it is worth nothing. It will be hated and destroyed by fire.

⁹Dear friends, even as we tell you this, we are sure of better things for you. These things go along with being saved from the punishment of sin. ¹⁰God always does what is right. He will not forget the work you did to help the Christians and the work you are still doing to help them. This shows your love for Christ. ¹¹We want each one of you to keep on working to the end. Then what you hope for, will happen. ¹²Do not be lazy. Be like those who have faith and have not given up. They will receive what God has promised them.

God's Promise

¹³When God made a promise to Abraham, He made that promise in His own name because no one was greater. ¹⁴He said, "I will make you happy in so many ways. For sure, I will give you many children." (Genesis 22:16-17) ¹⁵Abraham was willing to wait and God gave to him what He had promised.

¹⁶When men make a promise, they use a name greater than themselves. They do this to make sure they will do what they promise. In this way, no one argues about it. ¹⁷And so God made a promise. He wanted to show Abraham that He would never change His mind. So He made the promise in His own name.

¹⁸God gave these two things that cannot be changed and God cannot lie. We who have turned to Him can have great comfort knowing that He will do what He has promised. ¹⁹This hope is a safe anchor for our souls. It will never move. This hope goes into the Holiest Place of All behind the curtain of heaven. ²⁰Jesus has already gone there. He has become our Religious Leader forever and has made the way for man to go to God. He is like Melchizedek.

Melchizedek — Like Christ

7 Melchizedek was king of Salem. He was a religious leader for God. When Abraham was coming back from the war where many kings were killed, Melchizedek met Abraham and showed respect to him. ²Abraham gave Melchizedek one-tenth part of all he had. Melchizedek's name means king of what is right. Salem means peace. So he is king of peace. ³Melchizedek was without a father or mother or any family. He had no beginning of life or end of life. He is a religious leader forever like the Son of God.

⁴We can see how great Melchizedek was. Abraham gave him one-tenth part of all he had taken in the war. ⁵The Jewish Law made the family of Levi the Jewish religious leaders. The Law said that the religious leaders were to take one-tenth part of everything from their own people. ⁶Melchizedek was not even from the family group of Levi but Abraham paid him. Melchizedek showed respect to Abraham who was the one who had received God's promises. ⁷The one who shows respect is always greater than the one who receives it. ⁸Jewish religious leaders receive one-tenth part. They are men and they all die. But here Melchizedek received one-tenth part and is alive. ⁹We might say that Levi, the head of the family group of Jewish religious leaders, received one-tenth part through Abraham. ¹⁰Levi was not yet born. He was still inside Abraham's body when Abraham paid Melchizedek.

¹¹The Jewish Law was given during the time when Levi and his sons were the religious leaders. If the work of those religious leaders had been perfect in taking away the sins of the people, there would have been no need for another religious leader. But one like Melchizedek was needed and not one from the family

group of Aaron. ¹²For when the family group of religious leaders
changed, the Jewish Law had to be changed also. ¹³These things
speak of Christ Who is from another family group. That family
group never had a religious leader who killed animals and gave
gifts at the altar for the sins of the people. ¹⁴Our Lord came from
the family group of Judah. Moses did not write anything about
religious leaders coming from that family group.

A Different Religious Leader Has Come

¹⁵We can see that a different Religious Leader has come. This
One is like Melchizedek. ¹⁶Christ did not become a Religious
Leader by coming from the family group of Levi as the Jewish
Law said had to be. He became the Religious Leader by the power
of a life that never ends. ¹⁷The Holy Writings say this about
Christ, "You are a Religious Leader forever like Melchizedek."
(Psalm 110:4)

¹⁸God put the Law of Moses aside. It was weak and could not be
used. ¹⁹For the Law of Moses could not make men right with God.
Now there is a better hope through which we can come near to
God.

²⁰God made a promise when Christ became the Religious Leader
Who made the way for man to go to God. ²¹God did not make such
a promise when Levi's family group became religious leaders. But
when Christ became a Religious Leader, this is the promise God
made, "The Lord has made a promise. He will never change His
mind. You will be a Religious Leader forever." (Psalm110:4)
²²Christ makes this New Way of Worship sure for us because of
God's promise. ²³There had to be many religious leaders during
the time of the Old Way of Worship. They died and others had to
keep on in their work. ²⁴But Jesus lives forever. He is the
Religious Leader forever. It will never change. ²⁵And so Jesus is
able, now and forever, to save from the punishment of sin all who
come to God through Him because He lives forever to pray for
them.

²⁶We need such a Religious Leader Who made the way for man
to go to God. Jesus is holy and has no guilt. He has never sinned
and is different from sinful men. He has the place of honor above
the heavens. ²⁷Christ is not like other religious leaders. They had

to give gifts every day on the altar in worship for their own sins first and then for the sins of the people. Christ did not have to do that. He gave one gift on the altar and that gift was Himself. It was done once and it was for all time. ²⁸The Jewish Law makes religious leaders of men. These men are not perfect. After the Law was given, God spoke with a promise. He made His Son a perfect Religious Leader forever.

We have such a Religious Leader Who has made the way for man to go to God.

8 Now the important thing is this: We have such a Religious Leader Who has made the way for man to go to God. He is the One Who sits at the right side of the All-powerful God in the heavens. ²He is the Religious Leader of that holy place in heaven which is the true place of worship. It was built by the Lord and not by men's hands. ³Every religious leader of the Old Way of Worship had the work of killing animals and of giving gifts on the altar to God. So Christ had to have something to give also. ⁴If Christ were on the earth, He would not be a religious leader such as these. The religious leaders on earth give gifts like the Jewish Law says. ⁵Their work shows us only a picture of the things in heaven. When Moses was putting up the tent to worship in, God told him, "Be sure you make the tent for worship like I showed you on the Mountain of Sinai." (Exodus 25:40)

⁶But Christ has a more perfect work. He is the One Who goes between God and man in this new and better way. The New Way of Worship promises better things. ⁷If the Old Way of Worship had been perfect, there would have been no need for another one. ⁸God was not happy how the people lived by the Old Way of Worship. He said, "The day will come when I will make a New Way of Worship for the Jews and those of the family group of Judah. ⁹The New Way of Worship will not be like the Old Way of Worship I gave to their early fathers. That was when I took them by the hand and led them out of Egypt. But they did not follow the Old Way of Worship. And so I turned away from them. ¹⁰This is the New Way of Worship that I will give to the Jews. When that day comes, says the Lord, I will put My Laws into their minds. And I will write them in their hearts. I will be their God, and they will be My people. ¹¹No one will need to teach his neighbor or his brother to know the Lord. All of them will already know Me from the least to the greatest. ¹²I will show loving-

kindness to them because of their sins. I will remember their sins no more." (Jeremiah 31:31-34)

¹³When God spoke about a New Way of Worship, He showed that the Old Way of Worship was finished and of no use now. It will never be used again.

The New Way Of Worship Is Better

9 There were special ways of worship and a special holy place made by man for the Old Way of Worship. ²A big tent was built and set up. It was called the holy place. It had a light and a table, and the holy bread was on the table. ³Behind the second curtain there was another tent. This was called the Holiest Place of All. ⁴In the inside tent there was an altar where special perfume was burned. There was also a large box made of wood called the box of the Way of Worship. Both of these were covered with gold inside and out. Inside the box was a pot made of gold with the bread from heaven. It also had in it Aaron's stick that once started to grow. The stones on which the Law of Moses was written were in it. ⁵Above the box were two special bodies of honor. Their wings were spread up and over and met in the center. On the top of the box and under the shadow of their wings was the place where sins were forgiven. We cannot tell anymore about these things now.

⁶When everything was finished, the Jewish religious leaders went in and out of the outside tent to do the things which had to be done to worship God. ⁷Once each year the head religious leader would go into the inside tent alone. He would not go in without blood. He gave this blood to God as a gift in worship for his own sins and for the sins of all the people who sinned without knowing it.

⁸And so the Holy Spirit is teaching that, with the Old Way of Worship, the people could not go into the Holiest Place of All as long as the outside tent and its Old Way of Worship were being used. ⁹The outside tent is a picture of that day. With the Old Way of Worship, animals killed and gifts given in worship to God could not take away the guilty feeling of sin. ¹⁰The Old Way of Worship was made up of Laws about what to eat and drink. These Laws

told how to wash and other things to do with the body. These things had to be done until Christ came to bring a better way of worship.

The New Way Of Worship Has A Better Gift

[11]But Christ came as the Head Religious Leader of the good things God promised. He made the way for man to go to God. He was a greater and more perfect tent. He was not made by human hands and was not a part of this earth. [12]Christ went into the Holiest Place of All one time for all people. He did not take the blood of goats and young cows to give to God as a gift in worship. He gave His own blood. By doing this, He bought us with His own blood and made us free from sin forever. [13]With the Old Way of Worship, the blood and ashes of animals could make men clean after they had sinned. [14]How much more the blood of Christ will do! He gave Himself as a perfect gift to God through the Spirit that lives forever. Now your heart can be free from the guilty feeling of doing work that is worth nothing. Now you can work for the living God.

He gave His own blood.

[15]Christ is the One Who gave us this New Way of Worship. All those who have been called by God may receive life that lasts forever just as He promised them. Christ bought us with His blood when He died for us. This made us free from our sins which we did under the Old Way of Worship.

[16]When a man wants to give his money to someone after he dies, he writes it all down on paper. But that paper is worth nothing until the man is dead. [17]That piece of paper means nothing as long as he is alive. It is good only when he dies. [18]The Old Way of Worship had to have a death to make it good. The blood of an animal was used. [19]Moses told the people all the things they had to obey in the Jewish Law. Then he took the blood of animals together with water and put it on the Book of the Law and on all the people. He used special branches and red wool as he put it on them. [20]Moses said, "This is the blood of the Way of Worship which God said you must obey." (Exodus 24:8) [21]In the same way, Moses put the blood on the tent and on all the things used in worship. [22]The Jewish Law says that almost everything is made clean by blood. Sins are not forgiven unless blood is given.

One Perfect Gift

²³The tent to worship in and the things inside to worship with were like the things in heaven. They were made clean by putting blood on them. But the things in heaven were made clean by a much better gift of worship. ²⁴For Christ did not go into the Holiest Place of All that was made by men, even if it was like the true one in heaven. He went to heaven itself and He is in front of God for us. ²⁵Christ has not given Himself many times, as the head religious leader here on earth went into the Holiest Place of All each year with blood that was not his own. ²⁶For then Christ would have had to die many times since the world began. But He came once at the end of the Old Way of Worship. He gave Himself once for all time. He gave Himself to destroy sin. ²⁷It is in the plan that all men die once. After that, they will stand in front of God and He will say if they are guilty. ²⁸It is the same with Christ. He gave Himself once to take away the sins of many. When He comes the second time, He will not need to give Himself again for sin. He will save all those who are waiting for Him.

In The Old Way Of Worship Many Gifts Were Given

10 The Jewish Law is like a picture of the good things to come. The Jewish religious leaders gave gifts on the altar in worship to God all the time year after year. Those gifts could not make the people perfect who came to worship. ²If those gifts given to God could take away sins, they would no longer feel guilty of sin. They would have given no more gifts. ³When they gave the gifts year after year, it made them remember that they still had their sins. ⁴The blood of animals cannot take away the sins of men.

In The New Way Of Worship One Gift Was Given

⁵When Christ came to the world, He said to God, "You do not want animals killed or gifts given in worship. You have made My body ready to give as a gift. ⁶You are not pleased with animals that have been killed or burned and given as gifts on the altar to take away sin. ⁷Then I said, 'I have come to do what You want, O God. It is written in the Jewish Law that I would.'"

8Then Christ said, "You do not want animals killed or gifts given in worship to you for sin. You are not pleased with them." These things are done because the Jewish Law says they should be done. 9Then He said, "I have come to do what You want Me to do." And this is what He did when He died on a cross. God did away with the Old Way of Worship and made a New Way of Worship. 10Our sins are washed away and we are made clean because Christ gave His own body as a gift to God. He did this once for all time.

11All Jewish religious leaders stand every day killing animals and giving gifts on the altar. They give the same gifts over and over again. These gifts cannot take away sins. 12But Christ gave Himself once for sins and that is good forever. After that He sat down at the right side of God. 13He is waiting there for God to make of those who have hated Him a place to rest His feet. 14And by one gift He has made perfect forever all those who are being set apart for God-like living.

15The Holy Spirit tells us this: First He says, 16"This is the New Way of Worship that I will give them. When that day comes, says the Lord, I will put My Laws into their hearts. And I will write them in their minds." Then He says, 17"I will not remember their sins and wrong-doings anymore." (Jeremiah 31:33-34) 18No more gifts on the altar in worship are needed when our sins are forgiven.

We Can Go To God Through Christ

19Christian brothers, now we know we can go into the Holiest Place of All because the blood of Jesus was given. 20We now come to God by the new and living way. Christ made this way for us. He opened the curtain, which was His own body. 21We have a great Religious Leader over the house of God. 22And so let us come near to God with a true heart full of faith. Our hearts must be made clean from guilty feelings and our bodies washed with pure water. 23Let us hold on to the hope we say we have and not be changed. We can trust God that He will do what He promised. 24Let us help each other to love others and to do good. 25Let us not stay away from church meetings. Some people are doing this all the time. Comfort each other as you see the day of His return coming near.

Do Not Fall Back Into Sin

[26]If we keep on sinning because we want to after we have received and know the truth, there is no gift that will take away sins then. [27]Instead, we will stand in front of God and on that day He will say we are guilty. And the hot fires of hell will burn up those who work against God. [28]Anyone who did not obey the Old Way of Worship died without loving-kindness when two or three men spoke against him. [29]How much more will a man have to be punished if he walks on and hates the Son of God? How much more will he be punished if he acts as if the blood of God's New Way of Worship is worth nothing? This New Way of Worship is God's way of making him holy. How much more will he be punished if he laughs at the Holy Spirit Who wanted to show him loving-favor? [30]For we know God said, "I will pay back what is coming to them." And, "The Lord will say who is guilty among His people." (Deuteronomy 32:35-36) [31]The very worst thing that can happen to a man is to fall into the hands of the living God!

[32]Remember how it was in those days after you heard the truth. You suffered much. [33]People laughed at you and beat you. When others suffered, you suffered with them. [34]You had loving-pity for those who were in prison. You had joy when your things were taken away from you. For you knew you would have something better in heaven which would last forever.

[35]Do not throw away your trust, for your pay will be great. [36]You must be willing to wait without giving up. After you have done what God wants you to do, God will give you what He promised you. [37]The Holy Writings say, "In a little while, the One you are looking for will come. It will not be a long time now. [38]For the one right with God lives by faith. If anyone turns back, I will not be pleased with him." (Habakkuk 2:3-4) [39]We are not of those people who turn back and are lost. Instead, we have faith to be saved from the punishment of sin.

Faith

11 Now faith is being sure we will get what we hope for. It is being sure of what we cannot see. [2]God was pleased with the men who had faith who lived long ago.

Now faith is being sure we will get what we hope for. It is being sure of what we cannot see.

³Through faith we understand that the world was made by the Word of God. Things we see were made from what could not be seen.

⁴Because Abel had faith, he gave a better gift in worship to God than Cain. His gift pleased God. Abel was right with God. Abel died, but by faith he is still speaking to us.

⁵Because Enoch had faith, he was taken up from the earth without dying. He could not be found because God had taken him. The Holy Writings tell how he pleased God before he was taken up. ⁶A man cannot please God unless he has faith. Anyone who comes to God must believe that He is. That one must also know that God gives what is promised to the one who keeps on looking for Him.

⁷Because Noah had faith, he built a large boat for his family. God told him what was going to happen. His faith made him hear God speak and he obeyed. His family was saved from death because he built the boat. In this way, Noah showed the world how sinful it was. Noah became right with God because of his faith in God.

⁸Because Abraham had faith, he obeyed God when God called him to leave his home. He was to go to another country that God promised to give him. He left his home without knowing where he was going. ⁹His faith in God kept him living as a stranger in the country God had promised to him. Isaac and Jacob had received the same promise. They all lived in tents together. ¹⁰Abraham was looking to God and waiting for a city that could not be moved. It was a city planned and built by God.

¹¹Because Sarah had faith, she was able to have a child long after she was past the age to have children. She had faith to believe that God would do what He promised. ¹²Abraham was too old to have children. But from this one man came a family with as many in it as the stars in the sky and as many as the sand by the sea.

¹³These people all died having faith in God. They did not receive what God had promised to them. But they could see far ahead to

all the things God promised and they were glad for them. They knew they were strangers here. This earth was not their home. [14]People who say these things show they are looking for a country of their own. [15]They did not think about the country they had come from. If they had, they might have gone back. [16]But they wanted a better country. And so God is not ashamed to be called their God. He has made a city for them.

[17]Because Abraham had faith, when he was tested, he gave his son Isaac as a gift on the altar in worship. God had made a promise to Abraham that He would give him a son. And yet Abraham was willing to give his only son as a gift on the altar in worship. [18]God had said to Abraham, "Your family will come from Isaac." (Genesis 21:12) [19]Abraham believed God was able to bring Isaac back to life again. And so it may be said that Abraham did receive him back from death.

[20]Because Isaac had faith, he said that good would come to Jacob and Esau in the future. [21]Because Jacob had faith, he said that good would come to each of Joseph's sons as he was dying. He used his walking stick to hold him up as he prayed to God.

[22]Because Joseph had faith, he spoke of the Jews leaving the country of Egypt. He was going to die soon, and he told them to bury his body in the country where they were going.

[23]Because of faith, Moses, after he was born, was hidden by his parents for three months. They saw that he was a beautiful child. They were not afraid of the king when he said that all baby boys should be killed.

[24]Because Moses had faith, he would not be called the son of Pharoah's daughter when he grew up. [25]He chose to suffer with God's people instead of having fun doing sinful things for awhile. [26]Any shame that he suffered for Christ was worth more than all the riches in Egypt. He kept his eyes on the pay God was going to give him.

[27]Because Moses had faith, he left Egypt. He was not afraid of the king's anger. Moses did not turn from the right way but kept seeing God in front of him. [28]Because Moses had faith, he told all

the Jews to put blood over their doors. Then the angel of death would pass over their houses and not kill their oldest sons.

29Because the Jews had faith, they went through the Red Sea as if they were on dry ground. But when the people of Egypt tried to go through, they were all killed by the water.

30Because the Jews had faith, the walls of the city of Jericho fell down after the Jews had walked around the city for seven days. 31Because Rahab had faith, she was kept from being killed along with those who did not obey God. She was a woman who sold the use of her body. But she helped the men who had come in secret to look over the country.

There Were Many More Who Had Faith In God

32What more should I say? There is not enough time to tell of Gideon and of Barak and of Samson and of Jephthah and of David and of Samuel and of the early preachers. 33It was because these people had faith that they won wars over other countries. They were good leaders. They received what God promised to them. They closed the mouths of lions 34and stopped fire that was burning. They got away from being killed with swords. They were made strong again after they had been weak and sick. They were strong in war. They made fighting men from other countries run home. 35It was because some women had faith that they received their dead back to life. Others chose to be beaten instead of being set free, because they would not turn against God. In this way, they would be raised to a better life. 36Others were talked against. Some were beaten. Some were put in chains and in prison. 37They were killed by stones being thrown at them. People were cut into pieces. They were tested. They were killed with swords. They wore skins of sheep and goats and had nothing they could call their own. They were hungry and sick. Everyone was bad to them. 38They walked through places where no people live and over mountains. They looked for holes in the ground to live in. They were too good for this world. 39It was because of their faith that God was pleased with them. But they did not receive what God had promised. 40God had planned something better for us. These men could not be made perfect without us.

It was because of their faith that God was pleased with them.

Christ The Perfect One

12 All these many people who have had faith in God are now gathered around watching us. Let us put every thing out of our lives that keeps us from doing what we should. Let us keep running in the race that God has planned for us. ²Let us keep looking to Jesus. Our faith comes from Him and He is the One Who makes it perfect. He did not give up when He had to suffer shame and die on a cross. He knew of the joy that would be His later. Now He is sitting at the right side of God.

Let us keep looking to Jesus.

³Sinful men spoke words of hate against Christ. He was willing to take such shame from sinners. Think of this so you will not get tired and give up. ⁴In your fight against sin, you have not yet had to stand against sin with your blood. ⁵Do you remember what God said to you when He called you His sons? "My son, listen when the Lord punishes you. Do not give up when He tells you what you must do. ⁶The Lord punishes everyone He loves. He whips every son He receives." (Proverbs 3:11-12) ⁷Do not give up when you are punished by God. Be willing to take it, knowing that God is teaching you as a son. Is there a father who does not punish his son sometimes? ⁸If you are not punished as all sons are, it means that you are not a true son of God. You are not a part of His family and He is not your Father. ⁹Remember that our fathers on earth punished us. We had respect for them. How much more should we obey our Father in heaven and live? ¹⁰For a little while our fathers on earth punished us when they thought they should. But God punishes us for our good so we will be holy as He is holy. ¹¹There is no joy while we are being punished. It is hard to take, but later we can see that good came from it. And it gives us the peace of being right with God.

¹²So lift up your hands that have been weak. Stand up on your weak legs. ¹³Walk straight ahead so the weak leg will not be turned aside, but will be healed.

¹⁴Be at peace with all men. Live a holy life. No one will see the Lord without having that kind of life. ¹⁵See that no one misses

God's loving-favor. Do not let wrong thoughts about others get started among you. If you do, many people will be turned to a life of sin. [16]None of you should fall into sex sins or forget God like Esau did. He had a right to get all Isaac had because he was the oldest son. But for one plate of food he sold this right to his brother. [17]You know that later he would have received everything. But he did not get it even when he asked for it with tears. It was too late to make right the wrong he had done.

[18]For you have not come close to a mountain that you can touch. You have not come to worship where there is burning fire and darkness and storm and wind. [19]The sound of a horn was heard and God's voice spoke. The people cried out to Moses to have God stop speaking to them. [20]They could not stand to listen to His strong words, "Even if an animal comes to the mountain, it must be killed." (Exodus 19:12) [21]What Moses saw was so hard to look at that he said, "I am full of fear and am shaking." (Deuteronomy 9:19)

[22]But instead, you have come to the mountain of Jerusalem. It is the city of the living God. It is the Jerusalem of heaven with its thousands of angels. [23]You have gathered there with God's children who were born long ago. They are citizens of heaven. God is there. He will tell all men if they are guilty. The spirits of all those right with God are there. They have been made perfect. [24]Jesus is there. He has made a way for man to go to God. He gave His blood that men might worship God the New Way. The blood of Jesus tells of better things than that which Abel used.

[25]Be sure you listen to the One Who is speaking to you. The Jews did not obey when God's Law was given to them on earth. They did not go free. They were punished. We will be punished more if we do not listen to God as He speaks from heaven. [26]On the Mountain of Sinai, God's voice shook the earth. But now He has promised, saying, "Once more I will shake the earth and the heavens." (Exodus 19:18)

[27]When God says, "Once more," He means He will take away everything of this world that can be shaken so the things that cannot be shaken will be left.

28Since we have received a holy nation that cannot be moved, let us be thankful. Let us please God and worship Him with honor and fear. 29For our God is a fire that destroys everything.

Christian Living

13 Keep on loving each other as Christian brothers. 2Do not forget to be kind to strangers and let them stay in your home. Some people have had angels in their homes without knowing it. 3Remember those in prison. Think of them as if you were in prison with them. Remember those who are suffering because of what others have done to them. You may suffer in the same way.

I will never leave you or let you be alone.

4Marriage should be respected by everyone. God will punish those who do sex sins and are not faithful in marriage.

5Keep your lives free from the love of money. Be happy with what you have. God has said, "I will never leave you or let you be alone." (Deuteronomy 31:6) 6So we can say for sure, "The Lord is my Helper. I am not afraid of anything man can do to me." (Psalm 118:6)

Jesus Christ is the same yesterday and today and forever.

7Remember your leaders who first spoke God's Word to you. Think of how they lived, and trust God as they did. 8Jesus Christ is the same yesterday and today and forever.

9Do not let the many strange teachings lead you into the wrong way. Our hearts are made strong by God's loving-favor. Food does not make our hearts strong. Those who obey laws about eating certain foods are not helped by them. 10We have an altar from which those who work in the place of worship have no right to eat.

11The head religious leader takes the blood of animals into the holy place to give it on the altar for sins. But the bodies of the animals are burned outside the city. 12It was the same with Jesus. He suffered and died outside the city so His blood would make the people clean from sin. 13So let us go to Him outside the city to share His shame. 14For there is no city here on earth that will last forever. We are looking for the one that is coming. 15Let us give

thanks all the time to God through Jesus Christ. Our gift to Him is to give thanks. Our lips should always give thanks to His name. [16]Remember to do good and help each other. Gifts like this please God.

[17]Obey your leaders and do what they say. They keep watch over your souls. They have to tell God what they have done. They should have joy in this and not be sad. If they are sad, it is no help to you.

[18]Pray for us. Our hearts tell us we are right. We want to do the right thing always. [19]Pray for me all the more so that I will be able to come to you soon.

God is
a God of peace.

[20]God is a God of peace. He raised our Lord Jesus from the dead. Jesus is the Good Shepherd of the sheep. His blood made the New Way of Worship which will last forever. [21]May God give you every good thing you need so you can do what He wants. May He do in us what pleases Him through Jesus Christ. May Christ have all the shining greatness forever! Let it be so.

May God give you
every good thing
you need
so you can do
what He wants.

[22]Christian brothers, I beg of you to listen to these words that will help you. This has been a short letter. [23]I want you to know that Timothy is out of prison. If he comes soon, I will bring him with me when I come to see you. [24]Say hello to all of your leaders and to all those who belong to Christ. The Christians from the country of Italy say hello to you. [25]May all of you have God's loving-favor. Let it be so.

1 This letter is from James. I am a workman owned by God and the Lord Jesus Christ. I say hello to the twelve family groups of the Jewish nation living in many parts of the world.

Take Hope When Tests Come

²My Christian brothers, you should be happy when you have all kinds of tests. ³You know these prove your faith. It helps you to not give up. ⁴Learn well how to wait so you will be strong and complete and in need of nothing.

⁵If you do not have wisdom, ask God for it. He is always ready to give it to you and will never say you are wrong for asking. ⁶You must have faith as you ask Him. You must not doubt. Anyone who doubts is like a wave which is pushed around by the sea. ⁷Such a man will get nothing from the Lord. ⁸The man who has two ways of thinking changes in everything he does.

If you do not have wisdom, ask God for it.

⁹A Christian brother who has few riches of this world should be happy for what he has. He is great in the eyes of God. ¹⁰But a rich man should be happy even if he loses everything. He is like a flower that will die. ¹¹The sun comes up with burning heat. The grass dries up and the flower falls off. It is no longer beautiful. The rich man will die also and all his riches will be gone. ¹²The man who does not give up when tests come is happy. After the test is over, he will receive the prize of life. God has promised this to those who love Him.

God Does Not Tempt Us

¹³When you are tempted to do wrong, do not say, "God is tempting me." God cannot be tempted. He will never tempt anyone. ¹⁴A man is tempted to do wrong when he lets himself be led by what his bad thoughts tell him to do. ¹⁵When he does what his bad thoughts tell him to do, he sins. When sin completes its work, it brings death.

¹⁶My Christian brothers, do not be fooled about this. ¹⁷Whatever is good and perfect comes to us from God. He is the One Who made all light. He does not change. No shadow is made by His turning. ¹⁸He gave us our new lives through the truth of His Word only because He wanted to. We are the first children in His family.

¹⁹My Christian brothers, you know everyone should listen much and speak little. He should be slow to become angry. ²⁰A man's anger does not allow him to be right with God. ²¹Put out of your life all that is dirty and wrong. Receive with a gentle spirit the Word that was taught. It has the power to save your souls from the punishment of sin.

²²Obey the Word of God. If you hear only and do not act, you are only fooling yourself. ²³Anyone who hears the Word of God and does not obey is like a man looking at his face in a mirror. ²⁴After he sees himself and goes away, he forgets what he looks like. ²⁵But the one who keeps looking into God's perfect Law and does not forget it will do what it says and be happy as he does it. God's Word makes men free.

²⁶If a person thinks he is religious, but does not keep his tongue from speaking bad things, he is fooling himself. His religion is worth nothing. ²⁷Religion that is pure and good before God the Father is to help children who have no parents and to care for women whose husbands have died who have troubles. Pure religion is also to keep yourself clean from the sinful things of the world.

The Rich And The Poor

2 My Christian brothers, our Lord Jesus Christ is the Lord of shining greatness. Since your trust is in Him, do not look on one person as more important than another. ²What if a man comes into your church wearing a gold ring and good clothes? And at the same time a poor man comes wearing old clothes. ³What if you show respect to the man in good clothes and say, "Come and sit in this good place?" But if you say to the poor man, "Stand up over there," or "Sit on the floor by my feet," ⁴are you not thinking that one is more important than the other? This kind of thinking is sinful. ⁵Listen, my dear Christian brothers, God has chosen those who are poor in the things of this world to be rich in faith. The holy nation of heaven is theirs. That is what God promised to those who love Him. ⁶You have not shown respect to the poor man. Is it not the rich men who make it hard for you and take you to court? ⁷They speak against the name of Christ. And it was Christ Who called you. ⁸You do well when you obey the Holy Writings which say, "You must love your neighbor as you love yourself." ⁹But if you look on one man as more important than another, you are sinning. And the Law says you are sinning.

You must love your neighbor as you love yourself.

Keep The Whole Law

¹⁰If you obey all the Laws but one, you are as guilty as the one who has broken them all. ¹¹The One Who said, "You must not do any sex sins," also said, "You must not kill another person." If you do no sex sins but kill someone, you are guilty of breaking the Law. ¹²Keep on talking and acting as people who will be told they are guilty or not by the Law that makes men free. ¹³Anyone who shows no loving-kindness will have no loving-kindness shown to him when he is told he is guilty. But if you show loving-kindness, God will show loving-kindness to you when you are told you are guilty.

Faith Without Works Is Dead

¹⁴My Christian brothers, what good does it do if you say you have faith but do not do things that prove you have faith? Can that kind of faith save you from the punishment of sin? ¹⁵What if a Christian does not have clothes or food? ¹⁶And one of you says to him, "Goodby, keep yourself warm and eat well." But if you do not give him what he needs, how does that help him? ¹⁷A faith that does not do things is a dead faith.

¹⁸Someone may say, "You have faith, and I do things. Prove to me you have faith when you are doing nothing. I will prove to you I have faith by doing things." ¹⁹You believe there is one God. That is good! But even the demons believe that, and because they do, they shake.

²⁰You foolish man! Do I have to prove to you that faith without doing things is of no use? ²¹Was not our early father Abraham right with God by what he did? He obeyed God and put his son Isaac on the altar to die. ²²You see his faith working by what he did and his faith was made perfect by what he did. ²³It happened as the Holy Writings said it would happen. They say, "Abraham put his trust in God and he became right with God." He was called the friend of God. ²⁴A man becomes right with God by what he does and not by faith only. ²⁵The same was true with Rahab, the woman who sold the use of her body. She became right with God by what she did in helping the men who had been sent to look through the country and sent them away by another road. ²⁶The body is dead when there is no spirit in it. It is the same with faith. Faith is dead when nothing is done.

The Power Of The Tongue

3 My Christian brothers, not many of you should become teachers. If we do wrong, it will be held against us more than other people who are not teachers. ²We all make many mistakes. If anyone does not make a mistake with his tongue by saying the wrong things, he is a perfect man. It shows he is able to make his body do what he wants it to do. ³We make a horse go wherever we want it to go by a small bit in its mouth. We turn its whole body by this. ⁴Sailing ships are driven by strong winds. But a small rudder turns a large ship whatever way the man at the wheel wants the ship to go.

⁵The tongue is also a small part of the body, but it can speak big things. See how a very small fire can set many trees on fire. ⁶The tongue is a fire. It is full of wrong. It poisons the whole body. The tongue sets our whole lives on fire with a fire that comes from hell. ⁷Men can make all kinds of animals and birds and fish and snakes do what they want them to do. ⁸But no man can make his tongue say what he wants it to say. It is sinful and does not rest. It is full of poison that kills. ⁹With our tongue we give thanks to our Father in heaven. And with our tongue we speak bad words against men who are made like God. ¹⁰Giving thanks and speaking bad words come from the same mouth. My Christian brothers, this is not right! ¹¹Does a well of water give good water

and bad water from the same place? ¹²Can a fig tree give olives or can a grapevine give figs? A well does not give both good water and bad water.

Wisdom From Above

¹³Who among you is wise and understands? Let that one show from a good life by the things he does that he is wise and gentle. ¹⁴If you have jealousy in your heart and fight to have many things, do not be proud of it. Do not lie against the truth. ¹⁵This is not the kind of wisdom that comes from God. But this wisdom comes from the world and from that which is not Christian and from the devil. ¹⁶Wherever you find jealousy and fighting, there will be trouble and every other kind of wrong-doing. ¹⁷But the wisdom that comes from heaven is first of all pure. Then it gives peace. It is gentle and willing to obey. It is full of loving-kindness and of doing good. It has no doubts and does not pretend to be something it is not. ¹⁸Those who plant seeds of peace will gather what is right and good.

4 What starts wars and fights among you? Is it not because you want many things and are fighting to have them? ²You want something you do not have, so you kill. You want something but cannot get it, so you fight for it. You do not get things because you do not ask for them. ³Or if you do ask, you do not receive because your reasons for asking are wrong. You want these things only to please yourselves.

⁴You are as wives and husbands who are not faithful in marriage and do sex sins. Do you not know that to love the sinful things of the world and to be a friend to them is to be against God? Yes, I say it again, if you are a friend of the world, you are against God. ⁵Do you think the Holy Writings mean nothing when they said, "The Holy Spirit Whom God has given to live in us has a strong desire for us to be faithful to Him?"

⁶But He gives us more loving-favor. For the Holy Writings say, "God works against the proud but gives loving-favor to those who have no pride." (Proverbs 3:34) ⁷So give yourselves to God. Stand against the devil and he will run away from you. ⁸Come

So give yourselves to God. Stand against the devil and he will run away from you.

close to God and He will come close to you. Wash your hands, you sinners. Clean up your hearts, you who want to follow the sinful ways of the world and God at the same time. ⁹Be sorry for your sins and cry because of them. Be sad and do not laugh. Let your joy be turned into sorrow. ¹⁰Let yourself be brought low in front of the Lord. Then He will lift you up and help you.

Do Not Talk Against Each Other

¹¹Christian brothers, do not talk against anyone or speak bad things about each other. If a person says bad things about his brother, he is speaking against him. And he will be speaking against God's Law. If you say the Law is wrong, and do not obey it, you are saying you are better than the Law. ¹²Only God can say what is right or wrong. He made the Law. He can save or put to death. How can we say if our brother is right or wrong?

¹³Listen! You who say, "Today or tomorrow we will go into this city and stay a year and make money." ¹⁴You do not know about tomorrow. What is your life? It is like fog. You see it and soon it is gone. ¹⁵What you should say is, "If the Lord wants us to, we will live and do this or that." ¹⁶But instead you are proud. You talk loud and big about yourselves. All such pride is sin. ¹⁷If you know what is right to do but you do not do it, you sin.

If you know what is right to do but you do not do it, you sin.

5 Listen, you rich men! Cry about the troubles that will come to you. ²Your riches are worth nothing. Your fine clothes are full of moth holes. ³Your gold and silver have rusted. Their rust will speak against you and eat your flesh like fire. You have saved riches for yourselves for the last days. ⁴Listen! The men working in your fields are crying against you because you have kept back part of their pay. Their cries have been heard by the Lord Who hears His people. ⁵You have had everything while you lived on the earth and have enjoyed its fun. You have made your hearts fat and are ready to be killed as an animal is killed. ⁶You have killed the One right with God. He does not try to stop you.

The Lord Will Come Again

⁷Christian brothers, be willing to wait for the Lord to come again. Learn from the farmer. He waits for the good fruit from the

earth until the early and late rains come. ⁸You must be willing to wait also. Be strong in your hearts because the Lord is coming again soon. ⁹Do not complain about each other, Christian brothers. Then you will not be guilty. Look! The One Who says who is guilty is standing at the door. ¹⁰See how the early preachers spoke for the Lord by their suffering and by being willing to wait. ¹¹We think of those who stayed true to Him as happy even though they suffered. You have heard how long Job waited. You have seen what the Lord did for him in the end. The Lord is full of loving-kindness and pity.

Do Not Swear

¹²My Christian brothers, do not swear. Do not use heaven or earth or anything else to swear by. If you mean yes, say yes. If you mean no, say no. You will be guilty for saying anything more.

The Power Of Prayer In Healing

¹³Is anyone among you suffering? He should pray. Is anyone happy? He should sing songs of thanks to God. ¹⁴Is anyone among you sick? He should send for the church leaders and they should pray for him. They should pour oil on him in the name of the Lord. ¹⁵The prayer given in faith will heal the sick man, and the Lord will raise him up. If he has sinned, he will be forgiven. ¹⁶Tell your sins to each other. And pray for each other so you may be healed. The prayer from the heart of a man right with God has much power. ¹⁷Elijah was a man as we are. He prayed that it might not rain. It did not rain on the earth for three and one-half years. ¹⁸Then he prayed again that it would rain. It rained much and the fields of the earth gave fruit.

Bring Back Those Who Are Lost In Sin

¹⁹My Christian brothers, if any of you should be led away from the truth, let someone turn him back again. ²⁰That person should know that if he turns a sinner from the wrong way, he will save the sinner's soul from death and many sins will be forgiven.

The Living Hope

1 This letter is from Peter, a missionary of Jesus Christ. I am writing to those who were taken away from their homeland and are living in the countries of Pontus and Galatia and Cappadocia and Asia and Bithynia. ²You were chosen by God the Father long ago. He knew you were to become His children. You were set apart for holy living by the Holy Spirit. May you obey Jesus Christ and be made clean by His blood. May you be full of His loving-favor and peace.

³Let us thank the God and Father of our Lord Jesus Christ. It was through His loving-kindness that we were born again to a new life and have a hope that never dies. This hope is ours because Jesus was raised from the dead. ⁴We will receive the great things that we have been promised. They are being kept safe in heaven for us. They are pure and will not pass away. They will never be lost. ⁵You are being kept by the power of God because you put your trust in Him and you will be saved from the punishment of sin at the end of the world.

⁶With this hope you can be happy even if you need to have sorrow and all kinds of tests for awhile. ⁷These tests have come to prove your faith and to show that it is good. Gold, which can be destroyed, is tested by fire. Your faith is worth much more than gold and it must be tested also. Then your faith will bring thanks and shining greatness and honor to Jesus Christ when He comes again. ⁸You have never seen Him but you love Him. You cannot see Him now but you are putting your trust in Him. And you have joy so great that words cannot tell about it. ⁹You will get what your faith is looking for, which is to be saved from the punishment of sin.

Your faith is worth much more than gold and it must be tested also.

¹⁰The early preachers tried to find out how to be saved. They told of the loving-favor that would come to you. ¹¹The early

preachers wondered at what time or to what person this would happen. The Spirit of Christ in them was talking to them and told them to write about how Christ would suffer and about His shining greatness later on. [17]They knew these things would not happen during the time they lived but while you are living many years later. These are the very things that were told to you by those who preached the Good News. The Holy Spirit Who was sent from heaven gave them power and they told of things that even the angels would like to know about.

Holy Living

[13]Get your minds ready for good use. Keep awake. Set your hope now and forever on the loving-favor to be given you when Jesus Christ comes again. [14]Be like children who obey. Do not desire to sin like you used to when you did not know any better. [15]Be holy in every part of your life. Be like the Holy One Who chose you. [16]The Holy Writings say, "You must be holy, for I am holy." (Leviticus 11:44-45) [17]The Father is the One Who says if you are guilty by what you do. He does not respect one person more than another. If you call Him Father, be sure you honor Him with love and fear all the days of your life here on earth. [18]You know you were not bought and made free from sin by paying gold or silver which comes to an end. And you know you were not saved from the punishment of sin by the way of life that you were given from your early fathers. That way of life was worth nothing. [19]The blood of Christ saved you. This blood is of great worth and no amount of money can buy it. Christ was given as a lamb without sin and without spot. [20]Long before the world was made, God chose Christ to be given to you in these last days. [21]Because of Christ, you have put your trust in God. He raised Christ from the dead and gave Him great honor. So now your faith and hope are in God.

The Living Word

[22]You have made your souls pure by obeying the truth through the Holy Spirit. This has given you a true love for the Christians. Let it be a true love from the heart. [23]You have been given a new birth. It was from a seed that cannot die. This new life is from the

Word of God which lives forever. ²⁴All people are like grass. Their greatness is like the flowers. The grass dries up and the flowers fall off. ²⁵But the Word of the Lord will last forever. That Word is the Good News which was preached to you.

Food For Christians

2 Put out of your life hate and lying. Do not pretend to be someone you are not. Do not always want something someone else has. Do not say bad things about other people. ²As new babies want milk, you should want to drink the pure milk which is God's Word so you will grow up and be saved from the punishment of sin. ³If you have tasted of the Lord, you know how good He is.

The Living Stone

⁴Come to Christ as to a living stone. Men have put Him aside, but He was chosen by God and is of great worth in the sight of God. ⁵You are to be as living stones in the building God is making also. You are His religious leaders giving yourselves to God through Jesus Christ. This kind of gift pleases God. ⁶The Holy Writings say, "Look, I lay down in Jerusalem a Stone of great worth, worth far more than any amount of money. Anyone who puts his trust in Him will not be ashamed." (Isaiah 28:16) ⁷This Stone is of great worth to you who have your trust in Him. But to those who have not put their trust in Him, the Holy Writings say, "The Stone which the workmen put aside has become the most important part of the building." (Psalm 118:22) ⁸The Holy Writings say, also, "Christ is the Stone that some men will trip over and the Rock over which they will fall." When they do not obey the Word of God, they trip over it. This is what happens to such men. ⁹But you are a chosen group of people. You are the King's religious leaders. You are a holy nation. You belong to God. He has done this for you so you can tell others how God has called you out of darkness into His great light. ¹⁰At one time you were a people of no use. Now you are the people of God. At one time you did not have loving-kindness. Now you have God's loving-kindness.

[11]Dear friends, your real home is not here on earth. You are strangers here. I ask you to keep away from all the sinful desires of the flesh. These things fight to get hold of your soul. [12]When you are around people who do not know God, be careful how you act. Even if they talk against you as wrong-doers, in the end they will give thanks to God for your good works when Christ comes again.

Obey The Leaders

[13]Obey the head leader of the country and all other leaders over you. This pleases the Lord. [14]Obey the men who work for them. God sends them to punish those who do wrong and to show respect to those who do right. [15]This is what God wants. When you do right, you stop foolish men from saying bad things. [16]Obey as men who are free but do not use this to cover up sin. Live as workmen owned by God at all times. [17]Show respect to all men. Love the Christians. Honor God with love and fear. Respect the head leader of the country.

Workmen Who Are Not Paid

[18]You who are owned by someone should respect your owners and do what they say. Do this if you have a good and kind owner. You must do it even if your owner is hard to work for. [19]This shows you have received loving-favor when you are even punished for doing what is right because of your trust in God. [20]What good is it if, when you are beaten for doing something wrong, you do not try to get out of it? But if you are beaten when you have done what is right, and do not try to get out of it, God is pleased. [21]These things are all a part of the Christian life to which you have been called. Christ suffered for us. This shows us we are to follow in His steps. [22]He never sinned. No lie or bad talk ever came from His lips. [23]When people spoke against Him, He never spoke back. When He suffered from what people did to Him, He did not try to pay them back. He left it in the hands of the One Who is always right in saying who is guilty. [24]He carried our sins in His own body when He died on a cross. In doing this, we may be dead to sin and alive to all that is right and good. His wounds have healed you! [25]You were like lost sheep. But now you have come back to Him Who is your Shepherd and the One Who cares for your soul.

He carried our sins
in His own body
when He died on a cross.

Teaching For Married Christians

3 Wives, obey your own husbands. Some of your husbands may not obey the Word of God. By obeying your husbands, they may become Christians by the life you live without you saying anything. ²They will see how you love God and how your lives are pure. ³Do not let your beauty come from the outside. It should not be the way you comb your hair or the wearing of gold or the wearing of fine clothes. ⁴Your beauty should come from the inside. It should come from the heart. This is the kind that lasts. Your beauty should be a gentle and quiet spirit. In God's sight this is of great worth and no amount of money can buy it. ⁵This was the kind of beauty seen in the holy women who lived many years ago. They put their hope in God. They also obeyed their husbands. ⁶Sarah obeyed her husband Abraham. She respected him as the head of the house. You are her children if you do what is right and do not have fear.

⁷In the same way, husbands should understand and respect their wives, because women are weaker than men. Remember, both husband and wife are to share together the gift of life that lasts forever. If this is not done, you will find it hard to pray.

Teaching For All Christians

⁸Last of all, you must share the same thoughts and the same feelings. Love each other with a kind heart and with a mind that has no pride. ⁹When someone does something bad to you, do not do the same thing to him. When someone talks about you, do not talk about him. Instead, pray that good will come to him. You were called to do this so you might receive good things from God. ¹⁰For "If you want joy in your life and have happy days, keep your tongue from saying bad things and your lips from talking bad about others. ¹¹Turn away from what is sinful. Do what is good. Look for peace and go after it. ¹²The Lord watches over those who are right with Him. He hears their prayers. But the Lord is against those who sin." (Psalm 34:12-16) ¹³Who will hurt you if you do what is right? ¹⁴But even if you suffer for doing what is

Turn away from what is sinful.

right, you will be happy. Do not be afraid or troubled by what they may do to make it hard for you. [15]Your heart should be holy and set apart for the Lord God. Always be ready to tell everyone who asks you why you believe as you do. Be gentle as you speak and show respect. [16]Keep your heart telling you that you have done what is right. If men speak against you, they will be ashamed when they see the good way you have lived as a Christian. [17]If God wants you to suffer, it is better to suffer for doing what is right than for doing what is wrong.

Christ Suffered For Us

[18]Christ suffered and died for sins once for all. He never sinned and yet He died for us who have sinned. He died so He might bring us to God. His body died but His spirit was made alive. [19]Christ went and preached to the spirits in prison. [20]Those were the spirits of the people who would not obey in the days of Noah. God waited a long time for them while Noah was building the big boat. But only eight people were saved from dying when the earth was covered with water. [21]This is like baptism to us. Baptism does not mean we wash our bodies clean. It means we are saved from the punishment of sin and go to God in prayer with a heart that says we are right. This can be done because Christ was raised from the dead. [22]Christ has gone to heaven and is on the right side of God. Angels and powers of heaven are obeying Him.

Following Christ Will Mean Suffering

4 Since Christ has suffered in His body, we must be ready to suffer also. Suffering puts an end to sin. [2]You should no longer spend the rest of your life giving in to the sinful desires of the flesh. But do what God wants as long as you live in this world. [3]In the past you gave enough of your life over to living like the people who do not know God. You gave your life to sex sins and to sinful desires. You got drunk and went to wild parties and to drinking parties and you worshiped false gods. [4]Those who do not know God are surprised you do not join them in the sinful things they do. They laugh at you and say bad things against you. [5]Remember, they will give an answer to Him Who says who is

If God
wants you to suffer,
it is better to suffer for
doing what is right than
for doing what is wrong.

guilty from all who are living or dead. ⁶For this reason, the Good News was preached to the dead. They stood in the flesh in front of the One Who says who is guilty so they might live in the Spirit as God wants.

Love Each Other

Keep awake so you can pray.

⁷The end of the world is near. You must be the boss over your mind. Keep awake so you can pray. ⁸Most of all, have a true love for each other. Love covers many sins. ⁹Be happy to have people stay for the night and eat with you. ¹⁰God has given each of you a gift. Use it to help each other. This will show God's loving-favor. ¹¹If a man preaches, let him do it with God speaking through him. If a man helps others, let him do it with the strength God gives. So in all things God may be honored through Jesus Christ. Shining greatness and power belong to Him forever. Let it be so.

Stay True During Suffering

¹²Dear friends, your faith is going to be tested as if it were going through fire. Do not be surprised at this. ¹³Be happy that you are able to share some of the suffering of Christ. When His shining greatness is shown, you will be filled with much joy. ¹⁴If men speak bad of you because you are a Christian, you will be happy because the Holy Spirit is in you. ¹⁵None of you should suffer as one who kills another person or as one who steals or as one who makes trouble or as one who tries to be the boss of other peoples' lives. ¹⁶But if a man suffers as a Christian, he should not be ashamed. He should thank God that he is a Christian. ¹⁷The time has come for Christians to stand in front of God and He will say who is guilty. If this happens to us, what will happen to those who do not obey the Good News of God? ¹⁸If it is hard for a man who is right with God to be saved, what will happen to the sinner? ¹⁹So if God wants you to suffer, give yourself to Him. He will do what is right for you. He made you and He is faithful.

He will do what is right for you. He made you and He is faithful.

5 I want to speak to the church leaders among you. I am a church leader also. I saw Christ suffer and die on a cross. I will also share His shining greatness when He comes again. ²Be good shepherds of the flock God has put in your care. Do not care for the flock as if you were made to. Do not care for the flock for money, but do it because you want to. ³Do not be bosses over the people you lead. Live as you would like to have them live. ⁴When the Head Shepherd comes again, you will get the prize of shining greatness that will not come to an end.

⁵In the same way, you younger men must obey the church leaders. Be gentle as you care for each other. God works against those who have pride. He gives His loving-favor to those who do not try to honor themselves. ⁶So put away all pride from yourselves. You are standing under the powerful hand of God. At the right time He will lift you up. ⁷Give all your worries to Him because He cares for you.

⁸Keep awake! Watch at all times. The devil is working against you. He is walking around like a hungry lion with his mouth open. He is looking for someone to eat. ⁹Stand against him and be strong in your faith. Remember, other Christians over all the world are suffering the same as you are. ¹⁰After you have suffered for awhile, God Himself will make you perfect. He will keep you in the right way. He will give you strength. He is the God of all loving-favor and has called you through Christ Jesus to share His shining greatness forever. ¹¹God has power over all things forever. Let it be so.

¹²I have known Silvanus as a faithful Christian brother and it is by him I have written this short letter to help you. It tells you of the true loving-favor of God. Stay true in His loving-favor. ¹³The church which is in the city of Babylon says hello. It has been chosen by God the same as you have been. My son, Mark, says hello also. ¹⁴Say hello to each other with a kiss of holy love. May all of you Christians have peace.

1 This letter is from Simon Peter. I am a missionary of Jesus Christ and a workman owned by Him. I am writing to those who have received the same faith as ours which is of great worth and which no amount of money can buy. This faith comes from our God and Jesus Christ, the One Who saves. ²May you have more and more of His loving-favor and peace as you come to know God and our Lord Jesus Christ better.

Christians Are To Grow

He gives us everything we need for life and for holy living.

³He gives us everything we need for life and for holy living. He gives it through His great power. As we come to know Him better, we learn that He called us to share His own shining greatness and perfect life. ⁴Through His shining greatness and perfect life, He has given us promises. These promises are of great worth and no amount of money can buy them. Through these promises you can have God's own life in you now that you have gotten away from the sinful things of the world which came from wrong desires of the flesh.

⁵Do your best to add holy living to your faith. Then add to this a better understanding. ⁶As you have a better understanding, be able to say no when you need to. Do not give up. And as you wait and do not give up, live God-like. ⁷As you live God-like, be kind to Christian brothers and love them. ⁸If you have all these things and keep growing in them, they will keep you from being of no use and from having no fruit when it comes to knowing our Lord Jesus Christ. ⁹But if you do not have these things, you are blind and cannot see far. You forget God saved you from your old life of sin.

¹⁰Christian brothers, make sure you are among those He has chosen and called out for His own. As long as you do these things, you will never trip and fall. ¹¹In this way, the road will be made wide open for you. And you will go into the holy nation that lasts forever of our Lord Jesus Christ, the One Who saves.

¹²You already know about these things but I want to keep telling you about them. You are strong in the faith now. ¹³I think

it is right as long as I am alive to keep you thinking about these things. [14]I know that I will soon be leaving this body. Our Lord Jesus Christ has told me this. [15]I will try to make a way for you to remember these things after I am gone.

[16]We had nothing to do with man-made stories when we told you about the power of our Lord Jesus Christ and of His coming again. We have seen His great power with our own eyes. [17]When He received honor and shining greatness from God the Father, a voice came to Him from the All-powerful God, saying, "This is My much-loved Son. I am very happy with Him." [18]We heard this voice come from heaven when we were with Christ on the holy mountain.

[19]All this helps us know that what the early preachers said was true. You will do well to listen to what they have said. Their words are as lights that shine in a dark place. Listen until you understand what they have said. Then it will be like the morning light which takes away the darkness. And the Morning Star (Christ) will rise to shine in your hearts.

[20]Understand this first: No part of the Holy Writings was ever made up by any man. [21]No part of the Holy Writings came long ago because of what man wanted to write. But holy men who belonged to God spoke what the Holy Spirit told them.

Watch For False Teachers

2 But there were false teachers among the people. And there will be false teachers among you also. These people will work in secret ways to bring false teaching to you. They will turn against Christ Who bought them with His blood. They bring fast death on themselves. [2]Many people will follow their wrong ways. Because of what they do, people will speak bad things against the way of truth. [3]They will tell lies and false stories so they can use you to get things for themselves. But God said they were guilty long ago and their death is on the way.

[4]God did not hold back from punishing the angels who sinned, but sent them down to hell. They are to be kept there in the deep

hole of darkness until they stand in front of Him Who tells them they are guilty. ⁵God did not hold back from punishing the people of the world who sinned long ago. He brought the flood on the world of sinners. But Noah was a preacher of right living. He and his family of seven were the only ones God saved. ⁶God said that the cities of Sodom and Gomorrah were guilty, and He destroyed them with fire. This was to show people who did not worship God what would happen to them. ⁷Lot was taken away from Sodom because he was right with God. He had been troubled by the sins that bad men did in wild living. ⁸He saw and heard how the people around him broke the Law. Everyday his own soul which was right with God was troubled because of their sinful ways. ⁹But the Lord knows how to help men who are right with God when they are tempted. He also knows how to keep the sinners suffering for their wrong-doing until the day they stand in front of God Who will say they are guilty. ¹⁰This is true about those who keep on wanting to please their own bodies in sinful desires and those who will not obey laws. They want to please themselves and are not afraid when they laugh and say bad things about the powers in heaven. ¹¹Angels are greater in strength and power than they. But angels do not speak against these powers in front of the Lord.

¹²Men like this are like animals who are not able to think but are born to be caught and killed. They speak bad words against that which they do not understand. They will die in their own sinful ways. ¹³This is the pay they will suffer for their sinful lives. They are not ashamed when they sin in the daylight. They are sores and dirty spots among you while they eat and drink big meals with you. ¹⁴Their eyes are full of sex sins. They never have enough sin. They get weak people to go along with them. Their hearts are always wanting something. They are people who will end up in hell because ¹⁵they have left the right way and have gone the wrong way. They have followed the way of Balaam, who was the son of Beor. He loved the money he got for his sin. ¹⁶But he was stopped in his sin. A donkey spoke to him with a man's voice. It stopped this early preacher from going on in his crazy way.

¹⁷Such people are like wells without water. They are like clouds before a storm. The darkest place below has been kept for them. ¹⁸They speak big-sounding words which show they are proud. They get men who are trying to keep away from sinful men to give

in to the sinful desires of the flesh. [19]They promise that these men will be free. But they themselves are chained to sin. For a man is chained to anything that has power over him.

[20]There are men who have been made free from the sins of the world by learning to know the Lord Jesus Christ, the One Who saves. But if they do these sins again, and are not able to keep from doing them, they are worse than they were before. [21]After knowing the holy Law that was given to them, they turned from it. It would have been better for them if they had not known how to be right with God. [22]They are like the wise saying, ''A dog turns back to what he has thrown up.'' (Proverbs 26:11) And, ''A pig that has been washed goes back to roll in the mud.''

The World Will Be Destroyed

3 Dear friends, this is the second letter I have written to you. In both of them I have tried to get you to remember some things. [2]You should remember the words that were spoken before by the holy early preachers. Do not forget the teaching of the Lord, the One Who saves. This was given to you by your missionaries.

[3]First of all, I want you to know that in the last days men will laugh at the truth. They will follow their own sinful desires. [4]They will say, "He promised to come again. Where is He? Since our early fathers died, everything is the same from the beginning of the world." [5]But they want to forget that God spoke and the heavens were made long ago. The earth was made out of water and water was all around it. [6]Long ago the earth was covered with water and it was destroyed. [7]But the heaven we see now and the earth we live on now have been kept by His word. They will be kept until they are to be destroyed by fire. They will be kept until the day men stand in front of God and sinners will be destroyed.

[8]Dear friends, remember this one thing, with the Lord one day is as 1,000 years. And 1,000 years are as one day. [9]The Lord is not slow about keeping His promise as some people think. He is waiting for you. The Lord does not want any person to be punished forever. He wants all people to be sorry for their sins and

Remember this one thing, with the Lord one day is as 1,000 years. And 1,000 years are as one day.

turn from them.   ¹⁰The day of the Lord will come as a robber comes. The heavens will pass away with a loud noise. The sun and moon and stars will burn up. The earth and all that is in it will be burned up.

¹¹Since all these things are to be destroyed in this way, you should think about the kind of life you are living. It should be holy and God-like. ¹²You should look for the day of God to come. You should do what you can to make it come soon. At that time the heavens will be destroyed by fire. And the sun and moon and stars will melt away with much heat. ¹³We are looking for what God has promised, which are new heavens and a new earth. Only what is right and good will be there.

¹⁴Dear friends, since you are waiting for these things to happen, do all you can to be found by Him in peace. Be clean and free from sin. ¹⁵You can be sure the long waiting of our Lord is part of His plan to save men from the punishment of sin. God gave our dear brother Paul the wisdom to write about this also. ¹⁶He wrote about these things in all of his writings. Some of these things are hard to understand. People who do not have much understanding and some who are not strong in the faith change the meaning of his letters. They do this to the other parts of the Holy Writings also. They are destroying themselves as they do this.

¹⁷And so, dear friends, now that you know this, watch so you will not be led away by the mistakes of these sinful people. Do not be moved by them. ¹⁸Grow in the loving-favor that Christ gives you. Learn to know our Lord Jesus Christ better. He is the One Who saves. May He have all the shining greatness now and forever. Let it be so.

Christ — The Word Of Life

1 Christ is the Word of Life. He was from the beginning. We have heard Him and have seen Him with our own eyes. We have looked at Him and put our hands on Him. ²Christ Who is Life was shown to us. We saw Him. We tell you and preach about the Life that lasts forever. He was with the Father and He has come down to us. ³We are preaching what we have heard and seen. We want you to share together with us what we have with the Father and with His Son, Jesus Christ. ⁴We are writing this to you so our joy may be full.

Christians Are To Live In The Light

⁵This is what we heard Him tell us. We are passing it on to you. God is light. There is no darkness in Him. ⁶If we say we are joined together with Him but live in darkness, we are telling a lie. We are not living the truth. ⁷If we live in the light as He is in the light, we share what we have in God with each other. And the blood of Jesus Christ, His Son, makes our lives clean from all sin. ⁸If we say that we have no sin, we lie to ourselves and the truth is not in us. ⁹If we tell Him our sins, He is faithful and we can depend on Him to forgive us our sins. He will make our lives clean from all sin. ¹⁰If we say we have not sinned, we make God a liar. And His Word is not in our hearts.

> If we tell Him our sins, He is faithful and we can depend on Him to forgive us our sins. He will make our lives clean from all sin.

Christ Is Our Helper

2 My dear children, I am writing this to you so you will not sin. But if anyone does sin, there is One Who will go between him and the Father. He is Jesus Christ, the One Who is right with God. ²He paid for our sins with His own blood. He did not pay for ours only, but for the sins of the whole world.

> He paid for our sins with His own blood.

³We can be sure that we know Him if we obey His teaching. ⁴Anyone who says, "I know Him," but does not obey His

teachings is a liar. There is no truth in him. ⁵But whoever obeys His Word has the love of God made perfect in him. This is the way to know if you belong to Christ. ⁶The one who says he belongs to Christ should live the same kind of life Christ lived.

⁷Dear friends, I am not writing a new Law for you to obey. It is an old Law you have had from the beginning. The old Law is the Word that you have heard. ⁸And yet it is a new Law that I am writing to you. It is truth. It was seen in Christ and it is seen in you also. The darkness is passing away and the true Light shines instead. ⁹Whoever says he is in the light but hates his brother is still in darkness. ¹⁰But whoever loves his brother is in the light. And there will be no reason to sin because of him. ¹¹Whoever hates his brother is not in the light but lives in darkness. He does not know where he is going because the darkness has blinded his eyes.

Do Not Love The World

¹²I am writing to you, my children, for your sins have been forgiven because of Christ's name. ¹³I am writing to you, fathers, because you know Him Who has been from the beginning. I am writing to you, young men, because you have power over the devil. I have written to you, young boys and girls, because you have learned to know the Father. ¹⁴I have written to you, fathers, because you know Him Who has been from the beginning. I have written to you, young men, because you are strong. You have kept God's Word in your hearts. You have power over the devil.

Do not love the world or anything in the world.

¹⁵Do not love the world or anything in the world. If anyone loves the world, the Father's love is not in him. ¹⁶For everything that is in the world does not come from the Father. The desires of our flesh and the things our eyes see and want and the pride of this life come from the world. ¹⁷The world and all its desires will pass away. But the man who obeys God and does what He wants done will live forever.

¹⁸My children, we are near the end of the world. You have heard that the false-christ is coming. Many false-christs have already come. This is how we know the end of the world is near. ¹⁹These left us. But they never belonged to us. If they had been a part of us, they would have stayed with us. Because they left, it is known they did not belong to us. ²⁰The Holy Spirit has been given to you

and you all know the truth. ²¹I have not written to you because you do not know the truth. I have written because you do know the truth and you know that no lie comes from the truth.

²²Who is a liar? He is a person who says that Jesus is not the Christ. The false-christ will have nothing to do with the Father and the Son and he will turn away from Them. ²³A person who will have nothing to do with the Son and turns against Him does not have the Father. The one who says he knows the Son has the Father also.

²⁴Keep in your heart what you have heard from the beginning. Then you will belong to the Son and to the Father if what you have heard from the beginning is in you. ²⁵And He has promised us life that lasts forever!

²⁶I have written to you about those who are trying to lead you in the wrong way. ²⁷Christ gave you the Holy Spirit and He lives in you. You do not need anyone to teach you. The Holy Spirit is able to teach you all things. What He teaches you is truth and not a lie. Live by the help of Christ as the Holy Spirit has taught you. ²⁸And now, my children, live by the help of Him. Then when He comes again, we will be glad to see Him and not be ashamed. ²⁹You know that Christ is right with God. Then you should know that everyone who is right with God is a child of His.

We Are God's Children

3 See what great love the Father has for us that He would call us His children. And that is what we are. For this reason the people of the world do not know who we are because they did not know Him. ²Dear friends, we are God's children now. But it has not yet been shown to us what we are going to be. We know that when He comes again, we will be like Him because we will see Him as He is. ³The person who is looking for this to happen will keep himself pure because Christ is pure.

⁴The person who keeps on sinning is guilty of not obeying the Law of God. For sin is breaking the Law of God. ⁵You know that Christ came to take away our sins. There is no sin in Him. ⁶The person who lives by the help of Christ does not keep on sinning.

The person who keeps on sinning has not seen Him or has not known Him. [7]My children, let no one lead you in the wrong way. The man who does what is right, is right with God in the same way as Christ is right with God. [8]The person who keeps on sinning belongs to the devil. The devil has sinned from the beginning. But the Son of God came to destroy the works of the devil. [9]No person who has become a child of God keeps on sinning. This is because the Holy Spirit is in him. He cannot keep on sinning because God is his Father. [10]This is the way you can know who are the children of God and who are the children of the devil. The person who does not keep on doing what is right and does not love his brother does not belong to God. [11]This is what you have heard from the beginning, that we should love each other. [12]Do not be like Cain. He was a child of the devil and killed his brother. Why did he kill him? It was because he did what was sinful and his brother did what was right.

[13]Do not be surprised if the world hates you, Christian brothers. [14]We know we have passed from death into life. We know this because we love the Christians. The person who does not love has not passed from death into life. [15]A man who hates his brother is a killer in his heart. You know that life which lasts forever is not in one who kills.

[16]We know what love is because Christ gave His life for us. We should give our lives for our brothers. [17]What if a person has enough money to live on and sees his brother in need of food and clothing? If he does not help him, how can the love of God be in him? [18]My children, let us not love with words or in talk only. Let us love by what we do and in truth. [19]This is how we know we are Christians. It will give our heart comfort for sure when we stand in front of Him. [20]Our heart may say that we have done wrong. But remember, God is greater than our heart. He knows everything. [21]Dear friends, if our heart does not say that we are wrong, we will have no fear as we stand in front of Him. [22]We will receive from Him whatever we ask if we obey Him and do what He wants. [23]This is what He said we must do: Put your trust in the name of His Son, Jesus Christ, and love each other. Christ told us to do this. [24]The person who obeys Christ lives by the help of God and God lives in him. We know He lives in us by the Holy Spirit He has given us.

The Spirits Must Be Tested

4 Dear Christian friends, do not believe every spirit. But test the spirits to see if they are from God for there are many false preachers in the world. ²You can tell if the spirit is from God in this way: Every spirit that says Jesus Christ has come in a human body is from God. ³And every spirit that does not say Jesus has come in a human body is not from God. It is the teaching of the false-christ. You have heard that this teaching is coming. It is already here in the world. ⁴My children, you are a part of God's family. You have stood against these false preachers and had power over them. You had power over them because the One Who lives in you is stronger than the one who is in the world. ⁵Those false teachers are a part of the world. They speak about the things of the world. The world listens to them. ⁶We are a part of God's family. The person who knows God will listen to us. The person who is not a part of God's family will not listen to us. In this way, we can tell what is the spirit of truth and what is the spirit of false teaching.

Loving God Makes Us Love our Christian Brothers

⁷Dear friends, let us love each other, because love comes from God. Those who love are God's children and they know God. ⁸Those who do not love do not know God because God is love. ⁹God has shown His love to us by sending His only Son into the world. God did this so we might have life through Christ. ¹⁰This is love! It is not that we loved God but that He loved us. For God sent His Son to pay for our sins with His own blood.

¹¹Dear friends, if God loved us that much, then we should love each other. ¹²No person has ever seen God at any time. If we love each other, God lives in us. His love is made perfect in us. ¹³He has given us His Spirit. This is how we know we live by His help and He lives in us.

Love Gives Us More Faith In Christ

¹⁴We have seen and are able to say that the Father sent His Son to save the world from the punishment of sin. ¹⁵The person who

tells of Him in front of men and says that Jesus is the Son of God, God is living in that one and that one is living by the help of God. [16]We have come to know and believe the love God has for us. God is love. If you live in love, you live by the help of God and God lives in you.

The Love Of God Has Power Over Fear And Hate

[17]Love is made perfect in us when we are not ashamed as we stand in front of Him on the day He says who is guilty. For we know that our life in this world is His life lived in us. [18]There is no fear in love. Perfect love puts fear out of our hearts. People have fear when they are afraid of being punished. The man who is afraid does not have perfect love. [19]We love Him because He loved us first. [20]If a person says, "I love God," but hates his brother, he is a liar. If a person does not love his brother whom he has seen, how can he love God Whom he has not seen? [21]We have these words from Him. If you love God, love your brother also.

5 The person who believes that Jesus is the Christ is a child of God. The person who loves the Father loves His children also. [2]This is the way we know we love God's children. It is when we love God and obey His Word. [3]Loving God means to obey His Word, and His Word is not hard to obey. [4]Every child of God has power over the sins of the world. The way we have power over the sins of the world is by our faith. [5]Who could have power over the world except by believing that Jesus is the Son of God? [6]Jesus Christ came by water and blood. He did not come by water only, but by water and blood. The Holy Spirit speaks about this and He is truth. [7]There are Three Who speak of this *(in heaven, the Father and the Word and the Holy Spirit. These Three are one. [8]There are three that speak of this on the earth,) the Holy Spirit and the water and the blood. These three speak the same thing. [9]If we believe what men say, we can be sure what God says is more important. God has spoken as He has told us about His Son. [10]The person who puts his trust in God's Son knows in his own heart that Jesus is the Son of God. The person who does not have his trust in God's Son makes God a liar. It is because he has not believed the word God spoke about His Son. [11]This is the word He spoke: God gave us life that lasts forever, and this life is in His

Son. ¹²He that has the Son has life. He that does not have the Son of God does not have life.

He who has the Son
has life.
He who does not have
the Son of God
does not have life.

¹³I have written these things to you who believe in the name of the Son of God. Now you can know you have life that lasts forever. ¹⁴We are sure that if we ask anything that He wants us to have, He will hear us. ¹⁵If we are sure He hears us when we ask, we can be sure He will give us what we ask for. ¹⁶You may see a Christian brother sinning in a way that does not lead to death. You should pray for him. God will give him life unless he has done that sin that leads to death. There is a sin that leads to death. There is no reason to pray for him if he has done that sin. ¹⁷Every kind of wrong-doing is sin. But there is a sin that does not lead to death.

I have written
these things to you
who believe in the name
of the Son of God.
Now you can know
you have life
that lasts forever.

¹⁸We know that no child of God keeps on sinning. The Son of God watches over him and the devil cannot get near him. ¹⁹We know that we belong to God, but the whole world is under the power of the devil. ²⁰We know God's Son has come. He has given us the understanding to know Him Who is the true God. We are joined together with the true God through His Son, Jesus Christ. He is the true God and the life that lasts forever. ²¹My children, keep yourselves from false gods.

1 The church leader writes to the chosen lady and to her children. I love you because of the truth. I am not the only one who loves you. All who know the truth love you. ²It is because the truth is in us and will be with us forever. ³Loving-favor and loving-kindness and peace are ours as we live in truth and love. These come from God the Father and from the Lord Jesus Christ, Who is the Son of the Father.

⁴I am happy to find some of your children living in the truth as the Father has said we should. ⁵And now I ask you, lady, that we have love one for the other. I am not writing to you about a new Law but an old one we have had from the beginning. ⁶Love means that we should live by obeying His Word. From the beginning He has said in His Word that our hearts should be full of love.

⁷There are many false teachers in the world. They do not say that Jesus Christ came in a human body. Such a person does not tell the truth. He is the false-christ. ⁸Watch yourselves! You do not want to lose what we have worked for. You want to get what has been promised to you.

⁹Anyone who goes too far and does not live by the teachings of Christ does not have God. If you live by what Christ taught, you have both the Father and the Son. ¹⁰If a person comes to you with some other kind of teaching, do not take him into your home. Do not even say hello to him. ¹¹The person who does has a share in his sins.

¹²I have many things to write to you. I do not want to write them in this letter. But I hope to come to you soon. Then we can talk about these things together that your joy may be full. ¹³The children of your sister who was chosen by God say hello to you.

1 The church leader writes to the much-loved Gaius. I love you because of the truth. ²Dear friend, I pray that you are doing well in every way. I pray that your body is strong and well even as your soul is. ³I was very happy when some Christians came and told me about how you are following the truth. ⁴I can have no greater joy than to hear that my children are following the truth.

⁵Dear friend, you are doing a good work by being kind to the Christians, and for sure, to the strangers. ⁶They have told the church about your love. It will be good for you to help them on their way as God would have you. ⁷These people are working for the Lord. They are taking nothing from the people who do not know God. ⁸So we should help such people. That way we will be working with them as they teach the truth.

⁹I wrote a letter to the church. But Diotrephes wants to be the leader and put himself first. He will have nothing to do with us. ¹⁰So if I come, I will show what he is doing by the bad things he is saying about us. Not only that, he will not take the Christian brothers into his home. He keeps others from doing it also. When they do, he puts them out of the church. ¹¹Dear friend, do not follow what is bad, but follow what is good. The person who does what is good belongs to God. The person who does what is bad has not seen God. ¹²Everyone speaks good things about Demetrius. The truth itself speaks for him. We say the same thing also and you know we are speaking the truth. ¹³I have much to write about but I do not want to write them in this letter. ¹⁴I hope to see you soon and then we can talk together. May you have peace. The friends here say hello to you. Say hello to each friend there by name.

Follow what is good.

1 This letter is from Jude, a brother of James. I am a workman owned by Jesus Christ. I am writing to you who have been chosen by God the Father. You are kept for Jesus Christ. ²May you have much of God's loving-kindness and peace and love.

³Dear friends, I have been trying to write to you about what God did for us when He saved us from the punishment of sin. Now I must write to you and tell you to fight hard for the faith which was once and for all given to the holy people of God. ⁴Some sinful men have come into your church without anyone knowing it. They are living in sin and they speak of the loving-favor of God to cover up their sins. They have turned against our only Leader and Lord, Jesus Christ. Long ago it was written that these people would die in their sins.

⁵You already know all this, but think about it again. The Lord saved His people out of the land of Egypt. Later He destroyed all those who did not put their trust in Him. ⁶Angels who did not stay in their place of power, but left the place where they were given to stay, are chained in a dark place. They will be there until the day they stand in front of God to be told they are guilty. ⁷Do you remember about the cities of Sodom and Gomorrah and the towns around them? The people in those cities did the same things. They were full of sex sins and strong desires for sinful acts of the body. Those cities were destroyed by fire. They still speak to us of the fire of hell that lasts forever.

What False Teachers Are Like

⁸In the same way, these men go on dreaming and sinning against their bodies. They respect no leaders. They speak bad against those who live in the heavens. ⁹Michael was one of the head angels. He argued with the devil about the body of Moses. But Michael would not speak sharp words to the devil, saying he was guilty. He said, "The Lord speak sharp words to you." ¹⁰But these men speak against things they do not understand. They are

like animals in the way they act. By these things they destroy themselves. ¹¹It is bad for them! They have followed the way of Cain who killed his brother. They have chosen the way of Balaam and think only about making money. They were destroyed as Korah was destroyed who would not show respect to leaders. ¹²When you come together to eat the Christians' love suppers, these people are like hidden rocks that wreck a ship. They only think of themselves. They are like clouds without rain carried along by the wind and like trees without fruit in the fall of the year. They are pulled out by the roots and are dead now and never can live again. ¹³They are like the waves of a wild sea. Their sins are like the dirty water along the shore. They look like stars moving here and there. But the darkest place has been kept for them forever.

¹⁴Enoch was the head of the seventh family born after Adam. He said this about such people, "The Lord comes with many thousands of His holy ones. ¹⁵He comes to say that all are guilty for all the sin they have done and all the bad things these sinners have spoken against God." ¹⁶These men complain and are never happy with anything. They let their desires lead them into sin. When they talk about themselves, they make it sound as if they are great people. They show respect to people only to get something out of them.

¹⁷Dear friends, you must remember the words spoken by the missionaries of our Lord Jesus Christ. ¹⁸They said, "In the last days there will be men who will laugh at the truth and will be led by their own sinful desires." ¹⁹They are men who will make trouble by dividing people into groups against each other. Their minds are on the things of the world because they do not have the Holy Spirit.

²⁰Dear friends, you must become strong in your most holy faith. Let the Holy Spirit lead you as you pray. ²¹Keep yourselves in the love of God. Wait for life that lasts forever through the loving-kindness of our Lord Jesus Christ. ²²Have loving-kindness for those who doubt. ²³Save some by pulling them out of the fire. Have loving-kindness for others but also fear them. Be afraid of being led into doing their sins. Hate even the clothes that have touched sinful bodies.

Christ can bring you
in front of Himself
free from all sin.

24There is One Who can keep you from falling. Christ can bring you in front of Himself free from all sin. He can give you great joy as you stand in front of Him in His shining greatness. 25He is the only God. He is the One Who saves from the punishment of sin through Jesus Christ our Lord. May He have shining greatness and honor and power and the right to do all things. He had this before the world began, He has it now, and He will have this forever. Let it be so.

1 The things that are written in this Book are made known by Jesus Christ. God gave these things to Christ so He could show them to the workmen He owns. These are things which must happen very soon. Christ sent His angel to John who is a workman owned by Him. Christ made these things known to John. ²John tells that the Word of God is true. He tells of Jesus Christ and all that he saw and heard of Him. ³The man who reads this Book and listens to it being read and obeys what it says will be happy. For all these things will happen soon.

John Says Hello To The Seven Churches In The Countries Of Asia

⁴This is John writing to the seven churches in the countries of Asia. May you have loving-favor and peace from God Who was and Who is and Who is to come. May you have loving-favor and peace from the seven Spirits who are in front of the place where God sits. ⁵May you have loving-favor and peace from Jesus Christ Who is faithful in telling the truth. Jesus Christ is the first to be raised from the dead. He is the head over all the kings of the earth. He is the One Who loves us and has set us free from our sins by His blood. ⁶Christ has made us a holy nation of religious leaders who can go to His God and Father. He is the One to receive honor and power forever! Let it be so. ⁷Look! He is coming in the clouds. Every eye will see Him. Even the men who killed Him will see Him. All the people on the earth will cry out in sorrow because of Him. Yes, let it be so.

⁸The Lord God says, "I am the First and the Last, the beginning and the end of all things. I am the All-powerful One Who was and Who is and Who is to come."

What God Wanted To Show John Of Christ

⁹I, John, am your Christian brother. I have shared with you in suffering because of Jesus Christ. I have also shared with you His holy nation and we have not given up. I was put on the island

called Patmos because I preached the Word of God and told about Jesus Christ. ¹⁰I was worshiping on the Lord's Day when I heard a loud voice behind me like the loud sound of a horn. ¹¹It said, "*(I am the First and the Last). Write in a book what you see and send it to the seven churches. They are in the cities of Ephesus and Smyrna and Pergamum and Thyatira and Sardis and Philadelphia and Laodicea."

¹²I turned around to see who was speaking to me. As I turned, I saw seven lights made of gold. ¹³Among the lights stood One Who looked like the Son of Man. He had on a long coat that came to His feet. A belt of gold was around His chest. ¹⁴His head and His hair were white like white wool. They were as white as snow. His eyes were like fire. ¹⁵His feet were like shining brass as bright as if it were in a fire. His voice sounded like powerful rushing water. ¹⁶He held seven stars in His right hand. A sharp sword that cuts both ways came out of His mouth. His face was shining as bright as the sun shines at noon. ¹⁷When I saw Him, I fell down at His feet like a dead man. He laid His right hand on me and said, "Do not be afraid. I am the First and the Last. ¹⁸I am the Living One. I was dead. But look, I am alive forever. I have power over death and hell. ¹⁹So write the things you have seen and the things that are and the things that will happen later. ²⁰This is what the seven stars and the seven lights made of gold mean that you saw in My right hand. The seven stars are the angels of the seven churches. The seven lights are the seven churches.

Words To The Church In Ephesus

2 "Write this to the angel of the church in the city of Ephesus: 'The One Who holds the seven stars in His right hand and the One Who walks among the seven lights made of gold, says this: ²I know what you have done and how hard you have worked. I know how long you can wait and not give up. I know that you cannot put up with sinful men. I know that you have put men to the test who call themselves missionaries. You have found they are not missionaries but are false. ³You have waited long and have not given up. You have suffered because of Me. You have kept going on and have not become tired. ⁴But I have this one thing against you. You do not love Me as you did at first. ⁵Remember how you

once loved Me. Be sorry for your sin and love Me again as you did at first. If you do not, I will come to you and take your light out of its place. I will do this unless you are sorry for your sin and turn from it.   6But you have this: You hate what the Nicolaitans do. I hate what they do also.   7You have ears! Then listen to what the Spirit says to the churches. I will give the fruit of the tree of life in the garden of God to everyone who has power and wins.'

Words To The Church In Smyrna

8"Write this to the angel of the church in the city of Smyrna: 'The One Who is First and Last, the One Who died and came to life again, says this: 9I know of your troubles. I know you are poor. But still you are rich! I know the bad things spoken against you by those who say they are Jews. But they are not Jews. They belong to the devil.   10Do not be afraid of what you will suffer. Listen! The devil will throw some of you into prison to test you. You will be in trouble for ten days. Be faithful even to death. Then I will give you the prize of life.   11You have ears! Then listen to what the Spirit says to the churches. The person who has power and wins will not be hurt by the second death!'

Be faithful even to death. Then I will give you the prize of life.

Words To The Church In Pergamum

12"Write this to the angel of the church in the city of Pergamum: 'The One Who has the sharp sword that cuts both ways, says this: 13I know where you live. It is the place where Satan sits. I know that you are true to Me. You did not give up and turn away from your faith in Me, even when Antipas was killed. He was faithful in speaking for Me. He was killed in front of you where Satan is.   14But I have a few things against you. You have some people who follow the teaching of Balaam. He taught Balak to set a trap for the Jews. He taught them to eat food that had been given as a gift in worship to false gods and to do sex sins.   15You also have some who follow the teaching of the Nicolaitans in the same way.   16Be sorry for your sins and turn from them. If you do not, I will come to you right away. I will fight against them with the sword of My mouth.   17You have ears! Then listen to what the Spirit says to the churches. I will give the hidden bread from heaven to everyone who has power and wins. I will give each of them a white stone also. A new name will be

written on it. No one will know the name except the one who receives it!'

Words To The Church In Thyatira

¹⁸"Write this to the angel of the church in the city of Thyatira: 'The Son of God Who has eyes like fire and Whose feet are like shining brass, says this: ¹⁹I know what you are doing. I know of your love and faith. I know how you have worked and how you have waited long and have not given up. I know that you are working harder now than you did at first. ²⁰But I have this against you: You are allowing Jezebel who calls herself a preacher to teach the workmen I own. She is leading them in the wrong way and they are doing sex sins. And they are eating food that has been given as a gift in worship to false gods. ²¹I gave her time to be sorry for her sins and turn from them. She does not want to turn from her sex sins. ²²Listen! I will throw her on a bed. Those who do sex sins with her will suffer much trouble and pain. I will let them suffer unless they are sorry for the sins they have done with her and turn from them. ²³And I will kill her children. All the churches will know that I am the One Who looks deep into the hearts and minds. I will give you whatever is coming to you because of your work. ²⁴But the rest of you there in the city of Thyatira have not followed this false teaching. You have not learned what they call the secrets of Satan. So I will put no other load on you. ²⁵But hold on to what you have until I come. ²⁶To the one who has power and wins and does what I want him to do, I will give the right and the power over the nations. ²⁷He will be leader over them using a piece of iron. And they will be broken in pieces like pots of clay. My Father has given Me this right and power. ²⁸And I will give him the Morning Star. ²⁹You have ears! Then listen to what the Spirit says to the churches!'

Words To The Church In Sardis

3 "Write this to the angel of the church in the city of Sardis: 'The One Who has the seven Spirits of God and the seven stars, says this: I know what you are doing. I know people think you are alive, but you are dead. ²Wake up! Make stronger what you have before it dies. I have not found your work complete in

God's sight.   ³So remember what you have received and heard. Keep it. Be sorry for your sins and turn from them. If you will not wake up, I will come as a robber. You will not know at what time I will come.   ⁴But there are a few people in the church in the city of Sardis whose clothes are not dirty with sins. They will walk with Me wearing white clothes. They have done what they should. ⁵Everyone who has power and wins will wear white clothes. I will not take his name from the book of life. I will speak of his name in front of My Father and His angels.   ⁶You have ears! Then listen to what the Spirit says to the churches.'

Words To The Church In Philadelphia

⁷"Write this to the angel of the church in the city of Philadelphia: 'He Who is holy and true, Who holds the key of David, Who opens and no man can shut, Who shuts and no man can open, says this: ⁸I know what you are doing. Listen! You do not have much power, but you have obeyed My Word. You have not turned against Me. So I have given you an open door that no man can shut.   ⁹Listen! There are some who belong to Satan. They say they are Jews, but they are not. They are liars. Listen! I will make them come to you and get down at your feet. Then they will know that I love you.   ¹⁰I will keep you from the time of trouble. The time to test everyone is about to come to the whole world. I will do this because you have listened to Me and have waited long and have not given up.   ¹¹I am coming very soon. Hold on to what you have so no one can take your prize.   ¹²I will make the one who has power and wins an important part that holds up the house of God. He will never leave it again. I will write on him the name of My God and the name of the city of My God. It is the new Jerusalem. The new Jerusalem will come down from My God out of heaven. I will write My new name on him.   ¹³You have ears! Then listen to what the Spirit says to the churches.'

I am coming very soon.

Words To The Church In Laodicea

¹⁴"Write this to the angel of the church in the city of Laodicea: 'The One Who says, Let it be so, the One Who is faithful, the One Who tells what is true, the One Who made everything in God's world, says this: ¹⁵I know what you are doing. You are not cold or hot. I wish you were one or the other.   ¹⁶But because you are warm,

and not hot or cold, I will spit you out of My mouth. ¹⁷You say that you are rich and that you need nothing, but you do not know that you are so troubled in mind and heart. You are poor and blind and without clothes. ¹⁸You should buy gold from Me that has been tested by fire that you may be rich. Buy white clothes to dress yourself so the shame of not wearing clothes will be taken away. Buy medicine to put on your eyes so you can see. ¹⁹I speak strong words to those I love and I punish them. Have a strong desire to please the Lord. Be sorry for your sins and turn from them. ²⁰Listen! I stand at the door and knock. If anyone hears My voice and opens the door, I will come in to him and we will eat together. ²¹I will allow the one who has power and wins to sit with me on the place where I sit. I had power and won also. Then I sat down beside My Father Who is sitting in His place of power. ²²You have ears! Then listen to what the Spirit says to the churches.' "

Listen! I stand at the door and knock.

The King's Place Of Power In Heaven

4 After this, I looked and saw a door standing open in heaven. The first voice I heard was like the loud sound of a horn. It said, "Come up here. I will show you what must happen after these things." ²At once I was under the Spirit's power. Listen! The place where the King sits was in heaven. There was One sitting on that place. ³The One Who sat there looked as bright as jasper and sardius stones. The colors like those of an emerald stone were all around that place. ⁴There were twenty-four smaller places to sit around the place where the King sits. And on these places twenty-four leaders were sitting dressed in white clothes. They had headbands of gold on their heads. ⁵Lightning and noise and thunder came from the place where He sits. Seven lights of fire were burning in front of the place where He sits. These were the seven Spirits of God.

⁶In front of the place where He sits there was what looked like a sea of glass, shining and clear. Around that place and on each side there were four living beings that were full of eyes in front and in back. ⁷The first living being was like a lion. The second one was like a young cow. The third one had a face like a man. The fourth one was like a very large bird with its wings spread. ⁸Each one of

the four living beings had six wings. They had eyes all over them, inside and out. Day and night they never stop saying, "Holy, holy, holy is the Lord God, the All-powerful One. He is the One Who was and Who is and Who is to come."

⁹The four living beings speak of His shining greatness and give honor and thanks to Him Who sits on His place as King. It is He Who lives forever. ¹⁰The twenty-four leaders get down in front of Him and worship Him Who lives forever. They lay their headbands in front of Him and say, ¹¹"Our Lord and our God, it is right for You to have the shining greatness and the honor and the power. You made all things. They were made and have life because You wanted it that way."

The Book In Heaven

5 I saw a book in the right hand of the One Who sits on His place as King. It had writing on the inside and on the back side. It was locked with seven locks. ²I saw a powerful angel calling with a loud voice, "Who is able to open the book and to break its locks?" ³No one in heaven or on the earth or under the earth was able to open the book or to look into it. ⁴Then I began to cry with loud cries. I cried because no one was good enough to open the book or to look into it.

⁵One of the leaders said to me, "Stop crying. Listen! The Lion from the family group of Judah has power and has won. He can open the book and break its seven locks. He is of the family of David."

⁶I saw a Lamb standing in front of the twenty-four leaders. He was in front of the place where the King sits and in front of the four living beings. He looked as if He had been killed. He had seven horns and seven eyes. These are the seven Spirits of God. They have been sent out into all the world. ⁷The Lamb came and took the book from the right hand of the One Who sat there as King. ⁸When the Lamb had taken the book, the four living beings and the twenty-four leaders got down in front of Him. Each one had a music box with strings. They all had pots made of gold, full of special perfume, which are the prayers of the people who belong to God. ⁹They sang a new song, saying, "It is right for You to

take the book and break its locks. It is because You were killed. Your blood has bought men for God from every family and from every language and from every kind of people and from every nation. ¹⁰You have made them to be a holy nation of religious leaders to work for our God. They will be the leaders on the earth."

¹¹I looked again. I heard the voices of many thousands of angels. They stood around the place where the King sits and around the four living beings and the leaders. ¹²They said with a loud voice, "The Lamb Who was killed has the right to receive power and riches and wisdom and strength and honor and shining greatness and thanks."

The Lamb Who was killed has the right to receive power and riches and wisdom and strength and honor and shining greatness and thanks.

¹³Then I heard every living thing in heaven and on the earth and under the earth and in the sea and all that are in them. They were saying, "Thanks and honor and shining greatness and all power are to the One Who sits on His place as King and to the Lamb forever." ¹⁴The four living beings kept saying, "Let it be so!" And the twenty-four leaders got down and worshiped Him.

The Seven Locks [The First Lock] — Power To Win

6 I saw the Lamb break open the first of the seven locks. I heard one of the four living beings cry out like the sound of thunder, "Come and see!" ²I looked and saw a white horse. The one who sat on it had a bow. A headband was given to him. He went out to win and he won.

The Second Lock — Fighting

³He broke open the second lock. Then I heard the second living being say, "Come and see!" ⁴Another horse came out. This one was red. The one who sat on it was given a long sword. He was given power to take peace from the earth so men would kill each other.

The Third Lock — No Food

⁵He broke open the third lock. Then I heard the third living being say, "Come and see!" I looked and saw a black horse. The

one who sat on it had something in his hand with which to weigh things. ⁶I heard a voice from among the four living beings saying, "A small jar of wheat for a day's pay. Three small jars of barley for a day's pay. Do not hurt the olive oil and wine."

The Fourth Lock — Death

⁷He broke open the fourth lock. Then I heard the fourth living being say, "Come and see!" ⁸I looked and saw a light colored horse. The one who sat on it had the name of Death. Hell followed close behind him. They were given the right and the power to kill one-fourth part of everything on the earth. They were to kill with the sword and by people having no food and by sickness and by the wild animals of the earth.

The Fifth Lock — Killed For Telling Of Jesus

⁹He broke open the fifth lock. Then I saw under the altar all the souls of those who had been killed for telling the Word of God. They had also been killed for being faithful in telling about Christ. ¹⁰All those who had been killed cried out with a loud voice saying, "How long will it be yet before You will punish those on the earth for killing us? Lord, You are holy and true." ¹¹White clothes were given to each one of them. They were told to rest a little longer. They were to wait until all the other workmen owned by God and their Christian brothers would be killed as they had been. Then the group would be complete.

The Sixth Lock — God's Anger On The Earth

¹²I looked as the Lamb broke the sixth lock. The earth shook as if it would break apart. The sun became black like dark cloth. The moon became like blood. ¹³The stars of the sky fell to the earth. They were like figs falling from a tree that is shaken by a strong wind. ¹⁴The sky passed away like paper being rolled up. Every mountain and island moved from its place. ¹⁵The kings and the leaders of the earth hid themselves in the holes and among the rocks of the mountains. All the head soldiers and rich men and strong men and men who were free and those who were owned by someone hid themselves also. ¹⁶They called to the mountains and to the rocks, "Fall on us! Hide us from the face of the One Who

sits in His place as King. Hide us from the anger of the Lamb, [17]because the special day of Their anger has come! Who is able to stand against it?''

The Workmen God Owns Are Marked

7 After this I saw four angels. They were standing at the four corners of the earth. They were holding back the four winds of the earth so no wind would blow on the earth or the sea or on any tree. [2]I saw another angel coming from the east. He was carrying the mark of the living God. He called with a loud voice to the four angels who had been given power to hurt the earth and sea. [3]The angel from the east said, ''Do not hurt the earth or the sea or the trees until we have put the mark of God on the foreheads of the workmen He owns.''

[4]I heard how many there were who received the mark of God. There were 144,000 people of the twelve family groups of Israel. [5]These received the mark of God: 12,000 from the family group of Judah, 12,000 from the family group of Reuben, 12,000 from the family group of Gad, [6]12,000 from the family group of Asher, 12,000 from the family group of Naphtali, 12,000 from the family group of Manasseh, [7]12,000 from the family group of Simeon, 12,000 from the family group of Levi, 12,000 from the family group of Issachar, [8]12,000 from the family group of Zebulun, 12,000 from the family group of Joseph, and 12,000 from the family group of Benjamin.

The Many People Who Belonged To God

They were from every nation.

[9]After this I saw many people. No one could tell how many there were. They were from every nation and from every family and from every kind of people and from every language. They were standing in front of the place where the King sits and in front of the Lamb. They were wearing white clothes and they held branches in their hands. [10]And they were crying out with a loud voice, ''We are saved from the punishment of sin by our God Who sits on His place as King and by the Lamb!'' [11]Then all of the angels standing around the place where the King sits and around the leaders and the four living beings got down on their faces in

front of God and worshiped Him. ¹²They said, "Let it be so! May our God have worship and shining greatness and wisdom and thanks and honor and power and strength forever. Let it be so!"

¹³Then one of the twenty-four leaders asked me, "Who are these people dressed in white clothes? Where did they come from?" ¹⁴I answered him, "Sir, you know." Then he said to me, "These are the ones who came out of the time of much trouble. They have washed their clothes and have made them white in the blood of the Lamb. ¹⁵For this reason they are in front of the place where God sits as King. They help Him day and night in the house of God. And He Who sits there will care for them as He is among them. ¹⁶They will never be hungry or thirsty again. The sun or any burning heat will not shine down on them. ¹⁷For the Lamb Who is in the center of the place where the King sits will be their Shepherd. He will lead them to wells of the water of life. God will take away all tears from their eyes."

The Seventh Lock — No Sound In Heaven

8 When the Lamb broke the seventh lock, there was not a sound in heaven for about one-half hour.

²Then I saw the seven angels standing in front of God. They were given seven horns.

³Another angel came and stood at the altar. He held a cup made of gold full of special perfume. He was given much perfume so he could mix it in with the prayers of those who belonged to God. Their prayers were put on the altar made of gold in front of the place where the King sits. ⁴Smoke from burning the special perfume and the prayers of those who belong to God went up in front of God out of the angel's hand. ⁵Then the angel took the cup of gold. He filled it with fire from the altar and threw it down on the earth. There was thunder and noise and lightning and the earth shook.

⁶The seven angels that had the seven horns got ready to blow them.

The First Horn — Hail And Fire

[7]So the first angel blew his horn. Hail and fire mixed with blood came down on the earth. One-third part of the earth was burned up. One-third part of the trees was burned up. All the green grass was burned up.

The Second Horn — The Burning Mountain

[8]The second angel blew his horn. Something like a large mountain was burning with fire. It was thrown into the sea. One-third part of the sea turned into blood. [9]One-third part of all sea life died. One-third part of all the ships was destroyed.

The Third Horn — The Star Of Poison

[10]The third angel blew his horn. A large star fell from heaven. It was burning with a fire that kept burning like a bright light. It fell on one-third part of the rivers and on the places where water comes out of the earth. [11]The name of the star is Wormwood. One-third part of the water became poison. Many men died from drinking the water because it had become poison.

The Fourth Horn — Not As Much Light

[12]The fourth angel blew his horn. One-third part of the sun and one-third part of the moon and one-third part of the stars were hurt. One-third part of them was made dark so that one-third part of the day and night had no light.

[13]Then I looked and saw a very large bird flying in the sky. It said with a loud voice, "It is bad! It is bad! It is bad for those who live on the earth when the sound comes from the horns that the other three angels will blow!"

The Fifth Horn — The Hole Without A Bottom

9 The fifth angel blew his horn. I saw a star from heaven which had fallen to earth. The key to the hole without a bottom was given to the angel. [2]He opened the hole and smoke came out like the smoke from a place where there is much fire. The sun and the air became dark because of the smoke from the hole. ³Locusts came down to the earth out of the smoke. They were given power to hurt like small animals that sting. ⁴They were told not to hurt the grass or any green plant or any tree. They were to hurt only the men who did not have the mark of God on their foreheads. ⁵The locusts were not allowed to kill these men. They were to give them much pain for five months like the pain that comes from a small animal that stings. ⁶Men will look for ways to die during those days, but they will not find any way. They will want to die, but death will be kept from them. ⁷The locusts looked like horses ready for war. They had on their heads what looked like headbands of gold. Their faces were like men's faces. ⁸Their hair was like the hair of women. Their teeth were like the teeth of lions. ⁹Their chests were covered with what looked like pieces of iron. The sound their wings made was like the sound of many wagons rushing to war. ¹⁰They had tails like a small animal that stings. The sting came from their tails. They were given power to hurt men for five months. ¹¹These locusts have a king over them. He is the head angel of the hole that has no bottom. His name in the Hebrew language is Abbadon. In the Greek language it is Apollyon. (It means the one who destroys.)

¹²The first time of trouble is past. But listen, there are two more times of trouble coming after this.

The Sixth Horn — The Killing Angels

¹³The sixth angel blew his horn. I heard a voice coming from the four corners of the altar made of gold that is in front of God. ¹⁴The voice said to the sixth angel who had the horn, "Let the four angels loose that have been chained at the big river Euphrates." ¹⁵They had been kept ready for that hour and day and month and year. They were let loose so they could kill one-third part of all men that were living. ¹⁶The army had 200 million soldiers on horses. I heard them say how many there were.

¹⁷I saw, as God wanted to show me, the horses and the men on them. The men had pieces of iron over their chests. These were red like fire and blue like the sky and yellow like sulphur. The heads of the horses looked like the heads of lions. Fire and smoke and

sulphur came out of their mouths. ¹⁸One-third part of all men was killed by the fire and smoke and sulphur that came out of their mouths. ¹⁹The power of the horses was in their mouths and in their tails. Their tails were like the heads of snakes and with them they could bite and kill. ²⁰The men that were still living after these troubles were past would not turn away from worshiping demons. They would not turn away from false gods made from gold and silver and brass and stone and wood. None of these false gods can see or hear or walk. ²¹These men were not sorry for their sins and would not turn away from all their killing and their witchcraft. They would not stop their sex sins and their stealing.

The Angel And The Little Book

10 Then I saw another strong angel coming down from heaven covered with a cloud. He had many colors around his head. His face was like the sun. His feet were like long flames of fire. ²He had in his hand a little book that was open. The angel put his right foot on the sea. He put his left foot on the land. ³He cried with a loud voice like the sound of a lion. The seven thunders sounded. ⁴I was ready to write when the seven thunders had spoken. Then I heard the voice from heaven saying, "Lock up the things which the seven thunders have spoken. Do not write them!"

⁵Then the strong angel that I saw standing on the sea and on the land lifted his right hand to heaven. ⁶He made a promise in the name of God Who lives forever, Who made the heaven and the earth and the sea and everything in them. He promised that there will be no more waiting. ⁷And when the seventh angel blows his horn, God will put His secret plan into action. It will be done just as He told it to the early preachers He owned.

⁸Then the voice I heard from heaven spoke to me again. It said, "Go and take the little book that is open. It is in the hand of the angel who is standing on the sea and on the land."

⁹I went to the angel and asked him to give me the little book. He said, "Take it and eat it. It will taste like honey in your mouth. But after you have eaten it, it will make your stomach sour." ¹⁰Then I took it from the angel's hand and ate it. It was sweet as

honey in my mouth, but it made my stomach sour after I had eaten it.

¹¹Then they said to me, "You must tell what will happen again in front of many people and nations and families and kings."

The House Of God

11 I was given a stick that is used to see how big things are. Someone said, "Go up to the house of God and find out how big it is. Find out about the altar also. See how many people are worshiping. ²Do not find out about the porch of the house of God. It has been given over to the nations who do not know God. They will walk over all the Holy City to wreck it for forty-two months. ³I will give power to my two men who tell what they know. They will speak for God for 1,260 days (forty-two months). They will be dressed in clothes made from the hair of animals."

The Two Men Who Tell What They Know

⁴These two men who tell what they know are the two olive trees and the two lights that stand in front of the Lord of the earth. ⁵If anyone hates them and tries to hurt them, fire comes out of the mouths of these two men. The fire kills those who try to hurt them. ⁶They have power to shut up the sky. During the time they speak for God, there will be no rain. They have power to change all waters into blood. They can send every kind of trouble to the earth whenever they want to.

The Death Of The Two Men Who Speak For God

⁷When they have finished speaking for God, the wild animal will make war with them. It will come up out of the hole without a bottom. This wild animal will have power over them and kill them. ⁸Their dead bodies will lie in the street of the city of Jerusalem. It is where their Lord was nailed to a cross. The city is sometimes called Sodom and Egypt. ⁹For three and one-half days those from every people and from every family and from every language and from every nation will look at their dead bodies. People will not allow the dead bodies of these two men to be put into a grave.

¹⁰Those who are living on the earth will be happy because of the death of these two men. They will do things to show they are happy. They will send gifts to each other. They will do this because these two men brought much trouble and suffering to the people of the earth.

The Two Men Come To Life Again

¹¹After three and one-half days, life from God came into them again. They stood on their feet. Those who saw them were very much afraid. ¹²Then the two men who told what they knew heard a loud voice from heaven. It said, "Come up here." And they went up to heaven in a cloud. All those who hated them watched them go. ¹³At the same time the earth shook. One-tenth part of the buildings of the city fell down. 7,000 people were killed. The rest of the people were afraid and gave honor to the God of heaven.

¹⁴The second time of trouble is past. But look, the third time of trouble is coming soon.

The Seventh Horn — Worship In Heaven

¹⁵The seventh angel blew his horn. There were loud voices in heaven saying, "The nations of the world have become the holy nation of our Lord and of His Christ. He will be the Leader forever." ¹⁶Then the twenty-four leaders who sat on the places given them in front of God fell to the ground on their faces and worshiped God. ¹⁷They said, "All-powerful Lord God, the One Who is and Who was and Who is to come, we thank You because You are using Your great power and have become Leader. ¹⁸The people who do not know God have become angry with You. Now it is time for You to be angry with them. It is time for the dead to stand in front of You and to be told they are guilty. It is time for the workmen You own who are the early preachers and those who belong to You to get the pay that is coming to them. It is time for the important people and those not important who honor Your name to get the pay that is coming to them. It is time to destroy those who have made every kind of trouble on the earth."

¹⁹God's house in heaven was opened. The special box which held the Old Way of Worship was seen in the house of God. There was

lightning and thunder and noise. The earth shook and large hail stones fell.

The Woman And The Snake-Like Animal

12 Something very special was seen in heaven. A woman was there dressed with the sun. The moon was under her feet. A headband with twelve stars in it was on her head. ²She was about to become a mother. She cried out with pain waiting for the child to be born.

³Something else special was seen in heaven. A large snake-like animal was there. It was red and had seven heads and ten horns. There was a headband on each head. ⁴With his tail he pulled one-third part of the stars out of heaven. He threw them down to the earth. This snake-like animal stood in front of the woman as she was about to give birth to her child. He was waiting to eat her child as soon as it was born. ⁵Then the woman gave birth to a son. He is to be the leader of the world using a piece of iron. But this child was taken away to God and to the place where He sits. ⁶The woman ran away into the desert. God had made the place ready for her. He will care for her there 1,260 days.

War In Heaven

⁷Then there was war in heaven. Michael and his angels fought against this snake-like animal. This animal and his angels fought back. ⁸But the snake-like animal was not strong enough to win. There was no more room in heaven for them. ⁹The snake-like animal was thrown down to earth from heaven. This animal is the old snake. He is also called the Devil or Satan. He is the one who has fooled the whole world. He was thrown down to earth and his angels were thrown down with him.

¹⁰Then I heard a loud voice in heaven saying, "Now God has saved from the punishment of sin! God's power as King has come! God's holy nation has come! God's Christ is here with power! The one who spoke against our Christian brothers has been thrown down to earth. He stood in front of God speaking against them day and night. ¹¹They had power over him and won because of the

God's power as King has come!

blood of the Lamb and by telling what He had done for them. They did not love their lives but were willing to die. ¹²For this reason, O heavens and you who are there, be full of joy. It is bad for you, O earth and sea. For the devil has come down to you. He is very angry because he knows he has only a short time."

War On Earth

¹³When the snake-like animal which is the devil saw that he had been thrown down to the earth, he began to hunt for the woman who had given birth to the boy baby. ¹⁴The woman was given two wings like the wings of a very large bird so she could fly to her place in the desert. She was to be cared for there and kept safe from the snake, which is the devil, for three and one-half years. ¹⁵Then the snake spit water from his mouth so the woman might be carried away with a flood. ¹⁶The earth helped the woman by opening its mouth. It drank in the flood of water that this snake-like animal spit from his mouth. ¹⁷This snake-like animal was very angry with the woman. He went off to fight with the rest of her children. They are the ones who obey the Laws of God and are faithful to the teachings of Jesus.

The Two Animals — The First One From The Sea

13 I stood on the sand by the seashore. There I saw a wild animal coming up out of the sea. It had seven heads and ten horns with a headband on each horn. There were names on each head that spoke bad words against God. ²The wild animal I saw was covered with spots. It had feet like those of a bear. It had a mouth like that of a lion. The snake-like animal gave this wild animal his own power and his own place to sit as king. The wild animal was given much power. ³One of the heads of the wild animal looked as if it had been killed. But the bad cut given to kill him was healed. The whole world was surprised and wondered about this, and they followed after the wild animal. ⁴They worshiped the snake-like animal for giving this wild animal such power. And they worshiped this wild animal. They said, "Who is like this wild animal? Who can fight against it?"

⁵The animal was given a mouth which spoke words full of pride and it spoke very bad things against the Lord. It was given much

power for forty-two months. ⁶And it opened its mouth speaking very bad things against God. It spoke against God's name and His house and against those living in heaven. ⁷It was allowed to fight against the people who belong to God, and it had power to win over them. It had power over every family and every group of people and over people of every language and every nation. ⁸Every person on the earth from the beginning of the world whose name has not been written in the book of life of the Lamb Who was killed will worship this animal.

⁹You have ears! Then listen. ¹⁰Whoever is to be tied and held will be held. Whoever kills with a sword must himself be killed with a sword. Now is when God's people must have faith and not give up.

Now is when God's people must have faith and not give up.

The Second Animal — From The Land

¹¹Then I saw another wild animal coming out of the earth. He had two horns like those of a lamb. His voice was like that of the snake-like animal. ¹²He used the power of the first wild animal who was there with him. He made all the people on earth worship the first wild animal who had received the bad cut to kill him but was healed. ¹³The second wild animal did great powerful works. It spoke and made those who did not worship the first wild animal to be killed. ¹⁴He fooled the men of the earth by doing powerful works. He did these things in front of the first wild animal. He told those who live on the earth to make a god that looks like the first wild animal. The first wild animal was the one that was cut by the sword but lived. ¹⁵The second wild animal was given power to give life to the false god. This false god was the one that was made to look like the first wild animal. It was given power to talk. All those who did not worship it would die. ¹⁶The second wild animal made every person have a mark on their right hand or on their forehead. It was given to important men and to those not important, to rich men and poor men, to those who are free and to those who are owned by someone. ¹⁷No one could buy or sell anything unless he had the mark on him. This mark was the name of the first wild animal or another way to write his name. ¹⁸This is wisdom. Let the person who has good understanding learn the meaning of the other way to write the name of the first wild animal. This name is a man's name. It is 666.

The Lamb Stands In Jerusalem

14 Then I looked and saw the Lamb standing on the Mountain of Zion. There were 144,000 people with Him. These people had His name and His Father's name written on their foreheads. ²I heard a voice coming from heaven. It was like the sound of rushing water and of loud thunder. The voice I heard was like people playing music from boxes with strings. ³This large group sang a new song. They sang in front of the place where the King sits and in front of the four living beings and the twenty-four leaders. Only the 144,000 could learn this song. They had been bought by the blood of Christ and made free from the earth. ⁴These are men who have kept themselves pure by not being married. They follow the Lamb wherever He goes. They have been bought by the blood of Christ and have been made free from among men. They are the first ones to be given to God and to the Lamb. ⁵No lie has come from their mouths. They are without blame.

The Three Angels

⁶Then I saw another angel flying in the heavens. He was carrying the Good News that lasts forever. He was preaching to every nation and to every family group and to the people of every language and to all the people of the earth. ⁷He said with a loud voice, "Honor God with love and fear. The time has come for Him to say who is guilty among men. Worship Him Who made heaven and earth and the sea and the places where water comes out of the earth."

⁸A second angel followed, saying, "Babylon has fallen! The great city Babylon has fallen! She made all the nations drink of the wine of her dirty life of sex sin."

⁹A third angel followed, saying with a loud voice, "If anyone worships the wild animal and his false god and receives a mark on his forehead or hand, ¹⁰he will drink of the wine of the anger of God. It is mixed in full strength in the cup of God's anger. They

will be punished with fire and burning sulphur in front of the holy angels and in front of the Lamb. ¹¹The smoke of those who are being punished will go up forever. They have no rest day or night. It is because they have worshiped the wild animal and his false god and have received the mark of his name. ¹²This is why God's people need to keep true to God's Word and stay faithful to Jesus.

¹³Then I heard a voice from heaven, saying, "Write these words: 'From now on those who are dead who died belonging to the Lord will be happy.' " "Yes," says the Spirit, "they will have rest from all their work. All the good things they have done will follow them."

The War Of Armageddon

¹⁴I looked and saw a white cloud. Sitting on the cloud was One like the Son of Man. He had a headband of gold on His head. In His hand He had a sharp knife for cutting grain. ¹⁵Then another angel came out from the house of God and called to Him with a loud voice. He said, "Use Your knife and gather in the grain. The time has come to gather the grain because the earth is ready." ¹⁶He Who sat on the cloud raised His knife over the earth. And the grain was gathered in.

¹⁷Then another angel came out from the house of God in heaven. He had a sharp knife for cutting grain also. ¹⁸Another angel who has power over fire came out from the altar. He said with a loud voice to the angel who had the sharp knife, "Use your knife and gather in the grapes from the vine of the earth. For they are ready to gather." ¹⁹The angel used his sickle on the earth. He gathered from the vine of the earth and put the fruit into the large place for making wine. It was full of God's anger. ²⁰They walked on it outside the city and blood came out of the place where wine is made. The blood ran as far as a man could walk in seven days. It came up as high as a horse's head.

Seven Angels With Seven Troubles

15 Then I saw something else special in heaven that was great and made me wonder. There were seven angels with the seven last kinds of trouble. With these, God's anger is finished.

²Then I saw something that looked like a sea of glass mixed with fire. I saw many standing on the sea of glass. They were those who had won their fight with the wild animal and his false god and with his mark. All of them were holding music boxes with strings that God had given to them. ³They were singing the song of Moses, who was a workman owned by God, and the song of the Lamb, saying, "The things You do are great and powerful. You are the All-powerful Lord God. You are always right and true in everything You do. You are King of all nations. ⁴Who will not honor You, Lord, with love and fear? Who will not tell of the greatness of Your name? For You are the only One Who is holy. All nations will come and worship in front of You. Everyone sees that You do the right things."

⁵After this I looked and saw that the Holiest Place of All in the house of God was opened. ⁶The seven angels who had the seven last kinds of trouble came out of the house of God. They were wearing clothes made of clean white linen. They were wearing belts made of gold around their chests. ⁷Then one of the four living beings gave to each of the seven angels a jar made of gold. These jars were filled with the anger of God Who lives forever. ⁸The house of God was filled with smoke from the shining greatness and power of God. No one was able to go into the house of God until the seven angels had completed the seven kinds of trouble.

The First Jar — Sinful Sores

16 Then I heard a loud voice coming from the house of God. The voice said to the seven angels, "Go and pour out the seven jars of God's anger onto the earth!"

²The first angel poured out his jar of God's anger onto the earth. Painful sores were given to everyone who had the mark of the wild animal and who worshiped his god.

The Second Jar — Death In The Sea

³The second angel poured out his jar of God's anger onto the sea. The water became like the blood of a dead man. Every living thing in the sea died.

The Third Jar — Water Turns To Blood

4The third angel poured out his jar of God's anger onto the rivers and places where water comes out of the earth. The water turned to blood. 5I heard the angel of the waters saying, "You are right in punishing by sending this trouble. You are the Holy One Who was and is and will be. 6They have poured out the blood of God's people and of the early preachers. You have given them blood to drink. They are getting the pay that is coming to them." 7I heard a voice from the altar saying, "Lord God, the All-powerful One! What You decide about people is right and true."

You are the Holy One
Who was and is
and will be.

Lord God,
the All-powerful One!
What You decide
about people
is right and true.

The Fourth Jar — Burning Heat

8The fourth angel poured out his jar of God's anger onto the sun. It was allowed to burn men with its fire. 9Men were burned with the heat of this fire and they called God bad names even when He had the power over these kinds of trouble. They were not sorry for their sins and did not turn from them and honor Him.

The Fifth Jar — Darkness

10The fifth angel poured out his jar of God's anger onto the place where the wild animal sits as king. The whole nation of the wild animal was turned into darkness. Those who worshiped him bit their tongues because of the pain. 11They called the God of heaven bad names because of their pain and their sores. They were not sorry for what they had done.

The Sixth Jar — The Euphrates River Dries Up

12The sixth angel poured out his jar of God's anger onto the great Euphrates River. The water dried up. In this way, the kings of the countries of the east could cross over. 13Then I saw three demons that looked like frogs. They came out of the mouths of the snake-like animal and the second wild animal and the false preacher. 14These are demons that do powerful works. These demons go to all the kings of all the earth. They bring them together for the war of the great day of the All-powerful God.

15(Listen! I will come like a robber. The man is happy who stays awake and keeps his clothes ready. He will not be walking around

without clothes and be ashamed.) 16Then the demons brought the kings together in the place called Armageddon in the Hebrew language.

The Seventh Jar — The Earth Shakes And Hail Falls

17The seventh angel poured out his jar of God's anger into the air. A loud voice came from the place where the King sits in the house of God, saying, "It is all done!" 18Then there were voices and lightning and thunder and the earth shook. The earth shook much more than it had ever shaken before. 19The big and strong city of Babylon was split in three parts. The cities of other nations fell to the ground. Then God remembered the strong city of Babylon. He made her drink the wine from His cup of much anger. 20Every island went down into the sea. No mountain could be found. 21Large pieces of hail fell from heaven on men. These pieces were about as heavy as a small man. But men called God bad names because of so much trouble from the hail.

The Sinful Woman

17 Then one of the seven angels who had the seven jars came to me. He said, "Come! I will show you how the powerful woman who sells the use of her body will be punished. She sits on the many waters of the world. 2The kings of the earth have done sex sins with her. People of the world have been made drunk with the wine of her sex sins."

3My spirit was carried away by the angel to a desert. I saw a woman sitting on a red wild animal. It had seven heads and ten horns. All over the red wild animal was written bad names which spoke against God. 4The woman was wearing purple and red clothes. She was wearing gold and pearls and stones worth much money. She had in her hand a gold cup full of sinful things from her sex sins. 5There was a name written on her forehead which had a secret meaning. It said, "The big and powerful Babylon, mother of all women who sell the use of their bodies and mother of everything sinful of the earth." 6I looked at the woman. She was drunk with the blood of God's people and those who had been killed for telling about Jesus. When I saw her. I wondered very much.

7The angel asked me, "Why do you wonder? I will tell you the secret about this woman and the red wild animal that carries her. It is the red wild animal with seven heads and ten horns. 8The red wild animal you saw was alive but is now dead. It is about to come up from the hole without a bottom and be destroyed. The people of the earth, whose names have not been written in the book of life from the beginning of the world, will be surprised as they look at the red wild animal. It was alive. Now it is dead, but it will come back again.

9"Here is where we need wisdom. The seven heads of the animal are mountains where the woman sits. 10They are seven kings also. Five of them are no longer kings. The sixth one is now king. The seventh one will be king, but only for a little while. 11The red wild animal that died is the eighth king. He belongs to the first seven kings, but he will be destroyed also.

12"The ten horns of the red wild animal which you saw are ten kings. They have not become leaders yet. But they will be given the right and the power to lead their nations for one hour with the red wild animal. 13They agree to give the right and the power to the red wild animal. 14These kings will fight and make war with the Lamb. But the Lamb will win the war because He is Lord of lords and King of kings. His people are the called and chosen and faithful ones."

He is Lord of lords and King of kings.

15Then the angel said to me, "You saw the waters where the woman who sold the use of her body is sitting. The waters are people and large groups of people and nations and languages. 16The ten horns you saw and the red wild animal will hate the woman who sold the use of her body. They will take everything from her and even her clothes. They will eat her flesh and burn her with fire. 17God put into their minds a plan that would carry out His desire. They will agree to give their nation to the red wild animal until the words of God have been completed. 18The woman you saw is the big and powerful city that has power over the kings of the earth."

Babylon Is Destroyed

18 Then I saw another angel coming down from heaven. He had much power. The earth was made bright with his shining greatness. ²He cried out with a loud voice, "The big and powerful city of Babylon is destroyed. Demons and every kind of dirty spirit live there. Dirty birds that are hated are there. ³For she gave her wine to the nations of the world. It was the wine of her desire for sex sins. The kings of the earth have done these sex sins with her. The men of the earth who buy and sell have become rich from the riches she received while living in sin."

⁴I heard another voice from heaven saying, "Come out from her, my people. Do not be a part of her sins so you will not share her troubles. ⁵For her sins are as high as heaven. God is ready to punish her for her sins. ⁶Pay her back for what she has paid you. Give back to her twice as much as she has done. Give back to her in her own cup twice as much as she gave you. ⁷Give her as much trouble and suffering as the fun and the rich living she chose for herself. In her heart she says, 'I sit here like a queen. I am not a woman whose husband has died. I will never have sorrow.' ⁸Because of this, troubles of death and sorrow and no food will come to her in one day. She will be burned with fire. For the Lord God is powerful. He is the One Who says she is guilty.

The Lord God is powerful.

Kings Cry Because Of Babylon

⁹"Then the kings of the earth will cry for her and be sorry when they see the smoke of her burning. They are the ones who did sex sins with her and lived as rich people. ¹⁰They stand a long way from her because they are afraid of her sufferings. They say, 'It is bad! It is bad for the big and powerful city of Babylon. For in one hour she is destroyed.' ¹¹The men of the earth who buy and sell are sorry for her and cry. They cry because there is no one to buy their things anymore. ¹²They sold gold and silver and stones worth much money and pearls. They sold fine linen and purple and red silk cloth. They sold all kinds of perfumed wood. They sold things made from the teeth of animals and things made from wood that costs much money. They sold brass and iron and stone.

¹³They sold spices and perfumes of all kinds. They sold wine and olive oil and fine flour and wheat. They sold cows and sheep and horses and wagons. They sold men who are not free and they sold the lives of men. ¹⁴They say to her, 'All the good things you wanted so much are gone from you. Your riches are gone. The things you liked so much are gone. You will never have them again.' ¹⁵The men of the earth who became rich by buying and selling in that city will stand a long way back because they are afraid of her sufferings. They will cry and have sorrow. ¹⁶They will say, 'It is bad! It is bad for that powerful city. She dressed in fine linen of purple and red. She covered herself with gold and pearls and stones worth much money. ¹⁷For in one hour her riches are destroyed.' The captain of every ship and all who traveled on ships and all who worked on ships stood a long way back. ¹⁸They cried out as they saw the smoke of her burning, saying, 'Has there ever been such a city as powerful as this one?' ¹⁹They threw dirt on their heads. They cried out with much sorrow and said. 'It is bad! It is bad for the powerful city! She is the place where all those who owned ships on the sea became rich from all her riches. For in one hour everything is gone!'

²⁰"Be full of joy because of her, O heaven! Be full of joy, you who belong to God and missionaries and early preachers! For God has punished her for what she did to you."

²¹Then a strong angel picked up a large stone like those used for grinding wheat. He threw it into the sea, saying, "The big and strong city of Babylon will be thrown down like this. It will never be found again. ²²The sound of those playing music on boxes with strings and on flutes and on horns will not be heard in you again. No workman doing any kind of work will be found in you again. The sound of the grinding stone will not be heard in you again. ²³No light will ever shine in you again. There will be no more happy voices from a wedding heard in you. Your men who bought and sold were the most powerful on earth. You fooled people over all the world by your witchcraft. ²⁴And in this city was found the blood of the early preachers and of those who belonged to God and of all those who had been killed on the earth."

Giving Thanks In Heaven

19 After this I heard what sounded like the voices of many people in heaven, saying, "Thanks to our God, the One Who saves. Honor and power belong to Him. ²For the way He punishes people is right and true. He has punished the powerful woman who sold the use of her body. She was making the earth sinful with her sex sins. She killed those who worked for God. He has punished her for it." ³Again they said, "Thanks to our God. The smoke from her burning goes up forever." ⁴The twenty-four leaders and the four living beings got down and worshiped God Who was sitting on His place as King. They said, "Let it be so. Thanks to our God!"

⁵A voice came from the place where the King sits, saying, "Give thanks to our God, you workmen who are owned by Him. Give thanks to our God, you who honor Him with love and fear, both small and great."

The Wedding Supper Of The Lamb

⁶Then I heard what sounded like the voices of many people. It was like the sound of powerful rushing water. And it was like loud thunder. It said, "Thanks to our God. For the Lord our God is King. He is the All-powerful One. ⁷Let us be full of joy and be glad. Let us honor Him, for the time has come for the wedding supper of the Lamb. His bride has made herself ready. ⁸She was given clean, white, fine linen clothes to wear. The fine linen is the right living of God's people."

The Lord our God is King.

⁹The angel said to me, "Write this: 'Those who are asked to the wedding supper of the Lamb are happy.' " And he said, "These are the true words of God." ¹⁰Then I got down at his feet to worship him. But he said to me, "No! Do not worship me. I am a workman together with you and your Christian brothers who tell of their trust in Christ. Worship God. For the truth about Jesus makes the early preachers know what to preach about."

The King Of Kings On The White Horse

¹¹Then I saw heaven opened. A white horse was standing there. The One Who was sitting on the horse is called Faithful and True. He is the One Who punishes in the right way. He makes war. ¹²His eyes are a flame of fire. He has many headbands on His head. His name is written on Him but He is the only One Who knows what it says. ¹³The coat He wears has been put in blood. His name is The Word of God. ¹⁴The armies in heaven were dressed in clean, white, fine linen. They were following Him on white horses. ¹⁵Out of His mouth comes a sharp sword to punish the nations. He will be the Leader over them using a piece of iron. He walks on the grapes where wine is made. From it will come the anger of God, the All-powerful One. ¹⁶On His coat and on His leg is the name written, "KING OF KINGS AND LORD OF LORDS."

¹⁷Then I saw an angel standing in the sun. He cried out with a loud voice to all the birds flying in the sky, "Come and gather together for the great supper of God! ¹⁸Come and eat the flesh of kings and of captains of soldiers and of strong men and of the flesh of horses and of those sitting on them. Come and eat the flesh of all men, small and great. Some are free and some are not free."

¹⁹Then I saw the wild animal and the kings of the earth and their armies gather together. They were ready to fight against the One Who is sitting on the white horse and against His army. ²⁰The wild animal was taken. The false preacher was taken with it. It was the false preacher who had done powerful works in front of the wild animal. In this way, he fooled those who had received the mark of the wild animal and those who worshiped his false god. These two were thrown alive into the lake of fire that burns with sulphur. ²¹The rest were killed with the sword that came out of the mouth of the One Who sat on the horse. All the birds were filled by eating the flesh of these who were killed.

Satan Is Chained For One Thousand Years

20 Then I saw an angel coming down from heaven. He had in his hand a key to the hole without a bottom. He also had a strong chain. ²He took hold of the snake-like animal, that old snake, who is the Devil, or Satan, and chained him for 1,000 years.   ³The angel threw the devil into the hole without a bottom. He shut it and locked him in it. He could not fool the nations anymore until the 1,000 years were completed. After this he must be free for awhile.

⁴Then I saw places where kings sit. Those who were sitting there were given the power to say who is guilty. I saw the souls of those who had been killed because they told about Jesus and preached the Word of God. They had not worshiped the wild animal or his false god. They had not received his mark on their foreheads or hands. They lived again and were leaders along with Christ for 1,000 years. ⁵The rest of the dead did not come to life again until the 1,000 years were finished. This is the first time many people are raised from the dead at the same time. ⁶Those who are raised from the dead during this first time are happy and holy. The second death has no power over them. They will be religious leaders of God and of Christ. They will be leaders with Him for 1,000 years.

Satan Is Destroyed Forever

⁷When the 1,000 years are finished, Satan will be free to leave his prison. ⁸He will go out and fool the nations who are over all the world. They are Gog and Magog. He will gather them all together for war. There will be as many as the sand along the seashore. ⁹They will spread out over the earth and all around the place where God's people are and around the city that is loved. Fire will come down from God out of heaven and destroy them. ¹⁰Then the devil who fooled them will be thrown into the lake of fire burning with sulphur. The wild animal and the false preacher are already there. They will all be punished day and night forever.

The Guilty Will Be Punished

¹¹Then I saw the place where God sits. It was a great white seat. I saw the One Who sat on it. The earth and the heaven left Him in a hurry and they could be found no more. ¹²I saw all the dead people standing in front of God. There were great people and small people. The books were opened. Then another book was opened. It was the book of life. The dead people were told they were guilty by what they had done as it was written in the books. ¹³The sea gave

Another book was opened.
It was the book of life.

up the dead people who were in it. Death and hell gave up the dead people who were in them. Each one was told he was guilty by what he had done. ¹⁴Then death and hell were thrown into the lake of fire. The lake of fire is the second death. ¹⁵If anyone's name was not written in the book of life, he was thrown into the lake of fire.

All Things New

21 Then I saw a new heaven and a new earth. The first heaven and the first earth had passed away. There was no more sea. ²I saw the Holy City, the new Jerusalem. It was coming down out of heaven from God. It was made ready like a bride is made ready for her husband. ³I heard a loud voice coming from heaven. It said, "Look! God's home is with men. He will live with them. They will be His people. God Himself will be with them. He will be their God. ⁴God will take away all their tears. There will be no more death or sorrow or crying or pain. All the old things have passed away." ⁵Then the One sitting on His place as King said, "Look! I am making all things new. Write, for these words are true and faithful." ⁶Then He said to me, "These things have happened! I am the First and the Last. I am the beginning and the end. To anyone who is thirsty, I will give the water of life. It is a free gift. ⁷He who has power and wins will receive these things. I will be his God and he will be My son. ⁸But those who are afraid and those who do not have faith and the sinful-minded people and those who kill other people and those who do sex sins and those who follow witchcraft and those who worship false gods and all those who tell lies will be put into the lake of fire and sulphur. This is the second death."

The New Jerusalem

⁹Then one of the seven angels who had the seven jars full of the seven last troubles came to me and said, "Come! I will show you the bride, the wife of the Lamb." ¹⁰My spirit was carried away by the angel to a very high mountain. He showed me the Holy City of Jerusalem. It was coming out of heaven from God. ¹¹It was filled with the shining greatness of God. It shone like a stone worth much money, like a jasper stone. It was clear like glass. ¹²It had a very high wall, and there were twelve gates. Twelve angels stood by the gates. The names of the twelve family groups of the Jewish

nation were written on the gates. [13]There were three gates on each side. There were three on the east side and three on the north side and three on the south side and three on the west side. [14]The walls were on twelve stones. The names of the twelve missionaries of the Lamb were written on the stones.

[15]The angel had a stick in his hand. It was used to find out how big the city and its gates and the walls were. [16]He found out that the city was as wide as it was long and it was as high as it was wide. It was as long as a man could walk in fifty days. It was the same each way. [17]The angel found out that the walls were the same as a man taking seventy-two long steps. The angel used the same way to find out about the city as a man would have used. [18]The wall was made of jasper. The city was made of pure gold. This gold was as clear as glass. [19]The city was built on every kind of stone that was worth much money. The first stone was jasper. The second was sapphire. The third was chalcedony. The fourth was emerald. [20]The fifth was sardonyx. The sixth was sardius. The seventh was chrysolite. The eighth was beryl. The ninth was topaz. The tenth was chrysoprase. The eleventh was jacinth and the twelfth was amethyst. [21]The twelve gates were twelve pearls. Each gate was made from one pearl. The street of the city was pure gold. It was as clear as glass.

[22]I did not see a house of God in the city. The All-powerful Lord God and the Lamb are the house of God in this city. [23]There is no need for the sun and moon to shine in the city. The shining greatness of God makes it full of light. The Lamb is its light. [24]The nations will walk by its light. The kings of the earth will bring their greatness into it. [25]The gates are open all day. They will never be shut. There will be no night there. [26]The greatness and honor of all the nations will be brought into it. [27]Nothing sinful will go into the city. No one who is sinful-minded or tells lies can go in. Only those whose names are written in the Lamb's book of life can go in.

More About The New Jerusalem

22 Then the angel showed me the river of the water of life. It was as clear as glass and came from the place where God and the Lamb sit. [2]It runs down the center of the street in the city. On each side of the river was the tree of life. It gives twelve different kinds of fruit. It gives this fruit twelve times a year, new fruit each month. Its leaves are used to heal the nations.

³There will be nothing in the city that is sinful. The place where God and the Lamb sit will be there. The workmen He owns will work for Him. ⁴They will see His face and His name will be written on their foreheads. ⁵There will be no night there. There will be no need for a light or for the sun. Because the Lord God will be their light. They will be leaders forever.

Jesus Is Coming Soon

⁶Then the angel said to me, "These words are faithful and true. The Lord God of the early preachers has sent His angel to show the workmen He owns what must happen soon. ⁷Listen! I am coming soon. The one who obeys what is written in this Book is happy!"

The one who obeys
what is written
in this Book
is happy!

⁸It was I, John, who heard and saw these things. Then I got down at the feet of the angel who showed me these things. I was going to worship him. ⁹But he said to me, "No! You must not do that. I am a workman together with you and with your Christian brothers and the early preachers and with all those who obey the words in this Book. You must worship God!" ¹⁰Then he said to me, "Do not lock up the words of this Book. These things will happen soon. ¹¹And let the sinful people keep on being sinful. Let the dirty-minded people keep on being dirty-minded. And let those right with God keep on being right with God. Let the holy people keep on being holy.

¹²"Listen! I am coming soon. I am bringing with Me the pay I will give to everyone for what he has done. ¹³I am the First and the Last. I am the beginning and the end. ¹⁴Those who wash their clothes clean are happy (who are washed by the blood of the Lamb). They will have the right to go into the city through the gates. They will have the right to eat the fruit of the tree of life. ¹⁵Outside the city are the dogs. They are people who follow witchcraft and those who do sex sins and those who kill other people and those who worship false gods and those who like lies and tell them.

[16]"I am Jesus. I have sent My angel to you with these words to the churches. I am the beginning of David and of his family. I am the bright Morning Star."

[17]The Holy Spirit and the Bride say, "Come!" Let the one who hears, say, "Come!" Let the one who is thirsty, come. Let the one who wants to drink of the water of life, drink it. It is a free gift.

[18]I am telling everyone who hears the words that are written in this book: If anyone adds anything to what is written in this book, God will add to him the kinds of trouble that this book tells about. [19]If anyone takes away any part of this book that tells what will happen in the future, God will take away his part from the tree of life and from the Holy City which are written in this book.

[20]He Who tells these things says, "Yes, I am coming soon!" Let it be so. Come, Lord Jesus. [21]May all of you have the loving-favor of the Lord Jesus Christ. Let it be so.

Yes, I am coming soon!

WORD LIST

Words Used In Other Translations	Words Used In This Translation
	A
abominable	sinful-minded people
adultery	sex sins
	not faithful in marriage
almighty	All-powerful
Amen	let it be so
anointed	He put His hand on Me
	chosen
anointed (with oil)	poured oil on
antichrist	false-christ
apostle	missionary
archangel	head angel
ark of the covenant	special box that held the Old Way of Worship
	box of the Way of Worship
armour	things God gives you to fight with
astonished	surprised and wondered
authority	the right and the power
	B
beasts	living beings
	wild animals
behold	look
	listen
believe	have faith
	put his trust in
beloved	much-loved
	dear friends
beseech	ask you from my heart
besought	asked
betray	hand Him over to them
bitterness	bad feelings about other people
blameless	without blame
blaspheme	speaks like he is God
	speaks against God
bless, blessed, blessing	respect and give thanks
	give honor to Him and thank God
bondwoman	woman who is owned by someone and who has to do what she is told

bottomless pit	hole without a bottom
bridegroom	man to be married soon

C

centurion	captain of the army
charged	told them with strong words
chariot	wagon
cheer	take hope
circumcise	religious act of becoming a Jew
clamour	noise
command	told them with strong words
commandment	teaching
	Law
	God's Word
compassion	loving-pity
concupiscence	desire for sex sin
condemn	guilty and be punished forever
confess	told their sins
conscience	their own hearts tell them they are guilty
corruptible	that which dies
counsel (take)	talk about what to do
courage	strength of heart
Covenant (Testament)	New Way of Worship
	Old Way of Worship
covetousness	wanting something that belongs to someone
create	made
	something is made out of nothing
creation	the whole world
crown	headband
	prize
crown of life	prize which is life
crucify	nail Him on a cross
curse	keep from being with God
	say bad things against

D

day of judgment	the day men stand in front of God to be told they are guilty
deacons	church helpers
deceit	lying
deceive	fools you and turns you to the wrong way
defend	proving

deliver	hand Him over
	give, gave
	set us free
	be free
deny, denied	lied and said he did not know Me
	troubled and turn away
	turn your backs against
	act as if you never knew Him
despise	hate
diligence	do your best
disciple	follower
discipline	punish
divisions	dividing people into groups against each other
doctrine	teaching

E

earnestly	deep feelings
ears to hear	if you have ears, then listen
effeminate	men who act like women
elders	church leaders
elect	the people of God
emulations	jealousy
encouragement	comfort
enemy	one who hates
	one who works against you
endure	keeps on
enmity	fighting
envying	wanting something someone else has
escape	get away from it
eternal life	life that lasts forever
evangelist	a preacher who goes from town to town
everlasting fire	fire that never goes out
everlasting life	life that lasts forever
evil	bad
	sinful
evil speaking	bad talk
example	I have done this to show you

F

false witness	tell a lie about someone else
fasting	not eating so you can pray better
favored	special

fear (of the Lord)	respect
	honor
feast	religious gathering
	religious supper
	special supper
fellowship	share together
	joined together
flesh (worldly)	old self
	sinful things of this life (world)
foolishness	doing foolish things
for My sake	because of Me
	because you trust in Me
fornication	sex sins
forsake	leave alone
forswear	make a promise you cannot keep
foundation	the part on which the building stands
foundation of the world	before the world was made
fulfilled	it happened as the early preacher said it would happen

G

gain	use you to get things for themselves
generation	people of this day
	family
Gentiles	people who do not know God
	people who are not Jews
glory	shining greatness
	honor
glorify, glorified	receive great honor
	honors
gnashing of teeth	grinding of teeth
godliness	God-like
	holy living
Gospel	Good News
grace	loving-favor
	God's love
greed	always wanting something
greeting	saying hello
groan	we cry inside ourselves with sounds that cannot be put into words
guests	those who ate with Him
guile	speaking words of hate
	talking bad about others

H

hark	Listen!
harlot	a woman who sells the use of her body
harps	music boxes of strings
harvest	gathering time
heathen	people who do not know God
heresy	false teaching
high priest	head religious leader
homosexual	people who do sex sins with their own sex
Host (Lord of)	Lord of all
hostility	fighting
House (of David)	Family of David
humble	no pride
hypocrisy	saying one thing but thinking something else
hypocrite	you who pretend to be someone you are not

I

idol	a god
idolatry	worshiping false gods
immortality	life that never dies
imperishable	will never die
incense	special perfume
incorruptible	never dies
indeed	for sure
inn	place where people stay for the night
inordinate affection	a strong and bad desire to please the body
intercedes	prays to God for us

J

judge	punish
	says he is guilty or not
	says what is right or wrong
judged	told he is guilty
	told he is wrong
judgment	they will stand in front of God and He will say if they are guilty
justified	made right with God

K

kingdom	holy nation
kingdom of God	holy nation of God

kingdom of heaven	holy nation of heaven
knowledge	much learning

L

lasciviousness	desire for sex sins
	desire for wrong things
law (God's Law)	Law
law (of the land)	law
lawful	right with the law
lawyer (see scribe)	man who knew the law
leper	a man with a bad skin disease
longsuffering	being able to wait
lots (casting)	drawing names
lunatic	those who lose the use of their minds for awhile
lust	a desire for sex sins

M

majesty	great power
malice	bad talk which hurts other people
manifested	shown
manna	bread from heaven
market place	the center of town where people gather
marvelled	surprised and wondered
master	teacher
	owner
measure	what you go by
meekness	not having pride
mercy	loving-kindness
message	news
messenger	man to carry news
	helper
midst	among
minister (serve)	care for
miracles	powerful works
mock	make fun of
mourn	have sorrow
multitude	many people
murder	kill other people
murmur	talk among themselves against Him
	talk against
mystery	hidden truth
	secret
	great truth that is hidden

O

offend	ashamed of Me and leave Me
	ashamed and turns away
oppression	bad power held over them
ordain	set apart
overcome	power over the devil
	won the fight
overcomer	have power over

P

partiality	to respect one person more than another
Passover	a special religious gathering to remember how the Jews left Egypt
pastor	church leader
patience	not give up
	being willing to wait
Pentecost	fifty days after the special religious gathering to remember how the Jews left Egypt
	that special day to remember how the Holy Spirit came on the church
perish	lost
	lost from God forever
persecute	make it hard for them
perseverance	faith stays strong even when people make it very hard for you
Pharisee	proud religious law-keeper
plagues	troubles
pleasures	to please ourselves
praise	thank
	respect
	words of greatness
precious	of great worth
	no amount of money can buy it
priests	religious leaders
(Christ as High Priest)	Religious Leader Who stands between God and man
	Religious Leader Who made the way for men to go to God
(High Priest)	head Jewish religious leader
prophesy	preach
	speaking God's Word
	tell what will happen in the future

prophet	special preacher
	early preacher
	one who speaks for God
	one who tells what is going to happen
propitiation	paid for our sins with His own blood

R

ransom	He gave His life so they could go free
rebuked	spoke sharp words
reconcile	turn from your sins and come to God
redeem (redemption)	bought by the blood of Christ and made free
regeneration	new life
reign	has power
reject	have nothing to do with
	turn away from
rejoice	be happy
	be full of joy
remission	forgiveness
rend	tear to pieces
repent	be sorry for your sins and turn from them
reproach	have no honor
	shame
reprobate	person in sin on his way to hell
reprove	speak strong words to
resist	stand against
resurrection	raised from the dead
	come up from the grave
revelation	some things the Lord has shown me
	some special words from God
revellings	wild parties
reverence	honor God with love and fear
reward	pay
righteousness	right with God

S

Sabbath	Day of Rest
sackcloth	clothes made from hair
sacrifice (offering)	a gift given on the altar in worship
	give a gift
	kill animals and give gifts
Sadducees	religious group of people who believe no one will be raised from the dead
saints	true Christians
	those who belong to Christ

sake (for your sake)	for your good
sanctify	set apart
	made holy
	right with God
	set apart for God-like living and to do His work
Sanhedrin	religious leaders' court
scribe (see lawyer)	teacher of the Law
Scripture	Holy Writings
	God's Written Word
season	time of the year
seditions	dividing into little groups and thinking the other group is wrong
seeks	looks for
self-control	being the boss over our own desires
sigh	breathe deep within
sign	something special to see
	something to look for
slander	talk that hurts people
slave	one who is sold to work
sober	be careful how they act
	keep our minds awake
spiritual	full-grown Christians
	strong Christians
spiritual gifts	gifts of the Holy Spirit
steadfast	not to be moved by others
straightway	at once
stumble	trip
	fall
swear	promise
sword (two-edged)	sword that cuts both ways

T

tabernacle	tent to worship in
temperance	the right use of what we have
temple	house of God
temptation	causes you to sin
tender	kind
Testament (Covenant)	New Way of Worship
	Old Way of Worship
throne	king's seat
	place where kings sit
tongues	languages
	special sounds

tradition	teaching that was given by our fathers (man-made)
trample	break them under their feet
treasures	riches
tribes	early families, family groups
tribulation	time of much trouble
triumph	power over the devil
	win the fight
tumult (commotion)	making much noise

V

vain (not in vain)	that I did not work with you for nothing
verily	for sure
virgin	a woman who has never had a man
virtue	the power to stand against sin
vision	saw in a dream what God wanted him to see
	special dream

W

watch	look and listen
	look out
weeping	loud crying
welcome	receive him and make him happy
	say hello
wicked	sinful
widow	woman whose husband has died
will (God's will)	what God wants done
winepress	a place for making wine
withered	dried up
	dying
witness	tells what he knows
	tell of what you have seen happen
woe	it is bad for you
	sorrow and trouble
	time of trouble
wonderful	great
worthy	has the right to
	good enough
wrath	anger
	bad temper
	God's anger

TOPICAL VERSE FINDER

Afraid
Matt. 14:25-27
John 14:27
Heb. 13:6
I John 4:18

Angels
Matt. 28:2-5
Acts 5:17-20; 8:26; 12:7-9; 27:21-26
I Cor. 6:3
Col. 2:18
Heb. 13:2

Anger
Eph. 4:26,31
Col. 3:5-8
James 1:20

Baptism
Matt. 3:13-17
Rom. 6:3-5
Col. 2:12
Eph. 4:5

Becoming Full-Grown Christians
Eph. 3:16-19
Col. 1:9-11; 3:12-17
I Tim. 4:11-16
II Tim. 2:14-19
I Peter 2:1-3
II Peter 1:5-9; 3:17-18

Being Pure
Phil. 2:13-15
I Tim. 5:22
James 3:16-18; 4:8
I John 3:3

Being The Boss Over Your Own Desires [*Self-Control*]
Rom. 13:14
I Cor. 9:24-25
I Tim. 6:11-12
II Tim. 2:3-5

Being Tempted
Matt. 26:41
I Cor. 10:11-13
Heb. 2:18; 4:14-16
James 1:14; 4:7
II Pet. 2:9

Christ: One Of The Three-In-One God
Matt. 26:62-64
John 1:1-4,18; 10:30; 14:8-10
Col. 1:15-19; 2:9
Titus 2:13
Heb. 1:3,8
I John 5:20

Church
Matt. 16:18; 18:15-17
Acts 2:42-47; 14:23; 16:4-5
Rom. 16:5
Eph. 1:21-22

Comfort and Help
Matt. 5:4; 11:28-30
Rom. 15:1-6
II Cor. 1:3-5
I Thess. 5:14
II Thess. 2:16-17

Death
Rom. 14:7-9
II Cor. 5:1-9
Phil. 1:21-22
I Thess. 5:9-10
II Tim. 4:6-8
Heb. 9:27
Rev. 21:1-4

Death Of A Loved One
John 5:28-29
I Cor. 15:12-57
I Thess. 4:13-18

Divorce
Matt. 5:31-32; 19:3-9
Mark 10:2-12
Luke 16:18
Rom. 7:1-3
I Cor. 7:10-16

Doubtful Things
Rom. 14:1-23
I Cor. 8:1-13
Phil. 2:12-15
Col. 3:1-10,17
I Thess. 5:21-22
Titus 2:12-14
James 4:4-5
I John 2:15-17

Doing The Right Things
Matt. 7:12
James 1:5-6; 4:17

Debts
Rom. 13:8

Faith
Rom. 10:17
Eph. 2:8
Heb. 11:1-40; 12:1-2
James 1:2-8
I Peter 1:7
I John 5:4

Fear
John 14:27
Rom. 8:28,31,35-39
II Tim. 1:7
Heb. 13:5-6
I John 4:18

Feeling Bad Over Something That Happened [*Disappointment*]
John 14:27; 16:31-33
Rom. 8:28
I Thess. 5:18
Heb. 4:16
I Peter 1:3-9

Foolish Son [*Prodigal Son*]
Luke 15:11-32

Forgiveness Of Sin
Matt. 6:14-15
Col. 1:14
I John 1:7-9

Forgiving Others
Matt. 6:12,14-15; 18:15-17,21-22,35
Mark 11:25-26
Luke 17:3-4
Eph. 4:32
Col. 3:12-13

Free Because Of Christ [*Liberty*]
John 8:31-32,36
Rom. 6:6-11,15-23; 7:6; 8:1-2
Gal. 5:1,13-14

Friends, and Being Friendly
John 13:34-35; 15:12-14
Gal. 6:1-5,10

Fruit Of The Spirit
Gal. 5:22-23

Gifts Of The Holy Spirit
Rom. 12:6-8
I Cor. 12-14
Eph. 4:11-12
I Peter 4:10

Giving With A Heart Of Love
Matt. 5:42
Luke 6:38
Rom. 12:8
II Cor. 9:6-7

God Meets The Needs Of His Children [*Provision*]
Matt. 6:25-34
II Cor. 9:8
Eph. 3:20
I Peter 1:4
II Peter 1:3-4

God's Care
Eph. 3:20
Phil. 4:14-19
Heb. 4:14-16; 13:5-6
I Peter 5:5-7
I John 4:14-16

God's Will
Eph. 5:15-21
Phil. 2:12-18
I Thess. 4:3
I Peter 3:17

Going Without Food [*Fasting*]
Matt. 6:16-18
Mark 9:28-29
Acts 14:23

God's Word
Col. 3:16
Heb. 4:12
I Peter 1:23;2:2-3

Golden Rule
Matt. 7:12
Luke 6:31

Good Samaritan
Luke 10:30-37

Hard Things That Come Your Way
Rom. 8:28
II Cor. 4:16-18
Heb. 5:8; 12:6-11
Rev. 3:19

Happiness
Matt. 5:2-12
Rom. 14:22
James 5:11
I Peter 3:14; 4:14

Having No Pride [*Humility*]
Acts 20:19
Rom. 12:3,16
Phil. 2:1-4
I Peter 5:5-7

Heaven
Acts 7:44-50
I Cor. 2:9
Heb. 8:1
I Peter 1:4
Rev. 21:3-4,27

Hell
Matt. 5:22; 18:8-9; 22:13; 25:41,46
Mark 9:48
II Thess. 1:8-9
Jude 6-7
Rev. 20:15

Helping Other Christians
Matt. 5:13-16; 10:37-42
Luke 3:10-14
Gal. 6:1-5,10
James 2:1-9
I John 3:17-18

Holy Spirit
John 14:15-18
Acts 2:1-4; 5:1-11
I Cor. 3:16-17; 6:18-20; 12:1-3
II Cor. 13:14
I Peter 1:2

Hope
Rom. 5:5; 8:24; 15:4,13
I Cor. 13:7
Gal. 5:5
II Thess. 2:16
Titus 1:2
Heb. 11:1
I Peter 1:3

How To Know You Are Saved
John 5:24; 6:37; 10:27-30; 20:31
Rom. 8:16-17; 10:8-13
I John 5:11-13

Husbands
I Cor. 7:1-4
Eph. 5:25-33
Col. 3:19
I Peter 3:7

Jesus' Teachings On The Mountain [*Beatitudes*]
Matt. 5:3-12
Luke 6:20-26

Jesus: As Lord
Luke 4:40-41
Rom. 10:9
I Cor. 6:19-20
Phil. 2:5-11

Jesus: The One Who Saves
Matt. 1:21
Luke 19:10
John 3:16-17; 14:6
Acts 4:12
Rom. 5:8
Eph. 1:7
I John 5:12

Knowing All Is Well
Gal. 6:9
Eph. 3:12
Phil. 1:6
Heb. 10:35-36
I Peter 2:9-10

Living For Christ
II Cor. 5:17
Col. 2:6-7
II Tim. 2:19
I Peter 2:2-3

Living Water
John 4:7-14; 7:37-39
Rev. 7:17; 22:17

Lord's Day
Matt. 12:1-14
Mark 2:27-28
Luke 6:5; 13:14-17
John 7:23
Acts 20:7
I Cor. 16:2

Lord's Prayer
Matt. 6:9-13
Luke 11:2-4

Lord's Supper
Matt. 26:26-30
Acts 2:42; 20:7
I Cor. 11:23-32

Love
John 3:16; 13:34-35; 15:12-14
Rom. 5:8; 8:35-39
I Cor. 13
I John 3:1

Man's Need To Be Saved
  Rom. 3:10-12,23; 5:12; 6:23
  I John 1:9-10

Marriage
  Matt. 19:3-9
  I Cor. 7
  Eph. 5:22-33
  Heb. 13:4
  I Peter 3:1-8

Never Alone
  Matt. 18:20; 28:20
  Acts 18:10
  Heb. 13:5

New Heaven And Earth
  Rev. 21-22

Obeying Christ And His Word
  John 14:21
  II Cor. 10:5-6
  James 2:10
  I John 3:22

Obeying The Laws And Leaders Of Your Nation
  Rom. 13:1-7
  I Tim. 2:1-3
  I Peter 2:13-17

Parents
  Eph. 6:1-4
  Col. 3:20-21
  I Tim. 5:4

Pay For Doing Good [*Rewards*]
  I Cor. 9:24-27; 15:58
  Gal. 6:9
  Eph. 6:8
  II Tim. 4:6-8

Peace
  John 14:27; 16:33
  Rom. 5:1
  II Cor. 1:3-5
  Phil. 4:4-9
  Col. 3:12-15

Poor
Matt. 26:11
II Cor. 8:9
Gal. 2:10
James 2:1-9

Power Over Satan
James 4:7
I John 4:4

Power Over Temptation [*Overcoming*]
Matt. 26:41
I Cor. 10:11-13
Phil. 1:6,10
I Thess. 3:2-3
James 4:7-10
II Peter 2:9
I John 4:4

Praise and Being Thankful
Eph. 5:15-20
Phil. 4:4-6
Col. 3:15-17
I Thess. 5:18
Heb. 13:15
I Peter 1:6-9

Prayer
Matt. 6:5-13; 7:7-11; 21:22
John 14:13-14; 15:7
Eph. 6:18-19
Phil. 4:6
Heb. 4:14-16
James 5:16-18
I John 5:14-15

Prize Of Life [*Crown*]
I Cor. 9:24-27
I Thess. 2:19-20
II Tim. 4:6-8
James 1:9-12
I Peter 5:1-4
Rev. 2:9-10

Satan
James 4:7
I John 4:4

Second Coming Of Christ
Matt. 24:35-44; 25:1-13
Luke 21:33-36
Acts 1:11
I Thess. 4:13-18
Titus 2:13
Heb. 10:25
II Peter 3:8-15
I John 3:2-3

Sex Sins [*Adultery and Fornication*]
Matt. 5:27-28; 19:18
Gal. 5:19
I Thess. 4:1-8
Heb. 13:4

Sharing The Good News [*Witnessing*]
Matt. 5:16; 28:18-20
Mark 5:18-20
Luke 24:48
John 17:18
Acts 1:8
Rom. 1:16-17
II Cor. 5:18-21
II Tim. 4:2
I Peter 3:15-17; 4:11

Sharing Together [*Fellowship*]
Matt. 18:20
John 13:34
Acts 2:42-47
I Cor. 1:9
II Cor. 13:14
Col. 1:12; 2:19
Heb. 10:24-25
I John 1:3,7

Sickness
Matt. 4:23
John 11:4
James 5:13-16

Sin
John 8:33-36
Rom. 3:23; 5:12; 6:23; 14:23b
Gal. 6:7-8

Sinful Desires
Matt. 5:27-30
Gal. 5:17-21

Sin That Cannot Be Forgiven [*Unpardonable Sin*
Matt. 12:30-32
Mark 3:22-30
Luke 12:10
Heb. 10:26-27
I John 5:16-17

Sorrow
Matt. 11:28-30
John 16:22
Rom. 8:26-28
II Cor. 1:3-5; 4:17-18; 6:10

Strength
II Cor. 12:7-10
Phil. 4:10-13

Studying and Teaching
Acts 17:11; 20:29-31
II Tim. 2:15; 3:14-17
Heb. 4:12-13
I Peter 2:2-3

Suffering
Rom. 8:18
II Cor. 1:3-5; 4:17; 12:7-10
Phil. 1:29; 3:10
II Tim. 2:12
Heb. 12:3-13
I Peter 3:14-17; 4:12-16; 5:8-11

Suffering For Christ [*Persecution*]
Matt. 5:10-11; 10:22
Mark 10:30
Acts 5:40-42; 9:10-16
Rom. 8:17
II Tim. 3:10-13
Heb. 11:24-26
James 1:2-3
I Peter 2:20

Tell The Good News To Those Who Have Not Heard
Matt. 28:18-20
Mark 16:15-16
Luke 24:47-49
John 20:21
Acts 1:8

The Way To Be Saved
John 3:3,16-17; 5:24; 14:6
Acts 16:31
Rom. 10:9-10,13
II Cor. 5:17
Eph. 2:8-9
Titus 3:4-7
I John 5:11-13

Things God Gives Christians To Stand Against Satan [*Armor*]
Eph. 6:10-18

Things That Will Happen Before Christ Comes Again
Matt. 24:3-14
Luke 21:25-28
I Thess. 4:13-18; 5:2-3
II Thess. 2:1-11
I Tim. 4:1
II Tim. 3:1-5
James 5:7-8
I Peter 4:7
II Peter 3:3-13

Time Of Much Trouble [*Tribulation*]
Matt. 24:21
Rev. 7:14; 11:2-3; 13:5

Trust
John 3:16-18; 20:30-31
Rom. 1:16; 3:22
Gal. 3:22

Way Of Life
Rom. 8:5-11
Eph. 5:18
II Tim. 3:10
I Peter 1:15
II Peter 3:11

Wedding Supper Of The Lamb [*Christ*]
Rev. 19:7-10

When Guilty
Rom. 8:1-17
II Cor. 5:20-21
Col. 2:11-18

When Tired
Matt. 11:28-30

When Discouraged
Matt. 11:28-30
John 14:27; 16:33
Heb. 4:16
I Peter 1:3-9
I John 5:14-15

Winning The Battle Over Satan [*Victory*]
Rom. 8:31-39
I Cor. 15:57
II Cor. 2:14
II Tim. 2:19
I John 5:4
Rev. 3:5; 21:7

Wives
I Cor. 11:2-16
Eph. 5:22-24
Col. 3:18
I Tim. 3:11
Titus 2:3-5
I Peter 3:1-6

Working For A Living
Rom. 12:11
Eph. 4:28
II Thess. 3:10-12

Worry
Matt. 6:25-34
Phil. 4:6
I Peter 5:7

Worship
Matt. 4:10
John 4:19-24
Rev. 19:10; 22:8-9

THINGS THAT HAPPENED WHILE JESUS WAS ON EARTH

THINGS THAT HAPPENED WHILE JESUS WAS ON EARTH	PLACE	MATTHEW	MARK	LUKE	JOHN
Luke Writes To Theophilus				1:1-4	
Before The Earth Was Made					1:1-14
The Family Of Jesus	Jerusalem	1:1-17		3:23-38	
An Angel Tells Of The Birth Of John The Baptist				1:5-25	
Mary Learns Of Jesus' Birth	Nazareth			1:26-38	
Mary Visits Elizabeth	A city of Judah			1:39-56	
Birth Of John The Baptist	A city of Judah			1:57-66	
Zacharias' Song	A city of Judah			1:67-80	
Birth Of Jesus	Bethlehem	1:18-25		2:1-7	
Shepherds Learn Of Jesus' Birth	Near Bethlehem			2:8-14	
Shepherds Go To Bethlehem	Near Bethlehem			2:15-20	
Jesus Taken To The House Of God	Jerusalem			2:21-38	
Visit Of The Men Who Learned From The Stars	Bethlehem	2:1-12			
Joseph Takes Mary And Jesus To Egypt	Bethlehem to Egypt	2:13-15			
Boys Killed By Herod	Bethlehem	2:16-18			
Joseph Takes Mary And Jesus To Nazareth	Egypt to Nazareth	2:19-23		2:39-40	
Jesus In The House Of God	Jerusalem			2:41-52	
John The Baptist Preaches	Judea	3:1-12	1:1-8	3:1-18	1:15-28
Jesus Was Baptized	Jordan	3:13-17	1:9-11	3:21-22	1:29-34
Jesus Was Tempted	Judea	4:1-11	1:12-13	4:1-13	
Call Of Andrew And Peter	Jordan				1:35-42
Call Of Philip And Nathanael	Galilee				1:43-51
First Powerful Work — Water Changed To Wine	Cana				2:1-12

Event	Place	Matthew	Mark	Luke	John
Nicodemus Visits Jesus At Night	Jerusalem				3:1-21
Jesus Preaches In Judea	Judea				3:22
John The Baptist Tells More About Jesus	Judea				3:23-36
Jesus Talks To The Woman At The Well	Samaria				4:1-42
Jesus Goes To Galilee	Galilee				4:43-45
Healing Of The Dying Boy	Galilee				4:46-54
John The Baptist Put Into Prison	Macherus	14:1-5	6:14-20		
Jesus Preaches In Galilee	Galilee	4:12-17	1:14-15		
In Nazareth They Do Not Believe In Jesus	Nazareth			4:16-30	
Call Of Simon, Andrew, James And John	Capernaum	4:18-22	1:16-20	5:1-11	
A Demon Put Out	Capernaum		1:21-28	4:31-37	
Peter's Mother-in-law Healed	Capernaum	8:14-15	1:29-31	4:38-39	
Many People Healed	Capernaum	8:16-17	1:32-34	4:40-41	
Jesus Keeps On Preaching In Galilee	Galilee	4:23-25	1:35-39	4:42-44	
Man With Skin Disease Healed	Galilee	8:1-4	1:40-45	5:12-16	
The Man Let Down Through The Roof	Capernaum	9:1-8	2:1-12	5:17-26	
Call Of Matthew	Capernaum	9:9-13	2:13-17	5:27-32	
Man Healed At Pool Of Bethesda	Jerusalem				5:1-47
Followers Ate Grain On Day Of Rest	Capernaum	12:1-8	2:23-28	6:1-5	
Jesus Heals On The Day Of Rest	Capernaum	12:9-14	3:1-6	6:6-11	
Jesus Heals By The Side Of The Lake	Capernaum	12:15-21	3:7-12	6:17-19	
Jesus Teaches On The Mountain	Capernaum	5:1-27		6:20-49	
Healing Of The Captain's Helper	Capernaum	8:5-13		7:1-10	
The Widow's Son Raised From The Dead	Nain			7:11-17	
John The Baptist Asks About Jesus	Capernaum	11:1-6		7:18-23	
Jesus Tells About John The Baptist	Capernaum	11:7-19		7:24-35	

		MATTHEW	MARK	LUKE	JOHN
Jesus Teaches In Galilee	Galilee			8:1-3	
A Nation That Cannot Stand	Capernaum	12:22-37	3:22-30	11:14-23	
When Bad Goes From A Person	Capernaum	12:43-45		11:24-26	
Jesus Tells About Jonah	Capernaum	12:38-42		11:29-32	
The New Kind Of Family	Capernaum	12:46-50	3:31-35	8:19-21	
It Will Be Bad For The Proud Religious Law-keepers	Capernaum			11:37-54	
Jesus Teaches His Followers	Capernaum			12:1-59	
Everyone Should Be Sorry For Their Sins And Turn From Them	Capernaum			13:1-5	
Picture-stories—Seed, Yeast, Pearl, Fish Net	Capernaum	12:1-52	4:1-34	8:4-18	
Testing Of Some Followers	Galilee	8:18-22		9:57-62	
The Wind And Waves Obey Jesus	Galilee	8:23-27	4:35-41	8:22-25	
Demons Ask To Live In Pigs	Galilee	8:28-34	5:1-20	8:26-39	
Jesus Teaches About Not Eating	Capernaum	9:14-17	2:18-22	5:33-35	
Two Healed Through Faith	Capernaum	9:18-26	5:21-43	8:40-56	
Two Blind Men Healed	Capernaum	9:27-31			
A Demon Put Out	Capernaum	9:32-34			
They Do Not Believe In Nazareth	Nazareth	13:53-58	6:1-6		
The Twelve Sent Out	Galilee	10:1-42	6:7-13	9:1-6	
John The Baptist Is Killed	Galilee	14:6-12	6:21-29	9:7-9	
Feeding Of Five Thousand	Galilee	14:13-21	6:30-44	9:10-17	6:1-14
Jesus Walks On Water	Galilee	14:22-33	6:45-52		6:15-21
People Are Healed At Gennesaret	Gennesaret	14:34-36	6:53-56		
Teaching On Bread Of Life	Capernaum				6:22-71
Jesus Speaks Sharp Words To Leaders	Capernaum	15:1-20	7:1-23		
Demon Put Out Of Girl	Tyre, Sidon	15:21-28	7:24-30		
Man Who Could Not Hear Or Speak Healed	Decapolis		7:31-37		

Event	Location	Matthew	Mark	Luke	John
Feeding Of The Four Thousand	Decapolis	15:32-39	8:1-9		
Jesus Speaks Sharp Words To Proud Religious Law-keepers	Magadan	16:1-4	8:10-13		
Jesus Teaches Against Proud Religious Law-keepers	Galilee	16:5-21	8:14-21		
A Blind Man Is Healed	Bethsaida		8:22-26		
Peter Says Jesus Is The Christ	Caesarea	16:13-20	8:27-30	9:18-20	
Jesus Tells Of His Death, First Time	Caesarea	16:21-28	8:31-38	9:21-27	
A Look At What Jesus Will Be Like	Caesarea	17:1-13	9:1-13	9:28-36	
A Boy Is Healed	Caesarea	17:14-21	9:14-29	9:37-42	
Jesus Tells Of His Death, Second Time	Galilee	17:22-23	9:30-32	9:43-45	
House Of God Tax	Capernaum	17:24-27			
Teaching About Faith As A Child	Capernaum	18:1-35	9:33-50	9:46-50	
Jesus And Followers Leave Galilee	Judea			9:51-56	
The Seventy Sent Out To Preach	Judea			10:1-24	
Jesus Teaches At Religious Gathering	Jerusalem				7:1-52
Jesus Talks To The Woman Found In Sin	Jerusalem				8:1-11
Jesus Talks To The Jews	Jerusalem				8:12-59
Picture-story Of Good Samaritan	Judea			10:25-37	
Jesus Visits Mary And Martha	Bethany			10:38-42	
The Followers Taught How To Pray	Judea			11:1-13	
The Blind Man Healed	Jerusalem				9:1-41
The Shepherd And The Door	Jerusalem				10:1-39
Many People Believe In Jesus	East of the Jordan River				10:40-42
Picture-story Of The Fig Tree	East of the Jordan River			13:6-9	
Woman Healed On The Day Of Rest	East of the Jordan River			13:10-17	
Jesus Teaches On Way To Jerusalem	East of the Jordan River			13:22-35	
Jesus Heals, Teaches, Picture-story Of Big Supper	East of the Jordan River			14:1-24	

Event	Place	MATTHEW	MARK	LUKE	JOHN
Giving Up Things Of This Earth	East of the Jordan River	10:37-39		14:25-35	
Picture-story Of Lost Sheep, Lost Money, Son Who Spent All His Money	East of the Jordan River			15:1-32	
Picture-story Of The Boss Who Stole	East of the Jordan River			16:1-13	
Jesus Teaches The Law Is Not Finished	East of the Jordan River			16:14-31	
Jesus Teaches About Forgiving	East of the Jordan River			17:1-10	
Ten Men With Skin Disease Healed	Samaria			17:11-19	
Jesus Tells Of His Second Coming	East of the Jordan River			17:20-37	
Picture-story Of The Woman Whose Husband Had Died	East of the Jordan River			18:1-8	
Picture-story Of The Proud Religious Law-keepers And Tax Gatherers	East of the Jordan River			18:9-14	
Lazarus Is Raised From The Dead	Bethany				11:1-44
Proud Religious Law-keepers Try To Kill Jesus	Jerusalem				11:45-54
Teaching On Divorce	East of the Jordan River	19:1-12	10:1-12		
Jesus Gives Thanks For Little Children	East of the Jordan River	19:13-15	10:13-16	18:15-17	
Jesus Teaches About Keeping The Law	East of the Jordan River	19:16-30	10:17-31	18:18-30	
Picture-story Of Workmen In Grape Field	East of the Jordan River	20:1-16			
Jesus Tells Of His Death, Third Time	East of the Jordan River	20:17-19	10:32-34	18:31-34	
James And John Ask Something Hard	East of the Jordan River	20:20-28	10:35-45		
Two Blind Men Healed Near Jericho	Jericho	20:29-34	10:46-52	18:35-43	
The Changed Life Of Zacchaeus	Jericho			19:1-10	
Picture-story Of Ten Workman And The Money	Jericho			19:11-28	
Proud Religious Law-keepers Look For Jesus	Jerusalem				11:55-57
Mary Of Bethany Puts Perfume On Jesus	Bethany	26:6-13	14:3-9		12:1-11
The Last Time Jesus Goes Into Jerusalem	Jerusalem	21:1-11	11:1-11	19:29-44	12:12-19

Event	Location	Matthew	Mark	Luke	John
Jesus Stops The Buying In The House Of God	Jerusalem	21:12-17	11:15-19	19:45-48	2:13-17
The Fig Tree Dries Up	Jerusalem	21:18-22	11:20-26		
They Ask Jesus Who Gave Him Power	Jerusalem	21:23-32	11:27-33	20:1-8	
Picture-story Of The Grape Field	Jerusalem	21:33-46	12:1-12	20:9-18	
Picture-story Of The Marriage Supper	Jerusalem	22:1-14			
Proud Religious Law-keepers Try To Trap Jesus	Jerusalem	22:15-22	12:13-17	20:19-26	
They Ask About Being Raised From The Dead	Jerusalem	22:23-33	12:18-27	20:27-40	
The Great Law	Jerusalem	22:34-40	12:28-34		
Jesus Asks Proud Religious Law-keepers About The Christ	Jerusalem	22:41-46	12:35-37	20:41-44	
False Teachers	Jerusalem	23:1-36	12:38-40	20:45-47	
Jesus Sorrows Over Jerusalem	Jerusalem	23:37-39			
A Woman Whose Husband Had Died Gave All She Had	Jerusalem		12:41-44	21:1-4	
The Greek People Want To See Jesus	Jerusalem				12:20-50
Jesus Tells Of The House Of God	Mountain of Olives	24:1-51	13:1-37	21:5-36	
Picture-story Of The Ten Young Women	Mountain of Olives	25:1-13			
Picture-story Of The Ten Men And The Money	Mountain of Olives	25:14-30			
Sheep And Goats	Mountain of Olives	25:31-46			
They Try To Find A Way To Kill Jesus	Jerusalem	26:1-5	14:1-2	22:1-6	
Judas Hands Jesus Over To Be Killed	Jerusalem	26:14-16	14:10-11		
Getting Ready For The Special Supper	Jerusalem	26:17-19	14:12-16	22:7-13	
The Last Special Supper	Jerusalem	26:20-25	14:17-21	22:14-18	13:21-35
They Argue Who Is Greatest	Jerusalem			22:24-30	
Jesus Washes His Followers' Feet	Jerusalem				13:1-20
The First Lord's Supper	Jerusalem	26:26-30	14:22-26	22:19-20	
Jesus Tells How Peter Will Lie About Him	Jerusalem	26:31-35	14:27-31	22:31-34	13:36-38

Event	MATTHEW	MARK	LUKE	JOHN	Location
Jesus Comforts His Followers				14:1-31	Jerusalem
The Vine And The Branches				15:1-27	Jerusalem
The Work Of The Holy Spirit				16:1-33	Jerusalem
Jesus' Prayer				17:1-26	Jerusalem
Jesus Prays In Gethsemane	26:36-46	14:32-42	22:39-46		Mountain of Olives
Jesus Handed Over To Sinners	26:47-56	14:43-52	22:47-51	18:1-11	Mountain of Olives
Jesus Stands In Front Of Caiaphas	26:57-58	14:53-54	22:52-54	18:19-24	Jerusalem
The Court Room	26:59-68	14:55-65			Jerusalem
Peter Lies About Jesus	26:69-75	14:66-72	22:55-62	18:15-18, 25-27	Jerusalem
Jesus Stands In Front Of Pilate	27:1-2, 11-14	15:1-5	23:1-5	18:28-37	Jerusalem
Death Of Judas	27:3-10				Jerusalem
Jesus Sent To Herod			23:6-12		Jerusalem
Jesus Or Barabbas Is To Go Free	27:15-26	15:6-14	23:17-25	18:38-40	Jerusalem
The Headband Of Thorns	27:27-32	15:15-21		19:1-5	Jerusalem
Pilate Tries To Let Jesus Go Free				19:6-16	Jerusalem
Jesus On The Cross	27:33-37	15:22-26	23:26-38	19:17-22	Jerusalem
The Two Robbers	27:38-44	15:27-32	23:39-43		Jerusalem
The Death Of Jesus	27:45-50	15:33-36	23:44-49	19:28-37	Jerusalem
The Powerful Works At His Death	27:51-54	15:37-39			Jerusalem
The Women At The Cross	27:55-56	15:40-41		19:25-27	Jerusalem
Jesus' Grave	27:57-66	15:42-47	23:50-56	19:38-42	Jerusalem
Jesus Is Raised From The Dead	28:1-10	16:1-8	24:1-12	20:1-18	Jerusalem
The Jews Make Up A Story	28:11-15				Jerusalem
Jesus' Followers Do Not Believe He Is Risen		16:9-14	24:13-43	20:24-29	Jerusalem
Jesus Sends His Followers To Preach	28:16-20	16:15-18	24:44-49	20:21-23	
Jesus Goes To Be Beside His Father		16:19-20	24:50-53		
The Risen Christ Talks To His Followers				21:1-23	Galilee